THE BOOK ®

Vauxhall/Opel Vectra
Service and Repair Manual

Peter T Gill and A K Legg LAE MIMI

Models covered

(3930 - 416 - 8AK2)

Vectra Saloon, Hatchback & Estate models, including special/limited editions
Petrol engines: 1.6 litre (1598cc), 1.8 litre (1796 & 1799cc), 2.0 litre (1998cc) & 2.2 litre (2198cc)
Turbo-Diesel engines: 2.0 litre (1994cc) & 2.2 litre (2171cc)

Does NOT cover 2.5 or 2.6 litre V6 petrol engines or dual fuel models

© Haynes Publishing 2004

ABCDE
FG

A book in the **Haynes Service and Repair Manual Series**

ISBN **978 1 85960 930 9**

British Library Cataloguing in Publication Data
A catalogue record for this book is available from

Printed in the USA

Haynes Publishing
Sparkford, Yeovil, Somerset BA22 7JJ, England

Haynes North America, Inc
861 Lawrence Drive, Newbury Park, California 91320, USA

Haynes Publishing Nordiska AB
A, Sverige

Contents

LIVING WITH YOUR VAUXHALL/OPEL VECTRA

MAINTENANCE

Routine Maintenance and Servicing

Contents

Advanced driving

Many people see the words 'advanced driving' and believe that it won't interest them or that it is a style of driving beyond their own abilities. Nothing could be further from the truth. Advanced driving is straightforward safe, sensible driving - the sort of driving we should all do every time we get behind the wheel.

An average of 10 people are killed every day on UK roads and 870 more are injured, some seriously. Lives are ruined daily, usually because somebody did something stupid. Something like 95% of all accidents are due to human error, mostly driver failure. Sometimes we make genuine mistakes - everyone does. Sometimes we have lapses of concentration. Sometimes we deliberately take risks.

For many people, the process of 'learning to drive' doesn't go much further than learning how to pass the driving test because of a common belief that good drivers are made by 'experience'.

Learning to drive by 'experience' teaches three driving skills:

- ☐ Quick reactions. (Whoops, that was close!)
- ☐ Good handling skills. (Horn, swerve, brake, horn).
- ☐ Reliance on vehicle technology. (Great stuff this ABS, stop in no distance even in the wet...)

Drivers whose skills are 'experience based' generally have a lot of near misses and the odd accident. The results can be seen every day in our courts and our hospital casualty departments.

Advanced drivers have learnt to control the risks by controlling the position and speed of their vehicle. They avoid accidents and near misses, even if the drivers around them make mistakes.

The key skills of advanced driving are **concentration,** effective all-round **observation, anticipation** and **planning.** When **good vehicle handling** is added to these skills, all driving situations can be approached and negotiated in a safe, methodical way, leaving nothing to chance.

Concentration means applying your mind to safe driving, completely excluding anything that's not relevant. Driving is usually the most dangerous activity that most of us undertake in our daily routines. It deserves our full attention.

Observation means not just looking, but seeing and seeking out the information found in the driving environment.

Anticipation means asking yourself what is happening, what you can reasonably expect to happen and what could happen unexpectedly. (One of the commonest words used in compiling accident reports is 'suddenly'.)

Planning is the link between seeing something and taking the appropriate action. For many drivers, planning is the missing link.

If you want to become a safer and more skilful driver and you want to enjoy your driving more, contact the Institute of Advanced Motorists at www.iam.org.uk, phone 0208 996 9600, or write to IAM House, 510 Chiswick High Road, London W4 5RG for an information pack.

Working on your car can be dangerous. This page shows just some of the potential risks and hazards, with the aim of creating a safety-conscious attitude.

General hazards

Scalding

• Don't remove the radiator or expansion tank cap while the engine is hot.
• Engine oil, automatic transmission fluid or power steering fluid may also be dangerously hot if the engine has recently been running.

Burning

• Beware of burns from the exhaust system and from any part of the engine. Brake discs and drums can also be extremely hot immediately after use.

Crushing

• When working under or near a raised vehicle, always supplement the jack with axle stands, or use drive-on ramps. *Never venture under a car which is only supported by a jack.*
• Take care if loosening or tightening high-torque nuts when the vehicle is on stands. Initial loosening and final tightening should be done with the wheels on the ground.

Fire

• Fuel is highly flammable; fuel vapour is explosive.
• Don't let fuel spill onto a hot engine.
• Do not smoke or allow naked lights (including pilot lights) anywhere near a vehicle being worked on. Also beware of creating sparks (electrically or by use of tools).
• Fuel vapour is heavier than air, so don't work on the fuel system with the vehicle over an inspection pit.
• Another cause of fire is an electrical overload or short-circuit. Take care when repairing or modifying the vehicle wiring.
• Keep a fire extinguisher handy, of a type suitable for use on fuel and electrical fires.

Electric shock

• Ignition HT voltage can be dangerous, especially to people with heart problems or a pacemaker. Don't work on or near the ignition system with the engine running or the ignition switched on.

• Mains voltage is also dangerous. Make sure that any mains-operated equipment is correctly earthed. Mains power points should be protected by a residual current device (RCD) circuit breaker.

Fume or gas intoxication

• Exhaust fumes are poisonous; they often contain carbon monoxide, which is rapidly fatal if inhaled. Never run the engine in a confined space such as a garage with the doors shut.
• Fuel vapour is also poisonous, as are the vapours from some cleaning solvents and paint thinners.

Poisonous or irritant substances

• Avoid skin contact with battery acid and with any fuel, fluid or lubricant, especially antifreeze, brake hydraulic fluid and Diesel fuel. Don't syphon them by mouth. If such a substance is swallowed or gets into the eyes, seek medical advice.
• Prolonged contact with used engine oil can cause skin cancer. Wear gloves or use a barrier cream if necessary. Change out of oil-soaked clothes and do not keep oily rags in your pocket.
• Air conditioning refrigerant forms a poisonous gas if exposed to a naked flame (including a cigarette). It can also cause skin burns on contact.

Asbestos

• Asbestos dust can cause cancer if inhaled or swallowed. Asbestos may be found in gaskets and in brake and clutch linings. When dealing with such components it is safest to assume that they contain asbestos.

Special hazards

Hydrofluoric acid

• This extremely corrosive acid is formed when certain types of synthetic rubber, found in some O-rings, oil seals, fuel hoses etc, are exposed to temperatures above 400°C. The rubber changes into a charred or sticky substance containing the acid. *Once formed, the acid remains dangerous for years. If it gets onto the skin, it may be necessary to amputate the limb concerned.*
• When dealing with a vehicle which has suffered a fire, or with components salvaged from such a vehicle, wear protective gloves and discard them after use.

The battery

• Batteries contain sulphuric acid, which attacks clothing, eyes and skin. Take care when topping-up or carrying the battery.
• The hydrogen gas given off by the battery is highly explosive. Never cause a spark or allow a naked light nearby. Be careful when connecting and disconnecting battery chargers or jump leads.

Air bags

• Air bags can cause injury if they go off accidentally. Take care when removing the steering wheel and/or facia. Special storage instructions may apply.

Diesel injection equipment

• Diesel injection pumps supply fuel at very high pressure. Take care when working on the fuel injectors and fuel pipes.

⚠ *Warning: Never expose the hands, face or any other part of the body to injector spray; the fuel can penetrate the skin with potentially fatal results.*

Remember...

DO

• Do use eye protection when using power tools, and when working under the vehicle.

• Do wear gloves or use barrier cream to protect your hands when necessary.

• Do get someone to check periodically that all is well when working alone on the vehicle.

• Do keep loose clothing and long hair well out of the way of moving mechanical parts.

• Do remove rings, wristwatch etc, before working on the vehicle – especially the electrical system.

• Do ensure that any lifting or jacking equipment has a safe working load rating adequate for the job.

DON'T

• Don't attempt to lift a heavy component which may be beyond your capability – get assistance.

• Don't rush to finish a job, or take unverified short cuts.

• Don't use ill-fitting tools which may slip and cause injury.

• Don't leave tools or parts lying around where someone can trip over them. Mop up oil and fuel spills at once.

• Don't allow children or pets to play in or near a vehicle being worked on.

The Vauxhall/Opel Vectra was introduced in the UK in October 1995 as a replacement for the Cavalier. It was originally available in Saloon and Hatchback versions with 1.6, 1.8, 2.0 and 2.5 litre petrol engines and 1.7 litre normally aspirated diesel engines. The Estate range was launched in October 1996. This Manual covers the facelifted models introduced in March 1999 which were available with 1.6, 1.8, 2.0 and 2.2 litre petrol engines, and 2.0 and 2.2 litre diesel engines. The 1.6 litre petrol engines are available with both single and double overhead belt-driven camshafts, the 1.8, and 2.0 litre petrol engines have belt-driven double overhead camshafts, and the 2.2 litre petrol engine has chain-driven double overhead camshafts. All the diesel engines have a single overhead belt-driven camshaft and are of direct injection design.

Models may be fitted with a five-speed manual, or four-speed automatic transmission mounted on the left-hand side of the engine.

All models have front-wheel-drive with fully-independent front and rear suspension.

Power steering (PAS) and Anti-Lock Braking (ABS) are fitted as standard to all models.

All models have a driver's airbag, and side airbags may be fitted as an option. Air conditioning is also available as an option.

For the home mechanic, the Vauxhall/Opel Vectra is a straight-forward vehicle to maintain and repair since design features have been incorporated to reduce the actual cost of ownership to a minimum, and most of the items requiring frequent attention are easily accessible.

Your Vauxhall/Opel Vectra manual

The aim of this manual is to help you get the best value from your vehicle. It can do so in several ways. It can help you decide what work must be done (even should you choose to get it done by a garage), provide information on routine maintenance and servicing, and give a logical course of action and diagnosis when random faults occur. However, it is hoped that you will use the manual by tackling the work yourself. On simpler jobs, it may even be quicker than booking the car into a garage and going there twice, to leave and collect it. Perhaps most important, a lot of money can be saved by avoiding the costs a garage must charge to cover its labour and overheads.

The manual has drawings and descriptions to show the function of the various components, so that their layout can be understood. Then the tasks are described and photo-graphed in a clear step-by-step sequence.

References to the 'left' or 'right' are in the sense of a person in the driver's seat, facing forward.

Project vehicles

The main vehicle used in the preparation of this manual, and which appears in many of the photographic sequences, was a Vauxhall Vectra Hatchback with a 2.2 litre petrol engine. Other vehicles included a Hatchback 2.0 litre diesel engine model.

Acknowledgements

Certain illustrations are the copyright of Vauxhall Motors Limited, and are used with their permission. Thanks are also due to Draper Tools Limited, who provided some of the workshop tools, and to all those people at Sparkford who helped in the production of this manual.

We take great pride in the accuracy of information given in this manual, but vehicle manufacturers make alterations and design changes during the production run of a particular vehicle of which they do not inform us. No liability can be accepted by the authors or publishers for loss, damage or injury caused by any errors in, or omissions from, the information given.

Vauxhall Vectra 2.2 LS Saloon

The following pages are intended to help in dealing with common roadside emergencies and breakdowns. You will find more detailed fault finding information at the back of the manual, and repair information in the main chapters.

If your car won't start and the starter motor doesn't turn

- ☐ If it's a model with automatic transmission, make sure the selector is in P or N.
- ☐ Open the bonnet and make sure that the battery terminals are clean and tight.
- ☐ Switch on the headlights and try to start the engine. If the headlights go very dim when you're trying to start, the battery is probably flat. Get out of trouble by jump starting (see next page) using a friend's car.

If your car won't start even though the starter motor turns as normal

- ☐ Is there fuel in the tank?
- ☐ Is there moisture on electrical components under the bonnet? Switch off the ignition, then wipe off any obvious dampness with a dry cloth. Spray a water-repellent aerosol product (WD-40 or equivalent) on ignition and fuel system electrical connectors like those shown in the photos. Pay special attention to the ignition coil wiring connector and HT leads.

A Check the condition and security of the battery connections.

B Check the wiring to the spark plugs and ignition coils.

Check that electrical connections are secure (with the ignition switched off) and spray them with a water dispersant spray like WD40 if you suspect a problem due to damp

C Check the engine wiring loom connectors for security.

D Check the wiring to the map sensor (where fitted).

Jump starting

When jump-starting a car using a booster battery, observe the following precautions:

✔ Before connecting the booster battery, make sure that the ignition is switched off.

✔ Ensure that all electrical equipment (lights, heater, wipers, etc) is switched off.

✔ Take note of any special precautions printed on the battery case.

✔ Make sure that the booster battery is the same voltage as the discharged one in the vehicle.

✔ If the battery is being jump-started from the battery in another vehicle, the two vehicles MUST NOT TOUCH each other.

✔ Make sure that the transmission is in neutral (or PARK, in the case of automatic transmission).

 HAYNES HiNT Jump starting will get you out of trouble, but you must correct whatever made the battery go flat in the first place. There are three possibilities:

1 The battery has been drained by repeated attempts to start, or by leaving the lights on.

2 The charging system is not working properly (alternator drivebelt slack or broken, alternator wiring fault or alternator itself faulty).

3 The battery itself is at fault (electrolyte low, or battery worn out).

1 Connect one end of the red jump lead to the positive (+) terminal of the flat battery

2 Connect the other end of the red lead to the positive (+) terminal of the booster battery.

3 Connect one end of the black jump lead to the negative (-) terminal of the booster battery

4 Connect the other end of the black jump lead to a bolt or bracket on the engine block, well away from the battery, on the vehicle to be started.

5 Make sure that the jump leads will not come into contact with the fan, drive-belts or other moving parts of the engine.

6 Start the engine using the booster battery and run it at idle speed. Switch on the lights, rear window demister and heater blower motor, then disconnect the jump leads in the reverse order of connection. Turn off the lights etc.

Wheel changing

Some of the details shown here will vary according to model. For instance, the location of the spare wheel and jack is not the same on all cars. However, the basic principles apply to all vehicles.

 Warning: Do not change a wheel in a situation where you risk being hit by another vehicle. On busy roads, try to stop in a lay-by or a gateway. Be wary of passing traffic while changing the wheel - it is easy to become distracted by the job in hand.

Preparation

☐ When a puncture occurs, stop as soon as it is safe to do so.
☐ Park on firm level ground, if possible, and well out of the way of other traffic.
☐ Use hazard warning lights if necessary.

☐ If you have one, use a warning triangle to alert other drivers of your presence.
☐ Apply the handbrake and engage first or reverse gear (or Park on models with automatic transmission).

☐ Chock the wheel diagonally opposite the one being removed – a couple of large stones will do for this.
☐ If the ground is soft, use a flat piece of wood to spread the load under the jack.

Changing the wheel

1 On Saloon and Hatchback models the jack and wheelbrace are stowed at the right-hand side of the luggage compartment, behind a cover. On Estate models they are beneath a cover in a compartment on the left-hand side of the luggage compartment.

2 The spare wheel is stored beneath a cover in the luggage compartment. Raise the cover, remove the securing screw and lift out the spare wheel. Place it beneath the sill as a precaution against the jack failing.

3 On models with steel wheels, use the special tool to pull the wheel trim from the wheel. On models with alloy wheels, use the screwdriver provided inserted at the wheel bolt holes to prise off the trim. Where an anti-theft device is fitted, use the tool provided to remove the trim.

4 Loosen each wheel bolt by half a turn.

5 Locate the jack head below the jacking point nearest the wheel to be changed. Pull out the cover; the jacking point is indicated by cut-outs in the sill. Turn the handle until the base of the jack touches the ground ensuring that the jack is vertical. Raise the vehicle until the wheel is clear of the ground. If the tyre is flat make sure that the vehicle is raised sufficiently to allow the spare wheel to be fitted.

7 Lower the vehicle to the ground, then finally tighten the wheel bolts in a diagonal sequence. Refit the wheel trim. Note that the wheel bolts should be tightened to the specified torque at the earliest opportunity.

6 Remove the bolts and lift the wheel from the vehicle. Place it beneath the sill in place of the spare as a precaution against the jack failing. Fit the spare wheel and tighten the bolts moderately with the wheelbrace.

Finally...

☐ Remove the wheel chocks.
☐ Stow the jack and tools in the correct locations in the car.
☐ Check the tyre pressure on the wheel just fitted. If it is low, or if you don't have a pressure gauge with you, drive slowly to the nearest garage and inflate the tyre to the right pressure.
☐ Have the damaged tyre or wheel repaired as soon as possible.

Identifying leaks

Puddles on the garage floor or drive, or obvious wetness under the bonnet or underneath the car, suggest a leak that needs investigating. It can sometimes be difficult to decide where the leak is coming from, especially if the engine bay is very dirty already. Leaking oil or fluid can also be blown rearwards by the passage of air under the car, giving a false impression of where the problem lies.

 Warning: Most automotive oils and fluids are poisonous. Wash them off skin, and change out of contaminated clothing, without delay.

 The smell of a fluid leaking from the car may provide a clue to what's leaking. Some fluids are distinctively coloured. It may help to clean the car carefully and to park it over some clean paper overnight as an aid to locating the source of the leak.
Remember that some leaks may only occur while the engine is running.

Sump oil

Engine oil may leak from the drain plug...

Oil from filter

...or from the base of the oil filter.

Gearbox oil

Gearbox oil can leak from the seals at the inboard ends of the driveshafts.

Antifreeze

Leaking antifreeze often leaves a crystalline deposit like this.

Brake fluid

A leak occurring at a wheel is almost certainly brake fluid.

Power steering fluid

Power steering fluid may leak from the pipe connectors on the steering rack.

Towing

When all else fails, you may find yourself having to get a tow home – or of course you may be helping somebody else. Long-distance recovery should only be done by a garage or breakdown service. For shorter distances, DIY towing using another car is easy enough, but observe the following points:
☐ Use a proper tow-rope – they are not expensive. The vehicle being towed must display an ON TOW sign in its rear window.
☐ Always turn the ignition key to the 'on' position when the vehicle is being towed, so that the steering lock is released, and that the direction indicator and brake lights will work.
☐ Only attach the tow-rope to the towing eyes provided.

☐ Before being towed, release the handbrake and select neutral on the transmission. On models with automatic transmission, special precautions apply. If in doubt, do not tow, or transmission damage may result.
☐ Note that greater-than-usual pedal pressure will be required to operate the brakes, since the vacuum servo unit is only operational with the engine running.
☐ Greater-than-usual steering effort will also be required.
☐ The driver of the car being towed must keep the tow-rope taut at all times to avoid snatching.
☐ Make sure that both drivers know the route before setting off.

☐ Only drive at moderate speeds and keep the distance towed to a minimum. Drive smoothly and allow plenty of time for slowing down at junctions.
☐ A towing eye is provided with the warning triangle and first aid kit in the luggage compartment.
☐ To fit the towing eye, prise the cover from the front bumper, then screw in the towing eye anti-clockwise as far as it will go using the handle of the wheel brace to turn the eye. **Note that the towing eye has a left-hand thread.** A rear towing eye is provided beneath the rear of the vehicle.

Introduction

There are some very simple checks which need only take a few minutes to carry out, but which could save you a lot of inconvenience and expense.

These *Weekly checks* require no great skill or special tools, and the small amount of time they take to perform could prove to be very well spent, for example;

☐ Keeping an eye on tyre condition and pressures, will not only help to stop them wearing out prematurely, but could also save your life.

☐ Many breakdowns are caused by electrical problems. Battery-related faults are particularly common, and a quick check on a regular basis will often prevent the majority of these.

☐ If your car develops a brake fluid leak, the first time you might know about it is when your brakes don't work properly. Checking the level regularly will give advance warning of this kind of problem.

☐ If the oil or coolant levels run low, the cost of repairing any engine damage will be far greater than fixing the leak, for example.

Underbonnet check points

◄ 1.6 litre DOHC petrol

A *Engine oil level dipstick*

B *Engine oil filler cap*

C *Coolant reservoir (expansion tank)*

D *Hydraulic fluid reservoir*

E *Washer fluid reservoir*

F *Battery*

G *Power steering fluid reservoir*

◄ 1.8 litre petrol

A *Engine oil level dipstick*

B *Engine oil filler cap*

C *Coolant reservoir (expansion tank)*

D *Hydraulic fluid reservoir*

E *Washer fluid reservoir*

F *Battery*

G *Power steering fluid reservoir*

◀ **2.2 litre petrol**

A *Engine oil level dipstick*

B *Engine oil filler cap*

C *Coolant reservoir (expansion tank)*

D *Hydraulic fluid reservoir*

E *Washer fluid reservoir*

F *Battery*

G *Power steering fluid reservoir*

◀ **2.0 litre diesel**

A *Engine oil level dipstick*

B *Engine oil filler cap*

C *Coolant reservoir (expansion tank)*

D *Hydraulic fluid reservoir*

E *Washer fluid reservoir*

F *Battery*

G *Power steering fluid reservoir*

Engine oil level

Before you start
✔ Make sure that your car is on level ground.
✔ Check the oil level before the car is driven, or at least 5 minutes after the engine has been switched off.

 HAYNES HiNT *If the oil is checked immediately after driving the vehicle, some of the oil will remain in the upper engine components, resulting in an inaccurate reading on the dipstick!*

The correct oil
Modern engines place great demands on their oil. It is very important that the correct oil for your car is used (See 'Lubricants and fluids').

Car Care
● If you have to add oil frequently, you should check whether you have any oil leaks. Place some clean paper under the car overnight, and check for stains in the morning. If there are no leaks, the engine may be burning oil.

● Always maintain the level between the upper and lower dipstick marks (see photo 3). If the level is too low severe engine damage may occur. Oil seal failure may result if the engine is overfilled by adding too much oil.

1 The dipstick is located on the front of the engine (see *Underbonnet Check Points* for exact location). Withdraw the dipstick.

3 Note the oil level on the end of the dipstick, which should be between the upper (MAX) mark and lower (MIN) mark. Approximately 1.0 litre of oil will raise the level from the lower mark to the upper mark.

2 Using a clean rag or paper towel remove all oil from the dipstick. Insert the clean dipstick into the tube as far as it will go, then withdraw it again.

4 Oil is added through the filler cap. Rotate the cap through a quarter-turn anti-clockwise and withdraw it. Top-up the level. A funnel may help to reduce spillage. Add the oil slowly, checking the level on the dipstick often. Do not overfill.

Coolant level

⚠ **Warning: DO NOT attempt to remove the expansion tank pressure cap when the engine is hot, as there is a very great risk of scalding. Do not leave open containers of coolant about, as it is poisonous.**

Car Care
● With a sealed-type cooling system, adding coolant should not be necessary on a regular basis. If frequent topping-up is required, it is likely there is a leak. Check the radiator, all hoses and joint faces for signs of staining or wetness, and rectify as necessary.

● It is important that antifreeze is used in the cooling system all year round, not just during the winter months. Don't top-up with water alone, as the antifreeze will become too diluted.

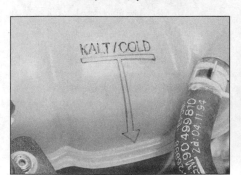

1 The coolant level varies with the temperature of the engine. When the engine is cold, the coolant level should be slightly above the KALT/COLD mark on the side of the tank. When the engine is hot, the level will rise.

2 If topping-up is necessary, **wait until the engine is cold**. Slowly unscrew the expansion tank cap, to release any pressure present in the cooling system, and remove it.

3 Add a mixture of water and antifreeze to the expansion tank until the coolant is up to the KALT/COLD level mark. Refit the cap and tighten it securely.

Brake & clutch fluid level

Warning:
● Hydraulic fluid can harm your eyes and damage painted surfaces, so use extreme caution when handling and pouring it.

● Do not use fluid that has been standing open for some time, as it absorbs moisture from the air, which can cause a dangerous loss of braking effectiveness.

● Make sure that your car is on level ground.
● The fluid level in the reservoir will drop slightly as the brake pads wear down, but the fluid level must never be allowed to drop below the MIN mark.

Safety First!
● If the reservoir requires repeated topping-up this is an indication of a fluid leak somewhere in the system, which should be investigated immediately.

● If a leak is suspected, the car should not be driven until the braking system has been checked. Never take any risks where brakes are concerned.

1 The MAX and MIN marks are indicated on the front of the reservoir. The fluid level must be kept between the marks at all times.

2 If topping-up is necessary, first wipe clean the area around the filler cap to prevent dirt entering the hydraulic system.

3 Carefully add fluid, taking care not to spill it onto the surrounding components. Use only the specified fluid; mixing different types can cause damage to the system. After topping-up to the correct level, securely refit the cap and wipe off any spilt fluid.

Power steering fluid level

Before you start
✔ Park the vehicle on level ground.
✔ Set the steering wheel straight-ahead.
✔ The engine should be turned off.

For the check to be accurate, the steering must not be turned once the engine has been stopped.

Safety First!
● The need for frequent topping-up indicates a leak, which should be investigated immediately.

1 The power steering fluid reservoir is located either on the power steering pump at the right- or left-hand front of the engine, or separately on the rear of the radiator. The fluid level should be checked with the engine stopped.

2 Unscrew the filler cap from the top of the reservoir, and wipe all fluid from the cap dipstick with a clean rag. Refit the filler cap, then remove it again. Note the fluid level on the dipstick.

3 When the engine is cold, the fluid level should be between the upper and lower marks on the dipstick where MIN and MAX marks are provided. Where only one mark is provided, the level should be between the bottom of the dipstick and the mark. Top up the fluid level using the specified type of fluid (do not overfill the reservoir), then refit and tighten the filler cap.

Tyre condition and pressure

It is very important that tyres are in good condition, and at the correct pressure - having a tyre failure at any speed is highly dangerous. Tyre wear is influenced by driving style - harsh braking and acceleration, or fast cornering, will all produce more rapid tyre wear. As a general rule, the front tyres wear out faster than the rears. Interchanging the tyres from front to rear ("rotating" the tyres) may result in more even wear. However, if this is completely effective, you may have the expense of replacing all four tyres at once! Remove any nails or stones embedded in the tread before they penetrate the tyre to cause deflation. If removal of a nail does reveal that the tyre has been punctured, refit the nail so that its point of penetration is marked. Then immediately change the wheel, and have the tyre repaired by a tyre dealer.

Regularly check the tyres for damage in the form of cuts or bulges, especially in the sidewalls. Periodically remove the wheels, and clean any dirt or mud from the inside and outside surfaces. Examine the wheel rims for signs of rusting, corrosion or other damage. Light alloy wheels are easily damaged by "kerbing" whilst parking; steel wheels may also become dented or buckled. A new wheel is very often the only way to overcome severe damage.

New tyres should be balanced when they are fitted, but it may become necessary to re-balance them as they wear, or if the balance weights fitted to the wheel rim should fall off. Unbalanced tyres will wear more quickly, as will the steering and suspension components. Wheel imbalance is normally signified by vibration, particularly at a certain speed (typically around 50 mph). If this vibration is felt only through the steering, then it is likely that just the front wheels need balancing. If, however, the vibration is felt through the whole car, the rear wheels could be out of balance. Wheel balancing should be carried out by a tyre dealer or garage.

1 Tread Depth - visual check
The original tyres have tread wear safety bands (B), which will appear when the tread depth reaches approximately 1.6 mm. The band positions are indicated by a triangular mark on the tyre sidewall (A).

2 Tread Depth - manual check
Alternatively, tread wear can be monitored with a simple, inexpensive device known as a tread depth indicator gauge.

3 Tyre Pressure Check
Check the tyre pressures regularly with the tyres cold. Do not adjust the tyre pressures immediately after the vehicle has been used, or an inaccurate setting will result.

Tyre tread wear patterns

Shoulder Wear

Underinflation (wear on both sides)
Under-inflation will cause overheating of the tyre, because the tyre will flex too much, and the tread will not sit correctly on the road surface. This will cause a loss of grip and excessive wear, not to mention the danger of sudden tyre failure due to heat build-up.
Check and adjust pressures
Incorrect wheel camber (wear on one side)
Repair or renew suspension parts
Hard cornering
Reduce speed!

Centre Wear

Overinflation
Over-inflation will cause rapid wear of the centre part of the tyre tread, coupled with reduced grip, harsher ride, and the danger of shock damage occurring in the tyre casing.
Check and adjust pressures

If you sometimes have to inflate your car's tyres to the higher pressures specified for maximum load or sustained high speed, don't forget to reduce the pressures to normal afterwards.

Uneven Wear

Front tyres may wear unevenly as a result of wheel misalignment. Most tyre dealers and garages can check and adjust the wheel alignment (or "tracking") for a modest charge.
Incorrect camber or castor
Repair or renew suspension parts
Malfunctioning suspension
Repair or renew suspension parts
Unbalanced wheel
Balance tyres
Incorrect toe setting
Adjust front wheel alignment
Note: *The feathered edge of the tread which typifies toe wear is best checked by feel.*

Screen washer fluid level

Screenwash additives not only keep the winscreen clean during foul weather, they also prevent the washer system freezing in cold weather - which is when you are likely to need it most. Don't top up using plain water as the screenwash will become too diluted, and will freeze during cold weather. *On no account use coolant antifreeze in the washer system - this could discolour or damage paintwork.*

1 The reservoir for the windscreen and rear window (where applicable) washer systems is located on the front left-hand side of the engine compartment. If topping-up is necessary, prise open the cap and lift out the dipstick attached to it.

2 When topping-up the reservoir a screen-wash additive should be added in the quantities recommended on the bottle.

Wiper blades

1 Check the condition of the wiper blades; if they are cracked or show any signs of deterioration, or if the glass swept area is smeared, renew them. Wiper blades should be renewed annually.

2 To remove a wiper blade, pull the arm fully away from the glass until it locks. Swivel the blade through 90°, then squeeze the locking clip, and detach the blade from the arm. When fitting the new blade, make sure that the blade locks securely into the arm, and that the blade is orientated correctly.

Battery

Caution: Before carrying out any work on the vehicle battery, read the precautions given in 'Safety first' at the start of this manual.

✔ Make sure that the battery tray is in good condition, and that the clamp is tight. Corrosion on the tray, retaining clamp and the battery itself can be removed with a solution of water and baking soda. Thoroughly rinse all cleaned areas with water. Any metal parts damaged by corrosion should be covered with a zinc-based primer, then painted.

✔ Periodically (approximately every three months), check the charge condition of the battery as described in Chapter 5A.

✔ If the battery is flat, and you need to jump start your vehicle, see *Roadside Repairs*.

1 The battery is located on the left-hand side of the engine compartment. Where fitted, unclip the fabric cover from the top of the battery for access to the terminals. The exterior of the battery should be inspected periodically for damage such as a cracked case or cover.

2 Check the tightness of battery clamps (A) to ensure good electrical connections. You should not be able to move them. Also check each cable (B) for cracks and frayed conductors.

HAYNES HINT

Battery corrosion can be kept to a minimum by applying a layer of petroleum jelly to the clamps and terminals after they are reconnected.

3 If corrosion (white, fluffy deposits) is evident, remove the cables from the battery terminals, clean them with a small wire brush, then refit them. Automotive stores sell a tool for cleaning the battery post . . .

4 . . . as well as the battery cable clamps

Electrical systems

✔ Check all external lights and the horn. Refer to the appropriate Sections of Chapter 12 for details if any of the circuits are found to be inoperative.

✔ Visually check all accessible wiring connectors, harnesses and retaining clips for security, and for signs of chafing or damage.

HAYNES HiNT *If you need to check your brake lights and indicators unaided, back up to a wall or garage door and operate the lights. The reflected light should show if they are working properly.*

1 If a single indicator light, stop-light or headlight has failed, it is likely that a bulb has blown and will need to be replaced. Refer to Chapter 12 for details. If both stop-lights have failed, it is possible that the switch has failed (see Chapter 9).

2 If more than one indicator light or headlight has failed, it is likely that either a fuse has blown or that there is a fault in the circuit (see Chapter 12). The main fuses are located beneath a cover on the driver's side of the facia. Pull up and remove the cover, then pull out the bottom of the fusebox.

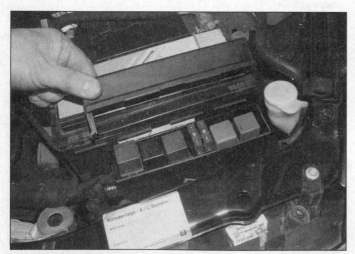

3 Additional fuses and relays are located in the left-hand side of the engine compartment.

4 To replace a blown fuse, remove it, where applicable, using the plastic tool provided. Fit a new fuse of the same rating, available from car accessory shops. It is important that you find the reason that the fuse blew (see *Electrical fault finding* in Chapter 12).

Lubricants and fluids

Engine

Petrol . . . . Multigrade engine oil, viscosity range SAE 10W/30 to 10W/50, to ACEA-A3/B3

Diesel . . . . Multigrade engine oil, viscosity SAE 5W/30 to 10W/50 to ACEA-A3/B3

Cooling system . . . . Ethylene-glycol based antifreeze*

Manual gearbox

F13, F17, F18 and F23 . . . . Vauxhall transmission fluid Cat.No.19 40 768

F35 up to MY2000 . . . . Vauxhall transmission fluid Cat.No.19 40 764

F35 from MY2001 . . . . Vauxhall transmission fluid Cat.No.19 40 768

Automatic transmission . . . . Dexron II type ATF

Power steering reservoir . . . . Dexron II type ATF

Hydraulic fluid reservoir . . . . Hydraulic fluid to SAE J1703, DOT 3 or DOT 4

* Vauxhall/Opel recommend the use of 'green' coolant (90 297 545) in vehicles manufactured before MY2001 (Model Year), and 'red' coolant (09 194 431/19 40 650) in vehicles manufactured from MY2001-on. Do not mix the two types of coolant.

Choosing your engine oil

Engines need oil, not only to lubricate moving parts and minimise wear, but also to maximise power output and to improve fuel economy.

HOW ENGINE OIL WORKS

• Beating friction

Without oil, the moving surfaces inside your engine will rub together, heat up and melt, quickly causing the engine to seize. Engine oil creates a film which separates these moving parts, preventing wear and heat build-up.

• Cooling hot-spots

Temperatures inside the engine can exceed 1000° C. The engine oil circulates and acts as a coolant, transferring heat from the hot-spots to the sump.

• Cleaning the engine internally

Good quality engine oils clean the inside of your engine, collecting and dispersing combustion deposits and controlling them until they are trapped by the oil filter or flushed out at oil change.

OIL CARE - FOLLOW THE CODE

To handle and dispose of used engine oil safely, always:

OIL CARE

OIL BANK LINE
0800 66 33 66
www.oilbankline.org.uk

• *Avoid skin contact with used engine oil. Repeated or prolonged contact can be harmful.*
• *Dispose of used oil and empty packs in a responsible manner in an authorised disposal site. Call 0800 663366 to find the one nearest to you. Never tip oil down drains or onto the ground.*

Note: *Pressures apply to original-equipment tyres only, and may vary if any other make or type of tyre is fitted; check with the tyre manufacturer or supplier for correct pressures if necessary. The pressures are also given on the inside of the fuel filler flap. Tyre pressures should be checked when the tyres are cold (before a journey); do not forget to check the spare.*

	Front	Rear

1999 and 2000 model year vehicles - 195/65R15, 205/60R15 and 205/55R16 tyres

1.6 and 1.8 litre petrol and 2.0 Di 16V engines

	Front	Rear
Up to 3 persons - all models	28 psi (1.9 bars)	28 psi (1.9 bars)
Full load:		
Saloon and Hatchback models	29 psi (2.0 bars)	38 psi (2.6 bars)
Estate models	29 psi (2.0 bars)	42 psi (2.9 bars)

2.0 litre petrol and 2.0 DTi 16V engines

	Front	Rear
Up to 3 persons - all models	30 psi (2.1 bars)	30 psi (2.1 bars)
Full load:		
Saloon and Hatchback models	32 psi (2.2 bars)	41 psi (2.8 bars)
Estate models	32 psi (2.2 bars)	45 psi (3.1 bars)

2001-on model year vehicles - 195/65R15, 205/60R15 and 205/55R16 tyres

1.6 and 1.8 litre petrol engines

	Front	Rear
Up to 3 persons - all models	28 psi (1.9 bars)	28 psi (1.9 bars)
Full load:		
Saloon and Hatchback models	30 psi (2.1 bars)	39 psi (2.7 bars)
Estate models	29 psi (2.0 bars)	42 psi (2.9 bars)

2.0 DTi 16V and 2.2 litre petrol and Diesel engines

	Front	Rear
Up to 3 persons - all models	32 psi (2.2 bars)	32 psi (2.2 bars)
Full load:		
Saloon and Hatchback models	33 psi (2.3 bars)	42 psi (2.9 bars)
Estate models	32 psi (2.2 bars)	45 psi (3.1 bars)

2001-on model year vehicles - 215/45ZR17 tyres

1.6 and 1.8 litre petrol engines

	Front	Rear
Up to 3 persons - all models	30 psi (2.1 bars)	33 psi (2.3 bars)
Full load:		
Saloon and Hatchback models	33 psi (2.3 bars)	42 psi (2.9 bars)
Estate models	32 psi (2.2 bars)	45 psi (3.1 bars)

2.0 DTi 16V and 2.2 litre Diesel engines

	Front	Rear
Up to 3 persons	35 psi (2.4 bars)	38 psi (2.6 bars)
Full load:		
Saloon and Hatchback models	36 psi (2.5 bars)	45 psi (3.1 bars)
Estate models	36 psi (2.5 bars)	49 psi (3.4 bars)

2.2 litre petrol engine

	Front	Rear
Up to 3 persons:		
Saloon and Hatchback models	33 psi (2.3 bars)	38 psi (2.6 bars)
Estate models	35 psi (2.4 bars)	38 psi (2.6 bars)
Full load:		
Saloon and Hatchback models	36 psi (2.5 bars)	45 psi (3.1 bars)
Estate models	36 psi (2.5 bars)	49 psi (3.4 bars)

Chapter 1 Part A:
Routine maintenance and servicing – petrol engine models

Contents

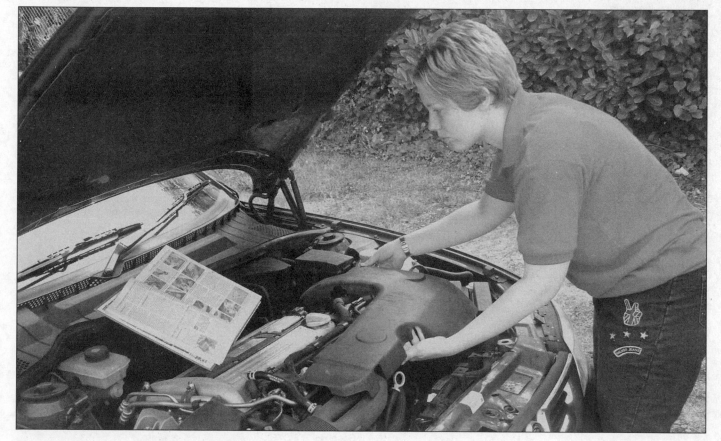

Degrees of difficulty

Easy, suitable for novice with little experience	**Fairly easy,** suitable for beginner with some experience	**Fairly difficult,** suitable for competent DIY mechanic	**Difficult,** suitable for experienced DIY mechanic	**Very difficult,** suitable for expert DIY or professional

Lubricants and fluids

Refer to *Weekly checks* on page 0•19

Capacities

Engine oil (including oil filter)

1.6 litre engine	3.25 litres
1.8 litre engine	4.25 litres
2.0 litre engine	4.25 litres
2.2 litre engine	5.0 litres
Difference between MIN and MAX on dipstick	1.0 litre

Cooling system

1.6 (X16SZR) engine:

Manual transmission without air conditioning	6.1 litres
Manual transmission with air conditioning	6.4 litres

1.6 (except X16SZR) and 1.8 litre engines:

Manual transmission without air conditioning	6.7 litres
Manual transmission with air conditioning	7.0 litres
Automatic transmission with or without air conditioning	6.9 litres

2.0 litre engine:

Manual transmission with or without air conditioning	7.2 litres
Automatic transmission with or without air conditioning	7.1 litres

2.2 litre engine:

Without air conditioning	6.9 litres
With air conditioning	7.0 litres

Transmission

Manual transmission:

F13 transmission unit	1.6 litres
F17 transmission unit	1.6 litres
F18 transmission unit	1.9 litres
F23 transmission unit	1.55 litres
Automatic transmission (at fluid change)	3.0 to 3.5 litres

Washer fluid reservoir

Without headlight washers	2.6 litres
With headlight washers	5.5 litres

Fuel tank

All models	60 litres

Engine Identification

Manufacturer's code	Engine type
X16SZR	1.6 litre SOHC petrol engine
X16XEL	1.6 litre DOHC petrol engine
X18XE	1.8 litre DOHC petrol engine
X18XE1	1.8 litre DOHC petrol engine
X20XEV	2.0 litre DOHC petrol engine
Z16XE	1.6 litre DOHC petrol engine
Z18XE	1.8 litre DOHC petrol engine
Z22SE	2.2 litre DOHC petrol engine

Cooling system

Antifreeze mixture:

50% antifreeze	Protection down to –37°C
55% antifreeze	Protection down to –45°C

Note: *Refer to antifreeze manufacturer for latest recommendations.*

Ignition system

Spark plugs:	Type	Gap
1.6, 1.8 and 2.0 litre	Bosch FLR8LD+U	1.0 mm
2.2 litre	Bosch HLR 8 STEX	1.1 mm

Brakes

Friction material minimum thickness (including backing plate):

Front brake pads	7.5 mm
Rear brake pads	6.7 mm
Rear brake shoes	1.0 mm lining thickness or 0.5 mm above rivet heads
Minimum handbrake shoe friction material thickness (lining only)	1.0 mm

Torque wrench settings

	Nm	lbf ft
Automatic transmission drain plug	40	30
Engine oil filter:		
Canister-type	15	11
Element-type retaining cap	25	18
Roadwheel bolts	110	81
Spark plug HT lead cover	3	2
Spark plugs	25	18
Sump drain plug:		
1.6, 1.8 and 2.0 litre engines:		
With rubber seal ring	10	7
With metal seal ring	45	33
2.2 litre engines	25	18

Maintenance schedule

The maintenance intervals in this manual are provided with the assumption that you, not the dealer, will be carrying out the work. These are the minimum maintenance intervals recommended by us for vehicles driven daily. If you wish to keep your vehicle in peak condition at all times, you may wish to perform some of these procedures more often. We encourage frequent maintenance, because it enhances the efficiency, performance and resale value of your vehicle.

If the vehicle is driven in dusty areas, used to tow a trailer, or driven frequently at slow speeds (idling in traffic) or on short journeys, more frequent maintenance intervals are recommended.

When the vehicle is new, it should be serviced by a factory-authorised dealer service department, in order to preserve the factory warranty.

Every 10 000 miles (15 000 km) or 6 months, whichever comes first

☐ Renew the engine oil and filter (Section 3)

Note: *Vauxhall recommends that the engine oil and filter are changed every 20 000 miles (30 000 km) or 12 months. However, oil and filter changes are good for the engine and we recommend that the oil and filter are renewed more frequently, especially if the vehicle is used on a lot of short journeys.*

Every 20 000 miles (30 000 km) or 12 months, whichever comes first

☐ Check the condition of the auxiliary drivebelt and tensioner (Section 4)
☐ Check the front/rear brake pads and discs for wear (Section 5)
☐ Check and adjust the handbrake (Section 6)
☐ Check the rear brake shoes for wear (Section 7)
☐ Check the steering and suspension components for condition and security (Section 8)
☐ Check the rear suspension level control system (where applicable) (Section 9)
☐ Check the body and underbody for corrosion protection (Section 10)
☐ Check all components, pipes and hoses for fluid leaks (Section 11)
☐ Check the condition of the driveshaft gaiters (Section 12)
☐ Check and if necessary adjust the headlight beam alignment (Section 13)
☐ Check the roadwheel bolts are tightened to the specified torque (Section 14)
☐ Lubricate all door locks and hinges, door stops, bonnet lock and release, and tailgate lock and hinges (Section 15)
☐ Check the operation of all electrical systems (Section 16)
☐ Carry out a road test (Section 17)

Every 20 000 miles (30 000 km) or 2 years, whichever comes first

☐ Renew the pollen filter element (Section 18)

Note: *If the vehicle is used in dusty conditions, the pollen filter should be renewed more frequently.*

Every 40 000 miles (60 000 km) or 2 years, whichever comes first

☐ Renew the remote control batteries (Section 19)

Every 2 years, regardless of mileage

☐ Renew the hydraulic fluid (Section 20)
☐ Renew the coolant (Section 21)
☐ Exhaust emission test (Section 22)

Every 40 000 miles (60 000 km) or 4 years, whichever comes first

☐ Renew the air cleaner element (Section 23)
☐ Renew the spark plugs and check the ignition system (Section 24)
☐ Renew the timing belt and tensioner roller (Section 25)
☐ Renew the fuel filter (Section 26)
☐ Renew the automatic transmission fluid (Section 27)
☐ Check the rear brake drums for wear (Section 28)

Underbonnet view of a 1.6 litre DOHC engine model

1 Engine oil filler cap
2 Air cleaner
3 Front suspension strut upper mounting
4 Hydraulic fluid reservoir
5 Auxiliary fuse and relay box
6 Cooling system expansion tank
7 Battery
8 Washer fluid reservoir
9 Radiator
10 Engine oil level dipstick
11 Air injection valve
12 Radiator top hose
13 Thermostat housing
14 Power steering fluid reservoir

Front underbody view of a 1.6 litre DOHC engine model

1 Exhaust front downpipe
2 Oil filter
3 Electric cooling fan motor
4 Engine oil drain plug
5 Front suspension lower arm
6 Steering track rod
7 Driveshaft
8 Subframe
9 Manual transmission
10 Washer fluid reservoir

Underbonnet view of a 1.8 litre engine model

1 Engine oil filler cap
2 Front suspension strut upper mounting
3 Hydraulic fluid reservoir
4 Air cleaner
5 Auxiliary fuse and relay box
6 Cooling system expansion tank
7 Battery
8 Washer fluid reservoir
9 Auxiliary fuse/relay box
10 Radiator
11 Auxiliary relay box
12 Power steering fluid reservoir
13 Radiator top hose
14 Engine oil level dipstick

Underbonnet view of a 2.2 litre engine model

1 Engine oil filler cap
2 Engine oil level dipstick
3 Inlet air temperature sensor
4 Air cleaner
5 Front suspension strut upper mountings
6 Hydraulic fluid reservoir
7 Auxiliary fuse and relay box
8 Cooling system expansion tank
9 Brake ABS unit
10 Spark plug low tension wiring connector
11 Exhaust gas recirculation (EGR) valve
12 Engine management ECU
13 Power steering pump hydraulic fluid reservoir
14 Windscreen/headlight washer fluid reservoir
15 Battery
16 Transmission
17 Alternator
18 Radiator top hose

Front underbody view of a 2.2 litre engine model

1 Air conditioning compressor
2 Engine oil drain plug
3 Electric cooling fan
4 Transmission
5 Windscreen/headlight washer fluid reservoir
6 Front brake calipers
7 Front suspension lower arms
8 Steering track rods
9 Front suspension subframe
10 Exhaust system downpipe
11 Driveshaft
12 Horn

Typical rear underbody

1 Exhaust rear silencer
2 Rear towing eye
3 Rear suspension crossmember
4 Rear suspension strut
5 Rear suspension lower arm
6 Fuel filter
7 Rear suspension trailing arm
8 Fuel tank

1 General information

1 This Chapter is designed to help the home mechanic maintain his/her vehicle for safety, economy, long life and peak performance.

2 The Chapter contains a master maintenance schedule, followed by Sections dealing specifically with each task in the schedule. Visual checks, adjustments, component renewal and other helpful items are included. Refer to the accompanying illustrations of the engine compartment and the underside of the vehicle for the locations of the various components.

3 Servicing your vehicle in accordance with the mileage/time maintenance schedule and the following Sections will provide a planned maintenance programme, which should result in a long and reliable service life. This is a comprehensive plan, so maintaining some items but not others at the specified service intervals, will not produce the same results.

4 As you service your vehicle, you will discover that many of the procedures can – and should – be grouped together, because of the particular procedure being performed, or because of the proximity of two otherwise-unrelated components to one another. For example, if the vehicle is raised for any reason, the exhaust can be inspected at the same time as the suspension and steering components.

5 The first step in this maintenance programme is to prepare yourself before the actual work begins. Read through all the Sections relevant to the work to be carried out, then make a list and gather all the parts and tools required. If a problem is encountered, seek advice from a parts specialist, or a dealer service department.

2 Regular maintenance

1 If, from the time the vehicle is new, the routine maintenance schedule is followed closely, and frequent checks are made of fluid levels and high-wear items, as suggested throughout this manual, the engine will be kept in relatively good running condition, and the need for additional work will be minimised.

2 It is possible that there will be times when the engine is running poorly due to the lack of regular maintenance. This is even more likely if a used vehicle, which has not received regular and frequent maintenance checks, is purchased. In such cases, additional work may need to be carried out, outside of the regular maintenance intervals.

3 If engine wear is suspected, a compression test (refer to the appropriate part of Chapter 2) will provide valuable information regarding the overall performance of the main internal components. Such a test can be used as a basis to decide on the extent of the work to be carried out. If, for example, a compression test indicates serious internal engine wear, conventional maintenance as described in this Chapter will not greatly improve the performance of the engine, and may prove a waste of time and money, unless extensive overhaul work is carried out first.

4 The following series of operations are those most often required to improve the performance of a generally poor-running engine:

Primary operations

a) Clean, inspect and test the battery (refer to 'Weekly checks').
b) Check all the engine-related fluids (refer to 'Weekly checks').
c) Check the condition and tension of the auxiliary drivebelt (Section 4).
d) Renew the spark plugs (Section 24).
e) Check the condition of the air filter, and renew if necessary (Section 23).
f) Renew the fuel filter (Section 26).
g) Check the condition of all hoses, and check for fluid leaks (Section 11).

5 If the above operations do not prove fully effective, carry out the following secondary operations:

Secondary operations

All items listed under *Primary operations*, plus the following:

a) Check the charging system (refer to Chapter 5A).
b) Check the ignition system (refer to Chapter 5B).
c) Check the fuel system (refer to the appropriate part of Chapter 4).

Every 10 000 miles (15 000 km) or 6 months

3 Engine oil and filter renewal

1 Frequent oil and filter changes are the most important preventative maintenance procedures which can be undertaken by the DIY owner. As engine oil ages, it becomes diluted and contaminated, which leads to premature engine wear.

2 Before starting this procedure, gather together all the necessary tools and materials. Also make sure that you have plenty of clean rags and newspapers handy, to mop up any spills. Ideally, the engine oil should be warm, as it will drain more easily, and more built-up sludge will be removed with it. Take care not to touch the exhaust or any other hot parts of the engine when working under the vehicle. To avoid any possibility of scalding, and to protect yourself from possible skin irritants and other harmful contaminants in used engine oils, it is advisable to wear gloves when carrying out this work.

3 Firmly apply the handbrake then jack up the front of the vehicle and support it on axle stands (see *Jacking and vehicle support*). Where necessary, remove the engine undertray.

4 Remove the oil filler cap **(see illustration)**.

5 Using a spanner, or preferably a suitable socket and bar, slacken the drain plug about half a turn. Position the draining container under the drain plug, then remove the plug completely **(see Haynes Hint)**.

6 Allow some time for the oil to drain, noting that it may be necessary to reposition the container as the oil flow slows to a trickle.

3.4 Removing the oil filler cap

HAYNES HINT

As the drain plug releases from the threads, move it away quickly so that the stream of oil running out of the sump goes into the drain pan and not up your sleeve.

3.8 Oil filter retaining cap (Z22SE engine)

3.9a Using an oil filter removal tool to slacken the filter (viewed from underneath the vehicle)

7 After all the oil has drained, wipe the drain plug and the sealing washer with a clean rag. Examine the condition of the sealing washer, and renew it if it shows signs of scoring or other damage which may prevent an oil-tight seal. Clean the area around the drain plug opening, and refit the plug complete with the washer and tighten it to the specified torque.

8 Move the container into position under the oil filter. On 1.6 litre models the canister-type oil filter is located on the front of the cylinder block. On X18XE and 2.0 litre engines the canister-type oil filter is located on the right-hand end of the rear of the engine, where it is screwed onto the oil pump housing. On X18XE1 and 2.2 litre engines, the element-type oil filter is located beneath a threaded cap on the front of the cylinder block, near the base of the oil level dipstick tube **(see illustration)**.

9 Where a canister-type oil filter is fitted, use an oil filter removal tool to slacken the filter initially, then unscrew it by hand the rest of the way. Empty the oil from the old filter into the container. Where an element-type oil filter is fitted, unscrew the filter cap and withdraw it,

together with the element, then separate the element, and remove the O-ring seal from the cap **(see illustrations)**.

10 Use a clean rag to remove all oil, dirt and sludge from the filter sealing area on the engine. Where applicable, clean the oil filter housing and cap, and inspect the sealing ring for condition.

11 On the canister-type filter, apply a light coating of clean engine oil to the sealing ring on the new filter, then screw the filter into position on the engine. Tighten the filter firmly by hand only – **do not** use any tools. If a genuine filter is being fitted and the special oil filter tool (a socket which fits over the end of the filter) is available, tighten the filter to the specified torque.

12 On the element-type filter, locate a new O-ring seal in the groove on the retaining cap, then locate the new element in the cap and insert them both in the filter housing. Screw on the cap and tighten to the specified torque.

13 Remove the old oil and all tools from under the vehicle then lower the vehicle to the ground.

14 Fill the engine through the filler hole, using the correct grade and type of oil (refer to *Weekly Checks* for details of topping-up). Pour in half the specified quantity of oil first, then wait a few minutes for the oil to drain into the sump. Continue to add oil, a small quantity at a time, until the level is up to the lower mark on the dipstick. Adding approximately a further 1.0 litre will bring the level up to the upper mark on the dipstick.

15 Start the engine and run it for a few minutes, while checking for leaks around the oil filter seal and the sump drain plug. Note that there may be a delay of a few seconds before the low oil pressure warning light goes out when the engine is first started, as the oil circulates through the new oil filter and the engine oil galleries before the pressure builds-up.

16 Stop the engine, and wait a few minutes for the oil to settle in the sump once more. With the new oil circulated and the filter now completely full, recheck the level on the dipstick, and add more oil as necessary.

17 Dispose of the used engine oil safely with reference to *General repair procedures*.

3.9b Unscrew the cap . . .

3.9c . . . and remove from the housing . . .

3.9d . . . then separate the element from the cap

Every 20 000 miles (30 000 km) or 12 months

4 Auxiliary drivebelt and tensioner – check and renewal

Checking

1 Due to their function and material make-up, drivebelts are prone to failure after a long period of time and should therefore be inspected regularly.

2 With the engine stopped, inspect the full length of the drivebelt for cracks and separation of the belt plies. It will be necessary to turn the engine (using a spanner or socket and bar on the crankshaft pulley bolt) in order to move the belt from the pulleys so that the belt can be inspected thoroughly. Twist the belt between the pulleys so that both sides can be viewed. Also check for fraying, and glazing which gives the belt a shiny appearance. Check the pulleys for nicks, cracks, distortion and corrosion.

3 Check the position of the drivebelt tensioner assembly arm, the arm should be in between the stops on the backplate and should be free to move (see illustration).

4.3 Check the auxiliary drivebelt tensioner arm indicator (2) is correctly positioned between the stops (1 and 3) on the backplate

4.10a Auxiliary drivebelt configuration on models without air conditioning

4 If the belt shows signs of wear or damage, or the tensioner arm is against the stop, the belt and tensioner must be renewed.

Renewal

5 To remove the drivebelt, first remove the air intake pipe, the intake hose, or air cleaner complete, according to model.

6 On X16SZR, X16XEL, Z16XE, X18XE1 and Z18XE engines disconnect the wiring from the coolant temperature sensor.

Models with air conditioning

7 Jack up the front of the vehicle and support it on axle stands (see *Jacking and vehicle support*).

8 Remove the engine top cover, then support the engine with a trolley jack until all tension is relieved from the right-hand engine mounting. Unscrew the upper bolt from the right-hand engine mounting bracket (note that the bolt cannot be removed completely), then unbolt the bracket from the engine so that there is sufficient clearance to remove the auxiliary drivebelt.

9 Remove the right-hand front roadwheel and the right-hand engine compartment side cover.

All models

10 Prior to removal, make a note of the correct routing of the belt around the various pulleys (see illustrations). If the belt is to be re-used, also mark the direction of rotation on the belt to ensure the belt is refitted the same way around.

11 Using a suitable spanner or socket fitted to the tensioner pulley centre bolt, lever the tensioner clockwise, away from the belt until there is sufficient slack to enable the belt to be slipped off the pulleys. Carefully release the tensioner pulley until it is against its stop then remove the belt from the vehicle.

12 To renew the tensioner, refer to the appropriate part of Chapter 2.

13 Fit the new tensioner and auxiliary drivebelt using a reversal of the removal procedure. Manoeuvre the belt into position,

4.10b Auxiliary drivebelt configuration on models with air conditioning

routing it correctly around the pulleys; if the original belt is being fitted, use the marks made prior to removal to ensure it is fitted the correct way around.

5 Front & rear brake pad and disc check

1 Firmly apply the handbrake, then jack up the front and rear of the vehicle and support it securely on axle stands (see *Jacking and vehicle support*). Remove the roadwheels.

2 For a quick check, the pad thickness can be carried out via the inspection hole on the caliper (see Haynes Hint). Using a steel rule, measure the thickness of the pad lining including the backing plate. This must not be less than that indicated in the Specifications.

3 The view through the caliper inspection hole gives a rough indication of the state of the brake pads. For a comprehensive check, the brake pads should be removed and cleaned. The operation of the caliper can then also be checked, and the condition of the brake disc itself can be fully examined on both sides. Chapter 9 contains a detailed description of how the brake disc should be checked for wear and/or damage.

4 If any pad's friction material is worn to the specified thickness or less, *all four pads must be renewed as a set*. Refer to Chapter 9 for details.

5 On completion, refit the roadwheels and lower the vehicle to the ground.

6 Handbrake check and adjustment

Refer to Chapter 9.

HAYNES HiNT

For a quick check, the thickness of friction material remaining on the inner brake pad can be measured through the aperture in the caliper body.

8.4 Check for wear in the hub bearings by grasping the wheel and trying to rock it

7 Rear brake shoe check

Note: *This Section applies only to models fitted with rear drum brakes.*
Refer to Chapter 9.

8 Suspension and steering check

Front suspension and steering

1 Raise the front of the vehicle, and securely support it on axle stands (see *Jacking and vehicle support*).
2 Visually inspect the balljoint dust covers and the steering rack-and-pinion gaiters for splits, chafing or deterioration. Any wear of these components will cause loss of lubricant, together with dirt and water entry, resulting in rapid deterioration of the balljoints or steering gear.
3 Check the power steering fluid hoses for chafing or deterioration, and the pipe and hose unions for fluid leaks. Also check for signs of fluid leakage under pressure from the steering gear rubber gaiters, which would indicate failed fluid seals within the steering gear.
4 Grasp the roadwheel at the 12 o'clock and 6 o'clock positions, and try to rock it **(see illustration)**. Very slight free play may be felt, but if the movement is appreciable, further investigation is necessary to determine the source. Continue rocking the wheel while an assistant depresses the footbrake. If the movement is now eliminated or significantly reduced, it is likely that the hub bearings are at fault. If the free play is still evident with the footbrake depressed, then there is wear in the suspension joints or mountings.
5 Now grasp the wheel at the 9 o'clock and 3 o'clock positions, and try to rock it as before. Any movement felt now may again be caused by wear in the hub bearings or the steering track rod balljoints. If the outer balljoint is worn, the visual movement will be obvious. If the inner joint is suspect, it can be felt by placing a hand over the rack-and-pinion

rubber gaiter and gripping the track rod. If the wheel is now rocked, movement will be felt at the inner joint if wear has taken place.
6 Using a large screwdriver or flat bar, check for wear in the suspension mounting bushes by levering between the relevant suspension component and its attachment point. Some movement is to be expected, as the mountings are made of rubber, but excessive wear should be obvious. Also check the condition of any visible rubber bushes, looking for splits, cracks or contamination of the rubber.
7 With the car standing on its wheels, have an assistant turn the steering wheel back-and-forth, about an eighth of a turn each way. There should be very little, if any, lost movement between the steering wheel and roadwheels. If this is not the case, closely observe the joints and mountings previously described. In addition, check the steering column universal joints for wear, and also check the rack-and-pinion steering gear itself.

Rear suspension

8 Chock the front wheels, then jack up the rear of the vehicle and support securely on axle stands (see *Jacking and vehicle support*).
9 Working as described previously for the front suspension, check the rear hub bearings, the suspension bushes and the strut or shock absorber mountings (as applicable) for wear.

Shock absorber

10 Check for any signs of fluid leakage around the shock absorber body, or from the rubber gaiter around the piston rod. Should any fluid be noticed, the shock absorber is defective internally, and should be renewed.
Note: *Shock absorbers should always be renewed in pairs on the same axle.*
11 The efficiency of the shock absorber may be checked by bouncing the vehicle at each corner. Generally speaking, the body will return to its normal position and stop after being depressed. If it rises and returns on a rebound, the shock absorber is probably suspect. Also examine the shock absorber upper and lower mountings for any signs of wear.

HAYNES HiNT

A leak in the cooling system will usually show up as white- or rust-coloured deposits on the area adjoining the leak.

9 Rear suspension level control system check

Where fitted on Estate models, check that the rear suspension self-levelling control system operates correctly. In the event of a suspected fault, have the system checked by a Vauxhall/Opel dealer.

10 Body corrosion check

This work should be carried out by a Vauxhall/Opel dealer in order to validate the vehicle warranty. The work includes a thorough inspection of the vehicle paintwork and underbody for damage and corrosion.

11 Hose and fluid leak check

1 Visually inspect the engine joint faces, gaskets and seals for any signs of water or oil leaks. Pay particular attention to the areas around the cylinder head cover, cylinder head, oil filter and sump joint faces. Bear in mind that, over a period of time, some very slight seepage from these areas is to be expected – what you are really looking for is any indication of a serious leak. Should a leak be found, renew the offending gasket or oil seal by referring to the appropriate Chapters in this manual. Similarly, check for leaks around the transmission casing.
2 Also check the security and condition of all the engine-related pipes and hoses, and all braking system pipes and hoses, and fuel lines. Ensure that all cable ties or securing clips are in place, and in good condition. Clips which are broken or missing can lead to chafing of the hoses, pipes or wiring, which could cause more serious problems in the future.
3 Carefully check the radiator hoses and heater hoses along their entire length. Renew any hose which is cracked, swollen or deteriorated. Cracks will show up better if the hose is squeezed. Pay close attention to the hose clips that secure the hoses to the cooling system components. Hose clips can pinch and puncture hoses, resulting in cooling system leaks. If the crimped-type hose clips are used, it may be a good idea to replace them with standard worm-drive clips.
4 Inspect all the cooling system components (hoses, joint faces, etc) for leaks **(see Haynes Hint)**.
5 Where any problems are found on system components, renew the component or gasket with reference to Chapter 3.
6 With the vehicle raised, inspect the fuel tank and filler neck for punctures, cracks and other damage. The connection between the

filler neck and tank is especially critical. Sometimes a rubber filler neck or connecting hose will leak due to loose retaining clamps or deteriorated rubber.

7 Carefully check all rubber hoses and metal fuel lines leading away from the fuel tank. Check for loose connections, deteriorated hoses, crimped lines, and other damage. Pay particular attention to the vent pipes and hoses, which often loop up around the filler neck and can become blocked or crimped. Follow the lines to the front of the vehicle, carefully inspecting them all the way. Renew damaged sections as necessary. Similarly, whilst the vehicle is raised, take the opportunity to inspect the exhaust system and all underbody brake fluid pipes and hoses.

8 From within the engine compartment, check the security of all fuel, vacuum and brake hose attachments and pipe unions, and inspect all hoses for kinks, chafing and deterioration.

9 Check the condition of the power steering and, where applicable, the automatic transmission fluid pipes and hoses.

12 Driveshaft gaiter check

1 With the vehicle raised and securely supported on stands, turn the steering onto full lock then slowly rotate the roadwheel. Inspect the condition of the outer constant velocity (CV) joint rubber gaiters while squeezing the gaiters to open out the folds (see illustration). Check for signs of cracking, splits or deterioration of the rubber which may allow the grease to escape and lead to water and grit entry into the joint. Also check the security and condition of the retaining clips. Repeat these checks on the inner CV joints. If any damage or deterioration is found, the gaiters should be renewed as described in Chapter 8.

2 At the same time, check the general condition of the CV joints themselves by first holding the driveshaft and attempting to rotate the wheel. Repeat this check by holding the inner joint and attempting to rotate the

12.1 Check the condition of the driveshaft gaiters (1) and the retaining clips (2)

driveshaft. Any appreciable movement indicates wear in the joints, wear in the driveshaft splines or loose driveshaft retaining nut.

13 Headlight beam alignment check

Refer to Chapter 12 for details

14 Wheel bolt tightness check

1 Remove the wheel trims and check the tightness of all the wheel bolts, using a torque wrench.

2 Refit the wheel trims on completion.

15 Hinge and lock lubrication

1 Work around the vehicle and lubricate the hinges of the bonnet, doors and tailgate with a light machine oil.

2 Lightly lubricate the bonnet release mechanism and exposed section of inner cable with a smear of grease.

3 Check the security and operation of all hinges, latches and locks, adjusting them where required. Check the operation of the central locking system.

4 Check the condition and operation of the tailgate struts, renewing them both if either is leaking or no longer able to support the tailgate securely when raised.

16 Electrical systems check

1 Check the operation of all electrical equipment, ie, lights, direction indicators, horn, wash/wipe system, etc. Refer to the appropriate Sections of Chapter 12 for details if any of the circuits are found to be inoperative.

2 Visually check all accessible wiring connectors, harnesses and retaining clips for security, and for signs of chafing or damage. Rectify any faults found.

17 Road test

Instruments/ electrical equipment

1 Check the operation of all instruments and electrical equipment.

2 Make sure that all instruments read correctly, and switch on all electrical

equipment in turn, to check that it functions properly.

Steering and suspension

3 Check for any abnormalities in the steering, suspension, handling or road 'feel'.

4 Drive the vehicle, and check that there are no unusual vibrations or noises.

5 Check that the steering feels positive, with no excessive 'sloppiness', or roughness, and check for any suspension noises when cornering and driving over bumps.

Drivetrain

6 Check the performance of the engine, clutch, transmission and driveshafts.

7 Listen for any unusual noises from the engine, clutch and transmission.

8 Make sure that the engine runs smoothly when idling, and that there is no hesitation when accelerating.

9 Check that, where applicable, the clutch action is smooth and progressive, that the drive is taken up smoothly, and that the pedal travel is not excessive. Also listen for any noises when the clutch pedal is depressed.

10 Check that all gears can be engaged smoothly without noise, and that the gear lever action is smooth and not abnormally vague or 'notchy'.

11 On automatic transmission models, make sure that all gearchanges occur smoothly, without snatching, and without an increase in engine speed between changes. Check that all of the gear positions can be selected with the vehicle at rest. If any problems are found, they should be referred to a Vauxhall/Opel dealer.

12 Listen for a metallic clicking sound from the front of the vehicle, as the vehicle is driven slowly in a circle with the steering on full-lock. Carry out this check in both directions. If a clicking noise is heard, this indicates wear in a driveshaft joint (see Chapter 8).

Braking system

13 Make sure that the vehicle does not pull to one side when braking, and that the wheels do not lock prematurely when braking hard.

14 Check that there is no vibration through the steering when braking.

15 Check that the handbrake operates correctly, without excessive movement of the lever, and that it holds the vehicle stationary on a slope.

16 Test the operation of the brake servo unit as follows. Depress the footbrake four or five times to exhaust the vacuum, then start the engine. As the engine starts, there should be a noticeable 'give' in the brake pedal as vacuum builds-up. Allow the engine to run for at least two minutes, and then switch it off. If the brake pedal is now depressed again, it should be possible to detect a hiss from the servo as the pedal is depressed. After about four or five applications, no further hissing should be heard, and the pedal should feel considerably harder.

Every 20 000 miles (30 000 km) or 2 years

18 Pollen filter renewal

1 Open the bonnet, and pull up the rubber weatherseal from the flange at the rear of the engine compartment **(see illustration)**.
2 Open the cover in the water deflector for access to the pollen filter **(see illustration)**.
3 Release the clips from each end, then lift

out the filter **(see illustration)**.
4 Fit the new filter using a reversal of the removal procedure; make sure that the marking is visible on the right-hand end of the filter, as viewed through the cover.

18.1 Pull up the rubber weatherseal ...

18.2 ... then open the cover ...

18.3 ... and lift out the pollen filter

Every 40 000 miles (60 000 km) or 2 years

19 Remote control battery renewal

Note: *The following procedure must be performed within 3 minutes, otherwise the remote control unit will have to be reprogrammed.*
1 Using a screwdriver, prise the battery cover from the ignition key fob **(see illustrations)**.
2 Note how the circular battery is fitted, then carefully remove it from the contacts.
3 Fit the new battery and refit the cover making sure that it clips fully onto the base.

19.1a Prise off the battery cover ...

19.1b ... and remove the circular battery

Every 2 years, regardless of mileage

20 Hydraulic fluid renewal

⚠️ **Warning: Hydraulic fluid can harm your eyes and damage painted surfaces, so use extreme caution when handling and pouring it. Do not use fluid that has been standing open for some time, as it absorbs moisture from the air. Excess moisture can cause a dangerous loss of braking effectiveness.**
Note: *The brake and clutch hydraulic systems share a reservoir.*

1 The procedure is similar to that for the bleeding of the hydraulic systems as described in Chapters 6 and 9. Renew the fluid in the braking system first, then the clutch fluid.
2 Working as described in Chapter 9, open the first bleed screw in the sequence, and pump the brake pedal gently until nearly all the old fluid has been emptied from the master cylinder reservoir. Top-up to the MAX level with new fluid, and continue pumping until only the new fluid remains in the reservoir, and new fluid can be seen emerging from the bleed screw. Tighten the screw, and top the reservoir level up to the MAX level line.

 Old hydraulic fluid is invariably much darker in colour than the new, making it easy to distinguish the two.

3 Work through all the remaining bleed screws in the sequence until new fluid can be seen at all of them. Be careful to keep the master cylinder reservoir topped-up to above the MIN level at all times, or air may enter the system and greatly increase the length of the task.
4 Bleed the fluid from the clutch hydraulic system as described in Chapter 6.

5 When the operation is complete, check that all bleed screws are securely tightened, and that their dust caps are refitted. Wash off all traces of spilt fluid, and recheck the master cylinder reservoir fluid level.

6 Check the operation of the brakes and clutch before taking the car on the road.

21 Coolant renewal

Cooling system draining

⚠️ **Warning: Wait until the engine is cold before starting this procedure. Do not allow antifreeze to come in contact with your skin, or with the painted surfaces of the vehicle. Rinse off spills immediately with plenty of water. Never leave antifreeze lying around in an open container, or in a puddle in the driveway or on the garage floor. Children and pets are attracted by its sweet smell, but antifreeze can be fatal if ingested.**

1 With the engine completely cold, remove the expansion tank filler cap. Turn the cap anti-clockwise, wait until any pressure remaining in the system is released, then unscrew it and lift it off.

2 Where applicable, remove the engine undershield, then position a suitable container beneath the left-hand side of the radiator.

3 Loosen the clip and disconnect the bottom hose from the radiator, and allow the coolant to drain into the container. On the Z22SE engine, also unscrew the drain plug from under the coolant pump housing **(see illustration).**

4 When the flow of coolant stops, refit the bottom hose and tighten the clip, and on the Z22SE engine, refit and tighten the coolant pump drain plug.

5 If the coolant has been drained for a reason other than renewal, then provided it is clean and less than two years old, it can be re-used, though this is not recommended.

Cooling system flushing

6 If coolant renewal has been neglected, or if the antifreeze mixture has become diluted, then in time, the cooling system may gradually lose efficiency, as the coolant passages become restricted due to rust, scale deposits, and other sediment. The cooling system efficiency can be restored by flushing the system clean.

7 The radiator should be flushed independently of the engine, to avoid unnecessary contamination.

Radiator flushing

8 Disconnect the top and bottom hoses and any other relevant hoses from the radiator, with reference to Chapter 3.

9 Insert a garden hose into the radiator top inlet. Direct a flow of clean water through the radiator, and continue flushing until clean water emerges from the radiator bottom outlet.

10 If after a reasonable period, the water still does not run clear, the radiator can be flushed with a good proprietary cleaning agent. It is important that the manufacturer's instructions are followed carefully. If the contamination is particularly bad, remove the radiator, insert the hose in the radiator bottom outlet, and reverse-flush the radiator.

Engine flushing

11 Remove the thermostat as described in Chapter 3 then, if the radiator top hose has been disconnected from the engine, temporarily reconnect the hose.

12 With the top and bottom hoses disconnected from the radiator, insert a garden hose into the radiator top hose. Direct a clean flow of water through the engine, and continue flushing until clean water emerges from the radiator bottom hose.

13 On completion of flushing, refit the thermostat and reconnect the hoses with reference to Chapter 3.

Cooling system filling

14 Before attempting to fill the cooling system, make sure that all hoses and clips are in good condition, and that the clips are tight. Note that an antifreeze mixture must be used all year round, to prevent corrosion of the engine components.

15 Remove the expansion tank filler cap.

16 On the X16SZR engine, remove the temperature gauge sender unit from the right-hand end of the inlet manifold with reference to Chapter 3; this is necessary to bleed the air from the system. Note that on other engines the system bleeds automatically during the warm-up period.

17 Slowly fill the system until the coolant level reaches the KALT/COLD mark on the side of the expansion tank. On the X16SZR engine, refit the temperature gauge sender unit to the inlet manifold as soon as bubble-free coolant emerges from the thermostat housing, then continue to fill the system until

21.3 Removing the coolant drain plug located under the coolant pump housing (Z22SE engine)

the coolant reaches the KALT/COLD mark on the expansion tank.

18 Refit and tighten the expansion tank filler cap.

19 Start the engine, and allow it to run until it reaches normal operating temperature (until the cooling fan cuts in and out).

20 Stop the engine, and allow it to cool, then re-check the coolant level with reference to *Weekly checks*. Top-up the level if necessary and refit the expansion tank filler cap. Where applicable, refit the engine undershield.

Antifreeze mixture

21 The antifreeze should always be renewed at the specified intervals. This is necessary not only to maintain the antifreeze properties, but also to prevent corrosion which would otherwise occur as the corrosion inhibitors become progressively less effective.

22 Always use an ethylene-glycol based antifreeze which is suitable for use in mixed-metal cooling systems. **Note:** *Vauxhall recommend the use of 'green' coolant (90 297 545) in vehicles manufactured before MY2001 (Model Year), and 'red' coolant (09 194 431/19 40 650) in vehicles manufactured from MY2001-on.* **Do not mix the two types of coolant.** The quantity of antifreeze and levels of protection are given in the Specifications.

23 Before adding antifreeze, the cooling system should be completely drained, preferably flushed, and all hoses checked for condition and security.

24 After filling with antifreeze, a label should be attached to the expansion tank, stating the type and concentration of antifreeze used, and the date installed. Any subsequent topping-up should be made with the same type and concentration of antifreeze.

25 Do not use engine antifreeze in the windscreen/tailgate washer system, as it will cause damage to the vehicle paintwork. A screenwash additive should be added to the washer system in the quantities stated on the bottle.

22 Exhaust emission check

1 The exhaust emission check is carried out initially after 3 years, then every 2 years, however, on vehicles which are subject to intensive use (eg, taxis/hire cars/ambulances) it must be carried out annually. The check involves checking the engine management system operation by plugging an electronic tester into the system diagnostic socket to check the electronic control unit (ECU) memory for faults (see Chapter 4A).

2 In reality, if the vehicle is running correctly and the engine management warning light in the instrument panel is functioning normally, then this check need not be carried out.

23.2a Release the retaining clips (arrowed) . . .

23.2b . . . then lift up the housing lid and remove the air cleaner filter element

Every 40 000 miles (60 000 km) or 4 years

23 Air cleaner element renewal

1 The air cleaner is located in the front right-hand corner of the engine compartment.
2 Release the securing clips, and lift the air cleaner cover sufficiently to enable removal of the filter element (see illustrations). Do not to

24.2 Undo the retaining screws (arrowed) and remove the cover from the engine

strain the wiring for the airflow meter/intake air temperature sensor wiring (as applicable) as the cover is lifted.
3 Lift out the filter element.
4 Wipe out the casing and the cover. Fit the new filter element, noting that the rubber locating flange should be uppermost, and secure the cover with the clips.

24 Spark plug renewal and ignition system check

Spark plug renewal

1 The correct functioning of the spark plugs is vital for the correct running and efficiency of the engine. It is essential that the plugs fitted are appropriate for the engine; suitable types are specified at the beginning of this Chapter, or in the vehicle's Owner's Handbook. If the correct type is used and the engine is in good condition, the spark plugs should not need attention between scheduled replacement intervals. Spark plug cleaning is rarely

necessary, and should not be attempted unless specialised equipment is available, as damage can easily be caused to the firing ends.
2 Where applicable, remove the engine top cover after removing the oil filler cap (see illustration). Refit the cap.
3 On X16XEL without a secondary air system, Z16XE, X18XE1, Z18XE and Z22SE engines, remove the ignition module from the spark plugs with reference to Chapter 5B (see illustration).
4 On X16XEL engines with a secondary air system, remove the upper part of the inlet manifold.
5 On X18XE and X20XEV engines, unbolt the ignition HT lead cover from the cylinder head cover (see illustration).
6 If the marks on the spark plug (HT) leads cannot be seen, mark the leads to correspond to the cylinder the lead serves. Pull the leads from the plugs by gripping the end fitting, not the lead, otherwise the lead connection may be fractured. Where applicable, use the tool clipped to one of the plug leads to pull the HT leads from the plugs (see illustrations).

24.3 Removing the ignition module (Z22SE engine)

24.5 On X18XE and X20XEV engines undo the retaining screws (arrowed) and remove the spark plug cover

24.6a HT leads should be numbered (1) for identification purposes. Note the HT lead removal tool (2) clipped to the cap

24.6b Use the removal tool to pull the HT leads from the plugs

24.8 Removing the spark plugs (Z22SE engine)

24.12 The multi-electrode plugs fitted as standard should not be adjusted

24.14a If single electrode plugs are being fitted, use check the electrode gap using a feeler gauge . . .

24.14b . . . or a wire gauge . . .

24.15 . . . and if necessary adjust the gap by bending the electrode

7 It is advisable to remove the dirt from the spark plug recesses using a clean brush, vacuum cleaner or compressed air before removing the plugs, to prevent dirt dropping into the cylinders.

8 Unscrew the spark plugs from the cylinder head using a spark plug spanner, suitable box spanner or a deep socket and extension bar **(see illustration)**. Keep the socket aligned with the spark plug – if it is forcibly moved to one side, the ceramic insulator may be broken off.

It is very often difficult to insert spark plugs into their holes without cross-threading them. To avoid this possibility, fit a short length of rubber hose over the end of the spark plug. The flexible hose acts as a universal joint to help align the plug with the plug hole. Should the plug begin to cross-thread, the hose will slip on the spark plug, preventing thread damage to the aluminium cylinder head.

9 Examination of the spark plugs will give a good indication of the condition of the engine. As each plug is removed, examine it as follows. If the insulator nose of the spark plug is clean and white, with no deposits, this is indicative of a weak mixture or too hot a plug (a hot plug transfers heat away from the electrode slowly, a cold plug transfers heat away quickly).

10 If the tip and insulator nose are covered with hard black-looking deposits, then this is indicative that the mixture is too rich. Should the plug be black and oily, then it is likely that the engine is fairly worn, as well as the mixture being too rich.

11 If the insulator nose is covered with light tan to greyish-brown deposits, then the mixture is correct and it is likely that the engine is in good condition.

12 Some engines are fitted with multi-electrode plugs as standard by Vauxhall **(see illustration)**. On these plugs, the electrode gaps are all preset and no attempt should be made to bend the electrodes.

13 If non-standard single electrode plugs are to be installed, the spark plug electrode gap is of considerable importance. If the gap is too large or too small, the size of the spark and its efficiency will be seriously impaired and it will not perform correctly under all engine speed and load conditions. The gap should be set to the value specified by the manufacturer.

14 To set the gap, measure it with a feeler blade or spark plug gap gauge and then carefully bend the outer plug electrode until the correct gap is achieved. The centre electrode should never be bent, as this may crack the insulator and cause plug failure, if nothing worse. If using feeler blades, the gap is correct when the appropriate-size blade is a firm sliding fit **(see illustrations)**.

15 Special spark plug electrode gap adjusting tools are available from most motor accessory shops, or from some spark plug manufacturers **(see illustration)**.

16 Before fitting the spark plugs, check that the threaded connector sleeves are tight, and that the plug exterior surfaces and threads are clean **(see Haynes Hint)**.

17 Remove the rubber hose (if used), and tighten the plug to the specified torque using the spark plug socket and a torque wrench **(see illustration)**. Refit the remaining spark plugs in the same manner.

18 Connect the HT leads to the spark plugs in their correct order, then refit the items removed in paragraphs 2 to 5.

24.17 Tighten the spark plugs to the specified torque

26.4 Release the retaining clip . . .

26.6a . . . then disconnect the clip . . .

26.6b . . . and disconnect the fuel hoses from the fuel filter.

Ignition system check

⚠ Warning: Voltages produced by an electronic ignition system are considerably higher than those produced by conventional ignition systems. Extreme care must be taken when working on the system with the ignition switched on. Persons with surgically-implanted cardiac pacemaker devices should keep well clear of the ignition circuits, components and test equipment.

19 Where applicable, the spark plug HT leads should be checked whenever new spark plugs are fitted.

20 Ensure that the leads are numbered before removing them, to avoid confusion when refitting. Pull the leads from the plugs by gripping the end fitting, not the lead, otherwise the lead connection may be fractured.

21 Check inside the end fitting for signs of corrosion, which will look like a white crusty powder. Push the end fitting back onto the spark plug, ensuring that it is a tight fit on the plug. If not, remove the lead again and use pliers to carefully crimp the metal connector inside the end fitting until it fits securely on the end of the spark plug.

22 Using a clean rag, wipe the entire length of the lead to remove any built-up dirt and grease. Once the lead is clean, check for burns, cracks and other damage. Do not bend the lead excessively, nor pull the lead length-wise – the conductor inside might break.

26.7 Removing the fuel filter from under the vehicle

23 Disconnect the other end of the lead and check for corrosion and a tight fit in the same manner as the spark plug end. Refit the lead securely on completion.

24 Check the remaining leads one at a time, in the same way.

25 If new spark plug (HT) leads are required, purchase a set for your car and engine.

26 Where applicable, check the ignition module with reference to Chapter 5B.

27 Even with the ignition system in first-class condition, some engines may still occasionally experience poor starting attributable to damp ignition components. To disperse moisture, a water-dispersant aerosol can be very effective.

25 Timing belt and tensioner roller renewal

Refer to the information given in the appropriate part of Chapter 2.

26 Fuel filter renewal

1 The fuel filter is located under the rear of the vehicle where it is clipped onto the fuel tank retaining strap.

2 Depressurise the fuel system as described in Chapter 4A.

3 Chock the front wheels, then jack up the rear of the vehicle and support on axle stands (see *Jacking and vehicle support*).

4 Release the retaining clip holding the filter to the underbody **(see illustration)**. Before removing the filter, note the orientation of the fuel flow direction arrow.

5 Be prepared for fuel spillage, and take adequate fire precautions. Position a suitable container below the fuel filter to catch spilt fuel.

6 Release the connectors and disconnect the fuel hoses from the fuel filter, noting their locations to ensure correct refitting. A Vauxhall/Opel special tool is available to disconnect the hose connectors, but provided care it taken, the connections can be released

using a pair of pliers or a screwdriver **(see illustrations)**.

7 Withdraw the filter from under the vehicle **(see illustration)**.

8 Fitting the new filter is a reversal of removal, bearing in mind the following points.

a) Ensure that the filter is fitted with the flow direction arrow on the filter body pointing in the direction of fuel flow.

b) Ensure that the hoses are reconnected to their correct locations, as noted before removal.

c) On completion, run the engine and check for leaks. If leakage is evident, stop the engine immediately and rectify the problem without delay.

27 Automatic transmission fluid renewal

1 Park the vehicle on level ground and firmly apply the handbrake.

2 Drain and renew the transmission fluid as described in Chapter 7B.

3 The fluid level is checked using the dipstick which is situated on the top of the transmission unit and is positioned between the battery and engine unit **(see illustration)**.

4 Start the engine and allow it to idle for a couple of minutes with the selector lever in the P position.

5 With the engine idling, withdraw the dipstick from the tube, and wipe all the fluid from its end with a clean rag or paper towel.

27.3 The automatic transmission fluid dipstick is located between the engine and battery

Insert the clean dipstick back into the tube as far as it will go, then withdraw it once more. Note the fluid level on the end of the dipstick and ensure it is between the upper (MAX) and lower (MIN) level markings **(see illustration)**. If the transmission fluid is cold, use the markings on the side of the dipstick marked +20°C and if the transmission fluid is at operating temperature, use the markings on the +80°C side of the dipstick.

6 If topping-up is necessary, add the required quantity of the specified fluid to the transmission via the dipstick tube. Use a funnel with a fine mesh gauze, to avoid spillage, and to ensure that no foreign matter enters the transmission. **Note:** *Never overfill the transmission so that the fluid level is above the relevant upper (MAX) mark.*

7 After topping-up, take the vehicle on a short run to distribute the fresh fluid, then recheck the level, topping-up if necessary.

8 Always maintain the level between the two dipstick marks. If the level is allowed to fall below the lower mark, fluid starvation may result, which could lead to severe transmission damage.

9 Frequent need for topping-up indicates that there is a leak, which should be found and corrected before it becomes serious.

28 Rear brake drum check

Refer to Chapter 9.

27.5 Automatic transmission fluid dipstick fluid level markings

A Markings for use when fluid is at operating temperature
B Markings for use when fluid is cold

Notes

Chapter 1 Part B:
Routine maintenance and servicing – diesel engine models

Contents

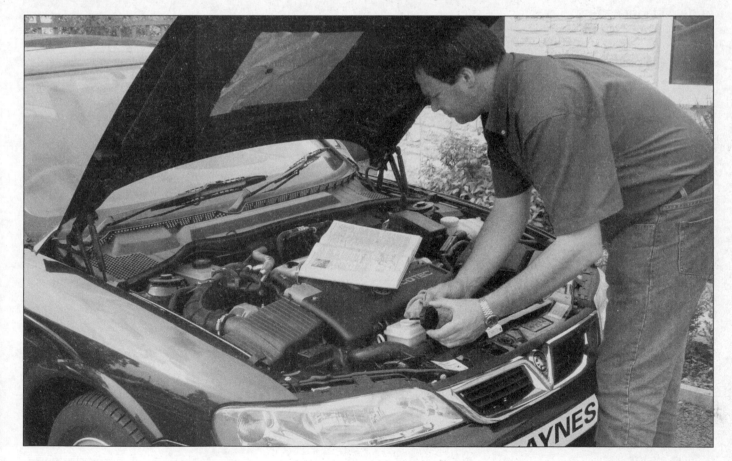

Degrees of difficulty

| Easy, suitable for novice with little experience | | Fairly easy, suitable for beginner with some experience | | Fairly difficult, suitable for competent DIY mechanic | | Difficult, suitable for experienced DIY mechanic | | Very difficult, suitable for expert DIY or professional |

Lubricants and fluids

Refer to *Weekly checks* on page 0•19

Capacities

Engine oil
Including oil filter . . . . 5.5 litres
Excluding oil filter:
   Y20DTH, Y22DTR . . . . 5.1 litres
   X20DTL, X20DTH . . . . 5.0 litres
Difference between MIN and MAX on dipstick . . . . 1.0 litre

Cooling system
X20DTH, Y20DTH and Y22DTR . . . . 7.2 litres
X20DTL . . . . 7.4 litres

Manual transmission
All models . . . . 1.6 litres

Washer fluid reservoir
Without headlight washers . . . . 2.6 litres
With headlight washers . . . . 5.5 litres

Fuel tank
All models . . . . 60 litres

Engine identification

Manufacturer's code	Engine type
X20DTH	2.0 litre high-pressure turbo diesel engine
X20DTL	2.0 litre low-pressure turbo diesel engine
Y20DTH	2.0 litre high-pressure turbo diesel engine
Y22DTR	2.2 litre high-pressure turbo diesel engine

Cooling system
Antifreeze mixture:
   50% antifreeze . . . . Protection down to –37°C
   55% antifreeze . . . . Protection down to –45°C
Note: *Refer to antifreeze manufacturer for latest recommendations.*

Pre-heating system
Glow plugs:
   X20DTL:
      From chassis number W1000001 . . . . Bosch 0 250 202 042
      From chassis number XL000001 . . . . Bosch 0 250 202 042
      From chassis number V7999999 . . . . Bosch 0 250 202 027
   X20DTH . . . . Bosch 0 250 202 042
   Y20DTH . . . . Bosch 0 250 202 043
   Y22DTR . . . . Bosch 0 250 202 043

Brakes
Friction material minimum thickness (including backing plate):
   Front brake pads . . . . 7.5 mm
   Rear brake pads . . . . 6.7 mm
   Rear brake shoes . . . . 1.0 mm lining thickness or 0.5 mm above rivet heads
   Minimum handbrake shoe friction material thickness (lining only) . . . 1.0 mm

Torque wrench settings

	Nm	lbf ft
Auxiliary drivebelt tensioner:		
Damper to tensioner	23	17
Tensioner mounting bolts:		
M10 bolt	42	31
M8 bolt	23	17
Engine oil filter housing cover	30	22
Fuel filter housing cover centre bolt	8	6
Roadwheel bolts	110	81
Sump drain plug	18	13

The maintenance intervals in this manual are provided with the assumption that you, not the dealer, will be carrying out the work. These are the minimum maintenance intervals recommended by us for vehicles driven daily. If you wish to keep your vehicle in peak condition at all times, you may wish to perform some of these procedures more often. We encourage frequent maintenance, because it enhances the efficiency, performance and resale value of your vehicle.

If the vehicle is driven in dusty areas, used to tow a trailer, or driven frequently at slow speeds (idling in traffic) or on short journeys, more frequent maintenance intervals are recommended.

When the vehicle is new, it should be serviced by a factory-authorised dealer service department, in order to preserve the factory warranty.

Every 10 000 miles (15 000 km) or 6 months, whichever comes first

☐ Renew the engine oil and filter (Section 3)

Note: *Vauxhall recommend that the engine oil and filter are changed every 20 000 miles (30 000 km) or 12 months. However, oil and filter changes are good for the engine and we recommend that the oil and filter are renewed more frequently, especially if the vehicle is used on a lot of short journeys.*

Every 20 000 miles (30 000 km) or 12 months, whichever comes first

☐ Check the condition of the auxiliary drivebelts and tensioner (Section 4)
☐ Check the front/rear brake pads and discs for wear (Section 5)
☐ Check and adjust the handbrake (Section 6)
☐ Check the rear brake shoes for wear (Section 7)
☐ Check the steering and suspension components for condition and security (Section 8)
☐ Check the rear suspension level control system (where applicable) (Section 9)
☐ Check the body and underbody for corrosion protection (Section 10)
☐ Check all components, pipes and hoses for fluid leaks (Section 11)
☐ Check the condition of the driveshaft gaiters (Section 12)
☐ Check and if necessary adjust the headlight beam alignment (Section 13)
☐ Check the roadwheel bolts are tightened to the specified torque (Section 14)
☐ Lubricate all door locks and hinges, door stops, bonnet lock and release, and tailgate lock and hinges (Section 15)
☐ Check the operation of all electrical systems (Section 16)
☐ Carry out a road test (Section 17)

Every 12 months, regardless of mileage

☐ Drain water from the fuel filter (Section 18)

Every 20 000 miles (30 000 km) or 2 years, whichever comes first

☐ Renew the pollen filter element (Section 19)

Note: *If the vehicle is used in dusty conditions, the pollen filter should be renewed more frequently.*

Every 40 000 miles (60 000 km) or 2 years, whichever comes first

☐ Renew the remote control batteries (Section 20)

Every 2 years, regardless of mileage

☐ Renew the hydraulic fluid (Section 21)
☐ Renew the coolant (Section 22)
☐ Exhaust emission test (Section 23)

Every 40 000 miles (60 000 km) or 4 years, whichever comes first

☐ Renew the air cleaner element (Section 24)
☐ Renew the fuel filter (Section 25)
☐ Check the rear brake drums for wear (Section 26)

Underbonnet view of a 2.0 litre diesel engine model

1   Front suspension strut
    upper mounting
2   Hydraulic fluid reservoir
3   Turbocharger and heat
    shield
4   Fuel filter
5   Auxiliary fuse and relay
    box
6   Battery
7   Auxiliary relay box
8   Power steering fluid
    reservoir
9   Engine oil level dipstick
10 Air cleaner

Front underbody view of a 2.0 litre diesel engine model

1   Front suspension lower
    arm
2   Front subframe
3   Electric cooling fan
4   Engine oil drain plug
5   Manual transmission
6   Steering track rod
7   Exhaust downpipe
8   Driveshaft

Typical rear underbody

1 Exhaust rear silencer
2 Rear towing eye
3 Rear suspension crossmember
4 Rear suspension strut
5 Rear suspension lower arm
6 Fuel filter (petrol versions only)
7 Rear suspension trailing arm
8 Fuel tank

1 General information

1 This Chapter is designed to help the home mechanic maintain his/her vehicle for safety, economy, long life and peak performance.
2 The Chapter contains a master maintenance schedule, followed by Sections dealing specifically with each task in the schedule. Visual checks, adjustments, component renewal and other helpful items are included. Refer to the accompanying illustrations of the engine compartment and the underside of the vehicle for the locations of the various components.
3 Servicing your vehicle in accordance with the mileage/time maintenance schedule and the following Sections will provide a planned maintenance programme, which should result in a long and reliable service life. This is a comprehensive plan, so maintaining some items but not others at the specified service intervals, will not produce the same results.
4 As you service your vehicle, you will discover that many of the procedures can – and should – be grouped together, because of the particular procedure being performed, or because of the proximity of two otherwise-unrelated components to one another. For example, if the vehicle is raised for any reason, the exhaust can be inspected at the same time as the suspension and steering components.

5 The first step in this maintenance programme is to prepare yourself before the actual work begins. Read through all the Sections relevant to the work to be carried out, then make a list and gather all the parts and tools required. If a problem is encountered, seek advice from a parts specialist, or a dealer service department.

2 Regular maintenance

1 If, from the time the vehicle is new, the routine maintenance schedule is followed closely, and frequent checks are made of fluid levels and high-wear items, as suggested throughout this manual, the engine will be kept in relatively good running condition, and the need for additional work will be minimised.
2 It is possible that there will be times when the engine is running poorly due to the lack of regular maintenance. This is even more likely if a used vehicle, which has not received regular and frequent maintenance checks, is purchased. In such cases, additional work may need to be carried out, outside of the regular maintenance intervals.
3 If engine wear is suspected, a compression test or leakdown test (refer to Chapter 2C) will provide valuable information regarding the overall performance of the main internal components. Such a test can be used as a basis to decide on the extent of the work to be carried out. If, for example, a compression

or leakdown test indicates serious internal engine wear, conventional maintenance as described in this Chapter will not greatly improve the performance of the engine, and may prove a waste of time and money, unless extensive overhaul work is carried out first.
4 The following series of operations are those most often required to improve the performance of a generally poor-running engine:

Primary operations

a) Clean, inspect and test the battery (refer to 'Weekly checks').
b) Check all the engine-related fluids (refer to 'Weekly checks').
c) Check the condition and tension of the auxiliary drivebelt (Section 4).
d) Check the condition of the air filter, and renew if necessary (Section 24).
e) Renew the fuel filter (Section 26).
f) Check the condition of all hoses, and check for fluid leaks (Section 11).

5 If the above operations do not prove fully effective, carry out the following secondary operations:

Secondary operations

All items listed under *Primary operations*, plus the following:

a) Check the charging system (refer to Chapter 5A).
b) Check the pre-heating system (refer to Chapter 5C).
c) Check the fuel system (refer to Chapter 4B).

Every 10 000 miles (15 000 km) or 6 months

3 Engine oil and filter renewal

1 Frequent oil and filter changes are the most important preventative maintenance procedures which can be undertaken by the DIY owner. As engine oil ages, it becomes diluted and contaminated, which leads to premature engine wear.

2 Before starting this procedure, gather together all the necessary tools and materials. Also make sure that you have plenty of clean rags and newspapers handy, to mop up any spills. Ideally, the engine oil should be warm, as it will drain more easily, and more built-up sludge will be removed with it. Take care not to touch the exhaust or any other hot parts of the engine when working under the vehicle. To avoid any possibility of scalding, and to protect yourself from possible skin irritants and other harmful contaminants in used engine oils, it is advisable to wear gloves when carrying out this work.

3 Firmly apply the handbrake then jack up the front of the vehicle and support it on axle stands (see *Jacking and vehicle support*). Remove the engine undertray where necessary.

4 Remove the oil filler cap (see illustration).

5 Using a spanner, or preferably a suitable socket and bar, slacken the drain plug about half a turn. Position the draining container under the drain plug, then remove the plug completely (see Haynes Hint).

6 Allow some time for the oil to drain, noting that it may be necessary to reposition the container as the oil flow slows to a trickle.

7 To gain access to the oil filter housing, undo the retaining screws and remove the plastic cover from the top of the engine (see illustration).

8 Using a large socket, unscrew the cover and remove it from the top of the oil filter housing (see illustration). Lift out the old filter element.

9 Fit the new filter element to the housing (see illustration).

10 Renew the sealing rings then refit the oil filter cover and tighten it to the specified torque (see illustration). Refit the plastic cover to the engine and securely tighten its screws.

11 After all the oil has drained, wipe the drain plug and the sealing washer with a clean rag. Examine the condition of the sealing washer, and renew it if it shows signs of scoring or other damage which may prevent an oil-tight seal. Clean the area around the drain plug

opening, and refit the plug complete with the washer and tighten it to the specified torque.

12 Remove the old oil and all tools from under the vehicle then lower the vehicle to the ground.

13 Fill the engine through the filler hole, using the correct grade and type of oil (refer to *Weekly Checks* for details of topping-up). Pour in half the specified quantity of oil first, then wait a few minutes for the oil to drain into the sump. Continue to add oil, a small quantity at a time, until the level is up to the lower mark on the dipstick. Adding approximately a further 1.0 litre will bring the level up to the upper mark on the dipstick.

14 Start the engine and run it for a few minutes, while checking for leaks around the oil filter seal and the sump drain plug. Note that there may be a delay of a few seconds before the low oil pressure warning light goes out when the engine is first started, as the oil circulates through the new oil filter and the engine oil galleries before the pressure builds-up.

15 Stop the engine, and wait a few minutes for the oil to settle in the sump once more. With the new oil circulated and the filter now completely full, recheck the level on the dipstick, and add more oil as necessary.

16 Dispose of the used engine oil safely with reference to *General repair procedures*.

3.4 Removing the oil filler cap

HAYNES HiNT

As the drain plug releases from the threads, move it away quickly so that the stream of oil running out of the sump goes into the drain pan and not up your sleeve.

3.7 Undo the retaining screws and remove the cover from the top of the engine

3.8 Unscrew the oil filter housing cover and lift out the old filter element

3.9 Fit the new filter element to the housing . . .

3.10 . . . then fit the new sealing rings to the cover recesses (arrowed) and refit the cover to the housing

Every 20 000 miles (30 000 km) or 12 months

4 Auxiliary drivebelt and tensioner – check and renewal

Note: *A single belt is used to drive all auxiliary components,*

Checking

1 Drivebelts are prone to failure after a long period of time and should therefore be inspected regularly.

2 With the engine stopped, inspect the full length of the drivebelt for cracks and separation of the belt plies. It will be necessary to turn the engine (using a spanner or socket and bar on the crankshaft pulley bolt) in order to move the belt from the pulleys so that the belt can be inspected thoroughly. Twist the belt between the pulleys so that both sides can be viewed. Also check for fraying, and glazing which gives the belt a shiny appearance. Check the pulleys for nicks, cracks, distortion and corrosion.

4.7a **Auxiliary drivebelt configuration on models without air conditioning**

4.7b **Auxiliary drivebelt configuration on models with air conditioning**

3 If the belt shows signs of wear or damage, it must be renewed.

4 To check the drivebelt tensioner, turn the tensioner anti-clockwise as far as possible using a socket on the special hexagon, then release it and check that it returns to its original position. If the tensioner has any tight spots or fails to return fully, it must be renewed.

Renewal

5 Remove the air cleaner housing as described in Chapter 4B.

6 Firmly apply the handbrake then jack up the front of the vehicle and support it on axle stands (see *Jacking and vehicle support*). Remove the engine undertray. To improve access, remove the right-hand front roadwheel and inner wheelarch liner.

7 Prior to removal make a note of the correct routing of the belt around the various pulleys **(see illustrations)**. If the belt is to be re-used, also mark the direction of rotation on the belt to ensure the belt is refitted the same way around.

8 Using a suitable spanner or socket fitted to the special hexagonal section on the tensioner pulley backplate, lever the tensioner anti-clockwise away from the belt until there is sufficient slack to enable the belt to be slipped off the pulleys **(see illustration)**. Carefully release the tensioner pulley until it is against its stop then remove the belt from the vehicle.

9 If the tensioner is being renewed, unbolt the bracket and damper from the timing cover.

10 Manoeuvre the belt into position, routing it correctly around the pulleys; if the original belt is being fitted, use the marks made prior to removal to ensure it is fitted the correct way around.

11 Lever the tensioner roller back against its spring, and seat the belt on the pulleys. Ensure the belt is centrally located on all pulleys then slowly release the tensioner pulley until the belt is correctly tensioned.

12 Refit the wheelarch cover, roadwheel and engine undertray, then lower the vehicle to the ground and tighten the wheel bolts to the specified torque

4.8 **Release the drivebelt tension and slip the belt off the pulleys**

13 Refit the air cleaner housing as described in Chapter 4B.

5 Front & rear brake pad and disc check

1 Firmly apply the handbrake, then jack up the front and rear of the vehicle and support it securely on axle stands (see *Jacking and vehicle support*). Remove the roadwheels.

2 For a quick check, the pad thickness can be carried out via the inspection hole on the caliper **(see Haynes Hint)**. Using a steel rule, measure the thickness of the pad lining including the backing plate. This must not be less than that indicated in the Specifications.

3 The view through the caliper inspection hole gives a rough indication of the state of the brake pads. For a comprehensive check, the brake pads should be removed and cleaned. The operation of the caliper can then also be checked, and the condition of the brake disc itself can be fully examined on both sides. Chapter 9 contains a detailed description of how the brake disc should be checked for wear and/or damage.

4 If any pad's friction material is worn to the specified thickness or less, *all four pads must be renewed as a set*. Refer to Chapter 9 for details.

5 On completion, refit the roadwheels and lower the vehicle to the ground.

6 Handbrake check and adjustment

Refer to Chapter 9.

For a quick check, the thickness of friction material remaining on the inner brake pad can be measured through the aperture in the caliper body.

8.4 Check for wear in the hub bearings by grasping the wheel and trying to rock it

7 Rear brake shoe check

Note: *This Section applies only to models fitted with rear drum brakes.*
Refer to Chapter 9.

8 Suspension and steering check

Front suspension and steering

1 Raise the front of the vehicle, and securely support it on axle stands (see *Jacking and vehicle support*).
2 Visually inspect the balljoint dust covers and the steering rack-and-pinion gaiters for splits, chafing or deterioration. Any wear of these components will cause loss of lubricant, together with dirt and water entry, resulting in rapid deterioration of the balljoints or steering gear.
3 Check the power steering fluid hoses for chafing or deterioration, and the pipe and hose unions for fluid leaks. Also check for signs of fluid leakage under pressure from the steering gear rubber gaiters, which would indicate failed fluid seals within the steering gear.

HAYNES HiNT

A leak in the cooling system will usually show up as white- or rust-coloured deposits on the area adjoining the leak.

4 Grasp the roadwheel at the 12 o'clock and 6 o'clock positions, and try to rock it **(see illustration)**. Very slight free play may be felt, but if the movement is appreciable, further investigation is necessary to determine the source. Continue rocking the wheel while an assistant depresses the footbrake. If the movement is now eliminated or significantly reduced, it is likely that the hub bearings are at fault. If the free play is still evident with the footbrake depressed, then there is wear in the suspension joints or mountings.
5 Now grasp the wheel at the 9 o'clock and 3 o'clock positions, and try to rock it as before. Any movement felt now may again be caused by wear in the hub bearings or the steering track rod balljoints. If the outer balljoint is worn, the visual movement will be obvious. If the inner joint is suspect, it can be felt by placing a hand over the rack-and-pinion rubber gaiter and gripping the track rod. If the wheel is now rocked, movement will be felt at the inner joint if wear has taken place.
6 Using a large screwdriver or flat bar, check for wear in the suspension mounting bushes by levering between the relevant suspension component and its attachment point. Some movement is to be expected, as the mountings are made of rubber, but excessive wear should be obvious. Also check the condition of any visible rubber bushes, looking for splits, cracks or contamination of the rubber.
7 With the car standing on its wheels, have an assistant turn the steering wheel back-and-forth, about an eighth of a turn each way. There should be very little, if any, lost movement between the steering wheel and roadwheels. If this is not the case, closely observe the joints and mountings previously described. In addition, check the steering column universal joints for wear, and also check the rack-and-pinion steering gear itself.

Rear suspension

8 Chock the front wheels, then jack up the rear of the vehicle and support securely on axle stands (see *Jacking and vehicle support*).
9 Working as described previously for the front suspension, check the rear hub bearings, the suspension bushes and the strut or shock absorber mountings (as applicable) for wear.

Shock absorber

10 Check for any signs of fluid leakage around the shock absorber body, or from the rubber gaiter around the piston rod. Should any fluid be noticed, the shock absorber is defective internally, and should be renewed.
Note: *Shock absorbers should always be renewed in pairs on the same axle.*
11 The efficiency of the shock absorber may be checked by bouncing the vehicle at each corner. Generally speaking, the body will return to its normal position and stop after being depressed. If it rises and returns on a rebound,

the shock absorber is probably suspect. Also examine the shock absorber upper and lower mountings for any signs of wear.

9 Rear suspension level control system check

Where fitted on Estate models, check that the rear suspension self-levelling control system operates correctly. In the event of a suspected fault, have the system checked by a Vauxhall/Opel dealer.

10 Body corrosion check

This work should be carried out by a Vauxhall/Opel dealer in order to validate the vehicle warranty. The work includes a thorough inspection of the vehicle paintwork and underbody for damage and corrosion

11 Hose and fluid leak check

1 Visually inspect the engine joint faces, gaskets and seals for any signs of water or oil leaks. Pay particular attention to the areas around the cylinder head cover, cylinder head, oil filter and sump joint faces. Bear in mind that, over a period of time, some very slight seepage from these areas is to be expected – what you are really looking for is any indication of a serious leak. Should a leak be found, renew the offending gasket or oil seal by referring to the appropriate Chapters in this manual. Similarly, check for leaks around the transmission casing.
2 Also check the security and condition of all the engine-related pipes and hoses, and all braking system pipes and hoses and fuel lines. Ensure that all cable ties or securing clips are in place, and in good condition. Clips which are broken or missing can lead to chafing of the hoses, pipes or wiring, which could cause more serious problems in the future.
3 Carefully check the radiator hoses and heater hoses along their entire length. Renew any hose which is cracked, swollen or deteriorated. Cracks will show up better if the hose is squeezed. Pay close attention to the hose clips that secure the hoses to the cooling system components. Hose clips can pinch and puncture hoses, resulting in cooling system leaks. If the crimped-type hose clips are used, it may be a good idea to replace them with standard worm-drive clips.
4 Inspect all the cooling system components (hoses, joint faces, etc) for leaks **(see Haynes Hint)**.

5 Where any problems are found on system components, renew the component or gasket with reference to Chapter 3.

6 With the vehicle raised, inspect the fuel tank and filler neck for punctures, cracks and other damage. The connection between the filler neck and tank is especially critical. Sometimes a rubber filler neck or connecting hose will leak due to loose retaining clamps or deteriorated rubber.

7 Carefully check all rubber hoses and metal fuel lines leading away from the fuel tank. Check for loose connections, deteriorated hoses, crimped lines, and other damage. Pay particular attention to the vent pipes and hoses, which often loop up around the filler neck and can become blocked or crimped. Follow the lines to the front of the vehicle, carefully inspecting them all the way. Renew damaged sections as necessary. Similarly, whilst the vehicle is raised, take the opportunity to inspect the exhaust system and all underbody brake fluid pipes and hoses.

8 From within the engine compartment, check the security of all fuel, vacuum and brake hose attachments and pipe unions, and inspect all hoses for kinks, chafing and deterioration.

9 Check the condition of the power steering fluid pipes and hoses.

12 Driveshaft gaiter check

1 With the vehicle raised and securely supported on stands, turn the steering onto full lock then slowly rotate the roadwheel. Inspect the condition of the outer constant velocity (CV) joint rubber gaiters while squeezing the gaiters to open out the folds (see illustration). Check for signs of cracking, splits or deterioration of the rubber which may allow the grease to escape and lead to water and grit entry into the joint. Also check the security and condition of the retaining clips. Repeat these checks on the inner CV joints. If any damage or deterioration is found, the gaiters should be renewed as described in Chapter 8.

2 At the same time, check the general condition of the CV joints themselves by first holding the driveshaft and attempting to rotate the wheel. Repeat this check by holding the inner joint and attempting to rotate the driveshaft. Any appreciable movement indicates wear in the joints, wear in the driveshaft splines or loose driveshaft retaining nut.

13 Headlight beam alignment check

Refer to Chapter 12 for details

14 Wheel bolt tightness check

1 Remove the wheel trims and check the tightness of all the wheel bolts, using a torque wrench.

2 Refit the wheel trims on completion.

15 Hinge and lock lubrication

1 Work around the vehicle and lubricate the hinges of the bonnet, doors and tailgate with a light machine oil.

2 Lightly lubricate the bonnet release mechanism and exposed section of inner cable with a smear of grease.

3 Check the security and operation of all hinges, latches and locks, adjusting them where required. Check the operation of the central locking system.

4 Check the condition and operation of the tailgate struts, renewing them both if either is leaking or no longer able to support the tailgate securely when raised.

16 Electrical systems check

1 Check the operation of all electrical equipment, ie, lights, direction indicators, horn, wash/wipe system, etc. Refer to the appropriate Sections of Chapter 12 for details if any of the circuits are found to be inoperative.

2 Visually check all accessible wiring connectors, harnesses and retaining clips for security, and for signs of chafing or damage. Rectify any faults found.

17 Road test

Instruments/ electrical equipment

1 Check the operation of all instruments and electrical equipment.

2 Make sure that all instruments read correctly, and switch on all electrical equipment in turn, to check that it functions properly.

Steering and suspension

3 Check for any abnormalities in the steering, suspension, handling or road 'feel'.

4 Drive the vehicle, and check that there are no unusual vibrations or noises.

5 Check that the steering feels positive, with no excessive 'sloppiness', or roughness, and check for any suspension noises when cornering and driving over bumps.

Drivetrain

6 Check the performance of the engine, clutch, transmission and driveshafts.

7 Listen for any unusual noises from the engine, clutch and transmission.

8 Make sure that the engine runs smoothly when idling, and that there is no hesitation when accelerating.

9 Check that, where applicable, the clutch action is smooth and progressive, that the drive is taken up smoothly, and that the pedal travel is not excessive. Also listen for any noises when the clutch pedal is depressed.

10 Check that all gears can be engaged smoothly without noise, and that the gear lever action is smooth and not abnormally vague or 'notchy'.

11 Listen for a metallic clicking sound from the front of the vehicle, as the vehicle is driven slowly in a circle with the steering on full-lock. Carry out this check in both directions. If a clicking noise is heard, this indicates wear in a driveshaft joint (see Chapter 8).

Braking system

12 Make sure that the vehicle does not pull to one side when braking, and that the wheels do not lock prematurely when braking hard.

13 Check that there is no vibration through the steering when braking.

14 Check that the handbrake operates correctly, without excessive movement of the lever, and that it holds the vehicle stationary on a slope.

15 Test the operation of the brake servo unit as follows. Depress the footbrake four or five times to exhaust the vacuum, then start the engine. As the engine starts, there should be a noticeable 'give' in the brake pedal as vacuum builds-up. Allow the engine to run for at least two minutes, and then switch it off. If the brake pedal is now depressed again, it should be possible to detect a hiss from the servo as the pedal is depressed. After about four or five applications, no further hissing should be heard, and the pedal should feel considerably harder.

12.1 Check the condition of the driveshaft gaiters (1) and the retaining clips (2)

Every 12 months, regardless of mileage

18 Fuel filter water draining

Caution: Before starting any work on the fuel filter, wipe clean the filter assembly and the area around it; it is essential that no dirt or other foreign matter is allowed into the system. Obtain a suitable container into which the filter can be drained and place rags or similar material under the filter assembly to catch any spillages. Do not allow diesel fuel to contaminate components such as the alternator and starter motor, the coolant hoses and engine mountings, and any wiring.

1 In addition to taking the precautions noted above to catch any fuel spillages, connect a tube to the drain screw on the base of the fuel filter/filter housing. Place the other end of the tube in a clean jar or can.
2 Unscrew the drain screw and allow the filter to drain until clean fuel, free of dirt or water, emerges from the tube (approximately 100 cc is usually sufficient) **(see illustration)**. Note that it maybe necessary to slacken the filter housing cover bolt to allow the fuel to drain.
3 Securely close the drain screw and remove the tube, containers and rag, mopping-up any spilt fuel. Where necessary, securely tighten the housing cover screw to the specified torque.
4 On completion, dispose safely of the drained fuel. Check carefully all disturbed components to ensure that there are no leaks

18.2 Draining water from the fuel filter

(of air or fuel) when the engine is restarted.
5 If necessary, bleed the fuel system as described in Chapter 4B.

Every 20 000 miles (30 000 km) or 2 years

19 Pollen filter renewal

1 Open the bonnet, and pull up the rubber weatherseal from the flange at the rear of the engine compartment **(see illustration)**.
2 Open the cover in the water deflector for access to the pollen filter **(see illustration)**.
3 Release the clips from each end, then lift

out the filter **(see illustration)**.
4 Fit the new filter using a reversal of the removal procedure; make sure that the marking is visible on the right-hand end of the filter, as viewed through the cover.

19.1 Pull up the rubber weatherseal . . .

19.2 . . . then open the cover . . .

19.3 . . . and lift out the pollen filter

Every 40 000 miles (60 000 km) or 2 years

20 Remote control battery renewal

Note: *The following procedure must be performed within 3 minutes, otherwise the remote control unit will have to be reprogrammed.*
1 Using a screwdriver, prise the battery cover from the ignition key fob **(see illustrations)**.
2 Note how the circular battery is fitted, then carefully remove it from the contacts.
3 Fit the new battery and refit the cover making sure that it clips fully onto the base.

20.1a Prise off the battery cover . . .

20.1b . . . and remove the circular battery

Every 2 years, regardless of mileage

21 Hydraulic fluid renewal

⚠ **Warning: Hydraulic fluid can harm your eyes and damage painted surfaces, so use extreme caution when handling and pouring it. Do not use fluid that has been standing open for some time, as it absorbs moisture from the air. Excess moisture can cause a dangerous loss of braking effectiveness.**

Note: *The brake and clutch hydraulic systems share a reservoir.*

1 The procedure is similar to that for the bleeding of the hydraulic systems as described in Chapters 6 and 9. Renew the fluid in the braking system first, then the clutch fluid.

2 Working as described in Chapter 9, open the first bleed screw in the sequence, and pump the brake pedal gently until nearly all the old fluid has been emptied from the master cylinder reservoir. Top-up to the MAX level with new fluid, and continue pumping until only the new fluid remains in the reservoir, and new fluid can be seen emerging from the bleed screw. Tighten the screw, and top the reservoir level up to the MAX level line.

HAYNES HINT *Old hydraulic fluid is invariably much darker in colour than the new, making it easy to distinguish the two.*

3 Work through all the remaining bleed screws in the sequence until new fluid can be seen at all of them. Be careful to keep the master cylinder reservoir topped-up to above the MIN level at all times, or air may enter the system and greatly increase the length of the task.

4 Bleed the fluid from the clutch hydraulic system as described in Chapter 6.

5 When the operation is complete, check that all bleed screws are securely tightened, and that their dust caps are refitted. Wash off all traces of spilt fluid, and recheck the master cylinder reservoir fluid level.

6 Check the operation of the brakes and clutch before taking the car on the road.

22 Coolant renewal

Cooling system draining

⚠ **Warning: Wait until the engine is cold before starting this procedure. Do not allow antifreeze to come in contact with your skin, or with the painted surfaces of the vehicle. Rinse off spills immediately with plenty of water.**

Never leave antifreeze lying around in an open container, or in a puddle in the driveway or on the garage floor. Children and pets are attracted by its sweet smell, but antifreeze can be fatal if ingested.

1 With the engine completely cold, remove the expansion tank filler cap. Turn the cap anti-clockwise, wait until any pressure remaining in the system is released, then unscrew it and lift it off.

2 Where applicable, remove the engine undershield, then position a suitable container beneath the left-hand side of the radiator.

3 Loosen the clip and disconnect the bottom hose from the radiator, and allow the coolant to drain into the container.

4 When the flow of coolant stops, refit the bottom hose and tighten the clip.

5 If the coolant has been drained for a reason other than renewal, then provided it is clean and less than two years old, it can be re-used, though this is not recommended.

Cooling system flushing

6 If coolant renewal has been neglected, or if the antifreeze mixture has become diluted, then in time, the cooling system may gradually lose efficiency, as the coolant passages become restricted due to rust, scale deposits, and other sediment. The cooling system efficiency can be restored by flushing the system clean.

7 The radiator should be flushed independently of the engine, to avoid unnecessary contamination.

Radiator flushing

8 Disconnect the top and bottom hoses and any other relevant hoses from the radiator, with reference to Chapter 3.

9 Insert a garden hose into the radiator top inlet. Direct a flow of clean water through the radiator, and continue flushing until clean water emerges from the radiator bottom outlet.

10 If after a reasonable period, the water still does not run clear, the radiator can be flushed with a good proprietary cleaning agent. It is important that the manufacturer's instructions are followed carefully. If the contamination is particularly bad, remove the radiator, insert the hose in the radiator bottom outlet, and reverse-flush the radiator.

Engine flushing

11 Remove the thermostat as described in Chapter 3 then, if the radiator top hose has been disconnected from the engine, temporarily reconnect the hose.

12 With the top and bottom hoses disconnected from the radiator, insert a garden hose into the radiator top hose. Direct a clean flow of water through the engine, and continue flushing until clean water emerges from the radiator bottom hose.

13 On completion of flushing, refit the thermostat and reconnect the hoses with reference to Chapter 3.

Cooling system filling

14 Before attempting to fill the cooling system, make sure that all hoses and clips are in good condition, and that the clips are tight. Note that an antifreeze mixture must be used all year round, to prevent corrosion of the engine components.

15 Remove the expansion tank filler cap.

16 Note that the system bleeds automatically during the warm-up period.

17 Slowly fill the system until the coolant level reaches the KALT/COLD mark on the side of the expansion tank.

18 Refit and tighten the expansion tank filler cap.

19 Start the engine, and allow it to run until it reaches normal operating temperature (until the cooling fan cuts in and out).

20 Stop the engine, and allow it to cool, then recheck the coolant level with reference to *Weekly checks*. Top-up the level if necessary and refit the expansion tank filler cap. Where applicable, refit the engine undershield.

Antifreeze mixture

21 The antifreeze should always be renewed at the specified intervals. This is necessary not only to maintain the antifreeze properties, but also to prevent corrosion which would otherwise occur as the corrosion inhibitors become progressively less effective.

22 Always use an ethylene-glycol based antifreeze which is suitable for use in mixed-metal cooling systems. **Note:** *Vauxhall recommend the use of 'green' coolant (90 297 545) in vehicles manufactured before MY2001 (Model Year), and 'red' coolant (09 194 431/19 40 650) in vehicles manufactured from MY2001-on. Do not mix the two types of coolant.* The quantity of antifreeze and levels of protection are given in the Specifications.

23 Before adding antifreeze, the cooling system should be completely drained, preferably flushed, and all hoses checked for condition and security.

24 After filling with antifreeze, a label should be attached to the expansion tank, stating the type and concentration of antifreeze used, and the date installed. Any subsequent topping-up should be made with the same type and concentration of antifreeze.

25 Do not use engine antifreeze in the windscreen/tailgate washer system, as it will cause damage to the vehicle paintwork. A screenwash additive should be added to the washer system in the quantities stated on the bottle.

23 Exhaust emission check

1 The exhaust emission check is carried out initially after 3 years, then every 2 years,

however, on vehicles which are subject to intensive use (eg, taxis/hire cars/ambulances) it must be carried out annually. The check involves checking the exhaust smoke density by accelerating the engine several times to its maximum unloaded speed.

2 Excessive smoke can be caused by a dirty air cleaner element, otherwise, professional advice may be needed to find the cause.

Every 40 000 miles (60 000 km) or 4 years

24 Air cleaner element renewal

1 The air cleaner is located in the front right-hand corner of the engine compartment.
2 Release the securing clips, and lift the air cleaner cover sufficiently to enable removal of the filter element **(see illustration)**. Take care not to strain the wiring for the airflow meter/intake air temperature sensor wiring (as applicable) as the cover is lifted.

3 Lift out the filter element **(see illustration)**.
4 Wipe out the casing and the cover **(see illustration)**. Fit the new filter, noting that the rubber locating flange should be uppermost, and secure the cover with the clips.

25 Fuel filter renewal

1 Drain the fuel filter housing (see Section 18).
2 Unscrew the centre bolt and remove the cover from the filter housing **(see illustrations)**.

3 Remove the filter element from the housing and discard it. Examine the housing cover and centre bolt sealing rings for signs of damage or deterioration and renew if necessary **(see illustrations)**.
4 Fit the new filter in the body, then fill the filter housing with fresh fuel. Ideally the fuel level should be just below the rim of the body.
5 Refit the cover to the housing then refit the centre bolt, ensuring the sealing is in position, tightening it to the specified torque **(see illustration)**. **Do not** overtighten the cover screw as the housing is easily damaged.
6 Start the engine and bleed the fuel system as described in Chapter 4B.

26 Rear brake drum check

Refer to Chapter 9.

24.2 Release the clips then lift the air cleaner cover . . .

24.3 . . . and remove the filter element

24.4 Wipe clean the air cleaner casing before fitting the new filter

25.2a Unscrew the centre bolt . . .

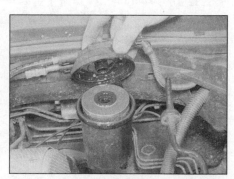

25.2b . . . and lift off the cover from the fuel filter housing

25.3a Remove the filter element . . .

25.3b . . . and check the cover sealing ring for signs of damage

25.5 Refit the centre bolt, ensuring the sealing ring (arrowed) is in position, and tighten it to the specified torque

Chapter 2 Part A:
1.6 litre SOHC petrol engine in-car repair procedures

Contents

Degrees of difficulty

Easy, suitable for novice with little experience	**Fairly easy,** suitable for beginner with some experience	**Fairly difficult,** suitable for competent DIY mechanic 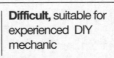	**Difficult,** suitable for experienced DIY mechanic	**Very difficult,** suitable for expert DIY or professional

Specifications

General

Engine type . . . . Four-cylinder, in-line, water-cooled. Single overhead camshaft, belt-driven, acting on hydraulic tappets

Manufacturer's engine code X16SZR
Bore . . . . 79.0 mm
Stroke . . . . 81.5 mm
Capacity . . . . 1598 cc
Firing order . . . . 1-3-4-2 (No 1 cylinder at timing belt end)
Direction of crankshaft rotation . . . . Clockwise (viewed from timing belt end of engine)
Compression ratio 9.6:1
Maximum power . . . . 55 kW at 5200 rpm
Maximum torque . . . . 128 Nm at 2800 rpm

Compression pressures

Standard . . . . 12 to 15 bar (174 to 218 psi)
Maximum difference between any two cylinders . . . . 1 bar (14.5 psi)

Camshaft

Endfloat . . . . 0.09 to 0.21 mm
Maximum permissible radial run-out . . . . 0.040 mm
Cam lift:
    Inlet valve . . . . 5.61 mm
    Exhaust valve . . . . 6.12 mm

Lubrication system

Oil pump type . . . . Gear type, driven directly from crankshaft
Minimum permissible oil pressure at idle speed, with engine
    at operating temperature (oil temperature of at least 80°C) . . . . 1.5 bar (22 psi)
Oil pump clearances:
    Gear teeth clearance . . . . 0.08 to 0.15 mm
    Gear endfloat . . . . 0.10 to 0.20 mm

Torque wrench settings

	Nm	lbf ft
Camshaft cover bolts	8	6
Camshaft housing end cover bolts	8	6
Camshaft sprocket bolt	45	33
Camshaft thrustplate bolts	8	6
Connecting rod big-end bearing cap bolt:		
Stage 1	25	18
Stage 2	Angle-tighten a further 30°	
Coolant pump bolts	8	6
Crankshaft pulley bolt*:		
Stage 1	55	41
Stage 2	Angle-tighten a further 45°	
Stage 3	Angle-tighten a further 15°	
Crankshaft sensor mounting bracket bolt	6	4
Cylinder head bolts*:		
Stage 1	25	18
Stage 2	Angle-tighten a further 60°	
Stage 3	Angle-tighten a further 60°	
Stage 4	Angle-tighten a further 60°	
Driveplate bolts	60	44
Driveplate lower cover plate bolts	8	6
Engine/transmission mounting bolts:		
Front (left- and right-hand) mounting:		
Bracket-to-engine/transmission bolts	60	44
Mounting-to-bracket/subframe nuts	45	33
Rear mounting:		
Mounting-to-bracket bolts	45	33
Mounting-to-subframe bolts	20	15
Bracket-to-transmission bolts	60	44
Torque support rod bolts	60	44
Engine-to-transmission unit bolts:		
M8 bolts	20	15
M10 bolts	40	30
M12 bolts	60	44
Flywheel bolts*:		
Stage 1	35	26
Stage 2	Angle-tighten a further 30°	
Stage 3	Angle-tighten a further 15°	
Flywheel lower cover plate bolts	8	6
Main bearing cap bolts:		
Stage 1	50	37
Stage 2	Angle-tighten a further 45°	
Stage 3	Angle-tighten a further 15°	
Oil pump:		
Retaining bolts	8	6
Pump cover screws	6	4
Oil pressure relief valve bolt	30	22
Oil pump pick-up/strainer bolts	8	6
Roadwheel bolts	110	81
Sump bolts:		
Models without air conditioning (steel sump):		
Sump-to-cylinder block/oil pump bolts	10	7
Drain plug	55	41
Models with air conditioning (alloy sump):		
Sump-to-cylinder block/oil pump bolts	8	6
Sump flange-to-transmission bolts:		
M8 bolts	20	15
M10 bolts	40	30
Drain plug	45	33
Timing belt cover bolts:		
Upper and lower covers	4	3
Rear cover	12	9
Timing belt tensioner bolt	20	15

1 General information

How to use this Chapter

1 This Part of Chapter 2 is devoted to in-car repair procedures for the engine. All procedures concerning engine removal and refitting, and engine block/cylinder head overhaul can be found in Chapter 2E.

2 Most of the operations included in this Part are based on the assumption that the engine is still installed in the car. Therefore, if this information is being used during a complete engine overhaul, with the engine already removed, many of the steps included here will not apply.

Engine description

3 The engine is a single overhead camshaft, four-cylinder, in-line unit, mounted transversely at the front of the car, with the clutch and transmission on its left-hand end.

4 The aluminium alloy cylinder block is of the dry-liner type. The crankshaft is supported within the cylinder block on five shell-type main bearings. Thrustwashers are fitted to number 3 main bearing, to control crankshaft endfloat.

5 The connecting rods are attached to the crankshaft by horizontally-split shell-type big-end bearings, and to the pistons by interference-fit gudgeon pins. The aluminium alloy pistons are of the slipper type, and are fitted with three piston rings, comprising two compression rings and a scraper-type oil control ring.

6 The camshaft runs directly in the camshaft housing, which is mounted on top of the cylinder head, and driven by the crankshaft via a toothed rubber timing belt (which also drives the coolant pump). The camshaft operates each valve via a follower. Each follower pivots on a hydraulic self-adjusting valve lifter (tappet) which automatically adjust the valve clearances.

7 Lubrication is by pressure-feed from a gear-type oil pump, which is mounted on the right-hand end of the crankshaft. It draws oil through a strainer located in the sump, and then forces it through an externally-mounted full-flow cartridge-type filter. The oil flows into galleries in the main bearing cap bridge arrangement and cylinder block/crankcase, from where it is distributed to the crankshaft (main bearings) and camshaft. The big-end bearings are supplied with oil via internal drillings in the crankshaft, while the camshaft bearings also receive a pressurised supply. The camshaft lobes and valves are lubricated by splash, as are all other engine components.

8 A semi-closed crankcase ventilation system is employed; crankcase fumes are drawn from the cylinder head cover, and passed via a hose to the inlet manifold.

Repair operations possible with the engine in the car

9 The following operations can be carried out without having to remove the engine from the vehicle:

a) Removal and refitting of the cylinder head.
b) Removal and refitting of the timing belt and sprockets.
c) Renewal of the camshaft oil seal.
d) Removal and refitting of the camshaft housing and camshaft.
e) Removal and refitting of the sump.
f) Removal and refitting of the connecting rods and pistons*.
g) Removal and refitting of the oil pump.
h) Renewal of the crankshaft oil seals.
i) Renewal of the engine mountings.
j) Removal and refitting of the flywheel/driveplate.

* Although the operation marked with an asterisk can be carried out with the engine in the car after removal of the sump, it is better for the engine to be removed, in the interests of cleanliness and improved access. For this reason, the procedure is described in Chapter 2E.

2 Compression test – description and interpretation

1 When engine performance is down, or if misfiring occurs which cannot be attributed to the ignition or fuel systems, a compression test can provide diagnostic clues as to the engine's condition. If the test is performed regularly, it can give warning of trouble before any other symptoms become apparent.

2 The engine must be fully warmed-up to normal operating temperature, the battery must be fully charged, and the spark plugs must be removed (see Chapter 1A). The aid of an assistant will also be required.

3 Disable the ignition system by disconnecting the wiring connector from the DIS module (see Chapter 5B) and the fuel system by removing the fuel pump relay from the engine compartment relay box (see Chapter 4A, Section 8).

4 Fit a compression tester to the number 1 cylinder spark plug hole. The type of tester which screws into the plug thread is to be preferred **(see illustration)**.

5 Have the assistant hold the throttle wide open and crank the engine on the starter motor; after one or two revolutions, the compression pressure should build-up to a maximum figure, and then stabilise. Record the highest reading obtained.

6 Repeat the test on the remaining cylinders, recording the pressure in each.

7 All cylinders should produce very similar pressures; any difference greater than that specified indicates the existence of a fault. Note that the compression should build-up

quickly in a healthy engine. Low compression on the first stroke, followed by gradually-increasing pressure on successive strokes, indicates worn piston rings. A low compression reading on the first stroke, which does not build-up during successive strokes, indicates leaking valves or a blown head gasket (a cracked head could also be the cause). Deposits on the undersides of the valve heads can also cause low compression.

8 If the pressure in any cylinder is reduced to the specified minimum or less, carry out the following test to isolate the cause. Introduce a teaspoonful of clean oil into that cylinder through its spark plug hole, and repeat the test.

9 If the addition of oil temporarily improves the compression pressure, this indicates that bore or piston wear is responsible for the pressure loss. No improvement suggests that leaking or burnt valves, or a blown head gasket, may be to blame.

10 A low reading from two adjacent cylinders is almost certainly due to the head gasket having blown between them; the presence of coolant in the engine oil will confirm this.

11 If one cylinder is about 20 per cent lower than the others, and the engine has a slightly rough idle, a worn camshaft lobe could be the cause.

12 If the compression reading is unusually high, the combustion chambers are probably coated with carbon deposits. If this is the case, the cylinder head should be removed and decarbonised.

13 On completion of the test, refit the spark plugs (see Chapter 1A), refit the fuel pump relay and reconnect the wiring connector to the DIS module.

3 Top dead centre (TDC) for No 1 piston – locating

1 In its travel up-and-down its cylinder bore, Top Dead Centre (TDC) is the highest point that each piston reaches as the crankshaft rotates. While each piston reaches TDC both at the top of the compression stroke and again at the top of the exhaust stroke, for the purpose of timing the engine TDC refers to the

2.4 Compression tester fitted to No 1 spark plug hole

3.5a Align the camshaft sprocket timing mark with the cut-out on the timing belt cover . . .

3.5b . . . and align the crankshaft pulley notch (A) with the timing belt pointer (B) to position No 1 piston at TDC on its compression stroke

piston position (usually number 1) at the top of its compression stroke.

2 Number 1 piston (and cylinder) is at the right-hand (timing belt) end of the engine, and its TDC position is located as follows. Note that the crankshaft rotates clockwise when viewed from the right-hand side of the car.

3 Disconnect the battery negative terminal. If necessary, remove all the spark plugs as described in Chapter 1A to enable the engine to be easily turned over.

4 To gain access to the camshaft sprocket timing mark, remove the timing belt upper cover as described in Section 6.

5 Using a socket and extension bar on the crankshaft pulley bolt, turn the crankshaft whilst keeping an eye on the camshaft sprocket. Rotate the crankshaft until the timing mark on the camshaft sprocket is correctly aligned with the cut-out on the top of the timing belt rear cover and the notch on the crankshaft pulley rim is correctly aligned with the pointer on the timing belt lower cover (see illustrations).

6 With the crankshaft pulley and camshaft sprocket timing marks positioned as described, the engine is positioned with No 1 piston at TDC on its compression stroke.

4 Camshaft cover – removal and refitting

Removal

1 Release the retaining clips and disconnect the breather hoses from the camshaft cover (see illustrations).

2 Slacken and remove the retaining bolts, noting the correct fitted location of any clips or brackets retained by the bolts (as applicable) then lift the camshaft cover from the camshaft housing (see illustration). If the cover is stuck, do not lever between the cover and camshaft housing mating surfaces – if necessary, gently tap the cover sideways to free it. Recover the gasket; if it shows signs of damage or deterioration it must be renewed.

Refitting

3 Prior to refitting, examine the inside of the cover for a build-up of oil sludge or any other contamination, and if necessary clean the cover with paraffin, or a water-soluble solvent. Examine the condition of the crankcase ventilation filter inside the camshaft cover, and clean as described for the inside of the cover if clogging is evident (if desired, the filter can be removed from the cover, after removing the securing bolts). Dry the cover thoroughly before refitting.

4 Ensure the cover is clean and dry and seat the gasket in the cover recess then refit the cover to the camshaft housing, ensuring the gasket remains correctly seated (see illustration).

5 Refit the retaining bolts, ensuring all relevant clips/brackets are correctly positioned, and tighten them to the specified torque working in a diagonal sequence (see illustration).

6 Reconnect the breather hoses securely to the cover.

4.1a Slacken the retaining clips and disconnect the large . . .

4.1b . . . and small breather hose from the rear of the camshaft cover

4.2 Removing the camshaft cover from the engine

4.4 Ensure the gasket is correctly located in the camshaft cover recess

4.5 On refitting ensure the wiring and HT lead clips (arrowed) are fitted to the correct bolts

5 Crankshaft pulley – removal and refitting

Note: A new pulley retaining bolt will be required on refitting.

Removal

1 Apply the handbrake, then jack up the front of the car and support it on axle stands. Remove the right-hand roadwheel.
2 Remove the auxiliary drivebelt as described in Chapter 1A. Prior to removal, mark the direction of rotation on the belt to ensure the belt is refitted the same way around.
3 Slacken the crankshaft pulley retaining bolt.

6.3 Timing belt upper cover retaining bolts (arrowed)

6.6 Timing belt lower cover retaining bolts (A)

There is no need to undo the timing belt tensioner bolt (B) to remove the cover

5.5 Refit the crankshaft pulley aligning the cut-out with the raised notch on the crankshaft sprocket (arrowed)

To prevent crankshaft rotation on manual transmission models, have an assistant select top gear and apply the brakes firmly. On automatic transmission models prevent rotation by removing one of the torque converter retaining bolts and bolting the driveplate to the transmission housing using a metal bar, spacers and suitable bolts (see Chapter 7B). If the engine is removed from the vehicle it will be necessary to lock the flywheel/driveplate (see Section 15).
4 Unscrew the retaining bolt and washer and remove the crankshaft pulley from the end of the crankshaft, taking care not to damage the crankshaft sensor.

Refitting

5 Refit the crankshaft pulley, aligning the pulley cut-out with the raised notch on the timing belt sprocket, then fit the washer and new retaining bolt **(see illustration)**.
6 Lock the crankshaft by the method used on removal, and tighten the pulley retaining bolt to the specified Stage 1 torque setting then angle-tighten the bolt through the specified Stage 2 angle, using a socket and extension bar, and finally through the specified Stage 3 angle. It is recommended that an angle-measuring gauge is used during the final stages of the tightening, to ensure accuracy **(see illustration)**. If a gauge is not available, use white paint to make alignment marks between the bolt head and pulley prior to tightening; the marks can then be used to check that the bolt has been rotated through the correct angle.

6.9 Slacken and remove the retaining bolts and remove the timing belt rear cover

5.6 Fit the new retaining bolt and tighten it as described in the text

7 Refit the auxiliary drivebelt as described in Chapter 1A using the mark made prior to removal to ensure the belt is fitted the correct way around.
8 Refit the roadwheel then lower the car to the ground and tighten the wheel bolts to the specified torque.

6 Timing belt covers – removal and refitting

Upper cover

Removal

1 Remove the air cleaner housing as described in Chapter 4A.
2 Remove the auxiliary drivebelt as described in Chapter 1A. Prior to removal, mark the direction of rotation on the belt to ensure the belt is fitted the same way around on refitting.
3 Undo the retaining screws then unclip the timing belt upper cover and remove it from the engine **(see illustration)**.

Refitting

4 Refitting is the reverse of removal, ensuring the auxiliary drivebelt is fitted the same way around as it was prior removal.

Lower cover

Removal

5 Remove the crankshaft pulley (see Section 5).
6 Remove the upper cover (see paragraphs 1 and 3) then undo the retaining screws and remove the lower cover from the engine **(see illustration)**.

Refitting

7 Refitting is the reverse of removal, using a new crankshaft pulley retaining bolt.

Rear cover

Removal

8 Remove the camshaft and crankshaft timing belt sprockets and the timing belt tensioner as described in Section 8.
9 Slacken and remove the bolts securing the rear cover to the camshaft housing and oil pump housing, and remove the cover from the engine **(see illustration)**.

7.5a Insert a tool (such as a punch) into the hole (arrowed) in the tensioner arm . . .

7.5b . . . then lever the arm clockwise and lock the tensioner in position by locating the tool in the backplate hole

7.7a Slacken the coolant pump bolts . . .

7.7b . . . and relieve the timing belt tension by rotating the pump with a suitable adapter

Refitting

10 Refitting is the reverse of removal, tightening the cover retaining bolts to the specified torque.

---

7 Timing belt – removal and refitting

Note: *The timing belt must be removed and refitted with the engine cold.*

Removal

1 Remove the timing belt upper cover as described in Section 6.

2 Position No 1 cylinder at TDC on its compression stroke as described in Section 3.

3 Remove the crankshaft pulley as described in Section 5.

7.8 Slip the timing belt off from the sprockets and remove it from the engine

4 Unbolt the timing belt lower cover and remove it from the engine (see Section 6).

5 Insert a suitable tool (such as a pin punch) into the hole in the timing belt tensioner arm, then lever the arm clockwise to its stop, and lock it in position by inserting the tool into the corresponding hole in the tensioner backplate (see illustrations). Leave the tool in position to lock the tensioner in position until the belt is refitted.

6 Check the camshaft and crankshaft sprocket timing marks are correctly aligned with the marks on the belt rear cover and oil pump housing.

7 Slacken the coolant pump retaining bolts then, using an open-ended spanner, carefully rotate the pump to relieve the tension in the timing belt. Adapters to fit the pump are available from most tool shops and allow the

7.10 Ensure the timing mark on the crankshaft sprocket is correctly aligned with the mark on the oil pump housing

pump to be easily turned using a ratchet or extension bar (see illustrations).

8 Slide the timing belt off from its sprockets and remove it from the engine (see illustration). If the belt is to be re-used, use white paint or similar to mark the direction of rotation on the belt. **Do not** rotate the crankshaft until the timing belt has been refitted.

9 Check the timing belt carefully for any signs of uneven wear, splitting or oil contamination, and renew it if there is the slightest doubt about its condition. If the engine is undergoing an overhaul and is approaching the manufacturers' specified interval for belt renewal (see Chapter 1A) renew the belt as a matter of course, regardless of its apparent condition. If signs of oil contamination are found, trace the source of the oil leak and rectify it, then wash down the engine timing belt area and all related components to remove all traces of oil.

Refitting

10 On reassembly, thoroughly clean the timing belt sprockets then check that the camshaft sprocket timing mark is still correctly aligned with the cover cut-out and the crankshaft sprocket mark is still aligned with the mark on the oil pump housing (see illustration).

11 Fit the timing belt over the crankshaft and camshaft sprockets, ensuring that the belt front run is taut (ie, all slack is on the tensioner pulley side of the belt), then fit the belt over the coolant pump sprocket and tensioner pulley. Do not twist the belt sharply while refitting it. Ensure that the belt teeth are correctly seated centrally in the sprockets, and that the timing marks remain in alignment. If a used belt is being refitted, ensure that the arrow mark made on removal points in the normal direction of rotation, as before.

12 Carefully remove the punch from the timing belt tensioner to release the tensioner spring.

13 Check the sprocket timing marks are still correctly aligned. If adjustment is necessary, lock the tensioner in position again then disengage the belt from the sprockets and make any necessary adjustments.

14 If the marks are still correctly positioned, tension the timing belt by rotating the coolant pump whilst observing the movement of the tensioner arm. Position the pump so that the tensioner arm is fully over against its stop, without exerting any excess strain on the belt, then tighten the coolant pump retaining bolts.

15 Temporarily refit the crankshaft pulley bolt then rotate the crankshaft smoothly through two complete turns (720°) in the normal direction of rotation to settle the timing belt in position.

16 Check that both the camshaft and crankshaft sprocket timing marks are realigned then slacken the coolant pump bolts. Adjust the pump so that the tensioner arm pointer is aligned with the cut-out on the

7.16 Rotate the coolant pump until the tensioner arm pointer (1) is correctly aligned with the cut-out (2) on the backplate

8.2 Using a home-made sprocket holding tool to retain the camshaft sprocket whilst the bolt is slackened

backplate then tighten the coolant pump bolts to the specified torque **(see illustration)**. Rotate the crankshaft smoothly through another two complete turns in the normal direction of rotation, to bring the sprocket timing marks back into alignment. Check that the tensioner arm pointer is still aligned with the backplate cut-out.

17 If the tensioner arm is not correctly aligned with the backplate, repeat the procedure in paragraph 16.

18 Once the tensioner arm and backplate remain correctly aligned, ensure the coolant pump bolts are tightened to the specified torque, then refit the timing belt covers and crankshaft pulley as described in Sections 5 and 6.

8 Timing belt tensioner and sprockets – removal and refitting

Camshaft sprocket

Removal

1 Remove the timing belt as described in Section 7.

2 The camshaft must be prevented from turning as the sprocket bolt is unscrewed, and this can be achieved in one of two ways as follows.

a) *Make up a sprocket-holding tool using two lengths of steel strip (one long, the other short), and three nuts and bolts; one nut and bolt forms the pivot of a forked tool, with the remaining two nuts and bolts at the tips of the 'forks' to engage with the sprocket spokes* **(see illustration)**.

b) *Remove the camshaft cover as described in Section 4 and hold the camshaft with an open-ended spanner on the flats provided.*

3 Unscrew the retaining bolt and washer and remove the sprocket from the end of the camshaft.

Refitting

4 Prior to refitting check the oil seal for signs of damage or leakage, if necessary, renewing it as described in Section 9.

5 Refit the sprocket to the end of the camshaft, aligning its cut-out with the camshaft locating pin, then refit the retaining bolt and washer **(see illustration)**.

6 Tighten the sprocket retaining bolt to the specified torque whilst preventing rotation using the method employed on removal **(see illustration)**.

7 Refit the timing belt as described in Section 7 then (where necessary) refit the camshaft cover as described in Section 4.

Crankshaft sprocket

Removal

8 Remove the timing belt (see Section 7).

9 Slide the sprocket off from the end of the crankshaft, noting which way around it is fitted.

Refitting

10 Ensure the Woodruff key is correctly fitted to the crankshaft.

11 Align the sprocket with the crankshaft groove then slide the sprocket into position, making sure its timing mark is facing outwards **(see illustration)**.

12 Refit the timing belt (see Section 7).

Tensioner assembly

Removal

13 Remove the timing belt (see Section 7).

8.5 Refit the camshaft sprocket making sure the locating pin (1) engages with the sprocket hole (2)

8.6 Use an open-ended spanner to retain the camshaft whilst the sprocket retaining nut is tightened to the specified torque

8.11 Refit the crankshaft sprocket making sure its timing marks are facing outwards

8.14 Slacken and remove the retaining bolt and remove the timing belt tensioner assembly

14 Slacken and remove the retaining bolt and remove the tensioner assembly from the oil pump **(see illustration)**.

Refitting

15 Fit the tensioner to the oil pump housing, making sure that the lug on the backplate is correctly located in the oil pump housing hole **(see illustration)**. Ensure the tensioner is correctly seated then refit the retaining bolt and tighten it to the specified torque.

9 Camshaft oil seal – renewal

1 Remove the camshaft sprocket as described in Section 8.

9.2 Removing the camshaft oil seal

9.4 Fitting a new camshaft oil seal

8.15 On refitting ensure the tensioner backplate lug (1) is correctly located in the oil pump housing hole (2)

2 Carefully punch or drill two small holes opposite each other in the oil seal. Screw a self-tapping screw into each, and pull on the screws with pliers to extract the seal **(see illustration)**.

3 Clean the seal housing, and polish off any burrs or raised edges which may have caused the seal to fail in the first place.

4 Lubricate the lips of the new seal with clean engine oil, and press it into position using a suitable tubular drift (such as a socket) which bears only on the hard outer edge of the seal **(see illustration)**. Take care not to damage the seal lips during fitting; note that the seal lips should face inwards.

5 Refit the camshaft sprocket as described in Section 8.

10 Camshaft – removal, inspection and refitting

Removal

Using service tool MKM 891

1 If access to the special service tool can be gained, the camshaft can be removed from the engine without disturbing the camshaft housing. The tool is fitted to the top of the camshaft housing, once the cover has been removed (see Section 4), and depresses the cam followers. This allows the camshaft to be withdrawn from the left-hand end of the

housing once the timing belt sprocket has been removed (see Section 8) and the cover and thrustplate have been unbolted (see paragraphs 3 to 6).

Caution: Prior to fitting the special tool, rotate the crankshaft another 90° past the TDC position (see Section 3). This will position the pistons approximately mid-way in the bores and prevent the valves contacting them when the tool is fitted.

Without service tool

2 Assuming that such a tool is not available, the camshaft can only be removed once the camshaft housing has been removed from the engine. Since the camshaft housing is secured in position by the cylinder head bolts, it is not possible to remove the camshaft without removing the cylinder head (see Section 12). **Note:** *In theory it is possible to remove the camshaft housing once the cylinder head bolts have been removed, and leave the head in position. However, this procedure carries a high risk of disturbing the head gasket, resulting in the head gasket 'blowing' once the camshaft and housing are refitted. If you wish to attempt this, remove the camshaft housing, as described in Section 12, noting that it will not be necessary to remove the manifolds, etc. Be warned though that, after refitting, you may find the head gasket will need renewing, meaning that the cylinder head will have to be removed after all and need another set of bolts. The decision is yours as to whether this is a chance worth taking.*

3 With the camshaft housing removed (where necessary), unbolt the DIS module and remove it from the end of the housing.

4 Undo the retaining bolts and remove the end cover from the left-hand end of the housing **(see illustration)**. Remove the sealing ring from the cover and discard it, a new one should be used on refitting.

5 Measure the camshaft endfloat by inserting feeler gauges between the thrustplate and the camshaft; if the endfloat is not within the limits given in the Specifications then the thrustplate will need to be renewed. Unscrew the two retaining bolts then slide out the camshaft thrustplate, noting which way round it is fitted **(see illustration)**.

10.4 Remove the cover from the left-hand end of the camshaft housing (sealing ring arrowed)

10.5 Undo the retaining bolts then remove the thrustplate (arrowed) . . .

6 Carefully withdraw the camshaft from the left-hand end of the housing, taking care not to damage the bearing journals (see illustration).

Inspection

7 With the camshaft removed, examine the bearings in the camshaft housing for signs of obvious wear or pitting. If evident, a new camshaft housing will probably be required. Also check that the oil supply holes in the camshaft housing are free from obstructions.

8 The camshaft itself should show no marks or scoring on the journal or cam lobe surfaces. If evident, renew the camshaft. If the camshaft lobes show signs of wear also examine the followers (see Section 11).

9 Check the camshaft thrustplate for signs of wear or grooves, and renew if necessary.

Refitting

10 Carefully prise the old seal out of from the camshaft housing, using a suitable screwdriver. Ensure the housing is clean then press the in new seal, ensuring its sealing lip is facing inwards, until it is flush with the housing.

11 Liberally lubricate the camshaft and housing bearings and the oil seal lip with fresh engine oil.

12 Carefully insert the camshaft into the housing, taking care not to mark the bearing surfaces or damage the oil seal lip.

13 Slide the thrustplate into position, engaging it with the camshaft slot, and tighten its retaining bolts to the specified torque. Check the camshaft endfloat (see paragraph 5).

14 Fit a new sealing ring to the end cover recess then refit the cover to the camshaft housing and tighten its retaining bolts to the specified torque. Refit the DIS module to the housing cover.

15 If work is being carried out using the special service tool, remove the tool and refit the camshaft sprocket. Return the crankshaft to TDC and refit the timing belt (see Sections 7 and 8).

16 If the tool is not being used, refit the camshaft housing as described in Section 12.

11 Camshaft followers and hydraulic tappets – removal, inspection and refitting

Using service tool KM-565

Removal

1 If access to the special tool or a suitable equivalent can be gained, the cam followers and tappets can be removed as follows, without disturbing the camshaft.

2 Firmly apply the handbrake then jack up the front of the vehicle and support it on axle stands. Remove the right-hand front roadwheel.

3 Remove the camshaft cover as described in Section 4.

4 Using a socket and extension bar, rotate the crankshaft in the normal direction of rotation until the camshaft lobe of the first follower/tappet to be removed is pointing straight upwards.

5 Fit the service tool to the top of the camshaft housing, making sure the tool end is correctly engaged with the top of the valve. Screw the tool stud into one of the housing cover bolt holes until the valve is sufficiently depressed to allow the follower to be slid out from underneath the camshaft. The hydraulic tappet can then also be removed as can the thrust pad from the top of the valve. Inspect the components (see paragraphs 10 and 11) and renew if worn or damaged.

Refitting

6 Lubricate the tappet and follower with fresh engine oil then slide the tappet into its bore in the cylinder head. Manoeuvre the follower into position, ensuring it is correctly engaged with the tappet and valve stem, then carefully remove the service tool.

7 Repeat the operation on the remaining followers and tappets.

Without service tool

Removal

8 Without the use of the special tool, it will be necessary to remove the camshaft housing to allow the followers and tappets to be removed (see Section 10, paragraph 2).

10.6 . . . and slide the camshaft out from the housing

9 With the housing removed, obtain eight small, clean plastic containers, and number them 1 to 8; alternatively, divide a larger container into eight compartments. Lift out each follower, thrust pad and hydraulic tappet in turn, and place them in their respective container. Do not interchange the cam followers, or the rate of wear will be much-increased (see illustrations).

Inspection

10 Examine the cam follower bearing surfaces which contact the camshaft lobes for wear ridges and scoring. Renew any follower on which these conditions are apparent. If a follower bearing surface is badly scored, also examine the corresponding lobe on the camshaft for wear, as it is likely that both will be worn. Also check the thrust pad for signs of wear or damage. Renew worn components as necessary.

11 If the hydraulic tappets are thought to be faulty they should be renewed; testing of the tappets is not possible.

Refitting

12 Lubricate the hydraulic tappets and their cylinder head bores with clean engine oil. Refit the tappets to the cylinder head, making sure they are fitted in their original locations.

13 Fit the thrust pads to the top of its respective valves.

14 Lubricate the followers with clean engine oil. Fit each follower, making sure it is correctly located with both the tappet and thrust pad, then refit the camshaft housing (see Section 12).

11.9a Remove each follower . . .

11.9b . . . thrust pad . . .

11.9c . . . and hydraulic tappet from the cylinder head

12.12 Removing the camshaft housing

12.13 Removing the cylinder head

12 Camshaft housing and cylinder head – removal and refitting

Removal

Note: *The engine must be cold when removing the cylinder head. New cylinder head bolts must be used on refitting.*

1 Depressurise the fuel system as described in Chapter 4A then disconnect the battery negative lead.

2 Drain the cooling system and remove the spark plugs as described in Chapter 1A.

3 Remove the timing belt as described in Section 7.

4 Remove the inlet and exhaust manifolds as described in Chapter 4A If no work is to be carried out on the cylinder head, the head can be removed complete with manifolds once the following operations have been carried out (see Chapter 4A).

 a) *Disconnect the various wiring connectors from the throttle body and manifold and free the wiring harness from the inlet manifold.*

 b) *Disconnect the fuel hoses from the throttle body and the various vacuum and coolant hoses from the inlet manifold.*

 c) *Unbolt the inlet manifold support bracket and the alternator upper bracket.*

 d) *Disconnect the accelerator cable.*

 e) *Unbolt the exhaust front pipe from manifold and disconnect the oxygen sensor wiring connector.*

5 Remove the camshaft cover as described in Section 4.

6 Remove the camshaft sprocket as described in Section 8.

7 Undo the retaining bolts securing the timing belt rear cover to the camshaft housing.

8 Disconnect the wiring connectors from the DIS module, purge valve and the coolant temperature sender unit and on the left-hand end of the cylinder head. Free the wiring from its retaining clips, noting its correct routing, and position it clear of the cylinder head.

9 Slacken the retaining clip and disconnect the coolant hose from the thermostat housing

10 Make a final check to ensure that all relevant hoses, pipes and wires, etc, have been disconnected.

11 Working in the **reverse** of the tightening sequence **(see illustration 12.29a)**, progressively slacken the cylinder head bolts by a third of a turn at a time until all bolts can be unscrewed by hand. Remove each bolt in turn, along with its washer.

12 Lift the camshaft housing from the cylinder head **(see illustration)**. If necessary, tap the housing gently with a soft-faced mallet to free it from the cylinder head, but **do not** lever at the mating faces. Note the fitted positions of the two locating dowels, and remove them for safe keeping if they are loose.

13 Lift the cylinder head from the cylinder block, taking care not to dislodge the cam followers or thrust pads **(see illustration)**. If necessary, tap the cylinder head gently with a soft-faced mallet to free it from the block, but

do not lever at the mating faces. Note the fitted positions of the two locating dowels, and remove them for safe keeping if they are loose.

14 Recover the cylinder head gasket, and discard it.

Preparation for refitting

15 The mating faces of the cylinder head and block must be perfectly clean before refitting the head. Use a scraper to remove all traces of gasket and carbon, and also clean the tops of the pistons. Take particular care with the aluminium surfaces, as the soft metal is damaged easily. Also, make sure that debris is not allowed to enter the oil and water channels – this is particularly important for the oil circuit, as carbon could block the oil supply to the camshaft or crankshaft bearings. Using adhesive tape and paper, seal the water, oil and bolt holes in the cylinder block. To prevent carbon entering the gap between the pistons and bores, smear a little grease in the gap. After cleaning the piston, rotate the crankshaft so that the piston moves down the bore, then wipe out the grease and carbon with a cloth rag. Clean the other piston crowns in the same way.

16 Check the block and head for nicks, deep scratches and other damage. If slight, they may be removed carefully with a file. More serious damage may be repaired by machining, but this is a specialist job.

17 If warpage of the cylinder head is suspected, use a straight-edge to check it for distortion. Refer to Chapter 2E if necessary.

18 Ensure that the cylinder head bolt holes in the crankcase are clean and free of oil. Syringe or soak up any oil left in the bolt holes. This is most important in order that the correct bolt tightening torque can be applied and to prevent the possibility of the block being cracked by hydraulic pressure when the bolts are tightened.

19 Renew the cylinder head bolts regardless of their apparent condition.

Refitting

20 Position number 1 piston at TDC, and wipe clean the mating faces of the head and block.

21 Ensure that the two locating dowels are in position at each end of the cylinder block/crankcase surface.

22 Fit the new cylinder head gasket to the block, making sure it is fitted with the correct way up with its OBEN/TOP mark uppermost **(see illustrations)**.

23 Carefully refit the cylinder head, locating it on the dowels.

24 Ensure the mating surfaces of the cylinder head and camshaft housing are clean and dry. Check the camshaft is still correctly positioned by temporarily fitting the camshaft sprocket and checking that the sprocket timing mark is still uppermost.

25 Apply a bead of suitable sealant to the cylinder head mating surface **(see illustration)**.

12.22a Fit the new gasket to the cylinder block, engaging it with the locating dowels (arrowed) . . .

12.22b . . . making sure its OBEN/TOP marking is uppermost

12.25 Apply sealant to the cylinder head upper mating surface then refit the camshaft housing

26 Ensure the two locating dowels are in position then lubricate the camshaft followers with clean engine oil.

27 Carefully lower the camshaft housing assembly into position, locating it on the dowels.

28 Fit the washers to the new cylinder head bolts then carefully insert them into position (**do not drop**), tightening them finger-tight only at this stage (**see illustration**).

29 Working progressively and in the sequence shown, first tighten all the cylinder head bolts to

12.28 Fit the washers to the new cylinder head bolts and screw the bolts into position

the Stage 1 torque setting (**see illustrations**).

30 Once all bolts have been tightened to the Stage 1 torque, again working in the sequence shown, tighten each bolt through its specified Stage 2 angle, using a socket and extension bar. It is recommended that an angle-measuring gauge is used during this stage of the tightening, to ensure accuracy (**see illustration**).

31 Working in the specified sequence, go around again and tighten all bolts through the specified Stage 3 angle.

32 Finally go around in the specified sequence again and tighten all bolts through the specified Stage 4 angle.

33 Refit the bolts securing the timing belt rear cover to the camshaft housing and tighten them to the specified torque.

34 Refit the camshaft sprocket as described in Section 8 then fit the timing belt as described in Section 7.

35 Reconnect the wiring connectors to the cylinder head components, ensuring all wiring is correctly routed, and secure it in position with the necessary clips.

36 Reconnect the coolant hose to the thermostat housing and securely tighten its retaining clip.

37 Refit/reconnect the manifolds as described in Chapter 4A (as applicable).

38 Refit the roadwheel then lower the vehicle to the floor and tighten the wheel bolts to the specified torque.

39 Ensure all pipes and hoses are securely reconnected then refill the cooling system and refit the spark plugs as described in Chapter 1A.

40 Reconnect the battery then start the engine and check for signs of leaks.

13 Sump –
removal and refitting

Removal

1 Disconnect the battery negative terminal.

2 Firmly apply the handbrake then jack up the front of the car and support it on axle stands.

3 Drain the engine oil as described in Chapter 1A, then fit a new sealing washer and refit the drain plug, tightening it to the specified torque.

4 Remove the exhaust system front pipe as described in Chapter 4A.

5 Where necessary, disconnect the wiring connector from the oil level sender unit on the sump.

No air conditioning (steel sump)

6 Slacken and remove the flywheel/driveplate lower cover retaining bolts and remove the cover from the base of the transmission unit (**see illustration**).

12.29a Cylinder head bolt tightening sequence

12.29b Working in the specified sequence, tighten the cylinder head bolts to the specified Stage 1 torque setting . . .

12.30 . . . and then through the various specified angles (see text)

13.6 Removing the flywheel/driveplate lower cover plate – models without air conditioning

**13.7 Removing the pressed-steel sump –
models without air conditioning**

**13.10 On models with air conditioning
remove the rubber plugs from the sump
flange to access the remaining bolts**

**13.12 Fit a new sealing ring to the oil
pump pick-up/strainer**

7 Progressively slacken and remove the bolts securing the sump to the base of the cylinder block/oil pump. Break the sump joint by striking the sump with the palm of the hand, then lower the sump away from the engine and withdraw it **(see illustration)**. Remove the gasket and discard it.

8 While the sump is removed, take the opportunity to check the oil pump pick-up/strainer for signs of clogging or splitting. If necessary, unbolt the pick-up/strainer and remove it from the base of the oil pump housing along with its sealing ring. The strainer can then be cleaned easily in solvent or renewed.

Air conditioned (alloy sump)

9 Slacken and remove the bolts securing the sump flange to the transmission housing.

10 Remove the sump and (where necessary) the oil pump pick-up/strainer as described in paragraphs 7 and 8. Note that the bolts securing the transmission end of the sump to the cylinder block are accessed through the cut-outs in the sump flange, once the rubber plugs have been removed **(see illustration)**.

Refitting

No air conditioning (steel sump)

11 Remove all traces of dirt and oil from the mating surfaces of the sump and cylinder block and (where removed) the pick-up/strainer and oil pump housing. Also remove all traces of locking compound from the pick-up bolts (where removed).

12 Where necessary, position a new sealing ring on top of the oil pump pick-up/strainer and fit the strainer **(see illustration)**. Apply locking compound to the threads of the retaining bolts then fit the bolts and tighten to the specified torque.

13 Apply a smear of suitable sealant to the areas of the cylinder block mating surface around the areas of the of the oil housing and rear main bearing cap joints **(see illustration)**.

14 Fit a new gasket to the sump then offer up the sump to the cylinder block and refit the retaining bolts. Working out from the centre in a diagonal sequence, progressively tighten the sump retaining bolts to their specified torque setting.

15 Refit the flywheel/driveplate cover plate to the transmission housing, tightening its retaining bolts to the specified torque.

16 Refit the exhaust front pipe (see Chapter 4A) and reconnect the oil level sender wiring connector (where fitted).

17 Lower the vehicle to the ground then fill the engine with fresh oil, with reference to Chapter 1A.

Air conditioned (alloy sump)

18 Where necessary, refit the oil pump pick-up/strainer as described in paragraphs 11 and 12.

19 Ensure the sump and cylinder block mating surfaces are clean and dry and remove all traces of locking compound from the sump bolts.

20 Apply a smear of suitable sealant to the areas of the cylinder block mating surface around the areas of the of the oil housing and rear main bearing cap joints.

21 Fit a new gasket to the sump and apply a few drops of locking compound to the threads of the sump to cylinder block/oil pump bolts.

22 Offer up the sump, ensuring the gasket remains correctly positioned, and loosely refit all the retaining bolts. Working out from the centre in a diagonal sequence, progressively tighten the bolts securing the sump to the cylinder block/oil pump to their specified torque setting.

23 Tighten the bolts securing the sump flange to the transmission housing to their specified torque settings. Refit the rubber plugs to the sump flange cut-outs.

24 Refit the exhaust front pipe (see Chapter 4A) and reconnect the oil level sender wiring connector (where fitted).

25 Lower the vehicle to the ground then fill the engine with fresh oil, with reference to Chapter 1A.

14 Oil pump –
removal, overhaul and refitting

Note: *The pressure relief valve can be removed with pump in position on the engine unit.*

Removal

1 Remove the timing belt (see Section 7).

**13.13 Apply sealant to the oil pump and rear main bearing cap joints (arrowed) before
the sump is refitted**

14.8 Undo the retaining screws and remove the oil pump cover

14.10 Removal of pump outer gear – outer face identification punch mark arrowed

14.11 Oil pressure relief valve components

1 Plunger	3 Sealing washer
2 Spring	4 Valve bolt

2 Remove the camshaft and crankshaft timing belt sprockets and the tensioner as described in Section 8.

3 Unbolt the timing belt rear cover from the camshaft housing and oil pump and remove it from the engine.

4 Remove the sump and oil pump pick-up/strainer as described in Section 13.

5 Disconnect the wiring connector from the oil pressure switch.

6 Unbolt the crankshaft sensor mounting bracket and position it clear of the oil pump.

7 Slacken and remove the retaining bolts then slide the oil pump housing assembly off of the end of the crankshaft, taking great care not to lose the locating dowels. Remove the housing gasket and discard it.

Overhaul

8 Undo the retaining screws and lift off the pump cover from the rear of the housing **(see illustration)**.

9 Using a suitable marker pen, mark the surface of both the pump inner and outer gears; the marks can then be used to ensure the rotors are refitted the correct way around.

10 Lift out the inner and outer gears from the pump housing **(see illustration)**.

11 Unscrew the oil pressure relief valve bolt from the front of the housing and withdraw the spring and plunger from the housing, noting which way around the plunger is fitted **(see illustration)**. Remove the sealing washer from the valve bolt.

12 Clean the components, and carefully examine the gears, pump body and relief valve plunger for any signs of scoring or wear. Renew any component which shows signs of wear or damage; if the gears or pump housing are marked then the complete pump assembly should be renewed.

13 If the components appear serviceable, measure the clearance between the inner gear and outer gear using feeler blades. Also measure the gear endfloat, and check the flatness of the end cover **(see illustrations)**. If the clearances exceed the specified tolerances, the pump must be renewed.

14 If the pump is satisfactory, reassemble the components in the reverse order of removal, noting the following:

a) *Ensure both gears are fitted the correct way around.*

b) *Fit a new sealing washer to the pressure relief valve bolt and tighten the bolt to the specified torque.*

c) *Remove all traces of locking compound from the cover screws. Apply a drop of fresh locking compound to each screw and tighten the screws to the specified torque.*

d) *On completion prime the oil pump by filling it with clean engine oil whilst rotating the inner gear.*

Refitting

15 Prior to refitting, carefully lever out the crankshaft oil seal using a flat-bladed screwdriver. Fit the new oil seal, ensuring its sealing lip is facing inwards, and press it squarely into the housing using a tubular drift which bears only on the hard outer edge of the seal **(see illustration)**. Press the seal into position so that it is flush with the housing and lubricate the oil seal lip with clean engine oil.

16 Ensure the mating surfaces of the oil pump and cylinder block are clean and dry and the locating dowels are in position.

17 Fit a new gasket to the cylinder block.

18 Carefully manoeuvre the oil pump into position and engage the inner gear with the crankshaft end **(see illustration)**. Locate the pump on the dowels, taking great care not to damage the oil seal lip.

19 Refit the pump housing retaining bolts in their original locations and tighten to the specified torque.

20 Refit the crankshaft sensor bracket to the pump housing and tighten its mounting bolt to the specified torque. Reconnect the oil pressure sensor wiring connector.

21 Refit the oil pump pick-up/strainer and sump as described in Section 13.

22 Refit the rear timing belt cover to the

14.13a Using a feeler blade to check gear clearance

14.13b Using a straight-edge and feeler blade to measure gear endfloat

14.15 Fitting a new crankshaft oil seal to the oil pump housing

14.18 Take care not to damage the oil seal on the crankshaft lip (1) and engage the inner gear with the crankshaft flats (2)

15.2 Lock the flywheel/driveplate ring gear with a tool similar to that shown

15.10a On manual transmission models, tighten the flywheel bolts to the specified Stage 1 torque setting . . .

15.10b . . . then tighten them through the specified Stage 2 and 3 angles

engine, tightening its retaining bolts to the specified torque.

23 Refit the timing belt sprockets and tensioner then refit the belt as described in Sections 7 and 8.

24 On completion refill the engine with clean oil as described in Chapter 1A.

15 Flywheel/driveplate – removal, inspection and refitting

Removal

Manual transmission models

Note: *New flywheel retaining bolts will be required on refitting.*

1 Remove the transmission as described in Chapter 7A then remove the clutch assembly as described in Chapter 6.

2 Prevent the flywheel from turning by locking the ring gear teeth with a similar arrangement to that shown **(see illustration)**. Alternatively, bolt a strap between the flywheel and the cylinder block/crankcase. Make alignment marks between the flywheel and crankshaft using paint or a suitable marker pen.

3 Slacken and remove the retaining bolts and remove the flywheel. Do not drop it, as it is very heavy.

Automatic transmission models

4 Remove the transmission as described in Chapter 7B then remove the driveplate as described in paragraphs 2 and 3, noting that there is a retaining plate fitted between the retaining bolts and driveplate.

Inspection

5 On manual transmission models, examine the flywheel for scoring of the clutch face. If the clutch face is scored, the flywheel may be surface-ground, but renewal is preferable. Check for wear or chipping of the ring gear teeth. Renewal of the ring gear is also possible is not a task for the home mechanic; renewal requires the new ring gear to be heated (up to 180° to 230°C) to allow it to be fitted.

6 On automatic transmission models closely

examine the driveplate and ring gear teeth for signs of wear or damage and check the driveplate surface for any signs of cracks.

7 If there is any doubt about the condition of the flywheel/driveplate, seek the advice of a Vauxhall dealer or engine reconditioning specialist. They will be able to advise if it is possible to recondition it or whether renewal is necessary.

Refitting

Manual transmission models

8 Clean the mating surfaces of the flywheel and crankshaft.

9 Offer up the flywheel and fit the new retaining bolts. If the original is being refitted align the marks made prior to removal.

10 Lock the flywheel by the method used on removal, and tighten the retaining bolts to the specified Stage 1 torque setting then angle-tighten the bolts through the specified Stage 2 angle, using a socket and extension bar, and finally through the specified Stage 3 angle. It is recommended that an angle-measuring gauge is used during the final stages of the tightening, to ensure accuracy **(see illustrations)**. If a gauge is not available, use white paint to make alignment marks between the bolt head and flywheel prior to tightening; the marks can then be used to check that the bolt has been rotated through the correct angle.

11 Refit the clutch as described in Chapter 6 then remove the locking tool, and refit the transmission as described in Chapter 7A.

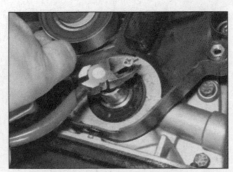

16.2 Removing the crankshaft oil seal

Automatic transmission models

12 Clean the mating surfaces of the drive-plate and crankshaft and remove all traces of locking compound from the driveplate retaining bolt threads.

13 Apply a drop of locking compound to each of the retaining bolt threads then offer up the driveplate, if the original is being refitted align the marks made prior to removal. Refit the retaining plate and screw in the retaining bolts.

14 Lock the driveplate using the method employed on dismantling then, working in a diagonal sequence, evenly and progressively tighten the retaining bolts to the specified torque.

15 Remove the locking tool and refit the transmission as described in Chapter 7B.

16 Crankshaft oil seals – renewal

Right-hand (timing belt end)

1 Remove the crankshaft sprocket as described in Section 8.

2 Carefully punch or drill two small holes opposite each other in the oil seal. Screw a self-tapping screw into each and pull on the screws with pliers to extract the seal **(see illustration)**.

Caution: Great care must be taken to avoid damage to the oil pump

3 Clean the seal housing and polish off any burrs or raised edges which may have caused the seal to fail in the first place.

4 Lubricate the lips of the new seal with clean engine oil and ease it into position on the end of the shaft. Press the seal squarely into position until it is flush with the housing. If necessary, a suitable tubular drift, such as a socket, which bears only on the hard outer edge of the seal can be used to tap the seal into position **(see illustration)**. Take great care not to damage the seal lips during fitting and ensure that the seal lips face inwards.

5 Wash off any traces of oil, then refit the crankshaft sprocket as described in Section 8.

16.4 Fitting a new crankshaft oil seal

Left-hand (flywheel/driveplate end)

6 Remove the flywheel/driveplate as described in Section 15.

7 Renew the seal as described in paragraphs 2 to 4.

8 Refit the flywheel/driveplate as described in Section 15.

17 Engine/transmission mountings – inspection and renewal

Inspection

1 If improved access is required, raise the front of the car and support it securely on axle stands. Where necessary, undo the retaining bolts and remove the undercover from beneath the engine/transmission unit.

2 Check the mounting rubber to see if it is cracked, hardened or separated from the metal at any point; renew the mounting if any such damage or deterioration is evident.

3 Check that all the mounting's fasteners are securely tightened; use a torque wrench to check if possible.

4 Using a large screwdriver or a pry bar, check for wear in the mounting by carefully levering against it to check for free play; where this is not possible, enlist the aid of an assistant to move the engine/transmission unit back-and-forth, or from side-to-side, while you watch the mounting. While some free play is to be expected even from new

components, excessive wear should be obvious. If excessive free play is found, check first that the fasteners are correctly secured, then renew any worn components as described below.

Renewal

Torque support rod

5 Undo the mounting bolts and remove the torque support rod from the right-hand end of the engine. If necessary, unbolt the mounting bracket and remove it from the engine unit.

6 On refitting tightening the mounting bolts to the specified torque.

Front mounting

7 Undo the mounting bolts and remove the torque support rod from the right-hand end of the engine unit.

8 Firmly apply the handbrake then jack up the front of the vehicle and support it on axle stands.

9 Support the weight of the engine/transmission using a trolley jack with a block of wood placed on its head.

10 Slacken and remove the nut and washer securing the mounting to the front subframe and the upper nut securing the mounting to its bracket.

11 Raise the engine/transmission unit slightly and manoeuvre the mounting out of position, noting which way up it is fitted. If necessary, undo the bolts securing the mounting bracket to the cylinder block/transmission (as applicable) then manoeuvre the mounting and bracket out of position. **Note:** *Take great care not to place any excess stress on the exhaust system when raising the engine. If necessary, disconnect the front pipe from the manifold (see Chapter 4A).*

12 Check all components for signs of wear or damage, and renew as necessary.

13 On reassembly, refit the mounting bracket (where removed) and tighten its bolts to the specified torque.

14 Locate the mounting in the subframe, ensuring it is fitted the correct way up, and lower the engine/transmission back down into position. Refit the mounting nuts and tighten them to the specified torque.

15 Lower the vehicle to the ground then refit

the torque support rod and tighten its mounting bolts to the specified torque.

Rear mounting

16 Undo the mounting bolts and remove the torque support rod from the right-hand end of the engine unit.

17 Firmly apply the handbrake then jack up the front of the vehicle and support it on axle stands.

18 On manual transmission models, referring to Chapter 7A, slacken the gearchange mechanism selector rod clamp bolt and disengage the selector rod from the transmission linkage.

19 On automatic transmission models, referring to Chapter 7B, detach the selector cable from the transmission.

20 Support the weight of the engine/transmission using a trolley jack with a block of wood placed on its head. Position the jack underneath the transmission and raise the transmission slightly to remove all load from the rear mounting.

21 Slacken and remove the bolts securing the rear mounting to the subframe and transmission then manoeuvre the assembly out from underneath the vehicle. If necessary, undo the retaining bolts and separate the mounting and mounting bracket.

22 On refitting, reassemble the mounting and mounting bracket (where necessary) then refit the mounting bolts and tighten them to the specified torque.

23 Manoeuvre the assembly into position and refit the bolts securing it to the subframe. Clean the threads of the bracket-to-transmission bolts and apply a few drops of locking compound to each one. Refit the bolts and tighten both the bracket and mounting bolts to their specified torque settings. Remove the jack from underneath the engine/transmission.

24 On manual transmission models, reconnect the selector rod and adjust the gearchange mechanism as described in Chapter 7A.

25 On automatic transmission models, reconnect and adjust the selector cable as described in Chapter 7B.

26 Lower the vehicle to the ground then refit the torque support rod and tighten its mounting bolts to the specified torque.

Notes

Chapter 2 Part B:
1.6, 1.8 and 2.0 litre DOHC petrol engine in-car repair procedures

Contents

Degrees of difficulty

Easy, suitable for novice with little experience	Fairly easy, suitable for beginner with some experience	Fairly difficult, suitable for competent DIY mechanic	Difficult, suitable for experienced DIY mechanic	Very difficult, suitable for expert DIY or professional

Specifications

General
Engine type . . . . Four-cylinder, in-line, water-cooled. Double overhead camshaft, belt-driven

Manufacturer's engine code:
1.6 litre X16XEL, Z16XE
1.8 litre X18XE
1.8 litre X18XE1, Z18XE
2.0 litre X20XEV
Bore:
1.6 litre . . . . 79.0 mm
1.8 litre:
    X18XE . . . . 81.6 mm
    X18XE1 and Z18XE . . . . 80.5 mm
2.0 litre . . . . 86.0 mm
Stroke:
1.6 litre . . . . 81.5 mm
1.8 litre:
    X18XE . . . . 86.0 mm
    X18XE1 and Z18XE . . . . 88.2 mm
2.0 litre . . . . 86.0 mm
Capacity:
1.6 litre . . . . 1598 cc
1.8 litre:
    X18XE . . . . 1799 cc
    X18XE1 and Z18XE . . . . 1796 cc
2.0 litre . . . . 1998 cc

General (continued)

Compression ratio:
  1.6 litre 10.5:1
  1.8 litre:
    X18XE 10.8:1
    X18XE1 and Z18XE 10.5:1
  2.0 litre 10.8:1
Maximum power (kW):
  1.6 litre:
    X16XEL .... 74 at 6200 rpm
    Z16XE .... 74 at 6000 rpm
  1.8 litre:
    X18XE .... 85 at 5400 rpm
    X18XE1 and Z18XE .... 85 at 5400 rpm
  2.0 litre .... 100 at 5600 rpm
Maximum torque (Nm):
  1.6 litre:
    16XEL .... 150 at 3200 rpm
    Z16XE .... 150 at 3600 rpm
  1.8 litre:
    X18XE .... 170 at 3600 rpm
    X18XE1 and Z18XE .... 170 at 3400 rpm
  2.0 litre .... 188 at 3200 rpm
Firing order .... 1-3-4-2 (No 1 cylinder at timing belt end)
Direction of crankshaft rotation .... Clockwise (viewed from timing belt end of engine)

Compression pressures

Standard .... 12 to 15 bar (174 to 218 psi)
Maximum difference between any two cylinders .... 1 bar (14.5 psi)

Camshaft

Endfloat .... 0.04 to 0.15 mm
Maximum permissible radial run-out .... 0.040 mm

Balancer shaft unit (X20XEV model)

Permissible backlash .... 0.02 to 0.06 mm
Shim code number: **Shim thickness**
  55 .... 0.535 to 0.565 mm
  58 .... 0.565 to 0.595 mm
  61 .... 0.595 to 0.625 mm
  64 .... 0.625 to 0.655 mm
  67 .... 0.655 to 0.685 mm
  70 .... 0.685 to 0.715 mm
  73 .... 0.715 to 0.745 mm
  76 .... 0.745 to 0.775 mm
  79 .... 0.775 to 0.805 mm
  82 .... 0.805 to 0.835 mm
  85 .... 0.835 to 0.865 mm

Lubrication system

Oil pump type – depending on engine code .... Rotor-type or crescent/gear-type driven directly from crankshaft
Minimum permissible oil pressure at idle speed, with engine
  at operating temperature (oil temperature of at least 80°C):
    1.6 litre engines .... 1.5 bar (22 psi)
    1.8 and 2.0 litre engines .... 2.0 bar (29 psi)
Oil pump clearances:
  Crescent/gear-type:
    Inner-to-outer gear teeth clearance .... 0.10 to 0.20 mm
    Gear endfloat:
      1.6 litre engines .... 0.08 to 0.15 mm
      1.8 and 2.0 litre engines .... 0.03 to 0.10 mm
  Rotor-type:
    Inner-to-outer rotor clearance .... 0.150 mm (max)
    Outer rotor-to-pump housing clearance .... 0.350 mm (max)
    Rotor endfloat .... 0.080 mm (max)

Torque wrench settings

	Nm	lbf ft
X16XEL, Z16XE, X18XE1 and Z18XE		
Baffle plate bolts	8	6
Camshaft bearing cap bolts	8	6
Camshaft cover bolts	8	6
Camshaft sprocket bolt*:		
Stage 1	50	37
Stage 2	Angle-tighten a further 60°	
Stage 3	Angle-tighten a further 15°	
Connecting rod big-end bearing cap bolt*:		
Stage 1	25	18
Stage 2	Angle-tighten a further 30°	
Crankshaft pulley bolt*:		
Stage 1	95	70
Stage 2	Angle-tighten a further 30°	
Stage 3	Angle-tighten a further 15°	
Crankshaft sensor mounting bracket bolt	8	6
Cylinder head bolts*:		
Stage 1	25	18
Stage 2	Angle-tighten a further 90°	
Stage 3	Angle-tighten a further 90°	
Stage 4	Angle-tighten a further 90°	
Stage 5	Angle-tighten a further 45°	
Driveplate bolts	60	44
Engine/transmission mounting bolts:		
Front (left- and right-hand) mounting:		
Bracket-to-engine/transmission bolts	60	44
Mounting-to-bracket/subframe nuts	45	33
Rear mounting:		
Mounting-to-bracket bolts	45	33
Mounting-to-subframe bolts	20	15
Bracket-to-transmission bolts	60	44
Torque support rod bolts	60	44
Engine-to-transmission unit bolts:		
M8 bolts	20	15
M10 bolts	40	30
M12 bolts	60	44
Flywheel bolts*:		
Stage 1	35	26
Stage 2	Angle-tighten a further 30°	
Stage 3	Angle-tighten a further 15°	
Main bearing cap bolts*:		
Stage 1	50	37
Stage 2	Angle-tighten a further 45°	
Stage 3	Angle-tighten a further 15°	
Oil level sensor Torx screws	8	6
Oil pump:		
Retaining bolts	6	4
Pump cover screws	6	4
Oil pressure relief valve bolt	30	22
Oil pump pick-up/strainer and baffle bolts	8	6
Roadwheel bolts	110	81
Sump bolts:		
Sump to cylinder block/oil pump bolts	10	7
Sump flange-to-transmission bolts:		
M8 bolts	20	15
M10 bolts	40	30
Drain plug	45	33
Timing belt cover bolts:		
Upper and lower covers	4	3
Rear cover	6	4
Timing belt idler pulley bolt	25	18
Timing belt tensioner bolt	20	15

*Use new fasteners

Torque wrench settings (continued)

	Nm	lbf ft
X18XE and X20XEV		
Baffle plate to balancer shaft unit bolts	8	6
Baffle plate to crankshaft housing bolts	20	15
Balancer unit-to-cylinder block bolts*:		
Stage 1	20	15
Stage 2	Angle-tighten a further 45°	
Camshaft bearing cap bolts	8	6
Camshaft cover bolts	8	6
Camshaft sprocket bolt*:		
Stage 1	50	37
Stage 2	Angle-tighten a further 60°	
Stage 3	Angle-tighten a further 15°	
Connecting rod big-end bearing cap bolt*:		
Stage 1	35	26
Stage 2	Angle-tighten a further 45°	
Stage 3	Angle-tighten a further 15°	
Crankshaft pulley bolts	20	15
Crankshaft sprocket bolt*:		
Stage 1	130	96
Stage 2	Angle-tighten a further 40 to 50°	
Cylinder head bolts*:		
Stage 1	25	18
Stage 2	Angle-tighten a further 90°	
Stage 3	Angle-tighten a further 90°	
Stage 4	Angle-tighten a further 90°	
Stage 5	Angle-tighten a further 15°	
Driveplate bolts*	65	48
Engine/transmission mounting bolts:		
Front (left- and right-hand) mounting:		
Bracket-to-engine/transmission bolts	60	44
Mounting-to-bracket/subframe nuts	45	33
Rear mounting:		
Mounting-to-bracket bolts	45	33
Mounting-to-subframe bolts	20	15
Bracket-to-transmission bolts	60	44
Torque support rod and bracket bolts	60	44
Engine-to-transmission unit bolts:		
M8 bolts	20	15
M10 bolts	40	30
M12 bolts	60	44
Flywheel bolts*:		
Stage 1	65	48
Stage 2	Angle-tighten a further 30°	
Stage 3	Angle-tighten a further 15°	
Main bearing cap bolts*:		
Stage 1	50	37
Stage 2	Angle-tighten a further 45°	
Stage 3	Angle-tighten a further 15°	
Main bearing ladder casting bolts	20	15
Oil pump:		
Retaining bolts	6	4
Pump cover screws	6	4
Oil pressure relief valve bolt	30	22
Oil pump pick-up/strainer bolts:		
Pick-up-to-oil pump housing bolts	8	6
Pick-up-to-main bearing cap casting bolt	20	15
Roadwheel bolts	110	81
Sump bolts:		
Lower sump pan bolts*:		
Stage 1	8	6
Stage 2	Angle-tighten a further 30°	
Upper sump casting bolts:		
Upper sump-to-cylinder block/oil pump bolts	20	15
Sump flange-to-transmission bolts:		
M8 bolts	20	15
M10 bolts	40	30
Drain plug	10	7

Torque wrench settings (continued)	Nm	lbf ft
Timing belt cover bolts	6	4
Timing belt idler pulley:		
Pulley bolt	25	18
Mounting bracket bolts	25	18
Timing belt tensioner bolt	20	15

*Use new fasteners

1 General information

How to use this Chapter

1 This Part of Chapter 2 is devoted to in-car repair procedures for the engine. All procedures concerning engine removal and refitting, and engine block/cylinder head overhaul can be found in Chapter 2E.

2 Most of the operations included in this Part are based on the assumption that the engine is still installed in the car. Therefore, if this information is being used during a complete engine overhaul, with the engine already removed, many of the steps included here will not apply.

Engine description

3 The engine is a double overhead camshaft, four-cylinder, in-line unit, mounted transversely at the front of the car, with the clutch and transmission on its left-hand end.

4 The aluminium alloy cylinder block is of the dry-liner type. The crankshaft is supported within the cylinder block on five shell-type main bearings. Thrustwashers are fitted to number 3 main bearing, to control crankshaft endfloat.

5 The connecting rods are attached to the crankshaft by horizontally-split shell-type big-end bearings, and to the pistons by interference-fit gudgeon pins. The aluminium alloy pistons are of the slipper type, and are fitted with three piston rings, comprising two compression rings and a scraper-type oil control ring.

6 The camshafts run directly in the cylinder head, and driven by the crankshaft via a toothed rubber timing belt (which also drives the coolant pump). The camshafts operate each valve via a follower. Each follower incorporates a hydraulic self-adjusting valve which automatically adjust the valve clearances.

7 Lubrication is by pressure-feed from either a crescent/gear-type or rotor-type oil pump, which is mounted on the right-hand end of the crankshaft. It draws oil through a strainer located in the sump, and then forces it through an externally mounted full-flow cartridge-type filter. The oil flows into galleries in the main bearing cap bridge arrangement and cylinder block/crankcase, from where it is distributed to the crankshaft (main bearings)

and camshafts. The big-end bearings are supplied with oil via internal drillings in the crankshaft, while the camshaft bearings also receive a pressurised supply. The camshaft lobes and valves are lubricated by splash, as are all other engine components.

8 A semi-closed crankcase ventilation system is employed; crankcase fumes are drawn from cylinder head cover, and passed via a hose to the inlet manifold.

Repair operations possible with the engine in the car

9 The following operations can be carried out without having to remove the engine from the vehicle.
a) Removal and refitting of the cylinder head.
b) Removal and refitting of the timing belt and sprockets.
c) Renewal of the camshaft oil seals.
d) Removal and refitting of the camshafts and followers.
e) Removal and refitting of the sump.
f) Removal and refitting of the connecting rods and pistons*.
g) Removal and refitting of the oil pump.
h) Renewal of the crankshaft oil seals.
i) Renewal of the engine mountings.
j) Removal and refitting of the flywheel/driveplate.

* Although the operation marked with an asterisk can be carried out with the engine in the car after removal of the sump, it is better for the engine to be removed, in the interests of cleanliness and improved access. For this reason, the procedure is described in Chapter 2E.

3.5 Align the camshaft sprocket timing marks so they are facing towards each other, an imaginary line can be drawn through the camshaft bolts and timing marks (as shown)

2 Compression test – description and interpretation

Refer to Chapter 2A, Section 2.

3 Top dead centre (TDC) for No 1 piston – locating

1 In its travel up and down its cylinder bore, Top Dead Centre (TDC) is the highest point that each piston reaches as the crankshaft rotates. While each piston reaches TDC both at the top of the compression stroke and again at the top of the exhaust stroke, for the purpose of timing the engine, TDC refers to the piston position (usually number 1) at the top of its compression stroke.

2 Number 1 piston (and cylinder) is at the right-hand (timing belt) end of the engine, and its TDC position is located as follows. Note that the crankshaft rotates clockwise when viewed from the right-hand side of the car.

3 Disconnect the battery negative terminal. If necessary, remove all the spark plugs as described in Chapter 1A to enable the engine to be easily turned over.

X16XEL, Z16XE, X18XE1 and Z18XE

4 To gain access to the camshaft sprocket timing marks, remove the timing belt upper cover as described in Section 6.

5 Using a socket and extension bar on the crankshaft pulley bolt, rotate the crankshaft until the timing marks on the camshaft sprockets are facing towards each and are both correctly aligned with the cylinder head upper surface. With the camshaft sprocket marks correctly positioned, align the notch on the crankshaft pulley rim with the mark on the timing belt lower cover (see illustration). The engine is now positioned with No 1 piston at TDC.

X18XE and X20XEV

6 To gain access to the camshaft sprocket timing marks, remove the timing belt outer cover as described in Section 6.

7 Using a socket and extension bar on the crankshaft sprocket bolt, rotate the crankshaft until the timing marks on the camshaft sprockets are both at the top and are correctly aligned with the marks on the

3.7 Align the camshaft sprocket timing marks with the marks (1) on the cylinder head cover, and the crankshaft pulley notch with the pointer (2) to position No 1 cylinder at TDC on its compression stroke

camshaft cover. With the camshaft sprocket marks correctly positioned, align the notch on the crankshaft pulley rim with the pointer on the cover **(see illustration)**. The engine is now positioned with No 1 piston at TDC.

4 Camshaft cover – removal and refitting

X16XEL and Z16XE

Removal

1 Remove the oil filler cap. Undo the retaining screws, disengage the engine cover from the locating lugs at the front of the camshaft cover, and remove the cover from the engine compartment **(see illustration)**.
2 Disconnect the wiring plug, remove the retaining screws, and remove the ignition module. If necessary, refer to Chapter 5B.
3 Release the retaining clips and disconnect the breather hoses from the left-hand end of the camshaft cover **(see illustration)**.
4 Evenly and progressively slacken and remove the camshaft cover retaining bolts.

4.1 Undo the two screws and disengage the locating lugs to remove the engine cover

5 Lift the camshaft cover away from the cylinder head and recover the cover's seals and the sealing rings which are fitted to each of the retaining bolt holes **(see illustration)**. Examine the seals and sealing rings for signs of wear or damage and renew if necessary.

Refitting

6 Ensure the cover and cylinder head surfaces are clean and dry then fit the camshaft seals securely to the cover grooves. Fit the sealing rings to the recesses around each retaining bolt hole, holding them in position with a smear of grease **(see illustrations)**.
7 Apply a smear of suitable sealant to areas of the cylinder head surface around the right-hand end inlet and exhaust camshaft bearing caps and also to the semi-circular cut-outs on the left-hand end of the head.
8 Carefully manoeuvre the camshaft cover into position, taking great care to ensure all the

4.5 Lift the camshaft cover away from the engine

4.6b . . . and fit the sealing rings to the recess around each retaining bolt hole

4.3 Disconnect the breather hoses

sealing rings remain correctly seated. Refit the cover retaining bolts and tighten the retaining bolts to the specified torque, working in a spiral pattern from the centre outwards.
9 Reconnect the breather hoses, securing them in position with the retaining clips.
10 Refit the ignition module with reference to Chapter 5B.
11 Refit the engine cover.

X18XE1 and Z18XE

Removal

12 Remove the engine cover as described in paragraph 1.
13 Slacken the retaining clips and disconnect the breather hoses from the left-hand rear of the cover **(see illustration)**.
14 Disconnect the wiring plug, undo the retaining screws, and remove the ignition module. Refer to Chapter 5B if necessary.

4.6a Ensure the seals are correctly seated in the cover recesses . . .

4.13 Disconnect the breather hoses

15 Disconnect the wiring plug from the coolant temperature sensor.

16 Disconnect the coolant pipe from the thermostat housing. Unbolt the retaining bracket from the camshaft cover and inlet manifold, release the retaining clip and move the pipe to one side **(see illustration)**. Be prepared for coolant spillage.

17 Evenly and progressively slacken and remove the camshaft cover retaining bolts.

18 Lift the camshaft cover away from the cylinder head and recover the rubber seal. Examine the seal for signs of wear or damage and renew if necessary.

Refitting

19 Ensure the cover and cylinder head surfaces are clean and dry then fit the camshaft seal securely to the cover groove **(see illustration)**.

20 Carefully manoeuvre the camshaft cover into position, taking great care to ensure the sealing ring remains correctly seated. Refit the cover retaining bolts and tighten the retaining bolts to the specified torque, working in a spiral pattern from the centre outwards.

21 Reconnect the coolant pipe to the thermostat housing, making sure it is secured by the retaining bracket on the camshaft cover and inlet manifold **(see illustration)**. Top-up the cooling system as described in Chapter 1A.

22 Refit the wiring plug to the coolant temperature sensor.

23 Reconnect the breather hoses, securing them in position with the retaining clips.

24 Refit the ignition module with reference to Chapter 5B.

25 Refit the engine cover.

X18XE and X20XEV

Removal

26 With reference to Chapter 4A, remove the air filter housing.

27 Remove the timing belt upper cover as described in Section 6.

28 Disconnect the engine breather hoses from the right-hand rear and left-hand front of the cover **(see illustration)**.

29 Undo the retaining screws and remove the spark plug cover. Disconnect the plug caps from the plugs then unclip the HT leads and position them clear of the cover.

30 Disconnect the wiring plug from the camshaft position sensor. Unclip the wiring harness from the cover.

31 Evenly and progressively slacken and remove the camshaft cover retaining bolts.

32 Lift the camshaft cover away from the cylinder head and recover the cover's seal and the sealing rings which are fitted to each of the retaining bolts holes. Examine the seal and sealing rings for signs of wear or damage and renew if necessary.

Refitting

33 Ensure the cover and cylinder head surfaces are clean and dry then fit the

4.16 Remove the bolt supporting the coolant pipe across the camshaft cover

camshaft seals securely to the cover grooves. Fit the sealing rings to the recesses around each retaining bolt hole, holding them in position with a smear of grease.

34 Apply a smear of suitable sealant to areas of the cylinder head surface around the right-hand end inlet and exhaust camshaft bearing caps and also to the semi-circular cut-outs on the left-hand end of the head.

35 Carefully manoeuvre the camshaft cover into position, taking great care to ensure all the sealing rings remain correctly seated. Refit the cover retaining bolts and tighten the retaining bolts to the specified torque, working in a spiral pattern from the centre outwards.

36 Reconnect the breather hoses, securing them in position with the retaining clips.

37 Refit the plug caps to the spark plugs, and reposition the HT leads.

38 Position the spark plug cover in the centre of the camshaft cover, and tighten the retaining screws securely.

39 Refit the timing belt upper cover as described in Section 6.

40 Refit the air filter housing (see Chapter 4A).

---

5 Crankshaft pulley – removal and refitting

X16XEL, Z16XE, X18XE1 and Z18XE

Note: *A new pulley retaining bolt will be required on refitting.*

4.21 Reconnect the pipe to the thermostat housing

4.19 Carefully fit the camshaft cover seal

Removal

1 Apply the handbrake, then jack up the front of the car and support it on axle stands. Remove the right-hand roadwheel.

2 Remove the auxiliary drivebelt as described in Chapter 1A. Prior to removal, mark the direction of rotation on the belt to ensure the belt is refitted the same way around.

3 Slacken the crankshaft pulley retaining bolt. To prevent crankshaft rotation on manual transmission models, have an assistant select top gear and apply the brakes firmly. On automatic transmission models prevent rotation by removing one of the torque converter retaining bolts and bolting the driveplate to the transmission housing using a metal bar, spacers and suitable bolts (see Chapter 7B). If the engine is removed from the vehicle it will be necessary to lock the flywheel/driveplate (see Section 15).

4 Unscrew the retaining bolt and washer and remove the crankshaft pulley from the end of the crankshaft, taking care not to damage the crankshaft sensor.

Refitting

5 Refit the crankshaft pulley, aligning the pulley cut-out with the raised notch on the timing belt sprocket, then fit the washer and new retaining bolt **(see illustration)**.

6 Lock the crankshaft by the method used on removal, and tighten the pulley retaining bolt to the specified Stage 1 torque setting then angle-tighten the bolt through the specified Stage 2 angle, using a socket and extension bar, and finally through the specified Stage 3 angle. It is recommended that an angle-

4.28 Disconnect the breather hoses from the camshaft cover (arrowed)

5.5 Align the pulley cut-out with the raised notch

measuring gauge is used during the final stages of the tightening, to ensure accuracy. If a gauge is not available, use white paint to make alignment marks between the bolt head and pulley prior to tightening; the marks can then be used to check that the bolt has been rotated through the correct angle.

7 Refit the auxiliary drivebelt as described in Chapter 1A using the mark made prior to removal to ensure the belt is fitted the correct way around.

8 Refit the roadwheel then lower the car to the ground and tighten the wheel bolts to the specified torque.

X18XE and X20XEV

Removal

9 Carry out the operations described in paragraphs 1 and 2.

10 Using a socket and extension bar on the

crankshaft sprocket bolt, turn the crankshaft until the notch on the pulley rim is correctly aligned with the pointer on the cover.

11 Slacken and remove the small retaining bolts securing the pulley to the crankshaft sprocket and remove the pulley from the engine. If necessary, prevent crankshaft rotation by holding the sprocket retaining bolt with a suitable socket.

Refitting

12 Check that the crankshaft sprocket mark is still aligned with the mark on the housing then manoeuvre the crankshaft pulley into position. Align the notch on the pulley rim with the pointer then seat the pulley on the sprocket and tighten its retaining bolts to the specified torque.

13 Carry out the operations described in paragraphs 7 and 8.

---

6 Timing belt covers – removal and refitting

X16XEL, Z16XE, X18XE1 and Z18XE

Upper cover

1 Remove the air cleaner housing as described in Chapter 4A.

2 Release the camshaft position sensor wiring (X16XEL and X18XE1) from the retaining clip on the upper cover. Undo the three retaining screws then unclip the upper

cover from the rear cover and remove it from the engine compartment **(see illustration)**.

3 Refitting is the reverse of removal, tighten the retaining bolts to the specified torque. On X16XEL and X18XE1 models, ensure that the camshaft position sensor wiring is correctly routed **(see illustration)**.

Lower cover

4 Remove the upper cover as described in paragraphs 1 and 2.

5 Hold the tensioner against the spring pressure, and disengage the auxiliary drivebelt from the pulleys (refer to Chapter 1A if necessary). Prior to removal, mark the direction of rotation on the belt to ensure the belt is refitted the same way around.

6 Apply the handbrake, then jack up the front of the car and support it on axle stands. Remove the right-hand roadwheel.

7 Remove the right-hand front lower wheelarch panel, as described in Chapter 11, Section 26.

8 Undo the retaining bolt and remove the auxiliary drivebelt tensioner **(see illustration)**.

9 Remove the crankshaft pulley as described in Section 5.

10 Undo the retaining bolt then unclip the cover from the rear cover and manoeuvre it out of position **(see illustrations)**.

11 Refitting is the reverse of removal, clip the cover into position and tighten the cover bolts to the specified torque **(see illustration)**.

Rear cover

12 Remove the timing belt as described in Section 7.

6.2 Undo the three screws and remove the timing belt upper cover

6.3 Ensure that the camshaft position sensor wiring is correctly routed

H32265

6.8 Remove the auxiliary drivebelt tensioner

6.10a Timing belt lower cover upper retaining bolt (arrowed) . . .

6.10b . . . and lower retaining bolt

6.11 Clip the cover back into position

6.15 Engine mounting-to-cylinder block bracket retaining bolts

6.16 Lift the rear cover away from the engine

13 Remove the camshaft cover as described in Section 4.

14 Remove the camshaft sprockets, crankshaft sprocket, timing belt tensioner, front idler pulley and the rear idler pulley as described in Section 8.

15 Slacken and remove the three retaining bolts, and withdraw the engine mounting bracket bolted to the cylinder block **(see illustration)**.

16 Undo the four retaining bolts and remove the rear cover upwards and away from the engine **(see illustration)**.

17 Refitting is the reverse of removal. Refit and tighten the cover bolts to the specified torque.

X18XE and X20XEV

Upper cover

18 Remove the air cleaner housing as described in Chapter 4A.

19 Slacken and remove the upper cover retaining bolts **(see illustration)**.

20 Lift away the upper cover.

21 Refitting is a reversal of removal **(see illustration)**. Tighten the cover retaining bolts to the specified torque.

Lower cover

22 Remove the upper cover as described in paragraphs 18 to 20.

23 Hold the tensioner against the spring pressure, and disengage the auxiliary drivebelt from the pulleys (refer to Chapter 1A if necessary). Prior to removal, mark the direction of rotation on the belt to ensure the belt is refitted the same way around.

24 On models with air conditioning, apply the handbrake, then jack up the front of the car and support it on axle stands. Remove the right-hand roadwheel. Remove the right-hand front lower wheelarch panel, as described in Chapter 11, Section 26.

25 Undo the retaining bolt(s), and remove the auxiliary drivebelt tensioner from the alternator support bracket.

26 Remove the crankshaft pulley, as described in Section 5.

27 Slacken and remove the two retaining bolts, release the retaining clips and remove the cover from the engine unit along with its seal **(see illustration)**.

6.19 Undo the timing belt cover retaining bolt(s) and recover the rubber spacers

28 Refitting is the reverse of removal, ensure the cover seal is correctly fitted. Tighten all bolts to the specified torque.

6.21 On refitting ensure the seal is correctly fitted to the outer cover

Rear cover

29 Remove the timing belt as described in Section 7.

H32264

6.27 Lower cover retaining bolts

7.4b Unbolt the camshaft sensor and position it clear of the timing belt

7.4a Camshaft and crankshaft sprocket timing marks – X16XEL, Z16XE, X18XE1 and Z18XE engines

I Camshaft sprocket timing marks aligned with the cylinder head upper surface

II Crankshaft sprocket timing mark aligned with mark on oil pump housing

30 With reference to Section 4, remove the camshaft cover.

31 Remove the camshaft sprockets, crankshaft sprocket, the timing belt tensioner and the idler pulleys as described in Section 8.

32 Unbolt the camshaft sensor from the cylinder head.

33 Unscrew the retaining bolts and remove the engine mounting bracket from the cylinder block.

34 Undo the four retaining bolts and remove the rear cover from the engine unit.

35 Refitting is the reverse of removal, tightening all bolts to the specified torque.

7 Timing belt – removal and refitting

Note: The timing belt must be removed and refitted with the engine cold.

Removal

1 Position No 1 cylinder at TDC on its compression stroke as described in Section 3.

2 Remove the crankshaft pulley as described in Section 5.

3 On X16XEL, Z16XE, X18XE1 and Z18XE engines, unbolt the timing belt lower cover and remove it from the engine (see Section 6).

4 On X16XEL, Z16XE, X18XE1 and Z18XE engines, check the camshaft sprocket timing marks are correctly aligned with the cylinder head surface and the crankshaft sprocket timing mark is aligned with the mark on the cover. Undo the two bolts securing the camshaft sensor to the cylinder head and position it clear of the engine (see illustrations).

5 On X18XE and X20XEV engines, check the camshaft sprocket timing marks are correctly aligned with the camshaft cover marks and the crankshaft sprocket timing mark is aligned with the pointer on the cover (see illustration).

6 On all models, slacken the timing belt tensioner bolt. Using an Allen key, rotate the tensioner arm clockwise to its stop, to relieve the tension in the timing belt, hold it in position and securely tighten the retaining bolt (see illustration).

7 Slide the timing belt from its sprockets and remove it from the engine (see illustration). If the belt is to be re-used, use white paint or similar to mark the direction of rotation on the belt. Do not rotate the crankshaft or camshafts until the timing belt has been refitted.

7.5 On X18XE and X20XEV engines ensure the camshaft sprocket marks are correctly aligned with the marks on the camshaft cover (arrowed)

7.6 Slacken the timing belt tensioner bolt (1) and rotate the tensioner clockwise using an Allen key in the arm cut-out (2)

7.7 Removing the timing belt

8 Check the timing belt carefully for any signs of uneven wear, splitting or oil contamination, and renew it if there is the slightest doubt about its condition. If the engine is undergoing an overhaul and is approaching the manufacturer's specified interval for belt renewal (see Chapter 1A) renew the belt as a matter of course, regardless of its apparent condition. If signs of oil contamination are found, trace the source of the oil leak and rectify it, then wash down the engine timing

belt area and all related components to remove all traces of oil.

Refitting

9 On reassembly, thoroughly clean the timing belt sprockets and tensioner/idler pulleys.
10 Check that the camshaft sprocket timing marks are still correctly aligned with the cylinder head surface (X16XEL, Z16XE, X18XE1 and Z18XE engines) or the camshaft cover marks (X18XE and X20XEV engines) and the crankshaft sprocket mark is still aligned with the mark on the cover (see illustration).
11 Fit the timing belt over the crankshaft and camshaft sprockets and around the idler pulleys, ensuring that the belt front run is taut (ie, all slack is on the tensioner side of the belt), then fit the belt over the coolant pump sprocket and tensioner pulley. Do not twist the belt sharply while refitting it. Ensure that the belt teeth are correctly seated centrally in the sprockets, and that the timing marks remain in alignment. If a used belt is being refitted, ensure that the arrow mark made on removal points in the normal direction of rotation, as before.

12 Slacken the timing belt tensioner bolt to release the tensioner spring. Rotate the tensioner arm anti-clockwise until the tensioner pointer is fully over against its stop, without exerting any excess strain on the belt. Hold the tensioner in position and securely tighten its retaining bolt (see illustration).
13 Check the sprocket timing marks are still correctly aligned. If adjustment is necessary, release the tensioner again then disengage the belt from the sprockets and make any necessary adjustments.
14 Using a socket on the crankshaft pulley/sprocket bolt (as applicable), rotate the crankshaft smoothly through two complete turns (720°) in the normal direction of rotation to settle the timing belt in position.
15 Check that both the camshaft and crankshaft sprocket timing marks are correctly realigned then slacken the tensioner bolt again.
16 If a new timing belt is being fitted, adjust the tensioner so that the pointer is aligned with the cut-out on the backplate (see illustration). Hold the tensioner in the correct position and tighten its retaining bolt to the

7.10 Crankshaft sprocket (A) and belt cover (B) timing marks – X16XEL, Z16XE, X18XE1 and Z18XE engines

7.12 Tension the belt by rotating the tensioner arm fully anti-clockwise until the pointer is positioned as shown

7.16 Timing belt tensioner pointer positions

I X16XEL, Z16XE, X18XE and X20XEV engines: Pointer (1) and backplate (2) for **new** belts

II X18XE1 and Z18XE engines: Pointer (1) and backplate (2) for **new** belts

7.17 Timing belt tensioner pointer positions

I   X16XEL, Z16XE, X18XE and X20XEV
engines: Pointer (1) and backplate (2) for
used belts

II   X18XE1 and Z18XE engines: Pointer (1)
and backplate (2) for used belts

specified torque. Rotate the crankshaft smoothly through another two complete turns in the normal direction of rotation, to bring the sprocket timing marks back into alignment. Check that the tensioner pointer is still aligned with the backplate cut-out.

17 If the original belt is being refitted, adjust the tensioner so that the pointer is positioned 4 mm to the left of the cut-out on the backplate **(see illustration)**. Hold the tensioner in the correct position and tighten

its retaining bolt to the specified torque. Rotate the crankshaft smoothly through another two complete turns in the normal direction of rotation, to bring the sprocket timing marks back into alignment. Check that the tensioner pointer is still correctly positioned in relation to the backplate cut-out.

18 If the tensioner pointer is not correctly positioned in relation to the backplate, repeat the procedure in paragraph 16 (new belt) or 17 (original belt) (as applicable).

8.2 Using an open-ended spanner to retain the camshaft whilst the sprocket retaining bolt is slackened

8.7 Ensure the camshaft sprocket cut-out (arrowed) is correctly engaged with the locating pin

19 Once the tensioner pointer and backplate remain correctly aligned, refit the timing belt covers and crankshaft pulley as described in Sections 5 and 6. On X16XEL, Z16XE, X18XE1 and Z18XE engines, it will be necessary to refit the camshaft sensor to the cylinder head prior to refitting the upper cover.

8   Timing belt sprockets, tensioner and idler pulleys – removal and refitting

Camshaft sprockets

Note: *New sprocket retaining bolt(s) will be required on refitting.*

Removal

1 Remove the timing belt as described in Section 7.

2 The camshaft must be prevented from turning as the sprocket bolt is unscrewed, and this can be achieved in one of two ways as follows.

a) *Make up a sprocket-holding tool using two lengths of steel strip (one long, the other short), and three nuts and bolts; one nut and bolt forms the pivot of a forked tool, with the remaining two nuts and bolts at the tips of the 'forks' to engage with the sprocket spokes* **(see illustration 8.2 in Chapter 2A).**

b) *Remove the camshaft cover as described in Section 4 and hold the camshaft with an open-ended spanner on the flats provided* **(see illustration).**

3 Unscrew the retaining bolt and washer and remove the sprocket from the end of the camshaft. If the sprocket locating pin is a loose fit in the camshaft end, remove it and store it with the sprocket for safe-keeping.

4 If necessary, remove the remaining sprocket using the same method. On X16XEL, Z16XE, X18XE1 and Z18XE engines the inlet and exhaust sprockets are different; the exhaust camshaft sprocket can be easily identified by the lugs which activate the camshaft position sensor.

Refitting

5 Prior to refitting check the oil seal(s) for signs of damage or leakage. If necessary, renew as described in Section 9.

6 Ensure the locating pin is in position in the camshaft end.

7 On X16XEL, Z16XE, X18XE1 and Z18XE engines refit the sprocket to the camshaft end, aligning its cut-out with the locating pin, and fit the washer and new retaining bolt **(see illustration)**. If both sprockets have been removed, ensure each sprocket is fitted to the correct shaft; the exhaust camshaft sprocket can be identified by the lugs on the sprocket outer face which trigger the camshaft position sensor.

8 On X18XE and X20XEV engines both inlet and exhaust camshaft sprockets are the same but each one is equipped with two locating

8.8 On X18XE and X20XEV engines ensure the locating pin is engaged in the correct sprocket hole on refitting (see text)

8.9 Using a spanner to prevent camshaft rotation

8.13 Refit the crankshaft sprocket with the timing mark facing outwards

pin cut-outs. If the sprocket is being fitted to the inlet camshaft engage the locating pin in the IN cut-out, and if the sprocket is being fitted to the exhaust camshaft engage the locating pin in the EX cut-out **(see illustration)**. Ensure the camshaft locating pin is engaged in the correct sprocket cut-out then fit the washer and new retaining bolt.

9 On all models, retain the sprocket by the method used on removal, and tighten the pulley retaining bolt to the specified Stage 1 torque setting then angle-tighten the bolt through the specified Stage 2 angle, using a socket and extension bar, and finally through the specified Stage 3 angle **(see illustration)**. It is recommended that an angle-measuring gauge is used during the final stages of the tightening, to ensure accuracy. If a gauge is not available, use white paint to make alignment marks between the bolt head and pulley prior to tightening; the marks can then be used to check that the bolt has been rotated through the correct angle.

10 Refit the timing belt as described in Section 7 then (where necessary) refit the camshaft cover as described in Section 4.

Crankshaft sprocket

X16XEL, Z16XE, X18XE1 and Z18XE

11 Remove the timing belt as described in Section 7.

12 Slide the sprocket off from the end of the crankshaft, noting which way around it is fitted.

13 Align the sprocket locating key with the crankshaft groove then slide the sprocket into

position, making sure its timing mark is facing outwards **(see illustration)**.

14 Refit the timing belt as described in Section 7.

X18XE and X20XEV

Note: *A new crankshaft sprocket retaining bolt will be required on refitting.*

15 Remove the timing belt as described in Section 7.

16 Slacken the crankshaft sprocket retaining bolt. To prevent crankshaft rotation on manual transmission models, have an assistant select top gear and apply the brakes firmly. On automatic transmission models prevent rotation by removing one of the torque converter retaining bolts and bolting the driveplate to the transmission housing using a metal bar, spacers and suitable bolts (see Chapter 7B). If the engine is removed from the vehicle it will be necessary to lock the flywheel/driveplate (see Section 15).

17 Unscrew the retaining bolt and washer and remove the crankshaft sprocket from the end of the crankshaft.

18 Align the sprocket location key with the crankshaft groove and slide the sprocket into position, ensuring its timing mark is facing outwards. Fit the washer and new retaining bolt.

19 Lock the crankshaft by the method used on removal, and tighten the sprocket retaining bolt to the specified Stage 1 torque setting then angle-tighten the bolt through the specified Stage 2 angle, using a socket and extension bar. It is recommended that an angle-measuring gauge is used during the

final stages of the tightening, to ensure accuracy. If a gauge is not available, use white paint to make alignment marks between the bolt head and sprocket prior to tightening; the marks can then be used to check that the bolt has been rotated through the correct angle.

20 Refit the timing belt as described in Section 7.

Tensioner assembly

Removal

21 Remove the timing belt as described in Section 7.

22 Slacken and remove the retaining bolt and remove the tensioner assembly from the engine.

Refitting

23 Fit the tensioner to the engine, making sure that the lug on the backplate is correctly located in the oil pump housing hole **(see illustrations)**. Ensure the tensioner is correctly seated then refit the retaining bolt. Using an Allen key, rotate the tensioner arm clockwise to its stop then securely tighten the retaining bolt.

24 Refit the timing belt as described in Section 7.

Idler pulleys

Removal

25 Remove the timing belt as described in Section 7.

26 Slacken and remove the retaining bolt(s) and remove the idler pulley(s) from the engine **(see illustration)**. On X18XE and X20XEV

8.23a Engage the tensioner backplate lug with the locating hole in the oil pump housing . . .

8.23b . . . and rotate the tensioner arm clockwise until the roller is as far away from the belt run as possible

8.26 Idler pulley retaining bolt

9.2 Camshaft oil seal removal method

engines, if necessary, unbolt the pulley mounting bracket and remove it from the cylinder block.

10.1 Prior to removing the timing belt, rotate the crankshaft 60° backwards to ensure the camshafts are correctly positioned (X18XE and X20XEV engine)

9.4 Using the old camshaft bolt and a socket to fit the new camshaft oil seal

Refitting

27 On X18XE and X20XEV engines refit the pulley mounting bracket (where removed) to the cylinder block and tighten its retaining bolts to the specified torque.

28 On all models, refit the idler pulley(s) and tighten the retaining bolt(s) to the specified torque.

29 Refit the timing belt (see Section 7).

9 Camshaft oil seals – renewal

1 Remove the relevant camshaft sprocket as described in Section 8.

2 Carefully punch or drill two small holes opposite each other in the oil seal. Screw a self-tapping screw into each, and pull on the screws with pliers to extract the seal (see illustration).

3 Clean the seal housing, and polish off any burrs or raised edges which may have caused the seal to fail in the first place.

4 Lubricate the lips of the new seal with clean engine oil, and press it into position using a suitable tubular drift (such as a socket) which bears only on the hard outer edge of the seal (see illustration). Take care not to damage the seal lips during fitting; note that the seal lips should face inwards.

5 Refit the camshaft sprocket as described in Section 8.

10 Camshaft and followers – removal, inspection and refitting

Removal

1 Prior to releasing the timing belt tension and removing the belt, rotate the crankshaft **backwards** by approximately 60° (4 teeth of movement); this will position the camshafts so that the valve spring pressure is evenly exerted along the complete length of the shaft, reducing the risk of the bearing caps being damaged on removal/refitting (see illustration). Remove the timing belt as described in Section 7.

2 Remove the camshaft sprockets as described in Section 8.

3 Starting on the inlet camshaft, working in a spiral pattern from the outside inwards, slacken the camshaft bearing cap retaining bolts by one turn at a time, to relieve the pressure of the valve springs on the bearing caps gradually and evenly (the reverse of illustration 10.15). Once the valve spring pressure has been relieved, the bolts can be fully unscrewed and removed along with the caps; the bearing caps and the cylinder head locations are numbered (inlet camshaft 1 to 5, exhaust camshaft 6 to 10) to ensure the caps are correctly positioned on refitting (see illustrations). Take care not to loose the locating dowels (where fitted).

Caution: If the bearing cap bolts are carelessly slackened, the bearing caps might break. If any bearing cap breaks then the complete cylinder head assembly must be renewed; the bearing caps are matched to the head and are not available separately.

10.3a Camshaft bearing cap numbering sequence

10.3b The identification numbers should be marked on both the bearing caps and the cylinder head (arrowed)

10.6 Using a rubber sucker to remove a camshaft follower

10.13 Apply a smear of sealant to the right-hand bearing caps

10.14 Refit the bearing caps using the identification markings to ensure each one is correctly fitted

4 Lift the camshaft out of the cylinder head and slide off the oil seal.

5 Repeat the operations described in paragraphs 3 and 4 and remove the exhaust camshaft.

6 Obtain sixteen small, clean plastic containers, and label them for identification. Alternatively, divide a larger container into compartments. Lift the followers out from the top of the cylinder head and store each one in its respective fitted position **(see illustration)**. **Note:** *Store all the followers the correct way up to prevent the oil draining from the hydraulic valve adjustment mechanisms.*

Inspection

7 Examine the camshaft bearing surfaces and cam lobes for signs of wear ridges and scoring. Renew the camshaft if any of these conditions are apparent. Examine the condition of the bearing surfaces both on the camshaft journals and in the cylinder head. If the head bearing surfaces are worn excessively, the cylinder head will need to be renewed.

8 Support the camshaft end journals on V-blocks, and measure the run-out at the centre journal using a dial gauge. If the run-out exceeds the specified limit, the camshaft should be renewed.

9 Examine the follower bearing surfaces which contact the camshaft lobes for wear ridges and scoring. Check the followers and their bores in the cylinder head for signs of wear or damage. If any follower is thought to be faulty or is visibly worn it should be renewed.

Refitting

10 Where removed, lubricate the followers with clean engine oil and carefully insert each one into its original location in the cylinder head.

11 Lubricate the camshaft followers with molybdenum disulphide paste (or clean engine oil) then lay the camshafts in position. Ensure the crankshaft is still positioned approximately 60° BTDC and position each camshaft so that the lobes of No 1 cylinder are pointing upwards. Temporarily refit the sprockets to the camshafts and position each one so that its sprocket timing mark is

approximately 4 teeth before its TDC alignment position.

12 Ensure the mating surfaces of the bearing caps and cylinder head are clean and dry and lubricate the camshaft journals and lobes with clean engine oil.

13 Apply a smear of sealant to the mating surfaces of both the inlet (No 1) and exhaust (No 6) camshaft right-hand bearing caps **(see illustration)**.

14 Ensure the locating dowels (where fitted) are in position then refit the camshaft bearing caps and the retaining bolts in their original locations on the cylinder head **(see illustration)**. The caps are numbered (inlet camshaft 1 to 5, exhaust camshaft 6 to 10) from right to left, and the corresponding numbers are marked on the cylinder head upper surface. All bearing cap numbers should be the right way up when viewed from the front of the engine.

15 Working on the inlet camshaft, tighten the bearing cap bolts by hand only then, working in a spiral pattern from the centre outwards, tighten the bolts by one turn at a time to

gradually impose the pressure of the valve springs on the bearing caps **(see illustration)**. Repeat this sequence until all bearing caps are in contact with the cylinder head then go around and tighten the camshaft bearing cap bolts to the specified torque.

Caution: If the bearing cap bolts are carelessly tightened, the bearing caps might break. If any bearing cap breaks then the complete cylinder head assembly must be renewed; the bearing caps are matched to the head and are not available separately.

16 Tighten the exhaust camshaft bearing cap bolts as described in paragraph 15.

17 Fit new camshaft oil seals as described in Section 9.

18 Refit the camshaft sprockets as described in Section 8.

19 Align all the sprocket timing marks to bring the camshafts and crankshaft back to TDC then refit the timing belt as described in Section 7.

20 Refit the camshaft cover and timing belt cover(s) as described in Sections 4 and 6.

H.28124

10.15 Camshaft bearing cap tightening sequence (exhaust camshaft shown – inlet the same)

11 Cylinder head –
removal and refitting

Note: *The engine must be cold when removing the cylinder head. New cylinder head bolts must be used on refitting.*

Removal

1 Depressurise the fuel system as described in Chapter 4A then disconnect the battery negative lead.

2 Drain the cooling system and remove the spark plugs as described in Chapter 1A.

3 Prior to releasing the timing belt tension and removing the belt, rotate the crankshaft **backwards** by approximately 60° (4 teeth of movement); this will position the camshafts so that the valve spring pressure is evenly exerted along the complete length of the shafts, preventing the shafts turning and reducing the risk of the valves contacting the pistons **(see illustration 10.1)**. Remove the timing belt as described in Section 7. Proceed as described under the relevant sub-heading.

X16XEL, Z16XE, X18XE1 and Z18XE

4 Remove the complete inlet manifold as described in Chapter 4A. Remove the exhaust manifold as described in Chapter 4A. If no work is to be carried out on the cylinder head, the head can be removed complete with the manifold once the following operations have been carried out (see Chapter 4A).

  a) *Unbolt the exhaust front pipe from manifold.*
  b) *Disconnect the oxygen sensor wiring connector.*
  c) *Disconnect the air hose and vacuum hose from the air injection valve.*

5 Remove the camshaft cover as described in Section 4.

6 Remove the camshaft sprockets and the timing belt idler pulleys as described in Section 8.

7 Undo the retaining bolts securing the timing belt rear cover to the cylinder head.

8 Referring to Chapter 10, unbolt the power steering pump and position it clear of the cylinder head.

9 Disconnect the wiring connectors from the DIS module and the coolant temperature sender units on the cylinder head. Free the wiring from its retaining clips, noting its correct routing, and position it clear of the cylinder head.

10 Release the retaining clips then disconnect and remove the upper coolant hose linking the cylinder head to the radiator. Release the retaining clip and disconnect the cylinder head coolant hose from the expansion tank.

11 Referring to Chapter 3, unclip the coolant hoses from the heater matrix unions on the engine compartment bulkhead to drain the coolant from the cylinder block. Once the flow of coolant has stopped, reconnect both hoses and mop up any spilt coolant.

12 Make a final check to ensure that all relevant hoses, pipes and wires, etc, have been disconnected.

13 Working in the **reverse** of the tightening sequence **(see illustration 11.32a)**, progressively slacken the cylinder head bolts by a third of a turn at a time until all bolts can be unscrewed by hand. Remove each bolt in turn, along with its washer.

14 Lift the cylinder head from the cylinder block. If necessary, tap the cylinder head gently with a soft-faced mallet to free it from the block, but **do not** lever at the mating faces. Note the fitted positions of the two locating dowels, and remove them for safe-keeping if they are loose.

15 Recover the cylinder head gasket, and discard it.

X18XE and X20XEV

16 Remove the inlet and exhaust manifolds as described in Chapter 4A. If no work is to be carried out on the cylinder head, the head can be removed complete with manifolds once all the hoses/wiring, etc, have been disconnected (see Chapter 4A).

17 Remove the camshaft cover as described in Section 4.

18 Remove the camshaft sprockets as described in Section 8.

19 Unbolt the torque support rod bracket from the end of the cylinder head.

20 Undo the retaining bolts securing the timing belt rear cover to the cylinder head.

21 Remove the cylinder head as described in paragraphs 10 to 15.

Preparation for refitting

22 The mating faces of the cylinder head and block must be perfectly clean before refitting the head. Use a scraper to remove all traces of gasket and carbon, and also clean the tops of the pistons. Take particular care with the aluminium surfaces, as the soft metal is damaged easily. Also, make sure that debris is not allowed to enter the oil and water channels – this is particularly important for the oil circuit, as carbon could block the oil supply to the camshaft or crankshaft bearings. Using adhesive tape and paper, seal the water, oil and bolt holes in the cylinder block. To prevent carbon entering the gap between the pistons and bores, smear a little grease in the gap. After cleaning the piston, rotate the crankshaft so that the piston moves down the bore, then wipe out the grease and carbon with a cloth rag. Clean the other piston crowns in the same way.

23 Check the block and head for nicks, deep scratches and other damage. If slight, they may be removed carefully with a file. More serious damage may be repaired by machining, but this is a specialist job.

24 If warpage of the cylinder head is suspected, use a straight-edge to check it for distortion. Refer to Chapter 2E if necessary.

25 Ensure that the cylinder head bolt holes in the crankcase are clean and free of oil. Syringe or soak up any oil left in the bolt holes. This is most important in order that the correct bolt tightening torque can be applied and to prevent the possibility of the block being cracked by hydraulic pressure when the bolts are tightened.

26 Renew the cylinder head bolts regardless of their apparent condition.

Refitting

27 Ensure the crankshaft is positioned approximately 60° BTDC and wipe clean the mating faces of the head and block.

28 Ensure that the two locating dowels are in position at each end of the cylinder block/crankcase surface.

29 Fit the new cylinder head gasket to the block, making sure it is fitted with the correct way up with its OBEN/TOP mark uppermost **(see illustrations)**.

30 Carefully refit the cylinder head, locating it on the dowels.

31 Fit the washers to the new cylinder head bolts then carefully insert them into position (**do not drop**), tightening them finger-tight only at this stage **(see illustration)**.

32 Working progressively and in the sequence shown, first tighten all the cylinder head bolts to the Stage 1 torque setting (**see illustrations**).

33 Once all bolts have been tightened to the Stage 1 torque, again working in the sequence shown, tighten each bolt through its specified Stage 2 angle, using a socket and extension bar. It is recommended that an angle-measuring gauge is used during this

11.29a Ensure the head gasket is fitted with its OBEN/TOP marking uppermost . . .

11.29b . . . over the locating dowels

11.31 Fit the new head bolts tightening them by hand only

11.32a Cylinder head bolt tightening sequence (all models)

stage of the tightening, to ensure accuracy (see illustration).

34 Working in the specified sequence, go around again and tighten all bolts through the specified Stage 3 angle.

35 Working again in the specified sequence, go around and tighten all bolts through the specified Stage 4 angle.

36 Finally go around in the specified sequence again and tighten all bolts through the specified Stage 5 angle.

X16XEL, Z16XE, X18XE1 and Z18XE

37 Reconnect the coolant hoses, securing them in position with the retaining clips.

38 Reconnect the wiring connectors to the cylinder head, ensuring the harness is correctly routed and retained by all the necessary clips.

39 Refit the power steering pump (see Chapter 10).

40 Refit the timing belt rear cover retaining bolts and tighten them to the specified torque.

41 Refit the camshaft sprockets and idler pulleys as described in Section 8.

42 Align all the sprocket timing marks to bring the camshafts and crankshaft back to TDC then refit the timing belt as described in Section 7.

43 Refit the camshaft cover and timing belt cover(s) as described in Sections 4 and 6.

44 Refit/reconnect the inlet and exhaust manifolds (see Chapter 4A).

45 Refit the roadwheel then lower the vehicle to the floor and tighten the wheel bolts to the specified torque.

46 Ensure all pipes and hoses are securely reconnected then refill the cooling system and refit the spark plugs as described in Chapter 1A.

47 Reconnect the battery then start the engine and check for signs of leaks.

X18XE and X20XEV

48 Reconnect the coolant hoses, securing them in position with the retaining clips.

49 Refit the timing belt rear cover retaining

11.32b Tighten the cylinder head bolts to the specified Stage 1 torque setting . . .

bolts and tighten them to the specified torque.

50 Refit the torque support rod bracket to the side of the cylinder head and securely tighten its retaining bolts.

51 Refit the camshaft sprockets as described in Section 8.

52 Carry out the procedures described in paragraphs 42 to 47.

12 Sump –
removal and refitting

X16XEL, Z16XE, X18XE1 and Z18XE

Removal

1 Disconnect the battery negative terminal (see Chapter 5A).

2 Firmly apply the handbrake then jack up the front of the car and support it on axle stands. Where necessary, undo the retaining screws and remove the undercover from beneath the engine/transmission unit.

3 Drain the engine oil as described in Chapter 1A, then fit a new sealing washer and refit the drain plug, tightening it to the specified torque.

4 Remove the exhaust system front pipe as described in Chapter 4A.

11.33 . . . and then through the various specified angles as described in the text

5 Disconnect the wiring connector from the oil level sensor (where fitted).

6 Slacken and remove the bolts securing the sump flange to the transmission housing.

7 Remove the rubber plugs from the transmission end of the sump flange to gain access to the sump end retaining bolts (see illustration).

8 Progressively slacken and remove the bolts securing the sump to the base of the cylinder block/oil pump. Break the sump joint by striking the sump with the palm of the hand, then lower the sump away from the engine and withdraw it. Where applicable, remove the gasket and discard it.

12.7 Remove the rubber plugs from the sump flange to access the remaining sump bolts

12.11 Fit new seal/gasket to the oil pump pick-up pipe

9 While the sump is removed, take the opportunity to check the oil pump pick-up/strainer for signs of clogging or splitting. If necessary, unbolt the pick-up/strainer and remove it from the engine along with its sealing ring. The strainer can then be cleaned easily in solvent or renewed.

Refitting

10 Remove all traces of sealer and oil from the mating surfaces of the sump and cylinder block and (where removed) the pick-up/strainer. Also remove all traces of locking compound from the pick-up bolts (where removed).

11 Where necessary, position a new gasket/seal on top of the oil pump pick-up/strainer and fit the strainer **(see illustration)**. Apply locking compound to the threads of the retaining bolts then fit the bolts and tighten to the specified torque.

12 Ensure the sump and cylinder block mating surfaces are clean and dry and remove all traces of locking compound from the sump bolts.

13 Apply a smear of suitable sealant (available form Vauxhall dealers) to the areas of the cylinder block mating surface around the areas of the of the oil pump housing and rear main bearing cap joints **(see illustration)**.

14 On models with a gasket, fit a new gasket to the sump and apply a few drops of locking compound to the threads of the sump to cylinder block/oil pump bolts.

15 On models with no gasket, apply a bead of suitable sealant (available from Vauxhall dealers) approximately 2.5 mm thick to the sealing surface of the oil pan. Around the No 5 main bearing cap area, increase the thickness of the bead to 3.5 mm **(see illustration)**.

16 Offer up the sump, ensuring the gasket sealer remains correctly positioned, and loosely refit all the retaining bolts. Working out from the centre in a diagonal sequence, progressively tighten the bolts securing the sump to the cylinder block/oil pump to their specified torque setting.

17 Tighten the bolts securing the sump flange to the transmission housing to their specified torque settings. Refit the rubber plugs to the sump flange cut-outs.

18 Refit the exhaust front pipe (see Chapter 4A) and reconnect the oil level sender wiring connector (where fitted).

12.13 Apply sealant to the oil pump and rear main bearing cap joints (arrowed) before the sump is refitted

19 Lower the vehicle to the ground then fill the engine with fresh oil, with reference to Chapter 1A.

X18XE and X20XEV

Note: *New lower sump retaining bolts will be required on refitting.*

Removal

20 Carry out the operations described in paragraphs 1 to 3.

21 If an oil level sensor is fitted, disconnect the wiring connector from the sensor then slide off the retaining clip and push the sensor connector into the sump.

22 Slacken and remove the bolts securing the lower sump pan to the main casting then free the sump pan from the main casting and remove it along with its gasket (where applicable). On models with an oil level sensor, take care not to damage the sensor wiring as the pan is removed.

23 To remove the main casting from the engine, remove the oil filter (see Chapter 1A). If the oil filter is damaged on removal (which is likely), a new one should be used on refitting and the engine should be filled with fresh oil.

24 Remove the exhaust system front pipe as described in Chapter 4A.

25 Slacken and remove the bolts securing the sump flange to the transmission housing.

26 Progressively slacken and remove the bolts securing the main casting to the base of

12.15 Apply a 2.5mm thick bead of sealant to the sump sealing surface – increase the thickness to 3.5mm around the No 5 main bearing cap area

the cylinder block/oil pump. Break the joint by striking the casting with the palm of the hand, then lower it away from the engine and withdraw it. Where applicable, remove the gasket and discard it. **Note:** *On some models it may be necessary to disconnect the right-hand driveshaft from the transmission in order to remove the main casting (see Chapter 8).*

27 If necessary, remove oil pump pick-up/strainer as described in paragraph 9.

Refitting

28 Remove all traces of sealer and oil from the mating surfaces of the sump main casting and pan, the cylinder block and (where removed) the pick-up/strainer. Also remove all traces of locking compound from the threads of the sump pan holes.

29 Where necessary, position a new gasket/seal on top of the oil pump pick-up/strainer. Fit the strainer to the engine and tighten its retaining bolts to their specified torque settings.

30 Ensure the main casting and cylinder block mating surfaces are clean and dry and remove all traces of locking compound from the retaining bolts.

31 Apply a smear of suitable sealant to the areas of the cylinder block mating surface around the areas of the of the oil housing and rear main bearing cap joints.

32 Fit a new gasket to the sump and apply a few drops of locking compound to the threads of the sump to cylinder block/oil pump bolts.

33 Offer up the main casting, ensuring the gasket remains correctly positioned, and loosely refit all the retaining bolts. Working out from the centre in a diagonal sequence, progressively tighten the bolts securing it to the cylinder block/oil pump to their specified torque setting.

34 Tighten the bolts securing the main casting flange to the transmission housing to their specified torque settings.

35 Refit the exhaust front pipe (see Chapter 4A) and, where necessary, refit the driveshaft (see Chapter 8).

36 Ensure the sump pan and main casting surfaces are clean and dry, place a new gasket on the top of the pan and offer it up to the main casting. On models with an oil level sensor, fit a new sealing ring to the wiring connector and seat the wiring connector in the main casting, securing it in position with the retaining clip, prior to seating the sump pan on the main casting.

37 Fit the new sump pan retaining bolts then go around in a diagonal sequence and tighten them to the specified Stage 1 torque setting. Once all bolts have been tightened go around again and angle-tighten them through the specified Stage 2 angle.

38 Fit a new oil filter and reconnect the oil level sender wiring connector (where necessary).

39 Lower the vehicle to the ground then fill the engine with fresh oil, with reference to Chapter 1A.

13 Oil level sensor – removal and refitting

X16XEL, Z16XE, X18XE1 and Z18XE

Removal

1 Firmly apply the handbrake then jack up the front of the car and support it on axle stands. Where necessary, undo the retaining screws and remove the undercover from beneath the engine/transmission unit.

2 Drain the engine oil as described in Chapter 1A, then fit a new sealing washer and refit the drain plug, tightening it to the specified torque.

3 Disconnect the oil level sensor wiring plug.

4 Slacken and remove the four screws, and manoeuvre the sensor out from the sump (**see illustration**).

Refitting

5 If the original sensor is to be re-used, renew the sealing ring.

6 Refit the sensor to the sump, apply a little locking compound to the retaining screws, and tighten the screws to the specified torque setting.

7 Lower the vehicle to the ground then fill the engine with fresh oil, with reference to Chapter 1A.

X18XE and X20XEV

Removal

8 Firmly apply the handbrake then jack up the front of the car and support it on axle stands. Where necessary, undo the retaining screws and remove the undercover from beneath the engine/transmission unit.

9 Drain the engine oil as described in Chapter 1A, then fit a new sealing washer and refit the drain plug, tightening it to the specified torque.

10 Disconnect the wiring connector from the oil level sensor then slide off the retaining clip and push the sensor connector into the sump.

11 Slacken and remove the bolts securing the lower sump pan to the main casting then free the sump pan from the main casting and remove it along with its gasket (see Section 12). Take care not to damage the oil level sensor wiring as the pan is removed.

12 Undo the two Torx screws and remove the sensor from the sump.

Refitting

13 Fit the sensor to the sump and tighten the Torx screws to the specified torque setting.

14 Ensure the sump pan and main casting surfaces are clean and dry, place a new gasket on the top of the pan and offer it up to the main casting. Fit a new sealing ring to the oil level sensor wiring connector and seat the wiring connector in the main casting, securing

13.4 Manoeuvre the oil level sensor from the sump and renew the seal

it in position with the retaining clip, prior to seating the sump pan on the main casting.

15 Fit the new sump pan retaining bolts then go around in a diagonal sequence and tighten them to the specified Stage 1 torque setting. Once all bolts have been tightened go around again and angle-tighten them through the specified Stage 2 angle.

16 Lower the vehicle to the ground then fill the engine with fresh oil, with reference to Chapter 1A.

14 Oil pump – removal, overhaul and refitting

Note: Depending on engine code the oil pump type could either be rotor-type or crescent/gear-type. At the time of writing, the X18XE1 and Z18XE were shown to have the rotor-type pump fitted, and all the other engines have the crescent/gear-type pump fitted.

Note: The pressure relief valve can be removed with pump in position on the engine unit, although on some models it will be necessary to unbolt the mounting bracket assembly from the block to allow the valve to be removed.

Removal

1 Remove the timing belt as described in Section 7.

2 Remove the rear timing belt cover as described in Section 6.

14.8 Oil pump rotors identifying marks (rotor-type pump)

14.7 Undo the retaining screws and remove the oil pump cover

3 Remove the sump and oil pump pick-up/strainer as described in Section 12.

4 Disconnect the wiring connector from the oil pressure switch.

5 On models, with the crankshaft sensor on the front pulley/vibration damper, unbolt the crankshaft sensor mounting bracket and position it clear of the oil pump.

6 Slacken and remove the retaining bolts then slide the oil pump housing assembly off of the end of the crankshaft, taking great care not to lose the locating dowels. Remove the housing gasket and discard it.

Overhaul

7 Undo the retaining screws and lift off the pump cover from the rear of the housing (**see illustration**).

8 Using a suitable marker pen, mark the surface of both the pump inner and outer gears/rotors; the marks can then be used to ensure the gears/rotors are refitted the correct way around (**see illustration**).

9 Lift out the inner and outer gears/rotors from the pump housing (**see illustration**).

10 Unscrew the oil pressure relief valve bolt from the front of the housing and withdraw the spring and plunger from the housing, noting which way around the plunger is fitted. Remove the sealing washer from the valve bolt (**see illustration**).

11 Clean the components, and carefully examine the gears/rotors, pump body and relief valve plunger for any signs of scoring or wear. Renew any component which shows signs of wear or damage; if the gears/rotors or

14.9 Removal of the pump outer gear – outer face identification punch mark arrowed (crescent/gear-type pump)

14.10 Oil pressure relief valve components

1 Plunger   *3 Sealing washer*
2 Spring   *4 Valve bolt*

pump housing are marked then the complete pump assembly should be renewed.

12 If the components appear serviceable, measure the clearance between the inner and outer gears/rotors using feeler blades. Also measure the gear/rotor endfloat, and check the flatness of the end cover **(see illustrations)**. If the clearances exceed the specified tolerances the pump must be renewed.

13 If the pump is satisfactory, reassemble the components in the reverse order of removal, noting the following.

a) *Ensure both gears/rotors are fitted the correct way around.*
b) *Fit a new sealing ring to the pressure relief valve bolt and tighten the bolt to the specified torque.*
c) *Apply a little locking compound to the*

14.13 Apply thread locking compound to the oil pump cover screws

14.14 Fitting a new crankshaft oil seal to the oil pump housing

14.12a Using a feeler blade to check gear clearance (crescent/gear-type pump)

threads, and tighten the pump cover screws to the specified torque **(see illustration)**.
d) *On completion prime the oil pump by filling it with clean engine oil whilst rotating the inner gear.*

Refitting

14 Prior to refitting, carefully lever out the crankshaft oil seal using a flat-bladed screwdriver. Fit the new oil seal, ensuring its sealing lip is facing inwards, and press it squarely into the housing using a tubular drift which bears only on the hard outer edge of the seal **(see illustration)**. Press the seal into position so that it is flush with the housing and lubricate the oil seal lip with clean engine oil.

15 Ensure the mating surfaces of the oil pump and cylinder block are clean and dry and the locating dowels are in position.

16 Fit a new gasket to the cylinder block.

17 Carefully manoeuvre the oil pump into position and engage the inner gear with the crankshaft end **(see illustration)**. Locate the pump on the dowels, taking great care not damage the oil seal lip.

18 Refit the pump housing retaining bolts in their original locations and tighten them to the specified torque.

19 On models with the crankshaft sensor on the front pulley/vibration damper, refit the crankshaft sensor bracket to the pump housing and tighten its mounting bolt to the specified torque.

20 Reconnect the oil pressure sensor wiring connector.

14.17 Take care not to damage the oil seal on the crankshaft lip (1) and engage the inner gear with the crankshaft flats (2)

14.12b Using a straight-edge and feeler blade to measure gear endfloat (crescent/gear-type pump)

21 Refit the oil pump pick-up/strainer and sump as described in Section 12.

22 Refit the rear timing belt cover to the engine, tightening its retaining bolts to the specified torque.

23 Refit the timing belt sprockets, idler pulleys and tensioner then refit the belt as described in Sections 7 and 8.

24 On completion, fit a new oil filter and fill the engine with clean oil as described in Chapter 1A.

15 Flywheel/driveplate – removal, inspection and refitting

Refer to Chapter 2A, Section 15.

16 Crankshaft oil seals – renewal

Right-hand (timing belt end)

1 Remove the crankshaft sprocket as described in Section 8.

2 Carefully punch or drill two small holes opposite each other in the oil seal. Screw a self-tapping screw into each and pull on the screws with pliers to extract the seal **(see illustration)**.

Caution: Great care must be taken to avoid damage to the oil pump

3 Clean the seal housing and polish off any

16.2 Removing the crankshaft oil seal

16.4 Fitting a new crankshaft oil seal

burrs or raised edges which may have caused the seal to fail in the first place.

4 Lubricate the lips of the new seal with clean engine oil and ease it into position on the end of the shaft. Press the seal squarely into position until it is flush with the housing. If necessary, a suitable tubular drift, such as a socket, which bears only on the hard outer edge of the seal can be used to tap the seal into position **(see illustration)**. Take great care not to damage the seal lips during fitting and ensure that the seal lips face inwards.

5 Wash off any traces of oil, then refit the crankshaft sprocket as described in Section 8.

Left-hand (flywheel/driveplate end)

6 Remove the flywheel/driveplate as described in Section 15.

7 Renew the seal as described in paragraphs 2 to 4 **(see illustration)**.

8 Refit the flywheel/driveplate as described in Section 15.

17 Engine/transmission mountings – inspection and renewal

Refer to Chapter 2A, Section 17.

18 Balancer unit (X20XEV engine) – removal and refitting

Removal

1 Some models fitted with the X20XEV engine are equipped with a balancer unit fitted between the cylinder block and the main sump casting. The unit consists of two counter-rotating balance shafts driven by the crankshaft **(see illustration)**.

2 Remove the sump main casting as described in Section 12.

3 Slacken the retaining bolts, and remove the balancer unit and shim.

Refitting

4 If operations have been carried out that might affect the backlash between the balancer shafts and the crankshaft (crankshaft, bearing cap or balancer unit replacement), then the backlash

16.7 Left-hand crankshaft oil seal – transmission and flywheel removed

must be measured and, if necessary, adjusted. If none of theses mentioned operations have been carried out, the original shim can be re-used.

5 In order to carry out the measurement and adjustment procedure, Vauxhall tool No KM 949 must be used. If this tool is not available, take the cylinder block and balancer unit to a Vauxhall dealer or specialist to have the backlash measured and adjusted. If the tool is available, proceed as follows.

6 With reference to Section 3 if necessary, set the crankshaft at TDC on No 1 cylinder at the end of the compression stroke.

7 Position the two balance shafts so that when viewed from the right-hand of the engine, the two flat machined surfaces are exactly horizontal **(see illustration)**.

8 Fit the existing shim and balancer unit to

18.1 Balancer unit (2) and shim (1)

18.7 Position the balancer shafts so that the two flat machined surfaces are horizontal

18.11 Dial gauge position – backlash adjustment

H32269

or cylinder block, so that the gauge probe acts vertically against the measuring arm between the notches of the flat machined surface **(see illustration)**.

12 Determine the 'beginning' and 'end' of the backlash by turning the exhaust side knurled bolt backwards and forwards. Position this balancer shaft at the 'beginning' of the backlash and zero the dial gauge.

13 Turn the exhaust side balancer shaft to the 'end' of the backlash, and read off the measurement from the dial gauge.

14 The backlash should be measured at four different balancer shaft positions. Using the crankshaft sprocket bolt, turn the crankshaft clockwise until the measuring arm on the inlet side balancer shaft points to the 6 o'clock position. Loosen the knurled bolt and reposition the arm back to the 9 o'clock position. Repeat the backlash measurement procedure in this position, and take two further readings repositioning the balancer shaft each time.

15 If any of the four reading are outside the value given in the Specifications, the backlash must be adjusted. Adjustment is achieved by inserting a shim of various thicknesses between the balancer unit and the cylinder block. Each shim is given a code number to represent its thickness (see Specifications). This code is also stamped onto the shim.

16 Having established the backlash, and the thickness of the existing shim (from the code number), it is then possible to determine the thickness (and code number) of the shim required to adjust the backlash to within the given tolerance. The next larger or smaller shim changes the backlash by approximately 0.02 mm. For example: The measured backlash with a shim code number '70' fitted was 0.08 mm. If this shim is replaced by one with the code number '67', the backlash is reduced to 0.06 mm. Only one shim may be fitted at a time.

17 After selecting the correct shim, and refitting the balancer unit and shim as described in paragraphs 6 to 8, repeat the measurement procedure to ensure the backlash is within tolerance.

18 Remove the dial gauge and the two knurled bolts of KM 949.

19 Refit the sump as described in Section 12.

the cylinder block. Insert the retaining bolts and tighten them to the specified torque.

9 Screw Vauxhall tool No KM 949 with the long knurled bolt into the end of the inlet side balancer shaft. Position the measuring arm so that it points to the 9 o'clock position, when viewed from the end of the engine. Hand tighten the bolt.

10 Screw the short knurled bolt of KM 949 into the exhaust side balancer shaft. Hand tighten the bolt.

11 Mount a dial gauge onto the balancer unit

Chapter 2 Part C:
2.2 litre DOHC petrol engine in-car repair procedures

Contents

Degrees of difficulty

Easy, suitable for novice with little experience	Fairly easy, suitable for beginner with some experience	Fairly difficult, suitable for competent DIY mechanic	Difficult, suitable for experienced DIY mechanic	Very difficult, suitable for expert DIY or professional

Specifications

General

Engine type	Four-cylinder, in-line, water-cooled. Chain-driven double overhead camshaft, acting on hydraulic tappets, 16 valves
Manufacturer's engine code	Z22SE
Bore	86.0 mm
Stroke	94.6 mm
Capacity	2198 cc
Injection sequence	1-3-4-2 (No 1 cylinder at timing chain end of engine)
Direction of crankshaft rotation	Clockwise (viewed from timing chain end of engine)
Compression ratio	10:1
Maximum power	108 kW at 5800 rpm
Maximum torque	203 Nm at 4000 rpm
Exhaust emissions standard	98/69/EC, Euro 4, Level B

Compression pressures

Standard	12 to 15 bar (174 to 218 psi)
Maximum difference between any two cylinders	1 bar (14.5 psi)
Pressure loss	Not more than 25% max per cylinder

Camshaft

Endfloat	0.04 to 0.14 mm
Maximum permissible radial run-out	0.06 mm
Cam lift (inlet and exhaust)	8.0 mm

Lubrication system

Oil pump type . . . . Rotor-type, driven by crankshaft pulley/vibration damper from crankshaft

Minimum permissible oil pressure at idle speed, with engine
  at operating temperature (oil temperature of at least 80°C) . . . . 1.5 bar (22 psi)
Oil pump clearances:
  Between outer rotor and oil pump housing . . . . 0.350 mm (max)
  Between inner and outer rotor . . . . 0.150 mm (max)
  Indentation/endfloat (rotor to upper edge of timing case cover) . . . . 0.080 mm (max)

Torque wrench settings

	Nm	lbf ft
Auxiliary drivebelt tensioner assembly bolts:		
Pulley backplate pivot bolt	42	31
Strut mounting bolts	23	17
Balance shaft retaining bracket bolts	10	7
Balance shaft sprocket bolts*:		
Stage 1	8	6
Stage 2	Angle-tighten a further 30°	
Camshaft bearing cap bolts	10	7
Camshaft bearing cap (for PAS pump mounting) bolts	25	18
Camshaft cover bolts	10	7
Camshaft sprocket bolt*:		
Stage 1	85	63
Stage 2	Angle-tighten a further 30°	
Connecting rod big-end bearing cap bolt*:		
Stage 1	25	18
Stage 2	Angle-tighten a further 50°	
Stage 3	Angle-tighten a further 50°	
Coolant drain bolt in coolant pump	20	15
Coolant pump sprocket access cover bolts	7	5
Coolant pump sprocket bolts	10	7
Coolant pump-to-cylinder block bolts	25	18
Crankshaft pulley/vibration damper bolt*:		
Stage 1	100	74
Stage 2	Angle-tighten a further 40°	
Stage 3	Angle-tighten a further 30°	
Cylinder block baseplate to cylinder block :		
M8 bolts	25	18
M10 bolts (main bearing bolts)*:		
Stage 1	20	15
Stage 2	Angle-tighten a further 70°	
Cylinder head x10 (main) bolts*:		
Stage 1	30	22
Stage 2	Angle-tighten a further 60°	
Stage 3	Angle-tighten a further 60°	
Stage 4	Angle-tighten a further 35°	
Cylinder head x4 (timing chain end) bolts*	35	26
Engine/transmission mounting bolts:		
Right-hand mounting (engine):		
Mounting-to-body nuts	60	44
Mounting-to-bracket bolt	60	44
Left-hand mounting:		
Mounting-to-body bolts	20	15
Bracket-to-transmission bolts	35	26
Mounting-to-bracket bolts	55	41
Rear mounting:		
Mounting-to-bracket bolts	45	33
Mounting-to-subframe bolts (x4)	60	44
Bracket-to-transmission bolts (x3)	60	44
Front mounting:		
Mounting-to-transmission bolts	60	44
Mounting to subframe	55	41
Flywheel bolts*:		
Stage 1	53	39
Stage 2	Angle-tighten a further 25°	
Sump-to-transmission bolts	40	30
Transmission-to-cylinder block bolts	60	44
Oil dipstick tube to intake manifold	10	7

Torque wrench settings (continued)

	Nm	lbf ft
Oil pump:		
Oil pressure control valve plug	40	30
Oil pump cover plate to timing cover bolts	6	4
Roadwheel bolts	110	81
Sump to cylinder block baseplate	25	18
Sump drain plug	25	18
Timing chain cover bolts	25	18
Timing chain guide bolts	10	7
Timing chain sliding rail bolt*	10	7
Timing chain tensioner rail pivot bolt	10	7
Timing chain oil spray/injector nozzle	10	7
Timing chain tensioner:		
Camshaft	75	55
Balance shafts	10	7

*Use new fasteners

1 General information

How to use this Chapter

1 This Part of Chapter 2 is devoted to in-car repair procedures for the engine. All procedures concerning engine removal and refitting, and engine block/cylinder head overhaul can be found in Chapter 2E.

2 Most of the operations included in this Part are based on the assumption that the engine is still installed in the car. Therefore, if this information is being used during a complete engine overhaul, with the engine already removed, many of the steps included here will not apply.

Engine description

3 The 2.2 litre (2198 cc) engine is a completely new engine designed by Vauxhall. It is of the sixteen-valve, in-line four-cylinder, double overhead camshaft (DOHC) type, mounted transversely at the front of the car with the transmission attached to its left-hand end.

4 The aluminium alloy cylinder block is of the dry-liner type. The crankshaft is supported within the cylinder block on five shell-type main bearings. Thrust washers are fitted to number 2 main bearing, to control crankshaft endfloat.

5 The connecting rods rotate on horizontally-split bearing shells at their big-ends. The pistons are attached to the connecting rods by gudgeon pins, which are an interference fit in the connecting rod small-end, and retained by circlips. The aluminium-alloy pistons are fitted with three piston rings – two compression rings and scraper-type oil control ring.

6 The inlet and exhaust valves are each closed by coil springs, and operate in guides pressed into the cylinder head.

7 The camshafts are driven by the crankshaft via a timing chain arrangement; there is also a lower timing chain which links the crankshaft to the balance shafts and coolant pump. The camshaft rotates directly in the head and operates the sixteen valves via followers and hydraulic tappets. The followers are situated directly below the camshaft, each one operating a separate valve. Valve clearances are automatically adjusted by the hydraulic tappets.

8 Lubrication is by means of an oil pump, which is driven off the right-hand end of the crankshaft. It draws oil from the sump, and then forces it through an externally-mounted filter into galleries in the cylinder block/crankcase. From there, the oil is distributed to the crankshaft (main bearings) and camshaft. The big-end bearings are supplied with oil via internal drillings in the crankshaft, while the camshaft bearings also receive a pressurised supply. The camshaft lobes and valves are lubricated by splash, as are all other engine components. The timing chain is lubricated by an oil spray nozzle.

9 A semi-closed crankcase ventilation system is employed; crankcase fumes are drawn from cylinder head cover, and passed via a hose to the inlet manifold.

Repair operations possible with the engine in the car

10 The following work can be carried out with the engine in the car:

a) Compression pressure testing.
b) Camshaft cover – removal and refitting.
c) Timing chain cover – removal and refitting.
d) Timing chains – removal and refitting.
e) Timing chain tensioners, guides and sprockets – removal and refitting.
f) Camshaft and followers – removal, inspection and refitting.
g) Cylinder head – removal and refitting.
h) Connecting rods and pistons – removal and refitting*.
i) Sump – removal and refitting.
j) Oil pump – removal, overhaul and refitting.
k) Crankshaft oil seals – renewal.
l) Engine/transmission mountings – inspection and renewal.
m) Flywheel – removal, inspection and refitting.

* Although the operation marked with an asterisk can be carried out with the engine in the car after removal of the sump, it is better for the engine to be removed, in the interests of cleanliness and improved access. For this reason, the procedure is described in Chapter 2E.

2 Compression test – description and interpretation

Refer to Chapter 2A, Section 2.

3 Top dead centre (TDC) for No 1 piston – locating

1 In its travel up and down its cylinder bore, Top Dead Centre (TDC) is the highest point that each piston reaches as the crankshaft rotates. While each piston reaches TDC both at the top of the compression stroke and again at the top of the exhaust stroke, for the purpose of timing the engine, TDC refers to the piston position (usually number 1) at the top of its compression stroke.

2 Number 1 piston is at the right-hand (timing chain) end of the engine, and its TDC position is located as follows. Note that the crankshaft rotates clockwise when viewed from the right-hand side of the car.

3 Disconnect the battery negative terminal (see Chapter 5A). To improve access to the crankshaft pulley, apply the handbrake, then jack up the front of the vehicle and support it on axle stands. Remove the retaining screws/clips and remove the right-hand wheelarch liner and engine undertray (where fitted).

4 To gain access to the camshaft sprocket timing marks, remove the camshaft cover as described in Section 5.

5 Using a socket and extension bar on the crankshaft sprocket bolt, rotate the crankshaft until the timing marks on the camshaft sprockets are both correctly aligned (see Section 4). With the camshaft sprocket alignment marks correctly positioned, the notch on the crankshaft pulley rim should align with the pointer on the timing chain cover. The engine is now positioned with No 1 piston at TDC.

4.0 Vauxhall camshaft locking tool (KM-6148)

A Camshaft sprocket locating pins

4.3 Locking the camshaft sprockets in position using the Vauxhall tool KM-6148

4 Valve timing – checking and adjustment

Note: *To check the valve timing, it will be necessary to use the following Vauxhall special tool (or suitable equivalent); the camshaft locking tool number is KM-6148 (see illustration). If access to this tool cannot be gained, this task must be entrusted to a Vauxhall dealer. The camshaft locking tool (pictured) has locating pins that locate in the holes in the camshaft sprockets, to ensures that the camshafts remain correctly positioned.*

1 Remove the camshaft cover as described in Section 5.
2 Position No 1 cylinder at TDC as described in Section 3, ensuring the crankshaft pulley notch is correctly aligned with the timing mark on the timing chain cover.
3 With the crankshaft in position, insert the camshaft locking tool into position on the right-hand end of the camshaft sprockets **(see illustration)**.
4 If the locking tool can be correctly fitted the valve timing is correctly set and no adjustment is necessary.
5 Refit the camshaft cover as described In Section 5
6 If the camshaft tool cannot be inserted

correctly into the camshaft sprockets, the timing will need to be reset. See Section 9 for the removal, inspection and refitting of the timing chain and sprockets.

5 Camshaft cover – removal and refitting

Removal

1 Unclip and remove the plastic cover from the top of the engine.
2 Release the securing clip from the wiring plug on the ignition module and disconnect.
3 Undo the four retaining bolts from the ignition module assembly and lift upwards **(see illustration)**.
4 Disconnect the breather hose from the front of the camshaft cover.
5 Unclip the wiring harness from along the front edge and left-hand side of the camshaft cover.
6 Disconnect the wiring plug from the EGR (exhaust gas recirculation) valve.
7 Unclip the brake servo vacuum pipe and coolant expansion tank hose from the wiring brackets along the front edge and left-hand side of the camshaft cover.
8 Undo the two retaining nuts and lift off the wiring trough from along the front of the camshaft cover **(see illustration)**.
9 Undo the two retaining nuts and remove the wiring bracket from the left-hand side of the camshaft cover. With the bracket removed, undo the right-hand stud to release the earth strap**(see illustrations)**.
10 On vehicles with air conditioning, undo the two retaining nuts from the timing chain end of the camshaft cover to release the refrigerant lines **(see illustration)**. Also unclip the fuel pipes from the bracket.
11 Slacken and remove the camshaft cover retaining bolts along with their sealing washers then lift the camshaft cover and

5.3 Removing the ignition module assembly from the spark plugs

5.8 Undo the two retaining nuts (arrowed) to remove the wiring trough

5.9a Remove the bracket from the left-hand end of the cam cover . . .

5.9b . . . then undo the earth strap retaining nut (arrowed)

gasket/seals away from the cylinder head. Renew the cover gasket/seals and retaining bolt sealing washers.

Refitting

12 Refitting is a reversal of removal noting the following points:

- a) *Use new camshaft cover gasket/seals*
- b) *Once the cover is in position, first tighten all the bolts hand-tight, then go around and tighten them all to the specified torque setting.*
- c) *Make sure the securing clip is fitted correctly to the wiring plug on the ignition module.*

6 Crankshaft pulley – removal and refitting

Note: *A new pulley retaining bolt will be required on refitting.*

Removal

1 Apply the handbrake, then jack up the front of the car and support it on axle stands. Remove the right-hand roadwheel.

2 Undo the retaining screws/clips and remove the engine undertray and wheel arch liner if required.

3 Remove the auxiliary drivebelt as described in Chapter 1A. Prior to removal, mark the direction of rotation on the belt to ensure the belt is refitted the same way around.

4 Slacken the crankshaft pulley retaining bolt. To prevent crankshaft rotation whilst the

6.6a Turn the pulley until the flat on the centre hub locates with the oil pump drive . . .

6.6b . . . then fit a new securing bolt to the pulley

5.10 Undo the two retaining nuts (arrowed) and release the air conditioning pipes

retaining bolt is slackened, have an assistant select top gear and apply the brakes firmly; if the engine is removed from the vehicle it will be necessary to lock the flywheel (see Section 16).

5 Unscrew the retaining bolt and washer and remove the crankshaft pulley from the end of the crankshaft. Whilst the pulley is removed check the oil seal for signs of wear or damage and, if necessary, renew as described in Section 15.

Refitting

6 Carefully locate the crankshaft pulley on the crankshaft end. Align the flats on the pulley with the oil pump, then turn the pulley to align the slot in the pulley with the crankshaft key. Slide the pulley fully into position, taking great care not to damage the oil seal, then fit the washer and new retaining bolt **(see illustrations)**.

7 Lock the crankshaft by the method used on removal, and tighten the pulley retaining bolt to the specified Stage 1 torque setting then angle-tighten the bolt through the specified Stage 2 angle, using a socket and extension bar, and finally through the specified Stage 3 angle. It is recommended that an angle-measuring gauge is used during the final stages of the tightening, to ensure accuracy **(see illustration)**. If a gauge is not available, use white paint to make alignment marks between the bolt head and pulley prior to tightening; the marks can then be used to check that the bolt has been rotated through the correct angle.

8 Refit the auxiliary drivebelt as described in Chapter 1A using the mark made prior to

6.7 Using an angle-measuring gauge to tighten the crankshaft pulley (engine removed for photo)

removal to ensure the belt is fitted the correct way around.

9 Position the engine undertray and wheel-arch liner, then refit the retaining clips/screws.

10 Refit the roadwheel then lower the car to the ground and tighten the wheel bolts to the specified torque.

7 Timing chain cover – removal and refitting

Removal

1 Firmly apply the handbrake then jack up the front of the car and support it on axle stands. Where necessary, undo the retaining clips/screws and remove the engine undertray.

2 Referring to Section 17, support the engine/transmission unit and unbolt the right-hand mounting assembly from the cylinder head.

3 Mark the running direction of the auxiliary belt, then slacken the tensioner and remove the belt as described in Chapter 1A.

4 Undo the securing bolt from the auxiliary belt tensioner and remove from the cylinder block.

5 For better access remove the right-hand side front wheelarch liner, then remove the crankshaft pulley/vibration damper (see Section 6).

6 Drain the engine oil as described in Chapter 1A.

7 Noting each bolt's correct fitted location (one bolt is also securing the coolant pump), slacken and remove all the bolts securing the timing chain cover to the cylinder block **(see illustration)**.

8 Carefully ease the timing cover squarely away from the cylinder block and manoeuvre it out of position, noting the correct fitted positions of its locating dowels. If the locating dowels are a loose fit, remove them and store with the cover for safe-keeping.

9 Remove the gasket and ensure the mating surfaces are clean, renew the gasket as required.

Refitting

10 Prior to refitting the cover, it is recommended that the crankshaft oil seal

7.7 Note retaining bolt (arrowed) on the inner part of the timing chain cover casing

7.10a Carefully lever the old crankshaft oil seal out of the cover . . .

7.10b . . . then using a suitable drift tap in the new oil seal

7.16 Refit the tensioner, making sure the dowel is located in the hole in the casing

should be renewed. Carefully lever the old seal out of the cover using a large flat-bladed screwdriver. Fit the new seal to the cover, making sure its sealing lip is facing inwards. Press/tap the seal into position until it is flush with the cover, using a suitable tubular drift, such as a socket, which bears only on the hard outer edge of the seal (see illustrations).

11 Ensure the mating surfaces of the cover and cylinder block are clean and dry and the locating dowels are in position.

12 Manoeuvre the gasket into position and locate it on the dowels.

13 Manoeuvre the timing cover into position, locating it on the dowels. Refit the cover retaining bolts, ensuring each one is fitted in its original location, and tighten them evenly and progressively to the specified torque.

14 Refit the crankshaft pulley as described in Section 6.

15 Refit the oil drain plug with new sealing

washer, and tighten to the specified torque.
16 Refit the auxiliary drivebelt tensioner making sure the dowel in the rear of the tensioner is aligned, then tighten the securing bolt to the specified torque (see illustration).
17 Refit the auxiliary drivebelt (see Chapter 1A).
18 Refit the engine/transmission right-hand mounting assembly (see Section 17).
19 Refit the undertray (where fitted) then lower the vehicle to the ground.
20 On completion refill the engine with oil as described in Chapter 1A. Start the engine and check for signs of oil leaks.

8 Timing chain tensioners –
   removal and refitting

Camshaft chain tensioner

Note: *If a new camshaft timing chain tensioner is being fitted, then a new tension rail should be fitted at the same time. Under no circumstances should the old tension rail be fitted with a new tensioner.*

Removal

1 Remove the camshaft cover as described in Section 5.
2 Unscrew the camshaft timing chain tensioner from the rear of the cylinder head, and remove the inner piston assembly (see illustration) Remove the sealing rings and discard them, new ones should be used on refitting.

Caution: Do not rotate the engine whilst the tensioner is removed.
3 Dismantle the tensioner (see illustration), and inspect the tensioner piston for signs of wear or damage and renew if necessary.

Refitting

4 Pretension the timing chain tensioner, by turning the inner piston clockwise (see illustrations) and allow it to lock in position. Lubricate the inner piston, then reassemble the timing chain tensioner.
5 Replace the sealing rings, then lubricate the timing chain tensioner/piston with clean engine oil and insert it into the cylinder head. **Note:** *Check the threads are clean on the tensioner and in the cylinder head before refitting.*
6 Tighten the tensioner to the specified torque.
7 Release the tensioner, by pressing on the tension rail/timing chain with a rounded bar (see illustration). This will press against the inner piston of the tensioner to unlock it, when it releases, the spring-loaded piston will take up the slack in the timing chain.
Caution: This procedure must be carried out correctly, otherwise the chain may be left slack and skip a tooth on the sprockets. This will result in engine damage.
8 Rotate the crankshaft through two complete rotations (720°) in the correct direction of rotation and check that all the timing marks re-align up at TDC, see Section 3.
9 Refit the camshaft cover as described in Section 5.

8.2 Removing the timing chain tensioner assembly

8.3 Inner piston removed to check for wear or damage

8.4a Turn the inner piston screw clockwise until it locks in position . . .

8.4b . . . then fit the inner piston to the outer tensioner assembly

8.7 Press the bar against the tension rail to release the tensioner inner piston

Balance shaft chain tensioner

Removal

10 Remove the timing chain cover as described in Section 7.

11 Undo the two retaining bolts and remove the balancer shaft chain tensioner from the cylinder block.

8.13 1.0 mm drill bit (arrowed) used to lock the tensioner piston in place

Caution: Do not rotate the engine whilst the tensioner is removed.

12 Inspect the tensioner piston for signs of wear or damage and renew if necessary.

Refitting

13 Pretension the balance shaft chain tensioner, by turning the piston clockwise approximately 45° and push it back into the

8.15 Removing the locking pin to release the tensioner

tensioner housing. Insert a 1.0 mm locking pin or drill bit into the hole in the piston housing, which will lock the piston in position **(see illustration)**.

14 Lubricate the tensioner piston with clean engine oil, then refit it onto the cylinder block tightening the bolts to there specified torque.

15 Once the tensioner is in position, remove the locking pin to release the tensioner piston **(see illustration)**. Make sure the piston engages with the tension rail correctly and takes up any slack in the balancer shaft timing chain.

Caution: This procedure must be carried out correctly, otherwise the chain may be left slack and skip a tooth on the sprockets. This could result in engine vibration or damage.

16 Refit the timing chain cover as described in Section 7.

Chain tensioner and guide rails

17 Tensioner and guide rail removal and refitting is part of the timing chain and sprockets removal and refitting procedure (see Section 9). They must be renewed if they show signs of wear or damage on their chain surfaces.

<table>
<tr><td>**9**</td><td>**Timing chains and sprockets** – removal, inspection and refitting</td><td></td></tr>
</table>

Note: *In order to set the valve timing accurately at TDC, a special Vauxhall service tool (or suitable alternative) is required (see Section 4). If the timing chain and sprockets are to be completely removed or refitted, then this task can be carried out without the tool. The timing can be re-aligned using the coloured links on the timing chain and the alignment marks on the sprockets (see illustrations).*

Caution: Prior to removal, ensure the camshaft sprockets are suitably marked as they are identical and can be refitted to either camshaft.

Note: *If there is any wear on the camshaft timing chain, tension rails, guides and crankshaft sprocket the components must always be renewed as a complete assembly.*

9.0a Align the silver link (arrowed) with the triangular timing mark on the exhaust sprocket . . .

9.0b . . . the copper coloured link (arrowed) with the diamond timing mark on the intake sprocket . . .

9.0c . . . and the second silver coloured link (arrowed) with the timing mark (white dot) on the crankshaft sprocket

9.5 Undo the two retaining bolts (arrowed) from the chain sliding rail

9.6a Remove the access plug from the cylinder head . . .

9.6b . . . and remove the guide rail upper securing bolt

Removal

Camshaft chain and sprockets

Note: *New camshaft sprocket retaining bolts and new timing chain sliding rail retaining bolts will be required on refitting.*

1 Disconnect the battery negative lead (see Chapter 5A) then remove the camshaft cover (see Section 5).

2 Position No 1 cylinder at TDC, as described in Section 3. The mark on the crankshaft pulley/vibration damper should be aligned with the mark on the timing cover casing.

3 Remove the timing chain cover as described in Section 7.

4 Remove the camshaft timing chain tensioner as described in Section 8.

5 Undo the two retaining bolts from the camshaft timing chain sliding rail on the top of the cylinder head **(see illustration)**.

6 Remove the access plug from the cylinder head and undo the upper securing bolt for the timing chain guide rail **(see illustrations)**.

7 Undo the lower securing bolt for the timing chain guide rail and remove downwards out from the engine **(see illustration)**.

8 Hold the camshafts in turn using an open-ended spanner on the flats provided, then slacken and remove the camshaft sprocket retaining bolts **(see illustration)**.

9 Remove the exhaust camshaft sprocket, making sure it is marked for refitting as they are both identical.

10 Undo the lower securing bolt from the timing chain tension rail, then remove it downwards and out from the engine **(see illustration)**.

11 Lift the timing chain off the crankshaft sprocket and remove the intake camshaft sprocket complete with timing chain out

through the top of the cylinder head.

12 Slide the crankshaft drivegear/sprocket (and spring washer, where fitted) off the Woodruff key on the crankshaft. **Note:** *FRONT is marked on the outer face of the gear.*

Balance shaft chain and sprockets

Note: *If there is any wear on the balancer shaft timing chain, tension rail and guides, balance shaft chain tensioner and all the drivegears/sprockets the components must always be renewed as a complete assembly.*

13 Remove the camshaft timing chain and sprockets as described in paragraphs 1 to 12.

14 Undo the two retaining bolts and remove the balancer shaft chain tensioner from the cylinder block.

15 Undo the securing bolts and remove the tension rail and the two guide rails from the cylinder block **(see illustration)**.

16 Lift the balancer shaft timing chain from the sprockets and remove.

17 Using a suitable drift, lock the balance shaft sprockets and undo the retaining bolts, then remove the sprocket from the balance shaft **(see illustration)**. Use new bolts when refitting.

18 Slide the crankshaft drivegear/sprocket (and spring washer, where fitted) off the Woodruff key on the crankshaft. **Note:** *FRONT is marked on the outer face of the gear.*

19 Lock the coolant pump drivegear with a suitable screwdriver, and undo the three securing bolts. Remove the drivegear from the coolant pump.

9.7 Undo the lower guide rail securing bolt (arrowed) and remove the guide rail downwards

9.8 Undo the camshaft sprocket retaining bolts – hold the camshafts using an open-ended spanner

9.10 Undo the retaining bolt and remove the tension rail from the engine

9.15 Undo the retaining bolts and remove the tension rail and guide rails

A Tension rail   B Guide rails

9.17 Using a drift to lock the balance shaft sprocket

Inspection

20 Examine the teeth on the sprockets for any sign of wear or damage such as chipped, hooked or missing teeth. If there is any sign of wear or damage on any sprocket/gear, all the sprockets/gears and the relevant chain should be renewed as a set.

21 Inspect the links of each timing chain for signs of wear or damage on the rollers. The extent of wear can be judged by checking the amount by which the chain can be bent sideways; a new chain will have very little sideways movement. If there is an excessive amount of side play in a timing chain, it must be renewed.

22 Note that it is a sensible precaution to renew the timing chains, regardless of their apparent condition, if the engine has covered a high mileage, or if it has been noted that the chain(s) have sounded noisy when the engine running. It is advised renewing the chains and sprockets as a matched set, since it is false economy to run a new chain on worn sprockets and *vice-versa*. If there is any doubt about the condition of the timing chains and sprockets, seek the advice of a Vauxhall dealer service department, who will be able to advise you as to the best course of action, based on their previous knowledge of the engine.

23 Examine the chain guide(s) and tensioner rail(s) for signs of wear or damage to their chain contact faces, renewing any which are badly marked.

Refitting

Camshaft chain and sprockets

24 If any new components are being fitted, transfer any alignment marks you have made from the original components to aid refitting. Ensure the crankshaft is still in the TDC position.

25 If not already fitted, refit the balance shaft timing chain and sprockets as described in paragraphs 40 to 47.

26 Slide the crankshaft drive sprocket (and spring washer, where fitted) onto the Woodruff key on the crankshaft. **Note:** *FRONT is marked on the outer face of the sprocket* **(see illustration)**.

27 Refit the intake camshaft sprocket complete with timing chain down through the top of the cylinder head. The copper coloured link should line up with the INT mark on the intake sprocket (a cable tie can be used to keep the chain in position – **see illustration 9.0b**). Attach the sprocket to the camshaft using a new securing bolt, tightening it hand-tight at this stage.

28 Insert the timing chain tension rail up through the engine casing into position for the tensioner. (Do not refit the lower securing bolt until the timing chain is in position.)

29 Insert the exhaust camshaft sprocket into the timing chain, making sure the silver link on the timing chain lines up with the EXH mark on the sprocket (a cable tie can be used

9.26 Refit the timing chain crankshaft sprocket, noting FRONT is marked on the outer face

to keep the chain in position – **see illustration 9.0a**). Attach the sprocket to the camshaft using a new securing bolt, tightening it hand-tight at this stage. **Note:** *One or both of the camshafts may have moved slightly, due to valve spring pressure. It may be necessary to turn the camshafts slightly to locate the sprockets in the correct position, use an open-ended spanner on the camshaft if required* **(see illustration)**. *Do not turn the camshafts too far as the engine is set at TDC and the valves could hit the pistons.*

30 Locate the timing chain onto the crankshaft drive sprocket, aligning the silver link with the mark on the sprocket **(see illustration 9.0c)**.

31 The lower securing bolt can now be fitted to the tension rail and tightened to its specified torque.

32 Insert the guide rail and fit lower securing bolt, tightening it to its specified torque.

33 Refit the guide rail upper securing bolt and access bolt in the cylinder head, tightening them to there specified torque.

Caution: All the timing marks (coloured chain links) must be aligned with the corresponding marks on the sprockets. This procedure must be carried out correctly, otherwise the timing being offset by one tooth will result in engine damage.

34 Refit the timing chain cover as described in Section 7.

35 Remove the cable ties from camshaft sprockets. Hold the camshafts in turn using an open-ended spanner on the flats provided,

9.36 Use new retaining bolts when refitting the sliding rail

9.29 Turning the camshaft slightly using an open-ended spanner to locate the sprocket in the correct position

then tighten the new securing bolts to there specified torque.

36 Attach the sliding rail for the camshaft timing chain to the top of the cylinder head, using new retaining bolts tighten them to the specified torque **(see illustration)**.

37 Refit the camshaft timing chain tensioner as described in Section 8.

38 Rotate the crankshaft through two complete rotations (720°) in the correct direction of rotation (to bring number 1 piston back to TDC on its compression stroke). If the special tool is available, check the valve timing as described in Section 4.

39 Refit the camshaft cover as described in Section 5. Reconnect the battery negative lead (see Chapter 5A).

Balance shaft chain and sprockets

40 Refit the drivegear to the coolant pump, and tighten the three securing bolts to the specified torque.

41 Slide the crankshaft drivegear/sprocket (and spring washer, where fitted) onto the Woodruff key on the crankshaft. **Note:** *FRONT is marked on the outer face of the gear (see illustration)*. The timing mark on the drivegear should be pointing downwards to align with the silver-coloured link on the timing chain.

42 Refit the exhaust sprocket to the balance shaft, using a new securing bolt **(see illustration)**. The sprocket is marked EXHAUST and has an arrow which points downwards to align with the silver-coloured link on the timing chain. Tighten the bolts to

9.41 Refit the balance shaft crankshaft sprocket, noting FRONT is marked on the outer face

9.42 Refit the balance shaft sprockets using new securing bolts

the specified torque, locking the balance shaft sprockets as on removal.

43 Refit the intake sprocket to the balance shaft, using a new securing bolt. The sprocket is marked INTAKE and has an arrow which points upwards to align with the copper-coloured link on the timing chain **(see illustration)**. Tighten the bolts to the specified torque, locking the balance shaft sprockets as on removal.

44 Refit the balancer shaft timing chain to the sprockets/gears and align the timing marks (coloured chain links) with the marks on the appropriate sprockets as mentioned above **(see illustration)**.

9.43 The arrow points upwards on the intake sprocket

45 Refit the tension rail and two guide rails to the cylinder block, tightening the securing bolts to the specified torque.

46 Refit the balancer shaft chain tensioner as described in Section 8.

47 Refit the camshaft timing chain and sprockets as described above.

10 Camshaft and followers – removal, inspection and refitting

Note: New camshaft sprocket retaining bolts and new timing chain sliding rail retaining bolts will be required on refitting.

Removal

1 Disconnect the battery negative lead (see Chapter 5A) then remove the camshaft cover as described in Section 5.

2 Remove the power steering pump as described in Chapter 10.

3 Position No 1 cylinder at TDC as described in Section 3.

4 Undo the two retaining bolts and remove the camshaft timing chain sliding rail on the top of the cylinder head **(see illustration 9.5)**.

5 If the special tool mentioned in Section 4 is not available, make sure No 1 cylinder is at TDC then cable tie the timing chain to the camshaft sprockets and mark the sprockets in relation to the cylinder head **(see illustration)**.

6 If the vehicle is still on axle stands, lower it back onto the ground making sure the handbrake is on and 1st gear is engaged. This is to prevent the engine being turned once TDC has been aligned.

7 Remove the camshaft timing chain tensioner as described in Section 8.

8 Hold the camshafts, using an open-ended spanner on the flats provided, then slacken and remove the camshaft sprocket retaining bolts **(see illustration 9.8)**.

Caution: Prior to removal ensure the camshaft sprockets are suitably marked as they are identical and can be refitted to either camshaft.

9 Disengage the camshaft sprockets (complete with chain) from the camshafts, keeping the chain under tension. Use a suitable screwdriver, bar or bolt to pass through the sprockets and rest on the upper surface of the cylinder head, to prevent the timing chain falling down and coming off the crankshaft drivegear/sprocket.

10 Note the identification markings on the camshaft bearing caps. The caps are numbered 1 to 10 with all numbers being the right way up when viewed from the driver's seat; numbers 1 to 5 on the exhaust camshaft starting from the timing chain end of the engine, and numbers 6 to 10 on the intake camshaft starting at the timing chain end. *Note: There is also an 11th cap on the intake camshaft, at the flywheel end of the cylinder head which the power steering pump is mounted to. If the markings are not clearly visible, make identification marks to ensure each cap is fitted correctly on refitting.*

11 Working in a spiral pattern from the outside inwards, slacken the camshaft bearing cap retaining bolts by one turn at a time, to relieve the pressure of the valve springs on the bearing caps gradually and evenly. Once the valve spring pressure has been relieved, the bolts can be fully unscrewed and removed, along with the caps. Take care not to loose any locating dowels which may be fitted to some of the bearing caps and lift the camshaft out from the head, noting the position of the lobes on the camshaft.

Caution: If the bearing cap bolts are carelessly slackened, the bearing caps might break. If any bearing cap breaks then the complete cylinder head assembly must be renewed; the bearing caps are matched to the head and are not available separately.

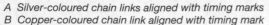

9.44 Balance shaft timing chain layout

A Silver-coloured chain links aligned with timing marks
B Copper-coloured chain link aligned with timing mark

10.5 Alignment marks made on camshaft sprockets for refitting

10.12 A container used to keep the followers and hydraulic tappets in order

10.13 Keep the hydraulic tappets in labelled containers with clean engine oil

10.18 Lubricate the tappets with clean engine oil before refitting

12 Obtain 16 small, clean plastic containers, and label them for identification. Alternatively, divide a larger container into compartments. Lift the followers out from the top of the cylinder head and store each one in its respective fitted position **(see illustration)**.

13 If the hydraulic tappets are also to be removed, withdraw each hydraulic tappet and place them in small containers with clean engine oil. This will keep them primed ready for refitting **(see illustration)**.

Inspection

14 Examine the camshaft bearing surfaces and cam lobes for signs of wear ridges and scoring. Renew the camshaft if any of these conditions are apparent. Examine the condition of the bearing surfaces both on the camshaft journals and in the cylinder head. If the head bearing surfaces are worn excessively, the cylinder head will need to be renewed.

15 Support the camshaft end journals on V-blocks, and measure the run-out at the centre journal using a dial gauge. If the run-out exceeds the specified limit, the camshaft should be renewed.

16 Examine the follower bearing surfaces which contact the camshaft lobes for wear ridges and scoring. Renew any followers on which these conditions are apparent.

17 Check the hydraulic tappets (where removed) and their bores in the cylinder head for signs of wear or damage. If any tappet is thought to be faulty it should be renewed.

Refitting

18 Where removed, lubricate the hydraulic tappets with clean engine oil and carefully insert each one into its original location in the cylinder head **(see illustration)**.

19 Refit the camshaft followers to the cylinder head, ensuring each follower is fitted in its original location **(see illustration)**.

20 Lubricate the camshaft followers with clean engine oil then lay the camshafts into position. Ensure the crankshaft is still aligned in position, and position the camshaft so that the lobes are pointing in the direction noted on removal.

21 Ensure the mating surfaces of the bearing caps and cylinder head are clean and dry and lubricate the camshaft journals and lobes with clean engine oil.

22 Apply a smear of sealant to the cylinder head mating surface at the flywheel end of the front camshaft (No 11) bearing cap **(see illustration)**. Re-fit the cap locating dowels to the cap if they have been removed.

23 Refit the camshaft bearing caps and the retaining bolts in their original locations on the cylinder head. The caps are numbered 1 to 10 with all numbers being the right way up when viewed from the driver's seat; numbers 1 to 5 on the exhaust camshaft starting from the timing chain end of the engine, and numbers 6 to 10 on the intake camshaft starting at the timing chain end. Refit the 11th cap on the front camshaft, at the flywheel end of the cylinder head which the power steering pump is mounted to **(see illustration)**.

24 Tighten all bolts by hand only then, working in a spiral pattern from the centre outwards, tighten the bolts by one turn at a time to gradually impose the pressure of the valve springs on the bearing caps. Repeat this sequence until all bearing caps are in contact with the cylinder head then go around and tighten the camshaft bearing cap bolts to the specified torque.

Caution: If the bearing cap bolts are carelessly tightened, the bearing caps might break. If any bearing cap breaks then the complete cylinder head assembly must be renewed; the bearing caps are matched to the head and are not available separately.

25 Using the marks made on removal, ensure that the timing chain is still correctly engaged with the sprockets then refit the camshaft sprockets to the camshaft. Locate the sprockets on the end of the camshaft and fit the new retaining bolts hand-tight at this stage **(see illustration)**. Remove the cable ties from the camshaft chain and sprockets.

10.19 Refit the camshaft followers in their original position

10.22 Apply silicone sealing compound thinly to the surface areas arrowed

10.23 Refitting No 11 cap to the power steering pump end of the intake camshaft

10.25 Refit new retaining bolts to the camshaft sprockets

11.7 Remove the two coolant hoses (arrowed) from the front of the cylinder head

26 Refit the camshaft timing chain tensioner as described in Section 8.

27 If the special tool is available, check that No 1 cylinder is correctly set at TDC as described in Section 3.

28 If the special tool is not available, align the marks made prior to removal on the camshaft and sprockets. Hold the camshaft with an open-ended spanner and tighten the sprocket bolt to the specified Stage 1 torque setting. Ensure the marks have remained in alignment then tighten the bolt through the specified Stage 2 angle. It is recommended that an angle-measuring gauge is used during the final stages of the tightening, to ensure accuracy. If a gauge is not available, use white paint to make alignment marks prior to tightening; the marks can then be used to check that the bolt has been rotated through the correct angle.

29 Refit the camshaft timing chain sliding rail using new retaining bolts, then tighten to the specified torque.

30 Refit the power steering pump as described in Chapter 10.

31 Turn the crankshaft pulley/vibration damper in the direction of rotation a two full revolutions. Check that the timing marks on the crankshaft pulley line up with the mark on the casing, and the special tool lines up with the camshaft sprockets (or the marks in relation to the cylinder head, made prior to removal).

32 Refit the camshaft cover as described in Section 5.

33 Reconnect the battery negative lead and lower the vehicle to the ground (where applicable)

11.22 Using a tap to clean out the threads in the cylinder block

11 Cylinder head – removal and refitting

Caution: Be careful not to allow dirt into the fuel injection pump or injector pipes during this procedure.
Note: *New cylinder head bolts, camshaft timing chain sliding rail bolts and camshaft sprocket retaining bolts will be required on refitting.*

Removal

1 Drain the cooling system as described in Chapter 1A.

2 Carry out the operations described in paragraphs 1 to 8 of Section 10.

3 Depressurise the fuel system as described in Chapter 4A.

4 Wipe clean the area around the fuel hose unions then slacken and remove the union bolts and sealing washers. Release the hoses from their retaining clips, and position them clear of the cylinder head.

5 Remove the inlet and exhaust manifolds as described in Chapter 4A.

6 Remove the air cleaner assembly as described in Chapter 4A.

7 Release the retaining clips and disconnect the coolant hoses from the front of the right-hand end of the cylinder head **(see illustration)**.

8 On vehicles with air conditioning, release the hoses/pipes from their retaining clips and move to one side. If the system requires disconnecting, see Chapter 3 for further information.

9 Remove the access bolt from the cylinder head and undo the upper securing bolt for the timing chain guide rail **(see illustrations 9.6a and 9.6b)**.

Caution: Prior to removal ensure the camshaft sprockets are suitably marked as they are identical and can be refitted to either camshaft.

10 Remove the camshaft sprockets from the timing chain. Hold the timing chain up, to prevent it dropping down into the cylinder block, keeping the timing chain located onto the crankshaft sprocket.

11 Slacken and remove the four retaining bolts from the timing chain end of the cylinder head **(see illustration 11.27)**.

12 Working in the **reverse** of the tightening sequence shown in illustration 11.27, progressively slacken the ten main cylinder head bolts by half a turn at a time, until all bolts can be unscrewed by hand.

13 Lift out the cylinder head bolts and where applicable recover the washers.

14 Lift the cylinder head away; seek assistance if possible, as it is a heavy assembly (especially if complete with manifolds). Also assistance will be required to guide the timing chain out through the cylinder head while keeping the chain under tension.

15 Remove the gasket, noting the locating dowels fitted to the top of the cylinder block. If they are a loose fit, remove the locating dowels and store them with the head for safe-keeping.

Caution: Do not lay the head on its lower mating surface; support the head on wooden blocks as it may be damaged if the head is placed directly onto a bench.

16 If the cylinder head is to be dismantled for overhaul, then refer to Part E of this Chapter.

Preparation for refitting

17 The mating faces of the cylinder head and cylinder block/crankcase must be perfectly clean before refitting the head. Use a hard plastic or wood scraper to remove all traces of gasket and carbon; also clean the piston crowns. Take particular care, as the surfaces are damaged easily. Also, make sure that the carbon is not allowed to enter the oil and water passages – this is particularly important for the lubrication system, as carbon could block the oil supply to any of the engine's components. Using adhesive tape and paper, seal the water, oil and bolt holes in the cylinder block/crankcase. To prevent carbon entering the gap between the pistons and bores, smear a little grease in the gap. After cleaning each piston, use a small brush to remove all traces of grease and carbon from the gap, then wipe away the remainder with a clean rag. Clean all the pistons in the same way.

18 Check the mating surfaces of the cylinder block/crankcase and the cylinder head for nicks, deep scratches and other damage. If slight, they may be removed carefully with a file, but if excessive, machining may be the only alternative to renewal (see your local specialist for machining).

19 Ensure that the cylinder head bolt holes in the crankcase are clean and free of oil. Syringe or soak up any oil left in the bolt holes. This is most important in order that the correct bolt tightening torque can be applied and to prevent the possibility of the block being cracked by hydraulic pressure when the bolts are tightened.

20 The cylinder head bolts must be discarded and renewed, regardless of their apparent condition.

21 If warpage of the cylinder head gasket surface is suspected, use a straight-edge to check it for distortion. Refer to Part E of this Chapter if necessary.

Refitting

22 Using a tap, clean out the thread in the four bolt holes at the timing chain end of the cylinder block **(see illustration)**. Wipe clean the mating surfaces of the cylinder head and cylinder block/crankcase.

23 Check that the locating dowels are in position then fit the new gasket to the cylinder block **(see illustrations)**.

24 Ensure the crankshaft is positioned approx 60° BTDC (this is to prevent any damage to the valves or pistons when refitting the cylinder head).

25 With the aid of an assistant, carefully refit the cylinder head assembly to the block, aligning it with the locating dowels. As the head is fitted, pass the timing chain up through the cylinder head, holding it in position by passing a suitable tool/screwdriver through the chain and resting it on the head upper surface. **Note:** *Keep the chain taut to prevent it coming off the crankshaft sprocket.*

26 Apply a smear of oil to the threads and the underside of the heads of the new cylinder head bolts and carefully enter each bolt into its relevant hole (*do not drop them in*). Screw all bolts in, by hand only, until finger-tight.

27 Working progressively and in the sequence shown, tighten the cylinder head bolts to their Stage 1 torque setting, using a torque wrench and suitable socket **(see illustration)**.

28 Once all bolts have been tightened to the Stage 1 torque, working again in the specified sequence, go around and tighten all bolts through the specified Stage 2 angle. It is recommended that an angle-measuring gauge is used to ensure accuracy **(see illustration)**. If a gauge is not available, use white paint to make alignment marks prior to tightening; the marks can then be used to check that the bolt has been rotated through the correct angle.

29 Go around again in the specified sequence and angle tighten the bolts through the specified Stage 3 angle.

30 Finally go around in the specified sequence and angle tighten the bolts through the specified Stage 4 angle.

31 Refit the four bolts securing the right-hand end of the cylinder head to the block (timing chain end) and tighten them to the specified torque setting **(see illustrations)**.

32 Re-align the camshaft sprockets, then turn the crankshaft carefully in the direction of engine rotation, to bring No 1 cylinder back to TDC.

33 Refit the camshaft sprockets to the camshafts as described in Section 10, paragraphs 25 to 33.

34 Reconnect the coolant hoses to the cylinder head and secure them in position with the retaining clips.

11.23a Check the dowels are in position to locate the cylinder head gasket . . .

11.23b . . . ensuring the gasket is fitted with its OBEN/TOP marking uppermost

11.27 Cylinder head bolt tightening sequence

35 Refit/reconnect the inlet and exhaust manifolds and associated components as described in Chapter 4A.

36 Position a new sealing washer on each side of the fuel hose unions then refit union bolts and tighten them to the specified torque (for further information refer to Chapter 4A).

37 On completion refill the cooling system (and air conditioning if required) as described in Chapters 1A and 3.

11.28 Tightening the cylinder head down through its stages, using an angle gauge

11.31a Fit four new retaining bolts to the timing chain end of the cylinder head . . .

11.31b . . . two of the bolts are inside the timing chain housing (bolt arrowed on exhaust side of head)

12.7 Undo the two sump to transmission bolts (A) and also the sump-to-lower cylinder block bolt (B)

12.11a Apply a continuous bead of silicone sealer around the sump . . .

12.11b . . . and also around the oil intake pipe area

12 Sump –
removal and refitting

Removal

1 Disconnect the battery negative terminal (see Chapter 5A).
2 Firmly apply the handbrake then jack up the front of the car and support it on axle stands. Where necessary, undo the retaining clips/screws and remove the engine undertray and right-hand wheelarch cover.
3 Drain the engine oil as described in Chapter 1A, then fit a new sealing washer and refit the drain plug, tightening it to the specified torque.
4 Where fitted, disconnect the wiring connector from the oil level sensor (see Chapter 5A).
5 Mark the running direction of the auxiliary belt, then slacken the tensioner and remove the belt as described in Chapter 1A.
6 Remove the lower mounting bolt for the air conditioning compressor. Slacken (do not remove) the upper two mounting bolts and use a block of wood (or similar) to wedge the compressor away from the sump. **Note:** *Take care not to damage the bolts or alloy mounting point when inserting the wedge; do not use excessive force.*
7 Slacken and remove the bolts securing the sump flange to the transmission housing **(see illustration)**.

8 Progressively slacken and remove the bolts securing the sump to the base of the cylinder block lower casing (there is one long bolt at the transmission end of the sump – **see illustration 12.7**). To break the sump joint it may be necessary to cut the silicone sealer using a suitable knife, taking care not to damage any surfaces. Lower the sump away from the engine.
9 While the sump is removed, take the opportunity to check the oil pump pick-up/strainer (if possible) for signs of clogging or splitting. **Note:** *The pick-up/strainer cannot be removed from the sump as it is riveted in position.*

Refitting

10 Remove all traces of silicone sealer and oil from the mating surfaces of the sump and cylinder block.
11 Apply a continuous bead of silicone sealing compound (available from your Vauxhall dealer) at approximately 1.0 mm from the inner edge of the sump. The bead of sealant should be between 2.0 and 2.5 mm in diameter. Also apply a bead of sealant (2.0 to 2.5 mm) around the oil intake pipe area of the sump mating surface **(see illustrations)**.
12 Offer up the sump to the cylinder block and loosely refit all the retaining bolts.
13 Working out from the centre in a diagonal sequence, progressively tighten the bolts securing the sump to the cylinder block lower casing. Tighten all the bolts to their specified torque setting.

14 Tighten the bolts securing the sump flange to the transmission housing to their specified torque settings.
15 Remove the wedge-shaped block from the air conditioning compressor and refit the lower mounting bolt. Tighten the three compressor mounting bolts to their specified torque (Chapter 3).
16 Refit the auxiliary drivebelt (see Chapter 1A).
17 Reconnect the oil level sensor wiring connector (as applicable). Where necessary refit the engine undertray and wheelarch cover.
18 Lower the vehicle to the ground then fill the engine with fresh engine oil (see Chapter 1A).

13 Oil pump –
removal, inspection and refitting

Note: *The oil pump pressure control valve can be removed with the timing chain cover in position on the engine (see paragraph 5 below).*

Removal

1 The oil pump assembly is built into the timing chain cover. Removal and refitting of the cover is as described in Section 7.

Inspection

2 Undo the retaining screws and lift off the pump cover plate from the inside of the timing chain cover **(see illustration)**.
3 Note any marks identifying the outer faces of the pump rotors. If none can be seen, use a suitable marker pen and mark the surface of both the pump inner and outer rotors; the marks can then be used to ensure the rotors are refitted the correct way around.
4 Lift out the inner and outer rotors from the cover **(see illustration)**.
5 Unscrew the oil pressure control valve plug from the timing chain cover and withdraw the spring and plunger, noting which way around the plunger is fitted. Remove the sealing ring from the valve bolt **(see illustrations)**.
6 Clean the components, and carefully examine the rotors, pump body and valve plungers for any signs of scoring or wear.

13.2 Undo the retaining screws and remove the pump cover plate

13.4 Removing the inner and outer rotors

13.5a Undo and remove the oil pressure control valve plug . . .

13.5b . . . and remove the oil pressure valve spring and plunger

13.7a Using a feeler blade to check the inner-to-outer rotor clearance . . .

13.7b . . . the outer rotor to oil pump housing . . .

13.7c . . . and also using a straight-edge to check the endfloat

Renew any component which shows signs of wear or damage; if the rotors or pump housing are marked then the complete pump assembly should be renewed.

7 If the components appear serviceable, measure the clearances (using feeler blades) between:

 a) The inner rotor and the outer rotor.
 b) The outer rotor and oil pump housing.
 c) The rotor endfloat.
 d) The flatness of the end cover.

If the clearances exceed the specified tolerances (see Specifications at the beginning of this Chapter), the pump must be renewed **(see illustrations)**.

8 If the pump is satisfactory, reassemble the components in the reverse order of removal, noting the following.

 a) *Ensure both rotors and the valve plunger are fitted the correct way around.*
 b) *Fit new sealing rings to the pressure*

control valve and tighten to the specified torque setting.
 c) *Refit the pump cover tightening the cover screws to the specified torque.*
 d) *On completion prime the oil pump by filling it with clean engine oil whilst rotating the inner rotor.*

Refitting

9 Refit the timing chain cover as described in Section 7.

14 Balance shaft – removal and refitting

Removal

1 Remove the balance shaft timing chain and sprockets as described in Section 9.

2 If the balance shaft sprockets are removed, mark the shafts to identify the intake shaft from the exhaust shaft for refitting.
3 Undo the securing nut from the balance shaft retaining plate and slide the balance shaft out from the cylinder block **(see illustrations)**.

Refitting

4 Refitting is the reverse of removal, tighten the retaining plate bolts to their specified torque.
5 Refit the balance shaft timing chain and sprockets as described in Section 9.

15 Crankshaft oil seals – renewal

Right-hand (timing chain end)

1 Remove the crankshaft pulley as described in Section 6.
2 Using a large flat-bladed screwdriver, carefully lever the seal out from the timing chain cover.
3 Clean the seal housing and polish off any burrs or raised edges which may have caused the seal to fail in the first place.
4 Lubricate the lips of the new seal with clean engine oil and press/tap it squarely into position until it sits into the recess in the cover **(see illustration)**. If necessary, a suitable tubular drift, such as a socket, which bears only on the hard outer edge of the seal can be

14.3a Undo the retaining bolt (arrowed) . . .

14.3b . . . and withdraw the balance shaft assembly

15.4 Make sure the seal seats squarely into the timing chain cover

15.7 Removing a crankshaft left-hand oil seal, using a pair of pliers and a screw

15.9 Carefully ease the oil seal over the end of the crankshaft and tap/press it squarely into position

16.2 Lock the flywheel/driveplate ring gear

used to tap the seal into position. Take great care not to damage the seal lips during fitting and ensure that the seal lips face inwards.

5 Wash off any traces of oil, then refit the crankshaft pulley as described in Section 6.

Left-hand (flywheel/driveplate end)

6 Remove the flywheel as described in Section 16.

7 Carefully punch or drill two small holes opposite each other in the oil seal. Screw a self-tapping screw into each and pull on the screws with pliers to extract the seal **(see illustration)**.

8 Clean the seal housing and polish off any burrs or raised edges which may have caused the seal to fail in the first place. **Note:** *Insulation tape can be put around the crankshaft flange to help fit the oil seal.*

9 Lubricate the lips of the new seal with clean engine oil and ease it into position on the end of the crankshaft. Press the seal squarely into position until it is flush with the bearing cap. If necessary, a suitable tubular drift, such as a socket, which bears only on the hard outer edge of the seal can be used to tap the seal into position. Take great care not to damage the seal lips during fitting and ensure that the seal lips face inwards **(see illustration)**.

10 If insulation tape was used around the crankshaft flange, remove it, taking care not to damage the oil seal. Refit the flywheel as described in Section 16.

16 Flywheel – removal, inspection and refitting

Note: *New flywheel retaining bolts will be required on refitting.*

Removal

1 Remove the transmission as described in Chapter 7A then remove the clutch assembly as described in Chapter 6.

2 Prevent the flywheel from turning by locking the ring gear teeth **(see illustration)**. Alternatively, bolt a strap between the flywheel and the cylinder block/crankcase. Make alignment marks between the flywheel and crankshaft using paint or a suitable marker pen.

3 Slacken and remove the retaining bolts and remove the flywheel. **Note:** *The flywheel is very heavy, take care not to drop it when removing.*

Inspection

4 Examine the flywheel for wear or chipping of the ring gear teeth.

5 Examine the flywheel for scoring of the clutch face. If the clutch face is scored, the flywheel may be surface-ground, but renewal is preferable.

6 If there is any doubt about the condition of the flywheel, seek the advice of a Vauxhall dealer or engine reconditioning specialist. They will be able to advise if it is possible to recondition it or whether renewal is necessary.

Refitting

7 Clean the mating surfaces of the flywheel and crankshaft and also clean out the threads in the crankshaft.

8 Offer up the flywheel and fit the new retaining bolts with locking compound. If the original is being refitted align the marks made prior to removal **(see illustration)**.

9 Lock the flywheel using the method employed on dismantling then, working in a diagonal sequence, evenly and progressively

16.8 Align the marks (arrowed) made on removal, then fit new retaining bolts with locking compound

tighten the retaining bolts to the specified Stage 1 torque setting.

10 Once all bolts have been tightened to the Stage 1 torque, go around and tighten all bolts through the specified Stage 2 angle. It is recommended that an angle-measuring gauge is used during the final stages of the tightening, to ensure accuracy. If a gauge is not available, use white paint to make alignment marks prior to tightening; the marks can then be used to check that the bolt has been rotated through the correct angle.

11 Refit the clutch as described in Chapter 6 then remove the flywheel locking tool (where applicable) and refit the transmission as described in Chapter 7A.

17 Engine/transmission mountings – inspection and renewal

Refer to Chapter 2A, Section 17.

Chapter 2 Part D:
Diesel engine in-car repair procedures

Contents

Degrees of difficulty

Easy, suitable for novice with little experience	**Fairly easy,** suitable for beginner with some experience	**Fairly difficult,** suitable for competent DIY mechanic	**Difficult,** suitable for experienced DIY mechanic	**Very difficult,** suitable for expert DIY or professional

Specifications

General

Engine type	Four-cylinder, in-line, water-cooled. Chain-driven, 16 valve – SOHC (single overhead camshaft), acting on hydraulic tappets
Manufacturer's engine code:	
2.0 litre low-pressure turbo model	X20DTL
2.0 litre high-pressure turbo model	X20DTH and Y20DTH
2.2 litre high-pressure turbo model	Y22DTR
Bore:	
2.0 litre	84 mm
2.2 litre	84 mm
Stroke:	
2.0 litre	90 mm
2.2 litre	98 mm
Capacity:	
2.0 litre	1994 cc
2.2 litre	2171 cc
Compression ratio:	
2.0 litre	18.5:1
2.2 litre	18.5:1
Maximum power:	
2.0 litre (X20DTL)	60 kW at 4300 rpm
2.0 litre (X20DTH and Y20DTH)	74 kW at 4300 rpm
2.2 litre (Y22DTR)	92 kW at 4000 rpm
Maximum torque:	
2.0 litre (X20DTL)	185 Nm at 1800 to 2500 rpm
2.0 litre (X20DTH)	205 Nm at 1600 to 2750 rpm
2.0 litre (Y20DTH)	230 Nm at 2000 to 2500 rpm
2.2 litre (Y22DTR)	270 Nm at 1500 to 2750 rpm
Injection sequence	1-3-4-2 (No 1 cylinder at timing chain end of engine)
Direction of crankshaft rotation	Clockwise (viewed from timing chain end of engine)

Compression pressures

Standard	25 to 28 bar (363 to 406 psi)
Maximum difference between any two cylinders	1 bar (14.5 psi)
Pressure loss	Not more than 25% max per cylinder

Camshaft
Endfloat . . . . 0.04 to 0.14 mm
Maximum permissible radial run-out . . . . 0.06 mm
Cam lift (inlet and exhaust) . . . . 8.0 mm

Lubrication system
Oil pump type . . . . Rotor-type, driven directly from crankshaft
Minimum permissible oil pressure at idle speed, with engine
   at operating temperature (oil temperature of at least 80°C) . . . . 1.5 bar (22 psi)

Torque wrench settings

	Nm	lbf ft
Auxiliary drivebelt tensioner assembly bolts:		
Pulley backplate pivot bolt	42	31
Strut mounting bolts	23	17
Balancer shaft to cylinder block*:		
Stage 1	20	15
Stage 2	Angle-tighten a further 45°	
Balancer shaft chain tensioner bolt	9	7
Balancer shaft sprocket bolt*:		
Stage 1	90	66
Stage 2	Angle-tighten a further 30°	
Camshaft bearing cap bolts:		
X20DTL and X20DTH	20	15
Y20DTH and Y22DTR	15	11
Camshaft cover bolts	8	6
Camshaft sprocket bolt*:		
Stage 1	90	66
Stage 2	Angle-tighten a further 60°	
Stage 3	Angle-tighten a further 30°	
Connecting rod big-end bearing cap bolt*:		
Stage 1	35	26
Stage 2	Angle-tighten a further 45°	
Stage 2	Angle-tighten a further 15°	
Cylinder block oil spray nozzle bolts	22	16
Crankshaft pulley bolt*:		
Stage 1	150	111
Stage 2	Angle-tighten a further 45°	
Stage 3	Angle-tighten a further 15°	
Cylinder head bolts*:		
Stage 1	25	18
Stage 2	Angle-tighten a further 65°	
Stage 3	Angle-tighten a further 65°	
Stage 4	Angle-tighten a further 65°	
Stage 5	Angle-tighten a further 65°	
Stage 6	Angle-tighten a further 15°	
Cylinder head-to-timing chain cover/block bolts:		
X20DTL and X20DTH	20	15
Y20DTH and Y22DTR*:		
Stage 1	20	15
Stage 2	Angle-tighten a further 30°	
Stage 3	Angle-tighten a further 5°	
Engine/transmission mounting bolts:		
Right-hand mounting:		
Mounting-to-bracket/subframe nuts	45	33
Bracket-to-engine bolts	60	44
Upper bracket nuts	45	33
Left-hand mounting:		
Mounting-to-bracket/subframe nuts	45	33
Bracket-to-transmission bolts	60	44
Rear mounting:		
Mounting-to-bracket bolts	45	33
Mounting-to-subframe bolts	20	15
Bracket-to-transmission bolts	60	44
Engine-to-transmission unit bolts:		
M8 bolts	20	15
M10 bolts	40	30
M12 bolts	60	44

Torque wrench settings (continued)

	Nm	lbf ft
Flywheel bolts*:		
Stage 1	45	33
Stage 2	Angle-tighten a further 30°	
Stage 3	Angle-tighten a further 15°	
Injection pump sprocket bolts:		
X20DTL and X20DTH	20	15
Y20DTH and Y22DTR	28	21
Injection pump sprocket cover bolts	6	4
Main bearing cap bolts*:		
Stage 1	90	66
Stage 2	Angle-tighten a further 60°	
Stage 3	Angle-tighten a further 15°	
Main bearing cap bridge bolts	20	15
Oil cooler-to-oil filter housing bolts	20	15
Oil filter housing cover:		
Metal cover	20 to 25	15 to 18
Plastic cover	25 to 30	18 to 22
Oil pump:		
Oil pressure relief valve bolt	60	44
Pump cover screws	8	6
Pump pick-up/strainer bolts	8	6
Safety valve bolt	45	33
Roadwheel bolts	110	81
Sump bolts:		
Sump to cylinder block/timing chain cover bolts	20	15
Sump flange-to-transmission bolts:		
M8 bolts	20	15
M10 bolts	40	30
Drain plug	18	13
Timing chain cover bolts	20	15
Timing chain guide bolts*	8	6
Timing chain tensioner blade pivot bolt	20	15
Timing chain tensioner cap	60	44

*Use new fasteners

1 General information

How to use this Chapter

1 This Part of Chapter 2 describes those repair procedures that can reasonably be carried out on the 2.0 litre and 2.2 litre diesel engines while it remains in the car. If the engine has been removed from the car and is being dismantled as described in Part E, any preliminary dismantling procedures can be ignored.

2 Note that, while it may be possible physically to overhaul items such as the piston/connecting rod assemblies while the engine is in the car, such tasks are not normally carried out as separate operations. Usually, several additional procedures (not to mention the cleaning of components and of oilways) have to be carried out. For this reason, all such tasks are classed as major overhaul procedures, and are described in Part E of this Chapter.

3 Part E describes the removal of the engine/transmission unit from the vehicle, and the full overhaul procedures that can then be carried out.

Engine description

4 The engines are of the sixteen-valve, in-line four-cylinder, single overhead camshaft (SOHC) type, mounted transversely at the front of the car with the transmission attached to its left-hand end.

5 The crankshaft runs in five main bearings. Thrustwashers are fitted to No 3 main bearing to control crankshaft endfloat.

6 The connecting rods rotate on horizontally-split bearing shells at their big-ends. The pistons are attached to the connecting rods by gudgeon pins, which are a sliding fit in the connecting rod small-end eyes being retained by circlips. The aluminium-alloy pistons are fitted with three piston rings – two compression rings and an oil control ring.

7 The cylinder block is made of cast iron and the cylinder bores are an integral part of the block. On this type of engine the cylinder bores are sometimes referred to as having dry liners.

8 The inlet and exhaust valves are each closed by coil springs, and operate in guides pressed into the cylinder head.

9 The camshaft is driven by the crankshaft via a dual timing chain arrangement; the lower timing chain links the crankshaft to the fuel injection pump and the upper chain links the injection pump to the camshaft. The camshaft rotates directly in the head and operates the sixteen valves via followers and hydraulic tappets. The followers are situated directly below the camshaft, each one operating two valves. Valve clearances are automatically adjusted by the hydraulic tappets.

10 Lubrication is by means of an oil pump, which is driven off the right-hand end of the crankshaft. It draws oil through a strainer located in the sump, and then forces it through an externally-mounted filter into galleries in the cylinder block/crankcase. From there, the oil is distributed to the crankshaft (main bearings) and camshaft. The big-end bearings are supplied with oil via internal drillings in the crankshaft, while the camshaft bearings also receive a pressurised supply. The camshaft lobes and valves are lubricated by splash, as are all other engine components. An oil cooler is fitted to keep the oil temperature stable under arduous operating conditions.

11 The high-pressure turbo models are fitted with an intercooler.

12 A balancer unit is fitted to the 2.2 litre (Y22DTR) engine, this consists of two balancer shafts which are driven via a chain from the crankshaft. The balancer shafts rotate in opposite directions at double the crankshaft speed. This unit is to help provide a vibration and noise-free running of the engine.

Repair operations possible with the engine in the car

13 The following work can be carried out with the engine in the car:
  a) *Compression pressure – testing.*
  b) *Camshaft cover – removal and refitting.*
  c) *Timing chain cover – removal and refitting.*
  d) *Timing chains – removal and refitting.*
  e) *Timing chain tensioners, guides and sprockets – removal and refitting.*
  f) *Camshaft and followers – removal, inspection and refitting.*
  g) *Cylinder head – removal and refitting.*
  h) *Connecting rods and pistons – removal and refitting*.*
  i) *Sump – removal and refitting.*
  j) *Oil pump – removal, overhaul and refitting.*
  k) *Oil cooler – removal and refitting.*
  l) *Crankshaft oil seals – renewal.*
  m) *Engine/transmission mountings – inspection and renewal.*
  n) *Flywheel – removal, inspection and refitting.*

* Although the operation marked with an asterisk can be carried out with the engine in the car after removal of the sump, it is better for the engine to be removed, in the interests of cleanliness and improved access. For this reason, the procedure is described in Chapter 2E.

2 Compression test – description and interpretation

Compression test

Note: *A compression tester specifically intended for diesel engines must be used, because of the higher pressures involved.*

1 When engine performance is down, or if misfiring occurs which cannot be attributed to the fuel system, a compression test can provide diagnostic clues as to the engine's condition. If the test is performed regularly, it can give warning of trouble before any other symptoms become apparent.

2 The tester is connected to an adapter which screws into the glow plug or injector hole. On these models, an adapter suitable for use in the glow plug holes will be required, due to the design of the injectors. It is unlikely to be worthwhile buying such a tester for occasional use, but it may be possible to borrow or hire one – if not, have the test performed by a garage.

3 Unless specific instructions to the contrary are supplied with the tester, observe the following points:
  a) *The battery must be in a good state of charge, the air filter must be clean, and the engine should be at normal operating temperature.*
  b) *All the glow plugs should be removed before starting the test (see Chapter 5C).*
  c) *Release the retaining clip and disconnect the wiring connector from the fuel injection pump control unit (see Chapter 4B, Section 8) to prevent the engine from running or fuel from being discharged.*

4 There is no need to hold the accelerator pedal down during the test, because the diesel engine air inlet is not throttled.

5 Crank the engine on the starter motor; after one or two revolutions, the compression pressure should build-up to a maximum figure, and then stabilise. Record the highest reading obtained.

6 Repeat the test on the remaining cylinders, recording the pressure in each.

7 All cylinders should produce very similar pressures; any difference greater than that specified indicates the existence of a fault. Note that the compression should build-up quickly in a healthy engine; low compression on the first stroke, followed by gradually-increasing pressure on successive strokes, indicates worn piston rings. A low compression reading on the first stroke, which does not build-up during successive strokes, indicates leaking valves or a blown head gasket (a cracked head could also be the cause). Deposits on the undersides of the valve heads can also cause low compression.

Note: *The cause of poor compression is less easy to establish on a diesel engine than on a petrol one. The effect of introducing oil into the cylinders ('wet' testing) is not conclusive, because there is a risk that the oil will sit in the swirl chamber or in the recess on the piston crown instead of passing to the rings.*

8 On completion of the test, reconnect the injection pump wiring connector then refit the glow plugs as described in Chapter 5C.

Leakdown test

9 A leakdown test measures the rate at which compressed air fed into the cylinder is lost. It is an alternative to a compression test, and in many ways it is better, since the escaping air provides easy identification of where pressure loss is occurring (piston rings, valves or head gasket).

10 The equipment needed for leakdown testing is unlikely to be available to the home mechanic. If poor compression is suspected, have the test performed by a suitably-equipped garage.

3 Top dead centre (TDC) for No 1 piston – locating

1 In its travel up and down its cylinder bore, Top Dead Centre (TDC) is the highest point that each piston reaches as the crankshaft rotates. While each piston reaches TDC both at the top of the compression stroke and again at the top of the exhaust stroke, for the purpose of timing the engine, TDC refers to the piston position (usually number 1) at the top of its compression stroke.

2 Number 1 piston (and cylinder) is at the right-hand (timing chain) end of the engine, and its TDC position is located as follows. Note that the crankshaft rotates clockwise when viewed from the right-hand side of the car.

3 Disconnect the battery negative terminal (see Chapter 5A). To improve access to the crankshaft pulley, apply the handbrake, then jack up the front of the vehicle and support it on axle stands. Remove the retaining screws/clips and remove the engine undertray.

4 To check the position of the camshaft either remove the camshaft cover (Section 5), so that the position of the cam lobes can be seen, or remove the braking system vacuum pump (Chapter 9) so the timing hole on the camshaft end can be seen.

5 Using a socket and extension bar on the crankshaft pulley bolt, rotate the crankshaft until the notch on the crankshaft pulley rim is aligned with the mark on the timing chain cover. Once the mark is correctly aligned, No 1 and 4 pistons are at TDC.

6 To determine which piston is at TDC on its compression stroke, check the position of the camshaft lobes/timing hole (as applicable). When No 1 piston is at TDC on its compression stroke, No 1 cylinder camshaft lobes will be pointing upwards and the timing hole on the left-hand of the camshaft will be at the top (12 o'clock position) with the camshaft slot parallel with the head surface **(see illustrations)**. If No 1 cylinder camshaft lobes are pointing downwards and the camshaft end timing mark is at the bottom (6 o'clock

3.6a When No 1 cylinder is at TDC on its compression stroke, its camshaft lobes (arrowed) will be pointing upwards . . .

3.6b . . . and the timing hole (arrowed) on the left-hand end of the camshaft will be at the top

position) then No 4 cylinder is at TDC on its compression stroke; rotate the crankshaft through a further complete turn (360°) to bring No 1 cylinder to TDC on its compression stroke.

7 With No 1 piston at TDC on its compression stroke, if necessary, the crankshaft can be locked in position by inserting a pin in through the crankshaft sensor bore on the front of the cylinder block. If access to the special Vauxhall tool (KM-929) cannot be gained, a home-made alternative will have to be manufactured (see Section 4). Remove the crankshaft sensor (see Chapter 4B, Section 8) and insert the pin, making sure it is correctly located in the crankshaft web slot **(see illustrations)**.

---

4 Valve timing – checking and adjustment

Note: To check the valve (and fuel injection pump) timing, it will be necessary to use the following Vauxhall special tools (or suitable equivalents); the camshaft locking tool (KM-932), the injection pump flange locking pin (KM-927), the crankshaft locking pin (KM-929) and the camshaft sprocket wrench (KM-933). If access to these tools cannot be gained, this task must be entrusted to a Vauxhall dealer. If the necessary facilities are available to manufacture home-made tools, the dimensions of the locking pins are given in the accompanying illustrations **(see illustrations)**. The camshaft locking tool (also pictured) ensures that the camshaft remains correctly positioned by keeping the camshaft slot parallel to the cylinder head surface.

1 Remove the auxiliary drivebelt as described in Chapter 1B. Undo the auxiliary drivebelt tensioner pulley strut lower mounting bolt and the pulley backplate pivot bolt and remove the tensioner assembly from the engine. **Note:** Store the assembly so the tensioner strut is the correct way up; if the strut is not stored properly it will have to be primed once it is refitted.

3.7a Remove the crankshaft sensor from the cylinder block and insert the locking pin . . .

2 Remove the braking system vacuum pump as described in Chapter 9.

3 To improve access to the injection pump sprocket cover and the pump, carry out the following.

a) Remove the air cleaner housing and exhaust system front pipe (see Chapter 4B).

b) Mark the position of the right-hand engine

3.7b . . . making sure it is correctly engaged with the crankshaft cut-out (arrowed – shown with sump removed)

4.0a Home-made tools necessary to check/adjust the valve timing

A Crankshaft locking pin
B Injection pump flange locking pin
C Camshaft locking tool

4.0b Crankshaft locking pin dimensions (in mm)

4.0c Injection pump flange locking pin dimensions (in mm)

4.8a Insert the locking pin in through the flange cut-out and engage it in the pump body hole

4.8a Engage the camshaft locking tool with the camshaft cut-out (arrowed)

4.14 Ensure the pump sprocket timing mark (arrowed) is correctly positioned then tighten the sprocket bolts

mounting bracket in relation to the cylinder head bracket. Undo the three bolts securing the right-hand engine mounting to the cylinder head bracket, and the three bolts securing the right-hand engine mounting to the inner wing, then raise the right-hand end of the engine using a jack/engine support bar (see Section 17). Raise the engine as high as possible without placing any excess strain on the remaining mountings or any pipes/hoses or wiring.

4 Remove the camshaft cover and position No 1 cylinder at TDC on it compression stroke as described in Section 3.

5 Remove the crankshaft sensor as described in Chapter 4B, Section 8.

6 Undo the retaining screws and remove the injection pump sprocket cover from the timing chain cover.

7 Ensure the crankshaft pulley notch is correctly aligned with the timing chain cover mark then insert the crankshaft locking pin into the crankshaft sensor aperture and engage it with the slot in the crankshaft web **(see illustrations 3.7a and 3.7b).**

8 With the crankshaft locked in position, insert the injection pump flange locking pin into the hole in the flange and engage it with hole in the pump body, then slide the camshaft locking tool into position on the left-hand end of the camshaft **(see illustrations).**

9 If all the locking tools can be correctly fitted the valve timing is correctly set and no adjustment is necessary, proceed as described in paragraphs 21 to 26. If either of the tools can not be inserted, adjust the timing as follows,

noting that a new camshaft sprocket bolt and tensioner bolt sealing ring will be required.

10 Remove the camshaft/injection pump sprocket locking tool (as applicable) then unbolt the right-hand mounting bracket assembly from the cylinder head.

11 Unscrew the upper timing chain tensioner cap from the rear of the cylinder head and remove the plunger, noting which way around it is fitted. Remove the sealing ring from the cap and discard it, a new one should be used on refitting.

12 Hold the camshaft, using an open-ended spanner on the flats provided, then slacken and remove the camshaft sprocket retaining bolt. Fit the new bolt, tightening it finger-tight only at this stage.

13 Slacken the bolts securing the injection pump sprocket to the pump flange.

14 With the crankshaft locked in position, ensure the timing mark on the injection pump upper timing chain sprocket is correctly aligned with the pump flange timing hole. Insert the flange locking pin, making sure it is correctly seated, then tighten the sprocket retaining bolts to the specified torque **(see illustration).**

15 Slide the camshaft locking tool into position making sure its pin engages centrally in the camshaft bore.

16 With all locking tools in position, fit the sprocket wrench to the camshaft sprocket; in the absence of the special wrench, pass two bolts through the sprocket holes and use a screwdriver to lever on the bolts. Have an assistant keep the timing chain taut on its

guide (upper) side by applying **slight** pressure to the sprocket; this will ensure all slack in the chain is on the tensioner side of chain.

17 With the upper timing chain tensioned as described, check that the injection pump locking pin slides in and out of position with only a slight amount of drag. If excessive force is needed to move the pin, have your assistant decrease the pressure on the sprocket or, if the pin moves easily, increase the pressure.

18 Once the upper timing chain is correctly tensioned, retain the camshaft with an open-ended spanner and tighten the camshaft sprocket retaining bolt to the specified Stage 1 torque setting **(see illustration).** Check the injection pump pin action then tighten the bolt through the specified Stage 2 angle and finally through the specified Stage 3 angle. It is recommended that an angle-measuring gauge is used during the final stages of the tightening, to ensure accuracy. If a gauge is not available, use white paint to make alignment marks between the bolt head and pulley prior to tightening; the marks can then be used to check that the bolt has been rotated through the correct angle.

19 Remove all the locking tools and fit a new sealing ring to the upper timing chain tensioner cap. Insert the plunger into the cylinder head, ensuring its closed end is facing the timing chain, then install the cap and tighten it to the specified torque. **Note:** *If a new tensioner is being fitted, release it by pushing the cap centre pin fully in until it is heard to 'click', the tensioner pin should then be able to be easily depressed and return smoothly.*

20 Rotate the crankshaft through two complete rotations (720°) in the correct direction of rotation (to bring number 1 piston back to TDC on its compression stroke) and check that all the locking tools can be inserted correctly.

21 Ensure the mating surfaces of the pump sprocket cover and timing chain cover are clean and dry. Where the cover was originally fitted with a gasket, fit the cover with a new gasket and tighten the retaining bolts to the specified torque. If no gasket was fitted, apply a bead of sealant (approximately 2 mm thick) to the cover mating surface then refit the cover and tighten its retaining bolts to the specified torque **(see illustration).**

4.18 Adjust the upper timing chain tension as described then tighten the camshaft sprocket bolt to the Stage 1 torque setting

4.21 Apply a bead of sealant to the mating surface of the injection pump sprocket cover mating surface

22 Refit the auxiliary drivebelt tensioner assembly to the engine unit, tightening the strut and backplate pivot bolts to their specified torque settings. If a new tensioner strut is being fitted, or the original was not stored properly, prime the strut by repeatedly compressing it using a socket on the backplate hexagonal section. Once the strut is functioning correctly, refit the auxiliary drivebelt as described in Chapter 1B.

23 Refit the right-hand mounting bracket assembly to the cylinder head (where removed) then lower the engine/transmission unit back down. Refit the right-hand engine mounting to the inner wing and align the mounting with the previously made marks on the cylinder head bracket, fit and tighten the bolts to the specified torque. Refit the camshaft cover (see Section 5).

24 Refit the exhaust front pipe and air cleaner housing as described in the Chapter 4B.

25 Refit the vacuum pump to the cylinder head (see Chapter 9).

26 Fit the crankshaft sensor to the cylinder block (see Chapter 4B, Section 8) and reconnect the battery.

5 Camshaft cover – removal and refitting

Removal

1 Undo the retaining screws and remove the plastic cover from the top of the camshaft cover **(see illustration).**

2 Slacken the retaining clip and disconnect the breather hose from the rear of the cover.

3 On low-pressure turbo (X20DTL) models slacken the clamp securing the metal pipe to the turbocharger, and the clamp securing the intake duct to the manifold. Undo the two retaining bolts and remove the duct assembly from the engine, along with the sealing ring which is fitted between the pipe and turbo-charger **(see illustration).** On high-pressure turbo models, release the retaining clips and bracket bolts, and remove the charge air pipe from the turbocharger to the intercooler.

4 On all models, carefully unclip and release the glow plug wiring guide from the rear of the cover. Undo the bolt securing the inlet manifold wiring harness tray to the cover. Where applicable, unclip the vacuum pipe and fuel hoses from the right-hand end of the cover.

5 Slacken and remove the camshaft cover retaining bolts along with their sealing washers then lift the camshaft cover and seal away from the cylinder head **(see illustration).** Examine the cover seal and retaining bolt sealing washers for signs of damage or deterioration and renew if necessary.

Refitting

6 Ensure the cover and cylinder head surfaces are clean and dry then fit the seal to the cover groove **(see illustration).**

5.1 Undo the retaining screws and remove the plastic cover from the engine

7 Fit the sealing washers to the retaining bolts, ensuring they are fitted the correct way up. Fit the retaining bolts to the cover making sure the cover seal is held firmly in position by the lower shoulder on each bolt.

8 Apply a smear of sealant to the circular cut-out on the right-hand end of the cylinder head mating surface and the areas of the cylinder head mating surface on either side of the left-hand end of the camshaft **(see illustrations).**

9 Carefully lower the cover into position and screw in the retaining bolts. Once all bolts are hand-tight, go around and tighten them all to the specified torque setting.

10 Clip the vacuum pipe and wiring back into position and reconnect the breather hose to the rear of the cover. Where applicable, reposition the fuel hoses into their retaining clips on the right-hand end of the cover.

11 On low-pressure turbo models refit the

5.5 Slacken and remove the camshaft cover retaining bolts noting the sealing washer (arrowed) which is fitted to each bolt

5.8a Apply a smear of sealant to the semi-circular cut-out on the right-hand end of the cylinder head . . .

5.3 On low-pressure turbo (X20DTL) models remove the metal pipe and intake duct linking the turbocharger to the manifold

intake duct and pipe, using a new sealing ring, and tighten its retaining clamps and bolts securely. On high-pressure models, refit the turbocharger-to-intercooler hose, tighten the mounting bracket bolt and retaining clips securely.

12 On all models, refit the plastic cover and securely tighten its retaining bolts.

6 Crankshaft pulley – removal and refitting

Note: *A new pulley retaining bolt will be required on refitting.*

Removal

1 Apply the handbrake, then jack up the front of the car and support it on axle stands.

5.6 Fit the seal to the camshaft cover groove

5.8b . . . and to the areas of the cylinder head surface on each side of the left-hand end camshaft cap (arrowed)

6.5a Slide the crankshaft pulley carefully into position engaging its slot (arrowed) with the Woodruff key . . .

Remove the right-hand roadwheel. Where applicable, undo the retaining screws/clips and remove the engine undertray.

2 Remove the auxiliary drivebelt as described in Chapter 1B. Prior to removal, mark the direction of rotation on the belt to ensure the belt is refitted the same way around.

3 Slacken the crankshaft pulley retaining bolt. To prevent crankshaft rotation whilst the retaining bolt is slackened, have an assistant select top gear and apply the brakes firmly; if the engine is removed from the vehicle it will be necessary to lock the flywheel (see Section 16).

4 Unscrew the retaining bolt and washer and remove the crankshaft pulley from the end of the crankshaft. Whilst the pulley is removed check the oil seal for signs of wear or damage and, if necessary, renew as described in Section 15.

Refitting

5 Carefully locate the crankshaft pulley on the crankshaft end, aligning the pulley slot with the crankshaft key. Slide the pulley fully into position, taking great care not to damage the oil seal, then fit the washer and new retaining bolt **(see illustrations)**.

6 Lock the crankshaft by the method used on removal, and tighten the pulley retaining bolt to the specified Stage 1 torque setting then angle-tighten the bolt through the specified

6.5b . . . then fit the retaining bolt and washer

Stage 2 angle, using a socket and extension bar, and finally through the specified Stage 3 angle. It is recommended that an angle-measuring gauge is used during the final stages of the tightening, to ensure accuracy **(see illustration)**. If a gauge is not available, use white paint to make alignment marks between the bolt head and pulley prior to tightening; the marks can then be used to check that the bolt has been rotated through the correct angle.

7 Refit the auxiliary drivebelt as described in Chapter 1B using the mark made prior to removal to ensure the belt is fitted the correct way around.

8 Refit the roadwheel and engine undertray, then lower the car to the ground and tighten the wheel bolts to the specified torque.

---

7 Timing chain cover – removal and refitting

Removal

1 Remove the upper timing chain and sprockets as described in Section 9.

2 Remove the cylinder head as described in Section 11. **Note:** *In theory it is possible to remove the timing chain cover without*

disturbing the cylinder head. However, this procedure carries a high risk of damaging the head gasket, resulting in oil/coolant leakage once the cover is refitted. If you wish to attempt this, leave the cylinder head in position and just undo the retaining bolts securing the head to the top of the timing chain cover. Be warned though that, after refitting, you may find the head gasket will need renewing, meaning that the cylinder head will have to be removed after all. The decision is yours as to whether this is a chance worth taking.

3 Remove the coolant pump as described in Chapter 3.

4 Remove the crankshaft pulley as described in Section 6. Prior to slackening the pulley bolt, temporarily remove the locking pin from the crankshaft to prevent damage. Refit the pin once the bolt is loose.

5 Remove the sump as described in Section 12.

6 Remove the alternator as described in Chapter 5A.

7 Remove the power steering pump as described in Chapter 10.

8 Unscrew the lower timing chain tensioner cap from the rear of the timing chain cover and remove the tensioner plunger, noting which way around it is fitted. Remove the sealing ring from the cap and discard it, a new one should be used on refitting.

9 Noting each bolt's correct fitted location (the bolts are not all the same length), slacken and remove all the bolts securing the timing chain cover to the cylinder block **(see illustration)**.

10 Carefully ease the timing cover squarely away from the cylinder block and manoeuvre it out of position, noting the correct fitted positions of its locating dowels. If the locating dowels are a loose fit, remove them and store with the cover for safe-keeping.

11 Undo the pivot bolt and remove the upper and lower timing chain tensioner blades from the cylinder block **(see illustration)**.

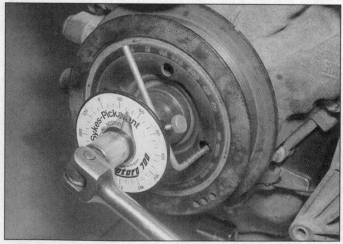

6.6 Lock the crankshaft then tighten the pulley retaining bolt

7.9 Timing chain cover retaining bolt locations (arrowed)

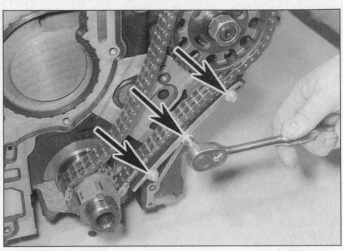

7.11 Unscrew the pivot bolt and remove the upper (1) and lower (2) timing chain tensioner blades

7.12 Undo the retaining bolts (arrowed) and remove the lower timing chain guide

12 Undo the retaining bolts and remove the lower timing chain guide from the cylinder block, noting which way around the guide is fitted **(see illustration)**.

13 Temporarily free the lower timing chain sprocket from the injection pump and manoeuvre the timing chain cover gasket away from the cylinder block. Once the gasket has been removed, seat the sprocket back on the injection pump flange **(see illustration)**.

Refitting

14 Prior to refitting the cover, it is recommended that the crankshaft oil seal should be renewed. Carefully lever the old seal out of the cover using a large flat-bladed screwdriver. Fit the new seal to the cover, making sure its sealing lip is facing inwards. Press/tap the seal into position until it is flush with the cover, using a suitable tubular drift, such as a socket, which bears only on the hard outer edge of the seal.

15 Ensure the mating surfaces of the cover and cylinder block are clean and dry and the locating dowels are in position.

16 Temporarily free the sprocket from the injection pump flange then manoeuvre the gasket into position and locate it on the dowels. Locate the sprocket back on the injection pump flange.

17 Refit the lower timing chain guide to the cylinder block and tighten its new retaining bolts to the specified torque. Ensure the guide is fitted the correct way around with its stepped face on the inside **(see illustration)**.

18 Manoeuvre the timing chain tensioner blades into position and refit the pivot bolt, tightening it to the specified torque setting **(see illustration)**.

19 Manoeuvre the timing cover into position. Align the oil pump drivegear with the crankshaft sprocket and slide the cover into position, locating it on the dowels.

20 Refit the timing chain cover retaining bolts, ensuring each one is fitted in its original location, and tighten them evenly and progressively to the specified torque.

21 Fit a new sealing ring to the lower timing chain tensioner cap. Insert the plunger, ensuring its closed end is facing the timing chain, then fit the cap to the timing chain cover and tighten to the specified torque. **Note:** *If a new tensioner is being fitted, release it by pushing the cap centre pin fully in until it is heard to 'click', the tensioner pin should then be able to be easily depressed and return smoothly.*

22 Refit the crankshaft pulley as described in Section 6.

23 Refit the cylinder head as described in Section 11.

24 Refit the upper timing chain and sprockets as described in Section 9.

25 Refit the sump as described in Section 12.

26 Refit the coolant pump, alternator and power steering pump (see Chapter 3, 5A and 10) and refit the auxiliary drivebelt (see Chapter 1B).

27 On completion refill the engine with oil and coolant as described in Chapter 1A. Start the engine and check for signs of oil leaks.

8 Timing chain tensioners – removal and refitting

Upper chain tensioner

Removal

1 Remove the air cleaner housing as described in Chapter 4B.

2 Referring to Section 17, support the engine/transmission unit and unbolt the right-hand mounting assembly from the cylinder head.

3 Unscrew the tensioner cap from the rear of the cylinder head and remove the plunger,

7.13 Free the sprocket from the injection pump and remove the timing chain cover gasket

7.17 Refit the lower timing chain guide and tighten its retaining bolts to the specified torque

7.18 Refit the pivot bolt to the tensioner blades and tighten to the specified torque

8.3a Unscrew the tensioner cap from the rear of the cylinder head . . .

8.3b . . . and withdraw the plunger, noting which way around it is fitted

8.6a Insert the plunger, making sure its closed end facing the timing chain, then fit tensioner cap and sealing washer (arrowed)

noting which way around it is fitted **(see illustrations)**. Remove the sealing ring from the cap and discard it, a new one should be used on refitting.

Caution: Do not rotate the engine whilst the tensioner is removed.

4 Inspect the tensioner plunger for signs of wear or damage and renew if necessary.

Refitting

5 Lubricate the tensioner plunger with clean engine oil and insert it into the cylinder head. Ensure the plunger is fitted the correct way around with its closed end facing the timing chain.

6 Fit a new sealing ring to the tensioner cap then fit the cap to the cylinder head, tightening it to the specified torque. **Note:** *If a new tensioner is being fitted, release it by*

pushing the cap centre pin fully in until it is heard to 'click', the tensioner pin should then be able to be easily depressed and return smoothly (see illustrations).

7 Refit the engine/transmission right-hand mounting assembly (see Section 17).

8 Refit the air cleaner housing as described in Chapter 4B.

Lower chain tensioner

Removal

9 Firmly apply the handbrake then jack up the front of the vehicle and support it on axle stands.

10 Undo the retaining bolts/clips and remove the engine/transmission undertray (where fitted).

11 Unscrew the tensioner cap from the rear

of the timing chain cover and remove the plunger, noting which way around it is fitted. Remove the sealing ring from the cap and discard it, a new one should be used on refitting **(see illustrations)**.

Caution: Do not rotate the engine whilst the tensioner is removed.

12 Inspect the tensioner plunger for signs of wear or damage and renew if necessary.

Refitting

13 Lubricate the tensioner plunger with clean engine oil and insert it into the timing chain cover. Ensure the plunger is fitted the correct way around with its closed end facing the timing chain **(see illustration)**.

14 Fit a new sealing ring to the tensioner cap then fit the cap to the cover, tightening it to the specified torque. **Note:** *If a new tensioner is being fitted, release it by pushing the cap centre pin fully in until it is heard to 'click', the tensioner pin should then be able to be easily depressed and return smoothly (see illustration).*

15 Refit the undertray (where fitted) then lower the vehicle to the ground.

Tensioner blades

16 Tensioner blade removal and refitting is part of the timing chain cover removal and refitting procedure (see Section 7). The blades must be renewed if they show signs of wear or damage on their chain surfaces.

8.6b If a new tensioner is being fitted, release it by depressing the cap centre pin until it is heard to click

8.11a Slacken and remove the lower timing chain tensioner cap and sealing washer from the rear of the timing chain cover . . .

8.11b . . . then withdraw the tensioner plunger

8.13 Ensure the plunger is fitted the correct way around with its closed end (arrowed) facing the timing chain

8.14 If a new tensioner is being fitted, release it by depressing the centre pin until it is heard to click

9 Timing chains and sprockets
– removal, inspection and refitting

Note: *In order to set the valve timing accurately, several special Vauxhall service tools (or suitable alternatives) are required (see Section 4). If access to suitable tools cannot be gained then it is recommended that this task is entrusted to a Vauxhall dealer or suitably-equipped garage. If the task is to be carried out without the tools then accurate alignment marks must be made between the sprocket(s), chain(s) and the shaft(s) prior to removal to ensure the valve timing is correctly set on refitting.*

Removal

Upper chain and sprockets

Note: *A new camshaft sprocket bolt and new timing chain guide retaining bolts will be required on refitting.*

1 Disconnect the battery negative lead then remove the camshaft cover (see Section 5).
2 Position No 1 cylinder at TDC on its compression stroke as described in Section 3 and lock the crankshaft in position.
3 To improve access to the injection pump sprocket cover, carry out the following.
 a) Remove the air cleaner housing and exhaust system front pipe (see Chapter 4B).
 b) Remove the auxiliary drivebelt (Chapter 1B).
 c) Mark the position of the right-hand engine mounting bracket in relation to the cylinder head bracket. Undo the three bolts securing the right-hand engine mounting to the cylinder head bracket, and the three bolts securing the right-hand engine mounting to the inner wing, then raise the right-hand end of the engine using a jack/engine support bar (see Section 17). Raise the engine as high as possible without placing any excess strain on the remaining mountings or any pipes/hoses or wiring.
4 Remove both the upper and lower timing chain tensioners as described in Section 8.
5 Undo the auxiliary drivebelt tensioner pulley strut lower mounting bolt and the pulley backplate pivot bolt and remove the tensioner

9.6a Undo the retaining screws . . .

9.6b . . . and remove the injection pump sprocket cover from the engine

9.8a To ease removal, heat the upper timing chain guide bolts with a hot air gun prior to removal

9.8b Unscrew both retaining bolts . . .

assembly from the engine. **Note:** *Store the assembly so the tensioner strut is the correct way up; if the strut is not stored properly it will have to be primed once it is refitted.*
6 Undo the retaining bolts and remove the injection pump sprocket cover from the timing chain cover **(see illustrations).**
7 If the special locking tools are available, lock the injection pump sprockets and camshaft in position (see Section 4). If the tools are not being used, make accurate alignment marks between the chain and sprockets, and the sprockets and the camshaft/pump flange.
8 Undo the retaining bolts then lift the upper chain guide out from the top of the cylinder head. **Note:** *The upper timing chain guide bolts should be heated with a hot air gun prior to removal; this loosens the locking compound on the bolt head and significantly*

eases removal of the bolts **(see illustrations).**
9 Hold the camshaft using an open-ended spanner on the flats provided, then slacken and remove the camshaft sprocket retaining bolt **(see illustration).** To ensure the camshaft sprocket and chain remain correctly mated, cable tie the chain to the sprocket. **Note:** *If the locking tools are being used, remove them prior to slackening the sprocket bolt and refit them once the bolt is loose.*
10 Remove the injection pump locking tool (where fitted) then slacken and remove the bolts securing the injection pump sprockets to the pump flange. Manoeuvre the injection pump upper chain sprocket out of position then free the camshaft sprocket from the camshaft end and lift the sprocket and upper timing chain out from the top of the cylinder head **(see illustration).**

9.8c . . . and lift the upper guide out from the top of the cylinder head

9.9 Retain the camshaft with an open-ended spanner and unscrew the sprocket retaining bolt

9.10 Unbolt the sprocket from the injection pump then free it from the chain and remove it through the cover aperture

9.14 Free the sprocket from the injection pump flange and remove it complete with the lower timing chain

9.15a Slide the sprocket off from the end of the crankshaft . . .

9.15b . . . and remove the Woodruff key

Lower chain and sprockets

11 Remove the upper timing chain and sprockets as described in paragraphs 1 to 10.
12 Remove the timing chain cover as described in Section 7.
13 Make alignment marks between the chain and sprockets and the injection pump sprocket and pump flange.
14 Free the pump sprocket from its flange and remove the sprocket and timing chain from the engine, noting which way around the sprocket is fitted **(see illustration)**.
15 Slide the crankshaft sprocket off from the crankshaft end and recover the Woodruff key from the crankshaft groove **(see illustrations)**.

Inspection

16 Examine the teeth on the sprockets for any sign of wear or damage such as chipped, hooked or missing teeth. If there is any sign of wear or damage on either sprocket, both sprockets and the relevant chain should be renewed as a set.
17 Inspect the links of each timing chain for signs of wear or damage on the rollers. The extent of wear can be judged by checking the amount by which the chain can be bent sideways; a new chain will have very little sideways movement. If there is an excessive amount of side play in a timing chain, it must be renewed.
18 Note that it is a sensible precaution to renew the timing chains, regardless of their apparent condition, if the engine has covered a high mileage, or if it has been noted that the

chain(s) have sounded noisy when the engine running. Although not strictly necessary, it is always worth renewing the chains and sprockets as a matched set, since it is false economy to run a new chain on worn sprockets and *vice-versa*. If there is any doubt about the condition of the timing chains and sprockets, seek the advice of a Vauxhall dealer service department, who will be able to advise you as to the best course of action, based on their previous knowledge of the engine.
19 Examine the chain guide(s) and tensioner blade(s) for signs of wear or damage to their chain contact faces, renewing any which are badly marked.

Refitting

Upper chain and sprockets

20 If any new components are being fitted, transfer the alignment marks from the original components to aid refitting. Ensure the crankshaft is still locked in the TDC position.
21 Engage the camshaft sprocket with the chain and lower the assembly into position.
22 Manoeuvre the injection pump sprocket into position and engage it with the timing chain.
23 Ensure the marks made prior to removal are all correctly aligned then engage the sprockets with the camshaft and injection pump flange. Where necessary, remove the cable tie from camshaft sprocket.
24 Align the injection pump sprocket timing mark with the hole in the pump flange then

refit the retaining bolts tightening them by hand only at this stage **(see illustration)**.
25 Fit the new sprocket retaining bolt to the camshaft end, tightening by hand only at this stage **(see illustration)**.
26 Refit the lower timing chain tensioner as described in Section 8.
27 Slide the upper timing chain guide into position, ensuring its locating lug is uppermost, then fit the new retaining bolts and tighten them to the specified torque **(see illustration)**.
28 If the special tools are available, fit all the tools to ensure the pump, camshaft and crankshaft are correctly positioned. If the tools are not being used, ensure the marks made prior to removal are realigned.
29 If the special tools are available, adjust the valve timing as described in Section 4, paragraphs 14 to 18. Remove all the locking tools.
30 If the tools are not available, align the marks made prior to removal then tighten the injection pump sprocket bolts to the specified torque. Tighten the camshaft sprocket bolt to the specified Stage 1 torque setting, whilst preventing the camshaft from rotating. Ensure the marks remain in alignment then tighten the bolt through the specified Stage 2 angle and finally through the specified Stage 3 angle. It is recommended that an angle-measuring gauge is used during the final stages of the tightening, to ensure accuracy. If a gauge is not available, use white paint to make alignment marks prior to tightening; the marks can then be used to check that the bolt has been rotated through the correct angle.

9.24 Align the injection pump sprocket timing mark (arrowed) with the pump flange hole and refit the retaining bolts

9.25 Fit the new camshaft sprocket retaining bolt and tighten it by hand only

9.27 Refit the upper timing chain guide to the cylinder head making sure its locating lug (arrowed) is uppermost

10.9 Remove the retaining bolts (arrowed) and lift out the upper timing chain guide

10.11a Free the camshaft sprocket from the timing chain . . .

10.11b . . . then pass a screwdriver or extension bar through the chain to prevent it falling down into the engine

31 Refit the upper timing chain tensioner as described in Section 8.

32 Ensure the mating surfaces of the pump sprocket cover and timing chain cover are clean and dry. Where the cover was originally fitted with a gasket, fit the cover with a new gasket and tighten the retaining bolts to the specified torque. If no gasket was fitted, apply a bead of sealant (approximately 2 mm thick) to the cover groove then refit the cover and tighten its retaining bolts to the specified torque.

33 Refit the auxiliary drivebelt tensioner assembly to the engine unit, tightening the strut and backplate pivot bolts to their specified torque settings. If a new tensioner strut is being fitted, or the original was not stored properly, prime the strut by repeatedly compressing it using a socket on the backplate hexagonal section. Once the strut is functioning correctly, refit the auxiliary drivebelt as described in Chapter 1B.

34 Refit the right-hand mounting assembly to the cylinder head then lower the engine/transmission unit back down. Refit the right-hand engine mounting to the inner wing and align the mounting with the previously made marks on the cylinder head bracket, fit and tighten the bolts to the specified torque.

35 Refit the camshaft cover as described in Section 5.

36 Refit the exhaust front pipe, air cleaner housing and crankshaft sensor (see Chapter 4B). Where the camshaft timing tool has have been used, refit the vacuum pump to the cylinder head (see Chapter 9).

Lower chain and sprockets

37 If any new components are being fitted transfer the alignment marks from the original components to aid refitting.

38 Refit the Woodruff key to the crankshaft then slide on the crankshaft sprocket, aligning the sprocket groove with the key.

39 Ensure the injection pump flange is still correctly positioned with the flange timing cut-out aligned with the hole in the pump body and the crankshaft is still locked at TDC.

40 Aligning the marks made prior to removal, engage the pump sprocket with the chain and manoeuvre the assembly into position. Engage the chain with the crankshaft sprocket and seat the pump sprocket on the

flange, ensuring the sprocket is fitted the correct way around. Check that all the marks made prior to removal are correctly aligned and that the injection pump flange timing cut-out is correctly position in the oblong slot in the sprocket.

41 Refit the timing cover as described in Section 7 then refit the upper timing chain as described earlier in this Section.

10 Camshaft and followers –
removal, inspection
and refitting

Note: A new camshaft sprocket retaining bolt and new upper timing chain guide retaining bolts will be required on refitting.

Removal

1 Disconnect the battery negative lead (see Chapter 5A) then remove the camshaft cover as described in Section 5.

2 Remove the braking system vacuum pump as described in Chapter 9.

3 Position No 1 cylinder at TDC on its compression stroke as described in Section 3 and lock the crankshaft in position.

4 To improve access to the injection pump sprocket cover, carry out the following.

a) *Remove the air cleaner housing and exhaust system front pipe (see Chapter 4B).*

b) *Remove the auxiliary drivebelt (see Chapter 1B).*

c) *Mark the position of the right-hand engine mounting bracket in relation to the cylinder head bracket. Undo the three bolts securing the right-hand engine mounting to the cylinder head bracket, and the three bolts securing the right-hand engine mounting to the inner wing, then raise the right-hand end of the engine using a jack/engine support bar (see Section 17). Raise the engine as high as possible without placing any excess strain on the remaining mountings or any pipes/hoses or wiring.*

5 Remove the upper timing chain tensioner as described in Section 8.

6 Undo the auxiliary drivebelt tensioner pulley strut lower mounting bolt and the pulley backplate pivot bolt and remove the tensioner assembly from the engine. **Note:** *Store the*

assembly so the tensioner strut is the correct way up; if the strut is not stored properly it will have to be primed once it is refitted.

7 Undo the retaining bolts and remove the injection pump sprocket cover from the timing chain cover.

8 Make accurate alignment marks between the upper timing chain and sprockets, and the camshaft sprocket and camshaft.

9 Undo the retaining bolts then lift the upper chain guide out from the top of the cylinder head **(see illustration)**. **Note:** *The upper timing chain guide bolts should be heated with a hot air gun prior to removal; this loosens the locking compound on the bolt head and significantly eases removal of the bolts.*

10 Hold the camshaft, using an open-ended spanner on the flats provided, then slacken and remove the camshaft sprocket retaining bolt. Remove the crankshaft locking tool prior to slackening the sprocket bolt and refit it once the bolt is loose.

11 Disengage the camshaft sprocket from the upper timing chain and remove it from the engine. Pass a screwdriver or extension bar through the upper chain, to prevent it falling down into the cylinder head, and rest it on the head upper surface **(see illustrations)**.

12 Note the identification markings on the camshaft bearing caps. The caps are numbered 1 to 5 with all numbers being the right way up when viewed from the front of the engine; number 1 cap being at the timing chain end of the engine and number 5 at the flywheel end **(see illustration)**. If the markings

10.12 Each camshaft bearing cap should be stamped with an identification number (arrowed)

10.14 Removing a camshaft follower

10.20 Lubricate the hydraulic tappets with clean engine oil and install them in the cylinder head

10.21 On refitting ensure that all followers are correctly positioned and that the punch marks (A) are facing towards the injector crosspipe (B)

are not clearly visible, make identification marks to ensure each cap is fitted correctly on refitting.

13 Working in a spiral pattern from the outside inwards, slacken the camshaft bearing cap retaining bolts by one turn at a time, to relieve the pressure of the valve springs on the bearing caps gradually and evenly. Once the valve spring pressure has been relieved, the bolts can be fully unscrewed and removed, along with the caps. Take care not to lose the locating dowels which are fitted to left-hand end (No 5) bearing cap and lift the camshaft out from the head.

Caution: If the bearing cap bolts are carelessly slackened, the bearing caps might break. If any bearing cap breaks then the complete cylinder head assembly must be renewed; the bearing caps are matched to the head and are not available separately.

14 Obtain eight (twenty-four if the tappets are also to be removed) small, clean plastic containers, and label them for identification. Alternatively, divide a larger container into compartments. Lift the followers out from the top of the cylinder head and store each one in its respective fitted position **(see illustration)**.

15 If the hydraulic tappets are also to be removed, remove the injector crosspipes as described in Chapter 4B, Section 11. Using a rubber sucker or magnet, withdraw each hydraulic tappet and place it in its container.

Inspection

16 Examine the camshaft bearing surfaces and cam lobes for signs of wear ridges and scoring. Renew the camshaft if any of these conditions are apparent. Examine the condition of the bearing surfaces both on the camshaft journals and in the cylinder head. If the head bearing surfaces are worn excessively, the cylinder head will need to be renewed.

17 Support the camshaft end journals on V-blocks, and measure the run-out at the centre journal using a dial gauge. If the run-out exceeds the specified limit, the camshaft should be renewed.

18 Examine the follower bearing surfaces which contact the camshaft lobes for wear ridges and scoring. Renew any followers on which these conditions are apparent.

19 Check the hydraulic tappets (where removed) and their bores in the cylinder head for signs of wear or damage. If any tappet is thought to be faulty it should be renewed.

Refitting

20 Where removed, lubricate the hydraulic tappets with clean engine oil and carefully insert each one into its original location in the cylinder head **(see illustration)**. Refit the injector crosspipes as described in Chapter 4.

21 Refit the camshaft followers to the cylinder head. Ensure each follower is fitted in its original location and the punch marks on

the follower upper surface are facing the injector crosspipe **(see illustration)**.

22 Lubricate the camshaft followers with clean engine oil then lay the camshaft in position. Ensure the crankshaft is still locked in position and position the camshaft so that the lobes of No 1 cylinder are pointing upwards and the slot on the left-hand end of the camshaft is parallel with the cylinder head surface (timing hole at the top) **(see illustrations)**.

23 Ensure the mating surfaces of the bearing caps and cylinder head are clean and dry and lubricate the camshaft journals and lobes with clean engine oil.

24 Apply a smear of sealant to the cylinder head mating surface of the left-hand (No 5) bearing cap and fit the cap locating dowels to the cylinder head **(see illustration)**.

25 Refit the camshaft bearing caps and the retaining bolts in their original locations on the cylinder head **(see illustration)**. The caps are numbered 1 to 5 from timing chain end of the cylinder head and all numbers should be the right way up when viewed from the front of the engine.

26 Tighten all bolts by hand only then, working in a spiral pattern from the centre outwards, tighten the bolts by one turn at a time to gradually impose the pressure of the valve springs on the bearing caps. Repeat this sequence until all bearing caps are in contact with the cylinder head then go around and

10.22a Refit the camshaft, positioning it so that No 1 cylinder lobes are pointing upwards (arrowed) . . .

10.22b . . . and the slot in its left-hand end is parallel to the cylinder head with the timing hole (arrowed) at the top

10.24 Apply sealant to the areas shown on the left-hand end of the cylinder head (arrowed)

10.25 Refit the camshaft bearing caps using the identification markings to ensure each one is correctly positioned

10.26 Working as described in text, tighten the bearing cap bolts to the specified torque

10.27 Refit the camshaft sprocket and install the new retaining bolt

tighten the camshaft bearing cap bolts to the specified torque **(see illustration)**.
Caution: If the bearing cap bolts are carelessly tightened, the bearing caps might break. If any bearing cap breaks then the complete cylinder head assembly must be renewed; the bearing caps are matched to the head and are not available separately.

27 Using the marks made on removal, ensure that the upper timing chain is still correctly engaged with the injection pump sprocket then refit the camshaft sprocket to the chain. Seat the sprocket on the end of the camshaft and fit the new retaining bolt **(see illustration)**.

28 Slide the upper timing chain guide into position, ensuring its locating lug is uppermost, then fit the new retaining bolts and tighten them to the specified torque.

29 If the special tools are available, adjust the valve timing as described in Section 4, paragraphs 14 to 18. Remove all the locking tools.

30 If the tools are not available, align the marks made prior to removal on the camshaft and sprocket. Hold the camshaft with an open-ended spanner and tighten the sprocket bolt to the specified Stage 1 torque setting. Ensure the marks have remained in alignment then tighten the bolt through the specified Stage 2 angle and finally through the specified Stage 3 angle. It is recommended that an angle-measuring gauge is used during the final stages of the tightening, to ensure accuracy **(see illustrations)**. If a gauge is not available, use white paint to make alignment marks prior to tightening; the marks can then be used to check that the bolt has been rotated through the correct angle.

31 Refit the upper timing chain tensioner as described in Section 8.

32 Ensure the mating surfaces of the pump sprocket cover and timing chain cover are clean and dry. Where the cover was originally fitted with a gasket, fit the cover with a new gasket and tighten the retaining bolts to the specified torque. If no gasket was fitted, apply a bead of sealant (approximately 2 mm thick) to the cover groove then refit the cover and tighten its retaining bolts to the specified torque.

33 Refit the auxiliary drivebelt tensioner assembly to the engine unit, tightening the strut and backplate pivot bolts to their specified torque settings. If a new tensioner strut is being fitted, or the original was not stored properly, prime the strut by repeatedly compressing it using a socket on the backplate hexagonal section. Once the strut is functioning correctly, refit the auxiliary drivebelt as described in Chapter 1B.

34 Refit the right-hand mounting assembly to the cylinder head, then lower the engine/transmission unit back down. Refit the right-hand engine mounting to the inner wing and align the mounting with the previously made marks on the cylinder head bracket, fit and tighten the bolts to the specified torque.

35 Refit the camshaft cover as described in Section 5.

36 Refit the exhaust front pipe, air cleaner housing and crankshaft sensor (see Chapter 4B).

37 Refit the vacuum pump as described in Chapter 9.

11 Cylinder head – removal and refitting

Caution: Be careful not to allow dirt into the fuel injection pump or injector pipes during this procedure.
Note: *New cylinder head bolts, upper timing*

10.30a If the timing tools are not available, align the marks made prior to removal then tighten the sprocket bolt to the Stage 1 torque setting . . .

chain guide bolts and a camshaft sprocket retaining bolt will be required on refitting.

Removal

1 Drain the cooling system as described in Chapter 1B.

2 Carry out the operations described in paragraphs 1 to 11 of Section 10, noting that it will be necessary to raise the engine on a jack. Support the engine by inserting stout block of wood in between the right-hand end of the sump and the subframe. **Note:** *If the sump needs to be removed at the same time as the head, it will be necessary to use the special Vauxhall service tool (KM-909-A) or fabricate a suitable alternative. The tool is bolted to the suspension subframe and locates in the hole on the right-hand rear corner of the cylinder block, this supports the weight of the engine whilst the right-hand mounting assembly is removed yet still allows access to the sump.*

3 Wipe clean the area around the fuel hose unions on the injection pump then slacken and remove the union bolts and sealing washers. Disconnect the return pipe from the pump union then release the hoses from their retaining clips, and position them clear of the cylinder head **(see illustrations)**.

4 Remove the inlet and exhaust manifolds as described in Chapter 4B. If no work is to be carried out on the cylinder head, the head can be removed complete with manifolds once the following operations have been carried out.

10.30b . . . and then through the specified Stage 2 and 3 angles

11.3a Unscrew the union bolts (arrowed) then disconnect the fuel feed and return hose unions from the injection pump . . .

11.3b . . . and disconnect the return pipe

11.5a Disconnect the coolant hoses (arrowed) from the front of the cylinder head . . .

a) *On high-pressure turbo models, remove the intake ducts and metal pipe from the turbocharger.*

b) *Unbolt the wiring harness tray from the top of the inlet manifold, disconnect the wiring connectors and position it clear of the engine. Unclip the crankshaft sensor wiring from the manifold.*

c) *Remove the injector pipes linking the pump to the injectors.*

d) *Disconnect the vacuum hoses from the inlet manifold switchover valve and the EGR valve.*

e) *Disconnect/unbolt the wiring connectors from the glow plugs then remove the turbocharger heat shields.*

f) *Disconnect the turbocharger oil pipes from the cylinder block. Disconnect the wastegate diaphragm vacuum hose.*

g) *Remove the starter motor heat shield and unbolt the wiring harness guide and exhaust manifold support bracket from the rear of the block.*

5 Release the retaining clips and disconnect the coolant hoses from the front and rear of the right-hand end of the cylinder head **(see illustrations)**.

6 Slacken and remove the alternator upper mounting bolt, and pivot the alternator to the rear to position it clear of the cylinder head **(see illustration)**.

7 Slacken and remove the three bolts securing the right-hand end of the cylinder

head to the top of the timing chain cover and the single bolt securing the head to the block **(see illustration)**.

8 Working in the **reverse** of the sequence shown in illustration 11.26, progressively slacken the ten main cylinder head bolts by half a turn at a time, until all bolts can be unscrewed by hand.

9 Lift out the cylinder head bolts and recover the washers.

10 Lift the cylinder head away; seek assistance if possible, as it is a heavy assembly (especially if complete with manifolds). Remove the gasket, noting the two locating dowels fitted to the top of the cylinder block. If they are a loose fit, remove the locating dowels and store them with the head for safe-keeping. Keep the head gasket for identification purposes (see paragraph 17). *Caution: Do not lay the head on its lower mating surface; support the head on wooden blocks, ensuring each block only contacts the head mating surface not the glow plugs or injector nozzles. The glow plugs and injector nozzles protrude out the bottom of the head and they will be damaged if the head is placed directly onto a bench.*

11 If the cylinder head is to be dismantled for overhaul, then refer to Part E of this Chapter.

Preparation for refitting

12 The mating faces of the cylinder head and cylinder block/crankcase must be perfectly

clean before refitting the head. Use a hard plastic or wood scraper to remove all traces of gasket and carbon; also clean the piston crowns. Take particular care, as the surfaces are damaged easily. Also, make sure that the carbon is not allowed to enter the oil and water passages – this is particularly important for the lubrication system, as carbon could block the oil supply to any of the engine's components. Using adhesive tape and paper, seal the water, oil and bolt holes in the cylinder block/crankcase. To prevent carbon entering the gap between the pistons and bores, smear a little grease in the gap. After cleaning each piston, use a small brush to remove all traces of grease and carbon from the gap, then wipe away the remainder with a clean rag. Clean all the pistons in the same way.

13 Check the mating surfaces of the cylinder block/crankcase and the cylinder head for nicks, deep scratches and other damage. If slight, they may be removed carefully with a file, but if excessive, machining may be the only alternative to renewal.

14 Ensure that the cylinder head bolt holes in the crankcase are clean and free of oil. Syringe or soak up any oil left in the bolt holes. This is most important in order that the correct bolt tightening torque can be applied and to prevent the possibility of the block being cracked by hydraulic pressure when the bolts are tightened.

11.5b . . . and the hose from the rear of the cylinder head

11.6 Remove the upper mounting bolt and pivot the alternator away from the cylinder head

11.7 Unscrew the bolts (arrowed) securing the right-hand end of the cylinder head to the timing chain cover/block

11.17 Cylinder head gasket thickness identification cut-outs (arrowed)

15 The cylinder head bolts must be discarded and renewed, regardless of their apparent condition.

16 If warpage of the cylinder head gasket surface is suspected, use a straight-edge to check it for distortion. Refer to Part E of this Chapter if necessary.

17 On this engine, the cylinder head-to-piston clearance is controlled by fitting different thickness head gaskets. The gasket thickness can be determined by looking at the tab situated directly in front of No 1 cylinder (see illustration).

Notches on tab	Gasket thickness
No notches	1.2 mm
One notch	1.3 mm
Two notches	1.4 mm

The correct thickness of gasket required is selected by measuring the piston protrusions as follows.

18 Ensure that the crankshaft is still locked in the TDC position. Mount a dial test indicator securely on the block so that its pointer can be easily pivoted between the piston crown and block mating surface. Zero the dial test indicator on the gasket surface of the cylinder block then carefully move the indicator over No 1 piston and measure its protrusion (see illustration). Repeat this procedure on No 4 piston.

19 Remove the crankshaft locking tool and rotate the crankshaft half a turn (180°) to bring No 2 and 3 pistons to TDC. Ensure the crankshaft is accurately positioned then measure the protrusions of No 2 and 3 pistons. Once both pistons have been measured, rotate the

crankshaft through a further one and a half turns (540°) to bring No 1 and 4 pistons back to TDC and lock the crankshaft in position again.

Caution: When rotating the crankshaft, keep the upper timing chain taut to prevent the chain jamming around the injection pump sprocket.

20 Using the largest protrusion measurement of the four pistons, select the correct thickness of head gasket required using the following table.

Piston protrusion measurement	Gasket thickness required
0.40 to 0.50 mm	1.2 mm
0.51 to 0.60 mm	1.3 mm
0.61 to 0.70 mm	1.4 mm

Refitting

21 Wipe clean the mating surfaces of the cylinder head and cylinder block/crankcase.

22 Check that the two locating dowels are in position then fit a new gasket to the cylinder block (see illustration).

23 Ensure the crankshaft is locked in the TDC position and the camshaft is correctly positioned with the lobes of No 1 cylinder pointing upwards and the slot on the left-hand end of the camshaft parallel with the cylinder head surface (timing hole at the top).

24 With the aid of an assistant, carefully refit the cylinder head assembly to the block, aligning it with the locating dowels. As the head is fitted, pass the upper timing chain up through the cylinder block, holding it in position by passing a screwdriver through the upper chain and resting it on the head upper surface.

25 Apply a smear of oil to the threads and the underside of the heads of the new cylinder head bolts and carefully enter each bolt into its relevant hole (*do not drop them in*). Screw all bolts in, by hand only, until finger-tight.

26 Working progressively and in the

11.18 Measuring piston protrusion using a dial gauge

sequence shown, tighten the cylinder head bolts to their Stage 1 torque setting, using a torque wrench and suitable socket (see illustration).

27 Once all bolts have been tightened to the Stage 1 torque, working again in the specified sequence, go around and tighten all bolts through the specified Stage 2 angle. It is recommended that an angle-measuring gauge is used to ensure accuracy. If a gauge is not available, use white paint to make alignment marks prior to tightening; the marks can then be used to check that the bolt has been rotated through the correct angle.

28 Go around again in the specified sequence and angle tighten the bolts through the specified Stage 3 angle.

29 Working again in the specified sequence, go around and tighten all bolts through the specified Stage 4 angle.

30 Go around again in the specified sequence and angle tighten the bolts through the specified Stage 5 angle.

31 Finally go around in the specified sequence and angle tighten the bolts through the specified Stage 6 angle.

32 Refit the bolts securing the right-hand end of the cylinder head to the block/timing cover and tighten them to the specified torque setting.

11.22 Ensure the locating dowels are in position (arrowed) and fit the new gasket

11.26 Cylinder head bolt tightening sequence

12.4 Disconnect the wiring connector from the oil temperature sensor (arrowed)

12.5 Slacken and remove the bolts securing the sump flange to the transmission housing (lower bolts arrowed)

12.7 Oil pump pick-up/strainer retaining bolts (arrowed)

33 Pivot the alternator back into position and tighten its upper mounting bolt to the specified torque (Chapter 5A).

34 Reconnect the coolant hoses to the cylinder head and secure them in position with the retaining clips.

35 Refit/reconnect the inlet and exhaust manifolds and associated components as described in Chapter 4B.

36 Refit the camshaft sprocket to the camshaft as described in paragraphs 27 to 37 of Section 10.

37 Position a new sealing washer on each side of the injection pump fuel hose unions then refit both union bolts and tighten them to the specified torque (Chapter 4B).

38 On completion refill the cooling system as described in Chapter 1B.

12 Sump –
removed and refitting

Removal

1 Disconnect the battery negative terminal (see Chapter 5A).

2 Firmly apply the handbrake then jack up the front of the car and support it on axle stands. Where necessary, undo the retaining screws and remove the undercover from beneath the engine/transmission unit.

3 Drain the engine oil as described in Chapter 1B, then fit a new sealing washer and refit the

drain plug, tightening it to the specified torque.

4 Disconnect the wiring connector(s) from the oil temperature sensor and (where fitted) the oil level sensor **(see illustration)**.

5 Slacken and remove the bolts securing the sump flange to the transmission housing **(see illustration)**.

6 Progressively slacken and remove the bolts securing the sump to the base of the cylinder block/oil pump. Break the sump joint by striking the sump with the palm of the hand, then lower the sump away from the engine and withdraw it. Remove the gasket and discard it.

7 While the sump is removed, take the opportunity to check the oil pump pick-up/strainer for signs of clogging or splitting. If necessary, unbolt the pick-up/strainer and remove it from the sump along with its sealing ring **(see illustration)**. The strainer can then be cleaned easily in solvent or renewed.

Refitting

8 Remove all traces of dirt and oil from the mating surfaces of the sump and cylinder block and (where removed) the pick-up/strainer.

9 Where necessary, position a new sealing ring on the oil pump pick-up/strainer flange and fit the strainer to the sump, tightening its retaining bolts to the specified torque.

10 Apply a smear of suitable sealant to the areas of the cylinder block mating surface around the oil pump housing and rear main

bearing cap joints **(see illustrations)**.

11 Fit a new gasket to the sump then offer up the sump to the cylinder block and loosely refit all the retaining bolts **(see illustration)**.

12 Working out from the centre in a diagonal sequence, progressively tighten the bolts securing the sump to the cylinder block/oil pump to their specified torque setting.

13 Tighten the bolts securing the sump flange to the transmission housing to their specified torque settings.

14 Reconnect the oil temperature/level sensor wiring connector(s) (as applicable). Where necessary refit the undercover.

15 Lower the vehicle to the ground then fill the engine with fresh oil (see Chapter 1B).

13 Oil pump –
removal, inspection and refitting

Note: *The oil pump safety valve can be removed with the timing chain cover in position on the engine and the pressure relief valve can be removed once the sump has been removed (see below).*

Removal

1 The oil pump assembly is built into the timing chain cover. Removal and refitting is as described in Section 7.

Inspection

2 Undo the retaining screws and lift off the

12.10a Apply a smear of sealant to the areas of the cylinder block/timing chain cover joints . . .

12.10b . . . and the rear main bearing cap/cylinder block joints

12.11 Fit a new gasket to the sump and manoeuvre it up into position

13.2 Remove the oil pump cover from the rear of the timing chain cover . . .

13.4a . . . then lift out the pump inner . . .

13.4b . . . and outer rotors

pump cover from the inside of the timing chain cover (see illustration).

3 Using a suitable marker pen, mark the surface of both the pump inner and outer rotors; the marks can then be used to ensure the rotors are refitted the correct way around.

4 Lift out the inner and outer rotors from the cover (see illustrations).

5 Unscrew the oil pressure relief valve bolt from the base of the timing chain cover and withdraw the spring, spring sleeve and plunger, noting which way around the plunger is fitted. Remove the sealing ring from the valve bolt (see illustrations).

6 Unscrew the safety valve bolt from the rear of the timing chain cover, the safety valve is the uppermost of the three bolts on the rear of the cover. Withdraw the spring and plunger from the cover, noting which way around the plunger is fitted (see illustrations). Remove the sealing ring from the valve bolt.

7 Clean the components, and carefully examine the rotors, pump body and valve plungers for any signs of scoring or wear. Renew any component which shows signs of wear or damage; if the rotors or pump housing are marked then the complete pump assembly should be renewed.

8 If the pump is satisfactory, reassemble the components in the reverse order of removal, noting the following.

a) Ensure both rotors and the valve plungers are fitted the correct way around.

b) Fit new sealing rings to the pressure relief valve and safety valve bolts and tighten both bolts to their specified torque settings.

c) Refit the pump cover tightening the cover screws to the specified torque (see illustration).

d) On completion prime the oil pump by filling it with clean engine oil whilst rotating the inner rotor.

Refitting

9 Refit the timing chain cover as described in Section 7.

14 Oil cooler – removal and refitting

Removal

1 The oil cooler/filter assembly is mounted onto the front, left-hand end of cylinder block and the cooler is bolted onto the front of the oil filter housing. To improve access, firmly apply the handbrake then jack up the front of the car and support it on axle stands. Where necessary, undo the retaining clips/screws and remove the engine/transmission under-tray.

13.5a Unscrew the oil pressure relief valve bolt and sealing washer . . .

13.5b . . . and withdraw the spring, spring sleeve (arrowed) . . .

13.5c . . . and plunger from the timing chain cover

13.6a Unscrew the safety valve bolt and washer . . .

13.6b . . . then remove the spring and valve plunger from the timing chain cover

13.8 On refitting tighten the pump cover screws to the specified torque

14.3 Undo the three retaining screws (arrowed) and remove the oil cooler from the oil filter housing

1 Cooler to oil filter housing oil seal

15.2 Lever the right-hand crankshaft oil seal out from the timing chain cover

15.7 Removing the crankshaft left-hand oil seal

2 To minimise coolant loss, clamp the coolant hoses on either side of the oil cooler then release the retaining clips and detach both hoses. Be prepared for some coolant loss and mop up any spilt coolant.

3 Wipe clean the area around the oil cooler then undo the retaining bolts and remove the cooler and sealing rings from the oil filter housing **(see illustration)**.

Refitting

4 Refitting is the reverse of removal, using new sealing rings. Check and top-up the coolant as described in Chapter 1B.

15 Crankshaft oil seals – renewal

Right-hand (timing chain end)

1 Remove the crankshaft pulley as described in Section 6.

2 Using a large flat-bladed screwdriver, carefully lever the seal out from the timing chain cover **(see illustration)**.

3 Clean the seal housing and polish off any burrs or raised edges which may have caused the seal to fail in the first place.

4 Lubricate the lips of the new seal with clean engine oil and press/tap it squarely into position until it is flush with the cover **(see illustration)**. If necessary, a suitable tubular drift, such as a socket, which bears only on the hard outer edge of the seal can be used to tap the seal into position. Take great care not

15.4 Press/tap the new seal squarely into position until it is flush with the cover

15.9 Carefully ease the new seal over the end of the crankshaft and tap/press it squarely into position

to damage the seal lips during fitting and ensure that the seal lips face inwards.

5 Wash off any traces of oil, then refit the crankshaft pulley as described in Section 6.

Left-hand (flywheel/driveplate end)

6 Remove the flywheel as described in Section 16.

7 Carefully punch or drill two small holes opposite each other in the oil seal. Screw a self-tapping screw into each and pull on the screws with pliers to extract the seal **(see illustration)**.

8 Clean the seal housing and polish off any burrs or raised edges which may have caused the seal to fail in the first place.

9 Lubricate the lips of the new seal with clean engine oil and ease it into position on the end of the crankshaft. Press the seal squarely into position until it is flush with the bearing cap. If necessary, a suitable tubular drift, such as a socket, which bears only on the hard outer edge of the seal can be used to tap the seal into position. Take great care not to damage the seal lips during fitting and ensure that the seal lips face inwards **(see illustration)**.

10 Refit the flywheel as described in Section 16.

16 Flywheel – removal, inspection and refitting

Note: *New flywheel retaining bolts will be required on refitting.*

Removal

1 Remove the transmission as described in Chapter 7A then remove the clutch assembly as described in Chapter 6.

2 Prevent the flywheel from turning by locking the ring gear teeth with a similar arrangement to that shown **(see illustration)**. Alternatively, bolt a strap between the flywheel and the cylinder block/crankcase. Make alignment marks between the flywheel and crankshaft using paint or a suitable marker pen.

3 Slacken and remove the retaining bolts and remove the flywheel **(see illustration)**. **Note:** *The flywheel is very heavy, take care not to drop it when removing.*

16.2 Lock the flywheel ring gear . . .

Inspection

4 Examine the flywheel for wear or chipping of the ring gear teeth. On some models, renewal of the ring gear is possible but it is not a task for the home mechanic; renewal requires the new ring gear to be heated (up to 180° to 230°C) to allow it to be fitted.

5 Examine the flywheel for scoring of the clutch face. If the clutch face is scored, the flywheel may be surface-ground, but renewal is preferable.

6 If there is any doubt about the condition of the flywheel, seek the advice of a Vauxhall dealer or engine reconditioning specialist. They will be able to advise if it is possible to recondition it or whether renewal is necessary.

Refitting

7 Clean the mating surfaces of the flywheel and crankshaft.

8 Offer up the flywheel and fit the new retaining bolts. If the original is being refitted align the marks made prior to removal.

9 Lock the flywheel using the method employed on dismantling then, working in a diagonal sequence, evenly and progressively tighten the retaining bolts to the specified Stage 1 torque setting.

10 Once all bolts have been tightened to the Stage 1 torque, go around and tighten all bolts through the specified Stage 2 angle. It is recommended that an angle-measuring gauge is used during the final stages of the tightening, to ensure accuracy. If a gauge is not available, use white paint to make alignment marks prior to tightening; the marks can then be used to check that the bolt has been rotated through the correct angle.

11 Finally go around again and angle tighten the bolts through the specified Stage 3 angle.

12 Refit the clutch as described in Chapter 6 then remove the locking tool and refit the transmission as described in Chapter 7A.

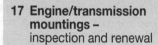

17 Engine/transmission mountings –
inspection and renewal

Note: *Vauxhall recommend that both the right-hand and left-hand mountings should be renewed if either one is damaged.*

Inspection

1 If improved access is required, raise the front of the car and support it securely on axle stands. Where necessary, undo the retaining bolts and remove the undercover from beneath the engine/transmission unit.

2 Check the mounting rubber to see if it is cracked, hardened or separated from the metal at any point; renew the mounting if any such damage or deterioration is evident.

3 Check that all the mounting fasteners are securely tightened; use a torque wrench to check if possible.

4 Using a large screwdriver or a pry bar,

16.3 . . . then unscrew the retaining bolts and remove the flywheel

check for wear in the mounting by carefully levering against it to check for free play; where this is not possible, enlist the aid of an assistant to move the engine/transmission unit back-and-forth, or from side-to-side, while you watch the mounting. While some free play is to be expected, even from new components, excessive wear should be obvious.

5 If excessive free play is found, check first that the fasteners are correctly secured, then renew any worn components as described below.

Renewal

Note: *Before slackening any of the engine mounting bolts/nuts, the relative positions of the mountings to their various brackets should be marked to ensure correct alignment upon refitting.*

Right-hand mounting

6 Remove the air cleaner housing and intake duct assembly as described in Chapter 4B.

7 Support the weight of the engine/transmission using a trolley jack with a block of wood placed on its head.

8 Slacken and remove the nuts securing the mounting bracket to the mounting and engine bracket and lift off the bracket. If necessary, the mounting bracket can then be unbolted from the side of the cylinder block.

9 Raise the engine/transmission unit slightly then unscrew the mounting lower retaining nut and remove the mounting from the body. **Note:** *Take great care not to place any excess stress on the exhaust system when raising the*

17.16 Left-hand mounting-to-subframe nut (arrowed)

engine. If necessary, disconnect the front pipe from the manifold (see Chapter 4B).

10 Check all components for signs of wear or damage, and renew as necessary.

11 On reassembly, fit the mounting to the vehicle body and tighten its nut to the specified torque.

12 Refit the engine bracket (where removed) to the cylinder block and tighten its bolts to the specified torque. Then refit the mounting bracket to the top of the mounting/engine bracket and tighten its nuts to the specified torque.

Left-hand mounting

13 Slacken and remove the nut securing the right-hand mounting bracket to the mounting.

14 Firmly apply the handbrake then jack up the front of the vehicle and support it on axle stands. Where necessary, unbolt and remove the undercover.

15 Support the weight of the engine/transmission using a trolley jack with a block of wood placed on its head.

16 Slacken and remove the nut and washer securing the left-hand mounting to the front subframe and the upper nut securing the mounting to its bracket **(see illustration)**.

17 Raise the engine/transmission unit slightly then undo the bolts securing the mounting bracket to the transmission unit and manoeuvre the mounting and bracket out of position. Remove the nut and separate the mounting and bracket, noting which way up the mounting is fitted. **Note:** *Take great care not to place any excess stress on the exhaust system when raising the engine. If necessary, disconnect the front pipe from the manifold (see Chapter 4B).*

18 Check all components for signs of wear or damage, and renew as necessary.

19 On reassembly, refit the mounting to the bracket, ensuring it is fitted the right way up, and lightly tighten its nut.

20 Manoeuvre the mounting assembly into position and refit the bolts securing it to the transmission, tightening them to the specified torque.

21 Lower the engine/transmission unit and locate the mounting correctly in the subframe. Refit the lower mounting nut then tighten both the upper and lower nuts to the specified torque.

22 Lower the vehicle to the ground then refit the nut to the right-hand mounting and tighten it to the specified torque.

Rear mounting

23 Remove the right-hand driveshaft as described in Chapter 8.

24 Remove the exhaust system front pipe as described in Chapter 4B.

25 Referring to Chapter 7A, slacken the gearchange mechanism selector rod clamp bolt and disengage the selector rod from the transmission linkage.

26 Undo the retaining nut securing the mounting bracket to the top of the right-hand mounting.

the mounting bolts and tighten them to the specified torque.

30 Manoeuvre the assembly into position and refit the bolts securing it to the subframe and transmission. Tighten the mounting bolts to their specified torque settings then remove the jack from underneath the engine/transmission.

31 Refit the nut to the right-hand mounting and tighten it to the specified torque.

32 Reconnect the selector rod and adjust the gearchange mechanism as described in Chapter 7A.

33 Refit the right-hand driveshaft as described in Chapter 8.

34 Refit the exhaust front pipe as described in Chapter 4B.

18 Balancer unit (Y22DTR engine) – general information

1 A balancer unit is fitted to the 2.2 litre (Y22DTR) engine, this is to help provide a vibration and noise-free running of the engine. It consists of two balancer shafts which are driven via a chain from the crankshaft, the chain is kept under tension by a hydraulic chain tensioner located inside the balancer unit housing **(see illustration)**. The balancer shafts rotate in opposite directions at double the crankshaft speed.

2 The balancer unit is mounted on the 2nd and 3rd crankshaft main bearings, and the oil supply to the balancer unit is also via these two main bearings.

3 Before the balancer unit is removed the engine must be set at TDC (see Section 3). **Note:** *The balancer shafts are set to the correct timing of the engine rotation, if the balancer shafts are removed they have to be refitted in the correct position or engine noise and vibration will occur.*

4 Two special tools are required for the removal and refitting of the balancer unit. In order to carry out the procedure, Vauxhall tool No KM-979 must be used to lock the balancer shafts in the TDC position and tool No KM-978 to reset the chain tensioner.

5 At the time of writing the removal and refitting procedure was not available, so no further information can be given.

18.1 Balancer unit layout – Y22DTR engines

1 Balancer unit
2 Crankshaft sprocket
3 Chain tensioner
4 Drive sprocket for balancer shaft

27 Support the weight of the engine/transmission using a trolley jack with a block of wood placed on its head. Position the jack underneath the transmission and raise the transmission slightly to remove all load from the rear mounting.

28 Slacken and remove the bolts securing the rear mounting to the subframe and transmission then manoeuvre the assembly out from underneath the vehicle. If necessary, undo the retaining bolts and separate the mounting and mounting bracket.

29 On refitting, reassemble the mounting and mounting bracket (where necessary) then refit

Chapter 2 Part E:
Engine removal and overhaul procedures

Contents

Degrees of difficulty

Easy, suitable for novice with little experience	**Fairly easy,** suitable for beginner with some experience	**Fairly difficult,** suitable for competent DIY mechanic 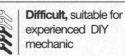	**Difficult,** suitable for experienced DIY mechanic	**Very difficult,** suitable for expert DIY or professional

Specifications

Note: *Where specifications are given as N/A, no information was available at the time of writing. Refer to your Vauxhall dealer for the latest information available.*
* Identification marking in brackets

Engine identification

Engine type	Manufacturer's code
1.6 litre SOHC petrol engine	X16SZR
1.6 litre DOHC petrol engine	X16XEL and Z16XE
1.8 litre DOHC petrol engine	X18XE, X18XE1 and Z18XE
2.0 litre DOHC petrol engine	X20XEV
2.2 litre DOHC petrol engine	Z22SE
2.0 litre low-pressure turbo diesel engine	X20DTL
2.0 litre high-pressure turbo diesel engine	X20DTH and Y20DTH
2.2 litre high-pressure turbo diesel engine	Y22DTR

Manufacturer's code	Engine type
X16SZR	1.6 litre SOHC petrol engine
X16XEL	1.6 litre DOHC petrol engine
X18XE	1.8 litre DOHC petrol engine
X18XE1	1.8 litre DOHC petrol engine
X20DTH	2.0 litre high-pressure turbo diesel engine
X20DTL	2.0 litre low-pressure turbo diesel engine
X20XEV	2.0 litre DOHC petrol engine
Y20DTH	2.0 litre high-pressure turbo diesel engine
Y22DTR	2.2 litre high-pressure turbo diesel engine
Z16XE	1.6 litre DOHC petrol engine
Z18XE	1.8 litre DOHC petrol engine
Z22SE	2.2 litre DOHC petrol engine

1.6 litre SOHC petrol engine (X16SZR)

Cylinder head
Maximum gasket face distortion	0.05 mm
Cylinder head height	95.90 to 96.10 mm

Valve seat width:
Inlet	1.3 to 1.5 mm
Exhaust	1.6 to 1.8 mm

Valves and guides
Valve guide height in cylinder head .... 80.85 to 81.25 mm

Valve stem diameter*:	Inlet	Exhaust
Standard (K)	6.998 to 7.012 mm	6.978 to 6.992 mm
1st oversize – 0.075 mm (K1)	7.073 to 7.087 mm	7.053 to 7.067 mm
2nd oversize – 0.150 mm (K2)	7.148 to 7.162 mm	7.128 to 7.142 mm
3rd oversize – 0.250 mm (A)	7.248 to 7.262 mm	7.228 to 7.262 mm

Valve stem run-out .... Less than 0.03 mm

Valve guide bore diameter*:
Standard (K)	7.030 to 7.050 mm
1st oversize – 0.075 mm (K1)	7.105 to 7.125 mm
2nd oversize – 0.150 mm (K2)	7.180 to 7.200 mm
3rd oversize – 0.250 mm (A)	7.280 to 7.300 mm

Stem-to-guide clearance:
Inlet	0.018 to 0.052 mm
Exhaust	0.038 to 0.072 mm

Valve length:
New	101.5 mm
Service limit	101.1 mm

Valve stem fitted height .... 13.75 to 14.35 mm

Valve head diameter:
Inlet	38 mm
Exhaust	31 mm

Cylinder block
Maximum gasket face distortion .... 0.05 mm

Cylinder bore diameter:
Standard:
Size group 6	78.955 to 78.965 mm
Size group 7	78.965 to 78.975 mm
Size group 8	78.975 to 78.985 mm
Oversize – 0.5 mm	79.465 to 79.475 mm
Maximum cylinder bore ovality	0.013 mm
Maximum cylinder bore taper	0.013 mm

Pistons and rings
Piston diameter:
Standard:
Size group 6	78.935 to 78.945 mm
Size group 7	78.945 to 78.955 mm
Size group 8	78.955 to 78.965 mm
Oversize – 0.5 mm; size group 7 + 0.5	79.445 to 79.455 mm
Piston-to-bore clearance	0.02 ± 0.01 mm

Piston ring end gaps (fitted in bore):
Top and second compression rings	0.3 to 0.5 mm
Oil control ring	0.4 to 1.4 mm

Piston ring thickness:
Top compression ring	1.2 mm
Second compression ring	1.5 mm
Oil control ring	3.0 mm
Piston ring-to-groove clearance	N/A

Gudgeon pins
Diameter	18 mm
Length	55 mm
Gudgeon pin-to-piston clearance	0.009 to 0.012 mm

Connecting rod
Big-end side clearance	0.07 to 0.24 mm

1.6 litre SOHC petrol engine (X16SZR) (continued)

Crankshaft

Endfloat	0.1 to 0.2 mm
Main bearing journal diameter:	
Standard	54.980 to 54.997 mm
1st undersize – 0.25 mm	54.730 to 54.747 mm
2nd undersize – 0.50 mm	54.482 to 54.495 mm
Big-end bearing journal (crankpin) diameter:	
Standard	42.971 to 42.987 mm
1st undersize – 0.25 mm	42.721 to 42.737 mm
2nd undersize – 0.50 mm	42.471 to 42.487 mm
Journal out-of round	0.04 mm
Journal taper	N/A
Crankshaft run-out	Less than 0.03 mm
Main bearing running clearance	0.017 to 0.047 mm
Big-end bearing (crankpin) running clearance	0.019 to 0.071 mm

Torque wrench settings

Refer to Chapter 2A Specifications

1.6 litre DOHC petrol engine (X16XEL and Z16XE)

Cylinder head

Maximum gasket face distortion	0.05 mm
Cylinder head height	134.90 to 135.10 mm
Cam lift:	
Inlet	8.50 mm
Exhaust	8.00 mm
Camshaft radial run-out	0.040 mm
Camshaft endfloat	0.040 to 0.144 mm
Valve seat angle in cylinder head	90° 30'
Valve seat width in cylinder head:	
Inlet	1.0 to 1.4 mm
Exhaust	1.4 to 1.8 mm

Valves and guides

	Inlet	Exhaust
Valve stem run-out	Less than 0.03 mm	
Valve guide bore diameter*:		
Standard	6.000 to 6.012 mm	
1st oversize – 0.075 mm	6.075 to 6.090 mm	
2nd oversize – 0.150 mm	6.150 to 6.165 mm	
Length of valve guide:		
Inlet	44.75 to 45.25 mm	
Exhaust	34.75 to 35.25 mm	
Installation height of valve guide	10.70 to 11.00 mm	
Installation height of valves:		
Standard	39.60 to 40.20 mm	
Oversize	39.20 to 39.80 mm	
Stem-to-guide clearance:		
Inlet	0.03 to 0.06 mm	
Exhaust	0.04 to 0.07 mm	
Valve length*:	Inlet	Exhaust
Standard	102.92 to 103.32	102.02 to 102.42
1st oversize – 0.075 mm (K1)	102.52 to 102.92	101.62 to 102.02
2nd oversize – 0.150 mm (K2)	102.52 to 102.92	101.62 to 102.02
Valve stem diameter*:	Inlet	Exhaust
Standard	5.955 to 5.970 mm	5.935 to 5.950 mm
1st oversize – 0.075 mm (K1)	6.030 to 6.045 mm	6.010 to 6.025 mm
2nd oversize – 0.150 mm (K2)	6.105 to 6.120 mm	6.085 to 6.100 mm
Valve head diameter:		
Inlet	31.0 mm	
Exhaust	27.5 mm	

1.6 litre DOHC petrol engine (X16XEL and Z16XE) (continued)

Gudgeon pins

Diameter	17.997 to 18.000 mm
Length	55 mm
Gudgeon pin clearance:	
In connecting rod (shrunk fit)	0.0 mm
In piston	0.09 to 0.012 mm

Crankshaft

Endfloat	0.100 to 0.202 mm
Main bearing journal diameter:	
Standard	54.980 to 54.997 mm
1st undersize – 0.25 mm	54.730 to 54.747 mm
2nd undersize – 0.50 mm	54.482 to 54.495 mm
Big-end bearing journal (crankpin) diameter:	
Standard	42.971 to 42.987 mm
1st undersize – 0.25 mm	42.721 to 42.737 mm
2nd undersize – 0.50 mm	42.471 to 42.487 mm
Big-end bearing journal shell thickness*:	
Standard (264N)	1.485 to 1.497 mm
1st undersize – 0.25 mm (blue – 265A)	1.610 to 1.622 mm
2nd undersize – 0.50 mm (white – 266B)	1.735 to 1.747 mm
Main bearing shell thickness (Nos 1, 2, 4 and 5)*:	
Standard (brown – 256N)	1.987 to 1.993 mm
Standard (green – 257N)	1.993 to 1.999 mm
1st undersize – 0.25 mm (brown/blue – 258A)	2.112 to 2.118 mm
1st undersize – 0.25 mm (green/blue – 259A)	2.118 to 2.124 mm
2nd undersize – 0.50 mm (brown/white – 260B)	2.237 to 2.243 mm
2nd undersize – 0.50 mm (green/white – 261B)	2.243 to 2.249 mm
Main bearing/thrust shell thickness (No 3)*:	
Standard (brown – 859N)	1.987 to 1.993 mm
Standard (green – 860N)	1.993 to 1.999 mm
1st undersize – 0.25 mm (brown/blue – 861A)	2.112 to 2.118 mm
1st undersize – 0.25 mm (green/blue – 862A)	2.118 to 2.124 mm
2nd undersize – 0.50 mm (brown/white – 863B)	2.237 to 2.243 mm
2nd undersize – 0.50 mm (green/white – 864B)	2.243 to 2.249 mm
Main bearing/thrust shell width (No 3)*:	
Standard (green/brown)	25.850 to 25.900 mm
1st undersize – 0.25 mm (brown/blue)	26.050 to 26.100 mm
2nd undersize – 0.50 mm (brown/white)	26.250 to 26.300 mm
Journal out-of round	0.04 mm
Journal taper	N/A
Crankshaft run-out	Less than 0.03 mm
Main bearing running clearance	0.013 to 0.043 mm
Big-end bearing (crankpin) running clearance	0.019 to 0.071 mm

Cylinder block

Maximum gasket face distortion	0.05 mm
Cylinder bore diameter:	
Standard:	
Size group 5	78.945 to 78.955 mm
Size group 6	78.955 to 78.965 mm
Size group 7	78.965 to 78.975 mm
Size group 8	78.975 to 78.985 mm
Size group 99	78.985 to 78.995 mm
Size group 00	78.995 to 79.005 mm
Size group 01	79.005 to 79.015 mm
Size group 02	79.015 to 79.025 mm
Size group 03	79.025 to 79.035 mm
Size group 04	79.035 to 79.045 mm
Size group 05	79.045 to 79.055 mm
Size group 06	79.055 to 79.065 mm
Size group 07	79.065 to 79.075 mm
Size group 08	79.075 to 79.085 mm
Size group 09	79.085 to 79.095 mm
Size group 1	79.095 to 79.105 mm
Oversize – 0.5 mm	79.465 to 79.475 mm
Maximum cylinder bore ovality and taper	0.013 mm

1.6 litre DOHC petrol engine (X16XEL and Z16XE) (continued)

Pistons and rings

Piston diameter:

Standard:

Size group 5	78.925 to 78.935 mm
Size group 6	78.935 to 78.945 mm
Size group 7	78.945 to 78.955 mm
Size group 8	78.955 to 78.965 mm
Size group 99	78.965 to 78.975 mm
Size group 00	78.975 to 78.085 mm
Size group 01	78.985 to 78.095 mm
Size group 02	78.995 to 79.005 mm
Size group 03	79.005 to 79.015 mm
Size group 04	79.015 to 79.025 mm
Size group 05	79.025 to 79.035 mm
Size group 06	79.035 to 79.045 mm
Size group 07	79.045 to 79.055 mm
Size group 08	79.055 to 79.065 mm
Size group 09	79.065 to 79.075 mm
Size group 1	79.075 to 79.085 mm
Oversize – 0.5 mm; size group 7 + 0.5	79.445 to 79.445 mm

Piston-to-bore clearance	0.02 to 0.04 mm

Piston rings:

Top (rectangular) compression ring:

Height (thickness)	1.20 mm
Gap	0.30 to 0.50 mm
Vertical play	0.02 to 0.04 mm

Middle (tapered) compression ring:

Height (thickness)	1.50 mm
Gap	0.30 to 0.50 mm
Vertical play	0.04 to 0.06 mm

Bottom oil scraper ring:

Height (thickness)	2.50 mm
Gap	0.40 to 1.40 mm
Vertical play	0.01 to 0.03 mm
Piston ring gap arrangement in cylinder	180°
Piston ring-to-groove clearance	N/A

Connecting rod

Big-end side clearance	0.11 to 0.24 mm

Torque wrench settings

Refer to Chapter 2B Specifications

1.8 litre DOHC petrol engine (X18XE1 and Z18XE)

Cylinder head

Maximum gasket face distortion	0.05 mm
Cylinder head height	135.00 to 136.00 mm

Cam lift:

Inlet	8.50 mm
Exhaust	8.00 mm
Camshaft radial run-out	0.040 mm
Camshaft endfloat	0.040 to 0.144 mm
Valve seat angle in cylinder head	90° 30'

Valve seat width in cylinder head:

Inlet	1.0 to 1.4 mm
Exhaust	1.4 to 1.8 mm

Valves and guides

Valve stem run-out	Less than 0.03 mm

Valve guide bore diameter:

Standard	5.000 to 5.012 mm
1st oversize – 0.075 mm	5.075 to 5.087 mm
2nd oversize – 0.150 mm	5.150 to 5.162 mm

Length of valve guide:

Inlet	38.70 to 39.30 mm
Exhaust	38.70 to 39.30 mm

1.8 litre DOHC petrol engine (X18XE1 and Z18XE) (continued)

Valves and guides (continued)

Installation height of valve guide	10.70 to 11.00 mm	
Installation height of valves	N/A	
Stem-to-guide clearance:		
Inlet	0.03 to 0.06 mm	
Exhaust	0.04 to 0.07 mm	
Valve length*:	**Inlet**	**Exhaust**
Standard	101.20 to 101.60	100.56 to 100.96
1st oversize – 0.075 mm (K1)	N/A	N/A
2nd oversize – 0.150 mm (K2)	N/A	N/A
Valve stem diameter*:	**Inlet**	**Exhaust**
Standard	4.955 to 4.970 mm	4.935 to 4.950 mm
1st oversize – 0.075 mm (K1)	N/A	N/A
2nd oversize – 0.150 mm (K2)	N/A	N/A
Valve head diameter:		
Inlet	31.2 mm	
Exhaust	27.5 mm	

Gudgeon pins

Diameter	17.997 to 18.000 mm
Length	55 mm
Gudgeon pin clearance:	
In connecting rod (shrunk fit)	0.0 mm
In piston	0.09 to 0.015 mm

Crankshaft

Endfloat	0.100 to 0.202 mm
Main bearing journal diameter:	
Standard	54.980 to 54.997 mm
1st undersize – 0.25 mm	54.730 to 54.747 mm
2nd undersize – 0.50 mm	54.482 to 54.495 mm
Big-end bearing journal (crankpin) diameter:	
Standard	42.971 to 42.987 mm
1st undersize – 0.25 mm	42.721 to 42.737 mm
2nd undersize – 0.50 mm	42.471 to 42.487 mm
Big-end bearing journal shell thickness*:	
Standard (264N)	1.485 to 1.497 mm
1st undersize – 0.25 mm (blue – 265A)	1.610 to 1.622 mm
2nd undersize – 0.50 mm (white – 266B)	1.735 to 1.747 mm
Main bearing shell thickness (Nos 1, 2, 4 and 5)*:	
Standard (brown – 256N)	1.987 to 1.993 mm
Standard (green – 257N)	1.993 to 1.999 mm
1st undersize – 0.25 mm (brown/blue – 258A)	2.112 to 2.118 mm
1st undersize – 0.25 mm (green/blue – 259A)	2.118 to 2.124 mm
2nd undersize – 0.50 mm (brown/white – 260B)	2.237 to 2.243 mm
2nd undersize – 0.50 mm (green/white – 261B)	2.243 to 2.249 mm
Main bearing/thrust shell thickness (No 3)*:	
Standard (brown – 859N)	1.987 to 1.993 mm
Standard (green – 860N)	1.993 to 1.999 mm
1st undersize – 0.25 mm (brown/blue – 861A)	2.112 to 2.118 mm
1st undersize – 0.25 mm (green/blue – 862A)	2.118 to 2.124 mm
2nd undersize – 0.50 mm (brown/white – 863B)	2.237 to 2.243 mm
2nd undersize – 0.50 mm (green/white – 864B)	2.243 to 2.249 mm
Main bearing/thrust shell width (No 3)*:	
Standard (green/brown)	25.850 to 25.900 mm
1st undersize – 0.25 mm (brown/blue)	26.050 to 26.100 mm
2nd undersize – 0.50 mm (brown/white)	26.250 to 26.300 mm
Journal out-of round	0.04 mm
Journal taper	N/A
Crankshaft run-out	Less than 0.03 mm
Main bearing running clearance	0.013 to 0.043 mm
Big-end bearing (crankpin) running clearance	0.019 to 0.071 mm

1.8 litre DOHC petrol engine (X18XE1 and Z18XE) (continued)

Cylinder block
Maximum gasket face distortion .... 0.05 mm
Cylinder bore diameter:
  Standard:
    Size group 5 .... 80.445 to 80.455 mm
    Size group 6 .... 80.455 to 80.465 mm
    Size group 7 .... 80.465 to 80.475 mm
    Size group 8 .... 80.475 to 80.485 mm
    Size group 99 .... 80.485 to 80.495 mm
    Size group 00 .... 80.495 to 80.505 mm
    Size group 01 .... 80.505 to 80.515 mm
    Size group 02 .... 80.515 to 80.525 mm
    Size group 03 .... 80.525 to 80.535 mm
    Size group 04 .... 80.535 to 80.545 mm
    Size group 05 .... 80.545 to 80.555 mm
    Size group 06 .... 80.555 to 80.565 mm
    Size group 07 .... 80.565 to 80.575 mm
    Size group 08 .... 80.575 to 80.585 mm
    Size group 09 .... 80.585 to 80.595 mm
    Size group 1 .... 80.595 to 80.605 mm
  Oversize – 0.5 mm .... 80.605 to 80.615 mm
Maximum cylinder bore ovality and taper .... 0.013 mm

Pistons and rings
Piston diameter:
  Standard:
    Size group 5 .... 80.415 to 78.955 mm
    Size group 6 .... 80.425 to 78.935 mm
    Size group 7 .... 80.435 to 78.945 mm
    Size group 8 .... 80.445 to 78.955 mm
    Size group 99 .... 80.455 to 80.465 mm
    Size group 00 .... 80.465 to 80.475 mm
    Size group 01 .... 80.475 to 80.485 mm
    Size group 02 .... 80.485 to 80.495 mm
    Size group 03 .... 80.495 to 80.505 mm
    Size group 04 .... 80.505 to 80.515 mm
    Size group 05 .... 80.515 to 80.525 mm
    Size group 06 .... 80.525 to 80.535 mm
    Size group 07 .... 80.535 to 80.545 mm
    Size group 08 .... 80.545 to 80.555 mm
    Size group 09 .... 80.555 to 80.565 mm
    Size group 1 .... 80.565 to 80.575 mm
  Oversize – 0.5 mm; size group 7 + 0.5 .... 80.965 to 80.975 mm
Piston-to-bore clearance .... 0.02 to 0.04 mm
Piston rings:
  Top (rectangular) compression ring:
    Height (thickness) .... 1.175 to 1.19 mm
    Gap .... 0.20 to 0.40 mm
    Vertical play .... N/A
  Middle (tapered) compression ring:
    Height (thickness) .... 1.175 to 1.19 mm
    Gap .... 0.40 to 0.60 mm
    Vertical play .... N/A
  Bottom oil scraper ring:
    Height (thickness) .... 1.88 to 1.96 mm
    Gap .... 0.25 to 0.75 mm
    Vertical play .... N/A
Piston ring gap arrangement in cylinder .... 180°
Piston ring-to-groove clearance .... N/A

Connecting rod
Big-end side clearance .... 0.11 to 0.24 mm

Torque wrench settings
Refer to Chapter 2B Specifications

1.8 and 2.0 litre DOHC petrol engines (X18XE and X20XEV)

Cylinder head

Maximum gasket face distortion	0.05 mm
Cam lift	9.20 mm
Camshaft radial run-out	0.06 mm
Camshaft endfloat	0.040 to 0.144 mm
Cylinder head height	134 mm

Valve seat width:

Inlet	1.0 to 1.5 mm
Exhaust	1.7 to 2.2 mm

Valves and guides

Valve guide height in cylinder head .... 13.70 to 14.00 mm

Valve stem diameter*:	**Inlet**	**Exhaust**
Standard (K)	5.955 to 5.970 mm	5.945 to 5.960 mm
1st oversize – 0.075 mm (K1)	6.030 to 6.045 mm	6.020 to 6.035 mm
2nd oversize – 0.150 mm (K2)	6.105 to 6.120 mm	6.095 to 6.110 mm

Valve stem run-out	Less than 0.03 mm
Valve seat angle in cylinder head	90° 40'

Valve guide bore diameter*:

Standard (K)	6.000 to 6.012 mm
1st oversize – 0.075 mm (K1)	6.075 to 6.090 mm
2nd oversize – 0.150 mm (K2)	6.150 to 6.165 mm

Stem-to-guide clearance:

Inlet	0.030 to 0.057 mm
Exhaust	0.040 to 0.067 mm

Valve length:

Inlet	101.90 to 102.30 mm
Exhaust	92.05 to 92.45 mm

Valve head diameter:

Inlet	31.9 to 32.1 mm
Exhaust	28.9 to 29.1 mm

Cylinder block

Maximum gasket face distortion .... 0.05 mm

Cylinder bore diameter:	**X18XE**	**X20XEV**
Standard:		
Size group 8	81.575 to 81.585 mm	85.975 to 85.985 mm
Size group 99	81.585 to 81.595 mm	85.985 to 85.995 mm
Size group 00	81.595 to 81.605 mm	85.995 to 86.005 mm
Size group 01	81.605 to 81.615 mm	86.005 to 86.015 mm
Size group 02	81.615 to 81.625 mm	86.015 to 86.025 mm
Oversize – 0.5 mm	82.065 to 82.075 mm	86.465 to 86.475 mm

Maximum cylinder bore ovality	0.013 mm
Maximum cylinder bore taper	0.013 mm

Pistons and rings

Piston diameter:	**X18XE**	**X20XEV**
Standard:		
Size group 8	81.555 to 81.565 mm	85.955 to 85.965 mm
Size group 99	81.565 to 81.575 mm	85.965 to 85.975 mm
Size group 00	81.575 to 81.585 mm	85.975 to 85.985 mm
Size group 01	81.585 to 81.595 mm	85.985 to 85.995 mm
Size group 02	81.595 to 81.605 mm	85.995 to 86.005 mm
Oversize – 0.5 mm; size group 7 + 0.5	82.045 to 82.055 mm	86.445 to 86.455 mm

Piston-to-bore clearance .... 0.02 to 0.04 mm

Piston ring end gaps (fitted in bore):

Top and second compression rings	0.3 to 0.5 mm
Oil control ring	0.4 to 1.4 mm

Piston ring thickness:

Top and second compression ring	1.5 mm
Oil control ring	3.0 mm

Piston ring-to-groove clearance .... N/A

Gudgeon pins

Diameter .... 21 mm

Length:

X18XE	56.0 mm
X20XEV	61.5 mm

Gudgeon pin-to-piston clearance .... 0.011 to 0.014 mm

1.8 and 2.0 litre DOHC petrol engines (X18XE and X20XEV) (continued)

Connecting rod

Big-end side clearance	0.07 to 0.24 mm

Crankshaft

Endfloat	0.05 to 0.15 mm
Main bearing journal diameter*:	
Standard:	
1st size group (white)	57.974 to 57.981 mm
2nd size group (green)	57.981 to 57.988 mm
3rd size group (brown)	57.988 to 57.995 mm
1st undersize – 0.25 mm	57.732 to 57.745 mm
2nd undersize – 0.50 mm	57.482 to 57.495 mm
Big-end bearing journal (crankpin) diameter:	
Standard	48.970 to 48.988 mm
1st undersize – 0.25 mm	48.720 to 48.738 mm
2nd undersize – 0.50 mm	48.470 to 48.488 mm
Journal out-of round	0.04 mm
Journal taper	N/A
Crankshaft run-out	Less than 0.03 mm
Main bearing running clearance	0.015 to 0.040 mm
Big-end bearing (crankpin) running clearance	0.006 to 0.031 mm

Torque wrench settings

Refer to Chapter 2B Specifications

2.2 litre DOHC petrol engine (Z22SE)

Cylinder head

Maximum gasket face distortion	0.05 mm
Cylinder head height (resurfacing is not permitted)	129 mm
Cam lift:	
Inlet	5.87 mm
Exhaust	5.99 mm
Valve seat angle in cylinder head	90°
Valve seat angle at valve head	90° 40'
Valve seat width in cylinder head:	
Inlet	1.1 to 1.3 mm
Exhaust	1.4 to 1.8 mm

Valves and guides

	Inlet	Exhaust
Installation height of valve guide	11.20 to 11.50 mm	
Installation height of valves	40.10	
Valve guide bore diameter:		
Standard	6.000 to 6.012 mm	
Oversize	N/A	
Length of valve guides	36mm	
Valve stem diameter*:	**Inlet**	**Exhaust**
Standard	5.955 to 5.970 mm	5.945 to 5.960 mm
Oversize – 0.075 mm (K1)	6.030 to 6.045 mm	6.020 to 6.035 mm
Valve length*:	**Inlet**	**Exhaust**
Standard	101.995 to 102.545	100.685 to 101.235
Oversize – 0.075 mm (K1)	101.595 to 102.145	100.285 to 100.835
Stem-to-guide clearance:		
Inlet	0.042 to 0.045 mm	
Exhaust	0.052 to 0.055 mm	
Valve stem run-out	Less than 0.03 mm	
Valve head diameter:		
Inlet	34.95 to 35.25 mm	
Exhaust	29.95 to 30.25 mm	

Cylinder block

Maximum gasket face distortion	0.05 mm
Cylinder bore diameter:	
Standard	85.992 to 86.008 mm
Oversize	86.117 to 86.133 mm
Maximum cylinder bore ovality	0.013 mm
Maximum cylinder bore taper	0.013 mm

2.2 litre DOHC petrol engine (Z22SE) (continued)

Pistons and rings

Piston diameter:	
Standard	85.967 to 85.982 mm
Oversize	86.092 to 86.107 mm
Piston-to-bore clearance	0.025 to 0.026 mm
Piston rings:	
Top (rectangular) compression ring:	
Height (thickness)	1.17 to 1.19 mm
Gap	0.20 to 0.40 mm
Vertical play	0.06 mm
Middle (tapered) compression ring:	
Height (thickness)	1.471 to 1.490 mm
Gap	0.35 to 0.55 mm
Vertical play	0.05 mm
Bottom oil scraper ring:	
Height (thickness)	2.348 to 2.477 mm
Gap	0.25 to 0.76 mm
Vertical play	0.063 to 0.172 mm
Piston ring gap arrangement in cylinder	120°
Piston ring-to-groove clearance	N/A

Gudgeon pins

Diameter	19.995 to 20.000 mm
Length	62.59 to 63.09 mm
Gudgeon pin clearance:	
In con-rod	0.012 to 0.021 mm
In piston	0.007 mm

Crankshaft

Main bearing journal diameter:	
Standard size	55.994 to 56.008 mm
1st undersize – 0.25 mm	55.744 to 55.758 mm
2nd undersize – 0.50 mm	55.494 to 55.508 mm
Main bearing shell thickness (Nos 1, 3, 4 and 5):	
Standard	4.030 to 4.037 mm
1st undersize – 0.25 mm	4.155 to 4.162 mm
2nd undersize – 0.50 mm	4.280 to 4.287 mm
Main bearing/thrust shell thickness (No 2):	
Standard	4.036 to 4.043 mm
1st undersize – 0.25 mm	4.161 to 4.168 mm
2nd undersize – 0.50 mm	4.268 to 4.293 mm
Main bearing/thrust shell width (No 2)	26.26 to 26.46 mm
Main bearing running clearance	0.007 to 0.014 mm
Big-end bearing journal (crankpin) diameter:	
Standard	49.000 to 49.014 mm
1st undersize – 0.25 mm	48.750 to 48.764 mm
2nd undersize – 0.50 mm	48.500 to 48.514 mm
Big-end bearing journal shell thickness:	
Standard	1.539 to 1.545 mm
1st undersize – 0.25 mm	1.664 to 1.670 mm
2nd undersize – 0.50 mm	1.795 to 1.798 mm
Big-end bearing (crankpin) running clearance	0.041 to 0.043 mm
Big-end side clearance	0.07 to 0.24 mm
Crankshaft endfloat	0.09 to 0.24 mm
Crankshaft run-out	Less than 0.03 mm
Journal out-of round	0.04 mm
Journal taper	N/A

Torque wrench settings

Refer to Chapter 2C Specifications

Diesel engines (X20DTL, X20DTH, Y20DTH and Y22DTR)

Cylinder head

Maximum gasket face distortion	N/A
Cam lift	8.5 mm
Cylinder head height	140 mm
Valve seat angle in cylinder head	90°
Valve seat width	1.4 to 1.8 mm

Diesel engines (X20DTL, X20DTH, Y20DTH and Y22DTR) (continued)

Valves and guides

Valve guide height in cylinder head . . . . 11.20 to 11.50 mm

Valve seat angle in at the valve head . . . . 90° 40'

	Inlet	Exhaust
Valve stem diameter*:		
Standard (K)	5.955 to 5.970 mm	5.945 to 5.960 mm
1st oversize – 0.075 mm (K1)	6.030 to 6.045 mm	6.020 to 6.035 mm
2nd oversize – 0.150 mm (K2)	6.105 to 6.120 mm	6.095 to 6.110 mm

Valve stem run-out . . . . Less than 0.03 mm

Valve guide bore diameter*:
  Standard (K) . . . . 6.000 to 6.012 mm
  1st oversize – 0.075 mm (K1) . . . . 6.075 to 6.090 mm
  2nd oversize – 0.150 mm (K2) . . . . 6.150 to 6.165 mm

Valve guide length
  Inlet . . . . 44.75 to 45.25 mm
  Exhaust . . . . 34.75 to 35.25 mm

Stem-to-guide clearance:
  Inlet . . . . 0.030 to 0.057 mm
  Exhaust . . . . 0.040 to 0.067 mm

Valve length:
  Standard . . . . 96.90 to 97.30 mm
  Oversize . . . . 96.50 to 96.90 mm

Valve head diameter:
  Inlet . . . . 28.9 to 29.1 mm
  Exhaust . . . . 25.9 to 26.1 mm

Cylinder block

Maximum gasket face distortion . . . . N/A

Cylinder bore diameter:
  Standard:
    Size group 8 . . . . 83.975 to 83.985 mm
    Size group 99 . . . . 83.985 to 83.995 mm
    Size group 00 . . . . 83.995 to 84.005 mm
    Size group 01 . . . . 84.005 to 84.015 mm
    Size group 02 . . . . 84.015 to 84.025 mm
    Oversize – 0.5 mm . . . . 84.475 to 84.485 mm

Maximum cylinder bore ovality . . . . N/A
Maximum cylinder bore taper . . . . N/A

Pistons and rings

Piston diameter:
  X20DTH, Y20DTH and Y22DTR:
    Standard:
      Size group 8 . . . . 83.885 to 83.895 mm
      Size group 99 . . . . 83.895 to 83.905 mm
      Size group 00 . . . . 83.905 to 83.915 mm
      Size group 01 . . . . 83.915 to 83.925 mm
      Size group 02 . . . . 83.925 to 83.935 mm
      Oversize – 0.5 mm . . . . 84.385 to 84.395 mm
  X20DTL:
    Standard:
      Size group 8 . . . . 83.905 to 83.915 mm
      Size group 99 . . . . 83.915 to 83.925 mm
      Size group 00 . . . . 83.925 to 83.935 mm
      Size group 01 . . . . 83.935 to 83.945 mm
      Size group 02 . . . . 83.945 to 83.955 mm
      Oversize – 0.5 mm . . . . 84.405 to 84.415 mm

Piston-to-bore clearance:
  X20DTH, Y20DTH and Y22DTR . . . . 0.08 to 0.10 mm
  X20DTL . . . . 0.06 to 0.08 mm

Piston ring end gaps (fitted in bore):
  Top and second compression rings . . . . 0.3 to 0.5 mm
  Oil control ring . . . . 0.4 to 1.4 mm

Piston ring-to-groove clearance:
  Top and second compression rings:
    X20DTL, X20DTH and Y22DTR . . . . 0.02 to 0.04 mm
    Y20DTH . . . . 0.11 to 0.15 mm

Diesel engines (X20DTL, X20DTH, Y20DTH and Y22DTR) (continued)

Pistons and rings (continued)

Oil control ring:	
X20DTL and X20DTH	0.01 to 0.03 mm
Y20DTH and Y22DTR	0.03 to 0.07 mm
Piston ring thickness:	
Top compression ring:	
X20DTL, Y20DTH and Y22DTR engine	2.00 mm
X20DTH engine	2.50 mm
Second compression ring	1.75 mm
Oil control ring	3.00 mm
Piston ring gap arrangement in cylinder	120°

Gudgeon pins

Diameter	29 mm
Length	68 mm

Connecting rod

Big-end side clearance	0.07 to 0.28 mm

Crankshaft

Endfloat	0.05 to 0.15 mm
Main bearing journal diameter*:	
Standard:	
1st size group (green)	67.966 to 67.974 mm
2nd size group (brown)	67.974 to 67.982 mm
1st undersize – 0.25 mm	67.716 to 67.732 mm
2nd undersize – 0.50 mm	67.466 to 67.482 mm
Big-end bearing journal (crankpin) diameter:	
Standard	48.971 to 48.990 mm
1st undersize – 0.25 mm	48.721 to 48.740 mm
2nd undersize – 0.50 mm	48.471 to 48.490 mm
Journal out-of round	0.03
Journal taper	N/A
Crankshaft run-out	Less than 0.03 mm
Main bearing running clearance	0.016 to 0.069 mm
Big-end bearing (crankpin) running clearance	0.010 to 0.061 mm

Torque wrench settings

Refer to Chapter 2D Specifications

1 General information

1 Included in this Part of Chapter 2 are details of removing the engine/transmission from the car and general overhaul procedures for the cylinder head, cylinder block and all other engine internal components.

2 The information given ranges from advice concerning preparation for an overhaul and the purchase of replacement parts, to detailed step-by-step procedures covering removal, inspection, renovation and refitting of engine internal components.

3 After Section 6, all instructions are based on the assumption that the engine has been removed from the car. For information concerning in-car engine repair, as well as the removal and refitting of those external components necessary for full overhaul, refer to the relevant in-car repair procedure section (Chapter 2A to 2D) of this Chapter and to Section 7. Ignore any preliminary dismantling operations described in the relevant in-car repair sections that are no longer relevant

once the engine has been removed from the car.

4 Apart from torque wrench settings, which are given at the beginning of the relevant in-car repair procedure Chapter 2A to 2D, all specifications relating to engine overhaul are at the beginning of this Part of Chapter 2.

2 Engine overhaul – general information

1 It is not always easy to determine when, or if, an engine should be completely over-hauled, as a number of factors must be considered.

2 High mileage is not necessarily an indication that an overhaul is needed, while low mileage does not preclude the need for an overhaul. Frequency of servicing is probably the most important consideration. An engine which has had regular and frequent oil and filter changes, as well as other required maintenance, should give many thousands of miles of reliable service. Conversely, a neglected engine may require an overhaul very early in its life.

3 Excessive oil consumption is an indication that piston rings, valve seals and/or valve guides are in need of attention. Make sure that oil leaks are not responsible before deciding that the rings and/or guides are worn. Perform a compression test, as described in the relevant Part A to D of this Chapter, to determine the likely cause of the problem.

4 Check the oil pressure with a gauge fitted in place of the oil pressure switch, and compare it with that specified. If it is extremely low, the main and big-end bearings, and/or the oil pump, are probably worn out.

5 Loss of power, rough running, knocking or metallic engine noises, excessive valve gear noise, and high fuel consumption may also point to the need for an overhaul, especially if they are all present at the same time. If a complete service does not remedy the situation, major mechanical work is the only solution.

6 An engine overhaul involves restoring all internal parts to the specification of a new engine. During an overhaul, the pistons and the piston rings are renewed. New main and big-end bearings are generally fitted; if

necessary, the crankshaft may be renewed, to restore the journals. The valves are also serviced as well, since they are usually in less-than-perfect condition at this point. While the engine is being overhauled, other components, such as the starter and alternator, can be overhauled as well. The end result should be an as-new engine that will give many trouble-free miles. **Note:** *Critical cooling system components such as the hoses, thermostat and coolant pump should be renewed when an engine is overhauled. The radiator should be checked carefully, to ensure that it is not clogged or leaking. Also, it is a good idea to renew the oil pump whenever the engine is overhauled.*

7 Before beginning the engine overhaul, read through the entire procedure, to familiarise yourself with the scope and requirements of the job. Overhauling an engine is not difficult if you follow carefully all of the instructions, have the necessary tools and equipment, and pay close attention to all specifications. It can, however, be time-consuming. Plan on the car being off the road for a minimum of two weeks, especially if parts must be taken to an engineering works for repair or reconditioning. Check on the availability of parts and make sure that any necessary special tools and equipment are obtained in advance. Most work can be done with typical hand tools, although a number of precision measuring tools are required for inspecting parts to determine if they must be renewed. Often the engineering works will handle the inspection of parts and offer advice concerning reconditioning and renewal. **Note:** *Always wait until the engine has been completely dismantled, and until all components (especially the cylinder block and the crankshaft) have been inspected, before deciding what service and repair operations must be performed by an engineering works. The condition of these components will be the major factor to consider when determining whether to overhaul the original engine, or to buy a reconditioned unit. Do not, therefore, purchase parts or have overhaul work done on other components until they have been thoroughly inspected. As a general rule, time is the primary cost of an overhaul, so it does not pay to fit worn or sub-standard parts.*

8 As a final note, to ensure maximum life and minimum trouble from a reconditioned engine, everything must be assembled with care, in a spotlessly-clean environment.

3 Engine removal – methods and precautions

1 If you have decided that the engine must be removed for overhaul or major repair work, several preliminary steps should be taken.
2 Locating a suitable place to work is extremely important. Adequate work space, along with storage space for the car, will be

needed. If a workshop or garage is not available, at the very least, a flat, level, clean work surface is required.
3 Cleaning the engine compartment and engine/transmission before beginning the removal procedure will help keep tools clean and organised.
4 An engine hoist or A-frame will also be necessary. Make sure the equipment is rated in excess of the combined weight of the engine and transmission. Safety is of primary importance, considering the potential hazards involved in lifting the engine/transmission out of the car.
5 If this is the first time you have removed an engine, an assistant should ideally be available. Advice and aid from someone more experienced would also be helpful. There are many instances when one person cannot simultaneously perform all of the operations required when lifting the engine out of the vehicle.
6 Plan the operation ahead of time. Before starting work, arrange for the hire of or obtain all of the tools and equipment you will need. Some of the equipment necessary to perform engine/transmission removal and installation safely and with relative ease (in addition to an engine hoist) is as follows: a heavy duty trolley jack, complete sets of spanners and sockets as described in the back of this manual, wooden blocks, and plenty of rags and cleaning solvent for mopping-up spilled oil, coolant and fuel. If the hoist must be hired, make sure that you arrange for it in advance, and perform all of the operations possible without it beforehand. This will save you money and time.
7 Plan for the car to be out of use for quite a while. An engineering works will be required to perform some of the work which the do-it-yourselfer cannot accomplish without special equipment. These places often have a busy schedule, so it would be a good idea to consult them before removing the engine, in order to accurately estimate the amount of time required to rebuild or repair components that may need work.
8 Always be extremely careful when removing and refitting the engine/transmission. Serious injury can result from careless actions. Plan ahead and take your time, and a job of this nature, although major, can be accomplished successfully.

4 Petrol engine and transmission unit – removal, separation and refitting

Removal

Note: *The engine can be removed from the car only as a complete unit with the transmission; the two are then separated for overhaul. The engine/transmission unit is lowered out of position, and withdrawn from under the vehicle. Bearing this in mind, ensure*

the vehicle is raised sufficiently so that there is enough clearance between the front of the vehicle and the floor to allow the engine/transmission unit to be slid out once it has been lowered out of position.

1 Park the vehicle on firm, level ground then remove the bonnet as described in Chapter 11.
2 Depressurise the fuel system (see Chapter 4A) then remove the battery and mounting plate as described in Chapter 5A.
3 Chock the rear wheels, then firmly apply the handbrake. Jack up the front of the vehicle. Securely support it on axle stands, bearing in mind the note at the start of this Section. Where necessary, undo the retaining screws and remove the undercover from beneath the engine/transmission unit.
4 If the engine is to be dismantled, working as described in Chapter 1A, first drain the engine oil and remove the oil filter. Also drain the cooling system.
5 Referring to Chapter 4A, carry out the following procedures.
  a) *Remove the air cleaner housing and associated components.*
  b) *Remove the exhaust front pipe.*
  c) *Disconnect the fuel feed and return hoses from the fuel rail/throttle housing.*
  d) *Disconnect the accelerator cable and position it clear of the engine.*
  e) *Disconnect the brake servo hose and various vacuum hoses and from the inlet manifold and exhaust manifolds, noting each hoses correct fitted location.*
  f) *Disconnect the wiring connectors from the inlet manifold electrical components and free the wiring so it can be positioned clear of the engine unit.*
6 Referring to Chapter 3, carry out the following procedures.
  a) *Release the retaining clips and disconnect the various coolant hoses from the cylinder head and the block.*
  b) *On models with air conditioning, unbolt the compressor and position it clear of the engine. Do not open the refrigerant circuit.*
  c) *Release the coolant/air-conditioning hoses/pipes (as applicable) from any relevant clips and ties and position them clear of the engine unit.*
7 Referring to Chapter 5A, disconnect the wiring from the starter motor, alternator, oil pressure warning light switch and (where fitted) the oil level sensor. Unbolt any relevant earth leads from the cylinder block/transmission then unbolt/unclip the wiring from the engine unit and position it clear.
8 Referring to Chapter 10, unbolt the power steering pump and position it clear of the engine unit with its hoses still attached.
9 On models with a manual transmission unit, carry out the following procedures.
  a) *Drain the transmission oil (see Chapter 7A) or be prepared for oil spillage as the engine/transmission unit is removed.*
  b) *Disconnect the wiring connector from the reversing light switch.*

c) Remove the gearchange linkage assembly from the top of the transmission unit (see Chapter 7A).

d) Slide out the retaining clip and disconnect the clutch hose end fitting from the top of the transmission bellhousing (see Chapter 6). Do not depress the clutch pedal whilst the hose is disconnected.

10 On models with an automatic transmission unit, carry out the following procedures as described in Chapter 7B.

a) Drain the transmission fluid.

b) Disconnect the selector cable and position it clear of the transmission.

c) Disconnect the transmission unit wiring connectors.

d) Disconnect the fluid cooler hoses from the transmission.

11 Manoeuvre the engine hoist into position, and attach it to the lifting brackets bolted onto the engine/transmission. Raise the hoist until it is supporting the weight of the engine.

12 With the engine securely supported, remove the front suspension subframe assembly as described in Chapter 10.

13 Referring to Chapter 8, free the driveshaft inner constant velocity joints from the transmission unit and position them clear. Note that it is not necessary to remove the driveshafts, they can be left attached to the hub assemblies. **Note:** *Do not allow the shafts to hang down under their own weight as this could damage the constant velocity joints/gaiters.*

14 Make a final check that any components which would prevent the removal of the engine/transmission from the car have been removed or disconnected. Ensure that components such as the driveshafts are secured so that they cannot be damaged on removal.

15 Slacken and remove the mounting bolts then remove the torque support rod from the right-hand end of the cylinder head.

16 If available, a low trolley should be placed under the engine/transmission assembly, to facilitate its easy removal from under the vehicle. Lower the engine/transmission assembly, making sure that nothing is trapped, taking great care not to damage the radiator/cooling fan assembly. Enlist the help of an assistant during this procedure, as it may be necessary to tilt the assembly slightly to clear the body panels. Great care must be taken to ensure that no components are trapped and damaged during the removal procedure.

17 Detach the hoist and withdraw the engine/transmission unit from under the vehicle.

Separation

Manual transmission models

18 With the engine/transmission assembly removed, support the assembly on suitable blocks of wood, on a workbench (or failing that, on a clean area of the workshop floor).

19 On models with a pressed-steel sump, undo the retaining bolts and remove the flywheel lower cover plate from the transmission.

20 Undo the retaining bolts and remove the starter motor from the transmission (see Chapter 5A).

21 Ensure that both engine and transmission are adequately supported, then slacken and remove the remaining bolts securing the transmission housing to the engine. Note the correct fitted positions of each bolt (and the relevant brackets) as they are removed, to use as a reference on refitting.

22 Carefully withdraw the transmission from the engine, ensuring that the weight of transmission is not allowed to hang on the input shaft while it is engaged with the clutch friction disc.

23 If they are loose, remove the locating dowels from the engine or transmission, and keep them in a safe place.

Automatic transmission models

24 With the engine/transmission assembly removed, support the assembly on suitable blocks of wood, on a workbench (or failing that, on a clean area of the workshop floor).

25 Undo the retaining bolts and remove the starter motor from the transmission (see Chapter 5A).

26 Remove the rubber cover(s) from the cylinder block/sump flange to gain access to the torque converter retaining bolts. Slacken and remove the visible bolt(s) then, using a socket and extension bar to rotate the crankshaft pulley, undo the remaining bolts securing the torque converter to the driveplate as they become accessible. Depending on model, there could be three or six bolts securing the torque converter to the driveplate. Discard the bolts, new ones must be used on refitting.

27 To ensure that the torque converter does not fall out as the transmission is removed, slide the converter along the shaft and fully into the transmission housing.

28 Separate the engine and transmission as described in paragraphs 21 to 23.

Refitting

Manual transmission models

29 If the engine and transmission have been separated, perform the operations described below in paragraphs 30 to 33. If not, proceed as described from paragraph 34 onwards.

30 Ensure the locating dowels are correctly positioned then carefully offer the transmission to the engine, until the locating dowels are engaged. Ensure that the weight of the transmission is not allowed to hang on the input shaft as it is engaged with the clutch friction disc.

31 Refit the transmission housing-to-engine bolts, ensuring that all the necessary brackets are correctly positioned, and tighten them to the specified torque setting.

32 Refit the starter motor and tighten its mounting bolts to the specified torque (see Chapter 5A).

33 On models with a pressed-steel sump, refit the flywheel lower cover plate to the

transmission, and tighten its retaining bolts to the specified torque.

34 Slide the engine/transmission unit into position and reconnect the hoist and lifting tackle to the engine lifting brackets.

35 With the aid of an assistant, carefully lift the assembly into position the engine compartment, manipulating the hoist and lifting tackle as necessary, taking great care not to trap any components.

36 Align the engine with the bracket on the right-hand side of the engine compartment then refit the torque support rod. Tighten the rod bolts by hand only at this stage.

37 Renew the driveshaft oil seals (see Chapter 7A) then carefully engage the driveshaft inner constant velocity joints with the transmission (see Chapter 8).

38 Refit the front suspension subframe as described in Chapter 10.

39 With the subframe assembly correctly installed, tighten the torque rod mounting bolts to the specified torque.

40 The remainder of the refitting procedure is a direct reversal of the removal sequence, noting the following points:

a) Ensure that all wiring is correctly routed and retained by all the relevant retaining clips and that all connectors are correctly and securely reconnected.

b) Ensure that all disturbed hoses are correctly reconnected, and securely retained by their retaining clips.

c) Fit a new sealing ring to the clutch hose end fitting on the transmission unit and reconnect the end fitting, ensuring it is securely retained by the clip. On completion, bleed the hydraulic system as described in Chapter 6.

d) Refit the gearchange linkage to the transmission and adjust as described in Chapter 7A.

e) Adjust the accelerator cable as described in the Chapter 4A.

f) Refill the transmission with correct quantity and type of oil, as described in Chapter 7A. If the oil was not drained, top-up the level as described in Chapter 7A.

g) Refill the engine with oil as described in Chapter 1A and also refill the cooling system.

Automatic transmission models

41 If the engine and transmission have been separated, perform the operations described below in paragraphs 42 to 46. If not, proceed as described from paragraph 47 onwards.

42 Remove all traces of old locking compound from the torque converter threads by running a tap of the correct thread diameter and pitch down the holes. In the absence of a suitable tap, use one of the old bolts with slots cut in its threads.

43 Ensure the engine/transmission locating dowels are correctly positioned and apply a smear of molybdenum disulphide grease to the torque converter locating pin and its centering bush in the crankshaft end.

5.3 Disconnect the coolant hoses (arrowed) from the right-hand end of the cylinder head (2.0 litre model)

5.4a Remove the bolt securing the earth lead to the rear of the cylinder block then disconnect the wiring from the oil pressure switch (arrowed) . . .

5.4b . . . alternator (A) and starter motor (B) then unbolt the wiring tray from the block (2.0 litre model)

44 Carefully offer the transmission to the engine, until the locating dowels are engaged. Refit the transmission housing-to-engine bolts, ensuring that all the necessary brackets are correctly positioned, and tighten them to the specified torque setting.

45 Fit the new torque converter-to-driveplate bolts and tighten them lightly only to start then go around and tighten them to the specified torque setting in a diagonal sequence. Refit the rubber covers to the sump flange.

46 Refit the starter motor and tighten its mounting bolts to the specified torque (see Chapter 5A).

47 Slide the engine/transmission unit into position and reconnect the hoist and lifting tackle to the engine lifting brackets.

48 With the aid of an assistant, carefully lift the assembly into position the engine compartment, manipulating the hoist and lifting tackle as necessary, taking great care not to trap any components.

49 Align the engine with the bracket on the right-hand side of the engine compartment then refit the torque support rod. Tighten the rod bolts by hand only at this stage.

50 Renew the driveshaft oil seals (see Chapter 7B) then carefully engage the driveshaft inner constant velocity joints with the transmission (see Chapter 8).

51 Refit the front suspension subframe as described in Chapter 10.

52 With the subframe assembly correctly installed, tighten the torque rod mounting bolts to the specified torque.

53 The remainder of the refitting procedure is a direct reversal of the removal sequence, noting the following points:

a) Ensure that all wiring is correctly routed and retained by all the relevant retaining clips and that all connectors are correctly and securely reconnected.

b) Ensure that all disturbed hoses are correctly reconnected, and securely retained by their retaining clips.

c) Fit new sealing rings to the transmission fluid cooler hose unions and ensure both unions are securely retained by their clips.

d) Adjust the accelerator cable as described in the Chapter 4A.

e) Refill the transmission with the specified

type and quantity of fluid and adjust the selector cable as described in Chapter 7B.

f) Refill the engine with correct quantity and type of oil, as described in Chapter 1A.

g) Refill the cooling system as described in Chapter 1A.

5 Diesel engine and transmission unit – removal, separation and refitting

Removal

Note: *The engine can be removed from the car only as a complete unit with the transmission; the two are then separated for overhaul. The engine/transmission unit is lowered out of position, and withdrawn from under the vehicle. Bearing this in mind, ensure the vehicle is raised sufficiently so that there is enough clearance between the front of the vehicle and the floor to allow the engine/transmission unit to be slid out once it has been lowered out of position.*

1 Carry out the operations described in paragraphs 1 to 4 of Section 4, noting that it is not necessary to depressurise the fuel system.

2 Referring to Chapter 4B, carry out the following procedures.

a) Remove the air cleaner housing and associated components.

b) Remove the exhaust front pipe.

c) Disconnect the fuel feed and return hoses from the injection pump.

d) Disconnect the brake servo hose and various vacuum hoses and from the inlet manifold and exhaust manifolds, noting each hoses correct fitted location.

e) Disconnect the wiring connectors from the inlet manifold electrical components and free the wiring so it can be positioned clear of the engine unit.

3 Referring to Chapter 3, carry out the following procedures.

a) Release the retaining clips and disconnect the various coolant hoses from the cylinder head and the block **(see illustration)**.

b) On models with air conditioning, unbolt the compressor and position it clear of

the engine. **Do not** open the refrigerant circuit.

c) Release the coolant/air-conditioning hoses/pipes (as applicable) from any relevant clips and ties and position them clear of the engine unit.

4 Referring to Chapter 5, disconnect the wiring from the starter motor, alternator, oil pressure warning light switch and (where fitted) the oil level/oil temperature sensor. Unbolt any relevant earth leads from the cylinder block/transmission then unbolt/unclip the wiring from the engine unit and position it clear **(see illustrations)**.

5 Referring to Chapter 10, unbolt the power steering pump and position it clear of the engine unit with its hoses still attached.

6 Referring to Chapter 7A, carry out the following procedures.

a) Drain the transmission oil or be prepared for oil spillage as the engine/transmission unit is removed.

b) Disconnect the wiring connector from the reversing light switch.

c) Remove the gearchange linkage assembly from the top of the transmission unit.

d) Slide out the retaining clip and disconnect the clutch hose end fitting from the top of the transmission bellhousing. Do not depress the clutch pedal whilst the hose is disconnected.

7 Manoeuvre the engine hoist into position, and attach it to the lifting brackets bolted onto the engine/transmission **(see illustration)**. Raise the hoist until it is supporting the weight of the engine.

5.7 Attach the engine hoist to the lifting brackets on the cylinder head

8 With the engine securely supported, remove the front suspension subframe assembly as described in Chapter 10.

9 Referring to Chapter 8, free the driveshaft inner constant velocity joints from the transmission unit and position them clear. Note that it is not necessary to remove the driveshafts, they can be left attached to the hub assemblies. **Note:** *Do not allow the shafts to hang down under their own weight as this could damage the constant velocity joints/gaiters.*

10 Make a final check that any components which would prevent the removal of the engine/transmission from the car have been removed or disconnected. Ensure that components such as the driveshafts are secured so that they cannot be damaged on removal.

11 Undo the retaining nuts and remove the bracket securing the right-hand engine mounting to the cylinder head.

12 If available, a low trolley should be placed under the engine/transmission assembly, to facilitate its easy removal from under the vehicle. Lower the engine/transmission assembly, making sure that nothing is trapped, taking great care not to damage the radiator/cooling fan assembly **(see illustration)**. Enlist the help of an assistant during this procedure, as it may be necessary to tilt the assembly slightly to clear the body panels. Great care must be taken to ensure that no components are trapped and damaged during the removal procedure.

13 Detach the hoist and withdraw the engine/transmission unit from under the vehicle.

Separation

14 Refer to Section 4.

Refitting

15 If the engine and transmission have been separated, perform the operations described below in paragraphs 16 to 18. If not, proceed as described from paragraph 19 onwards.

16 Ensure the locating dowels are correctly positioned then carefully offer the transmission to the engine, until the locating dowels are engaged. Ensure that the weight of the transmission is not allowed to hang on the input shaft as it is engaged with the clutch friction disc.

17 Refit the transmission housing-to-engine bolts, ensuring that all the necessary brackets are correctly positioned, and tighten them to the specified torque setting.

18 Refit the starter motor and tighten its mounting bolts to the specified torque (see Chapter 5A).

19 Slide the engine/transmission unit into position and reconnect the hoist and lifting tackle to the engine lifting brackets.

20 With the aid of an assistant, carefully lift the assembly into position the engine compartment, manipulating the hoist and

lifting tackle as necessary, taking great care not to trap any components.

21 Align the engine with the right-hand mounting then refit the mounting bracket, tightening its nuts by hand only at this stage.

22 Renew the driveshaft oil seals (see Chapter 7A) then carefully engage the driveshaft inner constant velocity joints with the transmission (see Chapter 8).

23 Refit the front suspension subframe as described in Chapter 10.

24 With the subframe assembly correctly installed, tighten the right-hand mounting bracket nuts to the specified torque.

25 The remainder of the refitting procedure is a direct reversal of the removal sequence, noting the following points:

a) *Ensure that all wiring is correctly routed and retained by all the relevant retaining clips and that all connectors are correctly and securely reconnected.*

b) *Ensure that all disturbed hoses are correctly reconnected, and securely retained by their retaining clips.*

c) *Fit new sealing washers to the injection pump fuel hose unions and tighten the union bolts to the specified torque (see Chapter 4B).*

d) *Fit a new sealing ring to the clutch fitting on the transmission unit and reconnect the end fitting, ensuring it is securely retained by the clip. On completion, check the bleed the hydraulic system as described in Chapter 6.*

e) *Refit the gearchange linkage to the transmission and adjust as described in Chapter 7A.*

f) *Refill the transmission with correct quantity and type of oil, as described in Chapter 7A. If the oil was not drained, top-up the level as described in Chapter 7A.*

g) *Refill the engine with oil as described in Chapter 1B and also refill the cooling system.*

5.12 Ensure all components are disconnected then carefully lower the engine/transmission unit and manoeuvre it out from underneath the vehicle

6 Engine overhaul – dismantling sequence

1 It is much easier to dismantle and work on the engine if it is mounted on a portable engine stand. These stands can often be hired from a tool hire shop. Before the engine is mounted on a stand, the flywheel/driveplate should be removed, so that the stand bolts can be tightened into the end of the cylinder block.

2 If a stand is not available, it is possible to dismantle the engine with it blocked up on a sturdy workbench, or on the floor. Be extra-careful not to tip or drop the engine when working without a stand.

3 If you are going to obtain a reconditioned engine, all the external components must be removed first, to be transferred to the replacement engine (just as they will if you are doing a complete engine overhaul yourself). These components include the following:

a) *Inlet and exhaust manifolds (Chapter 4).*
b) *Alternator/power steering pump/air conditioning compressor bracket(s) (as applicable).*
c) *Coolant pump (Chapter 3).*
d) *Fuel system components (Chapter 4).*
e) *Wiring harness and all electrical switches and sensors.*
f) *Oil filter (Chapter 1).*
g) *Flywheel/driveplate (relevant Part of this Chapter).*

Note: *When removing the external components from the engine, pay close attention to details that may be helpful or important during refitting. Note the fitted position of gaskets, seals, spacers, pins, washers, bolts, and other small items.*

4 If you are obtaining a 'short' engine (which consists of the engine cylinder block, crankshaft, pistons and connecting rods all assembled), then the cylinder head, sump, oil pump, and timing belt/chains (as applicable) will have to be removed also.

5 If you are planning a complete overhaul, the engine can be dismantled, and the internal components removed, in the order given below, referring to the relevant Part of this Chapter unless otherwise stated.

a) *Inlet and exhaust manifolds (Chapter 4).*
b) *Timing belt, sprockets and tensioner – all models except 2.2 litre petrol and all diesel engines.*
c) *Cylinder head.*
d) *Flywheel/driveplate.*
e) *Sump.*
f) *Oil pump.*
g) *Timing chains and sprockets – 2.2 litre petrol and all diesel engines.*
h) *Piston/connecting rod assemblies.*
i) *Crankshaft.*

6 Before beginning the dismantling and overhaul procedures, make sure that you have all of the correct tools necessary. Refer to the *Tools and working facilities* Section of this manual for further information.

7.5a Using a valve spring compressor . . .

7.5b . . . compress the valve spring until the collets can be removed from the valve

7.5c Remove the compressor then lift off the spring retainer . . .

7.5d . . . and remove the valve spring

7.5e Pull the seal off the top of the valve guide . . .

7.5f . . . then remove the spring seat

7 Cylinder head – dismantling

Note: *New and reconditioned cylinder heads are available from the manufacturer, and from engine overhaul specialists. Be aware that some specialist tools are required for the dismantling and inspection procedures, and new components may not be readily available. It may therefore be more practical and economical for the home mechanic to purchase a reconditioned head, rather than dismantle, inspect and recondition the original head.*

1 On 1.6 litre SOHC petrol engine, referring to Part A of this Chapter, remove the cylinder head from the engine then lift the camshaft followers, thrust pads and hydraulic tappets out from the cylinder head.

2 On 1.6, 1.8 and 2.0 litre DOHC petrol engines remove the camshafts and followers as described in Part B of this Chapter then remove the cylinder head from the engine.

3 On 2.2 litre DOHC petrol engines, working as described in Part C of this Chapter, remove the camshaft, followers and shims from the cylinder head then remove the cylinder head from the engine.

4 On 2.0 and 2.2 litre diesel engines, working as described in Part D of this Chapter, remove the camshaft, followers and hydraulic tappets from the cylinder head. Unscrew the glow plugs (Chapter 5C) then remove the cylinder head from the engine.

5 On all models, using a valve spring compressor, compress each valve spring in turn until the split collets can be removed. Release the compressor, and lift off the spring retainer and spring. Using a pair of pliers, carefully extract the valve stem seal from the top of the guide then slide off the spring seat **(see illustrations)**.

6 If, when the valve spring compressor is screwed down, the spring retainer refuses to free and expose the split collets, gently tap the top of the tool, directly over the retainer, with a light hammer. This will free the retainer.

7 Withdraw the valve through the combustion chamber. It is essential that each valve is stored together with its collets, retainer, spring, and spring seat **(see Haynes Hint)**. The valves should also be kept in their correct sequence, unless they are so badly worn that they are to be renewed.

8 Cylinder head and valves – cleaning and inspection

1 Thorough cleaning of the cylinder head and valve components, followed by a detailed inspection, will enable you to decide how much valve service work must be carried out during the engine overhaul. **Note:** *If the engine has been severely overheated, it is best to assume that the cylinder head is warped – check carefully for signs of this.*

Cleaning

2 Scrape away all traces of old gasket material from the cylinder head.

3 Scrape away the carbon from the combustion chambers and ports, then wash the cylinder head thoroughly with paraffin or a suitable solvent.

4 Scrape off any heavy carbon deposits that may have formed on the valves, then use a power-operated wire brush to remove deposits from the valve heads and stems.

Inspection

Note: *Be sure to perform all the following inspection procedures before concluding that the services of a machine shop or engine overhaul specialist are required. Make a list of all items that require attention.*

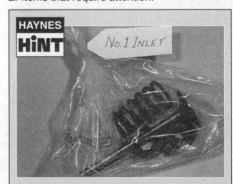

If the components are to be refitted, place each valve and its associated components in a labelled polythene bag or similar small container, and mark the bag/container with the relevant valve number to ensure that it is refitted in its original location.

8.6 Using a straight-edge and feeler gauge to check cylinder head surface distortion

8.12 Using a micrometer to measure valve stem diameter

8.15 Grinding-in a valve

Cylinder head

5 Inspect the head very carefully for cracks, evidence of coolant leakage, and other damage. If cracks are found, a new cylinder head should be obtained.

6 Use a straight-edge and feeler gauge blade to check that the cylinder head surface is not distorted **(see illustration)**. If it is, it may be possible to resurface it, provided that the cylinder head is not reduced to less than the minimum specified height.

7 Examine the valve seats in each of the combustion chambers. If they are severely pitted, cracked or burned, then they will need to be recut by an engine overhaul specialist. If they are only slightly pitted, this can be removed by grinding-in the valve heads and seats with fine valve-grinding compound, as described below.

8 If the valve guides are worn (indicated by a side-to-side motion of the valve, and accompanied by excessive blue smoke in the exhaust when running) new guides must be fitted. Measure the diameter of the existing valve stems (see below) and the bore of the guides, then calculate the clearance and compare the result with the specified value. If the clearance is not within the specified limits, renew the valves and/or guides as necessary.

9 The renewal of valve guides is best carried out by an engine overhaul specialist. If the work is to be carried out at home, however, use a stepped, double-diameter drift to drive out the worn guide towards the combustion chamber. On fitting the new guide, place it first in a deep-freeze for one hour, then drive it into its cylinder head bore from the camshaft side until it projects the specified amount above the cylinder head surface (where no measurement is given seek the advice of a Vauxhall dealer).

10 If the valve seats are to be recut this must be done only after the guides have been renewed.

Valves

11 Examine the head of each valve for pitting, burning, cracks and general wear, and check the valve stem for scoring and wear ridges. Rotate the valve, and check for any obvious indication that it is bent. Look for pitting and excessive wear on the tip of each valve stem. Renew any valve that shows any such signs of wear or damage.

12 If the valve appears satisfactory at this stage, measure the valve stem diameter at several points using a micrometer **(see illustration)**. Any significant difference in the readings obtained indicates wear of the valve stem. Should any of these conditions be apparent, the valve(s) must be renewed.

13 If the valves are in satisfactory condition, they should be ground (lapped) into their respective seats, to ensure a smooth gas-tight seal. If the seat is only lightly pitted, or if it has been recut, fine grinding compound **only** should be used to produce the required finish. Coarse valve-grinding compound should **not** be used unless a seat is badly burned or deeply pitted; if this is the case, the cylinder head and valves should be inspected by an expert to decide whether seat recutting, or even the renewal of the valve or seat insert, is required.

14 Valve grinding is carried out as follows. Place the cylinder head upside-down on a bench.

15 Smear a trace of the appropriate grade of valve-grinding compound on the seat face, and press a suction grinding tool onto the valve head. With a semi-rotary action, grind the valve head to its seat, lifting the valve occasionally to redistribute the grinding compound **(see illustration)**. A light spring placed under the valve head will greatly ease this operation.

16 If coarse grinding compound is being used, work only until a dull, matt even surface

9.1 Lubricate the valve stem with engine oil and insert the valve into the correct guide

is produced on both the valve seat and the valve, then wipe off the used compound and repeat the process with fine compound. When a smooth unbroken ring of light grey matt finish is produced on both the valve and seat, the grinding operation is complete. **Do not** grind in the valves any further than absolutely necessary, or the seat will be prematurely sunk into the cylinder head.

17 When all the valves have been ground-in, carefully wash off all traces of grinding compound using paraffin or a suitable solvent before reassembly of the cylinder head.

Valve components

18 Examine the valve springs for signs of damage and discoloration; if possible; also compare the existing spring free length with new components.

19 Stand each spring on a flat surface, and check it for squareness. If any of the springs are damaged, distorted or have lost their tension, obtain a complete new set of springs.

20 On 1.6 litre SOHC engines, the exhaust valve spring seats incorporate a bearing; the bearing rotates the valve which helps to keep the valve seat clean. If any spring seats bearing shows signs of wear or does not rotate smoothly then the seat should be renewed.

9 Cylinder head – reassembly

1 Lubricate the stems of the valves, and insert them into their original locations **(see illustration)**. If new valves are being fitted, insert them into the locations to which they have been ground.

2 Working on the first valve, refit the spring seat. Dip the new valve stem seal in fresh engine oil, then carefully locate it over the valve and onto the guide. Take care not to damage the seal as it is passed over the valve stem. Use a suitable socket or metal tube to press the seal firmly onto the guide. **Note:** *If genuine seals are being fitted, use the oil seal protector which is supplied with the seals; the protector fits over the valve stem and prevents the oil seal lip being damaged on the valve (see illustrations).*

9.2a Fit the spring seat . . .

9.2b . . . then fit the seal protector (where supplied) to the valve . . .

9.2c . . . and install the new valve guide oil seal . . .

9.2d . . . pressing it onto the valve guide with a suitable socket

9.3 Refit the valve spring and fit the spring retainer

9.4 Compress the valve and locate the collets in the recess on the valve stem

3 Locate the spring on the seat and fit the spring retainer (see illustration).

4 Compress the valve spring, and locate the split collets in the recess in the valve stem (see illustration and Haynes Hint). Release the compressor, then repeat the procedure on the remaining valves.

5 With all the valves installed, support the cylinder head on the bench and, using a hammer and interposed block of wood, tap the end of each valve stem to settle the components.

6 On 1.6 litre SOHC engine, working as described in Part A, refit the hydraulic tappets, thrust pads and followers to the head then refit the cylinder head.

7 On 1.6, 1.8 and 2.0 litre DOHC petrol

Use a little dab of grease to hold the collets in position on the valve stem while the spring compressor is released.

engines, working as described in Part B, refit the cylinder head to the engine and install the followers and camshafts.

8 On 2.2 litre DOHC petrol engines, working as described in Part C, refit the cylinder head to the engine and install the followers, shims and camshaft.

9 On 2.0 and 2.2 litre diesel engines, working as described in Part D, refit the cylinder head to the engine and install the hydraulic tappets, followers and camshaft.

10 Piston/connecting rod assembly – removal

Note: New connecting rod big-end cap bolts will be needed on refitting.

1 On 1.6 litre petrol engines, remove the cylinder head and sump then unbolt the pick-up/strainer from the base of the oil pump. Refer to Part A for information on SOHC engine and Part B for information on the DOHC engine.

2 On 1.8 and 2.0 litre DOHC engines, referring to Part B of this Chapter, remove the cylinder head and sump then unbolt the pick-up/strainer from the base of the oil pump. Undo the retaining screws and remove the baffle plate from the base of the cylinder block. To further improve access, evenly and progressively slacken the retaining bolts and remove the main bearing ladder casting from the base of the block.

3 On 2.2 litre petrol engines, referring to Part C

of this Chapter, remove the cylinder head and sump then remove the cylinder block lower casing.

4 On 2.0 and 2.2 litre diesel engines, working as described in Part D of this Chapter, remove the cylinder head and sump and unbolt the pick-up/strainer from the base of the oil pump.

5 On all models, if there is a pronounced wear ridge at the top of any bore, it may be necessary to remove it with a scraper or ridge reamer, to avoid piston damage during removal. Such a ridge indicates excessive wear of the cylinder bore.

6 Prior to removal, using feeler blades, measuring the connecting rod big-end side clearance of each rod (see illustration). If any rod exceeds the specified clearance, it must be renewed.

7 Using a hammer and centre-punch, paint or similar, mark each connecting rod and its

10.6 Checking connecting rod big-end side clearance

10.7 Prior to removal, make identification markings on the connecting rods and bearing caps (circled). Note that lug on the bearing cap faces towards the flywheel/driveplate end of the engine

bearing cap with its respective cylinder number on the flat machined surface provided; if the engine has been dismantled before, note carefully any identifying marks made previously **(see illustration)**. Note that No 1 cylinder is at the timing belt/chain (as applicable) end of the engine.

8 Turn the crankshaft to bring pistons 1 and 4 to BDC (bottom dead centre).

9 Unscrew the bolts from No 1 piston big-end bearing cap, then take off the cap and recover the bottom half-bearing shell. If the bearing shells are to be re-used, tape the cap and the shell together.

Caution: On some engines, the connecting rod/bearing cap mating surfaces are not machined flat; the big-end bearing caps are 'cracked' off from the rod during production and left untouched to ensure the cap and rod mate perfectly. Where this type of connecting rod is fitted, great care must be taken to ensure the mating surfaces of the cap and rod are not marked or damaged in anyway. Any damage to the mating surfaces will adversely affect the strength of the connecting rod and could lead to premature failure.

10 Using a hammer handle, push the piston up through the bore, and remove it from the top of the cylinder block. Recover the bearing shell, and tape it to the connecting rod for safe-keeping.

11 Loosely refit the big-end cap to the connecting rod, and secure with the nuts/bolts – this will help to keep the components in their correct order.

12 Remove No 4 piston assembly in the same way.

13 Turn the crankshaft through 180° to bring pistons 2 and 3 to BDC (bottom dead centre), and remove them in the same way.

11 Crankshaft – removal

Note: *New main bearing cap bolts will be required on refitting.*

1.6 litre petrol engine

1 Remove the oil pump and flywheel/driveplate. Refer to Part A for information on SOHC engine and Part B for information on the DOHC engine.

2 Remove the piston and connecting rod assemblies as described in Section 10. If no work is to be done on the pistons and connecting rods, unbolt the caps and push the pistons far enough up the bores that the connecting rods are positioned clear of the crankshaft journals.

3 Check the crankshaft endfloat as described in Section 14, then proceed as follows.

4 The main bearing caps should be numbered 1 to 5 from the timing belt end of the engine and all identification numbers should be the right way up when read from the rear of the cylinder block **(see illustration)**. **Note:** *On some engines the flywheel/driveplate end (number 5) bearing cap may not be numbered but is easily identified anyway.* If the bearing caps are not marked, using a hammer and punch or a suitable marker pen, number the caps from 1 to 5 from the timing belt end of the engine and mark each cap to indicate its correct fitted direction to avoid confusion on refitting.

5 Working in a diagonal sequence, evenly and progressively slacken the ten main bearing cap retaining bolts by half a turn at a time until all bolts are loose. Remove all bolts.

6 Carefully remove each cap from the cylinder block, ensuring that the lower main bearing shell remains in position in the cap.

7 Carefully lift out the crankshaft, taking care not to displace the upper main bearing shells **(see illustration)**. Remove the oil seal and discard it.

8 Recover the upper bearing shells from the cylinder block, and tape them to their respective caps for safe-keeping.

1.8 and 2.0 litre petrol engines

9 Remove the flywheel/driveplate and the oil pump as described in Part B of the Chapter.

10 Undo the retaining screws and remove the baffle plate from the base of the cylinder block. **Note:** *The oil baffle plate is only fitted to engines without a balancer unit.*

11 Evenly and progressively slacken the retaining bolts and remove the main bearing ladder casting (and balancer unit on 2.0 litre models – see Chapter 2B, Section 18) from the base of the block.

12 Remove the crankshaft as described in paragraphs 2 to 8.

2.2 litre petrol engines

13 Working as described in Part C of this Chapter, remove the flywheel and unbolt the oil pump cover from the right-hand end of the cylinder block.

14 Evenly and progressively slacken the retaining bolts and unbolt the lower main bearing cylinder block casing and remove it from the cylinder block **(see illustration)**. If the housing locating dowels are a loose fit, remove them and store them with the housing for safe-keeping.

15 Remove the piston and connecting rod assemblies as described in Section 10. If no work is to be done on the pistons and connecting rods, unbolt the caps and push the pistons far enough up the bores that the connecting rods are positioned clear of the crankshaft journals.

16 Check the crankshaft endfloat as described in Section 14, then remove the crankshaft and upper bearing shells as described in paragraphs 7 and 8

Diesel engines

17 Working as described in Part D of this Chapter, remove the crankshaft timing chain sprocket and the flywheel.

18 Evenly and progressively slacken and remove the retaining bolts then remove the

11.4 Main bearing cap identification markings (arrowed)

11.7 Removing the crankshaft

11.14 Lifting the lower main bearing cylinder block casing from the cylinder block

main bearing ladder casting or balancer unit (on 2.2 litre models) from the base of the bearing caps, noting which way around it is fitted.

19 Remove the crankshaft as described in paragraphs 2 to 8 noting that the bearing cap identification markings are different. On this engine, it will be necessary to make identification markings on each cap as only caps number 1 and 2 are marked by the manufacturer **(see illustration)**. Number the caps 1 to 5 from the timing chain end of the engine, marking each cap to indicate its correct fitted direction to avoid confusion on refitting.

12 Cylinder block – cleaning and inspection

Cleaning

1 Remove all external components and electrical switches/sensors from the block. For complete cleaning, the core plugs should ideally be removed. Drill a small hole in the plugs, then insert a self-tapping screw into the hole. Pull out the plugs by pulling on the screw with a pair of grips, or by using a slide hammer.

2 On diesel engines remove the piston oil spray nozzles from inside the cylinder block, the nozzles are retained by bolts **(see illustration)**.

3 Scrape all traces of gasket from the cylinder block, and from the main bearing casting (where fitted), taking care not to damage the gasket/sealing surfaces.

4 Remove all oil gallery plugs (where fitted). The plugs are usually very tight – they may have to be drilled out, and the holes retapped. Use new plugs when the engine is reassembled.

5 If any of the castings are extremely dirty, all should be steam-cleaned.

6 After the castings are returned, clean all oil holes and oil galleries one more time. Flush all internal passages with warm water until the water runs clear. Dry thoroughly, and apply a light film of oil to all mating surfaces, to prevent rusting. Also oil the cylinder bores. If you have access to compressed air, use it to speed up the drying process, and to blow out all the oil holes and galleries.

 Warning: Wear eye protection when using compressed air.

7 If the castings are not very dirty, you can do an adequate cleaning job with hot (as hot as you can stand), soapy water and a stiff brush. Take plenty of time, and do a thorough job. Regardless of the cleaning method used, be sure to clean all oil holes and galleries very thoroughly, and to dry all components well. Protect the cylinder bores as described above, to prevent rusting.

8 All threaded holes must be clean, to ensure accurate torque readings during reassembly.

11.19 On 2.0 litre diesel engines, only number 1 and 2 main bearing caps are marked by the manufacturer (arrowed)

To clean the threads, run the correct-size tap into each of the holes to remove rust, corrosion, thread sealant or sludge, and to restore damaged threads. If possible, use compressed air to clear the holes of debris produced by this operation. A good alternative is to inject aerosol-applied water-dispersant lubricant into each hole, using the long spout usually supplied.

 Warning: Wear eye protection when cleaning out these holes in this way.

9 Apply suitable sealant to the new oil gallery plugs, and insert them into the holes in the block. Tighten them securely.

10 On diesel engines refit the piston oil spray nozzles to the cylinder block, and tighten the retaining bolts to the specified torque **(see illustration)**.

11 If the engine is not going to be reassembled right away, cover it with a large plastic bag to keep it clean; protect all mating surfaces and the cylinder bores as described above, to prevent rusting.

Inspection

12 Visually check the castings for cracks and corrosion. Look for stripped threads in the threaded holes. If there has been any history of internal water leakage, it may be worthwhile having an engine overhaul specialist check the cylinder block/crankcase with special equipment. If defects are found, have them repaired if possible, or renew the assembly.

13 Check the bore of each cylinder for scuffing and scoring.

14 Measure the diameter of each cylinder bore at the top (just below the wear ridge), centre and bottom of the bore, both parallel to the crankshaft axis and at right angles to it, so that a total of six measurements are taken. Note that there are various size groups of standard bore diameter to allow for manufacturing tolerances; the size group markings are stamped on the cylinder block.

15 Compare the results with the Specifications at the beginning of this Chapter; if any measurement exceeds the service limit specified, the cylinder block must be rebored if possible, or renewed and new piston assemblies fitted.

16 If the cylinder bores are badly scuffed or scored, or if they are excessively worn, out-of-round or tapered, or if the piston-to-bore clearance is excessive (see Section 13), the cylinder block must be rebored (if possible) or renewed and new pistons fitted. Oversize (0.5 mm) pistons are available for all engines.

17 If the bores are in reasonably good condition and not worn to the specified limits, then the piston rings should be renewed. If this is the case, the bores should be honed to allow the new rings to bed in correctly and provide the best possible seal. The conventional type of hone has spring-loaded stones, and is used with a power drill. You will also need some paraffin (or honing oil) and rags. The hone should be moved up-and-down the bore to produce a crosshatch pattern, and plenty of honing oil should be used. Ideally, the crosshatch lines should intersect at approximately a 60° angle. Do not take off more material than is necessary to produce the required finish. If new pistons are being fitted, the piston manufacturers may specify a finish with a different angle, so their instructions should be followed. Do not withdraw the hone from the bore while it is still being turned – stop it first. After honing a bore, wipe out all traces of the honing oil. If equipment of this type is not available, or if you are not sure whether you are competent to undertake the task yourself, an engine overhaul specialist will carry out the work at moderate cost.

12.2 On diesel engines unscrew the retaining bolts and remove the piston oil spray nozzles from the cylinder block

12.10 On diesel engines refit the oil spray nozzles and tighten the retaining bolts to the specified torque

13.2 Using a feeler blade to remove a piston ring

13 Piston/connecting rod assembly – inspection

1 Before the inspection process can begin, the piston/connecting rod assemblies must be cleaned, and the original piston rings removed from the pistons.

2 Carefully expand the old rings over the top of the pistons. The use of two or three old feeler blades will be helpful in preventing the rings dropping into empty grooves **(see illustration)**. Be careful not to scratch the piston with the ends of the ring. The rings are brittle, and will snap if they are spread too far. They're also very sharp – protect your hands and fingers. Note that the third (oil control) ring consists of a spacer and two side rails. Always remove the rings from the top of the piston. Keep each set of rings with its piston if the old rings are to be re-used.

3 Scrape away all traces of carbon from the top of the piston. A hand-held wire brush (or a piece of fine emery cloth) can be used, once the majority of the deposits have been scraped away. The piston identification markings should now be visible.

4 Remove the carbon from the ring grooves in the piston, using an old ring. Break the ring in half to do this (be careful not to cut your fingers – piston rings are sharp). Be careful to remove only the carbon deposits – do not remove any metal, and do not nick or scratch the sides of the ring grooves.

5 Once the deposits have been removed,

clean the piston/connecting rod assembly with paraffin or a suitable solvent, and dry thoroughly. Make sure that the oil return holes in the ring grooves are clear.

6 If the cylinder bores are not damaged or worn excessively, and if the cylinder block does not need to be rebored (see Section 12), check the pistons as follows.

7 Carefully inspect each piston for cracks around the skirt, around the gudgeon pin holes, and at the piston ring 'lands' (between the ring grooves).

8 Look for scoring and scuffing on the piston skirt, holes in the piston crown, and burned areas at the edge of the crown. If the skirt is scored or scuffed, the engine may have been suffering from overheating, and/or abnormal combustion which caused excessively high operating temperatures. The cooling and lubrication systems should be checked thoroughly. Scorch marks on the sides of the pistons show that blow-by has occurred. A hole in the piston crown, or burned areas at the edge of the piston crown, indicates that abnormal combustion (pre-ignition, knocking, or detonation) has been occurring. If any of the above problems exist, the causes must be investigated and corrected, or the damage will occur again. The causes may include incorrect ignition/injection pump timing (as applicable), or a faulty injector.

9 Corrosion of the piston, in the form of pitting, indicates that coolant has been leaking into the combustion chamber and/or the crankcase. Again, the cause must be corrected, or the problem may persist in the rebuilt engine.

10 Measure the piston diameter at right angles to the gudgeon pin axis; compare the results with the Specifications at the beginning of this Chapter. Note that there are various size groups of standard piston diameter to allow for manufacturing tolerances; the size group markings are stamped on the piston crown.

11 To measure the piston-to-bore clearance, either measure the bore (see Section 12) and piston skirt as described and subtract the skirt diameter from the bore measurement, or insert each piston into its original bore, then select a feeler gauge blade and slip it into the bore along with the piston. The piston must be aligned exactly in its normal attitude, and the feeler gauge blade must be between the piston and bore, on one of the thrust faces, just up from the bottom of the bore. Divide the measured clearance by two, to provide the clearance when the piston is central in the bore. If the clearance is excessive, a new piston will be required. If the piston binds at the lower end of the bore and is loose towards the top, the bore is tapered. If tight spots are encountered as the piston/feeler gauge blade is rotated in the bore, the bore is out-of-round.

12 Repeat this procedure for the remaining pistons and cylinder bores. Any piston which is worn beyond the specified limits must be renewed.

Petrol engines

13 Examine each connecting rod carefully for signs of damage, such as cracks around the big-end and small-end bearings. Check that the rod is not bent or distorted. Damage is highly unlikely, unless the engine has been seized or badly overheated. Detailed checking of the connecting rod assembly can only be carried out by a Vauxhall dealer or engine repair specialist with the necessary equipment.

14 The gudgeon pins are an interference fit in the connecting rod small-end bearing. Therefore, piston and/or connecting rod renewal should be entrusted to a Vauxhall dealer or engine repair specialist, who will have the necessary tooling to remove and install the gudgeon pins. If new pistons are to be fitted, ensure that the correct size group pistons are fitted to each bore. **Note:** *Vauxhall state that the piston/connecting rod assemblies should not be disassembled. If any components requires renewal, then the complete assembly must be renewed. Do not fit a new piston to an old connecting rod or vice-versa.*

Diesel engines

15 The gudgeon pins are of the floating type, secured in position by two circlips. On these engines, the pistons and connecting rods can be separated as follows.

16 Using a small flat-bladed screwdriver, prise out the circlips, and push out the gudgeon pin **(see illustration)**. Hand pressure should be sufficient to remove the pin. Identify the piston and rod to ensure correct reassembly. Discard the circlips – new ones *must* be used on refitting.

17 Examine the gudgeon pin and connecting rod small-end bearing for signs of wear or damage **(see illustration)**. Wear will require the renewal of both the pin and connecting rod.

18 The connecting rods themselves should not be in need of renewal, unless seizure or some other major mechanical failure has occurred. Check the alignment of the connecting rods visually, and if the rods are not straight, take them to an engine overhaul specialist for a more detailed check.

19 Examine all components, and obtain any new parts from your Vauxhall dealer. If new pistons are purchased, they will be supplied

13.16 On diesel engines prise out the circlips then remove the gudgeon pin and separate the piston and connecting rod

13.17 Measuring gudgeon pin diameter with a micrometer

13.20 Piston/connecting rod assembly components

1 Circlip
2 Gudgeon pin
3 Arrow on piston crown
4 Piston
5 Connecting rod
6 Connecting rod assembly mark

complete with gudgeon pins and circlips. Circlips can also be purchased individually.

20 Assemble the piston and connecting rod so that the arrow on the piston crown is pointing away from the assembly mark which is cast onto one side of the connecting rod, on the top of the big-end bore **(see illustration)**.

21 Apply a smear of clean engine oil to the gudgeon pin. Slide it into the piston and through the connecting rod small-end. Check that the piston pivots freely on the rod, then secure the gudgeon pin in position with two new circlips, ensuring that each circlip is correctly located in its groove in the piston. Make sure that both circlips are positioned so that their end gaps are at the top **(see illustrations)**.

13.21a Ensure the piston and connecting rod are correctly assembled then insert the gudgeon pin . . .

14 Crankshaft – inspection

Checking endfloat

1 If the crankshaft endfloat is to be checked, this must be done when the crankshaft is still installed in the cylinder block, but is free to move (see Section 11).

2 Check the endfloat using a dial gauge in contact with the end of the crankshaft. Push the crankshaft fully one way, and then zero the gauge. Push the crankshaft fully the other way, and check the endfloat **(see illustration)**. The result can be compared with the specified amount, and will give an indication as to whether new main bearing shells are required.

3 If a dial gauge is not available, feeler gauges can be used. First push the crankshaft fully towards the flywheel/driveplate end of the engine, then use feeler gauges to measure the gap between the web of the crankpin and the side of thrustwasher **(see illustration)**. The thrustwashers are incorporated into number 2 main bearing shell on the 2.2 litre petrol engine, and number 3 main bearing shells on all other models.

Inspection

4 Clean the crankshaft using paraffin or a suitable solvent, and dry it, preferably with compressed air if available. Be sure to clean the oil holes with a pipe cleaner or similar probe, to ensure that they are not obstructed.

13.21b . . . and secure it in position with new circlips. On 2.0 litre engines position the circlip end gap at the top

⚠ *Warning: Wear eye protection when using compressed air.*

5 Check the main and big-end bearing journals for uneven wear, scoring, pitting and cracking.

6 Big-end bearing wear is accompanied by distinct metallic knocking when the engine is running (particularly noticeable when the engine is pulling from low speed) and some loss of oil pressure.

7 Main bearing wear is accompanied by severe engine vibration and rumble – getting progressively worse as engine speed increases – and again by loss of oil pressure.

8 Check the bearing journal for roughness by running a finger lightly over the bearing surface. Any roughness (which will be accompanied by obvious bearing wear) indicates that the crankshaft requires regrinding (where possible) or renewal.

9 Check for burrs around the crankshaft oil holes (the holes are usually chamfered, so burrs should not be a problem unless regrinding has been carried out carelessly). Remove any burrs with a fine file or scraper, and thoroughly clean the oil holes as described previously.

10 Using a micrometer, measure the diameter of the main and big-end bearing journals, and compare the results with the Specifications **(see illustration)**. By measuring the diameter at a number of points around each journal's circumference, you will be able to determine whether or not the journal is out-of-round. Take the measure-

14.2 Check the crankshaft endfloat using a dial gauge . . .

14.3 . . . or a feeler gauge

14.10 Using a micrometer to measure a crankshaft main bearing journal diameter

15.1 Typical main bearing shell identification markings

ment at each end of the journal, near the webs, to determine if the journal is tapered. Compare the results obtained with those given in the Specifications.

11 Check the oil seal contact surfaces at each end of the crankshaft for wear and damage. If the seal has worn a deep groove in the surface of the crankshaft, consult an engine overhaul specialist; repair may be possible, but otherwise a new crankshaft will be required.

12 Set the crankshaft up in V-blocks, and position a dial gauge on the top of the crankshaft number 1 main bearing journal. Zero the dial gauge, then slowly rotate the crankshaft through two complete revolutions, noting the journal run-out. Repeat the procedure on the remaining four main bearing journals, so that a run-out measurement is available for all main bearing journals. If the difference between the run-out of any two journals exceeds the service limit given in the Specifications, the crankshaft must be renewed.

13 Undersize (0.25 mm and 0.50 mm) big-end and main bearing shells are produced by

FATIGUE FAILURE

CRATERS OR POCKETS

IMPROPER SEATING

BRIGHT
(POLISHED) SECTIONS

SCRATCHED BY DIRT

DIRT EMBEDDED INTO
BEARING MATERIAL

LACK OF OIL

OVERLAY WIPED OUT

EXCESSIVE WEAR

OVERLAY WIPED OUT

TAPERED JOURNAL

RADIUS RIDE

H 28395

15.2 Typical bearing failures

Vauxhall for all engines. If the crankshaft journals have not already been reground, it may be possible to have the crankshaft reconditioned, and to fit undersize shells.

15 Main and big-end bearings – inspection

1 Even though the main and big-end bearings should be renewed during the engine overhaul, the old bearings should be retained for close examination, as they may reveal valuable information about the condition of the engine **(see illustration)**.

2 Bearing failure can occur due to lack of lubrication, the presence of dirt or other foreign particles, overloading the engine, or corrosion **(see illustration)**. Regardless of the cause of bearing failure, the cause must be corrected (where applicable) before the engine is reassembled, to prevent it from happening again.

3 When examining the bearing shells, remove them from the cylinder block, the main bearing caps, the connecting rods and the connecting rod big-end bearing caps. Lay them out on a clean surface in the same general position as their location in the engine. This will enable you to match any bearing problems with the corresponding crankshaft journal.

4 Dirt and other foreign matter gets into the engine in a variety of ways. It may be left in the engine during assembly, or it may pass through filters or the crankcase ventilation system. It may get into the oil, and from there into the bearings. Metal chips from machining operations and normal engine wear are often present. Abrasives are sometimes left in engine components after reconditioning, especially when parts are not thoroughly cleaned using the proper cleaning methods. Whatever the source, these foreign objects often end up embedded in the soft bearing material, and are easily recognised. Large particles will not embed in the bearing, and will score or gouge the bearing and journal. The best prevention for this cause of bearing failure is to clean all parts thoroughly, and keep everything spotlessly-clean during engine assembly. Frequent and regular engine oil and filter changes are also recommended.

5 Lack of lubrication (or lubrication breakdown) has a number of interrelated causes. Excessive heat (which thins the oil), overloading (which squeezes the oil from the bearing face) and oil leakage (from excessive bearing clearances, worn oil pump or high engine speeds) all contribute to lubrication breakdown. Blocked oil passages, which usually are the result of misaligned oil holes in a bearing shell, will also oil-starve a bearing, and destroy it. When lack of lubrication is the cause of bearing failure, the bearing material is wiped or extruded from the steel backing of the bearing. Temperatures may increase to

the point where the steel backing turns blue from overheating.

6 Driving habits can have a definite effect on bearing life. Full-throttle, low-speed operation (labouring the engine) puts very high loads on bearings, tending to squeeze out the oil film. These loads cause the bearings to flex, which produces fine cracks in the bearing face (fatigue failure). Eventually, the bearing material will loosen in pieces, and tear away from the steel backing.

7 Short-distance driving leads to corrosion of bearings, because insufficient engine heat is produced to drive off the condensed water and corrosive gases. These products collect in the engine oil, forming acid and sludge. As the oil is carried to the engine bearings, the acid attacks and corrodes the bearing material.

8 Incorrect bearing installation during engine assembly will lead to bearing failure as well. Tight-fitting bearings leave insufficient bearing running clearance, and will result in oil starvation. Dirt or foreign particles trapped behind a bearing shell result in high spots on the bearing, which lead to failure.

9 As mentioned at the beginning of this Section, the bearing shells should be renewed as a matter of course during engine overhaul; to do otherwise is false economy.

16 Engine overhaul – reassembly sequence

1 Before reassembly begins, ensure that all new parts have been obtained, and that all necessary tools are available. Read through the entire procedure to familiarise yourself with the work involved, and to ensure that all items necessary for reassembly of the engine are at hand. In addition to all normal tools and materials, thread-locking compound will be needed. A good quality tube of liquid sealant will also be required for the joint faces that are fitted without gaskets.

2 In order to save time and avoid problems, engine reassembly can be carried out in the following order:

a) Crankshaft.
b) Piston/connecting rod assemblies.
c) Timing chains and sprockets – 2.2 litre petrol and all diesel engines.
c) Oil pump.
d) Sump.
e) Flywheel/driveplate.
f) Cylinder head.
g) Timing belt tensioner and sprockets, and belts – all models except 2.2 litre petrol and all diesel engines.
h) Inlet and exhaust manifolds (Chapter 4).
i) Engine external components.

3 At this stage, all engine components should be absolutely clean and dry, with all faults repaired. The components should be laid out (or in individual containers) on a completely clean work surface.

17 Piston rings – refitting

1 Before fitting new piston rings, the ring end gaps must be checked as follows.
2 Lay out the pistotn/connecting rod assemblies and the new piston ring sets, so that the ring sets will be matched with the same piston and cylinder during the end gap measurement and subsequent engine reassembly.
3 Insert the top ring into the first cylinder, and push it down the bore using the top of the piston. This will ensure that the ring remains square with the cylinder walls. Push the ring down into the bore until it is positioned 15 to 20 mm down from the top edge of the bore, then withdraw the piston.
4 Measure the end gap using feeler gauges, and compare the measurements with the figures given in the Specifications **(see illustration)**.
5 If the gap is too small (unlikely if genuine Vauxhall parts are used), it must be enlarged, or the ring ends may contact each other during engine operation, causing serious damage. Ideally, new piston rings providing the correct end gap should be fitted. As a last resort, the end gap can be increased by filing the ring ends very carefully with a fine file. Mount the file in a vice with soft jaws, slip the ring over the file with the ends contacting the file face, and slowly move the ring to remove material from the ends. Take care, as piston rings are sharp, and are easily broken.
6 With new piston rings, it is unlikely that the end gap will be too large. If the gaps are too large, check that you have the correct rings for your engine and for the particular cylinder bore size.
7 Repeat the checking procedure for each ring in the first cylinder, and then for the rings in the remaining cylinders. Remember to keep rings, pistons and cylinders matched up.
8 Once the ring end gaps have been checked and if necessary corrected, the rings can be fitted to the pistons.
9 Fit the piston rings using the same technique as for removal. Fit the bottom (oil control) spacer first then install both the side rails, noting that both the spacer and side rails can be installed either way up.
10 The second and top compression rings are different and can be identified by their cross-sections; the top ring is square whilst the second ring is tapered. Fit the second and top compression rings ensuring that each ring is fitted the correct way up with its identification (TOP) mark uppermost **(see illustration)**. **Note:** *Always follow any instructions supplied with the new piston ring sets – different manufacturers may specify different procedures. Do not mix up the top and second compression rings. On some engines the top ring will not have an identification marking and can be fitted either way up.*

17.4 Measuring a piston ring end gap using a feeler gauge

17.11a Piston ring end gap positions (petrol engine)

I   Top and second compression rings
II Oil control ring side rails

11 With the piston rings correctly installed, check that each ring is free to rotate easily in its groove. Check the ring-to-groove clearance of each ring using feeler gauges and check that the clearance is within the specified range then position the ring end gaps as shown **(see illustrations)**.

18 Crankshaft – refitting and main bearing running clearance check

Note: *It is recommended that new main bearing shells are fitted regardless of the condition of the original ones.*

Selection of bearing shells

1 Although the original bearing shells fitted at the factory maybe of various grades, all new bearing shells sold are of the same grade. Vauxhall supply both standard size bearing shells and undersize shells for use when the crankshaft has been reground. The required size of shell required can be determined by measuring the crankshaft journals (see Section 14).

Main bearing clearance check

2 Clean the backs of the bearing shells and the bearing locations in both the cylinder block and the main bearing caps.

17.10 Sectional view of piston rings (1.6 litre engine)

17.11b Piston ring end gap positions (diesel engine)

I   Top compression ring
II Second compression ring
III Oil control ring

3 Press the bearing shells into their locations, ensuring that the tab on each shell engages in the notch in the cylinder block or main bearing cap **(see illustration)**. If the original bearing shells are being used for the check, ensure they are refitted in their original locations. The clearance can be checked in either of two ways.
4 One method (which will be difficult to achieve without a range of internal micrometers or internal/external expanding calipers) is to refit the main bearing caps to the cylinder block, with bearing shells in place. With the cap retaining bolts correctly tightened (use the original bolts for the check, not the new ones), measure the internal diameter of each assembled pair of bearing

18.3 Fit the bearing shells making sure their tabs are correctly located in the slots in the bearing cap/block (arrowed)

18.7 Plastigauge in place on a crankshaft main bearing journal

18.9 Measure the width of the deformed Plastigauge using the scale on the card

18.15 No 2 main bearing shell incorporates the thrust flanges (A) on the 2.2 petrol engine and No 3 main bearing shell on all other models – all the other shells are plain (B)

shells. If the diameter of each corresponding crankshaft journal is measured and then subtracted from the bearing internal diameter, the result will be the main bearing running clearance.

5 The second (and more accurate) method is to use a product known as Plastigauge. This consists of a fine thread of perfectly-round plastic which is compressed between the bearing shell and the journal. When the shell is removed, the plastic is deformed and can be measured with a special card gauge supplied with the kit. The running clearance is determined from this gauge. Plastigauge is sometimes difficult to obtain but enquiries at one of the larger specialist quality motor factors should produce the name of a stockist in your area. The procedure for using Plastigauge is as follows.

6 With the main bearing upper shells in place, carefully lay the crankshaft in position. Do not use any lubricant; the crankshaft journals and bearing shells must be perfectly clean and dry.

7 Cut several lengths of the appropriate size Plastigauge (they should be slightly shorter than the width of the main bearings) and place one length on each crankshaft journal axis **(see illustration)**.

8 With the main bearing lower shells in position, refit the main bearing caps, using the identification marks to ensure each one is correctly positioned. Refit the original retaining bolts and tighten them to the specified Stage 1 torque and then through the Stage 2 and 3 angles (see paragraphs 20 to 22). Take care not to disturb the

Plastigauge and **do not** rotate the crankshaft at any time during this operation. Evenly and progressively slacken and remove the main bearing cap bolts then lift off the caps again taking great care not to disturb the Plastigauge or rotate the crankshaft.

9 Compare the width of the crushed Plastigauge on each journal to the scale printed on the Plastigauge envelope to obtain the main bearing running clearance **(see illustration)**. Compare the clearance measured with that given in the Specifications at the start of this Chapter.

10 If the clearance is significantly different from that expected, the bearing shells may be the wrong size (or excessively worn if the original shells are being re-used). Before deciding that the crankshaft is worn, make sure that no dirt or oil was trapped between the bearing shells and the caps or block when the clearance was measured. If the Plastigauge was wider at one end than at the other, the crankshaft journal may be tapered.

11 Before condemning the components concerned, seek the advice of your Vauxhall dealer or suitable engine repair specialist. They will also be able to inform as to the best course of action or whether renewal will be necessary.

12 Where necessary, obtain the correct size of bearing shell and repeat the running clearance checking procedure as described above.

13 On completion, carefully scrape away all traces of the Plastigauge material from the crankshaft and bearing shells using a fingernail or other object which is unlikely to score the bearing surfaces.

Final crankshaft refitting

1.6 litre petrol engine

14 Carefully lift the crankshaft out of the cylinder block.

15 Place the bearing shells in their locations as described above in paragraphs 2 and 3 **(see illustration)**. If new shells are being fitted, ensure that all traces of the protective grease are cleaned off using paraffin. Wipe dry the shells and caps with a lint-free cloth.

16 Lubricate the upper shells with clean engine oil then lower the crankshaft into position **(see illustration)**.

17 Ensure the crankshaft is correctly seated then check the endfloat as described in Section 14.

18 On models with separate main bearing caps, ensure the bearing shells are correctly located in the caps and refit the caps to the cylinder block **(see illustration)**. Ensure the caps are fitted in their correct locations, with number 1 cap at the timing belt end, and are fitted the correct way around so that all the numbers are the correct way up when read from the rear of the cylinder block.

19 Ensure the rear (No 5) bearing cap is clean and dry then fill the groove on each side of the cap with sealing compound (Vauxhall recommend the use of sealant, part no 90485251, available from your Vauxhall dealer) **(see illustration)**. Fit the bearing cap to the engine, ensuring it is fitted the correct way around.

18.16 Lubricate the upper bearing shells with clean engine oil then fit the crankshaft

18.18 Lubricate the crankshaft journals then refit bearing caps Nos 1 to 4, ensuring each one is fitted in its original location

18.19 Fill the side grooves of the rear (No 5) bearing cap with sealant prior to refitting it to the engine

18.20 Apply a continuous bead of silicone sealing compound (arrowed) around the edge of the cylinder block

18.21 Lubricate the threads of the new main bearing cap bolts . . .

18.22 . . . then tighten the bolts to the specified Stage 1 torque setting . . .

20 On models with a lower main bearing cylinder block casing, remove all traces of silicone sealer and oil from the mating surfaces of the cylinder block and apply a continuous bead of silicone sealing compound (available from your Vauxhall dealer) around the edge of the cylinder block **(see illustration)**. The bead of sealant should be between 2.0 and 2.5 mm in diameter.

21 Apply a smear of clean engine to oil to the threads and underneath the heads of the new main bearing cap bolts. Fit the bolts, tightening them all by hand **(see illustration)**.

22 Working in a diagonal sequence from the centre outwards, tighten the main bearing cap/lower main bearing cylinder block casing bolts to the specified Stage 1 torque setting **(see illustration)**.

23 Once all bolts are tightened to the specified Stage 1 torque, go around again and tighten all bolts through the specified Stage 2 angle then go around for once more and tighten all bolts through the specified Stage 3 angle. It is recommended that an angle-measuring gauge is used during the final stages of the tightening, to ensure accuracy **(see illustrations)**. If a gauge is not available, use white paint to make alignment marks between the bolt head and cap prior to tightening; the marks can then be used to check that the bolt has been rotated through the correct angle.

24 Once all the bolts have been tightened, inject more sealant down the grooves in the rear main bearing cap until sealant is seen to be escaping through the joints. Once you are sure the cap grooves are full of sealant, wipe off all excess sealant using a clean cloth.

25 Check that the crankshaft is free to rotate smoothly; if excessive pressure is required to turn the crankshaft, investigate the cause before proceeding further.

26 Refit/reconnect the piston connecting rod assemblies to the crankshaft as described in Section 19.

27 Referring to Part A (SOHC engine) or Part B (DOHC engine), fit a new left-hand crank-shaft oil seal, then refit the flywheel/ driveplate, oil pump, cylinder head, timing belt sprocket(s) and fit a new timing belt.

18.23a . . . and then through the specified Stages 2 and 3 angles

1.8, 2.0 and 2.2 litre petrol engines

28 Refit the crankshaft as described in paragraphs 14 to 26.

29 Ensure the bearing cap and main bearing ladder casting or lower main bearing cylinder casing surfaces are clean and dry then refit (and balancer unit on 2.0 litre engines) to the cylinder block. Refit the retaining bolts and tighten them to the specified torque, working in a diagonal sequence from the centre outwards.

30 Refit the baffle plate to the base of the cylinder block assembly and tighten its retaining bolts to the specified torque. **Note:** *The oil baffle plate is only fitted to engines without a balancer unit.*

31 Working as described Part B of this Chapter, fit a new left-hand oil crankshaft oil seal then refit the flywheel/driveplate, oil

18.23b Tightening the lower main bearing cylinder block casing bolts to the specified Stages 2 and 3 angles (Z22SE engine)

pump, cylinder head, timing belt sprocket(s) and fit a new timing belt.

Diesel engines

32 Refit the crankshaft as described in paragraphs 14 to 26, using the marks made on removal to ensure the bearing caps are correctly positioned (see Section 11) **(see illustrations)**.

33 Ensure the bearing cap and main bearing ladder casting surfaces are clean and dry. Refit the casting to the engine (and balancer unit on 2.2 litre engines) ensuring that the arrow on the casting is pointing towards the timing chain end of the engine, then refit the retaining bolts and tighten them to the specified torque, working in a diagonal sequence from the centre outwards **(see illustrations)**.

18.32a With the rear bearing cap in position, inject sealant down the groove . . .

18.32b . . . until it is seen to be forced out through the hole in the cap (arrowed)

18.33a Refit the main bearing ladder casting . . .

34 Working as described Part D of this Chapter, fit a new left-hand oil crankshaft oil seal then refit the flywheel, timing chains and sprockets and cylinder head.

19 Piston/connecting rod assembly – refitting and big-end bearing running clearance check

Note: *It is recommended that new piston rings and big-end bearing shells are fitted regardless of the condition of the original ones.*

Selection of bearing shells

1 Although the original bearing shells fitted at the factory maybe of various grades, all new bearing shells sold are of the same grade. Vauxhall supply both standard size bearing shells and undersize shells for use when the crankshaft has been reground. The required

19.3 Fit the bearing shells making sure their tabs are correctly located in the connecting rod/cap groove (arrowed)

19.8 Ensure the piston ring end gaps are correctly spaced then fit the ring compressor

18.33b . . . ensuring its arrow is pointing towards the timing chain end of the engine, and tighten its retaining bolts to the specified torque

size of shell required can be determined by measuring the crankshaft journals (see Section 14).

Big-end bearing clearance check

2 Clean the backs of the bearing shells and the bearing locations in both the connecting rod and bearing cap.
3 Press the bearing shells into their locations, ensuring that the tab on each shell engages in the notch in the connecting rod and cap **(see illustration)**. If the original bearing shells are being used for the check ensure they are refitted in their original locations. The clearance can be checked in either of two ways.
4 One method is to refit the big-end bearing cap to the connecting rod, with bearing shells

19.7 Lubricate the piston rings with clean engine oil

19.9a Ensuring the arrow on the piston crown (circled) is pointing towards the timing belt end of the engine

in place. With the cap retaining bolts/nuts (use the original bolts for the check) correctly tightened, use an internal micrometer or vernier caliper to measure the internal diameter of each assembled pair of bearing shells. If the diameter of each corresponding crankshaft journal is measured and then subtracted from the bearing internal diameter, the result will be the big-end bearing running clearance.
5 The second method is to use Plastigauge as described in Section 18, paragraphs 5 to 13. Place a strand of Plastigauge on each (cleaned) crankpin journal and refit the (clean) piston/connecting rod assemblies, shells and big-end bearing caps. Tighten the bolts/nuts (as applicable) correctly taking care not to disturb the Plastigauge. Dismantle the assemblies without rotating the crankshaft and use the scale printed on the Plastigauge envelope to obtain the big-end bearing running clearance. On completion of the measurement, carefully scrape off all traces of Plastigauge from the journal and shells using a fingernail or other object which will not score the components.

Refitting

6 Ensure the bearing shells are correctly refitted as described above in paragraphs 2 and 3. If new shells are being fitted, ensure that all traces of the protective grease are cleaned off using paraffin. Wipe dry the shells and connecting rods with a lint-free cloth.
7 Lubricate the bores, the pistons and piston rings then lay out each piston/connecting rod assembly in its respective position **(see illustration)**.
8 Starting with assembly number 1, make sure that the piston rings are still spaced as described in Section 17, then clamp them in position with a piston ring compressor **(see illustration)**.

Petrol engines

9 Insert the piston/connecting rod assembly into the top of cylinder No 1, ensuring that the arrow marking on the piston crown is pointing towards the timing belt end of the engine. Using a block of wood or hammer handle against the piston crown, tap the assembly into the cylinder until the piston crown is flush with the top of the cylinder **(see illustrations)**.

19.9b Tap the piston gently into the bore using handle of a hammer

19.10 Make sure the lug (arrowed) is facing the flywheel/driveplate end of the engine

19.11a Tighten the big-end bearing cap bolts to the specified Stage 1 torque . . .

19.11b . . . and then through the specified angle(s)

10 Taking care not to mark the cylinder bore, liberally lubricate the crankpin and both bearing shells, then pull the piston/connecting rod assembly down the bore and onto the crankpin and refit the big-end bearing cap using the markings to ensure it is fitted the correct way around (the lug on the bearing cap base should be facing the flywheel/driveplate end of the engine) and screw in the new retaining bolts **(see illustration)**.

11 On 1.6 litre engines, tighten both bearing cap bolts to the specified Stage 1 torque setting and then tighten them through the specified Stage 2 angle. It is recommended that an angle-measuring gauge is used to ensure accuracy **(see illustrations)**. If a gauge is not available, use white paint to make alignment marks between the bolt head and cap prior to tightening; the marks can then be used to check that the bolt has been rotated through the correct angle.

12 On 1.8, 2.0 and 2.2 litre engines, tighten both bearing cap bolts to the specified Stage 1 torque setting then tighten them through the specified Stage 2 angle, and finally through the specified Stage 3 angle. It is recommended that an angle-measuring gauge is used during the final stages of the tightening, to ensure accuracy. If a gauge is not available, use white paint to make alignment marks between the bolt head and cap prior to tightening; the marks can then be used to check that the bolt has been rotated through the correct angle.

13 Refit the remaining three piston and connecting rod assemblies in the same way.

14 Rotate the crankshaft, and check that it turns freely, with no signs of binding or tight spots.

15 On 1.8, 2.0 and 2.2 litre engines, where removed, ensure the bearing cap and main bearing ladder casting surfaces are clean and dry. Refit the casting (and balancer unit on 2.0 litre engines) to the engine and tighten its retaining bolts to the specified torque, working in a diagonal sequence from the centre outwards. Refit the baffle plate to the base of the cylinder block and tighten its retaining bolts to the specified torque.

16 On all engines, refit the oil pump strainer, sump and the cylinder head as described in Part A or B (as applicable) of this Chapter.

19.17 On 2.0 litre diesel engines, tap the piston/connecting rod gently into the bore using handle of a hammer

Diesel engines

17 Insert the piston/connecting rod assembly into the top of cylinder No 1, ensuring that the arrow marking on the piston crown is pointing towards the timing chain end of the engine. Using a block of wood or hammer handle against the piston crown, tap the assembly into the cylinder until the piston crown is flush with the top of the cylinder **(see illustration)**.

18 Taking care not to mark the cylinder bore, liberally lubricate the crankpin and both bearing shells, then pull the piston/connecting rod assembly down the bore and onto the crankpin and refit the big-end bearing cap using the markings to ensure it is fitted the correct way around (the lug on the bearing cap base should be facing the flywheel end of the engine) and screw in the new retaining bolts **(see illustration)**.

19.19a . . . making sure its lug (arrowed) is facing the flywheel end of the engine. Tighten the bearing cap bolts to the specified Stage 1 torque . . .

19.18 Lubricate the bearing shell with clean engine oil and then refit the bearing cap to the connecting rod . . .

19 Tighten both bearing cap bolts to the specified Stage 1 torque setting then tighten them through the specified Stage 2 angle, and finally through the specified Stage 3 angle. It is recommended that an angle-measuring gauge is used during the final stages of the tightening, to ensure accuracy **(see illustrations)**. If a gauge is not available, use white paint to make alignment marks between the bolt head and cap prior to tightening; the marks can then be used to check that the bolt has been rotated through the correct angle.

20 Refit the remaining three piston and connecting rod assemblies in the same way.

21 Rotate the crankshaft, and check that it turns freely, with no signs of binding or tight spots.

22 Refit the oil pump strainer, sump and the cylinder head as described in Part D of this Chapter.

19.19b . . . and then through the specified Stages 2 and 3 angles

20 Engine –
initial start-up after overhaul

1 With the engine refitted in the vehicle, double-check the engine oil and coolant levels. Make a final check that everything has been reconnected, and that there are no tools or rags left in the engine compartment.

2 On petrol engine models, disable the ignition system by disconnecting the wiring connector from the ignition DIS module, and the fuel system by removing the fuel pump relay from the engine compartment relay box (see Chapter 4A, Section 8). Turn the engine on the starter until the oil pressure warning light goes out then stop and reconnect the wiring connector and refit the relay.

3 On diesel engine models, switch on the ignition and immediately turn the engine on the starter (without allowing the glow plugs to heat up) until the oil pressure warning light goes out.

4 On all models, start the engine as normal noting that this may take a little longer than usual, due to the fuel system components having been disturbed.

5 While the engine is idling, check for fuel, water and oil leaks. Don't be alarmed if there are some odd smells and smoke from parts getting hot and burning off oil deposits.

6 Assuming all is well, keep the engine idling until hot water is felt circulating through the top hose, then switch off the engine.

7 Allow the engine to cool then recheck the oil and coolant levels as described in *Weekly Checks*, and top-up as necessary.

8 If new pistons, rings or crankshaft bearings have been fitted, the engine must be treated as new, and run-in for the first 500 miles (800 km). *Do not* operate the engine at full-throttle, or allow it to labour at low engine speeds in any gear. It is recommended that the oil and filter be changed at the end of this period.

Chapter 3
Cooling, heating and air conditioning systems

Contents

Degrees of difficulty

| Easy, suitable for novice with little experience | | Fairly easy, suitable for beginner with some experience | | Fairly difficult, suitable for competent DIY mechanic | | Difficult, suitable for experienced DIY mechanic | | Very difficult, suitable for expert DIY or professional |

Specifications

General
System type . . . .   Pressurised, with remote expansion tank

Thermostat
Opening temperatures:
  Petrol engines:
    Except Z22SE:
      Starts to open . . . .   92°C
      Fully open . . . .   107°C
    Z22SE:
      Starts to open . . . .   82°C
      Fully open . . . .   97°C
  Diesel engines:
    Starts to open . . . .   92°C
    Fully open . . . .   107°C

Electric cooling fan operating temperature
Cooling fan on . . . .   100°C
Cooling fan off . . . .   95°C

Expansion tank cap
Opening pressure:
  Petrol engines . . . .   1.2 to 1.5 bars
  Diesel engines . . . .   1.4 to 1.5 bars
Boiling point . . . .   123°C

Torque wrench settings

	Nm	lbf ft
Air conditioning:		
Compressor mounting bolt	20	15
Refrigerant line to compressor:		
Except Z22SE	33	24
Z22SE	20	15
Refrigerant line to condenser:		
Except Z22SE	27	20
Z22SE	20	15
Refrigerant line to receiver-dryer:		
Except Z22SE	12 to 20	9 to 15
Z22SE	20	15
Coolant pump:		
X16SZR, X16XEL, Z16XE, X18XE1, Z18XE	8	6
X18XE, X20XEV, Z22SE	25	18
X20DTL, X20DTH, Y20DTH, Y22DTR	20	15
Coolant pump drain plug:		
Z22SE	20	15
Coolant pump pulley:		
X20DTL, X20DTH, Y20DTH, Y22DTR	20	15
Coolant pump sprocket:		
Z22SE	10	7
Coolant temperature sensor:		
X16SZR, X16XEL, Z16XE, Z18XE	14	10
X18XE, X20XEV	10	7
Z22SE	20	15
X20DTL, X20DTH:		
To thermostat housing	10	7
To cylinder head	18	13
Thermostat housing cover/thermostat:		
X16SZR, X16XEL, Z16XE	8	6
Z22SE	10	7
Thermostat housing (heat exchanger) to cylinder block:		
X20DTL, X20DTH	20	15
Thermostat housing to cylinder head:		
X16SZR, X16XEL, Z16XE, X18XE1	20	15
X18XE, X20XEV	15	11
Z22SE	10	7
X20DTL, X20DTH	8	6

1 General information and precautions

General information

The cooling system is of pressurised type, comprising a coolant pump, a crossflow radiator, electric cooling fan(s), and thermostat(s). On 1.6, 1.8 and 2.0 litre petrol engines, the coolant pump is driven by the timing belt. On the 2.2 litre petrol engine, the coolant pump is driven by the balancer shaft drive chain. On diesel engines the coolant pump is driven by the auxiliary drivebelt.

The system functions as follows. Cold coolant from the radiator passes through the bottom hose to the coolant pump, where it is pumped around the cylinder block, head passages and heater matrix. After cooling the cylinder bores, combustion surfaces and valve seats, the coolant reaches the underside of the thermostat, which is initially closed. The coolant passes through the heater, and is returned to the coolant pump.

When the engine is cold, the coolant circulates only through the cylinder block, cylinder head and heater. When the coolant reaches a predetermined temperature, the thermostat opens and the coolant also passes through to the radiator. As the coolant circulates through the radiator, it is cooled by the inrush of air when the car is in forward motion. Airflow is supplemented by the action of the electric cooling fan when necessary. Once the coolant has passed through the radiator, and has cooled, the cycle is repeated.

The electric cooling fan, mounted on the rear of the radiator, is controlled by a thermostatic switch. At a predetermined coolant temperature, the switch actuates the fan. An auxiliary electric cooling fan is fitted to models with air conditioning.

An expansion tank is fitted to the left-hand side of the engine compartment to accommodate expansion of the coolant when hot. The expansion tank is connected to the top of the radiator.

Precautions

 Warning: Do not attempt to remove the expansion tank filler cap, or disturb any part of the cooling system, while the engine is hot; there is a high risk of scalding. If the cap must be removed before the engine and radiator have fully cooled (even though this is not recommended) the pressure in the cooling system must first be relieved. Cover the cap with a thick layer of cloth, to avoid scalding, and slowly unscrew the filler cap until a hissing sound can be heard. When the hissing has stopped, indicating that the pressure has reduced, slowly unscrew the filler cap until it can be removed; if more hissing sounds are heard, wait until they have stopped before unscrewing the cap completely. At all times, keep well away from the filler cap opening.

Warning: Do not allow antifreeze to come into contact with the skin, or with the painted surfaces of the vehicle. Rinse off spills immediately, with plenty of water. Never leave antifreeze lying around in an open container, or in a puddle on the driveway or garage floor. Children and pets are attracted by its sweet smell, but antifreeze can be fatal if ingested.

Warning: If the engine is hot, the electric cooling fan may start rotating even if the engine is not running; be careful to keep hands, hair and loose clothing well clear when working in the engine compartment.

 Warning: Refer to Section 11 for precautions to be observed when working on models equipped with air conditioning.

2 Cooling system hoses – disconnection and renewal

Note: *Refer to the warnings given in Section 1 of this Chapter before proceeding. Do not attempt to disconnect any hose while the system is still hot.*

1 If the checks described in Chapter 1A or 1B reveal a faulty hose, it must be renewed as follows.

2 First drain the cooling system (see Chapter 1A or 1B). If the coolant is not due for renewal, it may be re-used if it is collected in a clean container.

3 Before disconnecting a hose, first note its routing in the engine compartment, and whether it is secured by any clips or ties. Use a screwdriver to slacken the clips, then move the clips along the hose, clear of the relevant inlet/outlet union. Carefully work the hose free.

4 Note that the radiator inlet and outlet unions are fragile; do not use excessive force when attempting to remove the hoses. If a hose proves to be difficult to remove, try to release it by rotating the hose ends before attempting to free it.

> **HAYNES HINT** *If all else fails, cut the coolant hose with a sharp knife, then slit it so that it can be peeled off in two pieces. Although this may prove expensive if the hose is otherwise undamaged, it is preferable to buying a new radiator.*

5 When fitting a hose, first slide the clips onto the hose, then work the hose into position. If clamp-type clips were originally fitted, it is a good idea to use screw-type clips when refitting the hose. If the hose is stiff, use a little soapy water (washing-up liquid is ideal) as a lubricant, or soften the hose by soaking it in hot water.

6 Work the hose into position, checking that it is correctly routed and secured. Slide each clip along the hose until it passes over the flared end of the relevant inlet/outlet union, before tightening the clips securely.

7 Refill the cooling system with reference to Chapter 1A or 1B.

8 Check thoroughly for leaks as soon as possible after disturbing any part of the cooling system.

3 Radiator – removal, inspection and refitting

Removal

X16SZR, X16XEL, Z16XE, Z18XE and X18XE1

1 Disconnect the battery negative (earth) lead (see Chapter 5A).

2 Drain the cooling system as described in Chapter 1A by disconnecting the bottom hose from the radiator **(see illustration)**.

3 Disconnect the wiring from the thermoswitch on the radiator.

4 On models with air conditioning, remove the main and auxiliary cooling fan housings complete as described in Section 5.

5 On models without air conditioning, unclip and remove the wiring connector from the cooling fan housing, then unbolt the cooling fan housing and withdraw it upwards from the radiator.

6 Loosen the clips and disconnect the expansion tank vent hose, then the upper hose from the radiator **(see illustration)**.

7 On models with automatic transmission, disconnect the fluid cooler hoses by extracting the spring clips. Be prepared for some loss of fluid by placing a suitable container beneath the hoses.

8 Unscrew the bolts and remove the mounting brackets from the top of the radiator. Examine the rubbers and if necessary obtain new ones.

9 Lift the radiator upwards from the rubber mountings in the subframe. Withdraw the radiator from the engine compartment.

X18XE and X20XEV

10 Disconnect the battery negative (earth) lead (see Chapter 5A).

11 Drain the cooling system as described in Chapter 1A by disconnecting the bottom hose from the radiator.

12 Remove the electric cooling fan assembly from the rear of the radiator as described in Section 5.

13 Loosen the clips and disconnect the expansion tank vent hose, then the upper hose from the radiator.

14 Disconnect the wiring from the cooling fan thermoswitch on models without air conditioning.

15 On models with automatic transmission, disconnect the fluid cooler hoses by extracting the spring clips. Be prepared for some loss of fluid by placing a suitable container beneath the hoses.

16 On models with air conditioning, unscrew and remove the bolt securing the dryer-receiver to the subframe near the bottom left-hand side of the radiator.

17 Remove the radiator grille as described in Chapter 11.

18 On models with air conditioning, remove

3.2 Disconnecting the bottom hose from the radiator

the front bumper complete (Chapter 11), then tie the condenser to the engine compartment front crossmember, and unscrew the condenser mounting bolts.

19 On models without air conditioning, unclip the power steering fluid cooling coil from its brackets on the front of the radiator.

20 Unscrew the bolts and remove the mounting brackets from the top of the radiator. Examine the rubbers and if necessary obtain new ones.

21 Lift the radiator upwards from the rubber mountings in the subframe. Withdraw the radiator from the engine compartment.

Z22SE

Note: *This sub-section describes models with air conditioning; the procedure is similar for models without air conditioning.*

22 Disconnect the battery negative (earth) lead (see Chapter 5A).

23 Apply the handbrake, then jack up the front of the vehicle and support it on axle stands (see *Jacking and vehicle support*).

24 Drain the cooling system as described in Chapter 1A by removing the drain plug from the bottom of the coolant pump, then refit and tighten the plug to the specified torque.

25 Unbolt the fuse/relay box from the battery support.

26 Disconnect the wiring from the air temperature sensor in the air intake.

27 Disconnect the crankcase ventilation hose from the camshaft cover, also disconnect the fuel pressure regulator vacuum line from the air intake. Unclip the vacuum line from the intake.

3.6 Disconnecting the expansion tank hose from the top of the radiator

3.29 Radiator top hose

3.30 Auxiliary fan wiring connector

3.32 Air conditioning refrigerant line and power steering return line on the cooling fan housing

28 Loosen the clips and remove the air intake ducting from the throttle body and from the air cleaner housing.

29 Loosen the clip and disconnect the top hose from the radiator (see illustration).

30 Disconnect the auxiliary fan wiring connector located on the engine compartment front crossmember (see illustration). Also disconnect the cooling fan motor wiring and unbolt the earth cable from the subframe.

31 Disconnect the wiring from the air conditioning compressor.

32 Release the air conditioning refrigerant line and power steering return line from the cooling fan housing (see illustration). Turn the line bracket fasteners a quarter turn anti-clockwise and remove from the housing.

33 Remove the radiator grille and front bumper as described in Chapter 11.

34 Disconnect the wiring from the air conditioning pressure switch behind the transmission.

35 On models with automatic transmission, position a container beneath the transmission then lever up the clips and disconnect the transmission fluid cooler lines from under the transmission. Allow the fluid to drain into the container.

36 Unscrew the mounting bolts and lift the electric cooling fan housing upwards from the rear of the radiator.

37 Loosen the clips, then disconnect the cooling expansion tank hose and bottom hose from the left-hand side of the radiator. Be prepared for some loss of coolant.

38 Unscrew the bolt securing the refrigerant line block connection.

39 Unscrew the mounting bolts and remove the brackets from the top of the radiator.

40 Where necessary, remove the right-hand headlight as described in Chapter 12, Section 7.

41 Unscrew the mounting bolts and remove the air intake pipe from under the engine compartment front crossmember.

42 Unscrew the condenser mounting bolts, then tie the auxiliary cooling fan housing and the air conditioning condenser to the engine compartment front crossmember (see illustrations).

43 Where necessary, unclip the engine oil cooler, then unscrew the auxiliary cooling fan housing from the front of the condenser, then carefully withdraw the radiator upwards (see illustration).

44 If a new radiator is to be fitted, remove the fan assembly and, where applicable, the automatic transmission fluid cooler pipes, and transfer them to the new radiator.

Y20DTH, Y22DTR and X20DTH

45 Remove the battery as described in Chapter 5A. This includes removing the battery insulation jacket and removing the front relay frame from the battery retaining plate.

46 Release the expansion tank coolant hose from the clip then unbolt the positive distribution unit from the battery support. Unbolt and remove the battery support.

47 Unscrew the bolts and remove the radiator mounting brackets from the engine compartment front crossmember.

48 Disconnect the electric cooling fan wiring from the thermoswitch and position to one side together with the front relay frame.

49 Disconnect the auxiliary fan wiring plugs, then unbolt the earth cable from the subframe.

50 Release the clips and remove the upper turbocharger air hose.

51 Unbolt the power steering pump fluid reservoir from the air cleaner housing and position to one side.

52 Apply the handbrake, then jack up the front of the vehicle and support it on axle stands (see *Jacking and vehicle support*). Remove the engine compartment lower cover.

53 Drain the cooling system as described in Chapter 1B by disconnecting the bottom hose from the radiator.

54 Remove the radiator grille and front bumper as described in Chapter 11.

55 On models with air conditioning, disconnect the wiring from both pressure switches.

56 Disconnect the wiring from the air conditioning compressor.

57 Unscrew the bolts securing the electric cooling fan housing to the rear of the radiator. Carefully push the radiator slightly forwards then withdraw the fan housing together with the fan motor from the engine compartment.

58 Release the clip and disconnect the turbocharger lower air hose from the intercooler.

59 Unclip the power steering fluid cooling coil from the brackets on the auxiliary fan housing.

60 On models with air conditioning, unbolt the receiver-dryer from the radiator.

61 Unbolt the auxiliary fan housing and withdraw downwards from the vehicle.

3.42a Air conditioning condenser mounting bolt

3.42b Tie the air conditioning condenser to the engine compartment front crossmember

3.43 Lifting the radiator from the engine compartment

62 Tie the air conditioning condenser to the front valance taking care not to bend the refrigerant lines.

63 Loosen the clips and disconnect the top hose, bottom hose and expansion tank hose from the radiator.

64 Lift the radiator from the rubber mountings in the subframe and withdraw upwards, together with the intercooler from the engine compartment.

65 Remove the intercooler from the radiator by unscrewing the upper mounting bolts, then tilting the unit and pushing it out of the lower guide.

66 Unscrew and remove the electric fan motor thermoswitch from the radiator. Discard the seal and obtain a new one for refitting.

X20DTL

67 Apply the handbrake, then jack up the front of the vehicle and support it on axle stands (see *Jacking and vehicle support*). Remove the engine compartment lower cover.

68 Drain the cooling system as described in Chapter 1B by disconnecting the bottom hose from the radiator.

69 Remove the front bumper as described in Chapter 11.

70 Remove the electric cooling fan and housing as described in Section 5.

71 Loosen the clips and disconnect the top and bottom hoses from the radiator.

72 Unscrew and remove the bolt securing the dryer flange to the bottom left-hand side of the radiator.

73 Tie the air conditioning condenser to the front valance taking care not to bend the refrigerant lines.

74 Unscrew the mounting bolts and carefully lift the radiator upwards from the engine compartment.

Inspection

75 If the radiator has been removed due to suspected blockage, reverse-flush it as described in Chapter 1A or 1B.

76 Clean dirt and debris from the radiator fins, using an air line (in which case, wear eye protection) or a soft brush.

Caution: Be careful, as the fins are easily damaged, and are sharp.

77 If necessary, a radiator specialist can perform a 'flow test' on the radiator, to establish whether an internal blockage exists.

78 A leaking radiator must be referred to a specialist for permanent repair. Do not attempt to weld or solder a leaking radiator.

79 In an emergency, minor leaks from the radiator can be cured by using a suitable radiator sealant (in accordance with its manufacturer's instructions) with the radiator fitted in the vehicle.

80 Inspect the radiator mounting rubbers, and renew them if necessary.

Refitting

81 Refitting is a reversal of removal, bearing in mind the following points.

a) *Ensure that the lower mounting rubbers are correctly located in the front subframe before locating the radiator in them (see illustration).*

b) *Ensure that all hoses are correctly reconnected, and their retaining clips securely tightened.*

c) *On completion, refill the cooling system as described in Chapter 1A or 1B and, on models with automatic transmission, check and if necessary top-up the automatic transmission fluid level as described in Chapter 1A.*

4 Thermostat – removal, testing and refitting

X16SZR

Removal

1 Disconnect the battery negative (earth) lead (see Chapter 5A).

2 Drain the cooling system as described in Chapter 1A.

3 Loosen the clip and disconnect the top hose from the thermostat cover on the right-hand side of the engine.

4 Remove the timing belt and idler, camshaft sprocket, and rear timing belt cover with reference to Chapter 2A.

5 Unscrew the mounting bolts and remove the thermostat cover from the cylinder head.

6 Carefully prise the thermostat from the cylinder head and remove the sealing ring.

Testing

7 A rough test of the thermostat's operation may be made by suspending it with a piece of string in a container full of water. Heat the water to bring it to the boil - the thermostat must open by the time the water boils. If not, renew it **(see illustration)**.

8 The opening temperature is usually marked on the thermostat. If a thermometer is available, the precise opening temperature of the thermostat may be determined, and compared with the value marked on the thermostat.

9 A thermostat which fails to close as the water cools must also be renewed.

Refitting

10 Thoroughly clean the mating faces of the thermostat cover and the cylinder head.

11 Locate the thermostat in the cylinder head together with a new sealing ring. Make sure that the spring and capsule end is facing into the head and position the thermostat with the outer bar vertical.

12 Refit the thermostat cover and tighten the bolts to the specified torque.

13 Refit the rear timing belt cover, camshaft sprocket, and timing belt and idler with reference to Chapter 2A.

14 Reconnect the top hose to the thermostat cover and tighten the clip.

3.81 Locating the pins on the bottom of the radiator in the rubber mountings

15 Refill and bleed the cooling system with reference to Chapter 1A.

16 Reconnect the battery negative (earth) lead.

X16SZR, X16XEL and Z16XE

Removal

17 The thermostat is located on the front right-hand end of the cylinder head. Disconnect the battery negative (earth) lead (see Chapter 5A).

18 Drain the cooling system as described in Chapter 1A by disconnecting the bottom hose from the radiator.

19 Remove the auxiliary drivebelt as described in Chapter 1A by turning the tensioner clockwise. Mark the drivebelt to indicate its direction of rotation before removing it.

20 Refer to Chapter 10 and unscrew the power steering pump mounting bolts from the auxiliary support. Suspend the pump to one side, without disconnecting the fluid lines. Note the different lengths of the mounting bolts.

21 Loosen the clip and disconnect the top hose from the thermostat housing cover.

22 Unbolt and remove the thermostat cover together with the integral thermostat. Remove the seal from the cover and obtain a new one **(see illustrations)**. Clean the cover and the housing surface.

23 If necessary, the thermostat housing may be removed from the cylinder head by first disconnecting the wiring from the coolant temperature sender and sensor, then

4.7 Testing the thermostat opening temperature

4.22a Removing the thermostat and cover on the 1.6 litre engine

4.22b Removing the sealing ring on the 1.6 litre engine

4.46 The top hose has a cut-out to locate on the thermostat cover lug

unscrewing the mounting bolts. Clean all remains of the gasket from the contact surfaces and obtain a new one.

Testing

24 A rough test of the thermostat's operation may be made by suspending it with a piece of string in a container full of water. Heat the water to bring it to the boil – the thermostat must open by the time the water boils. If not, renew it (see illustration 4.7).

25 The opening temperature is usually marked on the thermostat. If a thermometer is available, the precise opening temperature of the thermostat may be determined, and compared with the value marked on the thermostat.

26 A thermostat which fails to close as the water cools must also be renewed.

Refitting

27 Refitting is a reversal of removal, but fit a new seal to the thermostat, and where removed fit a new gasket to the housing. Refill the cooling system as described in Chapter 1A.

X18XE and X20XEV

Removal

28 The thermostat is located on the right-hand front of the cylinder head and is integral with the housing. First, disconnect the battery negative (earth) lead (see Chapter 5A).

29 Drain the cooling system as described in Chapter 1A by disconnecting the bottom hose from the radiator.

30 Loosen the clip and disconnect the top hose from the thermostat housing.

4.47 Removing the thermostat housing cover

31 Progressively unscrew the mounting bolts and remove the thermostat housing from the cylinder head. Clean all remains of the seal from the contact surfaces and obtain a new seal.

Testing

32 Refer to paragraphs 7 to 9.

Refitting

33 Refitting is a reversal of removal, but fit a new seal and tighten the mounting bolts to the specified torque. Refill the cooling system as described in Chapter 1A.

Z18XE and X18XE1

Removal

34 The thermostat is located on the right-hand front of the cylinder head, and it is integral with its housing. First, disconnect the battery negative (earth) lead (see Chapter 5A).

35 Apply the handbrake, then jack up the front of the vehicle and support it on axle stands (see *Jacking and vehicle support*). Remove the engine compartment undertray. Also remove the top cover from the engine.

36 Drain the cooling system as described in Chapter 1A by disconnecting the bottom hose from the radiator.

37 Loosen the clips and disconnect the top hose and expansion tank hose from the thermostat housing.

38 Disconnect the wiring from the coolant temperature sensor on the housing.

39 Unbolt and remove the housing from cylinder head, then remove the gasket.

4.48 Removing the thermostat from the housing

Thoroughly clean the contact surfaces of the housing and cylinder head.

Testing

40 Refer to paragraphs 7 to 9.

Refitting

41 Refitting is a reversal of removal, but fit a new gasket and tighten the mounting bolts securely. Refill the cooling system as described in Chapter 1A.

Z22SE

Removal

42 The thermostat is located on the left-hand rear of the cylinder head, over the transmission. First, disconnect the battery negative (earth) lead (see Chapter 5A).

43 Apply the handbrake, then jack up the front of the vehicle and support it on axle stands (see *Jacking and vehicle support*). Remove the engine compartment undertray.

44 Drain the cooling system as described in Chapter 1A. The drain plug is located in the bottom of the coolant pump.

45 Release the relay box from the ABS hydraulic modulator in the left-hand rear corner of the engine compartment, and position the box to one side.

46 Loosen the clip and disconnect the top hose from the thermostat cover. Note that the end of the hose has a cut-out which locates with a lug on the cover (see illustration).

47 Where applicable, unclip the coolant temperature sensor wiring from the cover, then unscrew the bolts and remove the cover from the thermostat housing (see illustration).

48 Lift the thermostat from the housing (see illustration). Remove the seal from the rim of the thermostat and discard it. Obtain a new one. Clean the contact surfaces of the cover and housing.

Testing

49 Refer to paragraphs 7 to 9.

Refitting

50 Refitting is a reversal of removal, but fit a new seal and tighten the cover bolts to the specified torque. Refill the cooling system as described in Chapter 1A.

Diesel models

Removal

51 The thermostat is located on the front right-hand end of the cylinder head, and is integral with the housing. First, disconnect the battery negative (earth) lead (see Chapter 5A).

52 Apply the handbrake, then jack up the front of the vehicle and support it on axle stands (see *Jacking and vehicle support*). Remove the engine compartment undertray, and also remove the top cover from the engine.

53 Drain the cooling system as described in Chapter 1B by disconnecting the bottom hose from the radiator.

54 Disconnect the wiring from the coolant temperature sensor on the thermostat housing.

55 Loosen the clips and disconnect the hoses from the thermostat housing (**see illustrations**).

56 Unbolt the thermostat housing from the cylinder head (**see illustrations**). Clean away all traces of gasket from the housing and cylinder head.

57 To remove the oil cooler thermostat located on the left-hand end of the cylinder block, first disconnect the hose then unscrew the bolts and remove the housing which includes the integral thermostat. Recover the gasket.

Testing

58 Refer to paragraphs 7 to 9.

Refitting

59 Refitting is a reversal of removal, but fit a new gasket and tighten the mounting bolts to the specified torque (where given). Refill the cooling system as described in Chapter 1B.

---

5 Electric cooling fan – testing, removal and refitting

> ⚠ **Warning: If the engine is hot, the cooling fan may start up at any time. Take extra precautions when working in the vicinity of the fan.**

Testing

1 The cooling fan is supplied with current via the ignition switch, relay(s) and a fuse (see Chapter 12). The circuit is completed by the cooling fan thermostatic switch, which is mounted in the right-hand end of the radiator. *Note: On models with air conditioning, there are two switches fitted to the radiator; both switches operate the cooling fan and the air conditioning auxiliary cooling fan simultaneously.*

2 If a fan does not work, run the engine until normal operating temperature is reached, then allow it to idle. If the fan does not cut in within a few minutes (or before the temperature gauge indicates overheating), switch off the ignition and disconnect the

4.55a Release the clip . . .

4.55b . . . and disconnect the top hose from the thermostat housing cover

4.56a Unscrew the mounting bolts . . .

4.56b . . . then remove the thermostat and cover together with the gasket

wiring plug from the cooling fan switch. Bridge the two contacts in the wiring plug using a length of spare wire, and switch on the ignition. If the fan now operates, the switch is probably faulty, and should be renewed.

3 If the fan still fails to operate, check that full battery voltage is available at the feed wire to the switch; if not, then there is a fault in the feed wire.

4 If the switch and the wiring are in good condition, the fault must be in the motor itself. The motor can be checked by disconnecting the motor wiring connector and connecting a 12-volt supply directly to the motor terminals. If the motor fails this test, it is proved faulty, and must be renewed complete.

Removal and refitting

Petrol models without air conditioning

5 Disconnect the wiring to the fan motor at the connector on the left-hand side of the fan housing.

6 Where necessary, disconnect the wiring from the thermoswitch on the right-hand side of the radiator.

7 Unclip the wiring holder from the housing.

8 Unscrew the two mounting bolts and lift the fan motor housing from the rear of the radiator.

9 Extract the clip and remove the fan wheel from the motor.

10 Unscrew the three nuts and remove the fan motor together with the fan wheel from the housing.

11 Refitting is a reversal of removal.

Petrol models with air conditioning (not Z22SE)

12 Apply the handbrake, then jack up the front of the vehicle and support it on axle stands (see *Jacking and vehicle support*). Remove the engine compartment undertray.

13 Drain the cooling system as described in Chapter 1A.

14 Disconnect both the positive and negative leads from the battery (see Chapter 5A).

15 Remove the relay and fusebox from the battery carrier.

16 Disconnect the wiring for the auxiliary fan.

17 Disconnect the multiplug with the rotary catch.

18 Unbolt the earth cable from the subframe.

19 Disconnect both wiring plugs from the air conditioning pressure switches.

20 Loosen the clips and disconnect the top hose from the radiator and thermostat housing.

21 Unbolt the refrigerant line bracket and disconnect the wiring from the thermoswitches.

22 Disconnect the wiring from the air conditioning compressor.

23 Unclip the refrigerant line from the bracket.

24 Remove the fan housing from the rear of the radiator and withdraw upwards from the engine compartment.

25 With the housing on the bench, disconnect the fan motor wiring and release it from the bracket.

26 Unscrew the three bolts and remove the fan motor and fan wheel from the housing.

5.38a Unscrew the mounting bolts from the radiator . . .

27 Refitting is a reversal of removal, but top-up the cooling system as required with reference to Chapter 1A.

Z22SE

28 Disconnect both the positive and negative leads from the battery (see Chapter 5A).
29 Remove the relay and fusebox from the battery carrier.
30 Disconnect the wiring for the auxiliary fan and position to one side.
31 Disconnect the multiple plug with the rotary catch.
32 Unbolt the earth cable from the subframe.
33 Disconnect the wiring from the air conditioning compressor.
34 Release the refrigerant line and the power steering return line from the cooling fan housing. Remove the two brackets from the housing by turning them 90° anti-clockwise.
35 Disconnect the wiring plug from the air conditioning pressure switch.
36 Unscrew the two upper mounting bolts then lift the cooling fan housing upwards from the engine compartment.
37 With the housing on the bench, disconnect the fan motor wiring and unclip from the bracket.
38 Unscrew the three bolts and remove the fan motor and fan wheel from the housing **(see illustrations)**.
39 Refitting is a reversal of removal.

X20DTL

40 Apply the handbrake, then jack up the front of the vehicle and support it on axle stands (see *Jacking and vehicle support*).

5.38b . . . and lift the assembly upwards from the engine compartment

Remove the engine compartment undertray and the engine top cover.
41 Drain the cooling system as described in Chapter 1B.
42 Remove the battery as described in Chapter 5A, then unbolt and remove the battery support bracket.
43 Unbolt the power steering hydraulic fluid reservoir from the cooling fan housing, unclip the fluid lines and position the reservoir to one side.
44 Disconnect the multiplug with the rotary catch for the auxiliary fan.
45 Unbolt the earth cable from the subframe.
46 Loosen the clip and disconnect the bottom hose from the radiator, then unclip the hose from the housing.
47 Loosen the clips and disconnect the top hose from the radiator and thermostat housing.
48 Loosen the clips and disconnect the air inlet duct from the upper inlet manifold and turbocharger pipe.
49 Disconnect the wiring from both air conditioning pressure switches.
50 Disconnect the wiring from the air conditioning compressor and both thermoswitches.
51 Detach the fan housing from the radiator and withdraw upwards from the engine compartment.
52 With the housing on the bench, unclip the fan motor wiring plug, then unscrew the three mounting bolts and detach the fan motor and fan wheel.
53 Extract the clip and remove the fan wheel from the motor.
54 Refitting is a reversal of removal, but refill the cooling system with reference to Chapter 1B.

X20DTH, Y20DTH and Y22DTR

55 Apply the handbrake, then jack up the front of the vehicle and support it on axle stands (see *Jacking and vehicle support*). Remove the engine compartment undertray and the engine top cover.
56 Remove the battery as described in Chapter 5A, then unbolt and remove the battery support bracket. Removal of the battery includes removing the insulation jacket, detaching the relay from the battery support bracket, unclipping the coolant hose and removing the distribution unit.
57 Loosen the clips and remove the upper air duct from the intercooler and inlet manifold.
58 Unbolt the power steering pump fluid reservoir from the air cleaner housing.
59 Unbolt the radiator upper mounting brackets from the engine compartment front crossmember.
60 Disconnect the fan motor thermoswitch wiring and position to one side, together with the front relay frame.
61 Disconnect the auxiliary fan wiring and multiplug.
62 Unbolt the earth cable from the subframe.
63 On models with air conditioning,

disconnect the wiring from both air conditioning pressure switches and from the air conditioning compressor.
64 Unscrew the four fan housing mounting bolts, then carefully push the radiator forwards and lift out the fan motor and housing.
65 With the housing on the bench, unclip the fan motor wiring plug, then unscrew the three mounting bolts and detach the fan motor and fan wheel.
66 Extract the clip and remove the fan wheel from the motor.
67 Refitting is a reversal of removal, but when refitting the upper air duct, observe the location cut-out for engagement with the intercooler stub.

6 Auxiliary electric cooling fan – testing, removal and refitting

Note: *The auxiliary electric cooling fan is fitted to models with X16XEL (without secondary air system), Y16XE, X18XE1 and Z18XE engines.*

Testing

1 Refer to Section 5.

Removal

2 Remove the radiator grille and front bumper (see Chapter 11).
3 Remove the right-hand headlight as described in Chapter 12, Section 7.
4 Undo the three screws and remove the air inlet duct from under the engine compartment front crossmember.
5 Disconnect the wiring from the auxiliary fan and remove the wiring from the fan housing.
6 Undo the four screws and carefully withdraw the fan housing downwards. On models with air conditioning tie the condenser to the body, taking care not to bend the refrigerant lines.
7 Undo the screws and remove the motor and fan from the housing.

Refitting

8 Refitting is a reversal of removal.

7 Cooling system electrical switches and sensors – testing, removal and refitting

Coolant temperature sensor

Testing

1 Testing of the coolant temperature sensor must be entrusted to a Vauxhall/Opel dealer, who will have the necessary specialist diagnostic equipment.

X18XE, X20XEV and Z22SE

2 Partially drain the cooling system with reference to Chapter 1A. Alternatively, it is possible to change the sensor quickly with minimal loss of coolant by first releasing any pressure from the cooling system. With the engine cold, temporarily remove the expansion tank cap.

3 Remove the DIS ignition module with reference to Chapter 5B.

4 Disconnect the wiring from the coolant temperature sensor located on the thermostat housing at the left-hand end of the cylinder head **(see illustration)**.

5 Unscrew and remove the sensor.

6 Fit the new sensor using a reversal of the removal procedure, but tighten the sensor to the specified torque and refill the cooling system with reference to Chapter 1A.

X16SZR, X16XEL and Z16XE

7 Partially drain the cooling system with reference to Chapter 1A. Alternatively, it is possible to change the sensor quickly with minimal loss of coolant by first releasing any pressure from the cooling system. With the engine cold, temporarily remove the expansion tank cap.

8 Disconnect the wiring from the sensor located on the inlet manifold on the X16SZR engine, or on the thermostat housing at the right-hand end of the cylinder head on other engines. On the X16SZR engine, remove the cover from the throttle body, disconnecting the air intake duct and the vacuum and breather hoses from the cover (see Chapter 4A).

9 Unscrew and remove the sensor.

10 Fit the new sensor using a reversal of the removal procedure, but tighten the sensor to the specified torque and refill the cooling system with reference to Chapter 1A.

Z18XE

11 Partially drain the cooling system with reference to Chapter 1A. Alternatively, it is possible to change the sensor quickly with minimal loss of coolant by first releasing any pressure from the cooling system. With the engine cold, temporarily remove the expansion tank cap.

12 Disconnect the wiring from the sensor located on the thermostat housing on the right-hand end of the cylinder head.

13 Unscrew and remove the sensor.

14 Fit the new sensor using a reversal of the removal procedure, but tighten the sensor to the specified torque and refill the cooling system with reference to Chapter 1A.

X20DTL, X20DTH and Y22DTH

15 Partially drain the cooling system with reference to Chapter 1B. Alternatively, it is possible to change the sensor quickly with minimal loss of coolant by first releasing any pressure from the cooling system. With the engine cold, temporarily remove the expansion tank cap.

16 Unbolt and remove the engine top cover.

17 Disconnect the wiring from the sensor located on the thermostat housing on the right-hand end of the cylinder head.

18 Unscrew and remove the sensor.

7.4 Coolant temperature sensor located on the thermostat housing (Z22SE engine)

19 Fit the new sensor using a reversal of the removal procedure, but tighten the sensor to the specified torque and refill the cooling system with reference to Chapter 1B.

Coolant temperature gauge sender

Note: *The temperature gauge sender unit can be distinguished by its single electrical wire, compared to the multi-pin connector for the fuel injection system's coolant temperature sensor.*

Testing

20 Testing of the coolant temperature sender is by the substitution of a unit known to be in good working order.

Removal

21 Partially drain the cooling system with reference to Chapter 1A or 1B. Alternatively, it is possible to change the sender quickly with minimal loss of coolant by first releasing any pressure from the cooling system. With the engine cold, temporarily remove the expansion tank cap.

22 Disconnect the single wire from the sender located on the thermostat housing **(see illustration)** on all engines except the X16SZR where it is screwed into the inlet manifold.

23 Unscrew and remove the sender.

Refitting

24 Fit the new sender using a reversal of the removal procedure, but tighten the sender to the specified torque and refill the cooling system with reference to Chapter 1A or 1B.

7.22 Coolant temperature sender located on the right-hand front of the cylinder head (diesel engines)

Cooling/auxiliary fan switch

Testing

25 Refer to Section 5.

Petrol engines

26 Drain the cooling system as described in Chapter 1A.

27 Loosen the clips and disconnect the top hose from the radiator and thermostat housing.

28 On models with air conditioning, unbolt the refrigerant line bracket from the radiator and refrigerant lines.

29 Unscrew the radiator top mounting bolts from the engine compartment front cross-member.

30 Disconnect the wiring from the fan motor temperature switch and, where applicable, the auxiliary fan motor temperature switch. The upper switch is for the cooling fan and the lower switch is for the auxiliary fan.

31 Unscrew and remove the switch from the radiator.

32 Refitting is a reversal of removal, but refill the cooling system with reference to Chapter 1A.

Diesel engines

33 Partially drain the cooling system with reference to Chapter 1B.

34 Disconnect the wiring from the switch located on the top left-hand side of the radiator.

35 Where the original top hose clip is fitted, it may be necessary to release the spring-type clip and reposition it away from the fan temperature switch.

36 Unscrew the switch from the radiator.

37 Refitting is a reversal of removal, but refill the cooling system with reference to Chapter 1B.

Coolant level warning switch

Testing

38 To test the coolant level warning switch, disconnect the wiring and connect an ohmmeter to the terminals. Check that with the switch immersed in coolant there is no continuity, and with the switch out of the coolant there is continuity.

Removal

39 The switch is located in the expansion tank. With the engine cold, unscrew the expansion tank filler cap to dissipate any remaining pressure.

40 Draw off the coolant from the expansion tank until its level is below the switch.

41 Disconnect the wiring, then unscrew the switch from the tank.

Refitting

42 Refitting is a reversal of removal.

Coolant shut-off valve

X18XE and X20XEV

43 Drain the cooling system as described in Chapter 1A by disconnecting the radiator bottom hose.

44 Disconnect the vacuum hose from the top of the valve.

45 Release or loosen the clips and disconnect the three hoses from the valve. To ensure the hoses are refitted correctly, mark them in relation to the valve.

46 Refitting is a reversal of removal, but refill the cooling system with reference to Chapter 1A.

Z22SE

47 Drain the cooling system as described in Chapter 1A by unscrewing the drain plug located on the bottom of the coolant pump. On completion, refit and tighten the plug.

48 Release or loosen the clips and disconnect the two coolant hoses (from the thermostat) from the top of the shut-off valve. Mark the hoses in relation to the valve to ensure correct refitting.

49 Remove the shut-off valve from the bracket on the brake servo unit and position to one side.

50 Disconnect the hoses from the heater matrix by releasing the quick-release fittings.

51 Disconnect the vacuum line and withdraw the shut-off valve from the engine compartment.

52 Refitting is a reversal of removal, but refill the cooling system with reference to Chapter 1A.

Solenoid valve for coolant shut-off

Z22SE

53 At the rear of the engine compartment, lift up the weatherstrip and open the service aperture in front of the windscreen.

54 Disconnect the vacuum hoses and wiring from the solenoid valve.

55 Unscrew the valve mounting bolt and remove the guide pin, then withdraw the shut-off valve.

56 Refitting is a reversal of removal.

8 Coolant pump – removal and refitting

X18XE and X20XEV

Removal

1 Disconnect the battery negative (earth) lead (see Chapter 5A).

2 Drain the cooling system as described in Chapter 1A by disconnecting the radiator bottom hose.

3 Remove the timing belt and tension roller with reference to the appropriate part of Chapter 2.

4 Unscrew and remove the three coolant pump securing bolts.

5 Withdraw the coolant pump from the cylinder block, noting that it may be necessary to tap the pump lightly with a soft-faced mallet to free it from the cylinder block.

8.22 On 1.6 litre engines align the flange edge with the mark on the cylinder block

6 Recover the pump sealing ring, and discard it; a new one must be used on refitting.

7 Note that it is not possible to overhaul the pump. If it is faulty, the unit must be renewed complete.

Refitting

8 Ensure that the pump and cylinder block mating surfaces are clean and dry, and apply a smear of silicone grease to the pump mating surface in the cylinder block.

9 Fit a new sealing ring to the pump, and install the pump in the cylinder block. Make sure that the lug on the pump aligns with the mark on the cylinder block.

10 Insert the securing bolts and tighten to the specified torque.

11 Refit the timing belt tensioner and timing belt as described in the appropriate part of Chapter 2.

12 Refit the radiator bottom hose, then refill the cooling system with reference to Chapter 1A.

13 Reconnect the battery negative lead (see Chapter 5A).

X16SZR, X16XEL, Z16XE, X18XE1 and Z18XE

Removal

14 Disconnect the battery negative (earth) lead (see Chapter 5A).

15 Drain the cooling system as described in Chapter 1A by disconnecting the radiator bottom hose.

16 Remove the timing belt and timing belt rear cover as described in the appropriate part of Chapter 2. **Note:** *The timing belt must*

8.35 Coolant pump drive sprocket access cover (Z22SE engine)

not come into contact with coolant.

17 Unscrew and remove the three coolant pump securing bolts.

18 Withdraw the coolant pump from the cylinder block, noting that it may be necessary to tap the pump lightly with a soft-faced mallet to free it from the cylinder block.

19 Recover the pump sealing ring, and discard it; a new one must be used on refitting.

20 Note that it is not possible to overhaul the pump. If it is faulty, the unit must be renewed complete.

Refitting

21 Ensure that the pump and cylinder block mating surfaces are clean and dry, and apply a smear of silicone grease to the pump mating surface in the cylinder block.

22 Fit a new sealing ring to the pump, and locate the pump in the cylinder block. On X18XE1 and Z18XE engines, make sure that the lug on the oil pump housing engages in the groove of the pump. On X16XEL and Z16XE engines, align the edge of the coolant pump flange with the mark on the cylinder block **(see illustration)**.

23 Insert the securing bolts and tighten to the specified torque.

24 Refit the timing belt rear cover and timing belt as described in the appropriate part of Chapter 2.

25 Refit the radiator bottom hose, then refill the cooling system with reference to Chapter 1A.

26 Reconnect the battery negative lead (see Chapter 5A).

Z22SE

Removal

27 Apply the handbrake, then jack up the front of the vehicle and support it on axle stands (see *Jacking and vehicle support*). Remove the engine compartment undertray.

28 Disconnect the battery negative (earth) lead (see Chapter 5A).

29 Unbolt the left-hand engine lifting eye from the cylinder head.

30 Unbolt the lower heatshield from the exhaust manifold, followed by the upper heat shield.

31 Drain the cooling system as described in Chapter 1A by unscrewing the drain plug from under the coolant pump. Refit and tighten the plug on completion.

32 Unclip the oxygen sensor wiring from the thermostat housing, then remove the cable retainer from the stud bolts.

33 Remove the relay box from the hydraulic modulator and position it to one side.

34 Separate the brake servo vacuum line at the quick-release connection.

35 Unbolt the coolant pump drive sprocket access cover from the timing cover on the right-hand side of the engine **(see illustration)**.

36 Vauxhall/Opel technicians use a special tool (KM-J-43651) to hold the sprocket stationary while the coolant pump is being

8.36a Home-made tool holding the coolant pump drive sprocket stationary (Z22SE engine)

8.36b Unscrew the two remaining bolts securing the coolant pump to the sprocket (Z22SE engine)

8.36c Vauxhall tool KM-J-43651 retaining the coolant pump sprocket while the pump is being removed (Z22SE engine)

1 Bolts holding the tool to the timing housing
2 Bolts holding the sprocket to the tool
Arrows indicate pump mounting bolts

removed. The tool consists of a flanged tube which is bolted to the sprocket and also to the timing housing, with holes to allow removal of the coolant pump bolts. It is possible to fabricate a simple home-made tool from a length of flat metal bar using two threaded rods screwed into the sprocket. First unscrew one of the pump mounting bolts from the sprocket taking care not to drop it into the timing case, then bolt the tool into position to hold the sprocket. With the tool in position, unscrew the two remaining bolts from the sprocket **(see illustrations)**. To prevent losing any of the bolts, temporarily place a cloth rag beneath the sprocket in the timing case.

37 Loosen the clip and disconnect the hose from the thermostat housing cover. Also disconnect the heater hoses from the thermostat housing and heater matrix. Remove the hoses.

38 Unclip the coolant temperature sensor wiring from the thermostat housing cover, then disconnect the wiring from the sensor.
39 Unscrew and remove the coolant temperature sensor from the thermostat housing.
40 Unclip the oxygen sensor wiring plug from the loom bracket and disconnect.
41 Unscrew the bolts and remove the thermostat housing and coolant pipe from the cylinder block and coolant pump. Note the lower bolt is a stud bolt, and note the location of the O-ring seal in the pump housing **(see illustrations)**.
42 Unscrew the pump mounting bolts noting that if you are using the Vauxhall/Opel tool, one of the bolts cannot be removed completely. There are two bolts at the front and two at the rear. Remove the pump from the timing housing and withdraw upwards from the engine **(see illustrations)**.

43 Recover the pump sealing ring, and discard it; a new one must be used on refitting.
44 Note that it is not possible to overhaul the pump. If it is faulty, the unit must be renewed complete.

Refitting

45 Ensure that the pump and timing housing mating surfaces are clean and dry, and apply a smear of silicone grease to the pump mating surface.
46 Fit a new sealing ring to the groove in the pump, then locate the pump in the timing housing, making sure that the three bolt holes are aligned with the holes in the sprocket.
47 Insert the pump mounting bolts and two of the sprocket bolts hand-tight to start with, then tighten them to the specified torque.
48 Remove the holding tool and refit the final sprocket bolt, tightening it to the specified torque.
49 Refit the coolant pump drive sprocket access cover to the timing cover together with a new gasket, and tighten the bolts securely.

8.41a Thermostat housing retaining bolts (Z22SE engine)

8.41b Removing the coolant pipe from the pump housing (Z22SE engine)

8.42a Unscrew the rear bolts . . .

8.42b . . . and the front bolts . . .

8.42c . . . and withdraw the coolant pump from the timing housing (Z22SE engine)

8.69 Unscrew the mounting bolts . . .

50 Refit the coolant pipe and thermostat housing together with new sealing rings, and tighten the bolts securely.

51 Reconnect the oxygen sensor wiring and refit the plug to the loom bracket.

52 Refit the coolant temperature sensor to the thermostat housing and tighten to the specified torque, then reconnect the wiring and secure.

53 Refit the hoses to the thermostat housing cover and tighten the clips.

54 Reconnect the brake servo vacuum line, and refit the relay box to the hydraulic modulator.

55 Refit the cable retainer and secure the oxygen sensor wiring.

56 Refit the exhaust manifold heatshields and engine lifting eye.

57 Reconnect the battery negative (earth) lead (see Chapter 5A).

58 Refill the cooling system with reference to Chapter 1A.

59 Refit the engine compartment undertray and lower the vehicle to the ground.

Diesel models

Removal

60 Disconnect the battery negative (earth) lead (see Chapter 5A).

61 Apply the handbrake, then jack up the front of the vehicle and support it on axle stands (see *Jacking and vehicle support*). Remove the engine compartment undertray.

62 Drain the cooling system as described in Chapter 1B.

63 Remove the auxiliary drivebelt as described in Chapter 1B.

8.71 . . . and recover the sealing ring

8.70 . . . withdraw the coolant pump from the cylinder block . . .

64 On models with air conditioning, remove the relay box from the air cleaner housing and position to one side.

65 Remove the air cleaner assembly as described in Chapter 4B.

66 Remove the engine top cover, then unscrew the centre nut(s) from the top of the right-hand engine mounting.

67 The engine must now be lifted slightly off the right-hand mounting to provide room to remove the coolant pump. To do this, either use a trolley jack and block of wood beneath the engine, or alternatively connect a hoist to the right-hand side of the engine. Whichever method is used, make sure the equipment is adequate for the job and can be used safely.

68 Hold the coolant pump pulley stationary using an old auxiliary drivebelt or an oil filter strap wrench, then unscrew and remove the bolts and remove the pulley from the drive flange on the coolant pump.

69 Unscrew and remove the three coolant pump securing bolts **(see illustration)**.

70 Withdraw the coolant pump from the cylinder block, noting that it may be necessary to tap the pump lightly with a soft-faced mallet to free it from the cylinder block **(see illustration)**.

71 Recover the pump sealing ring, and discard it; a new one must be used on refitting **(see illustration)**.

72 Note that it is not possible to overhaul the pump. If it is faulty, the unit must be renewed complete.

Refitting

73 Ensure that the pump and cylinder block mating surfaces are clean and dry, and apply a smear of silicone grease to the pump mating surface in the cylinder block.

74 Fit a new sealing ring to the pump, and install the pump in the cylinder block.

75 Insert the securing bolts and tighten to the specified torque.

76 Refit the pulley and tighten the securing bolts to the specified torque.

77 Lower the engine and refit the nut(s) to the top of the right-hand mounting. Tighten the nut(s) to the specified torque (see Chapter 2D).

78 Refit the engine top cover and the lower undertray, then lower the vehicle to the ground.

79 Refit the air cleaner assembly as described in Chapter 4B.

80 On models with air conditioning, refit the relay box to the air cleaner housing.

81 Refit the auxiliary drivebelt as described in Chapter 1B.

82 Reconnect the battery negative lead (see Chapter 5A).

83 Refill and bleed the cooling system as described in Chapter 1B.

9 Heating and ventilation system – general information

The heater/ventilation system consists of a four-speed blower motor (housed behind the facia), face-level vents in the centre and at each end of the facia, and air ducts to the front and rear footwells.

The heater controls are located in the centre of the facia, and the controls operate flap valves to deflect and mix the air flowing through the various parts of the heater/ventilation system. The flap valves are contained in the air distribution housing, which acts as a central distribution unit, passing air to the various ducts and vents.

Cold air enters the system through the grille at the rear of the engine compartment.

The air (boosted by the blower fan if required) then flows through the various ducts, according to the settings of the controls. Stale air is expelled through ducts at the rear of the vehicle. If warm air is required, the cold air is passed through the heater matrix, which is heated by the engine coolant.

A recirculation switch enables the outside air supply to be closed off, while the air inside the vehicle is recirculated. This can be useful to prevent unpleasant odours entering from outside the vehicle, but should only be used briefly, as the recirculated air inside the vehicle will soon deteriorate.

10 Heater/ventilation system components – removal and refitting

Air vents

Removal

1 To remove an air vent from the centre of the facia, insert a small screwdriver between the two vents and carefully lever out either one. On the driver's side it will be necessary to remove the sidelight switch assembly first. With the vents removed the housing can be removed by undoing the three retaining screws.

2 To remove the vent from the driver's side of the facia, first lever out the light control switch then remove the steering column shrouds. Undo the three screws and withdraw the vent assembly – the upper screw is located behind the vent grilles. Disconnect the wiring and remove the vent.

3 To remove the vent from the passenger's side of the facia, first remove the glovebox as described in Chapter 11. Undo the three screws and withdraw the vent assembly.

4 To remove the windscreen air duct panel located along the bottom of the windscreen first, on models fitted with Electronic Climate Control, remove the sun sensor as described later in this Section. Release the 10 clips and withdraw the aid duct panel taking care not to damage the facia panel. Vauxhall/Opel technicians use a special tool (KM-595-1) to release the clips, and if the clips are difficult to remove it may be possible to obtain the tool from a Vauxhall/Opel dealer.

Refitting

5 Refitting is a reversal of removal.

Blower motor resistor

Note: *The resistor is not fitted to models with electronic climate control.*

Removal

6 Remove the heater blower motor as described below.

7 Pull the resistor upwards then sideways then disconnect the wiring.

Refitting

8 Refitting is a reversal of removal.

Heater blower motor

Removal

9 Remove the pollen filter housing. This involves removing the windscreen wiper motor and disconnecting the vacuum hoses from the housing. On 2.0 litre diesel engine models also remove the ambient temperature sensor for the auxiliary heating.

10 Unscrew the bolts securing the heater blower motor cover, then release the clips and remove the cover.

11 Disconnect the wiring plug then withdraw the heater motor and disconnect the remaining wiring.

Refitting

12 Refitting is a reversal of removal.

Heater control assembly

Removal

13 Using a small screwdriver inserted at each bottom corner in turn, carefully prise out the panel from over the heater control knobs, then pull off the knobs **(see illustrations)**.

14 Undo the upper retaining screws and withdraw the heater control assembly by moving it slightly upwards then removing from the facia **(see illustration)**.

15 Disconnect the wiring from the rear of the control assembly.

16 Note the position of the cables then release the clips and disconnect the cables. To remove the cables completely, disconnect them from the heater housing **(see illustration)**.

10.13a Removing the heater control panel . . .

Refitting

17 Refitting is a reversal of removal. Before refitting the panel, make sure that the bulbs are correctly fitted. When refitting the knobs, make sure that the conductor engages with the lug on the spindle.

Heater housing

Note: *On models with air conditioning it is necessary to drain the refrigerant. This work must be carried out by qualified personnel.*

Removal

18 Remove the facia panel as described in Chapter 11.

19 Remove the front doors as described in Chapter 11.

20 Using a Torx key, unscrew the bolts securing the outer ends of the steering crossmember to the A-pillars on each side, then remove the two upper guides and unscrew the tolerance bolts from the ends of the crossmember, noting that they are **left-hand thread**.

21 Remove the rear footwell air distribution housing.

22 On models with air conditioning, the refrigerant must now be evacuated by a refrigerant engineer.

 Warning: Do not attempt to drain the refrigerant without the specialist equipment as this is potentially a dangerous job.

23 On models with air conditioning, working in the engine compartment disconnect the lines from the evaporator and remove the condensation drain flange.

10.13b . . . and heater control knobs

24 Working in the engine compartment, use two hose clamps to clamp the hoses leading to the heater matrix. The hoses are located on the bulkhead, just above the steering gear. Alternatively, drain the cooling system completely as described in Chapter 1A or 1B.

25 Disconnect the hoses from the heater matrix stubs by pressing the bar and pulling back the locking ring. Note that the connections are of quick-release design. Be prepared for some loss of coolant as the hoses are released, by placing cloth rags beneath them.

26 Unscrew the three bolts securing the heater housing to the bulkhead. The bolts are located in the engine compartment.

27 Remove the pollen filter housing. This involves removing the windscreen wiper motor and disconnecting the vacuum hoses from the housing. On 2.0 litre diesel engine models also remove the ambient temperature sensor for the auxiliary heating.

28 On models with electronic climate control, release the wiring harness plug for the power supply from the servo motors and fan.

29 Withdraw the heater housing from inside the vehicle.

Refitting

30 Refitting is a reversal of removal, but refill the cooling system as described in Chapter 1A or 1B. On models with air conditioning, have the system charged by the refrigerant engineer. When refitting the steering crossmember, make sure that the upper guides are located first before tightening the bolts.

10.14 Unscrewing the heater control assembly mounting screws

10.16 The heater control cables are clipped to the housing

10.31a For improved access to the heater hoses in the engine compartment on diesel models, disconnect the wiring . . .

10.31b . . . and remove the fuel filter

10.31c Using hose clamps to clamp the heater matrix hoses in the engine compartment

Heater matrix

Removal

31 Working in the engine compartment, use two hose clamps to clamp the hoses leading to the heater matrix. The hoses are located on the bulkhead, just above the steering gear. Alternatively, drain the cooling system completely as described in Chapter 1A or 1B. For improved access remove the fuel filter on diesel engine models (see illustrations).

32 Disconnect the hoses from the heater matrix stubs by pressing the bar and pulling back the locking ring. Note that the connections are of quick-release design. Tape over or plug the stubs to prevent dust or dirt entering the cooling system (see illustrations). Be prepared for some loss of coolant as the hoses are released, by placing cloth rags beneath them.

33 Remove the centre console as described in Chapter 11.

34 Remove the facia panel support bracket

from beneath the centre of the facia (see illustration).

35 Remove the rear footwell air distribution housing from beneath the centre of the facia. First pull up the extensions from the lower outlets, then undo the retaining screw and withdraw the housing. Finally remove the support bracket (see illustrations).

36 Release the clips and remove the cover to expose the heater matrix (see illustrations). On models with air conditioning, the cover is retained with bolts.

37 Carefully withdraw the heater matrix from the housing (see illustration). On models with air conditioning it is necessary to move the matrix to the right before removing it.

Refitting

38 Refitting is a reversal of removal. If the

10.32a Pull back the locking ring to disconnect the quick-release connections

10.32b Seal the ends of the matrix stubs before removing the matrix

10.34 Removing the facia panel support bracket (arrowed)

10.35a Pull up the extensions from the lower outlets . . .

10.35b . . . then undo the screw . . .

10.35c . . . and withdraw the rear footwell air distribution housing . . .

10.35d . . . followed by the support bracket

10.36a Use a screwdriver to release the clips . . .

10.36b . . . then remove the cover from the heater matrix

10.37 Carefully withdraw the heater matrix from the housing

matrix cover clips are damaged on removal, drill four holes in the cover and use self-tapping screws to secure the cover. Press the matrix firmly into the housing before refitting the cover **(see illustration)**. On completion refill the cooling system as described in Chapter 1A or 1B. Make sure that the quick-release hose fittings are correctly engaged by checking that the green lock ring is released.

Heater switch

Removal

39 Remove the heater control assembly as described in paragraphs 13 to 16.
40 Carefully release the lugs and remove the switch from the assembly.

Refitting

41 Refitting is a reversal of removal.

Facia-mounted heater switches

Removal

42 Using a small screwdriver, carefully prise the switch from the facia taking care not to damage the facia. Position a wad of cloth on the facia as a precaution.

Refitting

43 Refitting is a reversal of removal.

Vacuum tank

Removal

44 With the bonnet open, remove the water deflector from the right-hand (LHD models) or left-hand (RHD models) rear side of the engine compartment for access to the vacuum tank.

10.38 Press the heater matrix firmly into the housing before refitting the cover

45 Note the location of the vacuum hoses then disconnect them **(see illustration)**.
46 Unscrew the two mounting nuts and withdraw the vacuum tank.

Refitting

47 Refitting is a reversal of removal.

Vacuum unit

Removal

48 Remove the glovebox as described in Chapter 11.
49 On left-hand drive models remove the lower trim panel from the right-hand footwell.
50 Disconnect the wiring and vacuum hose from the vacuum unit.
51 Remove the air recirculation vacuum unit and lower it until the flap in the air distribution housing is open.
52 Press the linkage towards the front of the vehicle and withdraw the vacuum unit from inside the vehicle.

Refitting

53 Refitting is a reversal of removal.

Electronic Climate Control unit

Removal

54 On vehicles with a 'full' heater control panel (surrounding the radio as well as the heater controls), using a small screwdriver inserted at the top of the panel, carefully prise the heater control panel outwards from the facia until the four retaining clips are disengaged from the panel's upper edge, then lift the panel to withdraw it. Place a wad of cloth beneath the screwdriver to avoid damage to the facia.
55 On vehicles with a heater control panel surrounding only the heater controls, using small screwdriver inserted at each bottom corner in turn, carefully prise the heater control panel from the facia. Place a wad of cloth beneath the screwdriver to avoid damage to the facia – when the lower pair of retaining clips are disengaged, lift the panel and release the upper two clips &using a long, slim-bladed screwdriver, if required).
56 On all vehicles, remove the radio, then remove the hazard warning and other pushbutton switches from above the radio aperture – refer to the relevant Sections of

Chapter 12. Remove the radio mounting bracket and the switch mounting strip.
57 Using a small screwdriver to release their locking bars, unplug the two electrical connectors from the front (ie, engine compartment side) of the control assembly. On vehicles with a 'full' heater control panel, unscrew the control assembly's two upper mounting bolts. On all vehicles, use a screwdriver to release the control assembly's two lower retaining lugs (by pressing them in), then push the assembly towards the front of the vehicle (until the two locating pins have been disengaged from the facia) and lift it to withdraw it.

Refitting

58 Refitting is the reverse of removal, noting the following points:
 a) *Manoeuvre the control assembly into position and pull it against the facia so that the two location pins enter their respective apertures and the two lower retaining lugs engage correctly.*
 b) *Ensuring that the connections are clean and properly made, plug the two electrical connectors back into the front of the control assembly, then refit their locking bars to secure them.*
 c) *On vehicles with a 'full' heater control panel, tighten securely the control assembly's two upper mounting bolts.*
 d) *On all vehicles, refit all other components removed for access. On vehicles with a 'full' heater control panel, ensure that the panel is located from the top first, so that its four retaining clips are correctly seated*

10.45 The heater vacuum tank is located in the rear corner of the engine compartment

12.6 Seal the refrigerant inlet and outlet ports on the compressor

before the panel's lower end is pressed into place.
e) When reassembly is complete, synchronise the servomotors by switching on the ignition and depressing simultaneously the 'Auto On' and 'Auto Off' controls for approximately 5 seconds.

ECC air temperature sensor

Removal

59 Remove the climate control unit as described earlier.
60 Disconnect the wiring plug from the air outlet temperature sensor.
61 Twist the temperature sensor anti-clockwise and remove from the housing.

Refitting

62 Refitting is a reversal of removal.

ECC fan regulator

Removal

63 Remove the left-hand side footwell air duct.
64 Remove the cover from the side of the heater assembly.
65 On left-hand drive models, remove the accelerator pedal.
66 Unscrew the fan regulator retaining bolts.
67 Withdraw the fan regulator from the heater housing.

Refitting

68 Refitting is a reversal of removal.

12.7 Wiring plug on the compressor

ECC sun sensor

Removal

69 Carefully prise out the sensor from the top of the air duct panel taking care not to damage the panel. Use a wad of cloth when levering as a precaution.
70 Tape or clip the wiring to the facia to prevent it dropping inside.
71 Disconnect the wiring and remove the sensor.

Refitting

72 Refitting is a reversal of removal.

11 Air conditioning system – general information and precautions

General information

Air conditioning is standard on top of the range models, and optional on certain other models. It enables the temperature of incoming air to be lowered, and also dehumidifies the air, which makes for rapid demisting and increased comfort.

The cooling side of the system works in the same way as a domestic refrigerator. Refrigerant gas is drawn into a belt-driven compressor, and passes into a condenser mounted in front of the radiator, where it loses heat and becomes liquid. The liquid passes through an expansion valve to an evaporator, where it changes from liquid under high pressure to gas under low pressure. This change is accompanied by a drop in temperature, which cools the evaporator. The refrigerant returns to the compressor, and the cycle begins again.

Air blown through the evaporator passes to the heater assembly, where it is mixed with hot air blown through the heater matrix, to achieve the desired temperature in the passenger compartment.

The heating side of the system works in the same way as on models without air conditioning (see Section 10).

The operation of the system is controlled electronically. Any problems with the system should be referred to a Vauxhall/Opel dealer or an air conditioning specialist.

Precautions

It is necessary to observe special precautions whenever dealing with any part of the system, its associated components, and any items which necessitate disconnection of the system.

⚠️ **Warning: The refrigeration circuit contains a liquid refrigerant (Freon). This refrigerant is potentially dangerous, and should only be handled by qualified persons. If it is splashed onto the skin, it can cause frostbite. It is not itself poisonous, but in the presence of a naked flame it forms a**

poisonous gas; inhalation of the vapour through a lighted cigarette could prove fatal. Uncontrolled discharging of the refrigerant is dangerous, and potentially damaging to the environment. It is therefore dangerous to disconnect any part of the system without specialised knowledge and equipment. If for any reason the system must be disconnected, entrust this task to an authorised dealer or an air conditioning specialist.
Caution: Do not operate the air conditioning system if it is known to be short of refrigerant, as this may damage the compressor.

12 Air conditioning system components – removal and refitting

⚠️ *Warning: Read the precautions given in Section 11, and have the system discharged by a Vauxhall/Opel dealer or an air conditioning specialist. Do not carry out the following work unless the system has been discharged.*

Compressor

Removal

1 Have the air conditioning system evacuated by a qualified engineer. Seal the refrigerant circuit with suitable plugs.
2 Where necessary, remove the air filter housing as described in the appropriate part of Chapter 4.
3 Remove the auxiliary drivebelt as described in Chapter 1A or 1B.
4 Apply the handbrake, then jack up the front of the vehicle and support it on axle stands (see *Jacking and vehicle support*). Remove the splash guard from under the engine compartment.
5 On petrol engine models, remove the front exhaust downpipe as described in Chapter 4A.
6 Disconnect the refrigerant lines from the compressor, then tape over or plug the lines **(see illustration)**.
7 Disconnect the wiring plug from the compressor **(see illustration)**.
8 On models with the X20DTL diesel engine, disconnect the wiring plug at the sump.
9 Unscrew the mounting bolts and withdraw the compressor from the engine.

Refitting

10 Refitting is a reversal of removal but tighten the mounting bolts to the specified torque and tension the auxiliary drivebelt with reference to Chapter 1A or 1B. On completion, have the refrigerant engineer charge the system and fit new O-rings to the line connections. If a new compressor is being fitted, make sure that the oil level is checked and topped-up before fitting it, and initially run

12.21a Engine oil cooler right-hand retaining clip . . .

12.21b . . . and left-hand retaining clip

12.22a Auxiliary electric cooling fan assembly

the compressor for at least 2 minutes with the engine running at 1500 rpm, with the switch on maximum speed and all instrument panel flaps open. Note that the compressor lubricant is extremely hygroscopic, and must therefore always be stored in a sealed container; it must never be re-used.

Evaporator

Removal

11 Have the air conditioning system evacuated by a qualified engineer.
12 Remove the heater blower motor as described in Section 10.
13 Remove the expansion valve.
14 Remove the glovebox as described in Chapter 11.
15 On left-hand drive models, remove the trim panel from the right-hand footwell (see Chapter 11, Section 29).
16 Remove the coolant line cover, and on left-hand drive models the right-hand side footwell air duct.
17 Carefully cut around the edge of the housing and remove the evaporator. Note that the new evaporator is provided with a new cover which is screwed into position.

Refitting

18 Refitting is a reversal of removal, but before fitting the new evaporator apply sealing compound to the edge of the new cover. On completion, have the refrigerant engineer charge the system and fit new O-rings to the line connections.

Condenser

Removal

19 Have the air conditioning system evacuated by a qualified engineer.
20 Remove the radiator grille as described in Chapter 11.
21 Where applicable, unclip the engine oil cooler from the front of the condenser **(see illustrations)**.
22 Unbolt the auxiliary electric cooling fan assembly and disconnect the wiring **(see illustrations)**.
23 Detach the refrigerant lines from the

condenser and tape over or plug them.
24 Disconnect the radiator cooling fan wiring at the plug.
25 Carefully lift the condenser from the front of the radiator and withdraw from the vehicle **(see illustration)**.
26 If necessary, detach the receiver-dryer from the condenser.

Refitting

27 Refitting is a reversal of removal. On completion, have the refrigerant engineer charge the system and fit new O-rings to the line connections.

Receiver-dryer

Removal

28 Have the air conditioning system evacuated by a qualified engineer.

12.22b Unscrew the mounting bolts . . .

12.25 Air conditioning condenser on the front of the radiator

29 Remove the front bumper as described in Chapter 11.
30 The receiver-dryer is located on the front left-hand side of the radiator **(see illustration)**.
31 Detach the refrigerant lines and tape over or plug them.
32 Unbolt the receiver-dryer from the condenser.

Refitting

33 Refitting is a reversal of removal. On completion, have the refrigerant engineer charge the system and fit new O-rings to the line connections.

Auxiliary fan triple switch

Removal

34 The auxiliary fan switch is located on the left-hand rear of the radiator. First, have the

12.22c . . . and lift the cooling fan assembly from the condenser

12.30 The receiver-dryer is located on the front left-hand side of the radiator

air conditioning system evacuated by a qualified engineer.

35 Apply the handbrake, then jack up the front of the vehicle and support it on axle stands (see *Jacking and vehicle support*).

36 Disconnect the wiring from the switch, then unscrew the switch from the refrigerant line.

Refitting

37 Refitting is a reversal of removal. On completion, have the refrigerant engineer charge the system and fit new O-rings to the line connections.

Chapter 4 Part A:
Fuel and exhaust systems – petrol engine models

Contents

Degrees of difficulty

Easy, suitable for novice with little experience		Fairly easy, suitable for beginner with some experience		Fairly difficult, suitable for competent DIY mechanic		Difficult, suitable for experienced DIY mechanic		Very difficult, suitable for expert DIY or professional	

Specifications

System type

1.6 litre SOHC (X16SZR) models . . . . Multec (single-point injection)
1.6 litre DOHC (X16XEL and Z16XE) models . . . . Multec S (multi-point injection)
1.8 litre (X18XE1) models . . . . Simtec 70 (multi-point injection)
1.8 litre (Z18XE) models . . . . Simtec 71 (multi-point injection)
1.8 litre (X18XE) and 2.0 litre (X20XEV) models . . . . Simtec 56.5 (multi-point injection)
2.2 litre (Z22SE) models . . . . GMPT – E15 (multi-point injection)

Fuel system data

Fuel pump type . . . . Electric, immersed in tank
Fuel pump regulated constant pressure (approximate):
   Single-point injection system . . . . 0.8 bar
   Multi-point injection system* . . . . 3.0 to 3.5 bar
Specified idle speed . . . . Not adjustable – controlled by ECU
Idle mixture CO content . . . . Not adjustable – controlled by ECU
*Fuel pressure regulator vacuum hose disconnected and plugged (on X16XEL, X18XE and X20XEV models)

Recommended fuel

Minimum octane rating . . . . 95 RON* unleaded (UK premium unleaded).
   Leaded fuel (4-star/LRP) must **NOT** be used
*91 RON unleaded fuel can be used but a slight power loss maybe noticeable.

Torque wrench settings

	Nm	lbf ft
Accelerator pedal nuts	20	15
Accelerator pedal position sensor nuts	20	15
Braking system vacuum hose union nut	15	11
Camshaft sensor*:		
All engines except X18XE and X20XEV	8	6
X18XE and X20XEV engines	6	4
Crankshaft sensor bolt:		
All engines except X18XE, X20XEV and Z22SE	8	6
X18XE and X20XEV engines	6	4
Z22SE engine	10	7
Exhaust front pipe-to-manifold bolts*:		
X16XEL, Z16XE, Z18XE, and X18XE1 engines	25	18
X16SZR, X18XE and X20XEV engines	20	15
Z22SE engine	16	12
Exhaust manifold nuts*:		
All engines except Z22SE	22	16
Z22SE engine	12	9
Exhaust manifold shroud/heat shield bolts/nuts:		
All engines except Z22SE	8	6
Z22SE engine:		
Upper heat shield to cylinder block	25	18
Lower heat shield to upper heat shield	10	7
Fuel hose union nuts	15	11
Fuel pressure regulator clamp	5	4
Fuel rail bolts	8	6
Fuel tank retaining strap bolts	20	15
Inlet manifold nuts and bolts:		
X16XEL, Z16XE, Z18XE, and X18XE1 engines:		
Manifold to manifold flange	8	6
Manifold to cylinder head	20	15
Support bracket to manifold	20	15
Support bracket to cylinder block	35	26
X16SZR, X18XE and X20XEV engines	22	16
Z22SE engine	10	7
Knock sensor bolt:		
All engines except Z22SE	20	15
Z22SE engine	25	18
Spark plug heat shields – X16SZR engine	30	22
Throttle body – X16SZR engine:		
Retaining nuts	22	16
Upper body-to-lower body screws	6	4
Throttle housing:		
X16XEL, Z16XE, Z18XE, and X18XE1 engines	8	6
X18XE and X20XEV engines	9	7
Z22SE engines	10	7
Throttle potentiometer bolts – X16SZR engine	2	1

* Use new fasteners

1 General information and precautions

The fuel system consists of a fuel tank (which is mounted under the rear of the car, with an electric fuel pump immersed in it), a fuel filter and the fuel feed and return lines. On single-point injection models the fuel is supplied by a throttle body assembly which incorporates the single fuel injector and the fuel pressure regulator. On multi-point injection models the fuel pump supplies fuel to the fuel rail, which acts as a reservoir for the four fuel injectors which inject fuel into the inlet tracts. In addition, there is an Electronic control unit (ECU) and various sensors, electrical components and related wiring.

Refer to Section 7 for further information on the operation of each fuel injection system, and to Section 18 for information on the exhaust system.

⚠️ **Warning: Many of the procedures in this Chapter require the removal of fuel lines and connections, which may result in some fuel spillage. Before carrying out any operation on the fuel system, refer to the precautions given in 'Safety first!' at the beginning of this manual, and follow them implicitly. Petrol is a highly-dangerous and volatile liquid, and the precautions necessary when handling it cannot be overstressed.**

Note: *Residual pressure will remain in the fuel lines long after the vehicle was last used.*

Before disconnecting any fuel line, first depressurise the fuel system as described in Section 8.

2 Air cleaner assembly and intake ducts – removal and refitting

Removal

1 To remove the air cleaner housing, slacken the retaining clip securing the inlet trunking to the throttle body. Release the clips securing the trunking to the air cleaner housing by levering up the edge of the clip, then unscrew the retaining screw/nut(s) and remove the housing from the engine compartment **(see illustration)**.

2.1 Use a small screwdriver to release the trunking retaining clip

2.2a Disconnect any wiring connectors from the air intake trunking

2.2b Removing the intake pipe assembly (1.8 and 2.0 litre models

2 Where applicable, disconnect the wiring connector from the intake air temperature sensor and unclip the tank vent (canister purge) valve from the bracket on the housing **(see illustrations)**.

3 On single-point injection models, it will be necessary to disconnect the vacuum hose and the hot air intake hose from the housing as it is being removed.

4 The various air intake pipes/ducts can be disconnected and removed once the retaining clips have been slackened. In some cases it will be necessary to disconnect breather hoses, vacuum pipes and wiring connectors to allow the pipe/duct to be removed; the pipe/duct may also be bolted to a support bracket

Refitting

5 Refitting is the reverse of removal, making sure all the air intake ducts/hoses are securely reconnected.

---

3 Intake air temperature control system (single-point injection)

General information

1 The system is controlled by a heat-sensitive vacuum switch, mounted in the throttle body cover. When the temperature of the air passing through the cover is cold (below approximately 35°C), the vacuum switch is open, allowing inlet manifold depression to act on the air temperature control valve diaphragm in the base of the air cleaner housing. This vacuum causes the diaphragm to rise, drawing a flap valve across the cold-air intake, allowing only warmed air from the exhaust manifold shroud to enter the air cleaner.

2 As the temperature of the exhaust-warmed air entering the throttle body rises, the wax capsule in the vacuum switch deforms and closes the switch, cutting off the vacuum supply to the air temperature control valve assembly. As the vacuum supply is cut, the flap is gradually lowered across the hot-air intake until, when the temperature of the air in the duct is fully warmed-up (approximately

40°C), the control valve closes, allowing only cold air from the front of the car to enter the air cleaner.

Testing

3 To check the system, allow the engine to cool down completely, then detach the intake duct from the front of the air cleaner housing; the control valve assembly flap valve in the housing duct should be securely seated across the hot-air intake. Start the engine: the flap should immediately rise to close off the cold-air intake, and should then lower steadily as the engine warms-up, until it is eventually seated across the hot-air intake again.

4 To check the vacuum switch, disconnect the vacuum pipe from the control valve when the engine is running, and place a finger over the pipe end. When the engine is cold, full inlet manifold vacuum should be felt in the pipe, and when the engine is at normal operating temperature, there should be no vacuum in the pipe.

5 To check the air temperature control valve assembly, detach the intake duct from the air cleaner housing; the flap valve should be securely seated across the hot-air intake. Disconnect the vacuum pipe and, using a suitable length of hose, suck hard at the control valve stub; the flap should rise to shut off the cold-air intake.

6 If either component is faulty, it must be renewed. The vacuum switch is an integral part of the throttle body cover and the temperature control valve is an integral part of the air cleaner housing; neither component is available separately.

4.1 Remove the retaining clip then free the inner cable end fitting from its balljoint . . .

7 On completion of the check, ensure all disturbed items are securely reconnected.

---

4 Accelerator cable – removal, refitting and adjustment

Note: On Z16XE, Z18XE and Z22SE models, an electronic accelerator system is fitted (no accelerator cable), this consists of an accelerator pedal module and a throttle valve module. Each module has two potentiometers (sensors) which determine the position of the pedal, which then transmits a signal to the ECU. For the removal of the throttle valve module see Section 12, and for the accelerator pedal module removal see Section 16 or 17.

Removal

1 Working in the engine compartment, release the inner cable retaining clip then slide the clip out of the end fitting and release the cable from the throttle cam **(see illustration)**.

2 Free the accelerator outer cable from its mounting bracket, taking care not to lose the adjusting clip **(see illustration)**. Work back along the length of the cable, free it from any retaining clips or ties, noting its correct routing. On models with automatic transmission it will be necessary to disconnect the wiring from the kickdown switch which is built into the cable.

3 From inside the vehicle, unscrew the fasteners and remove the lower trim panel from underneath the driver's side of the facia to gain access to the accelerator pedal.

4.2 . . . and detach the outer cable from its bracket

4.4 Pull the cable grommet up and out from the end of the pedal

4.6 Accelerator cable grommet – pedal end

4.11 Removing the accelerator cable adjustment clip

4 Reaching up behind the facia, unclip the accelerator inner cable from the top of the accelerator pedal **(see illustration)**.

5 Return to the engine compartment then free the cable sealing grommet from the bulkhead and remove the cable and grommet from the vehicle.

6 Examine the cable for signs of wear or damage and renew if necessary. Check the rubber grommet for signs of damage or deterioration and renew it if necessary **(see illustration)**.

Refitting

7 Feed the cable into position from the engine compartment and seat the outer cable grommet in the bulkhead.

8 From inside the vehicle, clip the inner cable into position in the pedal end and check to make sure the grommet is correctly located in the bulkhead. Check that the cable is securely retained, then refit the trim panel to the facia.

9 From within the engine compartment, ensure the outer cable is correctly seated in the bulkhead, then work along the cable, securing it in position with the retaining clips and ties, ensuring that the cable is correctly routed. On models with automatic transmission, reconnect the wiring connector to the kickdown switch.

10 Connect the inner cable to the throttle cam and secure it in position with the retaining clip. Clip the outer cable into its mounting bracket and adjust the cable as described below.

Adjustment

11 Working in the engine compartment, slide the adjustment clip from accelerator outer cable **(see illustration)**.

12 With the clip removed, ensure that the throttle cam is fully against its stop. Gently pull the cable out of its grommet until all free play is removed from the inner cable.

13 With the cable held in this position, refit the spring clip to the last exposed outer cable groove in front of the rubber grommet. When the clip is refitted and the outer cable is released, there should be only a small amount of free play in the inner cable.

14 Have an assistant depress the accelerator pedal, and check that the throttle cam opens fully and returns smoothly to its stop.

5 Accelerator pedal – removal and refitting

Note: *On Z16XE, Z18XE and Z22SE models, an electronic accelerator system is fitted (no accelerator cable), this consists of an accelerator pedal module and a throttle valve module. Each module has two potentiometers (sensors) which determine the position of the pedal, which then transmit a signal to the ECU.*

1 From inside the vehicle, unscrew the fasteners and remove the lower trim panel from underneath the driver's side of the facia to gain access to the accelerator pedal.

2 On models with an accelerator cable, reach up behind the facia, unclip the accelerator inner cable from the top of the accelerator pedal **(see illustration 4.4)**.

3 On models with an electronic accelerator (no accelerator cable), disconnect the wiring connector from the pedal position sensor by sliding it towards the rear of the vehicle. Undo the retaining bolts and remove the pedal position sensor from the pedal assembly.

4 Unscrew the retaining nuts and remove the pedal assembly from the bulkhead **(see illustration)**.

5 Inspect the pedal assembly for signs of wear, paying particular attention to the pedal bushes, and renew as necessary. To dismantle the assembly, unhook the return spring then slide off the retaining clip and separate the pedal, mounting bracket, return spring and pivot bushes.

5.4 Undo the three pedal bracket retaining bolts

6 If the assembly has been dismantled, apply a smear of multi-purpose grease to the pedal pivot shaft and bushes. Fit the bushes and return spring to the mounting bracket and insert the pedal, making sure it passes through the return spring bore. Secure the pedal in position with the retaining clip and hook the return spring back behind the pedal.

7 Refit the pedal assembly and tighten its retaining nuts to the specified torque setting.

8 On models with an electronic accelerator (no accelerator cable), refit the pedal position sensor to the pedal assembly and reconnect the wiring connector.

9 On models with an accelerator cable, clip the accelerator cable into position on the pedal then refit the trim panel to the facia. On completion, adjust the accelerator cable as described in Section 4.

6 Unleaded petrol – general information and usage

Note: *The information given in this Chapter is correct at the time of writing. If updated information is thought to be required, check with a Vauxhall dealer. If travelling abroad, consult one of the motoring organisations (or a similar authority) for advice on the fuel available.*

1 The fuel recommended by Vauxhall is given in the Specifications Section of this Chapter, followed by the equivalent petrol currently on sale in the UK.

2 All petrol models are designed to run on fuel with a minimum octane rating of 95 RON. Lower octane fuel, down to minimum of rating 91 RON, can be safely used since the engine management system automatically adjusts the ignition timing to suit (using the information supplied by the knock sensor). However, a slight power loss is likely if fuel with a octane rating of less than 95 RON is used.

3 All models have a catalytic converter, and so must be run on unleaded fuel **only**. Under no circumstances should leaded fuel (UK 4-star/LRP) be used, as this may damage the converter.

4 Super unleaded petrol (98 octane) can also be used in all models if wished, though there is no advantage in doing so.

7 Fuel injection systems – general information

Multec single-point injection system

1 The Multec engine management (fuel injection/ignition) system **(see illustration)** incorporates a closed-loop catalytic converter, an evaporative emission control system and an exhaust gas recirculation (EGR) system, and complies with the latest emission control standards. The fuel injection side of the system operates as follows; refer to Chapter 5B for information on the ignition system.

2 The fuel pump, immersed in the fuel tank, pumps fuel from the fuel tank to the fuel injector, via a filter mounted underneath the rear of the vehicle. Fuel supply pressure is controlled by the pressure regulator in the throttle body assembly. The regulator operates by allowing excess fuel to return to the tank.

3 The electrical control system consists of the ECU, along with the following sensors.

a) *Throttle potentiometer – informs the ECU of the throttle position, and the rate of throttle opening or closing.*

b) *Coolant temperature sensor – informs the ECU of engine temperature.*

c) *Oxygen sensor – informs the ECU of the oxygen content of the exhaust gases (explained in greater detail in Part C of this Chapter).*

d) *Crankshaft sensor – informs the ECU of engine speed and crankshaft position.*

e) *Knock sensor – informs the ECU when pre-ignition ('pinking') is occurring.*

f) *Manifold absolute pressure (MAP) sensor – informs the ECU of the engine load by monitoring the pressure in the inlet manifold.*

g) *ABS control unit – informs the ECU of the vehicle speed.*

h) *Air conditioning system compressor switch (where fitted) – informs ECU when the air conditioning system is switched on.*

7.1 Multec single-point injection system components (X16SZR)

1 Crankshaft sensor	4 Throttle potentiometer	7 Evaporative emission system purge valve	9 Exhaust gas recirculation (EGR) valve	10 Oxygen sensor
2 Throttle body	5 Knock sensor			11 Idle speed control stepper motor
3 Fuel injector	6 MAP sensor	8 Ignition module		

7.8a Unclip the trim panel from the top of the centre console . . .

7.8b . . . to gain access to the diagnostic connector (arrowed)

4 All the above information is analysed by the ECU and, based on this, the ECU determines the appropriate ignition and fuelling requirements for the engine. The ECU controls the fuel injector by varying its pulse width – the length of time the injector is held open – to provide a richer or weaker mixture, as appropriate. The mixture is constantly varied by the ECU, to provide the best setting for cranking, starting (with either a hot or cold engine), warm-up, idle, cruising, and acceleration.

5 The ECU also has full control over the engine idle speed, via a stepper motor which is fitted to the throttle body. The motor

7.9a Multec S multi-point injection system components (X16XEL)

1 Crankshaft sensor	4 Throttle potentiometer	7 Evaporative emission system purge valve	10 Coolant temperature sensor
2 Knock sensor	5 Idle speed control stepper motor	8 Ignition module	11 Intake air temperature sensor
3 Exhaust gas recirculation (EGR) valve	6 MAP sensor	9 Oxygen sensor	12 Camshaft position sensor

pushrod controls the opening of an air passage which bypasses the throttle valve. When the throttle valve is closed (accelerator pedal released), the ECU uses the motor to vary the amount of air entering the engine and so controls the idle speed.

6 The ECU also controls the exhaust and evaporative emission control systems, which are described in detail in Part C of this Chapter.

7 If there is an abnormality in any of the readings obtained from any sensor, the ECU enters its back-up mode. In this event, the ECU ignores the abnormal sensor signal, and assumes a preprogrammed value which will allow the engine to continue running (albeit at reduced efficiency). If the ECU enters this back-up mode, the warning light on the instrument panel will come on, and the relevant fault code will be stored in the ECU memory.

8 If the warning light comes on, the vehicle should be taken to a Vauxhall dealer at the earliest opportunity. A complete test of the engine management system can then be carried out, using a special electronic diagnostic test unit which is simply plugged into the system's diagnostic connector. The connector is located behind the centre console; unclip the trim panel situated just in front of the handbrake lever to gain access (see illustrations).

Multec S multi-point injection system

9 The Multec S engine management (fuel injection/ignition) system (see illustrations) incorporates a closed-loop catalytic converter, an evaporative emission control system, an exhaust gas recirculation (EGR) system and a secondary air system, and complies with the latest emission control standards. The fuel injection side of the system operates as follows; refer to Chapter 5B for information on the ignition system.

10 The fuel pump, immersed in the fuel tank, pumps fuel from the fuel tank to the fuel rail, via a filter mounted underneath the rear of the vehicle. Fuel supply pressure is controlled by the pressure regulator which allows excess fuel to be returned to the tank. Note: On some later models the pressure regulator is located in the fuel tank as part of the fuel tank sender unit/pump.

11 The electrical control system consists of the ECU, along with the following sensors.

a) Throttle potentiometer – informs the ECU of the throttle position, and the rate of throttle opening or closing.

b) Coolant temperature sensor – informs the ECU of engine temperature.

c) Intake air temperature sensor – informs the ECU of the temperature of the air entering the manifold.

d) Oxygen sensor – informs the ECU of the oxygen content of the exhaust gases (explained in greater detail in Part C of this Chapter).

e) Crankshaft sensor – informs the ECU of engine speed and crankshaft position.

f) Camshaft sensor – informs the ECU of speed and position of the exhaust camshaft.

g) Knock sensor – informs the ECU when pre-ignition ('pinking') is occurring.

h) Manifold absolute pressure (MAP) sensor – informs the ECU of the engine load by monitoring the pressure in the inlet manifold.

i) ABS control unit – informs the ECU of the vehicle speed.

j) Air conditioning system compressor switch (where fitted) – informs ECU when the air conditioning system is switched on.

12 All the above information is analysed by the ECU and, based on this, the ECU determines the appropriate ignition and fuelling requirements for the engine. The ECU controls the fuel injector by varying its pulse width – the length of time the injector is held open – to provide a richer or weaker mixture, as appropriate. The mixture is constantly varied by the ECU, to provide the best setting

7.9b Multec S multi-point injection system components (Z16XE)

1	Evaporative emission system purge valve	5	Exhaust gas recirculation (EGR)
2	Oxygen sensor – catalytic converter control	6	Intake manifold pressure (MAP) sensor
3	Knock sensor	7	Engine control unit
4	Throttle body	8	Crankshaft sensor

9	Oxygen sensor – mixture regulation
10	Coolant temperature sensor
11	Coolant temperature sensor
12	Camshaft position sensor

H32944

for cranking, starting (with either a hot or cold engine), warm-up, idle, cruising, and acceleration. The Multec S system is a 'sequential' fuel injection system. This means that each of the four injectors is triggered individually just before the inlet valve of the relevant cylinder is about to open.

13 On early models, the ECU also has full control over the engine idle speed, via a stepper motor which is fitted to the throttle housing. The motor controls the opening of an air passage which bypasses the throttle valve. When the throttle valve is closed (accelerator pedal released), the ECU uses the motor to vary the amount of air entering the engine and so controls the idle speed.

14 On later models (Z16XE, Z18XE and Z22SE), the system has an electronic accelerator (no accelerator cable), this consists of an accelerator pedal module and a throttle valve module. Each module has two potentiometers (sensors) which determine the position of the pedal, which then transmitts a signal to the ECU. Also the crankshaft sensor has been moved to the cylinder block, where it picks up the signal from an increment disc on number eight web on the crankshaft.

15 The ECU also controls the exhaust and evaporative emission control systems, which are described in detail in Part C of this Chapter.

16 If there is an abnormality in any of the readings obtained from any sensor, the ECU enters its back-up mode. In this event, the ECU ignores the abnormal sensor signal, and assumes a preprogrammed value which will allow the engine to continue running (albeit at reduced efficiency). If the ECU enters this back-up mode, the warning light on the instrument panel will come on, and the relevant fault code will be stored in the ECU memory.

7.18a Simtec 56.5 and 70 multi-point fuel injection system components (X18XE, X18XE1 and X20XEV)

1 Intake air temperature sensor
2 Hot film mass airflow meter
3 Fuel pressure regulator
4 Throttle potentiometer
5 Crankshaft sensor
6 Idle speed control stepper motor
7 Camshaft position sensor
8 Knock sensor (on rear of the cylinder block)
9 Evaporative emission system purge valve
10 Ignition module
11 Coolant temperature sensor
12 Exhaust gas recirculation (EGR) valve

17 If the warning light comes on, the vehicle should be taken to a Vauxhall dealer at the earliest opportunity. A complete test of the engine management system can then be carried out, using a special electronic diagnostic test unit which is simply plugged into the system's diagnostic connector. The connector is located behind the centre console; unclip the trim panel situated just in front of the handbrake lever to gain access **(see illustrations 7.8a and 7.8b)**.

Simtec 56.5, 70 and 71 multi-point injection systems

18 The Simtec 56.5/70/71 engine manage-ment (fuel injection/ignition) systems **(see illustrations)** are almost identical in operation to the Multec S system (see paragraphs 9 to 17). The only major change to the system is that a Hot Film Mass airflow sensor is fitted in place of the manifold pressure (MAP) sensor. The airflow meter informs the ECU of the amount of air entering the inlet manifold.

19 Another additional feature of the Simtec system is that it incorporates a variable tract inlet manifold to help increase torque output at low engine speeds. Each inlet manifold tract is fitted with a valve. The valve is controlled by the ECU via a solenoid valve and vacuum diaphragm unit.

20 At low engine speeds (below approximately 3600 rpm) the valves remain closed. The air entering the engine is then forced to take the long inlet path through the manifold which leads to an increase in the engine torque output.

21 At higher engine speeds, the ECU switches the solenoid valve which then allows vacuum to act on the diaphragm unit. The diaphragm unit is linked to the valve assemblies and opens up each of the four valves allowing the air passing through the manifold to take the shorter inlet path which is more suited to higher engine speeds.

7.18b Simtec 71 multi-point fuel injection system components (Z18XE)

1 Camshaft position sensor	4 Oxygen sensor – catalytic	7 Engine control unit	10 Coolant temperature sensor
2 Hot film mass airflow	converter control	8 Crankshaft sensor	11 Coolant temperature sensor
meter	5 Knock sensor	9 Oxygen sensor – mixture	12 Evaporative emission system
3 Ignition module	6 Throttle body	regulation	purge valve

GMPT – E15 multi-point injection system

22 The GMPT – E15 engine management (fuel injection/ignition) system **(see illustrations)** is very similar in operation to the Multec S system (see paragraphs 9 to 17).

23 The only major change to the system is that special sensors are incorporated in the ignition module to replace the need for a camshaft sensor. The sensors read the injection impulse so as to determine the cylinder position.

24 This system also has an electronic accelerator (no accelerator cable), this consists of an accelerator pedal module and a throttle valve module. Each module has two potentiometers (sensors) which determine the position of the pedal, which then transmits a signal to the ECU. The throttle valve module consists of a throttle valve potentiometer and a throttle valve servo motor which actuates the throttle valve. **Note:** *The throttle valve module is an integrated unit and can only be renewed as a complete assembly.*

H32940

7.22a GMPT – E15 multi-point fuel injection system components (Z22SE)

1 *Evaporative emission system purge valve*
2 *Coolant temperature sensor*
3 *Accelerator pedal/accelerator pedal sensor*
4 *Injectors*
5 *Intake manifold pressure (MAP) sensor*

7.22b GMPT – E15 multi-point fuel injection system components (Z22SE)

1 Oxygen sensor – mixture regulation
2 Oxygen sensor – catalytic converter control
3 Exhaust gas recirculation (EGR) valve
4 Throttle body
5 DIS ignition module

7.22c GMPT – E15 multi-point fuel injection system components (Z22SE)

1 Engine control unit   3 Crankshaft sensor   5 Intake air temperature
2 Fuel pressure regulator   4 Knock sensor   sensor

8.2a Unclip the lid from the engine compartment main relay box . . .

8.2b . . . and remove the fuel pump relay

8.6a Fuel depressurisation valve (1.6 litre)

8.6b Fuel depressurisation valve (1.8 and 2.0 litre)

8.6c Fuel depressurisation valve (2.2 litre)

8.7 Unscrew the cap, and depress the valve core. Catch all the expelled fuel using a rag

8 Fuel injection system – depressurisation

⚠ **Warning: Refer to the warning note in Section 1 before proceeding. The following procedure will merely relieve the pressure in the fuel system – remember that fuel will still be present in the system components, and take precautions accordingly before disconnecting any of them.**

1 The fuel system referred to in this Section is defined as the tank-mounted fuel pump, the fuel filter, the fuel injector(s) and the pressure regulator, and the metal pipes and flexible hoses of the fuel lines between these components. All these contain fuel which will be under pressure while the engine is running, and/or while the ignition is switched on. The pressure will remain for some time after the ignition has been switched off, and it must be relieved in a controlled fashion when any of these components are disturbed for servicing work.

SOHC engines

2 Ensure the ignition is switched off then remove the cover from the engine compartment relay box, which is situated next to the battery. Remove the fuel pump relay (the relay should be coloured purple) from the box **(see illustrations)**.

3 Start the engine and allow it to idle until the engine starts to run roughly then switch the ignition off.

4 Disconnect the battery negative terminal then refit the relay and cover to the relay box.

DOHC engines

5 On these engines, the fuel system can either be depressurised as described above in paragraphs 2 to 4, or as follows.

6 Locate the valve assembly which is fitted to the fuel rail on the inlet manifold. On 1.6 litre engines the valve is on the right-hand end of the rail and on 1.8, 2.0 and 2.2 litre engines it can be found on the top of the rail **(see illustrations)**.

7 Unscrew the cap from the valve and position a container beneath the valve. Hold a wad of rag over the valve and relieve the pressure in the fuel system by depressing the valve core with a suitable screwdriver **(see illustration)**. Be prepared for the squirt of fuel as the valve core is depressed and catch it with the rag. Hold the valve core down until no more fuel is expelled from the valve.

9.3 Fuel pump access cover

8 Once all pressure is relieved, securely refit the valve cap.

9 Fuel pump – removal and refitting

⚠ **Warning: Refer to the warning note in Section 1 before proceeding.**

Note: On Z16XE, Z18XE, X18XE1 and Z22SE models the pressure regulator is located in the fuel tank as part of the fuel tank sender unit/pump.

Removal

1 Depressurise the fuel system as described in Section 8 then disconnect the battery negative lead.

2 Fold the rear seat cushion forwards and lift up the flap in the carpet to reveal the fuel pump access cover.

3 Using a screwdriver, carefully prise the plastic access cover from the floor to expose the fuel pump **(see illustration)**.

4 Disconnect the wiring connector from the fuel pump, and tape the connector to the vehicle body, to prevent it disappearing behind the tank **(see illustration)**.

5 Mark the fuel hoses for identification purposes. The hoses are equipped with quick-release fittings to ease removal. To disconnect each hose, compress the clips located on each side of the fitting and ease the fitting off of its union. Disconnect both hoses from the top of the pump, noting the

9.4 Fuel pump wiring connector (A) and fuel hoses (B)

9.6 Undo the locking ring

9.7 Disconnect the wiring connector from the underside of the fuel pump cover

9.8a Release the retaining clips (1) and lift the housing assembly upwards (use a hook engaged with the eye – 2) . . .

9.8b . . . and remove it from the vehicle

9.9 Removing the fuel filter from the base of the pump assembly

correct fitted position of the sealing rings and plug the hose ends to minimise fuel loss.

6 Unscrew the locking ring and remove it from the tank. This is best accomplished by using a screwdriver on the raised ribs of the locking ring. Carefully tap the screwdriver to turn the ring anti-clockwise until it can be unscrewed by hand **(see illustration)**.

7 Carefully lift the fuel pump cover away from tank until the wiring connector can be disconnected from its underside **(see illustration)**. Make alignment marks between the cover and hoses then release the retaining clips and remove the cover from the vehicle along with its sealing ring. Discard the sealing ring; a new one must be used on refitting.

8 Release the three retaining clips by pressing them inwards then lift the fuel pump housing assembly out of the fuel tank, taking great care not to drop the fuel filter which is fitted to the pump base **(see illustrations)**.

Also try not to spill fuel onto the interior of the vehicle.

9 Inspect the fuel filter for signs of damage or deterioration and renew if necessary **(see illustration)**.

10 If necessary the pump housing assembly can be dismantled and the pump removed, noting the wiring connectors correct locations.

Refitting

Note: *A new fuel pump cover sealing ring will be required on refitting.*

11 Where necessary, reassemble the pump and housing components ensuring the wiring connectors are correctly and securely reconnected.

12 Ensure the filter is securely fitted to the base of the pump then carefully manoeuvre the pump assembly into position, making sure it clips securely into position.

13 Fit a new sealing ring to the tank.

14 Reconnect the fuel hoses to the pump cover, using the marks made on removal, and securely tighten their retaining clips. Reconnect the wiring connector then seat the pump cover on the tank.

15 Refit the locking ring to the fuel tank and tighten it securely.

16 Reconnect the fuel hoses to the pump cover, ensuring each fitting clicks securely into position, and reconnect the wiring connector.

17 Reconnect the battery then start the engine and check for fuel leaks. If all is well, refit the access cover and fold the seat back into position.

10 Fuel gauge sender unit – removal and refitting

⚠ **Warning: Refer to the warning note in Section 1 before proceeding.**

Note: *A new fuel pump cover sealing ring will be required on refitting.*

1 Carry out the operations described in paragraphs 1 to 7 of Section 9 to remove the fuel pump cover.

2 The fuel gauge sender unit is clipped to the side of the fuel pump mounting reservoir. Carefully release the retaining clip then slide the sender unit upwards to release it from its mounting **(see illustration)**.

3 Manoeuvre the sender unit through the fuel tank aperture, taking great care not damage the float arm **(see illustration)**.

10.2 Unclip the fuel gauge sender unit . . .

10.3 . . . and manoeuvre it out from the tank

11.5a Remove the rubber cover from the fuel tank filler neck . . .

11.5b . . . then undo the retaining screw (arrowed)

11.9 Disconnect the fuel feed and return hoses (arrowed) at the unions in front of the tank

4 Manoeuvre the sender unit carefully in through the tank aperture and slide it into position on the side of the fuel pump reservoir.

5 Ensure the sender unit is clipped securely in position then refit the fuel pump cover as described in paragraphs 12 to 16 of Section 9.

11 Fuel tank – removal and refitting

 Warning: Refer to the warning note in Section 1 before proceeding.

1 Depressurise the fuel system as described in Section 8 then disconnect the battery negative terminal.

2 Before removing the fuel tank, all fuel must be drained from the tank. Since a fuel tank drain plug is not provided, it is therefore preferable to carry out the removal operation when the tank is nearly empty. The remaining fuel can then be syphoned or hand-pumped from the tank.

3 Remove the exhaust system and relevant heat shield(s) as described in Section 20.

4 Disconnect the wiring connector from the fuel pump as described in paragraphs 1 to 4 of Section 9.

5 Open up the fuel filler flap and remove the rubber cover from around the filler neck aperture. Slacken and remove the retaining bolt which secures the filler neck to the body **(see illustrations)**.

6 Remove the right-hand rear wheel then remove the retaining screws and clips and remove the plastic wheelarch liner.

7 Make alignment marks between the small hoses and the top of the filler neck assembly then release the retaining clips and disconnect both hoses.

8 Slacken the retaining clips and disconnect the main hoses from the base of the filler neck. Unscrew the filler neck lower retaining bolt and manoeuvre the assembly out from underneath the vehicle.

9 Trace the fuel feed and return hoses from the tank to their unions in front of the tank **(see illustration)**. Make alignment marks between the hoses then release the retaining

clips and disconnect both hoses. If the hoses are equipped with quick-release fittings, disconnect each hose by depressing the clips on each side of the fitting and easing the fitting of the pipe.

10 Unclip the fuel filter from the fuel tank retaining strap **(see illustration)**.

11 Place a trolley jack with an interposed block of wood beneath the tank, then raise the jack until it is supporting the weight of the tank.

12 Slacken and remove the retaining bolts and remove the two retaining straps from underneath the fuel tank **(see illustration)**.

13 Slowly lower the fuel tank out of position, disconnecting any other relevant vent pipes as they become accessible (where necessary), and remove the tank from underneath the vehicle.

14 If the tank is contaminated with sediment or water, remove the fuel pump cover (Section 9), and swill the tank out with clean fuel. The tank is injection-moulded from a synthetic material – if seriously damaged, it should be renewed. However, in certain cases, it may be possible to have small leaks or minor damage repaired. Seek the advice of a specialist before attempting to repair the fuel tank.

15 Refitting is the reverse of the removal procedure, noting the following points:

a) *When lifting the tank back into position, take care to ensure that none of the hoses become trapped between the tank and vehicle body. Refit the retaining straps and tighten the bolts to the specified torque.*

b) *Ensure all pipes and hoses are correctly routed and all hoses unions are securely joined.*

c) *On completion, refill the tank with a small amount of fuel, and check for signs of leakage prior to taking the vehicle out on the road.*

12 Throttle body/housing – removal and refitting

Note: *On Z16XE, Z18XE and Z22SE models, there is an electronic accelerator system fitted (no accelerator cable). The throttle valve potentiometer and servo motor are a combined part of the throttle body housing. Individual parts for the throttle body housing are not available separately and, if defective it must be renewed as a complete unit.*

 Warning: Refer to the warning note in Section 1 before proceeding.

X16SZR

1 Depressurise the fuel system as described in Section 8 then disconnect the battery negative terminal.

2 Slacken the retaining clip and disconnect the air intake duct from the throttle body cover. Disconnect the vacuum and breather hoses from the cover then undo the retaining screws and remove the cover and sealing ring from the top of the throttle body **(see illustrations)**.

11.10 Unclip the fuel filter from the fuel tank retaining strap

11.12 Fuel tank retaining strap bolt (arrowed)

12.2a Slacken and remove the retaining screws . . .

12.2b . . . and detach the intake duct and sealing ring from the throttle body

12.3 Disconnect the injector wiring connector and free it from the throttle body

12.5 Unclip the accelerator link rod (arrowed) from the throttle housing balljoint

12.7 Removing the throttle body assembly

12.8 Undo the retaining screws and separate the upper and lower sections of the throttle body

3 Depress the retaining clips and disconnect the wiring connectors from the throttle potentiometer, the idle control stepper motor and the injector and release the wiring from the throttle body (see illustration).

4 Disconnect the fuel hoses from the side of the throttle body.

5 Unclip the accelerator linkage link rod from the balljoint on the throttle housing (see illustration).

6 Disconnect the breather/vacuum hoses from the throttle body (as applicable).

7 Slacken and remove the nuts securing the throttle body assembly to the inlet manifold, then remove the assembly along with its gasket (see illustration). Discard the gasket, a new one should be used on refitting.

8 If necessary, undo the retaining screws and separate the upper and lower sections of the throttle body assembly (see illustration).

Remove the gasket and discard it, a new one should be used on refitting.

9 Where necessary, ensure the mating surfaces are clean and dry then fit a new gasket and rejoin the upper and lower sections of the throttle body. Apply locking compound to the retaining screw threads then fit the screws and tighten them evenly and progressively to the specified torque.

10 Ensure the throttle body and manifold mating surfaces are clean and dry and remove all traces of locking compound from the studs and nuts.

11 Fit the new gasket to the manifold then refit the throttle body. Apply a few drops of locking compound to the threads of each retaining nut then refit the nuts and tighten them evenly and progressively to the specified torque setting.

12 Reconnect the vacuum/breather hoses

(as applicable) and clip the accelerator linkage back onto its balljoint.

13 Reconnect the fuel hoses to the throttle body, tightening the union nuts to the specified torque, and reconnect the wiring connectors.

14 Ensure the sealing ring is in position then refit the cover to the throttle body. Securely tighten the cover retaining screws then reconnect the intake duct and vacuum hoses.

15 Reconnect the battery then start the engine and check for signs of fuel leaks before taking the vehicle on the road.

X16XEL and Z16XE

16 Depressurise the fuel system as described in Section 8 then disconnect the battery.

17 Remove the engine oil filler cap then undo the retaining screws and lift off the engine cover. Refit the oil filler cap.

18 Slacken and remove the bolts securing the wiring harness plastic tray to the rear of the inlet manifold. Starting at the front and working back, disconnect the wiring connectors from the oxygen sensor, DIS module, purge valve and the various connectors on the left-hand side of the manifold. Undo the nuts securing the earth leads to the cylinder head and manifold then unclip the plastic tray and position it clear of the manifold (see illustrations).

19 Remove the DIS module as described in Chapter 5B.

20 Unclip the evaporative emission system purge valve from the left-hand end of the

12.18a Undo the retaining bolts (arrowed) . . .

12.18b . . . then disconnect the various wiring connectors (arrowed) . . .

12.18c . . . and free the wiring harness tray from the manifold (X16XEL)

12.20 Unclip the purge valve from the left-hand end of the manifold

12.21 Disconnect the vacuum servo unit hose (1) and vacuum hose (2) from the manifold

manifold and disconnect the valve hose from the manifold **(see illustration)**.

21 Slacken the union nut and disconnect the braking system vacuum servo hose from the manifold. Also disconnect the breather/vacuum hoses which are situated next to the servo unit union **(see illustration)**.

22 Slacken the retaining clip and disconnect the intake duct from the throttle housing.

23 On X16XEL models, slacken and remove the bolts securing the accelerator cable mounting bracket to the manifold. Remove the retaining clip then free the cable end fitting from the throttle cam and position it clear of the housing.

24 Slacken and remove the throttle housing retaining bolts and free the housing from the manifold. Recover the housing gasket and discard it, a new one should be used on refitting.

25 Slacken the union nuts and disconnect the fuel hoses from the fuel rail. Retain the fuel rail adapters with an open-ended spanner whilst the union nuts are slackened.

26 On X16XEL models, rotate the throttle housing until access can be gained to the housing coolant hoses. Make alignment marks between the hoses and housing then release the retaining clips and disconnect both from the housing. Plug the hose ends to minimise coolant loss.

27 On Z16XE models, disconnect the wiring block connector from the electronic throttle valve module **(see illustration 12.36a and 12.36b)**. On X16XEL models, Disconnect the wiring connectors from the throttle valve potentiometer and the idle control stepper motor then manoeuvre the throttle housing assembly out from the engine compartment.

28 Refitting is the reverse of removal, bearing in mind the following points.

a) Ensure the wiring connectors and coolant hoses are correctly and securely reconnected before bolting the housing to the manifold.

b) Fit a new gasket and tighten the housing bolts to the specified torque.

c) Tighten the fuel hose union nuts to the specified torque setting.

d) Ensure all hoses are correctly and securely reconnected.

e) On completion adjust the accelerator cable as described in Section 4.

X18XE, X18XE1, Z18XE, X20XEV and Z22SE

29 Disconnect the battery negative terminal.

30 Where applicable, disconnect the wiring connectors from the intake air temperature sensor and the Hot Film Mass airflow meter **(see illustration)**.

31 Release the retaining clip and disconnect the breather hose from the cylinder head cover.

32 Slacken the retaining clips then disconnect the intake pipe from the air cleaner and throttle housing and remove the air intake pipe assembly from the engine compartment.

33 On models with an accelerator cable, remove the retaining clip and detach the accelerator cable from the throttle cam

balljoint and unclip the cable from its mounting bracket. On models with cruise control it will also be necessary to detach the cruise control cable.

34 On models with an accelerator cable, undo the retaining bolts and free the cable mounting bracket from the throttle housing.

35 On models with an accelerator cable, clamp the coolant hoses which are connected to the rear of the throttle body then release the retaining clips and disconnect both hoses **(see illustration)**. Wipe away any spilt coolant.

36 On electronic accelerator pedal models, disconnect the wiring block connector from the electronic throttle valve module **(see illustrations)**. On other models, disconnect the wiring connectors from the throttle potentiometer and the idle control stepper motor.

12.30 Disconnect the Hot Film Mass airflow sensor (except Z22SE)

12.35 Remove the throttle body coolant hoses (except Z18XE and Z22SE)

12.36a Release the securing clip . . .

12.36b . . . and disconnect the wiring connector (Z22SE)

37 Where applicable, disconnect the vacuum/breather hoses from the throttle body, noting their correct fitted locations, then undo the retaining nuts and remove the housing from the manifold. Remove the gasket and discard it, a new one should be used on refitting **(see illustration)**.

38 Refitting is the reverse of removal, bearing in mind the following points.

a) Ensure the mating surfaces are clean and dry then fit a new gasket and tighten the housing nuts to the specified torque.

b) Ensure all hoses are correctly and securely reconnected.

c) On completion adjust the accelerator cable as described in Section 4 (where applicable).

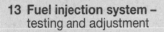

13 Fuel injection system – testing and adjustment

Testing

1 If a fault appears in the fuel injection system, first ensure that all the system wiring connectors are securely connected and free of corrosion. Ensure that the fault is not due to poor maintenance; ie, check that the air cleaner filter element is clean, the spark plugs are in good condition and correctly gapped, the cylinder compression pressures are correct, and that the engine breather hoses are clear and undamaged, referring to the appropriate part of Chapters 1, 2 and 5 for further information (as applicable).

14.3 Disconnect the wiring connector from the fuel injector . . .

14.4b . . . and remove the injector retaining plate

12.37 Renew the throttle body-to-manifold gasket

2 If these checks fail to reveal the cause of the problem, the vehicle should be taken to a suitably-equipped Vauxhall dealer for testing. A wiring block connector is incorporated in the engine management circuit, into which a special electronic diagnostic tester can be plugged (see Section 7). The tester will locate the fault quickly and simply, alleviating the need to test all the system components individually, which is a time-consuming operation that carries a risk of damaging the ECU.

Adjustment

3 Experienced home mechanics with a considerable amount of skill and equipment (including a tachometer and an accurately calibrated exhaust gas analyser) may be able to check the exhaust CO level and the idle speed. However, if these are found to be in

14.4a . . . then undo the retaining screw . . .

14.5 Remove the injector from the throttle body, noting the sealing rings (arrowed)

need of adjustment, the car will have to be taken to a suitably-equipped Vauxhall dealer who has access to the necessary diagnostic equipment required to test and adjust the settings.

14 Multec single-point injection system components – removal and refitting

Warning: Refer to the warning note in Section 1 before proceeding.

Fuel injector

Note: Before condemning an injector, if a faulty injector is suspected, it is worth trying the effect of one of the proprietary injector-cleaning treatments.

1 Depressurise the fuel system as described in Section 8 then disconnect the battery negative terminal.

2 Slacken the retaining clip and disconnect the air intake duct from the throttle body cover. Disconnect the vacuum and breather hoses from the cover then undo the retaining screws and remove the cover and sealing ring from the top of the throttle body.

3 Release the retaining clips and disconnect the wiring connector from the injector **(see illustration)**.

4 Undo the retaining screw and remove the injector retaining plate **(see illustrations)**.

5 Ease the injector out from the throttle body along with its sealing rings **(see illustration)**. Discard the sealing rings, they must be renewed whenever the injector is disturbed.

6 Refitting is a reversal of the removal procedure using new injector sealing rings. When refitting the retaining clip, ensure it is correctly engaged with the injector and securely tighten its retaining screw.

Fuel pressure regulator

Note: At the time of writing it appears that the regulator assembly is not available separately; if it is faulty the complete throttle body upper section must be renewed. Although the unit can be dismantled for cleaning, if required, it should not be disturbed unless absolutely necessary.

7 Depressurise the fuel system as described in Section 8 then disconnect the battery negative terminal.

8 Slacken the retaining clip and disconnect the air intake duct from the throttle body cover. Disconnect the vacuum and breather hoses from the cover then undo the retaining screws and remove the cover and sealing ring from the top of the throttle body.

9 Using a marker pen, make alignment marks between the regulator cover and throttle body, then slacken and remove the cover retaining screws **(see illustration)**.

10 Lift off the cover, then remove the spring seat and spring then withdraw the diaphragm, noting its correct fitted orientation **(see**

14.9 Fuel pressure regulator retaining screws (arrowed)

14.10 Fuel pressure regulator components

1 *Diaphragm*
2 *Spring*
3 *Spring seat*
4 *Cover*

14.14 Disconnecting the idle speed stepper motor

illustration). Remove all traces of dirt, and examine the diaphragm for signs of splitting. If damage is found, it will probably be necessary to renew the throttle body assembly.

11 Refitting is a reverse of the removal procedure, ensuring that the diaphragm and cover are fitted the correct way round, and that the retaining screws are securely tightened.

Idle speed control stepper motor

12 Disconnect the battery negative terminal.
13 To improve access to the motor, slacken the retaining clip and disconnect the air intake duct from the throttle body cover. Disconnect the vacuum and breather hoses from the cover then undo the retaining screws and remove the cover and sealing ring from the top of the throttle body.
14 Release the retaining clip and disconnect the wiring connector from the motor which is fitted to the front of the throttle body assembly (see illustration).
15 Undo the retaining screws and carefully manoeuvre the motor out of position, taking great care not to damage the motor plunger. Remove the sealing ring from the motor and discard it; a new one should be used on refitting (see illustration).
16 Refitting is the reverse of removal, using a new sealing ring. To ensure the motor plunger is not damaged on refitting, prior to installation, check that the plunger tip does not extend more than 28 mm from the motor mating flange (see illustration). If necessary, **gently** push the plunger into the body until it is correctly positioned.

Throttle potentiometer

17 Disconnect the battery negative terminal then release the retaining clip and disconnect the wiring connector from the throttle potentiometer which is fitted to the left-hand side of the throttle body (see illustration).
18 Slacken and remove the retaining screws and remove the potentiometer (see illustration).
19 Prior to refitting, clean the threads of the retaining bolts and apply a drop of fresh locking compound to each one. Ensure the potentiometer is correctly engaged with the throttle valve spindle then tighten its retaining

bolts to the specified torque and reconnect the wiring connector.

Coolant temperature sensor

20 The coolant temperature sensor is screwed into the rear of the inlet manifold. Refer to Chapter 3, Section 7, for removal and refitting details.

Manifold absolute pressure (MAP) sensor

21 The MAP sensor is mounted onto the engine compartment bulkhead, just to the left of the throttle body (see illustration). Ensure the ignition is switched off then disconnect the wiring connector and vacuum hose from the sensor. The MAP sensor can then be unclipped and removed from its mounting.
22 Refitting is the reverse of removal.

14.16 Ensure the plunger does not extend more than the specified distance (A) from the mating flange (see text)

14.18 . . . then undo the retaining screws and remove the potentiometer from the throttle housing

14.15 Remove the motor from the throttle body noting the sealing ring (arrowed)

Crankshaft sensor

23 The sensor is mounted on the rear of the cylinder block and is accessible from underneath the vehicle. Firmly apply the

14.17 Disconnect the wiring connector . . .

14.21 MAP (manifold absolute pressure) sensor

14.25 Crankshaft sensor retaining bolt (arrowed) – viewed from underneath the vehicle

handbrake then jack up the front of the vehicle and support it on axle stands.

24 Trace the wiring back from the sensor, releasing it from all the relevant clips and ties whilst noting its correct routing. Disconnect the wiring connector so the wiring is free to be removed with the sensor.

25 Unscrew the retaining bolt and remove the sensor from underneath the vehicle **(see illustration)**.

26 Refitting is the reverse of removal, tightening the retaining bolt to the specified torque. Ensure the wiring is correctly routed and retained by all the necessary clips and ties.

27 On completion, using feeler gauges, check that the clearance between the sensor tip and the crankshaft pulley teeth is 1.0 ± 0.7 mm. If the clearance is not within the specified range, renew the sensor mounting bracket.

Knock sensor

28 The knock sensor is mounted on the rear of the cylinder block and is accessible from underneath the vehicle. Firmly apply the handbrake then jack up the front of the vehicle and support it on axle stands.

29 Trace the wiring back from the sensor, noting its correct routing, and disconnect it at the connector.

30 Slacken and remove the retaining bolt and remove the sensor from the engine.

31 On refitting ensure the mating surfaces are clean and dry then fit the sensor and tighten its retaining bolt to the specified

15.9 On X16XEL engines the fuel pressure regulator (arrowed) is located on the left-hand end of the fuel rail

torque. Ensure the wiring is correctly routed and securely reconnected then lower the vehicle to the ground.

Electronic control unit (ECU)

32 The ECU is located behind the water deflector panel at the base of the windscreen.

33 Disconnect the battery negative terminal then remove both windscreen wiper arms as described in Chapter 12.

34 Peel off the rubber seal from the engine compartment bulkhead then unclip the water deflector panel from the base of the windscreen and remove it from the vehicle.

35 Undo the retaining nuts and remove the protective cover to gain access to the ECU.

36 Disconnect the wiring connectors then undo the retaining nuts and remove the ECU from the vehicle.

37 Refitting is the reverse of removal, ensuring the wiring connectors are securely reconnected and the ECU cover and water deflector are correctly seated.

Fuel pump relay

38 The fuel pump relay is located in the engine compartment main relay box.

39 Unclip the cover and remove it from the relay box, the fuel pump relay is coloured purple. Ensure the ignition is switched off then pull out the relay.

40 Refitting is the reverse of removal.

Air conditioning system switch

41 The air conditioning system switch is screwed into one of the refrigerant pipes and cannot be removed without first discharging the refrigerant (see Chapter 3). Renewal of the switch should therefore be entrusted to a suitably-equipped garage.

---

15 Multec-S injection system components – removal and refitting

> ⚠️ **Warning: Refer to the warning note in Section 1 before proceeding.**

Fuel rail and injectors

Note: *If a faulty injector is suspected, before condemning the injector, it is worth trying the effect of one of the proprietary injector-cleaning treatments.*

1 Depressurise the fuel system as described in Section 8 then disconnect the battery negative terminal.

2 Remove the upper section of the inlet manifold as described in Section 18.

3 Disconnect the wiring connectors from the four injectors then free the wiring harness from the fuel rail.

4 Unscrew the union nuts and disconnect the fuel hoses from the fuel rail. Whilst the unions are being slackened, retain the fuel rail adapters with an open-ended spanner.

5 Slacken and remove the three retaining bolts then carefully ease the fuel rail and injector

assembly out of position and remove it from the manifold. Remove the lower sealing rings from the injectors and discard them; they must be renewed whenever they are disturbed.

6 Slide off the relevant retaining clip and withdraw the injector from the fuel rail. Remove the upper sealing ring from the injector and discard it; all disturbed sealing rings must be renewed.

7 Refitting is a reversal of the removal procedure, noting the following points.
   a) Renew all disturbed sealing rings and apply a smear of engine oil to them to aid installation.
   b) Ease the injector(s) into the fuel rail, ensuring that the sealing ring(s) remain correctly seated, and secure in position with the retaining clips.
   c) On refitting the fuel rail, take care not to damage the injectors and ensure that all sealing rings remain in position. Once the fuel rail is correctly seated, tighten its retaining bolts to the specified torque.
   d) On completion start the engine and check for fuel leaks.

Fuel pressure regulator

Note: *On Z16XE models: Fuel pressure regulation is a function of the fuel tank pump module. The regulator is located under the fuel pump access cover. The regulator does not appear to be available as a separate part – check with your Vauxhall dealer. To remove the regulator, follow the procedure for fuel pump renewal, as described in Section 9, and disconnect the regulator from the fuel pipes and wiring connector located on the underside of the fuel pump access cover.*

8 On X16XEL models, depressurise the fuel system as described in Section 8 then disconnect the battery negative terminal.

9 Access to the fuel regulator is poor and can be improved slightly by freeing the wiring harness plastic tray from the inlet manifold (see Section 18) **(see illustration)**.

10 Retain the regulator with an open-ended spanner and unscrew the fuel hose union nut. Disconnect the fuel hose and the vacuum hose from the regulator.

11 Slacken and remove the retaining bolt and free the wiring bracket from the fuel rail.

12 Ease the regulator out from the end of the fuel rail and remove it along with its sealing ring.

13 Refitting is the reverse of removal, using a new sealing ring. On completion start the engine and check for fuel leaks.

Idle speed control stepper motor

Note: *On Z16XE models, there is an electronic accelerator system fitted (no accelerator cable). The throttle valve potentiometer and servo motor are a combined part of the throttle body housing. Individual parts for the throttle body housing are not available separately and, if defective, it must be renewed as a complete unit. Refer to Section 12 for the throttle body renewal procedure.*

15.15 Idle speed control motor retaining screws (arrowed) – shown with the throttle housing removed

15.18 Throttle potentiometer retaining screws (arrowed) – shown with the throttle housing removed

X16XEL

14 Access to the idle control stepper motor is very poor, to improve it remove the throttle housing as described in Section 12.

15 Undo the retaining screws and remove the motor from the housing along with its sealing ring **(see illustration)**.

16 Refitting is the reverse of removal, noting the following points.

a) *Prior to installation, check that the plunger tip does not extend more than 33 mm from the motor mating flange* **(see illustration 14.16)**. *If necessary, gently push the plunger into the body until it is correctly positioned. Failure to do this could lead to the motor being damaged.*

b) *Apply locking compound to the motor screws.*

Throttle potentiometer

Note: *On Z16XE models, there is an electronic accelerator system fitted (no accelerator cable). The throttle valve potentiometer and servo motor are a combined part of the throttle body housing. Individual parts for the throttle body housing are not available separately and, if defective, it must be renewed as a complete unit. Refer to Section 12 for the throttle body renewal procedure.*

15.25 MAP (manifold absolute pressure) sensor on the engine compartment bulkhead

X16XEL

17 Remove the throttle housing as described in Section 12.

18 Undo the retaining screws and remove the potentiometer from the side of the housing **(see illustration)**.

19 On refitting, fit the potentiometer, ensuring it is correctly engaged with the throttle valve spindle. Apply locking compound to the retaining screws and tighten them securely. Check the operation of the throttle valve then refit the housing as described in Section 12.

Coolant temperature sensor

20 The coolant temperature sensor is screwed into the thermostat housing. Refer to Chapter 3, Section 7, for removal and refitting details.

Intake air temperature sensor

21 The intake air temperature sensor is mounted in the intake duct which connects the air cleaner housing to the inlet manifold.

22 Ensure the ignition is switched off, then disconnect the wiring connector from the sensor.

23 Carefully ease the sensor out of position and remove its sealing grommet from the intake duct. If the sealing grommet shows signs of damage or deterioration it should be renewed.

24 Refitting is the reverse of removal, ensuring the sensor and grommet are correctly located in the duct.

Manifold absolute pressure (MAP) sensor

25 The MAP sensor is mounted onto the engine compartment bulkhead, just to the left of the inlet manifold **(see illustration)**.

26 Ensure the ignition is switched off then disconnect the wiring connector and vacuum hose from the sensor. The MAP sensor can then be unclipped and removed from its mounting.

27 Refitting is the reverse of removal.

Crankshaft sensor

28 On X16XEL engines, the sensor is mounted on a bracket at the rear of the right-hand end of the cylinder block and is accessible from underneath the vehicle **(see illustration)**. Firmly apply the handbrake then jack up the front of the vehicle and support it on axle stands.

29 On Z16XE engines, the sensor is mounted on the front of the cylinder block below the oil filter.

30 Trace the wiring back from the sensor, releasing it from all the relevant clips and ties whilst noting its correct routing. Disconnect the wiring connector so the wiring is free to be removed with the sensor. Unscrew the retaining bolt and remove the sensor.

31 Refitting is the reverse of removal, tightening the retaining bolt to the specified torque. Ensure the wiring is correctly routed and retained by all the necessary clips and ties.

32 On X16XEL engines, using feeler gauges, check that the clearance between the sensor tip and the crankshaft pulley teeth is 1.0 ± 0.7 mm. If the clearance is not within the specified range, renew the sensor mounting bracket.

15.28 Crankshaft position sensor (X16XEL)

15.35 Removing the camshaft sensor

Camshaft sensor

33 Remove the timing belt upper cover as described in Chapter 2B.

34 Trace the wiring back from the sensor, releasing it from all the relevant clips and ties whilst noting its correct routing. Disconnect the wiring connector so the wiring is free to be removed with the sensor.

35 Unscrew the retaining bolts and remove the sensor from the side of the cylinder head **(see illustration)**.

36 Refitting is the reverse of removal, tightening the retaining bolts to the specified torque. Ensure the wiring is correctly routed and retained by all the necessary clips and ties.

Knock sensor

37 Firmly apply the handbrake then jack up the front of the vehicle and support it on axle stands. The knock sensor is mounted onto the rear of the cylinder block, just to the right of the starter motor, and is accessible from underneath the vehicle.

38 Trace the wiring back from the sensor, noting its correct routing, and disconnect it at the connector.

39 Slacken and remove the retaining bolt and remove the sensor from the engine.

40 On refitting ensure the mating surfaces are clean and dry then fit the sensor and tighten its retaining bolt to the specified torque. Ensure the wiring is correctly routed and securely reconnected then lower the vehicle to the ground.

15.57 Release the retaining clips (arrowed) and disconnect the wiring cover assembly from the top of the injectors

15.55 Detach the accelerator cable from the throttle housing and its mounting bracket

Electronic control unit (ECU)

41 The ECU is located behind the water deflector panel at the base of the windscreen.

42 Disconnect the battery negative terminal then remove both windscreen wiper arms as described in Chapter 12.

43 Peel off the rubber seal from the engine compartment bulkhead then unclip the water deflector panel from the base of the windscreen and remove it from the vehicle.

44 Undo the retaining nuts and remove the protective cover to gain access to the ECU.

45 Release the retaining clip(s) then disconnect the wiring connector(s) from the ECU. Undo the retaining nuts and remove the ECU from the vehicle.

46 Refitting is the reverse of removal, ensuring the wiring connectors are securely reconnected and the ECU cover and water deflector are correctly seated.

Fuel pump relay

47 The fuel pump relay is located in the engine compartment main relay box.

48 Unclip the cover and remove it from the relay box, the fuel pump relay is coloured purple. Ensure the ignition is switched off then pull out the relay.

49 Refitting is the reverse of removal.

Air conditioning system switch

50 The air conditioning system switch is screwed into one of the refrigerant pipes and cannot be removed without first discharging the refrigerant (see Chapter 3). Renewal of the

15.59 Fuel supply pipe

switch should therefore be entrusted to a suitably-equipped garage.

16 Simtec injection system components – removal and refitting

Fuel rail and injectors

Note: *Before condemning an injector, if a faulty injector is suspected, it is worth trying the effect of one of the proprietary injector-cleaning treatments.*

1 Depressurise the fuel system as described in Section 8 then disconnect the battery negative terminal.

2 Disconnect the wiring connectors from the intake air temperature sensor and the Hot Film Mass airflow meter.

3 Release the retaining clips and disconnect the breather hoses from the rear of the cylinder head cover.

4 Slacken the retaining clips then disconnect the intake duct from the air cleaner and throttle housing and remove the duct assembly from the engine compartment, freeing it from the wiring harness.

5 On X18XE, X18XE1 and X20XEV models, remove the retaining clip and detach the accelerator cable from the throttle cam balljoint and unclip the cable from its mounting bracket. On models with cruise control it will also be necessary to detach the cruise control cable.

6 Disconnect the wiring connector from the idle control stepper motor then undo the retaining bolts and free the cable mounting bracket from the throttle housing.

7 Carefully release the retaining clips and lift the injector wiring cover assembly squarely away from the top of the injectors; the wiring connectors are an integral part of the cover.

8 Position the injector wiring cover assembly clear of the fuel rail.

9 Unscrew the union nuts and disconnect the fuel hoses from the fuel rail. Whilst the unions are being slackened, retain the fuel rail adapters with an open-ended spanner.

10 Slacken and remove the three retaining bolts then carefully ease the fuel rail and injector assembly out of position and remove it from the manifold. Remove the lower sealing rings from the injectors and discard them; they must be renewed whenever they are disturbed.

11 Slide off the relevant retaining clip and withdraw the injector from the fuel rail **(see illustration)**. Remove the upper sealing ring from the injector and discard it; all disturbed sealing rings must be renewed.

12 Refitting is a reversal of the removal procedure, noting the following points.

a) Renew all disturbed sealing rings and apply a smear of engine oil to them to aid installation.

b) Ease the injector(s) into the fuel rail, ensuring that the sealing ring(s) remain

16.11 Lever out the spring clip and carefully pull apart the connector

16.13 Fuel pressure regulator (Z18XE and X18XE1)

16.15 Fuel pressure regulator vacuum hose (1) and retaining clamp (2)

correctly seated, and secure in position with the retaining clips.

c) On refitting the fuel rail, take care not to damage the injectors and ensure that all sealing rings remain in position. Once the fuel rail is correctly seated, tighten its retaining bolts to the specified torque.

d) On completion start the engine and check for fuel leaks.

Fuel pressure regulator

13 On X18XE and X20XEV models, depressurise the fuel system as described in Section 8 then disconnect the battery negative terminal. **Note:** On Z18XE and X18XE1 models, fuel pressure regulation is a function of the fuel tank pump module. The regulator is located under the fuel pump access cover. However, the regulator does not appear to be available as a separate part – check with your Vauxhall dealer. To remove the regulator, follow the procedure for fuel pump renewal, as described in Section 9, and disconnect the regulator from the fuel pipes and wiring connector located on the underside of the fuel pump access cover **(see illustration)**.

14 To improve access to the regulator, release the retaining clips and disconnect the breather hose from the rear of the cylinder head cover.

15 Disconnect the vacuum hose from the regulator **(see illustration)**.

16 Slacken the retaining clamp then carefully ease the pressure regulator out from the top of the fuel rail. Remove the both sealing rings

from the regulator and discard them; new ones must be used on refitting.

17 Refitting is the reverse of removal, using new sealing rings. Lubricate the sealing rings with a smear of engine oil to ease installation and tighten the retaining clamp screw to the specified torque. On completion check for signs of fuel leakage.

Idle speed control stepper motor

Note: On Z18XE models, there is an electronic accelerator system fitted (no accelerator cable). The throttle valve potentiometer and servo motor are a combined part of the throttle body housing. Individual parts for the throttle body housing are not available separately and, if defective, it must be renewed as a complete unit. Refer to Section 12 for the throttle body renewal procedure.

Except Z18XE

18 Disconnect the wiring connectors from the intake air temperature sensor and the airflow meter. Release the retaining clip and disconnect the breather hose from the rear of the cylinder head cover then slacken the retaining clips and remove the intake duct assembly from the engine compartment.

19 Disconnect the wiring connector then undo the retaining screws and remove the motor assembly from the side of the throttle housing **(see illustrations)**. Remove the gasket and discard it; a new one should be used on refitting.

20 Refitting is the reverse of removal using a new gasket.

Throttle potentiometer

Note: On Z18XE models, there is an electronic accelerator system fitted (no accelerator cable). The throttle valve potentiometer and servo motor are a combined part of the throttle body housing. Individual parts for the throttle body housing are not available separately and, if defective, it must be renewed as a complete unit. Refer to Section 12 for the throttle body renewal procedure.

Except Z18XE

21 Ensure the ignition is switched off then disconnect the wiring connector from the throttle potentiometer which is fitted to the rear of the throttle housing.

22 Slacken and remove the retaining screws then remove the potentiometer from the housing.

23 Refitting is the reverse of removal, making sure the potentiometer is correctly engaged with the throttle valve spindle.

Coolant temperature sensor

24 The coolant temperature sensor is screwed into the housing on the left-hand end of the cylinder head. Refer to Chapter 3, Section 7, for removal and refitting details.

Intake air temperature sensor

25 Ensure the ignition is switched off then disconnect the wiring connector from the sensor **(see illustration)**.

26 Slacken the retaining clips then detach the intake duct from the airflow meter and air cleaner housing and remove it from the vehicle.

16.19a Disconnect the wiring connector . . .

16.19b . . . then undo the retaining screws (one hidden) and remove the idle speed control motor from the throttle housing

16.25 Disconnect the intake air temperature wiring connector

16.29 Disconnect the Hot Film Mass airflow meter wiring connector

27 Carefully ease the sensor out of position, taking great care not to damage the duct.
28 Refitting is the reverse of removal, noting that the sensor must be fitted so that its flat edge aligns with the flat on the intake duct.

Hot Film Mass airflow meter

29 Ensure the ignition is switched off then disconnect the wiring connector from the airflow meter **(see illustration)**.
30 Slacken the retaining clips then disconnect the intake ducts and remove the airflow meter from the vehicle. Inspect the meter for signs of damage and renew if necessary.
31 Refitting is the reverse of removal, ensuring the intake ducts are correctly engaged with the meter recesses.

Crankshaft sensor

32 On Z18XE engines, the sensor is mounted on the front of the cylinder block below the oil filter.
33 On X18XE1 engines, the sensor is mounted on a bracket at the rear of the right-hand end of the cylinder block. Follow the procedures as described in Section 15, paragraphs 28 to 32, for the X16XEL engine.
34 On X18XE and X20XEV engines, the sensor is mounted on the front of the cylinder block at the timing belt end. Remove the air cleaner housing with reference to Section 2, and unbolt the engine lifting shackle from the top of the engine. At the rear of the cylinder head, disconnect the wiring connector so the wiring is free to be removed with the sensor.
35 Trace the wiring back from the sensor,

16.46 Knock sensor retaining bolt

16.41 Remove the camshaft sensor – note the location dowel

releasing it from all the relevant clips and ties whilst noting its correct routing.
36 Unscrew the retaining bolt and remove the sensor from the front of the cylinder block, along with its sealing ring. Discard the sealing ring, a new one should be used on refitting.
37 Refitting is the reverse of removal using a new sealing ring and tightening the sensor bolt to the specified torque. Ensure the wiring cover assembly is clipped securely in position.

Camshaft sensor

38 Undo the retaining screws and remove the spark plug cover from the top of the cylinder head cover.
39 Ensure the ignition is switched off then disconnect the wiring connector from the camshaft sensor.
40 Remove the timing belt front cover as described in Chapter 2B.
41 Unscrew the retaining bolt and remove the camshaft sensor from the top of the cylinder head **(see illustration)**.
42 Refitting is the reverse of removal, tightening the sensor retaining bolt to the specified torque.

Knock sensor

43 The knock sensor is mounted on the rear of the cylinder block and is accessible from underneath the vehicle. Firmly apply the handbrake then jack up the front of the vehicle and support it on axle stands. Depending on model, it may be necessary to remove the starter motor as described in Chapter 5A to make access easier.

16.51 Inlet manifold valve switching solenoid and diaphragm

44 Trace the wiring back from the sensor, releasing it from all the relevant clips and ties whilst noting its correct routing.
45 Carefully release the retaining clips and lift the wiring cover assembly squarely away from rear of the cylinder head to gain access to the sensor wiring connector. Disconnect the connector so the wiring is free to be removed with the sensor.
46 Slacken and remove the retaining bolt and remove the sensor from the engine **(see illustration)**.
47 On refitting, ensure the mating surfaces are clean and dry then fit the sensor and tighten its retaining bolt to the specified torque. Ensure the wiring is correctly routed and securely reconnected then clip the wiring cover assembly back into position.

Electronic control unit (ECU)

48 Refer to Section 15, paragraphs 41 to 46.

Fuel pump relay

49 Refer to Section 15, paragraphs 47 to 49.

Air conditioning system switch

50 The air conditioning system switch is screwed into one of the refrigerant pipes and cannot be removed without first discharging the refrigerant (see Chapter 3). Renewal of the switch should therefore be entrusted to a suitably-equipped garage.

Inlet manifold valve switching solenoid

51 The solenoid which operates the inlet manifold valve assemblies is mounting on the left-hand end of the manifold **(see illustration)**.
52 Ensure the ignition is switched off then disconnect the wiring connector from the solenoid.
53 Disconnect both vacuum hoses then remove the solenoid from the manifold.
54 Refitting is the reverse of removal.

Inlet manifold valve vacuum diaphragm unit

55 The inlet manifold valve vacuum diaphragm unit is fitted to the left-hand end of the manifold **(see illustration 16.51)**.
56 Disconnect the vacuum hose, unclip the diaphragm rod from the its balljoint and remove the unit from the manifold.
57 Refitting is the reverse of removal.

---

17 GMPT – E15 injection system components – removal and refitting

Fuel rail and injectors

Note: *Before condemning an injector, it is worth trying the effect of one of the proprietary injector-cleaning treatments.*
1 Unclip the engine cover and depressurise the fuel system as described in Section 8 then disconnect the battery negative terminal.

2 Disconnect the wiring connector from the air temperature sensor in the air intake pipe **(see illustration)**.

3 Release the retaining clip and disconnect the breather hose from the cylinder head cover.

4 Release the retaining clips then disconnect the intake pipe from the air cleaner and throttle housing and remove the pipe assembly from the engine compartment, detach the vacuum pipe(s) from the intake pipe on removal.

5 Release the wiring harness from the oil dipstick guide tube, then remove the retaining bolt from the guide tube and twist it away from the intake manifold **(see illustration)**.

6 Undo the two retaining bolts and release the earth cables on the cylinder block below the intake manifold **(see illustration)**.

7 Release the wiring harness from the lower part of the intake manifold and the knock sensor wiring block connector from its retaining clip.

8 Disconnect the tank vent/purge valve (which is clipped onto the air filter housing) vacuum line from the intake manifold **(see illustration)**.

9 Release the two wiring harness plugs from the engine electronic control unit, then undo the securing bolts and remove the control unit from the intake manifold **(see illustration)**. Note the position of the earth cable on one of the securing bolts.

10 Unscrew the union nuts and disconnect the fuel pipes from the fuel rail, release the fuel pipes from the retaining clips and move to one side **(see illustration)**.

11 Disconnect the wiring connector from the throttle body, then undo the securing bolts and remove the throttle body unit from the intake manifold. Note the position of the cable retaining clip on one of the securing bolts.

12 Release the retaining clip for the EGR (exhaust gas recirculation) pipe, and disconnect it from the intake manifold **(see illustration)**.

13 Unclip the brake vacuum line and remove the securing nuts from the bracket on the EGR pipe to cylinder head retaining studs. Undo the two studs and remove the EGR pipe from the engine **(see illustration)**.

14 Disconnect the wiring connector from the air intake manifold pressure sensor.

15 Release the wiring harness plugs and disconnect them from the injectors, the ignition coil and the EGR valve.

16 Disconnect the brake servo vacuum pipe and release it from its retaining clips.

17 Unclip the coolant hose from the top of the wiring trough, undo the two retaining nuts and carefully unclip the wiring trough and move it to one side.

18 Slacken and remove the two retaining studs/bolts then carefully ease the fuel rail and injector assembly out of position and remove it from the manifold. Remove the lower sealing rings from the injectors and discard them; they must be renewed whenever they are disturbed.

17.2 Disconnecting the air temperature wiring connector

17.6 Undo the two earth cable retaining bolts (arrowed)

19 Slide off the relevant retaining clip and withdraw the injector from the fuel rail. Remove the upper sealing ring from the injector and discard it; all disturbed sealing rings must be renewed **(see illustration)**.

17.9 Releasing the wiring harness plugs from the engine control unit

17.12 Release the retaining clip and remove the EGR pipe from the intake manifold

17.5 Remove the retaining bolt from the oil dipstick guide tube

17.8 Unclip the vacuum pipe from the intake manifold

20 Refitting is a reversal of the removal procedure, noting the following points.

a) Renew all disturbed sealing rings and apply a smear of engine oil to them to aid installation.

17.10 Disconnecting the fuel pipes from the fuel rail

17.13 Remove the bracket and undo the studs (arrowed) to remove the EGR pipe from the engine

17.19 Release the retaining clip to remove the injector from the fuel rail

17.25a Disconnect the vacuum pipe, undo the bolts . . .

17.25b . . . and remove the pressure regulator from the fuel rail

b) *Ease the injector(s) into the fuel rail, ensuring that the sealing ring(s) remain correctly seated, and secure in position with the retaining clips.*

c) *On refitting the fuel rail, take care not to damage the injectors and ensure that all sealing rings remain in position. Once the fuel rail is correctly seated, tighten its retaining bolts to the specified torque.*

d) *Ensure that all the wiring connectors engage fully to make a good connection.*

e) *On completion start the engine and check for fuel leaks.*

Fuel pressure regulator

21 Unclip the engine cover and depressurise the fuel system as described in Section 8 then disconnect the battery negative terminal.

22 Release the retaining clip and disconnect the breather hose from the cylinder head cover.

23 Unclip the coolant hose from the top of the wiring trough, undo the two retaining nuts and carefully unclip the wiring trough and move it to one side.

24 Disconnect the vacuum line from the pressure regulator and from the intake manifold.

25 Slacken and remove the two retaining bolts, then carefully ease the pressure regulator from the end of the fuel rail along with its sealing rings **(see illustrations)**.

26 Refitting is the reverse of removal, using new sealing rings. On completion start the engine and check for fuel leaks.

Accelerator pedal position sensor

27 From inside the vehicle, unscrew the fasteners and remove the lower trim panel from underneath the driver's side of the facia to gain access to the accelerator pedal.

28 Disconnect the wiring connector from the pedal position sensor by sliding it to the rear of the vehicle.

29 Undo the retaining bolts and remove the pedal position sensor from the pedal assembly.

Throttle valve servo motor

30 The servo motor is a combined part of the throttle body housing. Individual parts for the throttle body housing are not available separately and, if defective, it must be renewed as a complete unit. Refer to Section 12 for the throttle body renewal procedure.

Throttle valve potentiometer

31 The throttle valve potentiometer is a combined part of the throttle body housing. Individual parts for the throttle body housing are not available separately and, if defective, it must be renewed as a complete unit. Refer to Section 12 for the throttle body renewal procedure.

Coolant temperature sensor

32 The coolant temperature sensor is screwed into the thermostat housing. Refer to Chapter 3, Section 7, for removal and refitting details.

Intake air temperature sensor

33 The intake air temperature sensor is mounted in the intake pipe which connects the air cleaner housing to the inlet manifold.

34 Ensure the ignition is switched off, then disconnect the wiring connector from the sensor **(see illustration 17.2)**.

35 Carefully ease the sensor out of position (note position for refitting) and remove its sealing grommet from the intake pipe. If the sealing grommet shows signs of damage or deterioration it should be renewed.

36 Refitting is the reverse of removal, ensuring the sensor and grommet are correctly located in the intake pipe.

Manifold Absolute Pressure (MAP) sensor

37 Unclip the engine cover and depressurise the fuel system as described in Section 8 then disconnect the battery negative terminal.

38 Disconnect the wiring connector from the air temperature sensor in the air intake pipe.

39 Release the retaining clip and disconnect the breather hose from the cylinder head cover.

40 Release the retaining clips then disconnect the intake pipe from the air cleaner and throttle housing and remove the pipe assembly from the engine compartment, detach the vacuum pipe(s) from the intake pipe on removal.

41 Disconnect the wiring connector from the throttle body, then undo the securing bolts/stud and remove the throttle body unit from the intake manifold. Note the position of the cable retaining clip on the securing stud.

42 Disconnect the wiring connector from the air intake manifold pressure sensor, turn the pressure sensor 1/4 of a turn clockwise and carefully pull out of the intake manifold **(see illustrations)**.

43 Refitting is the reverse of removal, using a new sealing ring.

Crankshaft sensor

44 The sensor is mounted on the front of the cylinder block above the starter motor. **Note:** *It may be necessary to remove the starter motor to gain better access to the sensor.*

45 Trace the wiring back from the sensor, releasing it from all the relevant clips and ties

17.42a Disconnect the wiring connector from the MAP sensor . . .

17.42b . . . and turn clockwise 1/4 of a turn, to release from the manifold

17.46 Unbolt the crankshaft sensor (arrowed) – starter removed

17.50 Unbolt the knock sensor (arrowed) – starter removed

17.59 Disconnecting the tank vent/purge valve from the air filter housing

whilst noting its correct routing. Disconnect the wiring connector from the sensor.

46 Unscrew the retaining bolt and remove the sensor from the cylinder block **(see illustration)**.

47 Refitting is the reverse of removal, tightening the retaining bolt to the specified torque. Ensure the wiring is correctly routed and retained by all the necessary clips and ties.

Knock sensor

48 The sensor is mounted on the front of the cylinder block above the starter motor. **Note:** *It may be necessary to remove the starter motor to gain better access to the sensor.*

49 Disconnect the wiring block connector at the bottom of the oil dipstick tube, so the wiring is free to be removed with the sensor.

50 Unscrew the retaining bolt and remove the sensor from the cylinder block **(see illustration)**.

51 On refitting ensure the mating surfaces are clean and dry then fit the sensor and tighten its retaining bolt to the specified torque. Ensure the wiring is correctly routed and retained by all the necessary clips and ties.

Electronic control unit (ECU)

52 Unclip the engine cover and depressurise the fuel system as described in Section 8 then disconnect the battery negative terminal.

53 Disconnect the wiring connector from the air temperature sensor in the air intake pipe.

54 Release the retaining clip and disconnect the breather hose from the cylinder head cover.

55 Release the retaining clips then disconnect the intake pipe from the air cleaner and throttle housing and remove the pipe assembly from the engine compartment, detach the vacuum pipe(s) from the intake pipe on removal.

56 Release the two wiring harness plugs from the engine control unit, then undo the securing bolts and remove the control unit from the intake manifold **(see illustration 17.9)**. Note the position of the earth cable on one of the securing bolts.

Fuel pump relay

57 Refer to Section 15, paragraphs 47 to 49.

Air conditioning system switch

58 The air conditioning system switch is screwed into one of the refrigerant pipes and cannot be removed without first discharging the refrigerant (see Chapter 3). Renewal of the switch should therefore be entrusted to a suitably-equipped garage.

Tank vent/purge valve

59 The tank vent/purge valve is clipped onto the side of the air filter housing **(see illustration)**.

60 Carefully detach the vacuum lines from the tank vent/purge valve, taking care not to damage the connections. If the valve is damaged in any way, then it must be renewed.

61 Disconnect the wiring connector from the tank vent/purge valve, then unclip the valve from the upper part of the air filter housing.

62 Refitting is the reverse of removal.

18 Inlet manifold – removal and refitting

SOHC engine

1 Depressurise the fuel system as described in Section 8 then disconnect the battery negative terminal.

2 Remove the auxiliary drivebelt then drain the cooling system as described in Chapter 1A.

3 Remove the air cleaner housing and intake duct as described in Section 2.

4 Disconnect the vacuum and breather hoses from the throttle body cover then undo the retaining screws and remove the cover and sealing ring from the top of the throttle body.

5 Disconnect the wiring connectors from the throttle potentiometer, the idle control motor, the throttle body injector, the coolant temperature sender and the exhaust gas recirculation (EGR) valve. Note the correct routing of the wiring then free it from all the relevant clips and ties. Unclip the wiring duct from the rear of the cylinder head and position it clear of the inlet manifold.

6 Undo the retaining bolts and remove the support bracket and alternator mounting bracket from the right-hand side of the manifold.

7 Slacken the unions nuts and disconnect the fuel hoses from the side of the throttle body. Whilst slackening the nuts, retain the throttle body adapters with an open-ended spanner.

8 Unclip and slide out the retaining clip securing the accelerator cable end fitting in position and detach the cable from the balljoint. Free the outer cable from its mounting bracket and position it clear of the manifold.

9 Disconnect the breather/vacuum hoses from the throttle body (as applicable) noting each ones correct fitted location.

10 Slacken the retaining clip and disconnect the coolant hose from the rear of the manifold.

11 Unscrew the union nut and disconnect the braking system servo unit hose from the manifold.

12 Check that all the necessary vacuum/breather hoses have been disconnected then slacken and remove the manifold retaining nuts.

13 Remove the manifold from the engine and recover the manifold gasket, noting which way around it is fitted.

14 Refitting is the reverse of removal bearing in mind the following points.

a) Prior to refitting, check the manifold studs and renew any that are worn or damaged.

b) Ensure the manifold and cylinder mating surfaces are clean and dry and fit the new gasket. Refit the manifold and tighten the retaining nuts evenly and progressively to the specified torque.

c) Ensure that all relevant hoses are reconnected to their original positions, and are securely held (where necessary) by their retaining clips.

d) Tighten the fuel hose and vacuum servo hose union nuts to their specified torque settings.

e) Refit the auxiliary drivebelt and refill the cooling system as described in Chapter 1A.

f) On completion, adjust the accelerator cable as described in Section 4.

1.6 litre DOHC

Removal

Note: *If only the upper section of the manifold is to be removed carry out the operations described in paragraphs 15 to 20.*

15 Remove the oil filler cap then undo the

18.16 Free the wiring harness from the rear of the manifold (X16XEL)

18.17 Unclip the purge valve (arrowed) from the left-hand end of the manifold (X16XEL)

retaining screws and lift off the cover from the top of the engine. Refit the oil filler cap. Drain the coolant system with reference to Chapter 1A.

16 Slacken and remove the bolts securing the wiring harness plastic tray to the rear of the inlet manifold. Starting at the front and working back, disconnect the wiring connectors from the oxygen sensor, DIS module, purge valve and the various connectors on the left-hand side of the manifold. Undo the nuts securing the earth leads to the cylinder head and manifold then unclip the plastic tray and position it clear of the manifold (see illustration).

17 Unclip the evaporative emission system purge valve from the left-hand end of the manifold and disconnect the valve hose from the manifold (see illustration).

18 Slacken the union nut and disconnect the braking system vacuum servo hose from the manifold. Also disconnect the breather/vacuum hoses which are situated next to the servo unit union. On X16XEL models, disconnect the vacuum hose from the fuel pressure regulator.

19 Release the retaining clips and disconnect the coolant pipes from the throttle housing.

20 Slacken and remove the retaining nuts and bolts from the front and rear of the manifold upper section (see illustration). Lift the manifold section out of position, freeing it from the connecting hose, and recover the gasket from the lower section.

21 To remove the lower section of the manifold, first depressurise the fuel system as described in Section 8.

22 Slacken the unions nuts and disconnect the fuel hoses from the fuel rail. Whilst slackening the nuts, retain the fuel rail adapters with an open-ended spanner.

23 Slacken the lower retaining clip and remove the connecting piece from the throttle housing.

24 Disconnect the crankshaft sensor wiring connector and free it from the manifold, noting its correct routing.

25 On X16XEL models, free the accelerator cable from the throttle housing and mounting bracket (see Section 4). On X16XEL and Z16XE models, disconnect the wiring connector(s) from the throttle valve body.

26 Undo the retaining bolts and remove the throttle housing from the its mounting flange. Recover the housing gasket and discard.

27 Unbolt the throttle housing mounting flange and remove it from the side of the manifold. Note each bolt's fitted location as they are different lengths.

28 Remove the auxiliary drivebelt (see Chapter 1A) then undo the retaining bolts and remove the alternator mounting bracket from the right-hand end of the manifold.

29 Release the retaining clip and disconnect the coolant hose from the base of the manifold.

30 Slacken and remove the retaining nuts then manoeuvre the lower section of the manifold away from the cylinder head and out of the engine compartment.

31 Unbolt the coolant housing from the right-hand end of the cylinder head then remove the manifold gasket and discard it.

32 Refitting is the reverse of removal bearing in mind the following points.

a) Prior to refitting, check the manifold studs and renew any that are worn or damaged.
b) Ensure the manifold and cylinder mating surfaces are clean and dry and fit the new gasket. Fit the manifold and coolant housing and tighten the retaining nuts and bolts evenly and progressively to the specified torque.
c) Fit the throttle housing using a new gasket and tighten its retaining bolts to the specified torque.
d) Ensure that all relevant hoses are reconnected to their original positions, and are securely held (where necessary) by their retaining clips.
e) Tighten the fuel hose and vacuum servo hose union nuts to their specified torque settings.
f) Refill the cooling system as described in Chapter 1A.
g) On completion, adjust the accelerator cable as described in Section 4.

1.8 and 2.0 litre engine

33 Remove the auxiliary drivebelt as described in Chapter 1A.

34 Depressurise the fuel system as described in Section 8 then disconnect the battery negative terminal.

35 Carry out the operations described in paragraphs 30 to 37 of Section 12 noting that it is not necessary to unbolt the throttle housing from the manifold.

36 Slacken the unions nuts and disconnect the fuel hoses from the fuel rail. Whilst slackening the nuts, retain the fuel rail adapters with an open-ended spanner.

37 Disconnect the wiring connectors from the DIS module, the purge valve, the manifold valve switchover solenoid, the coolant temperature sensor, the EGR valve and the oxygen sensor.

38 Carefully release the retaining clips and lift the wiring cover assembly squarely away from rear of the cylinder head. Disconnect the crankshaft sensor and knock sensor wiring connectors from the base of the cover then position the cover and wiring clear of the manifold.

39 Unscrew the union nut and disconnect the braking system servo unit hose from the manifold. Disconnect all remaining vacuum/breather hoses from the manifold, noting each ones correct fitted location.

40 Undo the retaining bolts and remove the alternator mounting brackets from the right-hand side of the inlet manifold (see illustration).

41 Undo the retaining bolts and remove the support bracket from the base of the manifold (see illustration).

42 Slacken and remove the retaining nuts and bolts and manoeuvre the manifold assembly away from the engine. Remove the gasket and discard it. Note: The manifold assembly must be treated as a sealed unit; do not attempt to dismantle it as no components, other than the switchover diaphragm and solenoid, are available separately.

18.20 Manifold upper section-to-camshaft cover bolts (arrowed)

18.40 Alternator support bracket (X18XE1) – note the earth connection

43 Refitting is the reverse of removal noting the following.
a) *Prior to refitting, check the manifold studs and renew any that are worn or damaged.*
b) *Ensure the manifold and cylinder mating surfaces are clean and dry and fit the new gasket. Refit the manifold and tighten the retaining nuts and bolts evenly and progressively to the specified torque.*
c) *Ensure that all relevant hoses are reconnected to their original positions, and are securely held (where necessary) by their retaining clips.*
d) *Tighten the fuel hose and vacuum servo hose union nuts to their specified torque settings.*
e) *Refit the auxiliary drivebelt as described in Chapter 1A.*
f) *On completion, adjust the accelerator cable as described in Section 4.*

2.2 litre engine

44 Carry out the operations described in Section 17, paragraphs 1 to 20, for the removal and refitting of the fuel rail and injectors.
45 Slacken and remove the retaining nuts and bolts and manoeuvre the manifold assembly away from the engine.
46 Refitting is the reverse of removal noting the following.
a) *Prior to refitting, check the manifold studs and renew any that are worn or damaged.*
b) *Ensure the manifold and cylinder mating surfaces are clean and dry and fit the new gasket. Refit the manifold and tighten the retaining nuts and bolts evenly and progressively to the specified torque.*
c) *Ensure that all relevant hoses are reconnected to their original positions, and are securely held (where necessary) by their retaining clips.*
d) *Tighten the fuel hose and vacuum servo hose union nuts to their specified torque settings.*

19 Exhaust manifold – removal and refitting

> ⚠ **Warning: When disconnecting the front pipe from the manifold, support the front pipe to prevent any damage to the exhaust system, catalytic converter or oxygen sensor wiring.**
> **Note:** *New manifold nuts will be required on refitting.*

X16SZR

1 Trace the wiring back from the oxygen sensor and disconnect its wiring connector. Free the wiring from all the necessary clips and ties so the sensor is free to be removed with the manifold.
2 Slacken and remove the bolts and springs securing the front pipe flange joint to the manifold.

18.41 Unbolt the manifold support bracket

3 Disconnect the hot air hose from the exhaust manifold shroud then undo the retaining bolts and remove the shroud from the manifold.
4 Remove the engine oil dipstick and pull the plug caps off from the centre (No 2 and 3) spark plugs. Unscrew the centre spark plug heat shields and remove them from the manifold (a special socket, number KM-834, is available to ease removal of the heat shields).
5 Undo the retaining nuts securing the manifold to the head. Manoeuvre the manifold out of the engine compartment, complete with the gasket.
6 Examine all the exhaust manifold studs for signs of damage and corrosion; remove all traces of corrosion, and repair or renew any damaged studs.
7 Ensure that the manifold and cylinder head sealing faces are clean and flat, and fit the new gasket.
8 Refit the manifold then fit the new retaining nuts and tighten them to the specified torque.
9 Apply a smear of high-temperature grease to the threads of the spark plug heat shields then refit the shields and tighten them to the specified torque. Reconnect the plug caps and refit the dipstick.
10 Refit the shroud to the manifold, tightening its retaining bolts to the specified torque, and reconnect the hot air hose.
11 Reconnect the oxygen sensor wiring connector making sure the wiring is correctly routed and retained by all the necessary clips.
12 Refit the front pipe as described in Section 20.

X16XEL

13 Where fitted, remove the secondary air injection system air valve and connecting pipe as described in Chapter 4C, Section 2.
14 Remove the oil filler cap, undo the retaining screws, and remove the engine cover. Trace the wiring back from the oxygen sensor and disconnect its wiring connector. Free the wiring from all the necessary clips and ties so the sensor is free to be removed with the manifold.
15 Where fitted, remove the heat shield, then slacken and remove the bolts securing the front pipe to the manifold and recover the gasket.

16 Undo the retaining nuts securing the manifold to the head. Manoeuvre the manifold out of the engine compartment, complete with the gasket.
17 Refit the manifold as described in paragraphs 6 to 8.
18 Fit a new gasket between the manifold and front pipe then refit the front pipe bolts and tighten them to the specified torque.
19 Reconnect the oxygen sensor wiring connector making sure the wiring is correctly routed and retained by all the necessary clips.
20 Refit the secondary air injection system connecting pipe and air valve as described in Chapter 4C.

X18XE1

21 Undo the retaining screws, remove the oil filler cap, and remove the engine cover. Slacken and remove the bolts securing the front pipe to the manifold and recover the gasket.
22 Drain the coolant system as described in Chapter 1A.
23 Release the retaining clip and disconnect the large coolant hose from the thermostat housing.
24 Undo the three bolts and remove the heat shield from the manifold.
25 Undo the engine oil dipstick guide bracket retaining bolt, and twist the dipstick guide tube to one side.
26 Slacken and remove the manifold retaining nuts, remove the manifold and recover the gasket.
27 Refit the manifold as described in paragraphs 6 to 8.
28 Realign the dipstick guide tube, and tighten the mounting bracket bolt securely.
29 Refit the heat shield to the manifold (noting that the lower bolt is the shorter of the three), and reconnect the coolant hose to the thermostat. Refill the cooling system as described in Chapter 1A.
30 Reconnect the front exhaust pipe to the manifold, using a new gasket.
31 Refit the engine cover.

X18XE and X20XEV

32 Remove the two engine transport brackets from the cylinder head. Slacken and remove the bolts securing the front pipe to the manifold and recover the gasket.
33 Loosen the front coolant hose from the cylinder head, but do not disconnect the pipe.
34 Undo the retaining screws and remove the heat shield from the manifold.
35 Slacken and remove the retaining nuts, and manoeuvre the manifold out of the engine compartment. Recover the gasket.
36 Refit the manifold as described in paragraphs 6 to 8.
37 Reconnect the front exhaust pipe, using a new gasket. Tighten the bolts to the specified torque.
38 Align the heat shield with the manifold, and tighten the screws to the specified torque.

19.43 Undo the front pipe mounting nut (Z16XE)

19.53 Unbolt the engine lifting shackle

58 Refit the manifold as described in paragraphs 6 to 8.
59 Reconnect the front exhaust pipe, using a new gasket. Tighten the bolts to the specified torque.
60 Align the heat shields with the manifold, and tighten the screws to the specified torque.
61 Make sure the oxygen sensor wiring is correctly routed and retained by all the necessary clips.

19.54 Removing the upper heat shield

19.57 Manoeuvre the manifold out from the engine

20 Exhaust system – general information, removal and refitting

General information

1 On most models, the exhaust system consists of three sections: the front pipe which incorporates the catalytic converter, the intermediate pipe and centre silencer, and the tailpipe and main silencer box. On models equipped with an automatic transmission unit, the exhaust system is split into four sections; the system is identical to that described above except that the catalytic converter is a separate item and not an integral part of the front pipe.
2 All exhaust sections are joined by flanged joints which are secured by bolts. Some of the joints are of the spring-loaded ball type, to allow for movement in the exhaust system. The system is suspended throughout its entire length by rubber mountings.

Removal – general

3 Each exhaust section can be removed individually, or alternatively, the complete system can be removed as a unit. Even if only one part of the system needs attention, it is often easier to remove the whole system and separate the sections on the bench.
4 To remove the system or part of the system, first jack up the front or rear of the car and support it securely on axle stands. Alternatively, position the car over an inspection pit or on car ramps.

Front pipe removal

X16SZR

5 Slacken and remove the bolts and springs securing the front pipe flange joint to the manifold.
6 Undo the bolts securing the front pipe to the intermediate pipe and remove the pipe from underneath the vehicle. Recover the gasket from the pipe-to-manifold joint.

Z16XE and X16XEL

7 Slacken and remove the bolts securing the front pipe flange joint to the manifold (see illustration).
8 On manual transmission models, unscrew the nut securing the front pipe to its mounting bracket and remove the washer, spacer and mounting rubber (see illustration 19.43).

39 Fasten the front coolant pipe to the cylinder head.
40 Re-attach the transport shackles to the cylinder head. Tighten the bolts securely.

Z16XE and Z18XE

41 Undo the retaining screws, remove the oil filler cap, and remove the engine cover.
42 Trace the wiring back from the oxygen sensor and disconnect its wiring connector. Free the wiring from all the necessary clips and ties so the sensor is free to be removed with the manifold.
43 On Z16XE engines, undo the retaining bolts and remove the bracket securing the front pipe under the engine (see illustration).
44 Slacken and remove the bolts securing the front pipe to the manifold and recover the gasket.
45 Undo the retaining screws and remove the heat shield from the manifold.
46 Slacken and remove the retaining nuts, and manoeuvre the manifold (complete with engine shackle) out of the engine compartment. Recover the gasket.
47 Refit the manifold as described in paragraphs 6 to 8.
48 Reconnect the front exhaust pipe, using a new gasket. Tighten the bolts to the specified torque.
49 Align the heat shield with the manifold, and tighten the screws to the specified torque.
50 Refit the exhaust front pipe securing bracket.
51 Reconnect the oxygen sensor wiring

connector making sure the wiring is correctly routed and retained by all the necessary clips.
52 Refit the engine cover.

Z22SE

53 Remove the engine transport shackle from the cylinder head (see illustration).
54 Undo the retaining screws and remove the lower and upper heat shield from the manifold (see illustration).
55 Trace the wiring back from the oxygen sensor and free the wiring from the rear engine mounting assembly.
56 Slacken and remove the bolts securing the front pipe to the manifold and recover the gasket.
57 Slacken and remove the retaining nuts, and manoeuvre the manifold out of the engine compartment (see illustration). Recover the gasket.

20.7 Exhaust front pipe-to-manifold bolts (arrowed)

20.18 Slacken and remove the bolts (arrowed) securing the intermediate pipe to the front pipe

20.19 Intermediate pipe rubber mountings

20.22 Intermediate pipe-to-tail pipe bolts and springs (arrowed)

Slacken and remove the bolts securing the front pipe to the intermediate pipe and remove the front pipe from the vehicle. Recover the gasket from the front pipe-to-manifold joint.

9 On automatic transmission models, unscrew the nuts securing the front pipe to its mounting bracket and remove the retaining plate. Slacken and remove the bolts and springs securing the front pipe to the catalytic converter and remove the front pipe from the vehicle. Recover the gaskets from the front pipe joints.

Z18XE, X18XE, X18XE1, X20XEV and Z22SE

10 Trace the wiring back from the oxygen sensor, noting its correct routing, and disconnect its wiring connector. Free the wiring from any clips so the sensor is free to be removed with the front pipe.

11 Slacken and remove the bolts securing the front pipe flange joint to the manifold.

12 Unscrew the nuts securing the front pipe to its mounting bracket and remove the retaining plate.

13 On manual transmission models, slacken and remove the bolts securing the front pipe to the intermediate pipe and remove the front pipe from the vehicle. Recover the gasket from the front pipe-to-manifold joint.

14 On automatic transmission models, slacken and remove the bolts and springs securing the front pipe to the catalytic converter and remove the front pipe from the vehicle. Recover the gaskets from the front pipe joints.

Catalytic converter removal

Automatic transmission models

15 Slacken and remove the bolts and springs securing the converter to the front pipe and bolts securing it to the intermediate pipe. Remove the catalytic converter from underneath the vehicle and recover the gasket from its front pipe joint.

Intermediate pipe removal

SOHC engines

16 Slacken and remove the bolts securing the intermediate pipe to the front pipe and slacken the clamp securing the pipe to the tailpipe.

17 Free the intermediate pipe from its mounting rubbers and manoeuvre it out from underneath the vehicle.

DOHC engines

18 Slacken and remove the bolts securing the intermediate pipe to the front pipe and the bolts and springs securing it to the tailpipe **(see illustration)**.

19 Free the intermediate pipe from its mounting rubbers and manoeuvre it out from underneath the vehicle **(see illustration)**. Recover the gasket from the rear tailpipe joint.

Tailpipe removal

SOHC engines

20 Slacken the clamp securing the tailpipe to the intermediate pipe.

21 Free the tailpipe from its mounting rubbers and remove it from the underneath the vehicle.

DOHC engines

22 Slacken and remove the bolts and springs securing the tailpipe joint to the intermediate pipe **(see illustration)**.

23 Free the tailpipe from its mounting rubbers and remove it along with its gasket.

Complete system removal

SOHC engines

24 Undo the bolts and spring securing the front pipe flange joint to the manifold.

25 Free the system from all its mounting rubbers and lower it from under the vehicle. Recover the gasket from the front pipe joint.

DOHC engines

26 Where applicable, trace the wiring back from the oxygen sensor, noting its correct routing, and disconnect its wiring connector. Free the wiring from any clips so the sensor is free to be removed with the front pipe.

27 Unscrew the nuts securing the front pipe to its mounting bracket and remove the retaining plate.

28 Slacken and remove the bolts securing the front pipe flange joint to the manifold and recover the gasket.

29 Free the exhaust system from all its mounting rubbers and lower it from underneath the vehicle.

Heat shield(s) removal

30 The heat shields are secured to the underside of the body by various nuts and bolts. Each shield can be removed once the relevant exhaust section has been removed. If a shield is being removed to gain access to a component located behind it, it may prove sufficient in some cases to remove the retaining nuts and/or bolts, and simply lower the shield, without disturbing the exhaust system.

Refitting

31 Each section is refitted by reversing the removal sequence, noting the following points:
  a) Ensure that all traces of corrosion have been removed from the flanges and renew all necessary gaskets.
  b) Inspect the rubber mountings for signs of damage or deterioration, and renew as necessary.
  c) Where no gasket is fitted to a joint, apply a smear of exhaust system jointing paste to ensure a gas-tight seal.
  d) Prior to tightening the exhaust system fasteners, ensure that all rubber mountings are correctly located, and that there is adequate clearance between the exhaust system and vehicle underbody.

Chapter 4 Part B:
Fuel and exhaust systems – diesel engine models

Contents

Degrees of difficulty

Easy, suitable for novice with little experience	Fairly easy, suitable for beginner with some experience	Fairly difficult, suitable for competent DIY mechanic	Difficult, suitable for experienced DIY mechanic	Very difficult, suitable for expert DIY or professional

Specifications

Engine identification

Manufacturer's code	**Engine type**
X20DTH	2.0 litre high-pressure turbo diesel engine
X20DTL	2.0 litre low-pressure turbo diesel engine
Y20DTH	2.0 litre high-pressure turbo diesel engine
Y22DTR	2.2 litre high-pressure turbo diesel engine

General
System type .... | EDC 15M direct injection system incorporating an electronically-controlled VP44 fuel injection pump. Turbocharger fitted to all models and intercooler fitted to high-pressure turbo models

Adjustment data
Idle speed:
  X20DTL and X20DTH .... | 790 to 890 rpm – controlled by ECU
  Y20DTH .... | 750 to 850 rpm – controlled by ECU
  Y22DTR .... | 760 to 920 rpm – controlled by ECU
Maximum speed:
  X20DTL and X20DTH .... | 4750 rpm – controlled by ECU
  Y20DTH .... | 4950 to 5050 rpm – controlled by ECU
  Y22DTR .... | 4930 to 5070 rpm – controlled by ECU

Injection pump
Direction of rotation .... | Clockwise, viewed from sprocket end
Pump timing (static) .... | Preset – controlled by ECU

Injectors
Opening pressure:
  X20DTL .... | 180 to 365 bar
  X20DTH, Y20DTH and Y22DTR .... | 220 to 380 bar

Torque wrench settings

	Nm	lbf ft
Accelerator pedal nuts	20	15
Auxiliary drivebelt tensioner assembly bolts:		
Pulley backplate pivot bolt	42	31
Strut mounting bolts	23	17
Camshaft sprocket bolt*:		
Stage 1	90	66
Stage 2	Angle-tighten a further 60°	
Stage 3	Angle-tighten a further 30°	
Charge (boost) pressure sensor bolt	8	6
Coolant temperature sensor	See Chapter 3	
Crankshaft sensor bolt	8	6
Exhaust front pipe:		
Pipe-to-intermediate pipe bolts	12	9
Pipe-to-turbocharger nuts	20	15
Exhaust manifold:		
Retaining nuts	22	16
Support bracket bolts	25	18
Fuel pipe union nuts	25	18
Injection pump:		
Front mounting bolts	25	18
Fuel pipe union bolts	15	11
Rear mounting bracket bolts	20	15
Sprocket cover bolts	6	4
Sprocket retaining bolts:		
X20DTL and X20DTH	20	15
Y20DTH and Y22DTR	28	21
Inlet manifold:		
Lower section-to-cylinder head nuts	22	16
Upper section-to-lower section bolts	8	6
Timing chain:		
Tensioner cap (upper and lower)	60	44
Upper chain guide bolts*	8	6
Turbocharger:		
Exhaust flange bolts	30	22
Oil feed pipe:		
Pipe-to-cylinder block union nut	20	15
Pipe-to-turbo charger union bolt	20	15
Oil return pipe:		
Pipe-to-cylinder block union nut	25	18
Pipe-to-turbocharger bolts	8	6
Turbocharger-to-manifold bolts	30	22

Use new fasteners

1 General information and precautions

General information

Note: *There are two versions of engine available; a low-pressure turbo (X20DTL) version and a high-pressure (X20DTH, Y20DTH and Y22DTR) version. Refer to 'Vehicle identification' for information on engine number location to determine which engine is fitted to your vehicle.*

1 The fuel system consists of a rear-mounted fuel tank, a fuel filter with integral water separator, a fuel injection pump, injectors and associated components.

2 Fuel is drawn from the fuel tank by the fuel injection pump. Before reaching the pump, the fuel passes through a fuel filter, where foreign matter and water are removed. Excess fuel lubricates the moving components of the pump, and is then returned to the tank.

3 The fuel injection pump is driven at half-crankshaft speed by the timing chain. The high pressure required to inject the fuel into the compressed air in the cylinder is achieved by a radial piston pump.

4 The injection pump is electronically-controlled to meet the latest emission standards. The system consists of the engine electronic control unit (ECU), the injection electronic control unit (ECU) and the following sensors.

a) Accelerator pedal position sensor – informs the ECU of the accelerator pedal position.

b) Coolant temperature sensor – informs the ECU of engine temperature.

c) Intake air temperature sensor – informs the ECU of the temperature of the air passing through the intake duct.

d) Oil temperature sensor – informs ECU of the temperature of the engine oil.

e) Airflow meter – informs the ECU of the amount of air passing through the intake duct.

f) Crankshaft sensor – informs the ECU of engine speed and crankshaft position.

g) Charge (boost) pressure sensor – informs ECU of the pressure in the inlet manifold.

h) ABS control unit – informs the ECU of the vehicle speed.

i) Atmospheric pressure sensor – informs the ECUs of the atmospheric pressure.

j) Fuel temperature sensor – informs the ECUs of the fuel temperature.

k) Injection pump shaft sensor – used by the ECUs to determine the exact injection timing.

l) Oil pressure switch – used by the engine ECU to control the instrument cluster oil warning lamp.

m) Clutch switch – used by the ECUs for cruise control functions.

n) Air conditioning system compressor switch (where fitted) – informs ECU when the air conditioning system is switched on.

5 All the above information is analysed by the ECU and, based on this, the ECU determines

the appropriate injection requirements for the engine. The ECU controls the injection pump timing, via the pump control unit, to provide the best setting for cranking, starting (with either a hot or cold engine), warm-up, idle, cruising, and acceleration.

6 Basic injection timing is determined when the pump is fitted. When the engine is running, it is varied automatically to suit the prevailing engine speed by a mechanism which turns the cam plate or ring – controlled by the ECU.

7 The ECU also controls the exhaust gas recirculation (EGR) system (see Chapter 4C) and the preheating system (see Chapter 5C).

8 The four fuel injectors produce a spray of fuel directly into the cylinders. The injectors are calibrated to open and close at critical pressures to provide efficient and even combustion. Each injector needle is lubricated by fuel, which accumulates in the spring chamber and is channelled to the injection pump return hose by leak-off pipes.

9 The inlet manifold is fitted with a butterfly valve arrangement to improve efficiency at low engine speeds. Each cylinder has two intake tracts in the manifold, one of which is fitted a valve; the operation of the valve is controlled by the ECU via a solenoid valve and vacuum diaphragm unit. At low engine speeds (below approximately 1500 rpm) the valves remain closed, meaning that air entering each cylinder is passing through only one of the two manifold tracts. At higher engine speeds, the ECU opens up each of the four valves allowing the air passing through the manifold to pass through both inlet tracts.

10 A turbocharger is fitted to increase engine efficiency by raising the pressure in the inlet manifold above atmospheric pressure. Instead of the air simply being sucked into the cylinders, it is forced in. Additional fuel is supplied by the injection pump in proportion to the increased air intake.

11 Energy for the operation of the turbocharger comes from the exhaust gas. The gas flows through a specially-shaped housing (the turbine housing) and in so doing, spins the turbine wheel. The turbine wheel is attached to a shaft, at the end of which is another vaned wheel known as the compressor wheel. The compressor wheel spins in its own housing, and compresses the inlet air on the way to the inlet manifold.

12 Between the turbocharger and the inlet manifold, the compressed air passes through an intercooler. This is an air-to-air heat exchanger is mounted next to the radiator, and supplied with cooling air from the front of the vehicle. The purpose of the intercooler is to remove some of the heat gained in being compressed from the inlet air. Because cooler air is denser, removal of this heat further increases engine efficiency.

13 Charge (boost) pressure which is the pressure in the inlet manifold, is limited by a wastegate. This diverts the exhaust gas away from the turbine wheel in response to a

pressure-sensitive actuator. A pressure-operated switch operates a warning light on the instrument panel in the event of excessive charge pressure developing.

14 The turbo shaft is pressure-lubricated by an oil feed pipe from the engine main oil so that the shaft 'floats' on a cushion of oil. A drain pipe returns the oil to the sump.

15 The charge (boost) pressure wastegate is controlled by the ECU via a solenoid valve. Note that an intercooler is only fitted to high-pressure turbo models.

16 If there is an abnormality in any of the readings obtained from any sensor, the ECU enters its back-up mode. In this event, the ECU ignores the abnormal sensor signal, and assumes a preprogrammed value which will allow the engine to continue running (albeit at reduced efficiency). If the ECU enters this back-up mode, the warning light on the instrument panel will come on, and the relevant fault code will be stored in the ECU memory.

17 If the warning light comes on, the vehicle should be taken to a Vauxhall dealer at the earliest opportunity. A complete test of the injection system can then be carried out, using a special electronic diagnostic test unit which is simply plugged into the system's diagnostic connector. The connector is located behind the centre console; unclip the trim panel situated just in front of the handbrake lever to gain access **(see illustration)**.

Precautions

⚠️ *Warning: It is necessary to take certain precautions when working on the fuel system components, particularly the fuel injectors. Before carrying out any operations on the fuel system, refer to the precautions given in 'Safety first!' at the beginning of this manual, and to any additional warning notes at the start of the relevant Sections.*

Caution: Do not operate the engine if any of air intake ducts are disconnected or the filter element is removed. Any debris entering the engine will cause severe damage to the turbocharger.

Caution: To prevent damage to the turbocharger, do not race the engine

1.13 Unclip the trim panel in front of the handbrake lever to gain access to the diagnostic plug

immediately after start-up, especially if it is cold. Allow it to idle smoothly to give the oil a few seconds to circulate around the turbocharger bearings. Always allow the engine to return to idle speed before switching it off – do not blip the throttle and switch off, as this will leave the turbo spinning without lubrication.

Caution: Observe the recommended intervals for oil and filter changing, and use a reputable oil of the specified quality. Neglect of oil changing, or use of inferior oil, can cause carbon formation on the turbo shaft, leading to subsequent failure.

---

2 Air cleaner assembly and intake ducts – removal and refitting

Removal

1 Disconnect the battery negative terminal then disconnect the wiring connector(s) from the airflow meter and (where fitted) the intake air temperature sensor **(see illustration)**.

2 Disconnect the breather hose from the intake duct then slacken the retaining clips and remove the duct assembly, complete with airflow meter, from the engine compartment **(see illustration)**.

3 Unclip the air cleaner housing lid and remove the filter element, noting which way up it is fitted. Undo the retaining nuts and remove the housing from the engine compartment, freeing it from its intake.

2.1 Disconnect the wiring connector from the airflow meter and (where fitted) the intake air temperature sensor (arrowed)

2.2 Removing the intake duct assembly complete with the air cleaner upper housing

2.4a On low-pressure turbo models slacken the retaining clamp securing the metal pipe to the turbocharger . . .

2.4b . . . then undo the two retaining bolts (arrowed) . . .

4 On low-pressure turbo models, to remove the ducts linking the turbocharger and inlet manifold, first undo the retaining screws and remove the plastic cover from the top of the engine. Slacken the retaining clip securing the duct connecting the metal pipe to the manifold. Undo the bolts securing the pipe to the cylinder head cover, then slacken the retaining clamp and detach the pipe from the turbocharger. Remove the pipe and duct assembly from the top of the engine and recover the sealing ring which is fitted between the pipe and turbocharger (**see illustrations**).

5 On high-pressure turbo models, the ducts linking the intercooler to the manifold and turbocharger pipe can be removed once their retaining clips have been slackened. To remove the metal pipe, detach the duct then slacken the clamp securing it to the turbocharger. Undo the retaining bolt and remove the pipe from the engine, noting the sealing ring which is fitted between the pipe and turbocharger (**see illustration**).

Refitting

6 Refitting is the reverse of removal, ensuring that all intake ducts are properly reconnected and their retaining clips securely tightened. Renew the sealing ring if the metal pipe has been disconnected from the turbocharger.

2.4c . . . and remove the metal pipe and intake duct . . .

2.4d . . . noting the sealing ring which is fitted to the turbocharger (arrowed)

2.4e Air cleaner and ducting – low-pressure models

1 Air cleaner housing lower part
2 Air cleaner housing upper part
3 Air intake hose
4 Hot Film Mass airflow meter
5 Air intake hose
6 Charge air pipe
7 Connecting hose
8 Air intake pipe
9 Connecting hose

H32432

2.5 Air cleaner and ducting – high-pressure models

1 Air cleaner housing lower part	3 Air intake hose	6 Charge air pipe	9 Charge air hose
2 Air cleaner housing upper part	4 Hot Film Mass airflow meter	7 Charge air hose	10 Air intake pipe
	5 Air intake hose	8 Intercooler	11 Connecting hose

H32433

3 Accelerator pedal – removal and refitting

1 From inside the vehicle, unscrew the fasteners and remove the lower trim panel from underneath the driver's side of the facia to gain access to the accelerator pedal (see illustrations).

2 Disconnect the wiring connector from the accelerator pedal position sensor.

3 Remove the retaining clip from the link rod balljoint then unclip the rod from the position sensor (see illustration).

3.1a Unscrew the fasteners . . .

3.1b . . . and remove the lower trim panel from underneath the driver's side of the facia

4 Unscrew the retaining nuts and remove the pedal assembly from the bulkhead.

5 Inspect the pedal assembly for signs of wear, paying particular attention to the pedal bushes, and renew as necessary. To dismantle the assembly, remove the position sensor (see Section 8) then unhook the return spring then slide off the retaining clip and separate the pedal, mounting bracket, return spring and pivot bushes.

6 If the assembly has been dismantled, apply a smear of multi-purpose grease to the pedal pivot shaft and bushes. Fit the bushes and return spring to the mounting bracket and insert the pedal, making sure it passes through the return spring bore. Secure the pedal in position with the retaining clip and

hook the return spring back behind the pedal. Refit the position sensor (see Section 8).

7 Refit the pedal assembly and tighten its retaining nuts to the specified torque setting.

8 Reconnect the wiring connector and actuating linkage, then refit the trim panel to the facia.

4 Fuel system – priming and bleeding

1 It is not necessary to manually prime and bleed the fuel system after any operation on the system components. Start the engine (this may take longer than usual, especially if the

fuel system has been allowed to run dry – operate the starter in ten second bursts with 5 seconds rest in between each operation) and run it a fast idle speed for a minute or so to purge any trapped air from the fuel lines. After this time the engine should idle smoothly at a constant speed.

2 If the engine idles roughly, then there is still some air trapped in the fuel system. Increase the engine speed again for another minute or so then recheck the idle speed. Repeat this procedure as necessary until the engine is idling smoothly.

5 Fuel gauge sender unit – removal and refitting

1 Refer to Section 10 of Chapter 4A, noting that there is no fuel pump in the tank reservoir, just a fuel pick-up filter.

6 Fuel tank – removal and refitting

1 Refer to Section 11 of Chapter 4A, noting that there is no fuel filter clipped to the tank strap. Plug the fuel hose ends to prevent the fuel draining from the system; this will enable the engine to be started more easily once the fuel tank has been refitted (see Section 4).

7 Maximum speed – checking and adjustment

Caution: The maximum speed is controlled by the ECU and cannot be adjusted by the home mechanic. The speed can be checked using a tachometer as described below, but if adjustment is needed it will have be necessary to take the vehicle to a Vauxhall dealer. They will have access to the necessary diagnostic equipment required to test and adjust the settings.

1 Run the engine to normal operating temperature.

2 Have an assistant fully depress the accelerator pedal, and check that the maximum engine speed is as given in the Specifications. Do not keep the engine at maximum speed for more than two or three seconds.

8 Injection system electrical components – removal and refitting

Airflow meter

1 Ensure the ignition is switched off then disconnect the wiring connector from the airflow meter (see illustration).

3.3 Accelerator pedal/sensor assembly
1 Retaining clip
2 Linkage rod
3 Accelerator position sensor
4 Accelerator pedal securing nuts

8.1 Disconnect the wiring connector then slacken the retaining clips (arrowed) and remove the airflow meter

8.9 Removing the accelerator pedal position sensor

8.13 Disconnect the wiring connector . . .

2 Slacken the retaining clips then free the airflow meter from the intake ducts and remove it from the engine compartment.

3 Refitting is the reverse of removal, ensuring the intake ducts are correctly seated and their retaining clips are securely tightened.

Intake air temperature sensor

Note: *On high-pressure turbo models, the air temperature sensor is built into the airflow meter.*

Low-pressure turbo models

4 Ensure the ignition is switched off, then disconnect the wiring connector and carefully ease the sensor out from the intake duct.

5 Refitting is the reverse of removal ensuring the sensor is correctly located in the duct.

Accelerator pedal position sensor

6 From inside the vehicle, unscrew the fasteners and remove the lower trim panel from underneath the driver's side of the facia to gain access to the accelerator pedal.

7 Disconnect the wiring connector from the sensor which is mounted onto the top of the accelerator pedal.

8 Remove the retaining clip from the link rod ball joint then unclip the rod from the sensor.

9 Undo the retaining screws and remove the sensor from the pedal bracket **(see illustration)**.

10 Refitting is the reverse of removal.

Crankshaft sensor

11 Undo the retaining screws and remove the plastic cover from the top of the cylinder head.

12 To gain access to the sensor from below, firmly apply the handbrake then jack up the front of the vehicle and support it on axle stands. Where necessary, undo the retaining bolts and remove the undercover from beneath the engine/transmission unit.

13 Trace the wiring back from the crankshaft sensor to its wiring connector then free the connector from its bracket and disconnect it from the main harness **(see illustration)**.

14 Wipe clean the area around the crankshaft sensor then slacken and remove the retaining bolt. Remove the sensor from the front of the cylinder block and recover the sealing ring **(see illustration)**.

15 Refitting is the reverse of removal, using a new sealing ring. Tighten the sensor retaining bolt to the specified torque.

Coolant temperature sensor

16 The coolant temperature sensor is screwed into the front of the cylinder head, at the right-hand end. Refer to Chapter 3, Section 7, for removal and refitting details.

Charge (boost) pressure sensor

17 Undo the retaining screws and remove the plastic cover from the top of the cylinder head.

18 Slacken and remove the screws securing the wiring harness tray to the top of the inlet manifold and disconnect the wiring connector from the charge pressure sensor **(see illustration)**.

19 Undo the retaining bolt and remove the sensor from the top of the inlet manifold, noting the sealing ring fitted to the sensor shaft.

20 Refitting is the reverse of removal, using a new sealing ring and tightening the retaining bolt to the specified torque.

Oil temperature sensor

21 Firmly apply the handbrake then jack up the front of the vehicle and support it on axle stands. Where necessary, undo the retaining bolts and remove the undercover from beneath the engine/transmission unit.

22 Drain the engine oil as described in Chapter 1B. Once the oil has finished draining, fit a new sealing ring then refit the drain plug and tighten it to the specified torque.

23 Disconnect the wiring connector then unscrew the sensor from the front of the sump **(see illustration)**.

24 On refitting is the reverse of removal, refilling the engine with oil as described in Chapter 1B.

Electronic control unit (ECU)

25 Remove the windscreen wiper arms as described in Chapter 12 then disconnect the battery negative terminal.

8.14 . . . then undo the retaining screw and remove the crankshaft sensor from the front of the cylinder block (sealing ring arrowed)

8.18 Disconnect the wiring connector then undo the retaining bolt (arrowed) and remove the charge pressure sensor

8.23 Disconnect the oil temperature sensor wiring connector

26 Unscrew the plastic nuts from the wiper arm spindles.

27 Peel off the rubber sealing strip from the top of the engine compartment bulkhead.

28 Carefully unclip the plastic vent panel from the base of the windscreen and remove it from the vehicle to gain access to the ECU.

29 Undo the retaining nuts and free the ECU protective cover from the body.

30 Release the retaining clip and disconnect the wiring connector from the ECU.

31 Undo the retaining nuts and remove the ECU from the vehicle.

32 Refitting is the reverse of removal, ensuring the wiring connector is securely reconnected.

Injection pump control unit

33 The control unit is an integral part of the injection pump and should not be disturbed. **Never** attempt to separate the control unit and pump.

Inlet manifold switchover solenoid

34 Remove the battery (see Chapter 5A) to gain access to the valve which is located in the front left-hand corner of the engine compartment. Note that there are two valves, the EGR system valve and the manifold switchover valve; the manifold switchover valve can be identified by its grey wiring connector **(see illustration)**.

35 Disconnect the wiring connector and vacuum hoses from the valve then undo the retaining screws and remove the valve from its mounting bracket.

36 Refitting is the reverse of removal.

Turbocharger wastegate solenoid

37 The wastegate (charge pressure) solenoid valve is located in the right-hand rear corner of the engine compartment **(see illustration 8.34)**.

38 To gain access to the valve, remove the intake duct assembly linking the air cleaner housing to the turbocharger (see Section 2).

39 Disconnect the wiring connector and vacuum hoses from the valve then undo the retaining screws and remove the valve from its mounting bracket.

40 Refitting is the reverse of removal.

9 Fuel injection pump – removal and refitting

Caution: Be careful not to allow dirt into the injection pump or injector pipes during this procedure.

Note: *Since it is necessary to remove the upper timing chain and sprockets to remove the injection pump, several special Vauxhall service tools (or suitable alternatives) will be required on refitting to enable the valve timing to be accurately adjusted (see Section 4 of Chapter 2D). If access to suitable tools cannot be gained then it is recommended that this task is entrusted to a Vauxhall dealer or suitably-equipped garage. If the task is to be carried out without the tools then accurate alignment marks must be made between the sprockets, camshaft and injection pump flange prior to removal. It is also likely that the special socket (MKM-604-30) will also be needed to unscrew the pump front mounting bolts.*

8.34 Vacuum pipe layout – high-pressure models

1 Charge pressure control solenoid valve
2 Charge pressure control actuator

3 Vacuum pump
4 EGR (exhaust gas recirculation) solenoid valve

5 Inlet manifold switchover solenoid valve
6 Inlet manifold switchover valve
7 EGR (exhaust gas recirculation) valve

9.2 Undo the union bolts (arrowed) and disconnect the feed and return pipes from the pump

Note: *A new camshaft sprocket bolt and upper timing chain guide bolts will be required on refitting.*

1 Remove the inlet manifold as described in Section 14.

2 Remove all traces of dirt from around the injection pump fuel feed and return pipe unions. Slacken and remove the union bolts and sealing washers then disconnect both pipes and position them clear of the pump **(see illustration)**.

3 Remove the upper timing chain and sprockets as described in Chapter 2D.

4 Working through the holes in the lower timing chain sprocket, slacken and remove the pump front mounting bolts **(see illustration)**.

5 Slacken and remove the retaining bolts and remove the pump rear mounting bracket. Manoeuvre the pump out of position along with its sealing ring. Discard the sealing ring, a new one must be used on refitting **(see illustrations)**.

Caution: Never attempt to dismantle the pump assembly. If there is a problem, take the pump to a Vauxhall dealer/diesel injection specialist for testing/repair.

6 Prior to refitting, ensure the timing cut-out in the pump sprocket flange is correctly aligned with the locating hole in the pump body and check that the camshaft and crankshaft are still correctly positioned.

7 Ensure the mating surfaces are clean and dry and fit a new sealing ring to the pump flange.

8 Manoeuvre the pump into position, engaging the lower timing chain sprocket with the pump flange. Refit the pump front mounting bolts and tighten them to the specified torque setting.

9 Refit the mounting bracket to the rear of the injection pump and tighten its retaining bolts to the specified torque.

10 Refit the upper timing chain and sprockets as described in Chapter 2D.

11 Position a new sealing washer on each side of the injection pump feed and return pipe unions then refit the union bolts, tightening them to the specified torque.

12 Refit the inlet manifold as described in Section 14.

13 Reconnect the battery negative lead then start the engine and bleed the fuel system as described in Section 4.

**10 Injection timing –
checking methods
and adjustment**

1 The injection timing is determined by the ECU using the information supplied by the various sensors. Checking of the injection system can only be carried out using specialist diagnostic equipment (see Section 1).

**11 Fuel injectors –
removal and refitting**

⚠️ *Warning: Exercise extreme caution when working on the fuel injectors. Never expose the hands*

or any part of the body to injector spray, as the high working pressure can cause the fuel to penetrate the skin, with possibly fatal results. You are strongly advised to have any work which involves testing the injectors under pressure carried out by a dealer or fuel injection specialist.
Caution: Be careful not to allow dirt into the injection pump, injectors or pipes during this procedure.
Caution: Take care not to drop the injectors, or allow the needles at their tips to become damaged. The injectors are precision-made to fine limits, and must not be handled roughly. In particular, never mount them in a bench vice.
Note: *If the injector nozzle is to be removed from the cylinder head, it is likely that the special Vauxhall puller (KM-928-B) and adapter (KM-931) will be needed. New injector crossover pipe bolts should be used on refitting.*

1 Remove the upper section of the inlet manifold as described in Section 14.

9.4 Slacken and remove the injection pump front mounting bolts (1) through the holes in the lower timing chain sprocket

9.5a Slacken and remove the retaining bolts (arrowed – one hidden) and remove the rear mounting bracket . . .

9.5b . . . then remove the pump from the engine, noting the sealing ring

11.4 Remove the injector crossover pipe from the cylinder head (sealing ring arrowed) . . .

11.5 . . . then remove the sealing ring from the top of the injector nozzle

11.7a Fit a new sealing washer to the base of the nozzle . . .

11.7b . . . then refit the nozzle to the cylinder head, aligning its locating pin with the head cut-out (arrowed)

2 Remove the camshaft and followers as described in Chapter 2D.

3 Disconnect the return pipe from the injector crossover pipe.

4 Unscrew the retaining bolt then carefully free the crossover pipe from the top of the injector nozzle and ease it from the cylinder head **(see illustration)**.

5 Remove the sealing rings from the crossover pipe and the top of the injector nozzle and discard, new ones must be used on refitting **(see illustration)**.

6 Fit the adapter and puller to the top of the injector nozzle and carefully pull the nozzle squarely out of the top of the cylinder head. Recover the sealing washer which is fitted to the base of the nozzle and discard it.

7 Fit a new sealing washer to the base of the injector nozzle then carefully ease the nozzle into position in the cylinder head, aligning its

locating pin with the cylinder head cut-out **(see illustrations)**.

8 Ensure the injector nozzle is pushed fully into the cylinder head then fit a new sealing ring to its upper end.

9 Fit a new sealing ring to the crossover pipe recess. Ease the crossover pipe into position in the cylinder head, seating it correctly on the top of the injector nozzle, fit the new retaining bolt. Tighten the retaining bolt as tight as possible by hand, then using a socket and extension bar, tighten it through a further complete rotation (360°) **(see illustrations)**.

10 Connect the return pipe to the crossover pipe then refit the inlet manifold section as described in Section 14.

11 Refit the camshaft and followers as described in Chapter 2D.

12 On completion start the engine and bleed the fuel system as described in Section 4.

11.9a Tighten the injector crossover pipe bolt as tight as possible by hand . . .

11.9b . . . then tighten the bolt by one complete turn

12 Turbocharger – removal and refitting

Note: *The Y22DTR has a turbocharger with variable geometry. At low engine speeds the vanes close to give less flow cross-section, then as the speed increases the vanes open to give an increased flow cross-section. This helps improve the efficiency of the turbocharger.*

Removal

1 Remove the exhaust manifold and turbocharger assembly as described in Section 15 and proceed as described under the relevant sub-heading.

2 With the assembly on bench, undo the retaining bolts and remove the exhaust connection flange and gasket from the turbocharger.

3 Unscrew the union bolt and remove the oil feed pipe. Recover the sealing washers fitted on each side of the pipe union.

4 Undo the retaining bolts and remove the oil return pipe and gasket.

5 Slacken and remove the mounting bolts then remove the turbocharger and gasket from the manifold.

6 Do not attempt to dismantle the turbocharger any further. If the unit is thought to be faulty take it to a turbo specialist or Vauxhall dealer for testing and examination. They will be able to inform you if the unit can be overhauled or will need renewing.

Refitting

7 Refitting is the reverse of removal, using new gaskets/sealing washers, and tightening the fasteners to their specified torque settings (where given). Refit the manifold and turbocharger assembly as described in Section 15.

13 Intercooler – removal and refitting

1 Remove the radiator as described in Chapter 3.

2 Undo the retaining bolts from the top of the intercooler, and hinge the top away from the radiator. Release the bottom of the intercooler from the radiator to remove **(see illustration opposite)**.

3 Refitting is the reverse of removal.

14 Inlet manifold – removal and refitting

Note: *New lower manifold section retaining nuts will be required on refitting.*

1 Disconnect the battery negative terminal then undo the retaining screws and remove the plastic cover from the top of the cylinder head.

13.2 Undo the retaining bolts (1) and unclip the intercooler from the radiator

2 Referring to Section 2, on low-pressure turbo models remove the metal pipe and duct linking the inlet manifold to the turbocharger, and on high-pressure turbo models remove the duct linking the manifold to the intercooler.

3 Undo the retaining screws securing the wiring harness tray to the top of the inlet manifold. Disconnect the wiring connectors from the coolant sensors, the fuel injection pump (slide out the retaining clip to release the connector), the crankshaft sensor and the manifold boost pressure sensor then position the tray clear of the manifold **(see illustrations)**.

4 Disconnect the vacuum pipe from the exhaust gas recirculation (EGR) valve on the top of the manifold **(see illustration)**.

5 Wipe clean the pipe unions then slacken the union nuts securing the injector pipes to the injectors and the four union nuts securing the pipes to the rear of the injection pump; as each pump union nut is slackened, retain the adapter with a suitable open-ended spanner to prevent it being unscrewed from the pump. With all the union nuts undone, remove the injector pipes from the engine unit and mop up any spilt fuel **(see illustrations)**. Seal the pipe end fittings to minimise fuel loss and prevent the entry of dirt.

6 Evenly and progressively slacken and remove the retaining bolts then lift off the

14.3a Slacken and remove the retaining bolts (arrowed) . . .

14.4 Disconnect the EGR valve vacuum pipe

upper part of the manifold **(see illustration)**. Recover the gasket and discard it.

7 To remove the lower section of the manifold, disconnect the vacuum pipe from the manifold switchover valve diaphragm unit

14.5b . . . and injection pump . . .

14.6 Slacken and remove the retaining bolts, then remove the upper section of the inlet manifold

14.3b . . . then disconnect the various wiring connectors and position the wiring harness tray clear of the manifold

14.5a Slacken the union nuts securing the injector pipes to the injectors . . .

and unbolt the wiring connector bracket from the manifold. Evenly and progressively slacken and remove the retaining nuts then remove the manifold lower section and gasket from the cylinder head **(see illustrations)**.

14.5c . . . and remove them from the engine

14.7a Disconnect the vacuum pipe from the manifold switchover valve . . .

14.7b . . . then remove the bolt securing the crankshaft sensor wiring to the manifold lower section

14.7c Unscrew the retaining nuts and remove the inlet manifold lower section from the engine

14.9 On refitting, use a new manifold gasket

8 Ensure that all mating surfaces are clean and dry.

9 Fit a new gasket to the cylinder head then refit the lower manifold section **(see illustration)**. Fit the new retaining nuts and, working in a diagonal sequence, evenly and progressively tighten them to the specified torque setting. Reconnect the switchover valve hose and refit the wiring bracket.

10 Fit a new gasket to the top of the manifold lower section then refit the upper section of the manifold, tightening its retaining bolts to the specified torque.

11 Refit the injector pipes, tightening the union nuts to the specified torque.

12 Refit the wiring harness tray to the top of the manifold, tightening its retaining bolts securely, and reconnect the wiring connectors. Reconnect the vacuum pipe to the EGR valve.

13 Refit the intake duct/pipe (see Section 2) then refit the plastic cover to the cylinder head.

14 Reconnect the battery then start the engine and bleed the fuel system as described in Section 4.

15 Exhaust manifold – removal and refitting

Note: *New manifold retaining nuts and exhaust front pipe nuts will be required on refitting.*

1 Disconnect the battery negative terminal then undo the retaining screws and remove the plastic cover from the top of the cylinder head. Jack up the front of the vehicle and support it on axle stands. Release the

retaining clips/screws and remove the engine undertray (where fitted)

2 Referring to Section 2, remove the air cleaner housing duct assembly and remove the metal pipe linking the turbocharger to the manifold/intercooler duct (as applicable).

3 Undo the retaining nuts and washers (where fitted) from the top of each glow plug then disconnect the wiring connectors and lift off the connector straps **(see illustration)**. On later models simply disconnect the connector from the top of the each glow plug.

4 Undo the retaining screws and remove the heat shields from the top of the manifold assembly **(see illustrations)**.

5 Undo the nuts securing the exhaust system front pipe to the manifold and free the pipe from the manifold **(see illustration)**.

6 Working underneath the vehicle, undo the retaining bolts and remove the heat shield from the rear of the starter motor.

7 Undo the retaining bolts and remove the wiring harness guide from the rear of the cylinder block.

8 Remove all traces of dirt from around the turbocharger oil feed and return pipe unions. Slacken the union nuts securing the pipes to the cylinder block and allow the oil to drain into a suitable container. Mop up any spilt oil.

9 Slacken and remove the retaining bolts and remove the manifold support bracket. Disconnect the vacuum hose from the turbocharger wastegate diaphragm **(see illustration)**.

15.3 Undo the retaining nuts (A) and remove the connector strap (B) from the glow plugs (left-hand arrangement shown)

15.4a Undo the retaining screws (arrowed) . . .

15.4b . . . and remove the heat shields from the manifold assembly

15.5 Separate the exhaust front pipe from the manifold and collect the gasket

15.9 Disconnect the vacuum hose from the turbocharger wastegate

10 Working in a diagonal sequence, evenly and progressively slacken and remove the exhaust manifold retaining nuts. Manoeuvre the manifold assembly out of position and recover the gasket **(see illustrations)**. If necessary, separate the turbocharger from the manifold as described in Section 12.

11 Refitting is the reverse of removal, noting the following points.

a) *Ensure all mating surfaces are clean and dry and renew all gaskets.*

b) *Fit the new manifold nuts and tighten them evenly and progressively to the specified torque, working in a diagonal sequence. Also tighten the support bracket bolts to the specified torque.*

c) *Tighten the turbocharger oil pipe union nuts to the specified torque.*

d) *Ensure the intake duct and metal pipe are securely reconnected (see Section 2).*

e) *Fit the exhaust front pipe as described in Section 16.*

f) *On completion check and, if necessary, top-up the oil and coolant levels as described in 'Weekly checks'.*

g) *On start the engine for the first time, allow the engine to idle for a few minutes before increasing the engine speed; this will allow oil to be circulated around the turbocharger bearings.*

---

16 Exhaust system –
general information, removal and refitting

General information

1 The exhaust system consists of three sections: the front pipe (which incorporates the catalytic converter), the intermediate pipe and the tailpipe. The front pipe is fitted with a flexible section to allow for movement in the exhaust system. The intermediate pipe-to-tailpipe joint is also spring-loaded to allow for movement in the system.

2 The system is suspended throughout its entire length by rubber mountings.

15.10a Remove the manifold assembly from the engine . . .

Removal

General

3 Each exhaust section can be removed individually, or the complete system can be removed as a unit. Even if only one part of the system needs attention, in some case it can be easier to remove the whole system and separate the sections on the bench.

4 To remove the system or part of the system, first jack up the front or rear of the car, and support it on axle stands. Alternatively, position the car over an inspection pit, or on car ramps. Where necessary, undo the retaining bolts and remove the undercover from beneath the engine/transmission unit.

Front pipe (with catalytic converter)

Note: *New pipe-to-manifold nuts should be used on refitting.*

5 Undo the nuts securing the front pipe to the turbocharger. Slacken and remove the bolts securing the front pipe to the intermediate pipe.

6 Free the front pipe from the turbocharger, recovering the gasket, and intermediate pipe then remove it from underneath the vehicle **(see illustration)**.

Intermediate pipe

7 Slacken and remove the bolts securing the intermediate pipe to the front pipe and the bolts and springs securing it to the tailpipe.

8 Remove the securing clips and release the intermediate pipe from its mounting rubbers

15.10b . . . and remove the gasket

(see illustration). Disengage the intermediate pipe from the front pipe and tailpipe and remove it from underneath the vehicle. Recover gasket which is fitted to the tailpipe joint.

Tailpipe

9 Slacken and remove the bolts and springs securing the tailpipe to the intermediate pipe joint **(see illustration)**.

10 Remove the securing clips then unhook the tailpipe from its mounting rubbers, and free it from the intermediate pipe. Recover the gasket from the joint.

Complete system

Note: *New pipe-to-manifold nuts should be used on refitting.*

11 Slacken and remove the nuts securing the front pipe flange joint to the turbocharger.

12 Remove the securing clips then free the system from its mounting rubbers and remove it from underneath the vehicle. Recover the gasket from the front pipe joint.

Heat shield(s)

13 The heat shields are secured to the underside of the body by various nuts and bolts. Each shield can be removed once the relevant exhaust section has been removed. If a shield is being removed to gain access to a component located behind it, it may prove sufficient in some cases to remove the retaining nuts and/or bolts, and simply lower the shield, without disturbing the exhaust system.

16.6 Free the front pipe from the turbocharger

16.8 Release the pipe from the mounting rubbers

16.9 Slacken and remove the bolts and springs securing the intermediate pipe to the tailpipe

Refitting

14 Each section is refitted by reversing the removal sequence, noting the following points:

a) Renew the front pipe nuts whenever they are disturbed.

b) Ensure that all traces of corrosion have been removed from the flanges, and renew all necessary gaskets. Where no gasket is fitted, apply a smear of exhaust system jointing paste to the joint to ensure a gas-tight seal.

c) Inspect the rubber mountings for signs of damage or deterioration, and renew as necessary.

d) Prior to tightening the exhaust system fasteners, ensure that all rubber mountings are correctly located, and that there is adequate clearance between the exhaust system and vehicle underbody.

Chapter 4 Part C:
Emission control systems

Contents

Degrees of difficulty

Easy, suitable for novice with little experience	**Fairly easy,** suitable for beginner with some experience	**Fairly difficult,** suitable for competent DIY mechanic

Difficult, suitable for experienced DIY mechanic

Very difficult, suitable for expert DIY or professional

Specifications

Engine identification

Engine type	Manufacturer's code
1.6 litre SOHC petrol engine	X16SZR
1.6 litre DOHC petrol engine	X16XEL and Z16XE
1.8 litre DOHC petrol engine	X18XE, X18XE1 and Z18XE
2.0 litre DOHC petrol engine	X20XEV
2.2 litre DOHC petrol engine	Z22SE
2.0 litre low-pressure turbo diesel engine	X20DTL
2.0 litre high-pressure turbo diesel engine	X20DTH and Y20DTH
2.2 litre high-pressure turbo diesel engine	Y22DTR

Manufacturer's code	Engine type
X16SZR	1.6 litre SOHC petrol engine
X16XEL	1.6 litre DOHC petrol engine
X18XE	1.8 litre DOHC petrol engine
X18XE1	1.8 litre DOHC petrol engine
X20DTH	2.0 litre high-pressure turbo diesel engine
X20DTL	2.0 litre low-pressure turbo diesel engine
X20XEV	2.0 litre DOHC petrol engine
Y20DTH	2.0 litre high-pressure turbo diesel engine
Y22DTR	2.2 litre high-pressure turbo diesel engine
Z16XE	1.6 litre DOHC petrol engine
Z18XE	1.8 litre DOHC petrol engine
Z22SE	2.2 litre DOHC petrol engine

Torque wrench settings

	Nm	lbf ft
Exhaust gas recirculation (EGR) valve bolts	20	15
Exhaust gas recirculation (EGR) solenoid bolts	4	3
Exhaust manifold shroud bolts	8	6
Oxygen sensor for catalytic converter (in front exhaust pipe):		
X16SZR and X16XEL	30	22
X18XE1	40	30
Z16XE, Z18XE, X18XE, X20XEV and Z22SE	55	41
Oxygen sensor for mixture regulation (in exhaust manifold):		
Z16XE and Z18XE	30	22
Z22SE	55	41
Secondary air injection system:		
Air valve connecting pipe bolts:		
M6 bolt	8	6
M8 bolt	20	15
Support bracket bolts (X16SZR, X16XEL and Z16XE)	8	6

1.7a Oxygen sensor location (Z16XE and Z18XE)

1 Mixture regulation oxygen sensor

2 Catalytic converter function oxygen sensor

1.7b Oxygen sensor location (Z22SE)

1 Mixture regulation oxygen sensor

2 Catalytic converter function oxygen sensor

1 General information

1 All petrol engine models use unleaded petrol and also have various other features built into the fuel system to help minimise harmful emissions. All models are equipped with a crankcase emission control system, a catalytic converter, an exhaust gas recirculation (EGR) system and an evaporative emission control system to keep fuel vapour/exhaust gas emissions down to a minimum.

2 All diesel engine models are also designed to meet strict emission requirements. All models are fitted with a crankcase emission control system and a catalytic converter to keep exhaust emissions down to a minimum. All models are also fitted with an exhaust gas recirculation (EGR) system to further decrease exhaust emissions.

3 The emission control systems function as follows.

Petrol models

Crankcase emission control

4 To reduce the emission of unburned hydrocarbons from the crankcase into the atmosphere, the engine is sealed and the blow-by gases and oil vapour are drawn from inside the crankcase, through a wire mesh oil separator, into the inlet tract to be burned by the engine during normal combustion.

5 Under all conditions the gases are forced out of the crankcase by the (relatively) higher crankcase pressure; if the engine is worn, the raised crankcase pressure (due to increased blow-by) will cause some of the flow to return under all manifold conditions.

Exhaust emission control

6 To minimise the amount of pollutants which escape into the atmosphere, all models are fitted with a catalytic converter in the exhaust system. The system is of the closed-loop type, in which a oxygen sensor(s) in the exhaust system provides the fuel injection/ignition system ECU with constant feedback, enabling the ECU to adjust the mixture to provide the best possible conditions for the converter to operate.

7 On Z16XE, Z18XE and Z22SE engines there are two heated oxygen sensors fitted to the exhaust system (see illustrations). The sensor nearest the engine (before the catalytic converter) determines the residual oxygen content of the exhaust gasses for mixture correction. The sensor in the exhaust front pipe (after the catalytic converter) monitors the function of the catalytic converter to give the driver a warning signal if there is a fault.

8 The oxygen sensor's tip is sensitive to oxygen and sends the ECU a varying voltage depending on the amount of oxygen in the exhaust gases; if the intake air/fuel mixture is too rich, the exhaust gases are low in oxygen so the sensor sends a low-voltage signal, the voltage rising as the mixture weakens and the amount of oxygen rises in the exhaust gases. Peak conversion efficiency of all major pollutants occurs if the intake air/fuel mixture is maintained at the chemically-correct ratio for the complete combustion of petrol of 14.7 parts (by weight) of air to 1 part of fuel (the 'stoichiometric' ratio). The sensor output voltage alters in a large step at this point, the ECU using the signal change as a reference point and correcting the intake air/fuel mixture accordingly by altering the fuel injector pulse width.

Evaporative emission control

9 To minimise the escape into the atmosphere of unburned hydrocarbons, an evaporative emissions control system is also fitted to all models. The fuel tank filler cap is sealed and a charcoal canister is mounted behind the right-hand front wing. The canister collects the petrol vapours generated in the tank when the car is parked and stores them until they can be cleared from the canister (under the control of the fuel injection/ignition system ECU) via the purge valve into the inlet tract to be burned by the engine during normal combustion.

10 To ensure that the engine runs correctly when it is cold and/or idling and to protect the catalytic converter from the effects of an over-rich mixture, the purge control valve is not opened by the ECU until the engine has warmed-up, and the engine is under load; the valve solenoid is then modulated on and off to allow the stored vapour to pass into the inlet tract.

Exhaust gas recirculation (EGR) system

11 This system is designed to recirculate small quantities of exhaust gas into the inlet tract, and therefore into the combustion process. This process reduces the level of unburnt hydrocarbons present in the exhaust gas before it reaches the catalytic converter. The system is controlled by the fuel injection/ignition ECU, using the information from its various sensors, via the EGR valve.

12 On 1.6 litre models the EGR valve is an electrically-operated valve mounted on the inlet manifold.

13 On 1.8, 2.0 and 2.2 litre models the EGR valve assembly is mounted on the left-hand end of the cylinder head. The valve assembly contains the vacuum-operated valve and the electrical solenoid valve which is used to switch the valve on and off.

Secondary air injection system

14 The purpose of the secondary air injection system is to decrease exhaust gas emissions when the engine is cold. The system achieves this by raising the temperature of the exhaust gases which has the effect of quickly warming the catalytic converter up to its normal operating temperature. Once the catalytic converter is up to temperature the air injection system is switched off.

15 The system consists of the pump, air cleaner, the air valve and the solenoid valve and is controlled by the fuel injection/ignition ECU. When the engine is cold, the solenoid valve switches the air valve to open and the pump injects a controlled amount of air into the cylinder head exhaust ports. The air then mixes with the exhaust gases, causing any unburned particles of the fuel in the mixture to be burnt in the exhaust port/manifold which effectively raises the temperature of the exhaust gases. Once the catalytic converter is up to temperature, the solenoid valve closes the air valve and the pump is switched off. A non-return valve prevents the exhaust gases passing through the air valve.

Diesel models

Crankcase emission control

16 Refer to paragraphs 4 and 5.

Exhaust emission control

17 To minimise the level of exhaust pollutants released into the atmosphere, a catalytic converter is fitted in the exhaust system.

18 The catalytic converter consists of a canister containing a fine mesh impregnated with a catalyst material, over which the hot exhaust gases pass. The catalyst speeds up the oxidation of harmful carbon monoxide, unburned hydrocarbons and soot, effectively reducing the quantity of harmful products released into the atmosphere via the exhaust gases.

Exhaust gas recirculation (EGR) system

19 This system is designed to recirculate small quantities of exhaust gas into the inlet tract, and therefore into the combustion process. This process reduces the level of unburnt hydrocarbons present in the exhaust gas before it reaches the catalytic converter. The system is controlled by the injection system ECU, using the information from its various sensors, via the EGR valve on the upper section of the inlet manifold. The EGR valve is vacuum operated and is switched on and off by an electrical solenoid valve.

2 Petrol engine emission control systems – testing and component renewal

Crankcase emission control

1 The components of this system require no attention other than to check that the hose(s) are clear and undamaged at regular intervals.

Evaporative emission control system

Testing

2 If the system is thought to be faulty, disconnect the hoses from the charcoal canister and purge control valve and check

2.8 Purge valve location (arrowed) (X18XE and X20XEV)

2.9 Unclip the purge valve from the air cleaner housing (Z18XE, X18XE1 and Z22SE)

that they are clear by blowing through them. Full testing of the system can only be carried out using specialist electronic equipment which is connected to the engine management system diagnostic wiring connector (see Chapter 4A). If the purge control valve or charcoal canister are thought to be faulty, they must be renewed.

Charcoal canister renewal

3 The charcoal canister is located behind the right-hand front wing. To gain access to the canister, firmly apply the handbrake then jack up the front of the vehicle and support it on axle stands.

4 Remove the retaining screws and fasteners and remove the wheelarch liner to gain access to the canister.

5 Slacken and remove the retaining clamp nut and free the canister from its mounting bracket. Mark the hoses for identification purposes then disconnect them and remove the canister from the vehicle.

6 Refitting is a reverse of the removal procedure, ensuring the hoses are correctly and securely reconnected.

Purge valve renewal

7 On 1.6 litre models, the purge valve is mounted onto the inlet manifold. On Z16XE engines it may be necessary to remove the air intake ducts as described in Chapter 4A to gain access to the valve. Unbolt the valve mounting bracket from the manifold then the valve and bracket can then be separated.

8 On X18XE and X20XEV engines, the purge valve is mounted on the left-hand end of the cylinder head. To improve access to the valve retaining bolts, remove the DIS module as described in Chapter 5B **(see illustration)**. Undo the retaining bolts and remove the purge valve and mounting bracket from the cylinder head.

9 On Z18XE, X18XE1 and Z22SE engines, the purge valve is mounted on the right-hand side of the engine compartment, behind the air cleaner housing. Unclip the valve from the air cleaner housing to remove **(see illustration)**.

10 To renew the valve, ensure the ignition is switched off then depress the retaining clip and disconnect the wiring connector from the valve.

11 Disconnect the hoses from the valve, noting their correct fitted locations and remove it from the engine.

12 Refitting is a reversal of the removal procedure, ensuring the valve is fitted the correct way around and the hoses are securely connected.

Exhaust emission control

Testing

13 The performance of the catalytic converter can be checked only by measuring the exhaust gases using a good-quality, carefully-calibrated exhaust gas analyser, as described in Chapter 1A.

14 If the CO level at the tailpipe is too high, the vehicle should be taken to a Vauxhall dealer so that the complete fuel injection and ignition systems, including the oxygen sensor,

can be thoroughly checked using the special diagnostic equipment. Once these have been checked and are known to be free from faults, the fault must be in the catalytic converter, which must be renewed.

Catalytic converter renewal

15 Refer to Chapter 4A, Section 20.

Oxygen sensor renewal

Note: On Z16XE, Z18XE and Z22SE engines there are two heated oxygen sensors fitted to the exhaust system. The sensor nearest the engine is for mixture regulation and the sensor furthest from the engine is to check the operation of the catalytic converter (see Section 1).

Note: The oxygen sensor is delicate and will not work if it is dropped or knocked, if its power supply is disrupted, or if any cleaning materials are used on it.

16 Warm the engine up to normal operating temperature then stop the engine and disconnect the battery negative terminal.

17 For sensors fitted in the exhaust front pipe, firmly apply the handbrake then jack up the front of the vehicle and support it on axle stands.

18 Trace the wiring back from the oxygen sensor which is to be replaced, and disconnect its wiring connector, freeing the wiring from any relevant retaining clips or ties and noting its correct routing **(see illustrations)**.

Caution: Take great care not burn yourself on the hot manifold/sensor.

19 Unscrew the sensor and remove it from the exhaust system front pipe/manifold. Where applicable recover the sealing washer and discard it; a new one should be used on refitting.

20 Refitting is a reverse of the removal procedure, using a new sealing washer (where applicable). Prior to installing the sensor, apply a smear of high temperature grease to the sensor threads (Vauxhall recommend the use of special grease 19 48 602, part no. 90 295 397 – available from your Vauxhall dealer). Tighten the sensor to the specified torque and ensure that the wiring is correctly routed and in no danger of contacting either the exhaust system or engine.

2.18a Oxygen sensor (arrowed) (X16XEL)

2.18b Oxygen sensor (X18XE and X20XEV)

2.18c Mixture regulation sensor (arrowed) fitted to the top of the manifold (Z16XE and Z18XE)

Exhaust gas recirculation (EGR) system

Testing

21 Comprehensive testing of the system can only be carried out using specialist electronic equipment which is connected to the engine management system diagnostic wiring connector (see Chapter 4A). If the EGR valve is thought to be faulty, it must be renewed.

EGR valve renewal

1.6 litre models

22 Ensure the ignition is switched off, then disconnect the wiring connector from the valve. On SOHC engines the valve is fitted to the centre of the inlet manifold and on DOHC engines it is mounted on the left-hand end of the manifold (see illustration).

23 Undo the retaining screws and remove the valve and its gasket from the manifold (see illustration).

24 Refitting is the reverse of removal, using a new gasket and tightening the valve bolts to the specified torque.

1.8, 2.0 and 2.2 litre models

25 Ensure the ignition is switched off then disconnect the wiring connector and vacuum hose from the EGR valve which is mounted on the left-hand end of the cylinder head (see illustrations).

26 Undo the retaining screws and remove the valve and its gasket from the end of the cylinder head (see illustration).

27 Refitting is the reverse of removal using a new gasket and tightening the valve bolts to the specified torque.

Secondary air injection system

Testing

28 Comprehensive testing of the system can only be carried out using specialist electronic equipment which is connected to the engine management system diagnostic wiring connector (see Chapter 4A). If any component is thought to be faulty, it must be renewed.

Air injection valve renewal

29 The air injection valve is located at the front of the cylinder head. On 1.6 litre engines the

2.22 On 1.6 litre SOHC petrol engines, disconnect the wiring connector . . .

2.25a EGR valve location (arrowed) (X18XE and X29XEV)

2.23 . . . then undo the retaining screws (arrowed) and remove the EGR valve from the inlet manifold

2.25b Disconnecting the wiring connector from the EGR valve (Z22SE)

valve is situated above the exhaust manifold, and on 1.8, 2.0 and 2.2 litre engines it is on the left-hand end of the head (see illustration).

30 Disconnect the vacuum pipe from the valve then release the retaining clip and disconnect the air hose (see illustration).

31 Slacken and remove the bolts securing the valve to the metal pipe and remove the valve and its gasket from the metal pipe.

32 Refitting is the reverse of removal, using a new gasket.

Air injection valve connecting pipe renewal

1.6 litre engine

33 Remove the air injection valve as described in paragraphs 29 to 31.

34 Undo the retaining bolts securing the pipe support bracket and the exhaust manifold

shroud in position and remove both items from the manifold.

35 Slacken and remove the pipe retaining bolts then remove the pipe and gasket from the front of the cylinder head.

36 Refitting is the reverse of removal, noting the following.

a) Ensure the mating surfaces are clean and dry and use a new gasket.

b) Apply a smear of high-temperature grease to the threads of the pipe retaining bolts prior to refitting.

c) Tighten all bolts to their specified torque settings (where given).

1.8, 2.0 and 2.2 litre engine

37 Remove the air injection valve as described in paragraphs 29 to 31.

38 Undo the retaining bolts and remove the shroud from the exhaust manifold.

2.26 Fit new metal gasket – note position of arrow for refitting

2.29 Air injection valve location (arrowed) (X18XE and X20XEV)

2.30 Air injection valve vacuum pipe (A) and air hose (B) (X16XEL)

2.41 The air injection pump (arrowed) is located beside the battery

39 Undo the retaining bolts and remove the connecting pipe from the front of the cylinder head. Recover the gaskets which are fitted between the pipe and cylinder head, and the gasket which is fitted between the pipe and cylinder head bracket.

40 Refitting is the reverse of removal, noting the following.
a) *Ensure the mating surfaces are clean and dry and use new gaskets.*
b) *Apply a smear of high-temperature grease to the threads of the pipe retaining bolts prior to refitting.*
c) *Tighten all bolts to their specified torque settings (where given).*

Air injection pump renewal

41 To gain access to the pump, remove the battery and mounting plate (see Chapter 5A) **(see illustration)**.

42 Disconnect the air hoses from the pump then undo the pump mounting bracket retaining nuts.

43 Remove the pump assembly from the engine compartment, disconnecting the wiring connector as it becomes accessible. If necessary the pump and mounting bracket can then be separated.

44 Refitting is the reverse of removal, tightening the retaining nuts securely.

Air injection pump filter renewal

45 To gain access to the filter, open up the bonnet then undo the retaining screws and remove the radiator grille (see Chapter 11). The filter is clamped to the centre of the vehicle front crossmember, behind the bumper **(see illustration)**.

46 Slacken the clamp bolt then disengage the filter from the clamp and disconnect it from the air hose.

47 Refitting is the reverse of removal.

Air injection solenoid valve renewal

48 The solenoid valve is mounted on the left-hand side of the engine compartment. To locate the valve, trace the vacuum hose back from the air valve on the front of the engine. On 1.8, 2.0 and 2.2 litre models it will be necessary to remove the battery to gain access to the valve.

49 Disconnect the wiring connector from the valve and detach the vacuum hoses, noting each ones correct fitted location.

50 Undo the retaining screws and remove the valve from the engine compartment.

51 Refitting is the reverse of removal, ensuring the vacuum hoses are correctly reconnected.

---

3 Diesel engine emission control systems – testing and component renewal

---

Crankcase emission control

1 The components of this system require no attention other than to check that the hose(s) are clear and undamaged at regular intervals.

Exhaust emission control

Testing

2 The performance of the catalytic converter can be checked only by measuring the exhaust gases using a good-quality, carefully-calibrated exhaust gas analyser as described in Chapter 1B.

3 If the catalytic converter is thought to be faulty, before assuming the catalytic converter is faulty, it is worth checking the problem is not due to a faulty injector(s). Refer to your Vauxhall dealer for further information.

Catalytic converter renewal

4 The catalytic converter is an integral part of the exhaust system front pipe/manifold. Refer to Chapter 4B, Section 16, for removal and refitting details.

Exhaust gas recirculation (EGR) system

Testing

5 Comprehensive testing of the system can only be carried out using specialist electronic equipment which is connected to the injection system diagnostic wiring connector (see Chapter 4B). If the EGR valve or solenoid valve are thought to be faulty, they must be renewed.

EGR valve renewal

6 If the EGR valve is to be renewed, it will be necessary to renew the complete upper section of the inlet manifold (see Chapter 4B). The valve assembly is not available separately and should not be removed from the manifold.

EGR solenoid valve renewal

7 Remove the battery (see Chapter 5A) to gain access to the valve which is located in the front left-hand corner of the engine compartment. Note that there are two valves, the EGR system valve and the inlet manifold switchover valve; the EGR system valve can be identified by its black wiring connector.

8 Disconnect the wiring connector and vacuum hoses from the valve then undo the retaining screws and remove the valve from its mounting bracket.

9 Refitting is the reverse of removal.

---

4 Catalytic converter – general information and precautions

---

1 The catalytic converter is a reliable and simple device which needs no maintenance in itself, but there are some facts of which an owner should be aware if the converter is to function properly for its full service life.

Petrol models

a) *DO NOT use leaded petrol in a car equipped with a catalytic converter – the lead will coat the precious metals, reducing their converting efficiency and will eventually destroy the converter.*
b) *Always keep the ignition and fuel systems well-maintained in accordance with the manufacturer's schedule.*
c) *If the engine develops a misfire, do not drive the car at all (or at least as little as possible) until the fault is cured.*

2.45 Location of secondary air injection system pump and filter

1 *Secondary air injection system pump*   2 *Secondary air injection system filter*

d) DO NOT push- or tow-start the car – this will soak the catalytic converter in unburned fuel, causing it to overheat when the engine does start.
e) DO NOT switch off the ignition at high engine speeds.
f) DO NOT use fuel or engine oil additives – these may contain substances harmful to the catalytic converter.
g) DO NOT continue to use the car if the engine burns oil to the extent of leaving a visible trail of blue smoke.
h) Remember that the catalytic converter operates at very high temperatures. DO NOT, therefore, park the car in dry undergrowth, over long grass or piles of dead leaves after a long run.
i) Remember that the catalytic converter is FRAGILE – do not strike it with tools during servicing work.
j) In some cases a sulphurous smell (like that of rotten eggs) may be noticed from the exhaust. This is common to many catalytic converter-equipped cars and once the car has covered a few thousand miles the problem should disappear.
k) The catalytic converter, used on a well-maintained and well-driven car, should last for between 50 000 and 100 000 miles – if the converter is no longer effective it must be renewed.

Diesel models

2 Refer to the information given in parts f, g, h, i and k of the petrol models information given above.

Chapter 5 Part A:
Starting and charging systems

Contents

Degrees of difficulty

| **Easy,** suitable for novice with little experience | 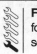 | **Fairly easy,** suitable for beginner with some experience | | **Fairly difficult,** suitable for competent DIY mechanic | | **Difficult,** suitable for experienced DIY mechanic | | **Very difficult,** suitable for expert DIY or professional | |

Specifications

Engine identification

Manufacturer's code	Engine type
X16SZR	1.6 litre SOHC petrol engine
X16XEL	1.6 litre DOHC petrol engine
X18XE	1.8 litre DOHC petrol engine
X18XE1	1.8 litre DOHC petrol engine
X20DTH	2.0 litre high-pressure turbo diesel engine
X20DTL	2.0 litre low-pressure turbo diesel engine
X20XEV	2.0 litre DOHC petrol engine
Y20DTH	2.0 litre high-pressure turbo diesel engine
Y22DTR	2.2 litre high-pressure turbo diesel engine
Z16XE	1.6 litre DOHC petrol engine
Z18XE	1.8 litre DOHC petrol engine
Z22SE	2.2 litre DOHC petrol engine

System type . . . . 12 volt, negative earth

Battery

Charge condition:
Poor	12.5 volts
Normal	12.6 volts
Good	12.7 volts

Torque wrench settings

	Nm	lbf ft
Alternator fixings:		
Diesel models:		
Alternator bracket (coolant flange) to cylinder head	20	15
Alternator bracket to cylinder head	20	15
Alternator lower fixing bolt	35	26
Petrol models:		
Alternator-to-bracket bolts	35	26
Alternator bracket -to-cylinder block bolts	35	26
Alternator bracket-to-cylinder block bolts (Z22SE engine)	20	15
Support bracket bolts	18	13
Engine torque support rod bolts	60	44
Knock sensor retaining bolt (Z22SE engine)	25	18
Oil level sensor to sump	8	6
Oil pressure switch:		
Diesel models	30	22
Petrol models:		
X16SZR, X16XEL, Z16XE, X18XE1 and Z18XE engines	30	22
X18XE and X20XEV engines	40	30
Z22SE engine	18	13
Oil temperature sensor in sump (diesels)	18	13
Starter motor bolts:		
Diesel models:		
Starter to cylinder block	45	33
Starter bracket to cylinder block	25	18
Starter bracket to starter	7	5
Petrol models:		
X16SZR engine:		
Starter fastening nut	45	33
Starter fastening bolt	25	18
X16XEL, Z16XE, X18XE1 and Z18XE engines:		
Starter to transmission	40	30
Starter to cylinder block	25	18
X18XE and X20XEV engines	60	44
Z22SE engine	40	30
Starter motor heat shield	6	4

1 General information and precautions

General information

1 The engine electrical system consists mainly of the charging and starting systems. Because of their engine-related functions, these components are covered separately from the body electrical devices such as the lights, instruments, etc (which are covered in Chapter 12). On petrol engine models refer to Part B for information on the ignition system, and on diesel models refer to Part C for information on the preheating system.

2 The electrical system is of the 12 volt negative earth type.

3 The battery is of the low maintenance or 'maintenance-free' (sealed for life) type and is charged by the alternator, which is belt-driven from the crankshaft pulley.

4 The starter motor is of the pre-engaged type incorporating an integral solenoid. On starting, the solenoid moves the drive pinion into engagement with the flywheel ring gear before the starter motor is energised. Once the engine has started, a one-way clutch prevents the motor armature being driven by the engine.

Precautions

5 Further details of the various systems are given in the relevant Sections of this Chapter. While some repair procedures are given, the usual course of action is to renew the component concerned. The owner whose interest extends beyond mere component renewal should obtain a copy of the *Automobile Electrical & Electronic Systems Manual*, available from the publishers of this manual.

6 It is necessary to take extra care when working on the electrical system to avoid damage to semi-conductor devices (diodes and transistors), and to avoid the risk of personal injury. In addition to the precautions given in *Safety first!* at the beginning of this manual, observe the following when working on the system:

7 *Always remove rings, watches, etc, before working on the electrical system.* Even with the battery disconnected, capacitive discharge could occur if a component's live terminal is earthed through a metal object. This could cause a shock or nasty burn.

8 *Do not reverse the battery connections.* Components such as the alternator, electronic control units, or any other components having semi-conductor circuitry could be irreparably damaged.

9 If the engine is being started using jump leads and a slave battery, connect the batteries *positive-to-positive* and *negative-to-negative* (see *Jump starting*). This also applies when connecting a battery charger.

10 Never disconnect the battery terminals, the alternator, any electrical wiring or any test instruments when the engine is running.

11 Do not allow the engine to turn the alternator when the alternator is not connected.

12 Never 'test' for alternator output by 'flashing' the output lead to earth.

13 Never use an ohmmeter of the type incorporating a hand-cranked generator for circuit or continuity testing.

14 Always ensure that the battery negative lead is disconnected when working on the electrical system.

15 Before using electric-arc welding equipment on the car, disconnect the battery, alternator and components such as the fuel injection/ignition electronic control unit to protect them from the risk of damage.

16 The radio/cassette unit fitted as standard equipment by Vauxhall is equipped with a built-in security code to deter thieves. If the power source to the unit is cut, the anti-theft system will activate. Even if the power source is immediately reconnected, the radio/

cassette unit will not function until the correct security code has been entered. Therefore, if you do not know the correct security code for the radio/cassette unit **do not** disconnect the battery negative terminal of the battery or remove the radio/cassette unit from the vehicle. Refer to *Radio/cassette unit anti-theft system* Section for further information.

2 Electrical fault finding – general information

Refer to Chapter 12.

3 Battery – testing and charging

Testing

Traditional-style and low maintenance battery

1 If the vehicle covers a small annual mileage, it is worthwhile checking the specific gravity of the electrolyte every three months to determine the state of charge of the battery. Use a hydrometer to make the check and compare the results with the following table. Note that the specific gravity readings assume an electrolyte temperature of 15°C (60°F); for every 10°C (18°F) below 15°C (60°F) subtract 0.007. For every 10°C (18°F) above 15°C (60°F) add 0.007.

| | Ambient temperature | |
	above 25°C (77°F)	below 25°C (77°F)
Fully-charged	1.210 to 1.230	1.270 to 1.290
70% charged	1.170 to 1.190	1.230 to 1.250
Discharged	1.050 to 1.070	1.110 to 1.130

2 If the battery condition is suspect, first check the specific gravity of electrolyte in each cell. A variation of 0.040 or more between any cells indicates loss of electrolyte or deterioration of the internal plates.
3 If the specific gravity variation is 0.040 or more, the battery should be renewed. If the cell variation is satisfactory but the battery is discharged, it should be charged as described later in this Section.

Maintenance-free battery

4 In cases where a 'sealed for life' maintenance-free battery is fitted, topping-up and testing of the electrolyte in each cell is not possible. The condition of the battery can therefore only be tested using a battery condition indicator or a voltmeter.
5 Certain models may be fitted with a 'Delco' type maintenance-free battery, with a built-in charge condition indicator. The indicator is located in the top of the battery casing, and indicates the condition of the battery from its colour **(see illustration)**. If the indicator shows green, then the battery is in a good

state of charge. If the indicator turns darker, eventually to black, then the battery requires charging, as described later in this Section. If the indicator shows clear/yellow, then the electrolyte level in the battery is too low to allow further use, and the battery should be renewed. **Do not** attempt to charge, load or jump start a battery when the indicator shows clear/yellow.

All battery types

6 If testing the battery using a voltmeter, connect the voltmeter across the battery and compare the result with those given in the Specifications under 'charge condition'. The test is only accurate if the battery has not been subjected to any kind of charge for the previous six hours. If this is not the case, switch on the headlights for 30 seconds, then wait four to five minutes before testing the battery after switching off the headlights. All other electrical circuits must be switched off, so check that the doors and tailgate are fully shut when making the test.
7 If the voltage reading is less than 12.2 volts, then the battery is discharged, whilst a reading of 12.2 to 12.4 volts indicates a partially-discharged condition.
8 If the battery is to be charged, remove it from the vehicle (Section 4) and charge it as described later in this Section.

Charging

Note: *The following is intended as a guide only. Always refer to the manufacturer's recommendations (often printed on a label attached to the battery) before charging a battery.*

Traditional-style and low maintenance battery

9 Charge the battery at a rate of 3.5 to 4 amps and continue to charge the battery at this rate until no further rise in specific gravity is noted over a four hour period.
10 Alternatively, a trickle charger charging at the rate of 1.5 amps can safely be used overnight.
11 Specially rapid 'boost' charges which are claimed to restore the power of the battery in 1 to 2 hours are not recommended, as they can cause serious damage to the battery plates through overheating.
12 While charging the battery, note that the temperature of the electrolyte should never exceed 37.8°C (100°F).

Maintenance-free battery

13 This battery type takes considerably longer to fully recharge than the standard type, the time taken being dependent on the extent of discharge, but it can take anything up to three days.
14 A constant voltage type charger is required, to be set, when connected, to 13.9 to 14.9 volts with a charger current below 25 amps. Using this method, the battery should be usable within three hours, giving a voltage reading of 12.5 volts, but this is for a partially-discharged

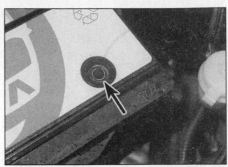

3.5 Battery charge condition indicator – 'Delco' type battery

battery and, as mentioned, full charging can take considerably longer.
15 If the battery is to be charged from a fully discharged state (condition reading less than 12.2 volts), have it recharged by your Vauxhall dealer or local automotive electrician, as the charge rate is higher and constant supervision during charging is necessary.

4 Battery – removal and refitting

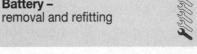

Removal

1 The battery is located on the left-hand side of the engine compartment. On some models the battery will be housed in a protective casing.
2 Unclip the cover (where fitted) then slacken the clamp nut and disconnect the clamp from the battery negative (earth) terminal **(see illustration)**. **Note:** *The battery must be disconnected within 15 seconds of the ignition switch being turned off, otherwise the alarm system will activate.*
3 Lift the insulation cover and disconnect the positive terminal lead in the same way.
4 Where applicable, unclip the relay/fusebox from the battery retaining bracket **(see illustration)**.
5 Unscrew the bolt and remove the battery retaining clamp and lift the battery out of the engine compartment **(see illustration)**.

4.2 Always disconnect the battery negative terminal (1) first and the positive terminal (2) second

4.4 Unclip the relay/fusebox from the battery retaining bracket

4.5 Unscrew the bolt (arrowed) and remove the battery retaining clamp

6 If necessary, unclip the fuse box/wiring bracket assembly from the rear of the battery mounting plate and unclip the relay box(es) from the front of the battery mounting plate (if not already removed).

7 Unbolt the battery mounting plate and remove it from the engine compartment, freeing all the relevant wiring from its retaining clips.

Refitting

8 Refitting is a reversal of removal, but smear petroleum jelly on the terminals after reconnecting the leads, and always reconnect the positive lead first, and the negative lead last.

5 Charging system – testing

Note: *Refer to the warnings given in 'Safety first!' and in Section 1 of this Chapter before starting work.*

1 If the ignition warning light fails to illuminate when the ignition is switched on, first check the alternator wiring connections for security. If satisfactory, check that the warning light bulb has not blown, and that the bulbholder is secure in its location in the instrument panel. If the light still fails to illuminate, check the

7.5 Undo the tensioner retaining bolt (1) and the tensioning strut mounting bolt (2)

continuity of the warning light feed wire from the alternator to the bulbholder. If all is satisfactory, the alternator is at fault and should be renewed or taken to an auto-electrician for testing and repair.

2 If the ignition warning light illuminates when the engine is running, stop the engine and check that the drivebelt is correctly tensioned (see Chapter 1A or 1B) and that the alternator connections are secure. If all is so far satisfactory, have the alternator checked by an auto-electrician for testing and repair.

3 If the alternator output is suspect even though the warning light functions correctly, the regulated voltage may be checked as follows.

4 Connect a voltmeter across the battery terminals and start the engine.

5 Increase the engine speed until the voltmeter reading remains steady; the reading should be approximately 12 to 13 volts, and no more than 14 volts.

6 Switch on as many electrical accessories (eg, the headlights, heated rear window and heater blower) as possible, and check that the alternator maintains the regulated voltage at around 13 to 14 volts.

7 If the regulated voltage is not as stated, the fault may be due to worn brushes, weak brush springs, a faulty voltage regulator, a faulty diode, a severed phase winding or worn or damaged slip-rings. The alternator should be renewed or taken to an auto-electrician for testing and repair.

6 Alternator drivebelt – removal, refitting and tensioning

Refer to the procedure given for the auxiliary drivebelt(s) in Chapter 1A or 1B.

7 Alternator drivebelt tensioner – removal and refitting

Removal

1 Firmly apply the handbrake then jack up the front of the vehicle and support it securely on axle stands. Remove the right-hand front

roadwheel and the lower wheelarch panel. If necessary, refer to Chapter 11.

2 With reference to the appropriate part of Chapter 4, remove the air cleaner housing.

3 Hold the tensioner arm against the spring pressure, and lift the drivebelt from the pulleys. Refer to the appropriate part of Chapter 1 if necessary.

4 On petrol models, undo the central mounting bolt, and remove the tensioner assembly from the alternator support bracket. On some models, the tensioner assembly is secured by two bolts.

5 On diesel models, undo the tensioner retaining bolt, and the lower tensioning strut mounting bolt (see illustration).

Refitting

6 On petrol models, align the tensioner assembly with the alternator support bracket. Ensure that the locating pins on the tensioner mounting surface engage correctly with the corresponding holes in the support bracket. Tighten the tensioner central mounting bolt to the specified torque (see illustration). On models where the tensioner is secured by two bolts, there are no locating pins to align.

7 On diesel models, tighten the tensioner retaining bolt, and the lower tensioning strut mounting bolt.

8 Hold the tensioner against the spring pressure, and refit the drivebelt around the pulleys (refer to the appropriate part of Chapter 1 if necessary).

9 Refit the wheelarch panel and the road wheel. Lower the vehicle to the ground, and refit the air cleaner housing.

8 Alternator – removal and refitting

Removal

1 Firmly apply the handbrake then jack up the front of the vehicle and support it securely on axle stands. Where necessary, undo the retaining bolts and remove the undercover from beneath the engine/transmission unit. Disconnect the battery negative lead and proceed as described under the relevant sub-heading.

7.6 Ensure the tensioner locating pins engage with the corresponding holes in the bracket

8.9 Remove the camshaft sensor wiring plug from the bracket

8.10 Remove the alternator upper mounting bolt

8.14 Alternator connections with the covers removed

2 Remove the air cleaner housing and air ducts as described in the appropriate part of Chapter 4.

3 Push the auxiliary drivebelt tensioner against the spring pressure, and disengage the belt from the pulleys (refer to the appropriate part of Chapter 1 if necessary)

S16SZR

4 Slacken and remove the mounting bolts and remove the support bracket from the alternator to the inlet manifold.

5 Undo the bolts and remove the support bracket securing the alternator to the cylinder head. Swing the alternator to the rear.

6 Unclip the wiring harness from the bracket, and remove the bracket.

7 Remove the rubber covers (where fitted) from the alternator terminals, then unscrew the retaining nuts and disconnect the wiring from the rear of the alternator.

8 Slacken and remove the lower alternator mounting bolt, and manoeuvre the alternator out of position.

X16XEL, Z16XE, X18XE1 and Z18XE

9 On 1.8 litre models, disconnect the camshaft sensor wiring plug and unclip it from the mounting bracket **(see illustration)**.

10 Remove the upper alternator mounting bolt **(see illustration)**.

11 Slacken the lower alternator bolt, and swing the alternator to the rear.

12 Undo the bolt(s) and remove the alternator drivebelt tensioner, as described in Section 7.

13 On 1.8 litre models, disconnect the wiring

plugs for the crankshaft sensor and oil pressure switch. Place the cables out of the way.

14 Remove the rubber covers (where fitted) from the alternator terminals, then unscrew the retaining nuts and disconnect the wiring from the rear of the alternator **(see illustration)**.

15 Slacken and remove the bolts securing the alternator mounting bracket to the cylinder block, then manoeuvre the alternator and bracket assembly upwards and out of position. On models fitted with air conditioning, manoeuvre the alternator and bracket assembly downwards and out of position **(see illustration)**.

16 Slacken and remove the bolts securing the alternator to its mounting bracket and separate the two components **(see illustration)**.

X18XE and X20XEV

17 Models without air conditioning: Remove the alternator drivebelt tensioner as described in Section 7.

18 Undo the retaining bolts and remove the alternator support brackets from the alternator to the inlet manifold and cylinder had.

19 Remove the rubber covers (where fitted) from the alternator terminals, then unscrew the retaining nuts and disconnect the wiring from the rear of the alternator.

20 Remove the three bolts securing the alternator mounting bracket to the cylinder

block, and manoeuvre the alternator and bracket assembly downwards and out of the engine compartment.

21 Slacken and remove the bolts securing the alternator to its mounting bracket and separate the two components.

Z22SE

22 Disconnect the wiring harness plug from the air intake temperature sensor.

23 Undo the retaining clips and remove the air intake pipe, disconnecting the air vent and vacuum pipes.

24 If not already done remove the lower part of the air cleaner housing and undo the bolt(s) and remove the alternator drivebelt tensioner, as described in Section 7.

25 Drain the cooling system as described in Chapter 1A, or be prepared for coolant spillage. Disconnect the coolant pipe from the right-hand end of the cylinder head.

26 Unclip the fuel feed line from the bracket on the cylinder head cover. It may be necessary to disconnect the fuel line from the fuel distributor pipe, see Chapter 4A for further information.

27 Unclip the refrigerant line for the air conditioning from the bracket on the cylinder head cover. It may be necessary to disconnect the refrigerant line to ease access, see Chapter 3 for further information.

28 Unscrew the retaining nut and disconnect the wiring terminal **(see illustrations)**, then unplug the wiring block connector from the rear of the alternator.

8.15 Alternator mounting bracket bolts (X18XE1)

8.16 Withdraw the alternator lower mounting bolt

8.28a Undo the retaining nut . . .

8.28b ... and disconnect the wiring terminal

8.29 Alternator mounting bracket bolts arrowed (Z22SE)

8.32 Lower alternator mounting bolt (3), upper mounting bolt (2), and coolant hose (1)

solenoid valve as described in Chapter 4B, Section 8.

34 Unscrew the nut and remove the upper alternator retaining bolt **(see illustration 8.32)**.

35 Drain the cooling system as described in Chapter 1B, or be prepared for coolant spillage. Disconnect the coolant flange from the right-hand end of the cylinder head.

36 Remove the lower retaining bolt, and remove the alternator upwards and out of the engine compartment.

Refitting

37 Refitting is the reverse of removal tightening all mounting bolts to their specified torque settings (where given). Ensure the drivebelt is correctly refitted and tensioned as described in the appropriate part of Chapter 1.

9 Alternator – brush renewal

Note: *If the alternator is thought to be suspect, it can be removed from the vehicle and taken to an auto-electrician for testing. Most auto-electricians will be able to supply and fit brushes at a reasonable cost. However, check on the cost of repairs and availability of parts before proceeding as it may prove more economical to obtain a new or exchange alternator.*

Procedure for a typical alternator

1 Remove the alternator, as described in Section 8.

2 Place the alternator on a clean work surface, with the pulley facing down.

3 Undo the retaining screws, and lift away the outer plastic cover **(see illustration)**.

4 Unscrew the two retaining screws and ease the wire from the connector **(see illustrations)**.

5 If the brushes are damaged or excessively worn, the brush pack must be renewed.

6 Clean and inspect the surfaces of the slip-rings, at the end of the alternator shaft. If they are excessively worn, or damaged, the alternator must be renewed.

29 Slacken and remove the four alternator mounting bolts, and manoeuvre the alternator out of position **(see illustration)**.

Diesel engines

30 With reference to Chapter 4B if necessary, remove the intake ducting complete with hot film mass airflow meter.

31 Unscrew the three bolts securing the rear wiring trough, and disconnect the wiring connections from the alternator.

32 Remove the starter motor and turbo-charger heat shields, and slacken the lower alternator retaining bolt **(see illustration)**.

33 Disconnect the vacuum pipe and wiring plug, and remove the turbocharger wastegate

9.3 Undo the screws and lift away the cover

9.4a Unscrew the brush pack screws ...

9.4b ... and ease the connector apart

9.7 Compress the brushes and refit the brush pack

11.7 Disconnect the wiring connectors from the starter solenoid

7 Reassemble the alternator by following the dismantling procedure in reverse, taking care to ease the brushes over the end of the slip-rings **(see illustration)**. On completion, refer to Section 8 and refit the alternator.

10 Starting system –
testing

Note: *Refer to the precautions given in 'Safety first!' and in Section 1 of this Chapter before starting work.*

1 If the starter motor fails to operate when the ignition key is turned to the appropriate position, the following possible causes may be to blame.

a) *The battery is faulty.*

b) *The electrical connections between the switch, solenoid, battery and starter motor are somewhere failing to pass the necessary current from the battery through the starter to earth.*

c) *The solenoid is faulty.*

d) *The starter motor is mechanically or electrically defective.*

2 To check the battery, switch on the headlights. If they dim after a few seconds, this indicates that the battery is discharged – recharge (see Section 3) or renew the battery. If the headlights glow brightly, operate the ignition switch and observe the lights. If they dim, then this indicates that current is reaching the starter motor, therefore the fault must lie in the starter motor. If the lights continue to glow brightly (and no clicking sound can be heard from the starter motor solenoid), this indicates that there is a fault in the circuit or solenoid – see following paragraphs. If the starter motor turns slowly when operated, but the battery is in good condition, then this indicates that either the starter motor is faulty, or there is considerable resistance somewhere in the circuit.

3 If a fault in the circuit is suspected, disconnect the battery leads (including the earth connection to the body), the starter/solenoid wiring and the engine/transmission earth strap. Thoroughly clean the connections, and reconnect the leads and wiring, then use a voltmeter or test lamp to check that full battery voltage is available at the battery positive lead connection to the solenoid, and that the earth is sound. Smear petroleum jelly around the battery terminals to prevent corrosion – corroded connections are amongst the most frequent causes of electrical system faults.

4 If the battery and all connections are in good condition, check the circuit by disconnecting the wire from the solenoid blade terminal. Connect a voltmeter or test lamp between the wire end and a good earth (such as the battery negative terminal), and check that the wire is live when the ignition switch is turned to the 'start' position. If it is, then the circuit is sound – if not the circuit wiring can be checked as described in Chapter 12.

5 The solenoid contacts can be checked by connecting a voltmeter or test lamp between the battery positive feed connection on the starter side of the solenoid, and earth. When the ignition switch is turned to the 'start' position, there should be a reading or lighted bulb, as applicable. If there is no reading or lighted bulb, the solenoid is faulty and should be renewed.

6 If the circuit and solenoid are proved sound, the fault must lie in the starter motor. In this event, it may be possible to have the starter motor overhauled by a specialist, but check on the cost of spares before proceeding, as it may prove more economical to obtain a new or exchange motor.

11 Starter motor –
removal and refitting

Removal

1 Disconnect the battery negative lead then firmly apply the handbrake then jack up the front of the vehicle and support it on axle stands. Where necessary, undo the retaining bolts and remove the undercover from beneath the engine/transmission unit. Proceed as described under the relevant sub-heading.

SOHC petrol engines

2 Slacken and remove the two retaining nuts and disconnect the wiring from the starter motor solenoid. Recover the washers under the nuts.

3 Unscrew the retaining nut and disconnect the earth lead from the starter motor upper bolt.

4 Slacken and remove the retaining bolts then manoeuvre the starter motor out from underneath the engine.

DOHC petrol engines

5 On X18XE and X20XEV engines, undo the retaining bolts and remove the support bracket from the underside of the inlet manifold.

6 Where necessary, disconnect the oil level sensor wiring connector.

7 Slacken and remove the two retaining nuts and disconnect the wiring from the starter motor solenoid **(see illustration)**. Recover the washers under the nuts.

8 Where applicable, unscrew the retaining nut and disconnect the earth lead from the starter motor upper bolt.

9 Slacken and remove the retaining bolts then manoeuvre the starter motor out from underneath the engine **(see illustration)**.

11.9 Remove the starter motor

Diesel engines

10 To improve access, remove the exhaust system front pipe as described in Chapter 4B.

11 Undo the retaining bolts and remove the heat shield from the rear of the starter motor.

12 Unscrew the wiring trough retaining bolts at the back of the cylinder block **(see illustration)**.

```
H32440
```

11.12 Starter motor fixings

1 Starter motor retaining bolts	4 Starter bracket and exhaust manifold support bolts
2 Wiring trough retaining bolts	
3 Wiring trough	5 Starter wiring connections

13 Slacken and remove the retaining bolts and remove the exhaust manifold/starter motor support bracket **(see illustration 11.12)**.

14 Slacken and remove the two retaining nuts and disconnect the wiring from the starter motor solenoid **(see illustration 11.12)**. Recover the washers under the nuts.

15 Where applicable, undo the retaining bolts and remove the turbocharger heat shield.

16 Undo the retaining nuts/bolt and remove the mounting bracket from the rear of the starter motor.

17 Slacken and remove the retaining bolts then manoeuvre the starter motor out from underneath the engine **(see illustration 11.12)**.

Refitting

18 Refitting is a reversal of removal tightening the retaining bolts to the specified torque. Ensure all wiring is correctly routed and its retaining nuts are securely tightened.

12 Starter motor – testing and overhaul

If the starter motor is thought to be suspect, it should be removed from the vehicle and taken to an auto-electrician for testing. Most auto-electricians will be able to supply and fit brushes at a reasonable cost. However, check on the cost of repairs before proceeding as it may prove more economical to obtain a new or exchange motor.

13 Ignition switch – removal and refitting

The ignition switch is integral with the steering column lock, and can be removed as described in Chapter 12, Section 4.

14 Oil pressure warning light switch – removal and refitting

Removal

Petrol engines except Z22SE

1 The switch is screwed into the rear of the oil pump housing which is located on the right-hand end of the engine, on the end of the crankshaft. To improve access to the switch, firmly apply the handbrake then jack up the front of the vehicle and support it on axle stands. Where necessary, undo the retaining bolts and remove the undercover from beneath the engine/transmission unit.

2 Disconnect the wiring connector then unscrew the switch and recover the sealing washer. Be prepared for oil spillage, and if the switch is to be left removed from the engine for any length of time, plug the switch aperture **(see illustration)**.

Z22SE

3 The switch is screwed into the front of the cylinder block, behind the starter motor **(see illustration)**. To gain access to the switch, it may be necessary to remove the starter motor as described in Section 11.

4 If a spanner (and not a deep socket) is to be used to remove the oil pressure switch, it may be necessary to undo the retaining bolt and remove the anti-knock sensor from the cylinder block **(see illustration)**.

5 Disconnect the wiring connector then unscrew the switch and recover the sealing washer. Be prepared for oil spillage, and if the switch is to be left removed from the engine for any length of time, plug the switch aperture.

Diesel engines

6 The switch is screwed into the rear of the cylinder block, above the right-hand drive-shaft **(see illustration)**. To gain access to the

14.2 Oil pressure warning light switch

14.3 Oil pressure warning light switch (Z22SE)

switch, firmly apply the handbrake then jack up the front of the vehicle and support it on axle stands. Where necessary, undo the retaining bolts and remove the undercover from beneath the engine/transmission unit. The switch can then be reached from underneath the vehicle.

7 Disconnect the wiring connector then unscrew the switch and recover the sealing washer. Be prepared for oil spillage, and if the switch is to be left removed from the engine for any length of time, plug the switch aperture.

Refitting

8 Examine the sealing washer for signs of damage or deterioration and if necessary renew.

9 Refit the switch and washer, tightening it to the specified torque, and reconnect the wiring connector.

10 Where applicable, refit the engine under tray.

11 Lower the vehicle to the ground (where necessary) then check and, if necessary, top-up the engine oil as described in *Weekly checks*.

15 Oil level sensor –
removal and refitting

X16XEL, Z16XE, X18XE1 and Z18XE

Removal

1 The oil level sensor (where fitted) is located on the front face of the engine sump.

2 To gain access to the sensor, firmly apply the handbrake then jack up the front of the vehicle and support it on axle stands. Where necessary, undo the retaining bolts and remove the undercover from beneath the engine/transmission unit.

3 Drain the engine oil into a clean container then refit the drain plug and tighten it to the specified torque setting (see Chapter 1A).

4 Disconnect the wiring connector(s) from the sensor.

5 Unscrew the retaining bolts then ease the sensor out from the sump and remove it along with its sealing ring/washer. Discard the sealing ring/washer, a new one should be used on refitting **(see illustration)**.

Refitting

6 Refitting is the reverse of removal ensuring the wiring is correctly routed and securely reconnected. On completion refill the engine with oil (see Chapter 1A).

All other engines

Removal

7 The oil level sensor (where fitted) is located inside the sump which must first be removed (see the appropriate part of Chapter 2).

8 With the sump removed, slide off the

14.4 Anti-knock sensor (arrowed) next to the oil pressure switch

retaining clip and free the sensor wiring connector from the sump.

9 Note the correct routing of the wiring then undo the retaining screws and remove the sensor assembly from the sump. Check the wiring connector seal for signs or damage and renew if necessary.

Refitting

10 Prior to refitting remove all traces of locking compound from the sensor retaining screw and sump threads. Apply a drop of fresh locking compound to the screw threads and lubricate the wiring connector seal with a smear of engine oil.

11 Fit the sensor, making sure the wiring is correctly routed, and securely tighten its retaining screws. Ease the wiring connector through the sump, taking care not to damage its seal, and secure it in position with the retaining clip **(see illustration)**.

12 Ensure the sensor is correctly refitted then

15.5 Remove the oil sensor and renew the seal

16.3 Disconnect the wiring connector from the sensor

14.6 Oil pressure warning light switch (2) and wiring connector (1) (diesel engines)

fit the sump as described in the appropriate part of Chapter 2.

16 Oil temperature sensor
(diesel engines) –
removal and refitting

Removal

1 Where fitted, release the retaining clips/ screws and remove the engine undertray.

2 Undo the sump plug and drain the engine oil as described in Chapter 1B.

3 The sensor (where fitted) is located at the front of the sump. Disconnect the wiring plug from the sensor **(see illustration)**.

4 Unscrew the sensor from the sump **(see illustration)**.

15.11 Secure the oil level sensor connector using the retaining clip (arrowed)

16.4 Unscrew the oil temperature sensor from the sump

Refitting

5 With a new sealing ring fitted, apply a few drops of locking compound to the threads of the sensor, securely refit the sensor to the sump. Take care not to overtighten.

6 Reconnect the sensor wiring plug.

7 Refit the engine undertray.

8 On completion refill the engine with oil (see Chapter 1B).

Chapter 5 Part B:
Ignition system – petrol models

Contents

Degrees of difficulty

Easy, suitable for novice with little experience	Fairly easy, suitable for beginner with some experience	Fairly difficult, suitable for competent DIY mechanic 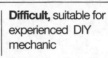	Difficult, suitable for experienced DIY mechanic	Very difficult, suitable for expert DIY or professional

Specifications

Engine identification

Manufacturer's code	Engine type
X16SZR	1.6 litre SOHC petrol engine
X16XEL	1.6 litre DOHC petrol engine
X18XE	1.8 litre DOHC petrol engine
X18XE1	1.8 litre DOHC petrol engine
X20XEV	2.0 litre DOHC petrol engine
Z16XE	1.6 litre DOHC petrol engine
Z18XE	1.8 litre DOHC petrol engine
Z22SE	2.2 litre DOHC petrol engine

General

System type	Distributorless ignition system controlled by engine management ECU
Firing order	1-3-4-2 (No 1 cylinder at timing belt end)

Torque wrench setting	Nm	lbf ft
DIS module screws	8	6

1 Ignition system – general information

1 The ignition system is integrated with the fuel injection system to form a combined engine management system under the control of one ECU (See Chapter 4A, Section 7, for further information). The ignition side of the system is of the distributorless type, and consists of the ignition module and the knock sensor.

2 On X16SZR, X18XE and X20XEV engines, the ignition module is a four output ignition coil. The module consists of two separate HT coils which supply two cylinders each (one coil supplies cylinders 1 and 4, and the other cylinders 2 and 3). Under the control of the ECU, the module operates on the 'wasted spark' principle, ie, each spark plug sparks twice for every cycle of the engine, once on the compression stroke and once on the exhaust stroke. On X16XEL, Z16XE, X18XE1, Z18XE and Z22SE engines, the ignition module consists of four ignition coils, one per

cylinder, in one casing mounted directly above the spark plugs. This module eliminates the need for any HT leads as the coils locate directly onto the relevant spark plug. The ECU uses its inputs from the various sensors to calculate the required ignition advance setting and coil charging time.

3 The knock sensor is mounted onto the cylinder block and informs the ECU when the engine is 'pinking' under load. The sensor is sensitive to vibration and detects the knocking which occurs when the engine starts to 'pink' (pre-ignite). The knock sensor sends an electrical signal to the ECU which in turn retards the ignition advance setting until the 'pinking' ceases.

⚠️ *Warning: Voltages produced by an electronic ignition system are considerably higher than those produced by conventional ignition systems. Extreme care must be taken when working on the system with the ignition switched on. Persons with surgically-implanted cardiac pacemaker devices should keep well clear of the ignition circuits, components and test equipment.*

2 Ignition system – testing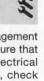

1 If a fault appears in the engine management (fuel injection/ignition) system first ensure that the fault is not due to a poor electrical connection or poor maintenance; ie, check that the air cleaner filter element is clean, the spark plugs are in good condition and correctly gapped, that the engine breather hoses are clear and undamaged, referring to Chapter 1A for further information. Also check that the accelerator cable is correctly adjusted as described in Chapter 4A. If the engine is running very roughly, check the compression pressures as described in the relevant part of Chapter 2.

2 If these checks fail to reveal the cause of the problem the vehicle should be taken to a suitably-equipped Vauxhall dealer for testing. A wiring block connector is incorporated in the engine management circuit into which a special electronic diagnostic tester can be plugged. The tester will locate the fault quickly

3.2a Ignition module (X16SZR)

3.2b Ignition module (X18XE and X20XEV)

1 HT leads   3 Retaining screws
2 Wiring connector

3.4 Unclip the engine cover (Z22SE)

3.6a Ignition module wiring plug (X16XEL, Z16XE, X18XE1 and Z18XE)

and simply, alleviating the need to test all the system components individually which is a time-consuming operation that carries a high risk of damaging the ECU.

3.6b Remove the securing clip . . .

3.6c . . . and disconnect the ignition module wiring plug (Z22SE)

3 The only ignition system checks which can be carried out by the home mechanic are those described in Chapter 1A, relating to the spark plugs. If necessary, the system wiring and wiring connectors can be checked as described in Chapter 12, ensuring that the ECU wiring connector(s) have first been disconnected.

3 DIS module – removal and refitting

Removal

X16SZR, X18XE and X20XEV

1 Disconnect the battery negative terminal.

3.7 Pull the ignition module up and off from the top of the spark plugs (Z22SE)

2 Disconnect the wiring connector and HT leads from the ignition module **(see illustrations)**. The module HT lead terminals are numbered (the leads should also be numbered) with their respective cylinder number to avoid confusion on refitting.
3 Slacken and remove the retaining screws and remove the ignition module from the end of the cylinder head.

X16XEL, Z16XE, X18XE1, Z18XE and Z22SE

4 On Z22SE unclip the engine cover and remove **(see illustration)**.
5 All other models, undo the retaining bolts, unscrew the oil filler cap, and remove the engine cover.
6 The ignition module is mounted at the top of the engine, between the inlet and exhaust camshaft casings. Disconnect the wiring plug at the left-hand end of the module **(see illustrations)**.
7 Undo the retaining screws, and lift the module up and out of position. If the module proves reluctant to separate from the spark plugs, insert two long 8 mm bolts into the threaded holes in the top of the module, and pull up on the bolts to free the module from the plugs **(see illustration)**.

Refitting

8 Refit the module to the cylinder head and tighten its retaining screws to the specified torque setting.
9 On X16SZR, X18XE and X20XEV models, reconnect each HT lead to its corresponding terminal on the ignition module using the numbers on the leads and modules.
10 Reconnect the wiring connector to the ignition module, making sure it is fitted securely
11 Refit the engine cover and reconnect the battery.

4 Ignition timing – checking and adjustment

1 There are no timing marks on the flywheel or crankshaft pulley. The timing is constantly being monitored and adjusted by the engine management ECU, and nominal values cannot be given. Therefore, it is not possible for the home mechanic to check the ignition timing.
2 The only way in which the ignition timing can be checked and (where possible) adjusted is by using special electronic test equipment, connected to the engine management system diagnostic connector (refer to Chapter 4A for further information). Refer to your Vauxhall dealer for further information.

Chapter 5 Part C:
Preheating system – diesel models

Contents

Degrees of difficulty

Easy, suitable for novice with little experience	Fairly easy, suitable for beginner with some experience	Fairly difficult, suitable for competent DIY mechanic	Difficult, suitable for experienced DIY mechanic	Very difficult, suitable for expert DIY or professional 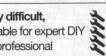

Specifications

Engine identification

Manufacturer's code	Engine type
X20DTH	2.0 litre high-pressure turbo diesel engine
X20DTL	2.0 litre low-pressure turbo diesel engine
Y20DTH	2.0 litre high-pressure turbo diesel engine
Y22DTR	2.2 litre high-pressure turbo diesel engine

Glow plug type . . . . See Chapter 1B

Torque wrench settings	Nm	lbf ft
Glow plugs	10	7

1 Preheating system – description and testing

Description

1 Each cylinder of the engine is fitted with a heater plug (commonly called a glow plug) screwed into it. The plugs are electrically-operated before and during start-up when the engine is cold. Electrical feed to the glow plugs is controlled via the injection system ECU.

2 A warning light in the instrument panel tells the driver that preheating is taking place. When the light goes out, the engine is ready to be started. The voltage supply to the glow plugs continues for several seconds after the light goes out. If no attempt is made to start, the timer then cuts off the supply, in order to avoid draining the battery and overheating the glow plugs.

3 The glow plugs also provide a 'post-heating' function, whereby the glow plugs remain switched on for a period after the engine has started. The length of time 'post-heating' takes place for is also determined by the control unit but it can be anything up to 6 minutes, depending on engine temperature.

4 The fuel filter is fitted with a heating element to prevent the fuel 'waxing' in extreme conditions and to improve combustion. The heating element is fitted between the filter and its housing and is controlled by the preheating system control unit (ECU). The heating element is switched on if the temperature of the fuel passing through the filter is less than 5°C (41°F) and switches off when the fuel temperature reaches 16°C (61°F).

Testing

5 If the system malfunctions, testing is ultimately by substitution of known good units, but some preliminary checks may be made as follows.

6 Connect a voltmeter or 12 volt test lamp between the glow plug supply cable and earth (engine or vehicle metal). Make sure that the live connection is kept clear of the engine and bodywork.

7 Have an assistant switch on the ignition, and check that voltage is applied to the glow plugs. Note the time for which the warning light is lit, and the total time for which voltage is applied before the system cuts out. Switch off the ignition.

8 At an under-bonnet temperature of 20°C (68°F), typical times noted should be approximately 3 seconds for warning light operation. Warning light time will increase with lower temperatures and decrease with higher temperatures.

9 If there is no supply at all, the control unit, relay or associated wiring is at fault.

10 To locate a defective glow plug, slacken and remove the nuts and washers (where fitted) then disconnect the main supply lead(s) and the electrical supply rail from the plugs. On later models simply pull off the wiring connector from each plug.

11 Use a continuity tester, or a 12 volt test lamp connected to the battery positive terminal, to check for continuity between each glow plug terminal and earth. The resistance of a glow plug in good condition is very low (less than 1 ohm), so if the test lamp does not light or the continuity tester shows a high resistance, the glow plug is certainly defective.

12 If an ammeter is available, the current draw of each glow plug can be checked. After an initial surge of 15 to 20 amps, each plug should draw 12 amps. Any plug which draws much more or less than this is probably defective.

13 As a final check, the glow plugs can be removed and inspected as described in the following Section.

2.2a Unscrew the retaining nut from each glow plug . . .

2.2b . . . then disconnect the wiring . . .

2.2c . . . and lift off the electrical connecting rails (where fitted)

2 Glow plugs – removal, inspection and refitting

Caution: If the preheating system has just been energised, or if the engine has been running, the glow plugs will be very hot.

Removal

1 Disconnect the battery negative lead. On high-pressure turbo models it will be necessary to remove the metal pipe that runs along the top of the exhaust manifold linking the turbocharger to the manifold/intercooler duct.

2 On early models undo the retaining nuts and washers from the top of each glow plug then disconnect the wiring connectors and lift off the electrical connecting rails **(see illustrations)**. On later models simply disconnect the connector from the top of the each glow plug.

3 Unscrew the glow plug(s) and remove them from the cylinder head.

Inspection

4 Inspect each glow plug for physical damage. Burnt or eroded glow plug tips can be caused by a bad injector spray pattern. Have the injectors checked if this sort of damage is found.

5 If the glow plugs are in good physical condition, check them electrically using a 12 volt test lamp or continuity tester as described in the previous Section.

6 The glow plugs can be energised by applying 12 volts to them to verify that they heat up evenly and in the required time.

3.4 Disconnect the glow plug ECU

Observe the following precautions.
a) *Support the glow plug by clamping it carefully in a vice or self-locking pliers. Remember it will become red-hot.*
b) *Make sure that the power supply or test lead incorporates a fuse or overload trip to protect against damage from a short-circuit.*
c) *After testing, allow the glow plug to cool for several minutes before attempting to handle it.*

7 A glow plug in good condition will start to glow red at the tip after drawing current for 5 seconds or so. Any plug which takes much longer to start glowing, or which starts glowing in the middle instead of at the tip, is defective.

Refitting

8 Carefully refit the plug(s) and tighten to the specified torque. Do not overtighten, as this can damage the glow plug element.

9 On early models, refit the supply rail(s) to the glow plugs, reconnect the wiring connector(s) then refit the washers and retaining nuts and tighten securely. On later models reconnect the connectors securely to the plugs.

10 Refit the metal pipe (where removed) to the turbocharger/duct then reconnect the battery and check the operation of the glow plugs.

3 Preheating system components – removal and refitting

Note: *Prior to attempting any repair procedure, check spares availability with your Vauxhall dealer.*

Pre-heating system ECU

Low-pressure turbo engines

1 The unit is located on the left-hand side of the engine compartment where it is mounted onto the left-hand side of the battery tray.

2 Disconnect the battery negative lead.

3 Slide the control unit up and off the battery tray.

4 Disconnect the wiring connector from the base of the unit. Remove the unit from the engine compartment **(see illustration)**.

5 Refitting is a reversal of removal.

High-pressure turbo engines

6 The operation of the preheating system is controlled by the injection system ECU and its sensors. Refer to Chapter 4B, Section 8, for further information.

Coolant temperature switch

7 The coolant temperature switch is screwed into the thermostat housing. Refer to Chapter 3, Section 7, for removal and refitting details.

Fuel filter heating element

8 Remove the fuel filter as described in Chapter 1B. If the filter is damaged on removal (which is likely), a new one should be used on refitting.

9 Disconnect the battery negative terminal then disconnect the wiring connector from the heating element.

10 Unscrew the centre bolt and remove the heating element from the filter housing. Recover the sealing ring and discard, a new one should be used on refitting.

11 Fit a new sealing ring the heating element recess then refit the element to the filter housing and securely tighten the centre bolt.

12 Reconnect the battery then fit the fuel filter as described in Chapter 1B.

Fuel filter heater switch

13 Disconnect the battery negative terminal then disconnect the wiring connector from the temperature switch which is screwed into the fuel filter housing.

14 Position a wad of rag beneath the filter housing to catch any spilt fuel then unscrew the switch and remove it from the housing. Plug the housing aperture to prevent the entry of dirt and minimise fuel loss. Remove the sealing ring from the switch and renew them.

15 Fit new sealing rings to the switch recesses then refit the switch to the filter housing and tighten securely. Reconnect the wiring connector to the switch then reconnect the battery.

Relays and fuses

16 The fuel heating element relays and fuses are located in the box in the engine compartment. Refer to Chapter 12 for further details.

Chapter 6
Clutch

Contents

Degrees of difficulty

| Easy, suitable for novice with little experience | | Fairly easy, suitable for beginner with some experience | | Fairly difficult, suitable for competent DIY mechanic | | Difficult, suitable for experienced DIY mechanic | | Very difficult, suitable for expert DIY or professional | |

Specifications

Engine identification

Manufacturer's code	Engine type
X16SZR	1.6 litre SOHC petrol engine
X16XEL	1.6 litre DOHC petrol engine
X18XE	1.8 litre DOHC petrol engine
X18XE1	1.8 litre DOHC petrol engine
X20DTH	2.0 litre high-pressure turbo diesel engine
X20DTL	2.0 litre low-pressure turbo diesel engine
X20XEV	2.0 litre DOHC petrol engine
Y20DTH	2.0 litre high-pressure turbo diesel engine
Y22DTR	2.2 litre high-pressure turbo diesel engine
Z16XE	1.6 litre DOHC petrol engine
Z18XE	1.8 litre DOHC petrol engine
Z22SE	2.2 litre DOHC petrol engine

Type . . . . Single dry friction disc with diaphragm spring, hydraulically operated

Friction disc

Diameter:
Petrol models:
  X16SZR and X16XEL . . . . 200 mm
  Z16XE . . . . 205 mm
  X18XE and X18XE1 . . . . 216 mm
  Z18XE . . . . 205 mm
  X20XEV . . . . 216 mm
  Z22SE . . . . 229 mm
Diesel models:
  X20DTL and X20DTH . . . . 228 mm
  Y20DTH . . . . 229 mm
  Y22DTR . . . . 240 mm

Torque wrench settings

	Nm	lbf ft
Hydraulic pipe union nut	14	10
Master cylinder retaining nuts	20	15
Pedal mounting bracket nuts	20	15
Pressure plate retaining bolts:		
Petrol models:		
1.6 and 1.8 litre engines	15	11
2.0 and 2.2 litre engines	28	21
Diesel models:		
2.0 and 2.2 litre engines	28	21
Release cylinder mounting bolts	5	4

1 General information

1 The clutch consists of a friction disc, a pressure plate assembly, and the hydraulic release cylinder (which incorporates the release bearing); all of these components are contained in the large cast-aluminium alloy bellhousing, sandwiched between the engine and the transmission **(see illustration)**.
2 The friction disc is fitted between the engine flywheel and the clutch pressure plate, and is allowed to slide on the transmission input shaft splines.
3 The pressure plate assembly is bolted to the engine flywheel. When the engine is running, drive is transmitted from the crank-shaft, via the flywheel, to the friction disc (these components being clamped securely together by the pressure plate assembly) and from the friction disc to the transmission input shaft.

4 To interrupt the drive, the spring pressure must be relaxed. This is achieved using a hydraulic release mechanism which consists of the master cylinder, the release cylinder and the pipe/hose linking the two components. Depressing the pedal pushes on the master cylinder pushrod which hydraulically forces the release cylinder piston against the pressure plate spring fingers. This causes the springs to deform and releases the clamping force on the friction disc.
5 The clutch is self-adjusting and requires no manual adjustment.
6 The clutch pedal support and clutch pedal are one assembly and must be renewed as a complete unit. In the event of a frontal collision, the clutch pedal is released from its bearing in the support bracket to prevent injury to the driver's feet and legs (this also applies to the brake pedal). If an airbag has been deployed, inspect the clutch pedal assembly and if necessary renew the complete unit.

2 Clutch hydraulic system – bleeding

⚠ *Warning: Hydraulic fluid is poisonous; wash off immediately and thoroughly in the case of skin contact, and seek immediate medical advice if any fluid is swallowed or gets into the eyes. Certain types of hydraulic fluid are flammable, and may ignite when allowed into contact with hot components; when servicing any hydraulic system, it is safest to assume that the fluid is flammable, and to take precautions against the risk of fire as though it is petrol that is being handled. Hydraulic fluid is also an effective paint stripper, and will attack plastics; if any is spilt, it should be washed off immediately, using copious quantities of fresh water. Finally, it is hygroscopic (it absorbs moisture from the*

1.1 Clutch components

1 Pressure line	5 Clutch control switch (where fitted)	8 Release cylinder pressure line	11 Pressure plate
2 Supply hose	6 O-ring	9 Sealing ring	12 Clutch (friction) disc
3 Master cylinder	7 Release cylinder	10 Pressure plate bolt	13 Fastening sleeve
4 Clutch pedal assembly			

air) – old fluid may be contaminated and unfit for further use. When topping-up or renewing the fluid, always use the recommended type, and ensure that it comes from a freshly-opened sealed container.

1 The correct operation of any hydraulic system is only possible after removing all air from the components and circuit; this is achieved by bleeding the system.

2 During the bleeding procedure, add only clean, unused hydraulic fluid of the recommended type; never re-use fluid that has already been bled from the system. Ensure that sufficient fluid is available before starting work.

3 If there is any possibility of incorrect fluid being already in the system, the hydraulic circuit must be flushed completely with uncontaminated, correct fluid.

4 If hydraulic fluid has been lost from the system, or air has entered because of a leak, ensure that the fault is cured before continuing further.

5 The bleed screw is screwed into the hose end fitting which is situated on the top of the transmission housing. On some models access to the bleed screw is limited and it may be necessary to jack up the front of the vehicle and support it on axle stands so that the screw can be reached from below.

6 Check that all pipes and hoses are secure, unions tight and the bleed screw is closed. Clean any dirt from around the bleed screw.

7 Unscrew the master cylinder fluid reservoir cap (the clutch uses the same fluid reservoir as the braking system), and top the master cylinder reservoir up to the upper (MAX) level line. Refit the cap loosely, and remember to maintain the fluid level at least above the lower (MIN) level line throughout the procedure, or there is a risk of further air entering the system.

8 There are a number of one-man, do-it-yourself bleeding kits currently available from motor accessory shops. It is recommended that one of these kits is used whenever possible, as they greatly simplify the bleeding operation, and reduce the risk of expelled air and fluid being drawn back into the system. If such a kit is not available, the basic (two-man) method must be used, which is described in detail below.

9 If a kit is to be used, prepare the vehicle as described previously, and follow the kit manufacturer's instructions, as the procedure may vary slightly according to the type being used; generally, they are as outlined below in the relevant sub-section.

Bleeding

Basic (two-man) method

10 Collect a clean glass jar, a suitable length of plastic or rubber tubing which is a tight fit over the bleed screw, and a ring spanner to fit the screw. The help of an assistant will also be required.

11 Remove the dust cap from the bleed screw. Fit the spanner and tube to the screw, place the other end of the tube in the jar, and pour in sufficient fluid to cover the end of the tube.

12 Ensure that the fluid level is maintained at least above the lower level line in the reservoir throughout the procedure.

13 Have the assistant fully depress the clutch pedal several times to build up pressure, then maintain it on the final downstroke.

14 While pedal pressure is maintained, unscrew the bleed screw (approximately one turn) and allow the compressed fluid and air to flow into the jar. The assistant should maintain pedal pressure and should not release it until instructed to do so. When the flow stops, tighten the bleed screw again, have the assistant release the pedal slowly, and recheck the reservoir fluid level.

15 Repeat the steps given in paragraphs 13 and 14 until the fluid emerging from the bleed screw is free from air bubbles. If the master cylinder has been drained and refilled allow approximately five seconds between cycles for the master cylinder passages to refill.

16 When no more air bubbles appear, tighten the bleed screw securely, remove the tube and spanner, and refit the dust cap. Do not overtighten the bleed screw.

Using a one-way valve kit

17 As their name implies, these kits consist of a length of tubing with a one-way valve fitted, to prevent expelled air and fluid being drawn back into the system; some kits include a translucent container, which can be positioned so that the air bubbles can be more easily seen flowing from the end of the tube.

18 The kit is connected to the bleed screw, which is then opened. The user returns to the driver's seat, depresses the clutch pedal with a smooth, steady stroke, and slowly releases it; this is repeated until the expelled fluid is clear of air bubbles.

19 Note that these kits simplify work so much that it is easy to forget the clutch fluid reservoir level; ensure that this is maintained at least above the lower level line at all times.

Using a pressure-bleeding kit

20 These kits are usually operated by the reservoir of pressurised air contained in the spare tyre. However, note that it will probably be necessary to reduce the pressure to a lower level than normal; refer to the instructions supplied with the kit.

21 By connecting a pressurised, fluid-filled container to the clutch fluid reservoir, bleeding can be carried out simply by opening the bleed screw and allowing the fluid to flow out until no more air bubbles can be seen in the expelled fluid.

22 This method has the advantage that the large reservoir of fluid provides an additional safeguard against air being drawn into the system during bleeding.

All methods

23 When bleeding is complete, and correct pedal feel is restored, tighten the bleed screw securely and wash off any spilt fluid. Refit the dust cap to the bleed screw.

24 Check the hydraulic fluid level in the master cylinder reservoir, and top-up if necessary (see *Weekly Checks*).

25 Discard any hydraulic fluid that has been bled from the system; it will not be fit for re-use.

26 Check the operation of the clutch pedal. If the clutch is still not operating correctly, air must still be present in the system, and further bleeding is required. Failure to bleed satisfactorily after a reasonable repetition of the bleeding procedure may be due to worn master cylinder/release cylinder seals.

3 Master cylinder – removal and refitting

Note: *A new hydraulic pipe union sealing ring will be required on refitting.*

Removal

Right-hand drive models

1 To gain access to the master cylinder, remove the braking system vacuum servo unit as described in Chapter 9.

2 Remove all traces of dirt from the outside of the master cylinder and position some cloth beneath the cylinder to catch any spilt fluid.

3 Slide out the retaining clip and free the hydraulic pipe from the connector in the end of the master cylinder at the engine compartment bulkhead. Plug the pipe end and master cylinder port to minimise fluid loss and prevent the entry of dirt. Recover the sealing ring from the union and discard it; a new one must be used on refitting **(see illustration)**. Refit the retaining clip to the master cylinder groove, ensuring its is correctly located.

4 From inside the vehicle, remove the driver's side footwell trim below the facia (see Chapter 11, Section 29), release the pedal return spring, slide off the retaining clip and remove the clevis pin securing the master cylinder pushrod to the pedal **(see illustration 5.2)**.

3.3 Slide out the retaining clip and free the hydraulic pipe from the connector

4.2 Clutch release cylinder hydraulic pipe union nut (A) and retaining bolts (B)

4.4 An O-ring seal (A) and oil seal (B) are supplied complete with the release cylinder (2.2 litre petrol engine)

5 Return to the engine compartment then undo the retaining nuts and remove the master cylinder from the vehicle, along with its gasket. If the master cylinder is faulty it must be renewed; overhaul of the unit is not possible.

Left-hand drive models

6 To gain access to the master cylinder, unclip the relay box from the top of the ABS hydraulic modulator unit and position it clear. Access is still poor but can be further improved by removing the braking system vacuum servo unit (see Chapter 9).

7 Minimise fluid loss by first removing the master cylinder reservoir cap, and then tightening it down onto a piece of polythene, to obtain an airtight seal.

8 Wipe away all traces of dirt around the clutch master cylinder pipe union on the side of the fluid reservoir. Release the retaining clip then disconnect the pipe, catching any spilt fluid with a cloth. Plug or tape over the reservoir union and pipe end to prevent dirt entry and minimise fluid loss. Wipe off any spilt fluid immediately.

9 From inside the vehicle, unscrew the fasteners and remove the lower trim panel from underneath the driver's side of the facia to gain access to the clutch pedal (see Chapter 11, Section 29).

10 Remove the master cylinder as described in paragraphs 2 to 6.

Refitting

Right-hand drive models

11 Ensure the cylinder and bulkhead mating surfaces are clean and dry and the gasket is in position.

12 Manoeuvre the master cylinder into position whilst ensuring that the pushrod clevis engages correctly with the pedal. Ensure the pushrod is correctly engaged then tighten the master cylinder retaining nuts to the specified torque.

13 Apply a smear of multi-purpose grease to the clevis pin then align the clevis and pedal

and insert the pin. Secure the clevis pin in position with the retaining clip, making sure it is correctly located in the pin groove.

14 Fit a new sealing ring to the hydraulic pipe union and ensure the retaining clip is correctly located in the master cylinder groove. Ease the pipe union into position until the retaining clip is heard to 'click' then check that the pipe is securely retained.

15 Refit the braking system servo unit and master cylinder and bleed the hydraulic braking system as described in Chapter 9.

16 Once the braking system has been correctly bled, bleed the clutch hydraulic system as described in Section 2.

Left-hand drive models

17 Carry out the operations described in paragraphs 11 to 14.

18 Refit the lower trim panel to the driver's side of the facia.

19 Reconnect the master cylinder hose to the fluid reservoir and secure it in position with the retaining clip.

20 Bleed the hydraulic system as described in Section 2 then refit the relay box to the top of the modulator unit.

4 Release cylinder – removal and refitting

Note: *Due to the amount of work necessary to remove and refit clutch components, it is usually considered good practice to renew the clutch friction disc, pressure plate assembly and release bearing as a matched set, even if only one of these is actually worn enough to require renewal. It is also worth considering the renewal of the clutch components on a preventative basis if the engine and/or transmission have been removed for some other reason.*

Removal

Note: *Refer to the warning concerning the*

dangers of asbestos dust at the beginning of Section 6.

1 Unless the complete engine/transmission unit is to be removed from the car and separated for major overhaul (see Chapter 2E), the clutch release cylinder can be reached by removing the transmission only, as described in Chapter 7A.

2 Wipe clean the outside of the release cylinder then slacken the union nut and disconnect the hydraulic pipe **(see illustration)**. Wipe up any spilt fluid with a clean cloth.

3 Unscrew the three retaining bolts and slide the release cylinder off from the transmission input shaft. If the sealing ring is separate from the release cylinder, remove it from the transmission housing and discard it; a new one must be used on refitting. Whilst the cylinder is removed, take care not to allow any debris to enter the transmission unit.

4 The release cylinder is a sealed unit and cannot be overhauled. If the cylinder seals have gone or the release bearing is noisy or rough in operation, then the complete unit must be renewed **(see illustration)**.

5 To remove the hydraulic pipe, unclip the fastening sleeve from the bellhousing and release it from the hydraulic pipe **(see illustration)**. Check the sealing ring on the bellhousing end of the hydraulic pipe.

4.5 The fastening sleeve which locates the end of the hydraulic pipe in the bellhousing

Refitting

6 Ensure the release cylinder and transmission mating surfaces are clean and dry and where required, fit the new sealing ring to the transmission recess.

7 Lubricate the release cylinder seal with a smear of transmission oil then carefully ease the cylinder along the input shaft and into position. Ensure the sealing ring is still correctly seated in its groove then refit the release cylinder retaining bolts and tighten them to the specified torque.

8 Reconnect the hydraulic pipe to the release cylinder, tightening its union nut to the specified torque.

9 Refit the fastening sleeve to the bellhousing and locate the hydraulic pipe, making sure the lug on the fastening sleeve locates correctly in the bellhousing **(see illustration)**. Fit new sealing ring to the bellhousing end of the hydraulic pipe.

10 Refit the transmission unit as described in Chapter 7A.

11 Bleed the clutch hydraulic system as described in Section 2.

<table>
<tr><td>**5**</td><td>**Clutch pedal –**
removal and refitting</td></tr>
</table>

Note: *The clutch pedal support and clutch pedal are one assembly and must be renewed as a complete unit. In the event of a frontal collision, the clutch pedal is released from its bearing in the support bracket to prevent injury to the driver's feet and legs (this also applies to the brake pedal). If an airbag has been deployed, inspect the clutch pedal assembly and if necessary renew the complete unit.*

Removal

1 Remove the braking system vacuum servo unit as described in Chapter 9. Ensure the clutch master cylinder fluid supply hose is securely clamped or plugged to prevent fluid loss and dirt entry.

2 Carefully prise the retaining clip open slightly, then slide it off the end of the clevis pin. Push the end of the clevis pin securing the master cylinder pushrod to the clutch pedal to remove **(see illustration)**.

3 Carefully unhook the return spring from behind the pedal to release all tension in the spring.

4 On models with cruise control, disconnect the wiring connector from the clutch switch then remove the switch from the pedal bracket.

5 Slacken and remove the nut(s) securing the top of the pedal mounting bracket to the facia frame.

6 Return to the engine compartment then slacken and remove the clutch master cylinder retaining nuts. Leave the master

4.9 Make sure the lug (arrowed) on the fastening sleeve is located correctly in the bellhousing

cylinder in position; there is no need to remove or disconnect it.

7 Slacken and remove the remaining nuts securing the pedal mounting bracket to the bulkhead. Return to the inside of the vehicle and manoeuvre the pedal and mounting bracket assembly out of position.

8 Check the pedal mounting brackets for signs of damage or deformation (the brackets are designed to bend easily as a safety feature in the event of a collision) and check the pedal mounting bushes for signs of wear. If any components is worn or damage it should be renewed; the pedal and brackets can be separated once the bracket bolts have been unscrewed.

Refitting

9 If the pedal and bracket assembly has been dismantled, apply a smear of multi-purpose grease to the pedal pivot shaft and bushes prior to reassembly. Reassemble all components, making sure the pedal return spring is correctly engaged with the bracket, then securely tighten the bracket bolts. Check that the pedal pivots smoothly before refitting the assembly to the vehicle.

10 Manoeuvre the pedal and bracket assembly into position, engaging the pedal with the master cylinder pushrod, then loosely refit the nuts securing it to the facia frame.

11 Working in the engine compartment, refit the nuts securing the pedal mounting bracket and master cylinder to the bulkhead and tighten them to the specified torque setting.

5.2 Slide of the retaining clip and remove the clevis pin (arrowed)

12 From inside the vehicle, apply a smear of multi-purpose grease to the clevis pin then align the pushrod with the clutch pedal hole and insert the pin. Secure the pin in position with the retaining clip, making sure it is correctly located in the groove.

13 Tighten the nuts securing the pedal bracket to the facia to the specified torque setting.

14 Hook the return spring into position behind the clutch pedal.

15 Refit the braking system servo unit and master cylinder then bleed the hydraulic system as described in Chapter 9.

16 On models with cruise control, ensure the switch plunger is fully depressed then refit the switch to the bracket and connect the wiring connector. Fully depress the clutch pedal and extend the switch plunger then release the pedal to set the switch adjustment.

17 Refit the lower cover to the facia and check the operation of the clutch before using the vehicle on the road.

<table>
<tr><td>**6**</td><td>**Clutch assembly –**
removal, inspection and refitting</td><td></td></tr>
</table>

⚠️ **Warning:** *Dust created by clutch wear and deposited on the clutch components may contain asbestos, which is a health hazard. DO NOT blow it out with compressed air, or inhale any of it. DO NOT use petrol or petroleum-based solvents to clean off the dust. Brake system cleaner or methylated spirit should be used to flush the dust into a suitable receptacle. After the clutch components are wiped clean with rags, dispose of the contaminated rags and cleaner in a sealed, marked container.*

Note: *Although some friction materials may no longer contain asbestos, it is safest to assume that they do, and to take precautions accordingly.*

Removal

1 Unless the complete engine/transmission unit is to be removed from the car and separated for major overhaul (see Chapter 2E), the clutch can be reached by removing the transmission as described in Chapter 7A.

2 Before disturbing the clutch, use chalk or a marker pen to mark the relationship of the pressure plate assembly to the flywheel.

3 Working in a diagonal sequence, slacken the pressure plate bolts by half a turn at a time, until spring pressure is released and the bolts can be unscrewed by hand.

4 Remove the pressure plate assembly and collect the friction disc, noting which way round the friction disc is fitted **(see illustration)**.

Inspection

Note: *Due to the amount of work necessary to remove and refit clutch components, it is usually considered good practice to renew the*

6.4 Note which way around the friction disc is fitted

6.14 The friction disc may be marked to show which way round the disc is to be fitted

6.17 Centralise the friction disc using a clutch aligning tool or similar

clutch friction disc, pressure plate assembly and release bearing as a matched set, even if only one of these is actually worn enough to require renewal. It is also worth considering the renewal of the clutch components on a preventative basis if the engine and/or transmission have been removed for some other reason.

5 Remove the clutch assembly.

6 When cleaning clutch components, read first the warning at the beginning of this Section; remove dust using a clean, dry cloth, and working in a well-ventilated atmosphere.

7 Check the friction disc facings for signs of wear, damage or oil contamination. If the friction material is cracked, burnt, scored or damaged, or if it is contaminated with oil or grease (shown by shiny black patches), the friction disc must be renewed.

8 If the friction material is still serviceable, check that the centre boss splines are unworn, that the torsion springs are in good condition and securely fastened, and that all the rivets are tight. If any wear or damage is found, the friction disc must be renewed.

9 If the friction material is fouled with oil, this must be due to an oil leak from the crankshaft oil seal, from the sump-to-cylinder block joint, or from the release cylinder assembly (either the main seal or the sealing ring). Renew the crankshaft oil seal or repair the sump joint as described in the appropriate part of Chapter 2, before installing the new friction disc. The clutch release cylinder is covered in Section 4.

10 Check the pressure plate assembly for obvious signs of wear or damage; shake it to check for loose rivets, or worn or damaged fulcrum rings, and check that the drive straps securing the pressure plate to the cover do not show signs of overheating (such as a deep yellow or blue discoloration). If the diaphragm spring is worn or damaged, or if its pressure is in any way suspect, the pressure plate assembly should be renewed.

11 Examine the machined bearing surfaces of the pressure plate and of the flywheel; they should be clean, completely flat, and free from scratches or scoring. If either is discoloured from excessive heat, or shows signs of cracks, it should be renewed – although minor damage of this nature can sometimes be polished away using emery paper.

12 Check that the release cylinder bearing rotates smoothly and easily, with no sign of noise or roughness. Also check that the surface itself is smooth and unworn, with no signs of cracks, pitting or scoring. If there is any doubt about its condition, the clutch release cylinder should be renewed (it is not possible to renew the bearing separately).

Refitting

13 On reassembly, ensure that the bearing surfaces of the flywheel and pressure plate are completely clean, smooth, and free from oil or grease. Use solvent to remove any protective grease from new components.

14 Fit the friction disc so that its spring hub assembly faces away from the flywheel; there may also be a marking showing which way round the disc is to be refitted **(see illustration)**.

15 Refit the pressure plate assembly, aligning the marks made on dismantling (if the original pressure plate is re-used). Fit the pressure plate bolts, but tighten them only finger-tight so that the friction disc can still be moved.

16 The friction disc must now be centralised so that, when the transmission is refitted, its input shaft will pass through the splines at the centre of the friction disc.

17 Centralisation can be achieved by passing a screwdriver or other long bar through the friction disc and into the hole in the crankshaft; the friction disc can then be moved around until it is centred on the crankshaft hole. Alternatively, a clutch-aligning tool can be used to eliminate the guesswork; these can be obtained from most accessory shops. A home-made aligning tool can be fabricated from a length of metal rod or wooden dowel which fits closely inside the crankshaft hole, and has insulating tape wound around it to match the diameter of the friction disc splined hole **(see illustration)**.

18 When the friction disc is centralised, tighten the pressure plate bolts evenly and in a diagonal sequence to the specified torque setting.

19 Refit the transmission as described in Chapter 7A.

Chapter 7 Part A:
Manual transmission

Contents

Degrees of difficulty

| **Easy,** suitable for novice with little experience | 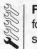 | **Fairly easy,** suitable for beginner with some experience | | **Fairly difficult,** suitable for competent DIY mechanic | | **Difficult,** suitable for experienced DIY mechanic | | **Very difficult,** suitable for expert DIY or professional | |

Specifications

Engine identification

Manufacturer's code	**Engine type**
X16SZR	1.6 litre SOHC petrol engine
X16XEL	1.6 litre DOHC petrol engine
X18XE	1.8 litre DOHC petrol engine
X18XE1	1.8 litre DOHC petrol engine
X20DTH	2.0 litre high-pressure turbo diesel engine
X20DTL	2.0 litre low-pressure turbo diesel engine
X20XEV	2.0 litre DOHC petrol engine
Y20DTH	2.0 litre high-pressure turbo diesel engine
Y22DTR	2.2 litre high-pressure turbo diesel engine
Z16XE	1.6 litre DOHC petrol engine
Z18XE	1.8 litre DOHC petrol engine
Z22SE	2.2 litre DOHC petrol engine

General

Type .... Manual, five forward speeds and reverse. Synchromesh on all forward speeds

Identification code*:
  Petrol models:

X16SZR	F13 WR
X16XEL	F17 WR/CR
Z16XE	F17 WR/CR
X18XE	F18 WR/CR
X18XE1	F17 WR/CR
Z18XE	F17 WR/CR
X20XEV	F23 SR (sports version available – with a final drive ratio of 3.95)
Z22SE	F23 SR

  Diesel models:

X20DTL	F23 SR/WR
X20DTH	F23 WR-SP/SL
Y20DTL	F23 WR
Y22DTR	F35 WR

WR = Wide Ratio (wide ratio gear set)
SR = Standard Ratio (standard ratio gear set)
CR = Close Ratio (close ratio gear set)
*The transmission identification code is cast onto the top of the transmission housing

Transmission ratios (:1):

	1st	2nd	3rd	4th	5th	Reverse
F13WR	3.55	1.96	1.30	0.95	0.76	3.31
F17 WR	3.72	1.96	1.32	0.94	0.75	3.30
F17 CR	3.72	2.13	1.41	1.12	0.89	3.30
F18 WR	3.58	1.87	1.23	0.92	0.74	3.33
F18 CR	3.58	2.14	1.48	1.12	0.89	3.33
F23 SR	3.58	2.02	1.35	0.98	0.81	3.31
F23 WR	3.58	1.89	1.19	0.85	0.69	3.31
F35 WR	3.38	1.76	1.12	0.89	0.70	3.17

Final drive ratio (:1)

F13 WR	3.94
F17 WR/CR	4.19
F18 WR	3.94
F18 CR	3.74
F23 SR	3.74
F23 WR-SP	3.74
F23 WR-SL	3.84
F35 WR	4.05

Lubrication

Oil type	See *Lubricants and fluids*
Oil capacity	See Chapter 1A or 1B

Torque wrench settings

	Nm	lbf ft
Differential lower cover plate bolts:		
F18 transmission unit	40	30
All other transmission units	30	22
Engine-to-transmission unit bolts:	18	13
M8 bolts	20	15
M10 bolts	40	30
M12 bolts	60	44
Engine/transmission left-hand mounting bolts	60	44
Flywheel cover plate	8	6
Gearchange mechanism:		
Selector rod clamp bolt:		
Stage 1	12	9
Stage 2	Angle-tighten a further 180°	
Lever mounting bolts	10	7
Level plug:		
F13 and F18 transmission unit:		
Stage 1	4	3
Stage 2	Angle-tighten a further 45 to 180°	
F17 transmission units	30	22
F23 transmission units	35	26
F35 transmission units	50	37
Reversing light switch	20	15
Roadwheel bolts	110	81
Shift assembly to transmission (F23 unit)	25	18
Shift Bowden cable bracket to transmission (F23 unit)	20	15
Speed sensor bolt	5	4

1 General information

1 The transmission is contained in a cast-aluminium alloy casing bolted to the engine's left-hand end, and consists of the gearbox and final drive differential – often called a transaxle.
2 Drive is transmitted from the crankshaft via the clutch to the input shaft, which has a splined extension to accept the clutch friction disc, and rotates in sealed ball-bearings. From the input shaft, drive is transmitted to the output shaft, which rotates in a roller bearing at its right-hand end, and a sealed ball-bearing at its left-hand end. From the output shaft, the drive is transmitted to the differential crown-wheel, which rotates with the differential case and planetary gears, thus driving the sun gears and driveshafts. The rotation of the planetary gears on their shaft allows the inner roadwheel to rotate at a slower speed than the outer roadwheel when the car is cornering.
3 The input and output shafts are arranged side-by-side, parallel to the crankshaft and driveshafts, so that their gear pinion teeth are in constant mesh. In the neutral position, the output shaft gear pinions rotate freely, so that drive cannot be transmitted to the crownwheel.

4 Gear selection is via a floor-mounted lever and selector linkage mechanism. The selector linkage cause the appropriate selector fork to move its respective synchro-sleeve along the shaft, to lock the gear pinion to the synchro-hub. Since the synchro-hubs are splined to the output shaft, this locks the pinion to the shaft, so that drive can be transmitted. To ensure that gearchanging can be made quickly and quietly, a synchromesh system is fitted to all forward gears, consisting of baulk rings and spring-loaded fingers, as well as the gear pinions and synchro-hubs. The synchromesh cones are formed on the mating faces of the baulk rings and gear pinions.

2.5 To drain the transmission oil undo the bolts and remove the cover plate

2.8 Using a funnel to fill the transmission via the reversing light switch aperture

2 Transmission oil – draining and refilling

1 This operation is much more efficient if the car is first taken on a journey of sufficient length to warm the engine/transmission up to normal operating temperature.

Caution: If the procedure is to be carried out on a hot transmission unit, take care not to burn yourself on the hot exhaust or the transmission/engine unit.

2 Park the car on level ground, switch off the ignition and apply the handbrake firmly. Jack up the front of the car and support it securely on axle stands. Where necessary, undo the retaining bolts/clip and remove the engine undertray.

F13, F17 and F18 transmissions

Note: A new differential lower cover plate gasket will be required for this operation.

3 Since the transmission oil is not renewed as part of the manufacturer's maintenance schedule, no drain plug is fitted to the transmission. If for any reason the transmission needs to be drained, the only way of doing so is to remove the differential lower cover plate.

4 Wipe clean the area around the differential cover plate and position a suitable container underneath the cover.

5 Evenly and progressively slacken and remove the retaining bolts then withdraw the cover plate and allow the transmission oil to drain into the container. Remove the gasket and discard it; a new one should be used on refitting **(see illustration)**.

6 Allow the oil to drain completely into the container. If the oil is hot, take precautions against scalding. Remove all traces of dirt and oil from the cover and transmission mating surfaces and wipe clean the inside of the cover plate.

7 Once the oil has finished draining, ensure the mating surfaces are clean and dry then refit the cover plate to the transmission unit,

complete with a new gasket. Refit the retaining bolts and evenly and progressively tighten them to the specified torque setting. Lower the vehicle to the ground.

8 The transmission is refilled via the reversing light switch aperture. Wipe clean the area around the reversing light switch, and remove the switch as described in Section 6. Refill the transmission with the specified type and amount of oil given in Chapter 1A, then refit the reversing light switch and tighten to the specified torque **(see illustration)**.

F23 and F35 transmission

9 Wipe clean the area around the drain plug and position a suitable container under the plug.

10 Undo the drain plug.

11 Once the oil has finished draining, refit the drain plug with a new sealing washer where applicable, and tighten the plug securely. Lower the vehicle to the ground.

12 The transmission is filled via the oil filler plug located on the top of the casing **(see illustration 9.4b)**. Wipe clean the area around the plug, and refill the transmission with the specified type and quantity of oil given in the appropriate part of Chapter 1. Then refit the filler plug, tightening it securely.

3.4 Lock the gearchange lever in position by inserting a 5 mm punch through the clamp and locating it in the hole on the left-hand side of the lever

All transmissions

13 Take the vehicle on a short journey so that the new oil is distributed fully around the transmission components.

14 On your return, park the vehicle on level ground and check the transmission oil level as described in Section 9.

3 Gearchange mechanism – adjustment

F13, F17, F18 and F35 transmissions

Note: A 5 mm drill or punch will be required to carry out this procedure.

1 Adjustment of the gearchange mechanism is not a routine operation and should only be needed if the mechanism has been removed. If the gearchange action is stiff or imprecise, check that it is correctly adjusted as follows.

2 The mechanism is adjusted via the clamp bolt which secures the selector rod to the transmission linkage (see Section 4). The bolt is located at the rear of the engine/transmission unit, just in front of the engine compartment bulkhead and, on most models, access to the bolt can be gained from above. If the bolt can not be reached from above, firmly apply the handbrake then jack up the front of the vehicle and support it securely on axle stands. Limited access can then be gained from underneath the vehicle.

3 Slacken the gearchange selector rod clamp bolt which is situated at the front of the rod. Do not remove the bolt completely.

4 From inside the vehicle, unclip the gearchange lever gaiter from the console and fold it back. Lock the gearchange lever in position by inserting a 5 mm drill or punch through the clamp on the left-hand side of the lever base and into its locating hole **(see illustration)**.

3.5 The selector mechanism locking pin is located on the top of the transmission unit

1 *Depress the pin to lock it in position*
2 *On completion, move the gearchange lever and check the pin springs back to its released position*

5 Lock the transmission selector mechanism in position by pressing in the spring-loaded locking pin on the selector mechanism cover, which is located on the top of the transmission unit **(see illustration)**.

6 With both the lever and transmission locked

3.10 Use a small screwdriver to release the cable clamping pieces (1)

3.12 Lock the gear lever in 'neutral' by pushing in the clamp with a screwdriver

3.13 Locking the cables by pushing down on the clamping pieces

4.3 Slacken the clamp bolt (arrowed) securing the transmission linkage to the selector rod

in position, tighten the selector rod clamp bolt to the specified torque Stage 1 setting then tighten it through the specified Stage 2 angle.

7 Remove the locking rod from the gearchange lever and check the operation of the gearchange mechanism; the transmission locking pin will automatically release when the lever is moved into the reverse position.

8 Ensure the transmission locking pin has released then (where necessary) lower the vehicle to the ground.

F23 transmission

9 The gearchange adjustment can be done without removing the centre console. If better access is required, remove the centre console as described in Chapter 11.

10 Using a small screwdriver, release both gearshift cable clamping pieces **(see illustration)**.

11 In the engine compartment, set the gearchange selector on the transmission to 'neutral' position.

12 Working back inside the vehicle, position the gear lever in the 'neutral' position, and lock it there by pushing in the clamp **(see illustration)**.

13 Lock both cable clamping pieces by pushing down **(see illustration)**.

14 Pull out the clamp locking the gear lever, and refit the gear lever gaiter and centre console cover. Check the gear selector mechanism for correct operation.

---

4 Gearchange mechanism – removal and refitting

F13, F17, F18 and F35 transmissions

1 The gearchange mechanism consists of the gearchange lever, the selector rod and the linkage assembly on the transmission. The lever and selector rod and the linkage assembly can be removed separately.

Gearchange lever and selector rod

2 Firmly apply the handbrake then jack up the front of the vehicle and support it on axle stands. Where necessary, undo the retaining bolts and remove the undercover from beneath the engine/transmission unit.

3 Using paint or a suitable marker pen, make alignment marks between the selector rod and the clamp on the front end of the rod. Loosen the clamp bolt by a couple of turns but do not remove it completely **(see illustration)**. Move the gearchange lever into the 4th gear position then free the selector rod from the clamp and slide off the rubber gaiter.

4 Remove the centre console as described in Chapter 11.

5 Undo the retaining screws and remove the switch panel from around the gearchange lever, disconnecting the wiring connectors as they become accessible (see Chapter 12).

4.15a Withdraw the pin connecting the linkage to the transmission unit selector lever . . .

4.15b . . . noting that it is necessary to depress the detent mechanism (arrowed) in order to release the pin

4.16 Carefully slide off the retaining clips securing the linkage bracket to its mounting and remove the assembly from the engine compartment

6 Slacken and remove the four bolts securing the gearchange lever to the floor then manoeuvre the lever and selector rod assembly out of position.

7 To dismantle the lever and rod assembly, carefully release the retaining clip from the base of the lever then separate the rod and lever and remove them from the housing. Examine all components for signs of wear or damage, paying particular attention to the selector rod and lever locating pivot bushes, and renew as necessary.

8 If necessary, reassemble the lever and rod, making sure the lever base is correctly located in the housing pivot, and secure them in position with the retaining clip.

9 Lubricate all pivot points and bearing surfaces with silicone grease then manoeuvre the assembly into position. Refit the housing retaining bolts and tighten them to the specified torque setting.

10 Refit the switch panel, making sure its wiring is correctly routed, then refit the centre console as described in Chapter 11.

11 From underneath the vehicle, slide the rubber gaiter onto the end of the selector rod and locate it securely in the bulkhead.

12 Engage the selector rod end with its linkage clamp. Align the marks made prior to removal and tighten the clamp bolt to the specified Stage 1 torque then tighten it through the specified Stage 2 angle.

13 Check the gearchange mechanism operation before lowering the vehicle to the

ground. If the mechanism seems notchy or imprecise, adjust it as described in Section 3.

Transmission linkage assembly

Note: *A new linkage to transmission lever pivot pin should be used on refitting.*

14 Separate the selector rod from its clamp as described in paragraph 3. The bolt is located at the rear of the engine/transmission unit, just in front of the engine compartment bulkhead and on most models access to the bolt can be gained from above. If the bolt can not be reached from above, firmly apply the handbrake then jack up the front of the vehicle and support it securely on axle stands. Limited access can then be gained from underneath the vehicle.

15 Depress the detent mechanism and remove the pivot pin connecting the linkage to the selector lever on the top of the transmission unit **(see illustrations)**. Discard the pivot pin, a new one should be used on refitting.

16 Slide off the retaining clips securing the linkage bracket to its mountings then manoeuvre the assembly upwards and out of position **(see illustration)**. If necessary, the mounting brackets can then be unbolted and removed.

17 Examine the linkage assembly closely for signs of wear or damage, renewing worn components as necessary **(see illustration)**.

18 Prior to refitting, lubricate the balljoints and pivot points with silicone grease.

19 Manoeuvre the assembly into position and locate the linkage bracket on its mountings. Secure the assembly in position with the retaining clips, ensuring they are correctly located in the mounting bracket pin grooves.

20 Align the linkage with the transmission selector lever and insert the new pivot pin. Ensure the pin is securely retained by its detent mechanism **(see illustration)**.

21 Engage the selector rod end with its linkage clamp. Align the marks made prior to removal and tighten the clamp bolt to the specified Stage 1 torque then tighten it through the specified Stage 2 angle.

22 Check the gearchange mechanism operation before lowering the vehicle to the ground. If the mechanism seems notchy or imprecise, adjust it as described in Section 3.

F23 transmission

23 The gearchange mechanism consists of the gear lever, selector cables, and linkage assembly on the transmission.

Gear lever

24 The gear lever assembly can be removed without removing the centre console. If better access is required, remove the centre console as described in Chapter 11.

25 Using a small screwdriver, open the selector cables clamping pieces as far as the notch. Opening them any further may damage the clamping pieces **(see illustration)**.

4.17 Examine the linkage assembly for signs of wear and renew worn components as necessary

4.20 Secure the linkage with a new pivot pin

4.25 Clamping piece unclipped to the first notch, to remove the inner cable

4.26 Unclip the outer cable from the gear lever assembly

4.29 The clamping pieces are attached to the bottom of the gear lever assembly by a ball and socket arrangement

4.42 Prise the gear linkage cables off the selector on the transmission

4.43 Unclip the outer cables from the bracket on the transmission casing

26 Note the fitted locations of the cables, then prise the ends of the cables from the gear lever assembly **(see illustration)**.
27 Slide the inner cables from the cable clamping pieces at the front of the gearchange assembly.
28 Undo the four retaining bolts and lift the gear lever assembly from the floor.
29 If required, the cable clamping pieces attached to the gear lever can be prised from their position. No further dismantling of the assembly is recommended **(see illustration)**.
30 If previously removed, attached the cable end fittings to the base of the lever using a pair of pliers.
31 Position the gear lever assembly on the floor, insert the securing bolts and tighten to the specified torque.
32 Refit the cable clamping pieces into the front of the gear lever housing. Do not lock the

clamping pieces at this stage.
33 Reconnect the ends of the cables to the cable end fittings attached to the base of the gear lever.
34 Carry out the *Gearchange mechanism adjustment* procedure, as described in the previous Section.
35 Refit the centre console.

Selector cables

36 With reference to Chapter 11, remove the centre console.
37 Using a small screwdriver, open the selector cables clamping pieces as far as the notch. Opening them any further may damage the clamping pieces **(see illustrations 3.10 and 4.25)**.
38 Note the fitted locations of the cables, then prise the ends of the cables from the gear lever assembly **(see illustrations 4.26)**.

39 Slide the inner cables from the cable clamping pieces at the front of the gearchange assembly.
40 Disconnect the battery.
41 Support the engine/transmission and remove the rear engine/transmission mounting as described in the appropriate part of Chapter 2.
42 Note the fitted locations of the cables, then prise the ends of the cables from the selector linkage assembly above/behind the transmission **(see illustration)**.
43 Release the outer cables from the linkage assembly bracket **(see illustration)**.
44 Pull the cables (complete with grommet) out of the bulkhead and into the engine compartment.
45 Push the selector cables through the bulkhead passage from the engine compartment.
46 Refit the outer cables to the retaining bracket at the transmission end.
47 Engage the cable end fittings with the selector linkage assembly, squeezing them together with pliers if necessary.
48 Check the cables are routed as noted during removal, and refit the outer cable clamping pieces with corresponding cut-outs in the front of the gear lever housing. Do not lock the clamping pieces at this stage.
49 Reconnect the cables to the end fittings attached to the base of the gear lever.
50 Carry out the *Gearchange mechanism adjustment* procedure, as described in the previous Section.
51 Refit the air distribution duct and centre console.

5 Oil seals – renewal

Driveshaft oil seals

1 Chock the rear wheels, apply the handbrake, then jack up the front of the car and support it on axle stands. Remove the appropriate front roadwheel.
2 Drain the transmission oil as described in Section 2 or be prepared for oil loss as the seal is changed.
3 Remove the driveshaft as described in Chapter 8.
4 Note the correct fitted depth of the seal in its housing then carefully prise it out of position using a large flat-bladed screwdriver **(see illustration)**.
5 Remove all traces of dirt from the area around the oil seal aperture, then apply a smear of grease to the outer lip of the new oil seal. Ensure the seal is correctly positioned, with its sealing lip facing inwards, and tap it squarely into position, using a suitable tubular drift (such as a socket) which bears only on the hard outer edge of the seal **(see illustration)**. Ensure the seal is fitted at the same depth in its housing that the original was.

5.4 Prising out a driveshaft oil seal

5.5 Fitting a new driveshaft oil seal using a socket as a tubular drift

6 Refit the driveshaft as described in Chapter 8.

7 If the transmission was drained, refill the transmission with the specified type and amount of oil, as described in Section 2. If the oil was not drained, top-up the transmission oil level and check as described in Section 9.

Input shaft oil seal

8 The input shaft oil seal is an integral part of the clutch release cylinder; if the seal is leaking the complete release cylinder assembly must be renewed. Before condemning the release cylinder, check that the leak is not coming from the sealing ring which is fitted between the cylinder and the transmission housing; the sealing ring can be renewed once the release cylinder assembly has been removed. Refer to Chapter 6 for removal and refitting details.

Selector rod oil seal

9 Renewal of the selector rod oil seal requires the selector mechanism cover to be unbolted from the transmission and dismantled. This is a difficult task and should therefore be entrusted to a Vauxhall dealer.

---

6 Reversing light switch –
testing, removal and refitting

Testing

F13, F17 and F18 transmissions

1 The reversing light circuit is controlled by a plunger-type switch that is screwed into the top of the transmission, towards the front of the housing. If a fault develops in the circuit, first ensure that the circuit fuse has not blown.
2 To test the switch, disconnect the wiring connector. Use a multimeter (set to the resistance function) or a battery-and-bulb test circuit to check that there is continuity between the switch terminals only when reverse gear is selected. If this is not the case, and there are no obvious breaks or other damage to the wires, the switch is faulty, and must be renewed.

F23 and F35 transmissions

3 The reversing light circuit is controlled by a plunger-type switch that is screwed into the rear of the transmission. If a fault develops in the circuit, first check that the circuit fuse has not blown.
4 To test the switch, disconnect the wiring connector. Use a multimeter (set to the resistance function) or a battery-and-bulb test circuit to check that there is continuity between the switch terminals only when the reverse gear is selected. If this is not the case, and there are no obvious breaks or other damage to the wires, the switch is faulty, and must be renewed.

6.6 The switch is located in the top/front of the transmission below the battery tray

Removal

F13, F17 and F18 transmissions

5 To improve access to the switch, remove the battery and mounting plate (see Chapter 5A).
6 Disconnect the wiring connector, then unscrew the switch and remove it from the transmission casing along with its sealing washer **(see illustration)**.

F23 and F35 transmissions

7 Apply the handbrake firmly. Jack up the front of the car and support it securely on axle stands. Where necessary, undo the retaining bolts/clip and remove the undertray from beneath the engine/transmission unit.
8 Disconnect the wiring connector, then unscrew the switch and remove it from the transmission casing along with its sealing washer **(see illustration)**.

Refitting

F13, F17 and F18 transmissions

9 Fit a new sealing washer to the switch, then screw it back into position in the top of the transmission housing and tighten it to the specified torque. Reconnect the wiring connector, then refit the battery (where removed) and test the operation of the circuit.

F23 and F35 transmissions

10 Fit a new sealing washer to the switch, then screw it back into position in the rear of the transmission housing and tighten it to the specified torque. Reconnect the wiring connector, then refit the engine undertray and lower the vehicle to the ground.

7.5a Use a small screwdriver to prise out the retaining clip . . .

6.8 The reversing light switch is positioned above the left-hand driveshaft

---

7 Transmission –
removal and refitting

Removal

1 Chock the rear wheels, then firmly apply the handbrake. Jack up the front of the vehicle, and securely support it on axle stands. Remove both front roadwheels then, where necessary, undo the retaining clips/screws and remove the engine undertray. Remove the air cleaner housing and intake trunking (see Chapter 4A or 4B)
2 Drain the transmission oil as described in Section 2 or be prepared for oil loss as the transmission is removed.
3 Remove the battery and mounting tray, and the starter motor (see Chapter 5A).
4 Disconnect the wiring connector from the reversing light switch and free the wiring from the transmission unit and retaining brackets.
5 Minimise clutch fluid loss by clamping the flexible hose next to the connection on the transmission housing. Prise out the retaining clip securing the clutch hydraulic pipe/hose end fitting to the top of the transmission bellhousing and detach the end fitting from the transmission **(see illustrations)**. Gently squeeze the two legs of the retaining clip together and re-insert the retaining clip back into position in the end fitting. Discard the sealing ring from the pipe end; a new sealing ring must be used on refitting. Plug/cover both the union and pipe ends to minimise fluid loss and prevent the entry of dirt into the

7.5b . . . and disconnect the clutch hydraulic pipe

7.9 Ensure that the engine unit is securely supported before removing the front suspension subframe

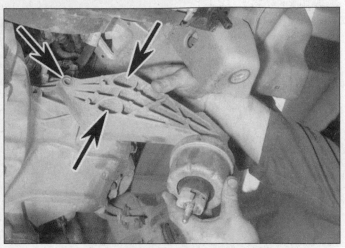

7.11 Undo the retaining bolts (locations arrowed) and remove the front left-hand mounting assembly

hydraulic system. **Note:** *Whilst the hose/pipe is disconnected, do not depress the clutch pedal.*

6 Remove the front exhaust downpipe, catalytic converter and centre silencer, as described in Chapter 4A or 4B.

7 On models fitted with F13, F17, F18 or F35 transmissions detach the gearchange mechanism linkage assembly from the top of the transmission unit as described in Section 4. On models quipped with F23 transmissions, prise the ends of the gearchange cables from the linkage on the top of the transmission, and unclip the outer cables from the retaining bracket as described in Section 4.

8 Referring to Chapter 8, remove both driveshafts. If the transmission has not been drained, be prepared for fluid loss.

9 Remove the front subframe assembly as described in Chapter 10, ensuring that the engine unit is securely supported by connecting a hoist to the engine assembly. If available, the type of support bar which locates in the engine compartment side channels is to be preferred **(see illustration)**.

10 Place a jack with a block of wood beneath the transmission, and raise the jack to take the weight of the transmission.

7.15 Free the transmission unit from the engine then lower it out of position and remove it from underneath the vehicle

11 Undo the retaining bolts and remove the front, left-hand engine/transmission mounting assembly from the front of the transmission housing **(see illustration)**.

12 Using the hoist or support bar, lower the transmission end of the assembly approximately 5 cm. Ensure that the various coolant hoses and wiring harnesses are not stretched.

13 On models where a pressed-steel sump is fitted to the engine, unbolt the flywheel cover plate and remove it from the base of the transmission unit.

14 Slacken and remove the upper and lower bolts securing the transmission housing to the engine. Note the correct fitted positions of each bolt, and the necessary brackets, as they are removed to use as a reference on refitting. Make a final check that all components have been disconnected, and are positioned clear of the transmission so that they will not hinder the removal procedure.

15 With the bolts removed, move the trolley jack and transmission, to free it from its locating dowels. Once the transmission is free, lower the jack and manoeuvre the unit out from under the car **(see illustration)**. Remove the locating dowels from the transmission or engine if they are loose, and keep them in a safe place.

Refitting

16 The transmission is refitted by a reversal of the removal procedure, bearing in mind the following points.

 a) Ensure the locating dowels are correctly positioned prior to installation.

 b) Tighten all nuts and bolts to the specified torque (where given).

 c) Renew the driveshaft oil seals (see Section 5) before refitting the driveshafts.

 d) Refit the front subframe assembly as described in Chapter 10.

 e) Fit a new sealing ring to the transmission clutch hydraulic pipe before clipping the hose/pipe end fitting into position. Ensure

the end fitting is securely retained by its clip then bleed the hydraulic system as described in Chapter 6.

 f) If the transmission was drained, refill the transmission with the specified type and amount of oil, as described in Section 2. If the oil was not drained, top-up the transmission oil and check the level as described in Section 9.

 g) On completion, adjust the gearchange mechanism/cables as described in Section 3.

8 Transmission overhaul – general information

1 Overhauling a manual transmission unit is a difficult and involved job for the DIY home mechanic. In addition to dismantling and reassembling many small parts, clearances must be precisely measured and, if necessary, changed by selecting shims and spacers. Internal transmission components are also often difficult to obtain, and in many instances, extremely expensive. Because of this, if the transmission develops a fault or becomes noisy, the best course of action is to have the unit overhauled by a specialist repairer, or to obtain an exchange reconditioned unit.

2 Nevertheless, it is not impossible for the more experienced mechanic to overhaul the transmission, provided the special tools are available, and the job is done in a deliberate step-by-step manner, so that nothing is overlooked.

3 The tools necessary for an overhaul include internal and external circlip pliers, bearing pullers, a slide hammer, a set of pin punches, a dial test indicator, and possibly a hydraulic press. In addition, a large, sturdy workbench and a vice will be required.

4 During dismantling of the transmission, make careful notes of how each component is fitted, to make reassembly easier and more accurate.

5 Before dismantling the transmission, it will help if you have some idea what area is malfunctioning. Certain problems can be closely related to specific areas in the transmission, which can make component examination and replacement easier. Refer to the *Fault finding* Section of this manual for more information.

9 Transmission oil level check

1 Position the vehicle over an inspection pit, on vehicle ramps, or jack it up, but make sure that it is level. The oil must be checked before the car is driven, or at least 5 minutes after the engine has been switched off. If the oil is checked immediately after driving the car, some of the oil will remain distributed around the transmission components, resulting in an inaccurate level reading.

2 Wipe clean the area around the level plug. The level plug is located behind the driveshaft inner joint on the left-hand side of the transmission (F13, F17 and F18 transmissions), or the rear of the differential housing (F23 and F35 transmissions) **(see illustrations)**. Unscrew the plug and clean it.

3 The oil level should reach the lower edge of the level plug hole. **Note:** *For some models fitted with the F23 transmission, the transmission is overfilled as part of a modification (see your local Vauxhall dealer). These transmissions have a yellow mark on the oil filler plug. On these vehicles, after filling up to the bottom of the level plug, fit and tighten the plug and add a further 0.5 litres of oil to the transmission.*

4 If topping-up is necessary, unscrew the reversing light switch (F13, F17 and F18 transmissions) or filler plug (F23 and F35 transmissions) and add the specified type of oil through the hole until oil begins to trickle out from the level plug hole **(see illustrations)**.

5 Allow the excess oil to drain out from the level plug hole then refit the plug, tightening it to the specified torque.

9.2a F13/17/18 transmission oil level hole

9.2b F23/35 transmission oil level checking plug (arrowed)

9.4a Top-up F13/17/18 transmissions through the reversing light switch aperture

9.4b F23/35 transmission oil filler plug (arrowed)

6 Refit the switch/filler plug, tightening it securely, and wash off any spilt oil.

7 If necessary (see paragraph 3) add the additional oil.

10 Speed sensor – removal and refitting

Note: *On some models the ABS system provides the engine ECU(s) with vehicle speed data, so a speed sensor is not fitted to the transmission.*

Removal

1 The sensor is located at the top of the transmission casing. Working in the engine compartment, reach down and disconnect the wiring plug from the top of the sensor.

2 Unscrew the retaining bolt and remove the sensor from the casing **(see illustration)**.

10.2 Unscrew the speed sensor retaining bolt (where fitted)

Refitting

3 With a new sealing ring fitted, insert the sensor into the transmission casing aperture. Ensure that the gear teeth engage correctly.

4 Tighten the retaining bolt to the specified torque and reconnect the wiring plug.

Notes

Chapter 7 Part B:
Automatic transmission

Contents

Degrees of difficulty

| Easy, suitable for novice with little experience | | Fairly easy, suitable for beginner with some experience | | Fairly difficult, suitable for competent DIY mechanic | | Difficult, suitable for experienced DIY mechanic | | Very difficult, suitable for expert DIY or professional | |

Specifications

Engine identification

Manufacturer's code	Engine type
X16XEL	1.6 litre DOHC petrol engine
X18XE	1.8 litre DOHC petrol engine
X18XE1	1.8 litre DOHC petrol engine
X20XEV	2.0 litre DOHC petrol engine
Z16XE	1.6 litre DOHC petrol engine
Z18XE	1.8 litre DOHC petrol engine
Z22SE	2.2 litre DOHC petrol engine

General

Type .... Electronically-controlled automatic, four forward speeds and a reverse, also three (economy, sport and winter) driving modes

Transmission type*:
X16XEL and Z16XE	AF13
X18XE, X18XE1 and Z18XE	AF17
X20XEV	AF20
Z22SE	AF22

Transmission code*:
X16XEL	YW
Z16XE	RH
X18XE, X18XE1 and Z18XE	RJ
X20XEV	JC
Z22SE	TD

Control unit code:
X16XEL	DP
Z16XE	CG
X18XE and X18XE1	DN
Z18XE	HQ
X20XEV	DM
Z22SE	AJ

*The transmission type/code is marked on the identification plate which is attached to the top of the transmission unit

Lubrication

Fluid type .... See *Lubricants and fluids*
Fluid capacity (after draining fluid) .... 3.0 to 3.5 litres (approximate)

Torque wrench settings

	Nm	lbf ft
Drain plug (main housing)	35	26
Drain screw	40	30
Engine-to-transmission unit bolts:		
M8 bolts	20	15
M10 bolts	40	30
M12 bolts	75	55
Engine/transmission left-hand mounting bolts	60	44
Fluid filler tube to transmission (AF13/17)	75	55
Fluid filler tube to selector lever position switch (AF20/22)	20	15
Fluid lines to transmission or fluid cooler	22	16
Fluid pump to transmission	25	18
Fluid temperature sensor:		
AF20	25	18
AF22	10	7
Input shaft speed sensor bolt	6	4
Output shaft speed sensor bolt	6	4
Selector lever:		
Actuation cable at transmission	20	15
Pivot crank nut	28	21
Position switch	25	18
Lever-to-vehicle body bolts	10	7
Torque converter-to-driveplate bolts*:		
AF13/17/20	55	41
AF22	45 + 30°	33 + 30°
Transmission selector shaft nuts:		
Main (starter/reversing light switch) nut	8	6
Selector lever nut	16	12

* Use new fasteners

1 General information

1 Most petrol-engined models covered in this manual were offered with the option of a four-speed, electronically-controlled automatic transmission, consisting of a torque converter, an epicyclic geartrain, and hydraulically-operated clutches and brakes. The unit is controlled by the electronic control unit (ECU) via four electrically-operated solenoid valves. The transmission unit has three driving modes; normal (economy), sport and winter modes.

2 The normal (economy) mode is the standard mode for driving in which the transmission shifts up at relatively low engine speeds to combine reasonable performance with economy. If the transmission unit is switched into sport mode, using the button on the selector lever, the transmission shifts up only at high engine speeds, giving improved acceleration and overtaking performance. When the transmission is in sport mode, the indicator light in the instrument panel is illuminated. If the transmission is switched into winter mode, using the button on the selector lever indicator panel, the transmission will select third gear as the vehicle pulls away from a standing start; this helps to maintain traction on very slippery surfaces.

3 The torque converter provides a fluid coupling between engine and transmission, which acts as an automatic clutch, and also provides a degree of torque multiplication when accelerating.

4 The epicyclic geartrain provides either of the four forward or one reverse gear ratios, according to which of its component parts are held stationary or allowed to turn. The components of the geartrain are held or released by brakes and clutches which are activated by the control unit. A fluid pump within the transmission provides the necessary hydraulic pressure to operate the brakes and clutches.

5 Driver control of the transmission is by a seven-position selector lever. The 'drive' D position, allows automatic changing throughout the range of all four gear ratios. An automatic kickdown facility shifts the transmission down a gear if the accelerator pedal is fully depressed. The transmission also has three 'hold' positions, 1 means only the first gear ratio can be selected, 2 allows both the first and second gear ratios position to be automatically selected and 3 allows automatic changing between the first three gear ratios. These 'hold' positions are useful for providing engine braking when traveling down steep gradients. Note, however, that the transmission should *never* be shifted down a position at high engine speeds.

6 Due to the complexity of the automatic transmission, any repair or overhaul work must be left to a Vauxhall dealer with the necessary special equipment for fault diagnosis and repair. The contents of the following Sections are therefore confined to supplying general information, and any service information and instructions that can be used by the owner.

2 Transmission fluid – draining and refilling

Draining

1 This operation is much quicker and more efficient if the vehicle is first taken on a journey of sufficient length to warm the engine/transmission up to normal operating temperature.

2 Park the vehicle on level ground, switch off the ignition, and apply the handbrake firmly. For improved access, jack up the front of the car and support it securely on axle stands.

3 Withdraw the dipstick, then position a container under the drain plug at the rear right-hand side of the transmission, below the driveshaft. Unscrew the plug and remove it along with its sealing washer **(see illustration)**.

2.3 Automatic transmission drain plug (1)

4 Allow the fluid to drain completely into the container. If the fluid is hot, take precautions against scalding.

5 When the fluid has finished draining, clean the drain plug threads and those of the transmission casing, fit a new sealing washer and refit the drain plug, tightening it to the specified torque wrench setting. Where applicable, lower the vehicle to the ground.

Refilling

6 Refilling the transmission is an awkward operation, adding the specified type and amount of fluid to the transmission a little at a time via the dipstick tube. Use a funnel with a fine mesh gauze, to avoid spillage, and to ensure that no foreign matter enters the transmission. Allow plenty of time for the fluid level to settle properly.

7 Start the engine, and allow it to idle for a few minutes whilst moving the selector lever through its various positions. Switch off the engine and add sufficient fluid to bring the level up to the lower mark on the dipstick. Take the car on a short run to fully distribute the new fluid around the transmission, then recheck the fluid level as described in Chapter 1A with the transmission at normal operating temperature.

3 Selector cable – adjustment

Note: *If the battery is disconnected with the selector lever in the P (park) position, the lever will be locked in position. To manually release the lever, carefully prise out the selector lever surround from the top of the centre console then, using a flat-bladed screwdriver, depress the detent lever on the left-hand side of the selector lever* (see illustration).

1 Operate the selector lever throughout its

3.0 To move the selector lever from the P position with the battery disconnected, manually release the detent lever

entire range and check that the transmission engages the correct gear indicated on the selector lever position indicator. If adjustment is necessary, continue as follows.

2 Position the selector lever in the P (park) position.

3 Working in the engine compartment, to gain access to the transmission end of the selector cable, remove the battery and mounting plate (see Chapter 5A).

4 Locate the selector cable mounting bracket on the top of the transmission unit and release the inner cable by carefully lifting the locking clip in the cable end fitting **(see illustration)**.

5 Ensure that the selector lever is locked in the P position and move the lever on the transmission selector mechanism fully forwards so that the transmission is also positioned in the P position **(see illustration)**. With both the selector lever and transmission correctly positioned, lock the cable adjuster in position by pushing the locking clip firmly down until it clicks in position.

6 Refit the battery then check the operation of the selector lever and, if necessary, repeat the adjustment procedure.

3.4 Release the selector cable inner cable by lifting the locking clip (inset)

4 Selector cable – removal and refitting

Removal

1 Remove the centre console as described in Chapter 11 then position the selector lever in the P (park) position.

2 Using a flat-bladed screwdriver, carefully lever the selector cable end fitting off from the balljoint from the base of the lever. Slide out the retaining clip and release the cable from the front of the lever mounting plate **(see illustration)**.

3 Working in the engine compartment, to gain access to the transmission end of the selector cable, remove the battery and mounting plate (see Chapter 5A).

4 Slide off the retaining clip (where fitted) then carefully unclip the selector cable end fitting from the transmission lever. Unclip the outer cable from its mounting bracket.

5 Work back along the cable, noting its

3.5 Move the transmission selector (1) fully forwards so that it is in the P position (2)

4.2 Remove the retaining clip (1) then lever the selector cable (2) off from the selector lever balljoint (3)

correct routing, and free it from all the relevant retaining clips. Free the cable grommet from the bulkhead and remove it from the vehicle.

6 Examine the cable, looking for worn end fittings or a damaged outer casing, and for signs of fraying of the inner cable. Check the cable's operation; the inner cable should move smoothly and easily through the outer casing. Remember that a cable that appears serviceable when tested off the car may well be much heavier in operation when curved into its working position. Renew the cable if it shows any signs of excessive wear or any damage.

Refitting

7 Manoeuvre the cable into position, ensuring it is correctly routed and pass it through the bulkhead. Ensure the cable passes through the selector lever mounting plate then locate the grommet securely in the bulkhead.

8 Pass the transmission end of the cable through its mounting bracket and clip the outer cable securely in position. Align the inner cable end fitting with the transmission lever then clip it on the lever and (where necessary) secure it in position with the retaining clip.

9 From inside the vehicle, secure the outer cable in position with the retaining clip, and clip the inner cable end fitting securely onto the selector lever balljoint.

10 Adjust the selector cable as described in Section 3.

11 Refit the centre console, as described in Chapter 11, and refit all components removed to gain access to the transmission end of the cable.

5 Selector lever assembly – removal and refitting

Note: *Renewal of the sport and winter mode switches is covered in Section 8.*

Removal

1 Remove the centre console, as described in Chapter 11, then position the selector lever in the P (park) position.

2 Disconnect the wiring connectors from the selector lever mode switches and free the bulbholder from the indicator panel.

3 Using a flat-bladed screwdriver, carefully lever the selector cable end fitting off from the balljoint from the base of the lever. Slide out the retaining clip and release the cable from the front of the lever mounting plate.

4 Slacken and remove the mounting bolts then manoeuvre the lever assembly out of position.

5 Inspect the selector lever mechanism for signs of wear or damage. To dismantle, slacken and remove the nut and washer then withdraw the pivot crank assembly. Unclip the

indicator panel then separate the lever assembly and mounting plate. No further dismantling is possible.

Refitting

6 Where necessary, reassemble the lever and mounting plate and insert the pivot crank. Ensure the crank is correctly engaged with the selector lever then refit the washer and tighten its retaining nut to the specified torque. Clip the indicator panel onto the mounting plate then check the operation of the lever before refitting it to the car.

7 Manoeuvre the lever assembly into position, engage it with the selector cable. Refit the retaining bolts and tighten them to the specified torque setting.

8 Secure the outer cable in position with the retaining clip and securely clip the cable end fitting onto the selector lever crank balljoint.

9 Ensuring the wiring is correctly routed, refit the bulbholder to the indicator panel and reconnect the switch wiring connectors.

10 Adjust the selector cable, as described in Section 3, then refit the centre console as described in Chapter 11.

6 Oil seals – renewal

Driveshaft

1 Refer to Chapter 7A, Section 5.

Torque converter

2 Remove the transmission as described in Section 9.

3 Carefully slide the torque converter off of the transmission shaft whilst being prepared for fluid spillage.

4 Note the correct fitted position of the seal in the oil pump housing then carefully lever the seal out of position taking care not to mark the housing or input shaft.

5 Remove all traces of dirt from the area around the oil seal aperture then press the new seal into position, ensuring its sealing lip is facing inwards.

6 Lubricate the seal with clean transmission fluid then carefully ease the torque converter into position.

7 Refit the transmission (see Section 9).

7 Fluid cooler – general information

The transmission fluid cooler is an integral part of the radiator assembly. Refer to Chapter 3 for removal and refitting details, if the cooler is damaged the complete radiator assembly must be renewed.

8 Transmission control system electrical components – removal and refitting

Starter inhibitor/ reversing light switch

1 The switch is a dual-function switch, performing the reversing light and starter inhibitor switch functions. The switch operates the reversing lights when reverse gear is selected and prevents the engine being started when the transmission is in gear. If at any time the reversing light operation becomes faulty, or it is noted that the engine can be started with the selector lever in any position other than P (park) or N (neutral), then it is likely that the switch is faulty. If adjustment fails to correct the fault then the complete switch must be renewed as a unit.

Removal

2 Position the selector lever in the N (neutral) position.

3 To gain access to the switch, remove the battery and mounting plate as described in Chapter 5A.

4 Slide off the retaining clip (where fitted) then carefully unclip the selector cable end fitting from the transmission lever **(see illustration 3.4)**. Unscrew the retaining nut and remove the lever from the transmission selector shaft.

5 Trace the wiring back from the switch and disconnect it at the wiring connector.

6 On 2.0 and 2.2 litre models, withdraw the transmission fluid dipstick then undo the retaining nut and ease the dipstick out from the transmission. Remove the dipstick seal and discard it; a new one should be used on refitting.

7 Bend back the lockwasher (where fitted) then slacken and remove the main nut and washer(s) from the transmission selector shaft.

8 Slacken and remove the switch and wiring retaining plate bolts, and manoeuvre the switch assembly upwards and away from the transmission unit.

Refitting

9 Prior to refitting, first make sure that the transmission selector shaft is still in the N (neutral) position. If there is any doubt, engage the selector lever with the transmission shaft and move the lever fully forwards (to the P position) then move it two notches backwards.

10 Locate the switch on the transmission shaft then refit the wiring retaining plate. Refit the retaining bolts, tightening them by hand only at this stage.

11 Refit the washer(s) and main nut to the selector shaft. Tighten the nut to the specified torque setting and secure it in position by bending up the locking washer against one of its flats.

12 Adjust the switch as described in paragraph 18.

13 Once the switch is correctly adjusted,

8.18 Starter inhibitor/reversing light switch adjustment details

1 Switch assembly marking   3 Selector shaft
2 Retaining bolt   4 Retaining bolt

8.22 Insert a welding rod (1) in through the base of the selector lever and push the sport mode switch out of position. The switch wires (2) can then be unsoldered

reconnect the wiring connector, ensuring that the wiring is correctly routed.

14 On 2.0 and 2.2 litre models, fit a new seal to the transmission aperture then ease the dipstick tube into position. Securely tighten the dipstick retaining nut then refit the dipstick.

15 Refit the selector lever to the shaft and tighten its retaining nut to the specified torque. Clip the selector cable end fitting securely onto the lever balljoint.

16 Refit the battery and check the operation of the switch. If necessary, adjust the selector cable as described in Section 3.

Adjustment

Note: *Before adjusting the switch first ensure the selector cable is correctly adjusted (see Section 3).*

17 Carry out the operations described in paragraphs 2 to 4.

18 With the transmission in neutral, the flats on the selector shaft should be parallel to the marking on the switch assembly **(see illustration)**. If adjustment is necessary, slacken the switch retaining bolts and rotate the switch assembly as necessary before retightening the bolts to the specified torque setting.

19 Refit the selector lever to the shaft and tighten its retaining nut to the specified torque. Refit the selector cable end fitting securely onto the lever and (where necessary) secure it in position with the retaining clip.

20 Refit the battery and check the operation of the switch. If adjustment of the switch has not been successful, then the switch must be faulty and should be renewed.

Sport mode switch

Note: *A soldering iron and solder will be required to renew the switch.*

Removal

21 Remove the selector lever assembly as described in Section 5.

22 Push the switch out of the top of the selector lever by inserting a length of welding rod up through the selector lever bore **(see illustration)**.

23 Make identification marks between the switch and wires then carefully unsolder the wires from the switch terminals and remove the switch. The wiring can then be withdrawn from the base of the lever.

Refitting

24 Feed the wiring up through the selector lever bore until it appears at the top. Solder the wires to the terminals of the switch, using the marks made prior to removal to ensure they are correctly connected.

25 Push the switch securely into position then refit the selector lever as described in Section 5.

Winter mode switch

Removal

26 Unclip the storage compartment from the centre console to gain access to the selector lever trim cover screws. Slacken and remove the two screws from the rear of the cover and lift the cover off of the lever.

27 Release the retaining clips and free the selector lever position indicator panel from the lever mounting plate.

28 Trace the wiring back from the switch and disconnect it at the wiring connector. Unclip the switch from the indicator panel and remove it from the vehicle.

Refitting

29 Refitting is the reverse of removal, ensuring the wiring is correctly routed.

Kickdown switch

30 The kickdown switch is an integral part of the accelerator cable and cannot be renewed separately. Refer to Chapter 4A for details of accelerator cable removal and refitting. **Note:** *On models with electronic throttle body and pedal sensor, the kickdown is controlled by the ECU.*

Electronic control unit (ECU)

Removal

31 The ECU is located in the front passenger footwell. Prior to removal, disconnect the battery negative terminal.

32 Prise out the retaining clips and remove the undercover from the passenger side of the facia. Remove the glovebox from the facia (see Chapter 11) to gain access to the ECU.

33 Release the retaining clip and disconnect the wiring connector from the ECU. Release the mounting bracket from the body and remove the ECU from the vehicle.

Refitting

34 Refitting is the reverse of removal, ensuring that the wiring is securely reconnected.

Shaft speed sensors

Removal

35 On 2.0 and 2.2 litre models, the speed sensors are fitted to the top of the transmission unit. The input shaft speed sensor is the front of the two sensors and is nearest to the left-hand end of the transmission. The output shaft sensor is the rear of the two **(see illustration)**. On 1.6 and 1.8 litre models, the

8.35 Transmission input shaft sensor (1) and output shaft speed sensor (2) locations (2.0 litre)

8.45 Undo the retaining bolts (arrowed) and remove the cover plate . . .

sensors are fitted to the top-rear of the transmission unit. The output shaft speed sensor is the uppermost of the two sensors.

36 On 1.6 and 1.8 litre models, firmly apply the handbrake, jack up the front of the vehicle and support it securely on axle stands. Remove the left front roadwheel and lower wheelarch liner (see Chapter 11, Section 26). On 2.0 and 2.2 litre models, to gain access to the sensors, remove the battery and mounting plate as described in Chapter 5A. Access can be further improved by unclipping the coolant expansion tank from its mountings and positioning it clear.

37 Disconnect the wiring connector and wipe clean the area around the relevant sensor.

38 Undo the retaining bolt and remove the sensor from the transmission. Remove the sealing ring from the sensor and discard it, a new one should be used on refitting.

Refitting

39 Fit the new sealing ring to the sensor groove and lubricate it with a smear of transmission fluid.

40 Ease the sensor into position then refit the retaining bolt and tighten it to the specified torque setting. Reconnect the wiring connector.

41 On 2.0 and 2.2 litre models, refit the battery and clip the expansion tank (where necessary) back into position. On 1.6 and 1.8 litre models, refit the wheelarch liner (where removed) and the roadwheel, then lower the vehicle to the ground.

8.46 . . . to gain access to the fluid temperature sensor (arrowed)

Fluid temperature sensor

Removal

Note: *On 1.6 and 1.8 litre models, the temperature sensor is not available separately from the transmission wiring harness. Also, in order to remove the sensor, it is necessary to remove the transmission side cover and expose the various shift valves and solenoids. This is a difficult task requiring the highest standards of cleanliness. For these reasons, the task of renewing the temperature sensor should be entrusted to a Vauxhall dealer or specialist. The procedure described below is applicable only to the AF20/22 transmission unit as fitted to 2.0 and 2.2 litre models.*

42 The fluid temperature sensor is screwed into the base of the transmission unit, at the front. Before removing the sensor, disconnect the battery negative terminal.

43 Firmly apply the handbrake then jack up the front of the vehicle and support it on axle stands.

44 Trace the wiring back from the sensor, noting its correct routing. Disconnect the wiring connector and free the wiring from its retaining clips.

45 Undo the retaining bolts and remove the cover plate from the sensor **(see illustration)**.

46 Wipe clean the area around the sensor and have a suitable plug ready to minimise fluid loss as the sensor is removed **(see illustration)**.

47 Unscrew the sensor and remove it from the transmission unit along with its sealing washer. Quickly plug the transmission aperture and wipe up any spilt fluid.

Refitting

48 Fit a new sealing washer to the sensor then remove the plug and quickly screw the sensor into the transmission unit. Tighten the sensor to the specified torque and wipe up any spilt fluid. Refit the cover plate and securely tighten its retaining bolts.

49 Ensure the wiring is correctly routed and retained by all the necessary clips then securely reconnect the wiring connector.

50 Lower the vehicle to the floor and reconnect the battery. Check the transmission fluid level as described in Chapter 1A.

---

9 Automatic transmission – removal and refitting

Note: *New torque converter-to-driveplate bolts and fluid cooler union sealing rings will be required on refitting.*

Removal

1 Chock the rear wheels, apply the handbrake, and place the selector lever in the N (neutral) position. Jack up the front of the vehicle, and securely support it on axle stands. Remove both front roadwheels then remove the retaining screws and fasteners

and (where necessary) remove the undercover from beneath the engine/transmission unit.

2 Drain the transmission fluid as described in Section 2, then refit the drain plug and tighten it to the specified torque.

3 Remove the battery and mounting plate, and the starter motor as described in Chapter 5A. To further improve access, unclip the coolant expansion tank from its mountings.

4 Depending on model, the DIS ignition module may need to be removed, as described in Chapter 5B.

5 Slide off the retaining clip (where fitted) then carefully unclip the selector cable end fitting from the transmission lever. Unclip the outer cable from its mounting bracket and position the cable clear of the transmission unit.

6 Trace the wiring back from the transmission switches and sensors and disconnect the various connectors by lifting their retaining clips. Release the main wiring harness from any clips or ties securing it to the transmission unit.

7 Disconnect the breather hose (where fitted) from the top of the transmission unit.

8 Make identification marks between the oil cooler hoses and their unions on the front of the transmission housing. Using a flat-bladed screwdriver, prise out the retaining clips from each hose end fitting and detach both hoses from the transmission. There are two types of fitting depending on model **(see illustrations)**. Clip the retaining clips back into position in the end fittings and discard the sealing rings; new sealing rings must be used on refitting. Plug/cover both the union and hose ends to prevent the entry of dirt.

9 Remove the front suspension subframe assembly as described in Chapter 10, ensuring that the engine unit is securely supported.

10 Referring to Chapter 8, free the driveshaft inner constant velocity joints from the transmission unit and position them clear. Note that it is not necessary to remove the driveshafts, then can be left attached to the hub assemblies. **Note:** *Do not allow the shafts to hang down under their own weight as this could damage the constant velocity joints/ gaiters.*

11 Undo the retaining bolts and remove the left-hand engine/transmission mounting assembly from the front of the transmission housing.

12 Remove the rubber cover(s) from the cylinder block/sump flange to gain access to the torque converter retaining bolts. Slacken and remove the visible bolt(s) then, using a socket and extension bar to rotate the crankshaft pulley, undo the remaining bolts securing the torque converter to the driveplate as they become accessible (on some there are three securing bolts and on others there are six). Discard the bolts, new ones must be used on refitting.

13 To ensure that the torque converter does not fall out as the transmission is removed, slide the converter along the shaft and fully into the transmission housing.

14 Place a jack with a block of wood beneath the transmission, and raise the jack to take the weight of the transmission.

15 With the jack positioned beneath the transmission taking the weight, slacken and remove the upper and lower bolts securing the transmission housing to the engine. Note the correct fitted positions of each bolt, and the necessary brackets, as they are removed, to use as a reference on refitting. Make a final check that all components have been disconnected, and are positioned clear of the transmission so that they will not hinder the removal procedure.

16 With all the bolts removed, move the trolley jack and transmission to the right, to free it from its locating dowels. Once the transmission is free, lower the jack and manoeuvre the unit out from under the car, taking care to ensure that the torque converter does not fall off. Remove the locating dowels from the transmission or engine if they are loose, and keep them in a safe place.

Refitting

17 The transmission is refitted by a reversal of the removal procedure, bearing in mind the following points.

a) Prior to refitting, remove all traces of old locking compound from the torque converter threads by running a tap of the correct thread diameter and pitch down the holes. In the absence of a suitable tap, use one of the old bolts with slots cut in its threads.

b) Prior to refitting, ensure the engine/transmission locating dowels are correctly positioned and apply a smear of molybdenum disulphide grease to the torque converter locating pin and its centering bush in the crankshaft end.

c) Once the transmission and engine are correctly joined, refit the securing bolts, tightening them to the specified torque setting.

d) Fit the new torque converter to driveplate bolts and tighten them lightly only to start then go around and tighten them to the specified torque setting in a diagonal sequence.

e) Tighten all nuts and bolts to the specified torque (where given).

f) Renew the driveshaft oil seals (see Chapter 7A) and refit the driveshafts to the transmission as described in Chapter 8.

g) Fit new sealing rings to the fluid cooler hose unions and ensure both unions are securely retained by their clips.

h) On completion, refill the transmission with the specified type and quantity of fluid as described in Section 2 and adjust the selector cable as described in Section 3.

10 Automatic transmission overhaul – general information
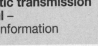

1 In the event of a fault occurring with the transmission, it is first necessary to determine whether it is of a mechanical or hydraulic nature, and to do this, special test equipment is required. It is therefore essential to have the work carried out by a Vauxhall dealer if a transmission fault is suspected.

2 Do not remove the transmission from the car for possible repair before professional fault diagnosis has been carried out, since most tests require the transmission to be in the vehicle.

9.8a Transmission fluid cooler hose connections – Type 1

| 1 Hose end fitting | 3 Transmission union |
| 2 Retaining clip | |

9.8b Transmission fluid cooler hose connections – Type 2

| 1 Hose end fitting | 3 Pipe end fitting |
| 2 Retaining clip | 4 Transmission unions |

Notes

Chapter 8
Driveshafts

Contents

Degrees of difficulty

Easy, suitable for novice with little experience	**Fairly easy,** suitable for beginner with some experience	**Fairly difficult,** suitable for competent DIY mechanic	**Difficult,** suitable for experienced DIY mechanic	**Very difficult,** suitable for expert DIY or professional

Specifications

General

Driveshaft type . . . . Solid steel shafts with inner and outer constant velocity (CV) joints. Right-hand driveshaft is fitted with a vibration damper on some models. An intermediate shaft is fitted to the right-hand side on models with the Y22DTR engine

Lubricant:

   Type/specification . . . . Special grease (Vauxhall part number 19 41 521 (90 094 176) supplied in sachets with gaiter kits – joints are otherwise prepacked with grease and sealed

   Quantity (per joint) . . . . 90 g

Torque wrench settings

	Nm	lbf ft
Front driveshaft/hub retaining nut:		
Stage 1	130	96
Stage 2	Loosen completely	
Stage 3	20	15
Stage 4	Angle-tighten a further 90°	
Stage 5	If necessary loosen to align split pin hole	
Front suspension lower arm balljoint to hub carrier	100	74
Roadwheel	110	81
Steering track rod end to steering arm on hub carrier	60	44
Vibration damper	10	7

2.2 Use a cold chisel to tap off the driveshaft nut cap

2.3 Removing the split pin from the castellated driveshaft nut

1 General information

Drive is transmitted from the differential to the front wheels by means of two, unequal-length driveshafts.

Each driveshaft is fitted with an inner and outer constant velocity (CV) joint. Each outer joint is splined to engage with the wheel hub, and is retained by a large nut. The inner joint is also splined to engage with the differential sunwheel and is held in place by an internal circlip.

A vibration damper is bolted to the right-hand driveshaft on some models.

The right-hand driveshaft on models fitted with the Y22DTR engine has an intermediate shaft attached to the rear of the cylinder block.

2 Driveshaft – removal and refitting

Removal

Note: *A new front hub nut and inner joint circlip will be required on refitting. The driveshaft outer joint splines may be a tight fit in the hub and it is possible that a puller/extractor will be required to draw the hub assembly off the driveshaft during removal.*

1 Apply the handbrake, then jack up the front of the vehicle and support it on axle stands (see *Jacking and vehicle support*). Remove the roadwheel. It is an advantage to only jack up one side of the vehicle as this will prevent loss of oil from the transmission when the driveshaft is withdrawn.

2 Using a cold chisel or screwdriver, tap off the hub nut cap **(see illustration)**.

3 Extract the split pin from the castellated hub nut on the end of the driveshaft **(see illustration)**.

4 The hub nut must now be loosened. The nut is extremely tight, and an extension bar will be required to loosen it. To prevent the driveshaft from turning, insert two roadwheel bolts, and insert a metal bar between them to counterhold the hub. Remove the hub nut and washer from the driveshaft **(see illustrations)**.

5 Unscrew the nut securing the track rod end to the steering arm on the hub carrier, then use a balljoint separator tool to remove the track rod end.

6 Unscrew and remove the clamp bolt securing the front lower suspension arm to the hub carrier. Note that the bolt head faces the rear of the vehicle **(see illustration)**.

7 Using a chisel or screwdriver as a wedge, expand the balljoint clamp at the bottom of the hub carrier **(see illustration)**.

8 Using a lever, push down on the suspension lower arm to free the balljoint from the hub carrier, then move the hub carrier to one side and release the arm, taking care not to damage the balljoint rubber boot.

9 The hub must now be freed from the end of the driveshaft. It should be possible to pull the hub off the driveshaft, but if the end of the driveshaft is tight in the hub, temporarily refit the hub nut to protect the driveshaft threads, then tap the end of the driveshaft with a soft-faced hammer while pulling outwards on the hub carrier **(see illustration)**. Alternatively, use a suitable puller to press the driveshaft through the hub.

10 With the driveshaft detached from the hub carrier, tie the suspension strut to one side and support the driveshaft on an axle stand.

11 On models without an intermediate shaft, use a lever to release the inner end of the driveshaft from the differential. Lever between the driveshaft and differential housing to release the driveshaft snap-ring. Where fitted, unbolt the heat shield from the inner end of the driveshaft **(see illustrations)**. On models with an intermediate shaft use a soft-metal drift to drive the inner end of the driveshaft from the intermediate shaft.

2.4a Removing the driveshaft nut . . .

2.4b . . . and washer

2.6 Unscrewing the clamp bolt securing the front lower suspension arm to the hub carrier

2.7 Using a cold chisel to expand the balljoint clamp at the bottom of the hub carrier

2.9 Use a soft-faced hammer to drive the driveshaft from the hub splines

2.11a Carefully lever between the driveshaft and differential housing to release the driveshaft

2.11b Heat shield protecting the inner end of the driveshaft

2.13 Vibration damper fitted to the right-hand driveshaft

12 Withdraw the driveshaft, ensuring that the constant velocity joints are not placed under excessive strain, and remove the driveshaft from beneath the vehicle. Whilst the driveshaft is removed from models without an intermediate shaft, plug or tape over the differential aperture to prevent dirt entry.

Caution: Do not allow the vehicle to rest on its wheels with one or both driveshafts removed, as damage to the wheel bearings(s) may result. If the vehicle must be moved on its wheels, clamp the wheel bearings using spacers and a long threaded rod to take the place of the driveshaft.

13 Most models have a vibration damper fitted to the right-hand driveshaft. If the damper is transferred to a new driveshaft, measure its fitted position before removing and locate it in the same position on the new driveshaft **(see illustration)**.

Refitting

Models without an intermediate shaft

14 Before refitting the driveshaft, examine the oil seal in the transmission housing and renew it if necessary as described in Chapter 7A or 7B.

15 Remove the circlip from the end of the driveshaft inner joint splines and discard it. Fit a new circlip, making sure it is correctly located in the groove.

16 Thoroughly clean the driveshaft splines, and the apertures in the transmission and hub assembly. Apply a thin film of grease to the oil

seal lips, and to the driveshaft splines and shoulders. Check that all gaiter clips are securely fastened.

17 Offer up the driveshaft, and engage the inner joint splines with those of the differential sun gear, taking care not to damage the oil seal. Push the joint fully into position, then check that the circlip is correctly located and securely holds the joint in position. If necessary, use a soft-faced mallet or drift to drive the driveshaft inner joint fully into position.

Models with an intermediate shaft

18 Using the soft-metal drift, drive the driveshaft inner joint onto the intermediate shaft.

All models

19 Align the outer constant velocity joint splines with those of the hub, and slide the joint back into position in the hub.

20 Using a lever, push down on the lower suspension arm, then relocate the balljoint and release the arm. Make sure that the balljoint stub is fully entered in the hub carrier.

21 Insert the clamp bolt with its head facing the rear of the vehicle, and tighten it to the specified torque.

22 Refit the track rod end to the steering arm on the hub carrier and tighten the nut to the specified torque.

23 Refit the washer to the end of the driveshaft, then screw on a new nut and tighten moderately at this stage.

24 Refit the roadwheel and lower the vehicle to the ground.

25 Tighten the hub nut in the stages given in the Specifications, and fit a new split pin. Bend the outer leg of the split pin over the end of the driveshaft, then cut the inner leg as necessary and bend it inwards **(see illustrations)**.

26 Tap the hub nut cap into position then refit the wheel trim.

27 Check and if necessary top-up the oil level in the transmission.

3 Intermediate shaft and bearing – removal and refitting

Note: *The intermediate shaft is fitted to models with the Y22DTR engine only.*

Removal

1 Apply the handbrake, then jack up the front of the vehicle and support it on axle stands (see *Jacking and vehicle support*). As a precaution against oil being spilt from the transmission, only jack up and support the right-hand side of the vehicle. Remove the right-hand front roadwheel.

2 Unscrew and remove the clamp bolt securing the front lower suspension arm to the hub carrier. Note that the bolt head faces the rear of the vehicle.

3 Using a chisel or screwdriver as a wedge, expand the balljoint clamp at the bottom of the hub carrier.

4 Using a lever, push down on the suspension lower arm to free the balljoint from the hub carrier, then move the hub carrier to one side and release the arm taking care not to damage the balljoint rubber boot.

5 Using a soft-metal drift, drive the inner joint of the driveshaft from the end of the intermediate shaft – the joint is retained by a circlip located in a groove in the shaft. Support the driveshaft to one side.

6 Unscrew the bolts securing the intermediate shaft bearing bracket to the rear of the cylinder block. Also unscrew the bolt securing the wiring loom support to the bracket.

7 Pull the intermediate shaft, together with

2.25a Insert the new split pin . . .

2.25b . . . and bend the legs to secure

4.3 Cut free the gaiter securing bands with a small hacksaw

4.4 Driveshaft joint retaining circlip (B) and circlip groove (A)

4.5 Tapping the joint from the driveshaft

the bracket, from the transmission. Be prepared for some loss of oil by placing a suitable container beneath the transmission.

8 Unbolt the bearing from the bracket.

9 If it is required to remove the bearing from the intermediate shaft, first grip the shaft in a soft-jawed vice, then remove the driveshaft retaining circlip and the bearing retaining circlip. It is now necessary to press the intermediate shaft out of the bearing. This is best achieved using a hydraulic press; support the bearing and press the shaft downwards.

Refitting

10 If a new bearing is being fitted, locate it on the intermediate shaft, then fully press on the bearing using the hydraulic press. Fit new circlips in the grooves. Refit the bearing to the bracket and tighten the bolts.

11 Before refitting the intermediate shaft, examine the oil seal in the transmission housing and renew it if necessary as described in Chapter 7A.

12 Insert the intermediate shaft into the transmission, engaging the splines with the differential sun gear, taking care not to damage the oil seal.

13 Refit the intermediate shaft bearing bracket to the cylinder block and tighten the bolts. Also refit the wiring loom support and tighten the bolt.

14 Locate the driveshaft inner joint on the intermediate shaft splines, then use a soft-metal drift to drive the joint onto the intermediate shaft until it is retained by the circlip.

5.2 Driveshaft inner securing band

15 Lever down on the suspension lower arm, and locate the balljoint in the hub carrier. Remove the wedge from the balljoint clamp.

16 Insert the clamp bolt with its head facing the rear of the vehicle, and tighten it to the specified torque.

17 Refit the roadwheel and lower the vehicle to the ground.

18 Check and if necessary top-up the transmission oil level.

4 Driveshaft joint – checking and renewal

Checking

1 Road test the vehicle, and listen for a metallic clicking noise from the front as the vehicle is driven slowly in a circle on full-lock. If evident, this indicates wear in the outer constant velocity joint which must be renewed.

2 To check for wear on the inner joint, apply the handbrake then jack up the front of the vehicle and support it on axle stands (see *Jacking and vehicle support*). Attempt to move the inner end of the driveshaft up-and-down, then hold the joint with one hand and attempt to rotate the driveshaft with the other. If excessive wear is evident, the joint must be renewed.

Renewal

3 With the driveshaft removed, as described in Section 2, release the metal securing bands

5.4a Locate the new inner securing band on the driveshaft . . .

and slide back the rubber gaiter from the worn joint. Where necessary, cut the bands free taking care not to damage the gaiter seating **(see illustration)**.

4 Using a screwdriver or circlip pliers, expand the circlip that secures the joint to the driveshaft **(see illustration)**.

5 Using a soft-faced mallet, tap the joint from the driveshaft **(see illustration)**.

6 Ensure that a new circlip is fitted to the new joint, then tap the new joint onto the driveshaft until the circlip engages in its groove.

7 Pack the joint with the specified type of grease.

8 Refit the rubber gaiter to the new joint, referring to Section 5, if necessary.

9 Refit the driveshaft to the vehicle, as described in Section 2.

5 Driveshaft joint gaiters – renewal

Renewal

1 With the driveshaft removed as described in Section 2, remove the relevant joint as described in Section 4. Note that if both gaiters on a driveshaft are to be renewed it is only necessary to remove one joint, however on the right-hand driveshaft it will also be necessary to remove the vibration damper after noting its location (where fitted).

2 Release the remaining securing band and slide the gaiter from the driveshaft. If the original Vauxhall band is fitted, use pincers to cut it free **(see illustration)**.

3 Clean the old grease from the joint, then repack the joint with the specified type of fresh grease. If excessively worn or damaged, the driveshaft joint should be renewed as described in Section 4.

4 Slide the new gaiter and new inner securing band onto the driveshaft so that the smaller diameter opening is located in the groove in the driveshaft **(see illustrations)**. Note: *Depending on model, there may be one or two grooves in the driveshaft; make sure that the gaiter is correctly located. On models with one groove, the inner end of the inner gaiter must be 135 mm from the end of the driveshaft. On*

5.4b ... followed by the new gaiter

5.5 Pack the joint with the specified type of grease

5.6 Fitting the joint to the splines on the driveshaft

models with two grooves, the inner end of the inner gaiter must be 123 mm from the end of the driveshaft.

5 Pack the joint with the specified type of grease **(see illustration)**.

6 Refit the joint, using a new inner securing circlip **(see illustration)**. Tap the joint onto the driveshaft until the circlip engages in its groove.

7 Slide the gaiter over the joint, then release any excess air by carefully lifting the gaiter from the joint with a screwdriver.

8 Secure the gaiter using new securing bands. To fit a loop-type band, locate it over the gaiter then squeeze the raised loop using pincers – note that Vauxhall technicians use a special tool to do this, however careful use of pincers or a similar tool will be sufficient **(see illustrations)**. To fit a lug-and-slot type band, wrap it around the gaiter and while pulling on

5.8a Fit the outer securing band . . .

5.8b ... and tighten using a pair of pincers

the band as tight as possible, engage the lug on the end of the band with one of the slots. Use a screwdriver if necessary to push the band as tight as possible before engaging the lug and slot. Finally tighten the band by

compressing the raised square portion of the band with pliers, taking care not to cut the gaiter.

9 Refit the driveshaft to the vehicle, as described in Section 2.

Chapter 9
Braking system

Contents

Degrees of difficulty

Easy, suitable for novice with little experience		Fairly easy, suitable for beginner with some experience		Fairly difficult, suitable for competent DIY mechanic		Difficult, suitable for experienced DIY mechanic		Very difficult, suitable for expert DIY or professional	

Specifications

Engine identification

Manufacturer's code	Engine type
X16SZR	1.6 litre SOHC petrol engine
X16XEL	1.6 litre DOHC petrol engine
X18XE	1.8 litre DOHC petrol engine
X18XE1	1.8 litre DOHC petrol engine
X20DTH	2.0 litre high-pressure turbo diesel engine
X20DTL	2.0 litre low-pressure turbo diesel engine
X20XEV	2.0 litre DOHC petrol engine
Y20DTH	2.0 litre high-pressure turbo diesel engine
Y22DTR	2.2 litre high-pressure turbo diesel engine
Z16XE	1.6 litre DOHC petrol engine
Z18XE	1.8 litre DOHC petrol engine
Z22SE	2.2 litre DOHC petrol engine

System type

All models .... Front discs and rear drums (X16SZR and X20DTL) or rear discs (except X16SZR and X20DTL) with vacuum servo assistance, 4-channel ABS (standard), operated via hydraulic modulator, dual hydraulic circuit split diagonally. Cable-operated handbrake on rear wheels. Traction control on certain models (X20XEV)

Front discs

Type	Ventilated
Diameter	288 mm
Minimum disc thickness after machining*	23 mm
Minimum pad friction material thickness (including backing plate)	7.5 mm
Maximum disc run-out	0.1 mm

* When this dimension is reached, only one further new set of brake pads is permissible, then renew the discs.

Rear discs

Type	Solid
Diameter	286 mm
Minimum disc thickness after machining*	9.0 mm
Minimum pad friction material thickness (including backing plate)	6.7 mm
Maximum disc run-out	0.1 mm
Minimum handbrake shoe friction material thickness (lining only)	1.0 mm

* When this dimension is reached, only one further new set of disc pads is permissible, then renew the discs.

Rear drums

Internal diameter	230 mm
Maximum internal diameter	231 mm
Minimum shoe friction material thickness	1.0 mm lining thickness or 0.5 mm above rivet heads

ABS system type

All models except X20XEV with traction control	ABS 415 single-diaphragm servo
X20XEV with traction control	ABS 5/TC and ABS 5.3/TC tandem-diaphragm servo

Torque wrench settings

	Nm	lbf ft
ABS control unit to hydraulic modulator body:		
Type ABS 415:		
Stage 1	6	4
Stage 2	7	5
Type ABS 5/TC and ABS 5.3/TC	3	2
ABS wheel speed sensor	8	6
Brake disc securing screw	4	3
Brake fluid line unions	16	12
Caliper bleed screw	6	4
Caliper hose banjo bolt	40	30
Front caliper mounting bracket to hub carrier	95	70
Front caliper to mounting bracket (apply thread lock fluid to threads) .	30	22
Handbrake lever mounting	10	7
Handbrake lever warning switch	3	2
Hydraulic modulator (ABS)	8	6
Master cylinder to servo	22	16
Pedal bracket and support	20	15
Rear brake drum securing screw	4	3
Rear caliper mounting	80	59
Rear wheel cylinder	9	7
Roadwheel bolts	110	81
Wheel cylinder bleed screw	6	4
Vacuum hose to vacuum pump (diesel engine models)	18	13
Vacuum hose to inlet manifold	18	13
Vacuum servo mounting nuts/bolts	20	15
Vacuum servo pushrod locknut	18	13

1 General information

The braking system is of servo-assisted, dual-circuit hydraulic type split diagonally. The arrangement of the hydraulic system is such that each circuit operates one front and one rear brake from a tandem master cylinder. Under normal circumstances, both circuits operate in unison. However, in the event of hydraulic failure in one circuit, full braking force will still be available at two wheels.

All models are fitted with front disc brakes, with rear drum brakes on models with the X16SZR petrol and X20DTL diesel engine, and rear disc brakes on all other models. The disc brakes are actuated by single-piston sliding type calipers, which ensure that equal pressure is applied to each disc pad. The rear drum brakes incorporate leading and trailing shoes, which are actuated by twin-piston wheel cylinders. A self-adjust mechanism is incorporated, to automatically compensate for brake shoe wear. As the brake shoe linings wear, the footbrake operation automatically operates the adjuster mechanism, which effectively lengthens the shoe strut and repositions the brake shoes, to reduce the lining-to-drum clearance.

All models are fitted with a 4-channel ABS (Anti-lock Braking System) incorporating a wheel speed sensor at each wheel. When the ignition is switched on, an ABS symbol illuminates in the instrument panel for a short time while the system performs a self-test. The system comprises an electronic control unit, roadwheel sensors, hydraulic modulator, and the necessary valves and relays. The purpose of the system is to stop wheels locking during heavy brake applications. This is achieved by automatic release of the brake on the locked wheel, followed by re-application of the brake. This procedure is carried out several times a second by the hydraulic modulator. The modulator is controlled by the electronic control unit, which itself receives signals from the wheel sensors, which monitor the locked or unlocked state of the wheels. The ABS unit is fitted between the brake master cylinder and the brakes.

If the ABS symbol in the instrument panel stays lit, or if it comes on whilst driving, there is a fault in the system and the vehicle must be taken to a Vauxhall/Opel dealer for assessment using specialist diagnostic equipment.

The handbrake is cable-operated on the rear brakes by a lever mounted between the front seats.

On diesel engine models, since there is no throttling of the inlet manifold, the manifold is not a suitable source of vacuum to operate the vacuum servo unit. The servo unit is therefore connected to a separate vacuum pump bolted to the left-hand end of the cylinder head and driven by the camshaft.

⚠️ **Warning: When servicing any part of the system, work carefully and methodically; also observe scrupulous cleanliness when overhauling any part of the hydraulic system. Always renew components (in axle sets, where applicable) if in doubt about their condition, and use only genuine Vauxhall/Opel replacement parts, or at least those of known good quality. Note the warnings given in 'Safety first!' and at relevant points in this Chapter concerning the dangers of asbestos dust and hydraulic fluid.**

2 Hydraulic system – bleeding

⚠️ **Warning: Hydraulic fluid is poisonous; wash off immediately and thoroughly in the case of skin contact, and seek immediate medical advice if any fluid is swallowed or gets into the eyes. Certain types of hydraulic fluid are inflammable, and may ignite when allowed into contact with hot components; when servicing any hydraulic system, it is safest to assume that the fluid is inflammable, and to take precautions against the risk of fire as though it is petrol that is being handled. Hydraulic fluid is also an effective paint stripper, and will attack plastics; if any is spilt, it should be washed off immediately, using copious quantities of fresh water. Finally, it is hygroscopic (it absorbs moisture from the air) – old fluid may be contaminated and unfit for further use. When topping-up or renewing the fluid, always use the recommended type, and ensure that it comes from a freshly-opened sealed container.**

General

1 The correct operation of any hydraulic system is only possible after removing all air from the components and circuit; this is achieved by bleeding the system.
2 During the bleeding procedure, add only clean, unused hydraulic fluid of the recommended type; never re-use fluid that has already been bled from the system. Ensure that sufficient fluid is available before starting work.
3 If there is any possibility of incorrect fluid being already in the system, the brake

components and circuit must be flushed completely with uncontaminated, correct fluid, and new seals should be fitted to the various components.
4 If hydraulic fluid has been lost from the system, or air has entered because of a leak, ensure that the fault is cured before proceeding further.
5 Park the vehicle over an inspection pit or on car ramps. Alternatively, apply the handbrake then jack up the front and rear of the vehicle and support it on axle stands (see *Jacking and vehicle support*). For improved access with the vehicle jacked up, remove the roadwheels.
6 Check that all pipes and hoses are secure, unions tight and bleed screws closed. Clean any dirt from around the bleed screws.
7 Unscrew the master cylinder reservoir cap, and top the master cylinder reservoir up to the MAX level line; refit the cap loosely, and remember to maintain the fluid level at least above the MIN level line throughout the procedure, otherwise there is a risk of further air entering the system.
8 There are a number of one-man, do-it-yourself brake bleeding kits currently available from motor accessory shops. It is recommended that one of these kits is used whenever possible, as they greatly simplify the bleeding operation, and also reduce the risk of expelled air and fluid being drawn back into the system. If such a kit is not available, the basic (two-man) method must be used, which is described in detail below.
9 If a kit is to be used, prepare the vehicle as described previously, and follow the kit manufacturer's instructions, as the procedure may vary slightly according to the type being used; generally, they are as outlined below in the relevant sub-section.
10 Whichever method is used, the same sequence should be followed (paragraphs 11 and 12) to ensure the removal of all air from the system.

Bleeding sequence

11 If the system has been only partially disconnected, and suitable precautions were taken to minimise fluid loss, it should only be necessary to bleed that part of the system (ie,

2.14 Dust cap on a bleed screw (arrowed)

the primary or secondary circuit). If the master cylinder or main brake lines have been disconnected, then the complete system must be bled.
12 The manufacturer does not give any sequence for bleeding the brake circuit, however, we recommend the following for right-hand drive models; for left-hand drive models, bleed the opposite sides:
  a) Left-hand rear brake.
  b) Right-hand front brake.
  c) Right-hand rear brake.
  d) Left-hand front brake.

Bleeding

Basic (two-man) method

13 Collect together a clean glass jar, a suitable length of plastic or rubber tubing which is a tight fit over the bleed screw, and a ring spanner to fit the screw. The help of an assistant will also be required.
14 Remove the dust cap from the first bleed screw in the sequence **(see illustration)**. Fit the spanner and tube to the screw, place the other end of the tube in the jar, and pour in sufficient fluid to cover the end of the tube.
15 Ensure that the master cylinder reservoir fluid level is maintained at least above the MIN level line throughout the procedure.
16 Have the assistant fully depress the brake pedal several times to build-up pressure, then maintain it on the final downstroke.
17 While pedal pressure is maintained, unscrew the bleed screw (approximately one turn) and allow the compressed fluid and air to flow into the jar. The assistant should maintain pedal pressure, following it down to the floor if necessary, and should not release it until instructed to do so. When the flow stops, tighten the bleed screw again, have the assistant release the pedal slowly, and recheck the reservoir fluid level.
18 Repeat the steps given in paragraphs 16 and 17 until the fluid emerging from the bleed screw is free from air bubbles. If the master cylinder has been drained and refilled, and air is being bled from the first screw in the sequence, allow approximately five seconds between cycles for the master cylinder passages to refill.
19 When no more air bubbles appear, securely tighten the bleed screw, remove the tube and spanner, and refit the dust cap. Do not overtighten the bleed screw.
20 Repeat the procedure on the remaining screws in the sequence, until all air is removed from the system and the brake pedal feels firm again.

Using a one-way valve kit

21 As the name implies, these kits consist of a length of tubing with a one-way valve fitted, to prevent expelled air and fluid being drawn back into the system; some kits include a translucent container, which can be positioned so that the air bubbles can be more easily seen flowing from the end of the tube.

2.22 Using a one-way valve kit to bleed the rear brake

22 The kit is connected to the bleed screw, which is then opened **(see illustration)**. The user returns to the driver's seat, depresses the brake pedal with a smooth, steady stroke, and slowly releases it; this is repeated until the expelled fluid is clear of air bubbles.

23 Note that these kits simplify work so much that it is easy to forget the master cylinder reservoir fluid level; ensure that this is maintained at least above the MIN level line at all times.

Using a pressure-bleeding kit

24 These kits are usually operated by a reservoir of pressurised air contained in the spare tyre. However, note that it will probably be necessary to reduce the pressure to a lower level than normal; refer to the instructions supplied with the kit.

25 By connecting a pressurised, fluid-filled container to the master cylinder reservoir, bleeding can be carried out simply by opening each screw in turn (in the specified sequence), and allowing the fluid to flow out until no more air bubbles can be seen in the expelled fluid.

26 This method has the advantage that the large reservoir of fluid provides an additional safeguard against air being drawn into the system during bleeding.

27 Pressure-bleeding is particularly effective when bleeding 'difficult' systems, or when bleeding the complete system at the time of routine fluid renewal.

All methods

28 When bleeding is complete, and firm pedal feel is restored, wash off any spilt fluid, securely tighten the bleed screws, and refit the dust caps.

29 Check the hydraulic fluid level in the master cylinder reservoir, and top-up if necessary (see *Weekly checks*).

30 Discard any hydraulic fluid that has been bled from the system; it will not be fit for re-use.

31 Check the feel of the brake pedal. If it feels at all spongy, air must still be present in the system, and further bleeding is required. Failure to bleed satisfactorily after a reasonable repetition of the bleeding procedure may be due to worn master cylinder seals. All models are fitted with ABS, and it may be found that air bubbles remain trapped in the ABS unit, causing a very poor-action brake pedal; in this instance, the manufacturers recommend that the TECH1 Vauxhall tester be used to operate the ABS pump while the system is being bled.

3 Hydraulic pipes and hoses – renewal

Note: Before starting work, refer to the note at the beginning of Section 2 concerning the dangers of hydraulic fluid.

1 If any pipe or hose is to be renewed, minimise fluid loss by first removing the master cylinder reservoir cap, and fitting a dummy cap without a vent hole. It is not possible to tighten the original cap onto a piece of polythene due to the location of the fluid level sender. Hose clamps can be fitted to flexible hoses to isolate sections of the circuit; metal brake pipe unions can be plugged (if care is taken not to allow dirt into the system) or capped immediately they are disconnected. Place a wad of rag under any union that is to be disconnected, to catch any spilt fluid.

2 If a flexible hose is to be disconnected, unscrew the brake pipe union nut before removing the spring clip which secures the hose to its mounting bracket. Where applicable, unscrew the banjo union bolt securing the hose to the caliper and recover the copper washers. When removing the front flexible hose, pull out the spring clip and disconnect it from the strut **(see illustrations)**.

3 To unscrew union nuts, it is preferable to obtain a brake pipe spanner of the correct size; these are available from most motor accessory shops. Failing this, a close-fitting open-ended spanner will be required, though if the nuts are tight or corroded, their flats may be rounded-off if the spanner slips. In such a case, a self-locking wrench is often the only way to unscrew a stubborn union, but it follows that the pipe and the damaged nuts must be renewed on reassembly. Always clean a union and surrounding area before disconnecting it. If disconnecting a component with more than one union, make a careful note of the connections before disturbing any of them.

4 If a brake pipe is to be renewed, it can be obtained, cut to length and with the union nuts and end flares in place, from Vauxhall/Opel dealers. All that is then necessary is to bend it to shape, following the line of the original, before fitting it to the car. Alternatively, most motor accessory shops can make up brake pipes from kits, but this requires very careful measurement of the original, to ensure that the replacement is of the correct length. The safest answer is usually to take the original to the shop as a pattern.

5 On refitting, do not overtighten the union nuts.

6 When refitting hoses to the calipers, always use new copper washers and tighten the banjo union bolts to the specified torque. Make sure that the hoses are positioned so that they will not touch surrounding bodywork or the roadwheels.

7 Ensure that the pipes and hoses are correctly routed, with no kinks, and that they are secured in the clips or brackets provided. After fitting, remove the dummy cap from the reservoir, and bleed the hydraulic system as described in Section 2. Wash off any spilt fluid, and check carefully for fluid leaks.

3.2a Pull out the spring clip . . .

3.2b . . . and disconnect the flexible hose from the front suspension strut

3.2c The rear flexible hose is connected to the rigid hydraulic line beneath the rear wheelarch

4.3 Removing the retaining spring from the front caliper

4.4 Remove the dust caps . . .

4.5a . . . then unscrew the guide bolts . . .

4 Front brake pads – renewal

⚠️ *Warning: Renew BOTH sets of front brake pads at the same time – NEVER renew the pads on only one wheel, as uneven braking may result. Note that the dust created by wear of the pads may contain asbestos, which is a health hazard. Never blow it out with compressed air, and do not inhale any of it. An approved filtering mask should be worn when working on the brakes. DO NOT use petroleum-based solvents to clean brake parts – use brake cleaner or methylated spirit only.*

1 Apply the handbrake, then jack up the front of the vehicle and support it on axle stands (see *Jacking and vehicle support*). Remove the front roadwheels.

2 Using a screwdriver lever out the brake pad warning sensor and unclip it from the retainer.

3 Prise the retaining spring from the outer edge of the caliper, noting its correct fitted position **(see illustration)**.

4 Remove the dust caps from the inner ends of the guide bolts **(see illustration)**.

5 Unscrew the guide bolts from the caliper, and lift the caliper and inner pad away from the mounting bracket. Tie the caliper to the suspension strut using a suitable piece of wire **(see illustrations)**. Do not allow the caliper to hang unsupported on the flexible brake hose.

6 Remove the inner pad from the caliper piston, noting that it is retained by a spring clip attached to the pad backing plate, and recover the outer pad from the mounting bracket **(see illustration)**.

7 Brush the dirt and dust from the caliper, but take care not to inhale it. Carefully remove any rust from the edge of the brake disc.

8 Measure the thickness of each brake pad (friction material and backing plate) **(see illustration)**. If either pad is worn at any point to the specified minimum thickness or less, all four pads must be renewed. The pads should also be renewed if any are fouled with oil or grease; there is no satisfactory way of degreasing friction material, once contaminated. If any of the brake pads are worn unevenly, or fouled with oil or grease,

trace and rectify the cause before reassembly.

9 If the brake pads are still serviceable, carefully clean them using a clean, fine wire brush or similar, paying particular attention to the sides and back of the metal backing. Clean out the grooves in the friction material, and pick out any large embedded particles of dirt or debris. Carefully clean the pad locations in the caliper body/mounting bracket.

10 Prior to fitting the pads, check that the guide bolts are a snug fit in the caliper bushes. Brush the dust and dirt from the caliper and piston. Apply a little high melting-point copper brake grease to the areas on the pad backing plates which contact the caliper and piston. Inspect the dust seal around the piston for damage, and the piston for evidence of fluid leaks, corrosion or damage. If attention to any of these components is necessary, refer to Section 10.

11 If new brake pads are to be fitted, the

caliper piston must be pushed back into the cylinder to make room for them. We recommend that the caliper bleed screw is loosened and the excess fluid drained into a container, rather than forcing the fluid through the circuit into the reservoir. This method will prevent any sediment being forced back into the master cylinder. Either use a G-clamp or similar tool, or use suitable pieces of wood as levers to move the piston fully into the caliper bore. Tighten the bleed screw.

12 Check that the cutaway recesses on the caliper piston are correctly positioned **(see illustration)**. If necessary, carefully turn the piston to its correct position.

13 Fit the inner pad to the caliper, ensuring that its clip is correctly located in the caliper piston **(see illustration)**.

14 Fit the outer pad to the caliper mounting bracket, ensuring that its friction material is facing the brake disc.

4.5b . . . and lift the caliper and inner pad away from the mounting bracket

4.5c Tie the caliper to the suspension strut, to avoid placing any strain on the hydraulic brake hose

4.6 Removing the outer pad from the mounting bracket

4.8 Measuring the brake pad thickness

4.12 Front brake caliper cutaway recess (arrowed) correctly positioned

4.13 Locate the clip in the front caliper piston when refitting the inner pad

4.16 Tightening the caliper guide bolts

4.18 Make sure the retaining spring ends are correctly located in the caliper holes

15 Slide the caliper and inner pad into position over the outer pad, and locate it in the mounting bracket.
16 Insert the caliper guide bolts, and tighten them securely **(see illustration)**.

17 Refit the guide bolt dust caps.
18 Refit the retaining spring to the caliper, ensuring that its ends are correctly located in the caliper holes **(see illustration)**.
19 Refit the brake pad warning sensor.

5.2 Driving out the pad retaining pins from the rear brake caliper

5.3 Removing a rear disc pad anti-rattle spring

5.4 Using a special removal tool to remove the rear brake disc pads

5.5 Using pliers to remove the inboard disc pad from the rear brake caliper

20 Depress the brake pedal repeatedly, until normal pedal pressure is restored.
21 Repeat the above procedure on the remaining front brake caliper.
22 Refit the roadwheels, then lower the vehicle to the ground and tighten the roadwheel bolts to the specified torque setting.
23 Check and top up the hydraulic fluid level as described in *Weekly checks*.
Caution: New pads will not give full braking efficiency until they have bedded-in. Be prepared for this, and avoid hard braking as far as possible for the first hundred miles or so after pad renewal.

5 Rear brake pads – renewal

⚠ *Warning: Renew BOTH sets of rear brake pads at the same time – NEVER renew the pads on only one wheel, as uneven braking may result. Note that the dust created by wear of the pads may contain asbestos, which is a health hazard. Never blow it out with compressed air, and do not inhale any of it. An approved filtering mask should be worn when working on the brakes. DO NOT use petroleum-based solvents to clean brake parts – use brake cleaner or methylated spirit only.*

1 Chock the front wheels, then jack up the rear of the vehicle and support it on axle stands (see *Jacking and vehicle support*). Remove the rear roadwheels, then release the handbrake lever.
2 Note how the anti-rattle spring is located, then drive out the upper and lower pad retaining pins from the outside of the caliper using a punch **(see illustration)**.
3 Remove the anti-rattle spring **(see illustration)**.
4 Push the pads away from the disc slightly, then using a pair of pliers or removal tool, withdraw the outboard pad from the caliper **(see illustration)**.
5 Withdraw the inboard pad from the caliper **(see illustration)**.
6 Brush the dust and dirt from the caliper, but take care not to inhale it. Carefully remove any rust from the edge of the brake disc.
7 Measure the thickness of each brake pad (friction material and backing plate). If either pad is worn at any point to the specified minimum thickness or less, all four pads must be renewed. The pads should also be renewed if any are fouled with oil or grease; there is no satisfactory way of degreasing friction material, once contaminated. If any of the brake pads are worn unevenly, or fouled with oil or grease, trace and rectify the cause before reassembly.
8 If the brake pads are still serviceable, clean them using a clean, fine wire brush or similar, paying particular attention to the sides and

...s, remove the spring
...up ...

6.11b ... then lift off the spring and
retainer pin

6.13 The left-hand adjuster strut assembly
is marked L (arrow)

It may be necessary to transfer the
...sting lever pivot pin and clip (arrowed)
...m the original shoes to the new ones

6.18 Apply a smear of anti-seize
compound to the contact surfaces of the
backplate (arrowed). Note the elastic band
wrapped around the wheel cylinder

6.19 Engage the rear brake shoe with the
handbrake cable, and locate the shoe on
the backplate

...hoes removed. As a precaution against the
wheel cylinder pistons dropping out, wrap a
strong elastic band around them.

13 If both brake assemblies are dismantled
at the same time, take care not to mix them
up. Note that the left-hand and right-hand
adjuster components are marked as such; the
threaded rod is marked L or R, and the other
'handed' components are colour-coded black
for the left-hand side, and silver for the right-
hand side **(see illustration)**.

14 Dismantle and clean the adjuster strut.
Apply a smear of silicone-based grease to the
adjuster threads.

15 Examine the return springs. If they are
distorted, or if they have seen extensive
service, renewal is advisable. Weak springs
may cause the brakes to bind.

16 If a new handbrake operating lever was
not supplied with the new shoes, transfer the
lever from the old shoes. The lever may be
secured with a pin and circlip, or by a rivet,
which will have to be drilled out. It may also
be necessary to transfer the adjusting lever
pivot pin and clip from the original front shoe
to the new shoe **(see illustration)**.

17 Peel back the rubber protective caps, and
check the wheel cylinder for fluid leaks or
other damage. Ensure that both cylinder
pistons are free to move easily. Refer to
Section 12, if necessary, for information on
wheel cylinder overhaul.

18 Prior to installation, clean the backplate
thoroughly. Apply a thin smear of high-
temperature copper-based brake grease or
anti-seize compound to the shoe contact

surfaces on the backplate and wheel cylinder
pistons **(see illustration)**. Do not allow the
grease to foul the friction lining material.

19 Ensure that the handbrake cable is
correctly retained by the clip on the lower
brake shoe pivot point, then engage the rear
shoe with the cable. Locate the shoe on the
backplate **(see illustration)**.

20 Install the rear shoe retainer pin and
spring, and secure it in position with the
spring cup.

21 Hook the lower return spring onto the rear
shoe, then engage the front shoe with the
return spring. Locate the front shoe on the
backplate, and secure it in position with its
retainer pin, spring and spring cup **(see
illustrations)**.

22 Screw the adjuster strut wheel fully onto
the forked end of the adjuster, so that the
adjuster strut is set to its shortest possible
length. Back the wheel off a half a turn, and
check that it is free to rotate easily.

23 Manoeuvre the adjuster strut assembly
into position between the brake shoes. Make
sure that both ends of the strut are correctly
engaged with the shoes, noting that the
forked end of the strut must be positioned so
that its longer, straight fork is to the rear of the
shoe **(see illustration)**.

24 Engage the adjusting lever return spring
with the front shoe and adjusting lever, and
locate the lever on its pivot pin **(see
illustration)**. Check that the lever and spring
are correctly located, and secure the lever in

6.21a Install the front shoe and lower
return spring ...

6.21b ... and secure it in position with the
retainer pin, spring and spring cup

5.11 Checking a rear caliper piston cut-away recess angle with a card template

back of the metal backing. Carefully clean the pad locations in the caliper body/mounting bracket.

9 Prior to fitting the pads, clean and check the pad retaining pins. Brush the dust and dirt from the caliper and piston (see Warning at the beginning of this Section). Apply a little high melting-point copper brake grease to the areas on the pad backing plates which contact the caliper and piston. Inspect the dust seal around the piston for damage, and the piston for evidence of fluid leaks, corrosion or damage. If attention to any of these components is necessary, refer to Section 11.

10 If new brake pads are to be fitted, the caliper piston must be pushed back into the cylinder to make room for them. We recommend that the caliper bleed screw is loosened and the excess fluid drained into a container, rather than forcing the fluid through the circuit into the reservoir. This method will prevent any sediment being forced back into the master cylinder. Either use a G-clamp or similar tool, or use suitable pieces of wood as levers to move the piston fully into the caliper bore. Tighten the bleed screw.

11 Check that the cutaway recesses in the pistons are positioned at approximately 23° to the horizontal. A template made of card may be used to check the setting **(see illustration)**. If necessary, carefully turn the pistons to their correct positions.

12 Locate the new pads and the anti-squeal shims in the caliper. Ensure that the friction material faces the disc, and check that the pads are free to move slightly.

13 Locate the anti-rattle spring on the pads, then insert the pad retaining pins from the inside edge of the caliper, while depressing the spring. Tap the pins firmly into the caliper.

14 Depress the brake pedal repeatedly until normal pedal pressure is restored.

15 Repeat the above procedure on the remaining rear brake caliper.

16 Refit the roadwheels, then apply the handbrake lever, lower the vehicle to the ground and tighten the roadwheel bolts to the specified torque setting.

17 Check and top up the hydraulic fluid level as described in *Weekly checks*.

Caution: New pads will not give full braking

efficiency until they have ▯
prepared for this, and a▯
as far as possible f▯
miles or so after p▯

6 Rear brake sh▯
renewal

Note: *This Section applies o▯
fitted with rear drum brakes.*

⚠️ **Warning: Brake shoes ▯
renewed on both rear w▯
the same time – never rene▯
shoes on only one wheel, as une▯
braking may result. Also, the dust create▯
by wear of the shoes may contain
asbestos, which is a health hazard. Never
blow it out with compressed air, and do not
inhale any of it. An approved filtering mask
should be worn when working on the
brakes. DO NOT use petrol or petroleum-
based solvents to clean brake parts; use
brake cleaner or methylated spirit only.**

1 Remove the rear brake drum as described in Section 9.

2 Taking precautions to avoid inhalation of dust, remove all traces of brake dust from the brake drum, shoes and backplate.

3 Measure the thickness of the friction material of each brake shoe at several points; if either shoe is worn at any point to the specified minimum thickness or less, **all four** shoes must be renewed as a set **(see illustration)**. The shoes should also be

6.11a Using plier▯

8 ▯
apan▯
betwee▯

9 Using a▯
retainer spr▯
it through 90▯
the spring and ▯

10 Detach the ▯
return spring, and r▯
return spring.

11 Remove the rear sho▯
spring and retainer pin▯
paragraph 9, then remove th▯
it from the handbrake ▯
illustrations).

12 Do not depress the brake pe▯

**6.16 ▯
adjus▯
fro▯**

6.3 Checking the wear of the rear brake shoe friction material

6.5 Note the correct fitted locations of all components, paying particular attention to the adjuster strut components

6.6 Unhook the upper return spring, and remove it from the brake shoes

6.7 Remove the retaining spring, followed by the lever and return spring (arrowed)

6.23 Refit the adjuster strut, noting that the longer, straight part of the fork (arrowed) must be behind the shoe

6.24 Refit the adjusting lever and spring, making sure that the spring is correctly engaged in the front brake shoe hole (arrowed)

6.25 Make sure that both shoes are correctly aligned with the wheel cylinder, then install the upper return spring

position with the retaining spring, making sure the spring ends are securely located in the retaining pin and shoe.

25 Remove the rubber band from the wheel cylinder. Make sure that both shoes are correctly positioned on the wheel cylinder pistons, then fit the upper return spring **(see illustration)**.

26 Ensure that the handbrake operating lever stop peg is correctly positioned against the edge of the shoe web, then refit the brake drum as described in Section 9.

27 Repeat the operation on the remaining brake.

28 Once both sets of rear shoes have been renewed, with the handbrake fully released, adjust the lining-to-drum clearance by repeatedly depressing the brake pedal at least 20 to 25 times. Whilst depressing the pedal,

7.6a Handbrake shoe hold-down spring and cup (arrowed)

have an assistant listen to the rear drums, to check that the adjuster strut is functioning correctly; if so, a clicking sound will be emitted by the strut as the pedal is depressed.

29 Check and, if necessary, adjust the handbrake as described in Section 17.

30 On completion, check the hydraulic fluid level as described in *Weekly checks*.

Caution: New shoes will not give full braking efficiency until they have bedded-in. Be prepared for this, and avoid hard braking as far as possible for the first hundred miles or so after shoe renewal.

7 Handbrake shoes (rear disc brakes) – inspection, removal and refitting

> ⚠️ *Warning: Brake shoes must be renewed on both rear wheels at the same time to ensure correct operation of the handbrake. Also, the dust created by wear of the shoes may contain asbestos, which is a health hazard. Never blow it out with compressed air, and do not inhale any of it. An approved filtering mask should be worn when working on the brakes. DO NOT use petrol or petroleum-based solvents to clean brake parts; use brake cleaner or methylated spirit only.*

Inspection

1 On models fitted with rear disc brakes, the

handbrake operates independently of the footbrake, using brake shoes on the inside of the disc in a similar way to rear drum brake models.

2 Remove the rear brake disc (see Section 8).

3 With the disc removed, check that the friction material has not worn down to less than the specified minimum.

4 If any one of the shoes has worn below the specified limit, all four handbrake shoes must be renewed as a set, as follows.

Removal

5 Clean the dust and dirt from the brake shoes and backplate (see Warning at the beginning of this Section).

6 Remove the shoe hold-down pins, springs and cups by depressing the cups and turning them through 90° using a pair of pliers **(see illustrations)**. This is a difficult task due to the strong spring tension and limited access, and an alternative method is to use a small socket through the holes in the hub flange to depress the springs. **Note:** *The front hold-down pin can be removed through the rear of the brake backplate, however the rear pin can only be removed after removing the rear hub and bracket (see Chapter 10).*

7 Note the fitted position of all components then remove the expander/adjuster from between the upper ends of the shoes **(see illustration)**.

8 Using a pair of pliers unhook the upper return spring from the shoes **(see illustration)**.

7.6b Using a pair of pliers . . .

7.6c . . . to remove the handbrake shoe hold-down springs

7.7 Removing the expander/adjuster from the top of the handbrake shoes

7.8 Unhook the upper return spring from the shoes with long-nosed pliers

7.9a Unhook the lower return spring and remove the leading . . .

7.9b . . . and trailing shoes from the backplate

7.10a Using a small screwdriver to prise the rear cable from the special clip

7.10b The return spring located on the rear of the backplate (arrowed)

12 Dismantle and clean all components. Examine the return springs. Renew worn or damaged components.

Refitting

13 Prior to installation, clean the backplate thoroughly. The handbrake shoes can be reassembled using a reversal of the dismantling procedure, however improved access is possible by removing the rear hub assembly as described in Chapter 10 and temporarily holding the backplate in position on the trailing arm using two bolts (see illustration). After reassembly the rear hub can then be refitted.

14 Reassemble the lever assembly and apply a little copper grease to the contact surfaces, then refit to the backplate and insert through the rubber grommet (see illustrations).

15 Refit the cable to the lever and connector and use a pair of pliers to squeeze the clip

9 Unhook the lower return spring and remove the leading and trailing shoes (see illustrations).
10 Disconnect the handbrake cable at the special clip using a small screwdriver then unhook the return spring from the backplate

and remove the lever assembly (see illustrations).
11 If both handbrake assemblies are dismantled at the same time, take care not to mix them up.

7.13 With the rear hub removed, temporarily hold the backplate in position using two bolts

7.14a The lever assembly dismantled

7.14b The lever assembled

7.14c Refitting the lever assembly to the backplate

7.15a Hooking the rear cable onto the lever . . .

7.15b . . . and connector . . .

7.15c . . . and squeezing the connector with a pair of pliers

7.15d Refitting the return spring

7.16 Apply copper-based grease to the contact surfaces on the backplate

7.17a Locate the front (trailing) shoe on the backplate . . .

7.17b . . . then refit the spring and cup . . .

7.17c . . . and use a pair of pliers to depress and turn the cup

together, then refit the return spring **(see illustrations)**.

16 Apply a thin smear of high-temperature copper-based brake grease or anti-seize compound to the shoe contact surfaces on

the backplate **(see illustration)**.

17 With the pins already fitted to the backplate, refit the front (trailing) shoe and secure with the hold-down spring and cup **(see illustrations)**.

18 Locate the rear (leading) shoe on the lever assembly and refit the lower return spring **(see illustrations)**.

19 Refit the hold-down spring and cup to secure the leading shoe to the backplate **(see illustration)**.

20 Refit the expander/adjuster between the upper ends of the shoes **(see illustration)**.

21 Hook the upper return spring on the shoes **(see illustration)**.

22 Where removed the rear hub can now be refitted **(see illustration)**.

23 Temporarily refit the disc over the shoes to determine the adjustment, then if necessary use a screwdriver to turn the serrated adjuster nut until it is just possible to refit the disc over the shoes without them binding **(see illustration)**.

24 Refit the brake disc with reference to Section 8.

7.18a Refit the rear (leading) shoe and the lower return spring

7.18b Engage the bottom of the shoe on the lever . . .

7.19 . . . then refit the hold-down spring and cup

7.20 Refit the adjuster between the upper ends of the shoes

7.21 Hook the upper return spring on the shoes

7.22 The handbrake shoes assembled ready for refitting of the rear hub

25 Adjust the handbrake as described in Section 17.
26 Refit the roadwheels and lower the vehicle to the ground.

8 Front/rear brake disc – inspection, removal and refitting

Note: *Before starting work, refer to the warning at the beginning of Section 4 or 5 concerning the dangers of asbestos dust. If either disc requires renewal, both should be renewed at the same time together with new pads, to ensure even and consistent braking.*

Inspection

1 Remove the wheel trim, then loosen the roadwheel bolts. If checking a front disc, apply the handbrake, and if checking a rear

8.3 The minimum thickness is stamped on the outer face of the rear disc

8.11a Using an impact driver to unscrew the front disc securing screw

7.23 Using a screwdriver through the hole in the drive flange to turn the serrated nut on the adjuster

disc, chock the front wheels and release the handbrake, then jack up the relevant end of the vehicle and support on axle stands (see *Jacking and vehicle support*). Remove the roadwheel.
2 Check that the brake disc securing screw is tight, then fit a spacer approximately 10.0 mm thick to one of the roadwheel bolts, and refit and tighten the bolt in the hole opposite the disc securing screw **(see illustration)**.
3 Rotate the brake disc, and examine it for deep scoring or grooving. Light scoring is normal, but if excessive, the disc should be removed and either renewed or machined (within the specified limits) by an engineering works. The minimum thickness is stamped on the outer face of the rear disc **(see illustration)**.
4 Using a dial gauge, or a flat metal block and feeler blades, check that the disc run-out does not exceed the figure given in the

8.10 Tie the front brake caliper to one side when removing the disc

8.11b Removing a front brake disc

8.2 Refit a wheel bolt and spacer (arrowed) opposite the disc securing screw (A) before checking the brake disc run-out

Specifications. Measure the run-out 10.0 mm (0.4 in) in from the outer edge of the disc.
5 If the rear disc run-out is excessive, check the rear wheel bearing adjustment, as described in Chapter 10.
6 If the front disc run-out is excessive, remove the disc as described later, and check that the disc-to-hub surfaces are perfectly clean. Refit the disc and check the run-out again.
7 If the run-out is still excessive, the disc should be renewed.
8 To remove a disc, proceed as follows.

Front disc

Removal

9 Remove the roadwheel bolt and spacer used when checking the disc.
10 Unbolt and remove the front brake caliper complete with disc pads and tie it to one side. Also remove the front brake caliper mounting bracket with reference to Section 10 **(see illustration)**.
11 Remove the securing screw and withdraw the disc from the hub. If available, use an impact driver to remove the screw **(see illustrations)**.

Refitting

12 Refitting is a reversal of removal, but make sure that the mating faces of the disc and hub are perfectly clean, and apply a little locking fluid to the threads of the securing screw.
13 Refit the disc pads, as described in Section 4.

Rear disc

Removal

14 Where applicable, remove the roadwheel bolt and spacer used when checking the disc.
15 Remove the rear brake pads, as described in Section 5.
16 Remove the rear brake caliper with reference to Section 11, but leave the hydraulic fluid pipe connected. Move the caliper to one side, and suspend it using wire or string to avoid straining the pipe.

17 Remove the securing screw and withdraw the disc from the hub **(see illustrations)**. If the disc is tight, back off the handbrake shoes by inserting a screwdriver through the adjuster hole in the disc and turning the adjuster wheel located at the top of the backplate. Alternatively, back off the handbrake cable at the adjustment on the handbrake lever (see Section 17).

Refitting

18 Refitting is a reversal of removal, but make sure that the mating faces of the disc and hub are perfectly clean, and apply a little locking fluid to the threads of the securing screw. Refit the disc pads, as described in Section 5, and adjust the handbrake as described in Section 17.

9 Rear brake drum – removal, inspection and refitting

Note: *Before starting work, refer to the warning at the beginning of Section 6 concerning the dangers of asbestos dust.*

Removal

1 Remove the relevant wheel trim, then loosen the rear roadwheel bolts and chock the front wheels. Jack up the rear of the vehicle, and support on axle stands positioned under the body sidemembers (see *Jacking and vehicle support*). Remove the roadwheel.
2 Fully release the handbrake.
3 Extract the drum securing screw and remove the drum. If the drum is tight, remove the plug from the inspection hole in the brake backplate, and push the handbrake operating lever away from the brake shoe web to allow the shoes to move away from the drums. If necessary, slacken the handbrake cable adjuster on the lever inside the vehicle.

Inspection

4 Brush the dust and dirt from the drum, taking care not to inhale it.
5 Examine the internal friction surface of the drum. If deeply scored, or so worn that the drum has become ridged to the width of the shoes, then both drums must be renewed.
6 Regrinding of the friction surface may be

10.5a Unscrew the bolts . . .

8.17a Undo the securing screw . . .

possible provided the maximum diameter given in the Specifications is not exceeded.

Refitting

7 Before refitting the drum, make sure that the handbrake operating lever is returned to its normal position behind the web on the trailing brake shoe.
8 Refit the brake drum and tighten the securing screw. If necessary, back off the adjuster wheel on the strut until the drum will pass over the shoes.
9 Adjust the brakes by operating the footbrake a number of times. A clicking noise will be heard at the drum as the automatic adjuster operates. When the clicking stops, adjustment is complete.
10 Refit the roadwheel and lower the vehicle to the ground.

10 Front brake caliper – removal, overhaul and refitting

Note: *New brake hose copper washers will be required when refitting. Before starting work, refer to the note at the beginning of Section 2 concerning the dangers of hydraulic fluid, and to the warning at the beginning of Section 4 concerning the dangers of asbestos dust.*

Removal

1 Apply the handbrake, then jack up the front of the vehicle and support it on axle stands (see *Jacking and vehicle support*). Remove the roadwheel.

10.5b . . . and remove the front brake caliper mounting bracket

8.17b . . . and remove the rear disc from the hub drive flange

2 Minimise fluid loss by first removing the master cylinder reservoir cap, then fitting a dummy cap without a vent hole. Alternatively, use a brake hose clamp to clamp the flexible hose leading to the brake caliper.
3 Clean the area around the caliper brake hose union. Unscrew and remove the union bolt, and recover the copper sealing washer from each side of the hose union. Discard the washers; new ones must be used on refitting. Plug the hose end and caliper hole, to minimise fluid loss and prevent the ingress of dust and dirt into the hydraulic system.
4 Remove the brake pads as described in Section 4, then remove the caliper from the vehicle.
5 If necessary, unbolt the caliper mounting bracket from the hub carrier **(see illustrations)**.

Overhaul

6 With the caliper on the bench, wipe it clean with a cloth rag.
7 Withdraw the partially-ejected piston from the caliper body, and remove the dust seal. The piston can be withdrawn by hand, or if necessary pushed out by applying compressed air to the brake hose union hole. Only low pressure should be required, such as is generated by a foot pump.
8 Using a small screwdriver, carefully remove the piston seal from the groove in the caliper, taking care not to mark the bore **(see illustration)**.
9 Carefully press the guide bushes out of the caliper body.

10.8 Removing the piston seal from the caliper body

10.16 The raised sectors (arrowed) must be positioned vertically when refitting the front brake caliper

10 Thoroughly clean all components, using only methylated spirit or clean hydraulic fluid. Never use mineral-based solvents such as petrol or paraffin, which will attack the rubber components of the hydraulic system. Dry the components using compressed air or a clean, lint-free cloth. If available, use compressed air to blow clear the fluid passages.

 Warning: Wear eye protection when using compressed air.

11 Check all components, and renew any that are worn or damaged. If the piston and/or cylinder bore are scratched excessively, renew the complete caliper body. Similarly check the condition of the guide bushes and bolts; both bushes and bolts should be undamaged and (when cleaned) a reasonably tight sliding fit. If there is any doubt about the condition of any component, renew it.
12 If the caliper is fit for further use, obtain the necessary components from your Vauxhall/Opel dealer. Renew the caliper seals and dust covers as a matter of course; these should never be re-used.
13 On reassembly, ensure that all components are absolutely clean and dry.
14 Dip the piston and the new piston seal in clean hydraulic fluid, and smear clean fluid on the cylinder bore surface.
15 Locate the new seal in the cylinder bore groove, using only the fingers to manipulate it into position.
16 Fit the new dust seal to the piston, then insert the piston into the cylinder bore using a

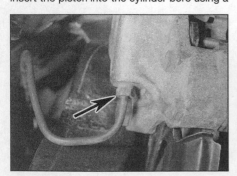

11.3 Hydraulic brake line union nut on the rear brake caliper

twisting motion to ensure it enters the seal correctly. Make sure the piston enters squarely into the bore with the raised sectors positioned vertically **(see illustration)**. Locate the dust seal in the body groove, and push the piston fully into the caliper bore.
17 Insert the guide bushes into position in the caliper body.

Refitting

18 Locate the caliper mounting bracket on the hub carrier, then insert and tighten the bolts (with locking fluid applied to their threads) to the specified torque **(see illustration)**.
19 Refit the brake pads as described in Section 4, together with the caliper which at this stage will not have the hose attached.
20 Position a new copper sealing washer on each side of the hose union, and connect the brake hose to the caliper. Ensure that the hose is correctly positioned against the caliper body lug, then install the union bolt and tighten it to the specified torque setting.
21 Remove the brake hose clamp or dummy cap, and bleed the hydraulic system as described in Section 2. Note that, providing the precautions described were taken to minimise brake fluid loss, it should only be necessary to bleed the relevant front brake circuit.
22 Refit the roadwheel, then lower the vehicle to the ground and tighten the roadwheel bolts to the specified torque.

10.18 Tightening the rear brake caliper mounting bracket bolts

11.5 Unscrewing the bolts securing the rear brake caliper to the trailing arm

11 Rear brake caliper – removal, overhaul and refitting

Note: *Before starting work, refer to the note at the beginning of Section 2 concerning the dangers of hydraulic fluid, and to the warning at the beginning of Section 5 concerning the dangers of asbestos dust.*

Removal

1 Chock the front wheels, then jack up the rear of the vehicle and support on axle stands (see *Jacking and vehicle support*). Remove the roadwheel.
2 Minimise fluid loss by first removing the master cylinder reservoir cap, then fitting a dummy cap without a vent hole. Alternatively, use a brake hose clamp to clamp the flexible hose leading to the brake caliper.
3 Clean the area around the hydraulic line union nut, then loosen the nut **(see illustration)**. Do not fully unscrew the nut at this stage.
4 Remove the brake pads as described in Section 5.
5 Unscrew and remove the mounting bolts securing the caliper to the trailing arm **(see illustration)**.
6 Fully unscrew the union nut and disconnect the hydraulic line from the caliper, then withdraw the caliper from the disc **(see illustration)**. Tape over or plug the hydraulic line to prevent entry of dust and dirt.

Overhaul

7 With the caliper on the bench, wipe it clean with a cloth rag.
8 Using a screwdriver, carefully prise out the lock collar retaining the dust seal in the caliper body.
9 Withdraw the partially-ejected pistons from the caliper body, and remove the dust seals. The pistons can be withdrawn by hand, or if necessary pushed out by applying compressed air to the brake line union hole. Only low pressure should be required, such as is generated by a foot pump.
10 Using a small screwdriver, carefully remove the piston seals from the caliper, taking care not to mark the bore.

11.6 Removing the rear brake caliper from the trailing arm and disc

11.18 Check that the piston (arrowed) is correctly positioned before refitting the rear brake caliper

11 Thoroughly clean all components, using only methylated spirit or clean hydraulic fluid. Never use mineral-based solvents such as petrol or paraffin, which will attack the rubber components of the hydraulic system.

12 Dry the components using compressed air or a clean, lint-free cloth. If available, use compressed air to blow clear the fluid passages.

 Warning: Wear eye protection when using compressed air.

13 Check all components, and renew any that are worn or damaged. If the pistons and/or cylinder bores are worn excessively, renew the complete caliper body.

14 If the caliper is fit for further use, obtain the necessary components from your Vauxhall/Opel dealer. Renew the caliper seals and dust covers as a matter of course; these should never be re-used.

15 On reassembly, ensure that all components are absolutely clean and dry.

16 Working on one piston at a time, dip the piston and the new piston seal in clean hydraulic fluid, and smear clean fluid on the cylinder bore surface.

17 Locate the new seal in the cylinder bore groove, using only the fingers to manipulate it into position.

18 Fit the new dust seal to the piston, then insert the piston into the cylinder bore using a twisting motion to ensure it enters the seal correctly. Make sure the piston enters squarely into the bore with the raised sectors positioned as described in Section 5 **(see illustration)**. Locate the dust seal in the body groove, and push the piston fully into the caliper bore. Press the dust seal lock collar into the caliper body.

Refitting

19 Locate the caliper over the disc, then insert the hydraulic line and screw in the union nut. Do not fully tighten the nut at this stage.

20 Apply a little locking fluid to the threads of the mounting bolts, then refit them and tighten to the specified torque.

21 Refit the brake pads as described in Section 5.

22 Fully tighten the hydraulic union nut.

23 Remove the dummy cap or hose clamp,

and bleed the hydraulic system as described in Section 2. Note that, providing the precautions described were taken to minimise brake fluid loss, it should only be necessary to bleed the relevant rear brake circuit.

24 Refit the roadwheel, then lower the vehicle to the ground and tighten the roadwheel bolts to the specified torque.

12 Rear wheel cylinder – removal, overhaul and refitting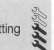

Note: *Before starting work, refer to the note at the beginning of Section 2 concerning the dangers of hydraulic fluid, and to the warning at the beginning of Section 6 concerning the dangers of asbestos dust.*

Removal

1 Remove the brake drum as described in Section 9.

2 Minimise fluid loss by first removing the master cylinder reservoir cap, then fitting a dummy cap without a vent hole, to obtain an airtight seal. Alternatively, use a brake hose clamp to clamp the flexible hose at the nearest convenient point to the wheel cylinder.

3 Carefully unhook the brake shoe upper return spring, and remove it from both brake shoes. Pull the upper ends of the shoes away from the wheel cylinder to disengage them from the pistons.

4 Wipe away all traces of dirt around the brake pipe union nut at the rear of the wheel cylinder, and unscrew the nut. Carefully ease the pipe out of the wheel cylinder, and plug or tape over its end to prevent dirt entry. Wipe off any spilt fluid immediately.

5 Unscrew the retaining bolt from the rear of the backplate, and remove the wheel cylinder, taking care not to allow surplus hydraulic fluid to contaminate the brake shoe linings.

Overhaul

6 Brush the dust and dirt from the wheel cylinder, but take care not to inhale it.

7 Pull the rubber dust seals from the ends of the cylinder body **(see illustration)**.

8 The pistons will normally be ejected by the pressure of the coil spring, but if they are not, tap the end of the cylinder body on a piece of wood, or apply low air pressure (eg, from a foot pump) to the hydraulic fluid union hole to eject the pistons from their bores. Remove the seals.

9 Thoroughly clean all components, using only methylated spirit or clean hydraulic fluid. Never use mineral-based solvents such as petrol or paraffin, which will attack the rubber components of the hydraulic system. Dry the components using compressed air or a clean, lint-free cloth. If available, use compressed air to blow clear the fluid passages.

10 Inspect the surfaces of the pistons and their bores in the cylinder body for scoring, or evidence of metal-to-metal contact. If evident, renew the complete wheel cylinder assembly. If the pistons and bores are in good condition, discard the seals and obtain a repair kit, which will contain all the necessary renewable items.

11 Lubricate the piston seals with clean brake fluid, and insert them into the cylinder bores, with the spring between them, using finger pressure only.

12 Dip the pistons in clean brake fluid, and insert them into the cylinder bores.

13 Fit the dust seals, and check that the pistons can move freely in their bores.

H.28158

12.7 Exploded view of the rear brake wheel cylinder

13.2 Brake master cylinder reservoir cap

13.4 Master cylinder mounting nuts (1), clutch hydraulic pipe (2) and brake line union nut (3)

13.7 Master cylinder mounting nuts

Refitting

14 Ensure that the backplate and wheel cylinder mating surfaces are clean, then spread the brake shoes and manoeuvre the wheel cylinder into position.

15 Insert the brake pipe, and screw in the union nut two or three turns to ensure that the thread has started.

16 Insert the wheel cylinder retaining bolt, and tighten to the specified torque setting. Now fully tighten the brake pipe union nut.

17 Remove the clamp from the flexible brake hose, or the dummy cap from the master cylinder reservoir.

18 Ensure that the brake shoes are correctly located on the cylinder pistons, then carefully refit the brake shoe upper return spring.

19 Refit the brake drum as described in Section 9.

20 Bleed the brake hydraulic system as described in Section 2. Providing suitable precautions were taken to minimise loss of fluid, it should only be necessary to bleed the relevant rear brake circuit.

13 Master cylinder – removal, overhaul and refitting

Note: *Before starting work, refer to the warning at the beginning of Section 2 concerning the dangers of hydraulic fluid.*

Removal

1 Exhaust the vacuum present in the brake servo unit by repeatedly depressing the brake pedal.

2 Disconnect the wiring from the brake fluid level sender and remove the reservoir cap. Syphon the hydraulic fluid from the reservoir **(see illustration)**. Alternatively, open any convenient bleed screw in the system, and gently pump the brake pedal to expel the fluid through a plastic tube connected to the bleed screw (see Section 2).

 Warning: Do not syphon the fluid by mouth, as it is poisonous; use a syringe or an old poultry baster.

3 Detach the relay box from the hydraulic modulator on the left-hand side of the engine compartment.

4 On models with manual transmission, release the clip and disconnect the clutch hydraulic pipe from the fluid reservoir **(see illustration)**. Tape over or plug the outlet.

5 Place cloth rags beneath the fluid reservoir then carefully prise it from the top of the master cylinder and withdraw from the engine compartment. If necessary, prise the reservoir seals from the top of the cylinder.

6 Identify the brake lines for position, then unscrew the union nuts and move the lines to one side. Tape over or plug the line outlets.

7 Unscrew the mounting nuts and withdraw the master cylinder **(see illustration)** from the front of the vacuum servo. Recover the seal. Take care not to spill fluid on the vehicle paintwork.

Overhaul

8 At the time of writing, master cylinder overhaul is not possible as no spares are available.

9 The only parts available individually are the fluid reservoir, its mounting seals, the filler cap and the master cylinder mounting seal.

10 If the master cylinder is worn excessively, it must be renewed.

Refitting

11 Ensure that the mating surfaces are clean and dry then fit the new seal to the rear of the master cylinder.

12 Fit the master cylinder to the servo unit, ensuring that the servo unit pushrod enters the master cylinder piston centrally. Fit the retaining nuts and tighten them to the specified torque setting.

13 Refit the brake lines and tighten the union nuts securely.

14 Smear a little brake fluid on the rubber seals in the top of the master cylinder, then press the fluid reservoir firmly into the seals.

15 On manual transmission models, reconnect the clutch hydraulic pipe and tighten the clip.

16 Refit the relay box to the hydraulic modulator.

17 Reconnect the wiring connector to the brake fluid level sender unit and refit the reservoir cap.

18 Top-up the reservoir with fresh hydraulic fluid to the MAX mark (see *Weekly checks*).

19 Bleed the hydraulic systems as described in Section 2 and Chapter 6 then refit the filler cap. Thoroughly check the operation of the brakes and clutch before using the vehicle on the road.

14 Brake pedal – removal and refitting

Note: *The brake pedal and bracket incorporates a safety feature. In the event of a frontal collision, the pedal is released from the bracket to protect the driver's foot and leg from injury.*

Removal

1 Remove the vacuum servo unit as described in Section 15.

2 Remove the stop-light switch from the pedal bracket by turning it through 180° (refer to Section 20). If preferred, leave the wiring connected and position the switch to one side.

3 Unbolt the brake pedal assembly from the bulkhead and support bracket. Withdraw the pedal assembly from inside the vehicle.

4 It is not possible to renew the pedal separately from the bracket, therefore if the pedal or bearings are worn excessively, the complete pedal and bracket must be renewed.

Refitting

5 Locate the pedal assembly on the bulkhead, then insert and tighten the bolts.

6 Refit the stop-light switch to the bracket.

7 Refit the vacuum servo unit as described in Section 15.

8 Check the operation of the brake pedal and stop-light switch before using the vehicle on the road.

15 Vacuum servo unit – testing, removal and refitting

Testing

1 To test the operation of the servo unit, with the engine off, depress the footbrake several times to exhaust the vacuum. Now start the engine, keeping the pedal firmly depressed. As the engine starts, there should be a noticeable 'give' in the brake pedal as the vacuum builds-up. Allow the engine to run for at least two minutes, then switch it off. The brake pedal should now feel normal, but further applications should result in the pedal feeling firmer, the pedal stroke decreasing with each application.

2 If the servo does not operate as described, first inspect the servo unit check valve as described in Section 16.

3 If the servo unit still fails to operate satisfactorily, the fault lies within the unit itself. Repairs to the unit are not possible; if faulty, the servo unit must be renewed.

Removal

Right-hand drive models

4 Remove the lower facia trim panel with reference to Chapter 11.

5 Working under the driver's side of the facia, prise out the clip and disconnect the pedal pushrod from the vacuum servo piston.

6 Remove the bonnet and the windscreen front deflector (see Chapter 11 and Chapter 12, Section 16).

7 Remove the air cleaner and duct assembly as described in the appropriate part of Chapter 4.

8 As applicable, unbolt the engine torque support brackets from the right-hand side of the engine.

9 Remove the brake master cylinder as described in Section 13.

10 Prise the vacuum non-return valve or adapter and elbow from the rubber grommet in the vacuum servo **(see illustration)**.

11 Remove the wiper motor as described in Chapter 12.

12 Unscrew the mounting nuts and bolt located on the right-hand side of the bulkhead and beneath the servo.

13 Release the hydraulic brake lines from the clips on the bulkhead, then withdraw the vacuum servo unit from the engine compartment.

Left-hand drive models

14 Remove the lower facia trim panel with reference to Chapter 11.

15 Working under the driver's side of the facia, prise out the locking plate then remove the pivot pin and disconnect the brake pedal from the servo piston rod.

16 Remove the rubber gaiter from the bulkhead.

17 Remove the brake master cylinder as described in Section 13.

18 Where necessary, remove the wiring harness conduit from above the servo unit in the engine compartment.

19 Remove the ABS hydraulic modulator and control unit as described in Section 23. Unbolt the modulator mounting bracket. On some models it may be necessary to disconnect the hydraulic lines from the modulator.

20 Carefully prise the non-return valve or adapter from the rubber grommet in the servo unit.

21 Unscrew the mounting nuts from the bracket and recover the washers, then withdraw the unit forwards and upwards from the engine compartment. On some models it may be necessary to remove the support as well.

Refitting

22 Before refitting the servo, check that the pushrod setting dimension is correct, as follows.

23 Measure the distance from the end face of the servo casing to the end of the pushrod **(see illustrations)**.

24 If adjustment is necessary, slacken the locknut, and turn the pushrod to give the specified dimension. Hold the pushrod and tighten the locknut to the specified torque.

25 Inspect the servo unit check valve sealing grommet for signs of damage or deterioration, and renew if necessary as described in Section 16.

Right-hand drive models

26 Ensure that the servo mounting faces are clean and dry.

27 Locate the servo unit on the bulkhead then refit the mounting nuts and bolt and tighten to the specified torque.

28 Refit the wiper motor (Chapter 12).

29 Refit the non-return valve or adapter and elbow to the rubber grommet in the vacuum servo.

30 Refit the brake master cylinder with reference to Section 13.

31 Refit the hydraulic brake lines in the clips on the bulkhead.

32 Refit the engine torque support brackets and tighten the mounting bolts to the specified torque (see the appropriate part of Chapter 2).

33 Refit the air cleaner and duct assembly with reference to the appropriate part of Chapter 4.

15.10 Vacuum hose adapter location in the vacuum servo unit

34 Refit the windscreen front deflector and bonnet (see Chapter 12, Section 16, and Chapter 11).

35 Refit the clip securing the pedal pushrod to the vacuum servo piston.

36 Refit the lower facia trim panel with reference to Chapter 11.

37 Bleed the brake hydraulic system as described in Section 2.

38 On completion, start the engine and check for air leaks at the vacuum hose-to-servo unit connection. Check the operation of the braking system.

Left-hand drive models

39 Ensure that the servo mounting faces are clean and dry.

40 Locate the servo on the bulkhead and align with the pedal pushrod, then refit the mounting nuts and tighten to the specified torque.

41 Refit the non-return valve or adapter in the rubber grommet.

42 Refit the ABS hydraulic modulator and control unit, together with the mounting bracket, with reference to Section 23. Reconnect the hydraulic lines where necessary.

43 Where necessary, refit the wiring harness conduit.

15.23a Pushrod setting dimension (1) and locknut (2) on RHD models

1 = 152.4 + 0.5 mm

15.23b Pushrod setting dimension (1) and locknut (2) on LHD models

1 = 149.5 + 0.5 mm

17.12 Adjusting the handbrake shoes using a screwdriver through the hole in the disc/flange

44 Refit the brake master cylinder with reference to Section 13.
45 Refit the rubber gaiter to the bulkhead.
46 Reconnect the brake pedal to the servo piston rod and refit the locking plate.
47 Refit the lower facia trim panel with reference to Chapter 11.
48 Bleed the brake hydraulic system as described in Section 2.
49 On completion, start the engine and check for air leaks at the vacuum hose-to-servo unit connection. Check the operation of the braking system.

16 Vacuum servo unit check valve and hose – removal, testing and refitting

Removal

1 Carefully ease the non-return valve or adapter from its rubber grommet on the front of the servo unit.
2 Disconnect the hose from the non-return valve/adapters as necessary and unscrew the union nut from the inlet manifold (petrol engines) or vacuum pump (diesel engines). If the hose is tight it may be necessary to cut it free.

Testing

3 Examine the check valve and hose(s) for signs of damage, and renew if necessary. The valve(s) may be tested by blowing through them in both directions. Air should flow through the valve in one direction only – when blown through from the servo unit end. Renew the valves and hoses as necessary.
4 Examine the servo unit rubber sealing grommet for signs of damage or deterioration, and renew as necessary.

Refitting

5 Refitting is a reversal of removal but make sure that the arrow on the non-return valve points towards the inlet manifold (petrol engines) or vacuum pump (diesel engines). Tighten the union nut on the inlet manifold to the specified torque.
6 On completion, start the engine and check that there are no air leaks.

17.13 Adjustment nut on the handbrake lever

17 Handbrake – adjustment

1 It is only necessary to adjust the handbrake after renewing or dismantling the rear brake shoes, or renewing the drum/disc.

Rear drum brake models

2 Chock the front wheels, then jack up the rear of the vehicle and support on axle stands (see *Jacking and vehicle support*).
3 Fully release the handbrake lever, then apply the footbrake firmly several times to ensure that the self-adjust mechanism is fully adjusted. Apply the handbrake lever to the 7th notch, and check that both rear wheels are locked firmly by attempting to rotate them by hand.
4 If adjustment is necessary, release the gaiter from the centre console and withdraw it over the handbrake lever for access to the adjustment nut.
5 Set the handbrake to the 4th notch, then tighten the adjustment nut on the handbrake lever (on the front of the primary cable) until the rear wheels can just be turned by hand. The braking effect must be the same for each rear wheel.
6 Apply the handbrake lever to the 7th notch and check that both rear wheels are locked firmly. If necessary, repeat the adjustment procedure.
7 Refit the gaiter and lower the vehicle to the ground.

18.6 Handbrake lever mounting nuts (arrowed)

Rear disc brake models

8 Chock the front wheels, then jack up the rear of the vehicle and support on axle stands (see *Jacking and vehicle support*).
9 Fully release the handbrake lever, then apply it to the 7th notch. Check that both rear wheels are locked firmly by attempting to rotate them.
10 If adjustment is necessary, first fully release the handbrake then release the gaiter from the centre console and withdraw it over the handbrake lever for access to the adjustment nut. Back off the nut to the end of the primary cable.
11 Remove both rear wheels.
12 Working on one side at a time, position the hole in the disc over the serrated adjustment nut on the adjuster at the top of the backplate. Using a screwdriver inserted through the hole, turn the nut to lock the disc then back it off until the disc just moves freely **(see illustration)**. Repeat the adjustment on the remaining rear brake.
13 Inside the vehicle, screw on the adjustment nut on the handbrake lever several turns then apply the lever to the 7th notch **(see illustration)**. Check that both rear wheels are firmly locked. If adjustment is necessary, release the handbrake and turn the adjustment nut as required, then recheck the adjustment.
14 After fitting new handbrake shoes, the shoes should be bedded-in by driving a short distance (approximately 300 meters) at low speed with the handbrake lever lightly applied. Check and if necessary adjust the handbrake again after completing the bedding-in.
15 Refit the rear wheels, refit the gaiter to the handbrake lever, and lower the vehicle to the ground.

18 Handbrake lever – removal and refitting

Removal

1 Jack up the vehicle and support on axle stands (see *Jacking and vehicle support*).
2 Remove the exhaust system as described in the appropriate part of Chapter 4.
3 Unbolt and remove the heat shield for access to the handbrake lever compensator. With the handbrake lever fully released, push the compensator forwards and unhook the primary cable from it.
4 Inside the vehicle, remove the centre console and handbrake lever gaiter as described in Chapter 11.
5 Unscrew the adjustment nut from the front end of the primary cable and withdraw the cable from the handbrake lever.
6 Unscrew and remove the lever mounting nuts, then disconnect the wiring from the warning light switch and withdraw the lever from inside the vehicle **(see illustration)**.

7 The handbrake 'on' warning lamp switch can be removed from the lever assembly after unscrewing the securing bolt.

Refitting

8 Refitting is a reversal of removal, but adjust the handbrake as described in Section 17.

19 Handbrake cables – removal and refitting

Removal

1 The handbrake cable consists of three main sections, a short front (primary) section which connects the lever to the equalizer plate and the left- and right-hand rear (secondary) sections which link the equalizer plate to the rear brakes. Short cables connect the rear of the secondary cables to the levers on the rear brake shoes with a special spring clip. Each section can be removed individually as follows.

Primary (front) cable

2 Firmly chock the front wheels, then jack up the rear of the vehicle and support it on axle stands (see *Jacking and vehicle support*).
3 Inside the vehicle, release the gaiter from the centre console and withdraw it over the handbrake lever.
4 With the handbrake lever fully released, unscrew the adjustment nut from the front end of the primary cable.
5 Working beneath the vehicle, remove the rear exhaust system from the catalytic converter as described in the appropriate part of Chapter 4.
6 Unbolt and remove the heat shield from the underbody for access to the handbrake compensator plate.
7 Turn the end stop of the primary cable through 90° and disconnect it from the compensator plate.
8 Disconnect the rubber boot from the underbody, and withdraw the primary cable. Remove the boot from the cable.

Secondary (rear) cable

Note: *The secondary cables are supplied as one part, together with the compensator plate.*
9 Firmly chock the front wheels, then jack up the rear of the vehicle and support it on axle stands (see *Jacking and vehicle support*). Fully release the handbrake lever.
10 Working beneath the vehicle, remove the rear exhaust system from the catalytic converter as described in the appropriate part of Chapter 4.
11 Unbolt and remove the heat shield from the underbody for access to the handbrake compensator plate.
12 Push the compensator plate forwards, then turn the end stop of the primary cable through 90° and disconnect it from the compensator plate.
13 Disconnect the rear of each secondary

cable from the rear cables at the connectors using a small screwdriver to prise them out **(see illustration)**. Examine the connectors and if necessary renew them.
14 Bend up the retaining clips and release the cable assembly from the guides on the underbody.
15 Withdraw the assembly from under the vehicle.

Rear cable

16 Firmly chock the front wheels, then jack up the rear of the vehicle and support it on axle stands (see *Jacking and vehicle support*). Fully release the handbrake lever.
17 Disconnect the rear cable from the connector using a small screwdriver to prise out the end fitting. Examine the connector and if necessary renew it.
18 Unhook the cable from the rear brake shoe lever.
19 If necessary, remove the rubber boot from the lever.

Refitting

20 Refitting is a reversal of the removal procedure, but adjust the handbrake as described in Section 17.

20 Stop-light switch – removal, refitting and adjustment

Removal

1 The stop-light switch is located on the pedal bracket in the driver's footwell.
2 To remove the switch, first remove the lower facia trim panel (see Chapter 11), then disconnect the heating duct for access to the switch.
3 Disconnect the wiring plug from the top of the switch, then twist the switch through 180° and remove it from the pedal bracket.

Refitting and adjustment

4 Before refitting the switch, push the actuation pin fully in.
5 Fit the switch into the pedal bracket and turn through 180° to secure.
6 Depress the brake pedal then pull the actuation pin fully out of the switch so that it contacts the pedal. Now release the pedal to set the pin.
7 Refit the heating duct and the lower facia trim panel. Check the operation of the stop-light.

21 Handbrake 'on' warning light switch – removal and refitting

Removal

1 Unclip the handbrake lever gaiter from the centre console and withdraw it over the handbrake lever.

19.13 Cable connector at the rear of the secondary cable

2 Disconnect the wiring then unscrew the mounting bolt and remove the switch from the handbrake lever bracket **(see illustration)**.

Refitting

3 Refitting is a reversal of removal.

22 Anti-lock Braking and Traction Control systems – general information

ABS is fitted as standard to all models. Traction control is fitted to certain models.

The ABS system comprises a hydraulic modulator and electronic control unit together with four roadwheel sensors. The hydraulic modulator contains the electronic control unit (ECU), the hydraulic solenoid valves (one set for each brake) and the electrically-driven pump. The purpose of the system is to prevent the wheel(s) locking during heavy braking. This is achieved by automatic release of the brake on the relevant wheel, followed by re-application of the brake.

The solenoid valves are controlled by the ECU, which itself receives signals from the four wheel sensors which monitor the speed of rotation of each wheel. By comparing these signals, the ECU can determine the speed at which the vehicle is travelling. It can then use this speed to determine when a wheel is decelerating at an abnormal rate, compared to the speed of the vehicle, and therefore predicts when a wheel is about to lock. During normal operation, the system functions in the same way as a non-ABS braking system.

21.2 Disconnect the wiring (arrowed) from the handbrake 'on' warning light switch

23.12a ABS hydraulic modulator and pipes (models with traction control)

23.12b Hydraulic line connections to the modulator (models with traction control)

If the ECU senses that a wheel is about to lock, it operates the relevant solenoid valve(s) in the hydraulic unit, which then isolates from the master cylinder the relevant brake(s) on the wheel(s) which is/are about to lock, effectively sealing-in the hydraulic pressure.

If the speed of rotation of the wheel continues to decrease at an abnormal rate, the ECU operates the electrically-driven pump which pumps the hydraulic fluid back into the master cylinder, releasing the brake. Once the speed of rotation of the wheel returns to an acceptable rate, the pump stops, and the solenoid valves switch again, allowing the hydraulic master cylinder pressure to return to the caliper/wheel cylinder (as applicable), which then re-applies the brake. This cycle can be carried out many times a second.

The action of the solenoid valves and return pump creates pulses in the hydraulic circuit. When the ABS system is functioning, these pulses can be felt through the brake pedal.

On some models, the ABS the hydraulic unit incorporates an additional set of solenoid valves which operate the traction control system. The system operates at speeds up to approximately 30 mph (60 km/h) using the signals supplied by the wheel sensors. If the ECU senses that a driving wheel is about to lose traction, it prevents this by momentarily applying the relevant front brake.

The operation of the ABS and the traction control system is entirely dependent on electrical signals. To prevent the system responding to any inaccurate signals, a built-in safety circuit monitors all signals received by the ECU. If an inaccurate signal or low battery voltage is detected, the system is automatically shut down, and the warning light on the instrument panel is illuminated, to inform the driver that the system is not operational. Normal braking is still available, however.

If a fault develops in the ABS/traction control system, the vehicle must be taken to a Vauxhall/Opel dealer for fault diagnosis and repair.

23 Anti-lock Braking and Traction Control system components – removal and refitting

Note: *Faults on the ABS system may be diagnosed by Vauxhall/Opel technicians using special diagnostic equipment not available to the home mechanic.*

Hydraulic modulator and ECU

Models without traction control

1 Remove the battery as described in Chapter 5A.

2 Remove the relay box and bracket from the hydraulic modulator.

3 Unscrew and remove the filler cap from the brake fluid reservoir, then draw out all of the hydraulic fluid using a poultry baster or old battery hydrometer.

4 Disconnect the special multiplug from the top of the hydraulic modulator by lifting the clip and unhooking the multiplug.

5 Unscrew the union nuts securing the hydraulic lines to the master cylinder and modulator and withdraw the lines a little way. Ideally, a special split ring spanner should be used to unscrew the nuts as they may be tight. Note the different thread sizes of the union nuts. Be prepared for some loss of fluid by placing cloth rags beneath the lines. Tape over or plug the ends of the lines and the fluid apertures to prevent entry of dust and dirt.

6 Unscrew and remove the mounting bolts, then withdraw the modulator and control unit upwards from the engine compartment. Take care not to spill any hydraulic fluid on the vehicle's paintwork.

7 Refitting is a reversal of removal, but finally bleed the hydraulic systems as described in Section 2 and Chapter 6.

Models with traction control

8 Disconnect the battery negative (earth) lead (see Chapter 5A).

9 Remove the relay box from the hydraulic modulator.

10 Unscrew and remove the filler cap from the brake fluid reservoir, then draw out all of the hydraulic fluid using a poultry baster or old battery hydrometer.

11 On left-hand drive models, remove the brake master cylinder completely as described in Section 13.

12 Unscrew the union nuts securing the hydraulic lines to the modulator and withdraw the lines a little way **(see illustrations)**. Ideally, a special split ring spanner should be used to unscrew the nuts as they may be tight. Note the different thread sizes of the union nuts. Be prepared for some loss of fluid by placing cloth rags beneath the lines. Tape over or plug the ends of the lines and the fluid apertures to prevent entry of dust and dirt.

13 Unscrew the modulator mounting nuts, and also unbolt the earth cable.

14 Disconnect the special multiplug from the top of the hydraulic modulator by lifting the clip and unhooking the multiplug. Also disconnect the wiring from the ABS control unit.

15 On the ABS 5/TC system, unclip the coolant expansion tank from its mounting and position it to one side.

16 Withdraw the modulator together with the control unit, while carefully pushing the hydraulic lines to one side.

17 Refitting is a reversal of removal, but finally bleed the hydraulic systems as described in Section 2 and Chapter 6.

Wheel sensor

Removal

18 To remove the rear wheel sensor, remove the wheel hub as described in Chapter 10. The complete rear wheel hub must be renewed in the event of a fault in the sensor.

19 To remove the front wheel sensor, first apply the handbrake, then jack up the front of the vehicle and support it on axle stands (see

23.21a Unscrew the bolt using a Torx key . . .

23.21b . . . and remove the wheel sensor

24.1 The vacuum pump is on the left-hand end of the cylinder head

Jacking and vehicle support). Remove the relevant roadwheel.

20 Disconnect the sensor wiring and release it from the clips on the front suspension strut and wheel arch.

21 Unscrew the mounting bolt using a Torx key and remove the sensor from the mounting bracket **(see illustrations)**. If necessary, the bracket may be unbolted from the hub carrier.

Refitting

22 Refitting is a reversal of removal, but tighten the mounting bolt to the specified torque.

Traction Control switch

Removal

23 Carefully prise the switch from the facia panel, using a small screwdriver. Use card or cloth to prevent damage to the facia.

Refitting

24 Refitting is a reversal of removal.

ABS Control Unit

Removal

25 Remove the hydraulic modulator and electronic control unit as previously described in this Section.

26 Disconnect the wiring then unscrew the mounting bolts and carefully remove the ABS control unit from the hydraulic body taking care not to damage the coil carrier.

27 Recover the seal from between the coil carrier and control unit.

Refitting

28 Insert the new seal, then carefully position the ABS control unit on the body and tighten the bolts to the specified torque in the stages given. **Note:** *Do not tilt the control unit when positioning it on the body.*

29 The remaining procedure is a reversal of the removal procedure; finally, bleed the brake hydraulic systems as described in Section 2 and Chapter 6.

24 Vacuum pump (diesel engine models) – removal and refitting

Removal

1 The vacuum pump is bolted directly to the left-hand end of the cylinder head **(see illustration)**. First, disconnect the air inlet hose from the inlet manifold, and unbolt the support bracket from the engine lifting bracket. Position the hose to one side.

2 Unbolt the engine wiring harness supports and move the harness downwards, away from the vacuum pump.

3 Disconnect the main brake servo vacuum line from the vacuum pump by counterholding the large union nut and unscrewing the small one **(see illustration)**.

4 Disconnect the small vacuum hose from the bottom of the vacuum pump.

5 Unscrew the mounting bolts, taking note of any cable clips/supports fitted beneath them, and withdraw the pump from the cylinder head.

6 Remove the O-ring from the groove in the pump. Discard the O-ring and obtain a new one.

Refitting

7 Refitting is a reversal of removal, but clean the mating faces of the pump and cylinder head, and fit a new O-ring.

24.3 Unscrew the union nut (arrowed) and disconnect the pipe from the vacuum pump

25 Vacuum pump (diesel engine models) – testing and overhaul

Note: *A vacuum gauge will be required for this check.*

1 The operation of the braking system vacuum pump can be checked using a vacuum gauge.

2 Disconnect the vacuum pipe from the pump, and connect the gauge to the pump union using a suitable length of hose.

3 Start the engine and allow it to idle, then measure the vacuum created by the pump. As a guide, after one minute, a minimum of approximately 500 mm Hg should be recorded. If the vacuum registered is significantly less than this, it is likely that the pump is faulty. However, seek the advice of a Vauxhall/Opel dealer before condemning the pump.

4 Overhaul of the vacuum pump is not possible, since no components are available separately for it. If faulty, the complete pump assembly must be renewed.

Notes

Chapter 10
Suspension and steering

Contents

Degrees of difficulty

Easy, suitable for novice with little experience	**Fairly easy,** suitable for beginner with some experience	**Fairly difficult,** suitable for competent DIY mechanic	**Difficult,** suitable for experienced DIY mechanic	**Very difficult,** suitable for expert DIY or professional

Specifications

General

Front suspension type	Independent, with MacPherson struts, gas-filled shock absorbers and anti-roll bar
Rear suspension type	Independent, with trailing arms, coil springs, gas-filled shock absorbers, upper and lower transverse arms and anti-roll bar
Steering type	Rack and pinion. Power steering standard on all models

Rear wheel bearings

Bearing radial run-out	0.05 mm
Bearing play (maximum)	0.3 mm
Bearing lateral run-out	0.05 mm

Front wheel alignment

Camber	–1°05' ± 45'
Max difference between sides	1°
Castor (non-adjustable):	
Saloon and Estate	+3°40' ± 1°
Max difference between sides	1°
Toe in	+0°10' ± 10'
Toe-in on turns (inner wheel turned in 20°)	1°10' ± 45'

Rear wheel alignment

Camber:	
Saloon	–1°27' ± 35'
Estate	–1°19' ± 35'
Max. difference between sides	0°35'
Toe in:	
Saloon	+0°27' ± 10'
Estate	+0°26' ± 10'
Max difference between sides	0°15'

Steering
Ratio . . . .   16.5 : 1

Wheels and tyres
Wheel size . . . .   6J x 15, 6J x 16 or 7J x 17
Tyre size:
  6J x 15 wheels . . . .   195/65 R15-91 T, 195/65 R15-91 H, 195/65 R15-91 V, 205/60 R15-91 V
  6J x 16 wheels . . . .   205/55 R16-91 V
  7J x 17 wheels (lowered suspension) . . . .   215/45 ZR17-91 W

Torque wrench settings

	Nm	lbf ft
Front suspension		
Anti-roll bar link:		
To strut	65	48
To anti-roll bar	65	48
Anti-roll bar to subframe	20	15
Brake splash guard	4	3
Fluid line to steering gear	28	21
Lower arm to subframe:		
Stage 1	90	66
Stage 2	Angle-tighten a further 75°	
Stage 3	Angle-tighten a further 15°	
Lower balljoint to hub carrier	100	74
Lower balljoint to lower arm	35	26
Strut to hub carrier:		
Stage 1	50	37
Stage 2	90	66
Stage 3	Angle-tighten a further 45°	
Stage 4	Angle-tighten a further 15°	
Strut upper mounting	55	41
Subframe:		
Bolts 1, 3, 4 and 5 (ie, all except engine mountings):		
Stage 1	100	74
Stage 2	Angle-tighten a further 45°	
Stage 3	Angle-tighten a further 15°	
Bolt 2 (ie, engine mountings)	60	44
Support bearing to shock absorber piston rod	70	52
Track rod end locknut	100	74
Track rod end to hub carrier	60	44
Rear suspension		
Anti-roll bar	55	41
Hub bracket to trailing arm:		
Stage 1	50	37
Stage 2	Angle-tighten a further 30°	
Stage 3	Angle-tighten a further 15°	
Lower arm to trailing arm and subframe:		
Stage 1	90	66
Stage 2	Angle-tighten a further 60°	
Stage 3	Angle-tighten a further 15°	
Shock absorber upper retaining nut	20	15
Strut to trailing arm:		
Stage 1	150	111
Stage 2	Angle-tighten a further 30°	
Stage 3	Angle-tighten a further 15°	
Strut upper mounting bracket to body	55	41
Subframe to underbody:		
Stage 1	90	66
Stage 2	Angle-tighten a further 60°	
Stage 3	Angle-tighten a further 15°	
Trailing arm front mounting bracket to underbody:		
Stage 1	90	66
Stage 2	Angle-tighten a further 30°	
Stage 3	Angle-tighten a further 15°	

Torque wrench settings (continued)

	Nm	lbf ft
Rear suspension (continued)		
Trailing arm to front mounting bracket:		
Stage 1	90	66
Stage 2	Angle-tighten a further 60°	
Stage 3	Angle-tighten a further 15°	
Upper arm to trailing arm and subframe:		
Stage 1	90	66
Stage 2	Angle-tighten a further 60°	
Stage 3	Angle-tighten a further 15°	
Steering		
Airbag unit to steering wheel	8	6
Fluid pressure line:		
To ancillary component support	7	5
To power steering pump:		
Petrol engines:		
Except Z22SE	38	28
Z22SE	28	21
Diesel engines	35	26
Fluid return line to reservoir	3	2
Power steering pump mounting (Z22SE)	25	18
Power steering pump pulley:		
Petrol engines:		
Stage 1	20	15
Stage 2	Angle-tighten a further 30°	
Stage 3	Angle-tighten a further 45°	
Diesel engines	20	15
Power steering pump tensioner	40	30
Power steering pump to ancillary component support (except Z22SE) .	25	18
Power steering pump to bracket (except Z22SE)	20	15
Rear engine mounting bracket to subframe	20	15
Steering column brace upper nut	22	16
Steering column intermediate shaft clamp bolt:		
Stage 1	22	16
Stage 2	Angle-tighten a further 45°	
Stage 3	Angle-tighten a further 15°	
Steering column to bulkhead	22	16
Steering gear to subframe	45	33
Steering wheel	20	15
Track rod end:		
To track rod	60	44
To hub carrier	60	44
Track rod to steering gear rack:		
Saginaw	100	74
Servotronic	80 ± 8	59 ± 6
Wheels		
All models	110	81

1 General information and precautions

General information

The front suspension is of independent type, with a subframe, MacPherson struts, lower arms, and an anti-roll bar. The struts, which incorporate coil springs and integral gas-filled shock absorbers, are attached at their upper ends to the reinforced strut mountings on the body shell. The lower end of each strut is bolted to the top of a cast hub carrier, which carries the hub, the brake disc and caliper. The hubs run within non-adjustable bearings in the hub carriers. The lower end of each hub carrier is attached, via a balljoint, to a pressed-steel lower arm assembly. The balljoints are bolted to the lower arms and attached to the hub carriers by a clamp bolt. Each lower arm is attached at its inboard end to the subframe with flexible rubber bushes, and controls both lateral and fore-and-aft movement of the front wheels. The anti-roll bar is mounted on the subframe, and is connected to the suspension struts by vertical drop links.

The rear suspension is of fully independent type, with a central crossmember, gas-filled shock absorbers incorporating coil springs, trailing arms, upper and lower transverse arms, and an anti-roll bar. The shock absorbers are attached at their upper ends to tower units located in the wheelarches; this design reduces the transfer of noise to the rear interior of the vehicle. The rear hub/stub axles are bolted to the trailing arms. The trailing arms and upper and lower transverse arms are located with flexible rubber bushes. The anti-roll bar is mounted on the central subframe, and is connected to the trailing arms by drop links. A rear suspension automatic self-levelling control system is fitted to certain Estate models.

1.3 Steering gear and column components

The steering is of conventional rack-and-pinion type, incorporating a collapsible safety column **(see illustration)**. The column is joined to the steering gear by an intermediate shaft incorporating two universal joints. The upper section of the column includes an outer slip coupling into which the steering lock engages. With the steering lock engaged, the coupling allows the column to turn at torques above 200 Nm (147 lbf ft) only, so making it impossible to break the steering lock shear pin. However, at this torque it is not possible to control the vehicle. The steering gear is mounted on the front suspension subframe. The steering gear track rods are attached to the steering arms on the hub carriers by track rod ends.

All models are fitted with power-assisted steering. On all engines except the Z22SE, the power steering pump is belt-driven from the crankshaft pulley; on the Z22SE it is driven from the left-hand end of the camshaft. The fluid reservoir is either incorporated in the pump or located remotely according to model.

As from June 1999, models with alloy wheels have 5-bolt fixing, however all other models remain with 4-bolt wheels.

Precautions

An airbag is fitted to the steering wheel. To ensure it operates correctly should it ever be needed, and to avoid the risk of personal injury from it being accidentally triggered, the following precautions must be observed. Also refer to Chapter 12 for more information:

a) *Before carrying out any operations on the airbag system, disconnect the battery negative terminal, and wait at least 1 minute to ensure that the system capacitor has been discharged.*

b) *Note that the airbag must not be subjected to temperatures in excess of 80°C (176°F). When the airbag is removed, ensure that it is stored with the pad facing upwards.*

c) *Do not allow any solvents or cleaning agents to contact the airbag assembly. The unit must be cleaned using only a damp cloth.*

d) *The airbag and control unit are both sensitive to impact. If either is dropped from a height of more than 50 cm (20 in), they must be renewed.*

e) *Disconnect the airbag control unit wiring plug prior to using arc-welding equipment on the vehicle.*

f) *On vehicles fitted with a passenger airbag, **do not** fit accessories in the airbag zone. Items like telephones, cassette storage boxes, additional mirrors, etc, can be ripped off and cause serious injury if the airbag inflates.*

2.5 Tie the brake caliper to the coil spring while removing the front hub carrier

g) *Note: The action of simply disconnecting and re-connecting any part of the airbag control system's wiring - even if no other work is done on any of the system's components - may cause the airbag warning light to illuminate. This will require the system to be re-set by a Vauxhall dealer.*

2 Front hub carrier – removal and refitting

Note: *It is recommended that all mounting nuts and bolts are renewed. A balljoint separator tool will be required for this operation.*
Caution: The front wheel camber setting is controlled by the bolts securing the hub carrier to the front suspension strut. Before removing the bolts, mark the hub carrier in relation to the strut accurately. On completion, the camber setting must be checked and adjusted by a suitably-equipped garage.

Removal

1 Apply the handbrake, then jack up the front of the vehicle and support it on axle stands (see *Jacking and vehicle support*). Remove the relevant front wheel.
2 Unscrew the nut securing the track rod end to the steering arm on the hub carrier. Using a balljoint separator, separate the track rod end from the steering arm.
3 Unscrew and remove the clamp bolt securing the front suspension lower arm balljoint in the hub carrier, noting which way round it is fitted.
4 Using a suitable lever, push down the lower arm and separate it from the hub carrier. When releasing the lower arm, take care not to damage the balljoint rubber boot on the bottom of the hub carrier; if necessary protect it with a piece of card or plastic. **Note:** *If the balljoint stub is tight in the hub carrier, use a screwdriver or cold chisel as a wedge to force the clamp apart.*
5 Remove the brake caliper with reference to Chapter 9, however, do not disconnect the hydraulic line from it. Tie the caliper to the coil on the front suspension strut using a length of wire or string **(see illustration)**.
6 Unscrew the mounting bolt and remove the wheel speed sensor from the top of the hub carrier. Tie it to one side.
7 Carefully tap the protective cap from the centre of the hub, then extract the split pin and unscrew the driveshaft retaining nut while holding the hub stationary with a bar positioned between two wheel bolts temporarily refitted to the hub. **Note:** *The nut is tightened to a high torque.* Remove the nut and spacer.
8 Pull the hub carrier out while pressing the driveshaft through the hub. If it is tight use a suitable puller.
9 Mark the position of the strut on the hub carrier. **Note:** *This is important to maintain the camber setting.*

2.10a The hub carrier-to-strut nuts face towards the rear

2.10b Removing the bolts securing the hub carrier to the strut

2.10c Withdrawing the hub from the driveshaft

10 Unscrew and remove the two bolts securing the hub carrier to the strut noting which way round they are fitted. Now lift the hub carrier from under the front wing while withdrawing the hub from the driveshaft **(see illustrations)**. If necessary, use a soft-faced mallet to drive the driveshaft through the hub.
11 Undo the screw and remove the front brake disc from the hub drive flange.
12 Undo the screws and remove the splash guard from the hub carrier **(see illustration)**.

Refitting

13 Refit the splash guard to the hub carrier and tighten the screws.
14 Refit the front brake disc to the hub drive flange and tighten the screw.
15 Ensure that the driveshaft outer constant velocity joint and hub splines are clean, then apply a little grease to the splines.
16 Lift the hub carrier into position and locate the hub on the splines on the end of the driveshaft. Locate the top of the hub carrier on the strut and insert the bolts making sure that the bolt heads are facing the front of the vehicle. With the hub carrier positioned as noted previously, tighten the bolts to the specified torque. If new components are being fitted, loosely tighten the bolts at this stage, and adjust the camber before using the vehicle on the road.
17 Refit the driveshaft retaining nut and spacer and hand-tighten the nut at this stage.
18 Refit the wheel speed sensor to the top of the hub carrier and tighten the mounting nut to the specified torque (see Chapter 9).
19 Refit the brake caliper with reference to Chapter 9.
20 Using a lever, push down the lower suspension arm then locate the balljoint in the bottom of the hub carrier and push the balljoint fully upwards. Insert the clamp bolt with its head facing to the rear and tighten to the specified torque.
21 Refit the track rod end to the steering arm and tighten the nut to the specified torque.
22 Refit the front wheel and lower the vehicle to the ground.
23 Fully tighten the driveshaft retaining nut to the specified torque in the stages given in the Specifications (see Chapter 8). Check that the castellated nut is aligned with the hole in the

driveshaft – if necessary, loosen the nut slightly to the next castellation. Fit a new split pin and bend over its ends to secure.
24 Tap the protective cap on the centre of the hub.
25 Check and if necessary adjust the camber angle setting at the earliest opportunity.

3 Front wheel bearings – checking and renewal

Note: *A press, a suitable puller, or similar improvised tools will be required for this operation. Obtain a bearing overhaul kit before proceeding. A new bearing retaining circlip should be used on refitting.*

Checking

1 To check the front wheel bearings for wear, apply the handbrake then jack up the front of the vehicle and support it on axle stands (see *Jacking and vehicle support*). Spin the wheel by hand and check for a noisy or rough bearing. Grip the wheel and rock it to check for excessive play in the bearing, however be careful not to confuse wear in the suspension or steering joints with wear in the bearing.

Renewal

2 With the hub carrier removed as described in Section 2, proceed as follows.
3 The hub must now be removed from the bearing/hub carrier assembly. It is preferable to use a press to do this, but it is possible to drive out the hub using a metal tube of

2.12 Front splash guard retaining screws

suitable diameter. Alternatively a suitable puller can be used.
4 Securely support the hub carrier, with the inner face uppermost then, using a metal bar or tube of suitable diameter, press or drive the hub from the hub bearing. Alternatively, use the puller to separate the hub from the bearing. Note that bearing inner race will remain on the hub.
5 Using a suitable puller, pull the half inner bearing race from the hub. Alternatively, support the bearing race on suitably thin metal bars, and press or drive the hub from the bearing race.
6 Remove the bearing retaining circlip from the inner face of the hub carrier – discard the circlip, a new one must be used on refitting.
7 Temporarily refit the half inner bearing race to the bearing, making sure that the bearing cage and the seal are in position then, using a puller, pull the bearing from the hub carrier, applying pressure to the inner race. Alternatively, support the hub carrier, and press or drive out the bearing.
8 Before fitting the new bearing, thoroughly clean the bearing location in the hub carrier.
9 Using a press or a suitable puller, fit the new bearing to the hub carrier. The outer face of the bearing should contact the shoulder in the hub carrier. It may be possible to improvise a suitable puller using a socket, nut, washers, and length of threaded bar.
10 Fit a new bearing retaining clip to the inner face of the hub carrier.
11 Press or draw the hub into the bearing. The bearing inner track must be supported during this operation. This can be achieved using a socket, nut washers, and a length of threaded bar.
12 Refit the hub carrier as described in Section 2.

4 Front subframe – removal and refitting

Note: *Vauxhall/Opel technicians use special jigs to ensure that the engine/transmission is correctly aligned. Without the use of these tools it is important to note the position of the engine/transmission accurately before removal.*

4.20a Front subframe side mounting bolt

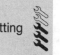

4.20b Subframe rear mounting bracket

Removal

1 Set the front wheels in the straight-ahead position, then remove the ignition key and lock the column by turning the steering wheel as required. Unlike earlier models which locked in the straight-ahead position, models from 1999 Model Year lock in a different position due to a modified intermediate shaft. Right-hand drive models lock with the steering wheel approximately 5° anti-clockwise, and left-hand drive models lock with the steering wheel approximately 45° clockwise.

2 In the driver's footwell, unscrew the bolt securing the bottom of the steering column intermediate shaft to the steering gear pinion. Pull the shaft from the pinion and position to one side.

3 Syphon all the fluid from the power steering fluid reservoir.

4 On manual transmission models, disconnect the gearchange rod from the transmission with reference to Chapter 7A. If preferred, the linkage can be disconnected at the bracket on the steering rack.

5 On petrol models, disconnect the oxygen sensor wiring and position to one side.

6 Connect a hoist to the engine/transmission assembly and support its weight. If available, the type of support bar which locates in the engine compartment side channels is to be preferred, as this will ensure correct repositioning during refitting.

7 Remove the radiator grille (Chapter 11) then use cable-ties to tie the radiator to the air deflector panel/crossmember on the front of the engine compartment.

8 Remove the front bumper as described in Chapter 11.

9 Apply the handbrake, then jack up the front of the vehicle and support it on axle stands (see *Jacking and vehicle support*). Remove both front wheels.

10 Unscrew the nuts and disconnect the anti-roll bar links from the struts on both sides. Use a further spanner to hold the studs while the nuts are being loosened.

11 Disconnect the steering track rod ends from the hub carriers by unscrewing the nuts and using a balljoint separator tool.

12 Unscrew and remove the clamp bolts securing the front suspension lower arm balljoints in the hub carriers, noting which way round they are fitted.

13 Using a suitable lever, push down the lower arms and separate them from the hub carriers. When releasing the lower arms, take care not to damage the balljoint rubber boots on the bottom of the hub carriers; if necessary protect them with a piece of card or plastic. **Note:** *If the balljoint stub is tight in the hub carrier, use a screwdriver or cold chisel as a wedge to force the clamp apart.*

14 Remove the front exhaust downpipe as described in the appropriate part of Chapter 4.

15 Unscrew the three bolts securing the rear engine mounting bracket to the transmission. If preferred, the bracket can be unbolted from the subframe.

16 On models with air conditioning, disconnect the coolant lines from the subframe.

17 Release the clips and disconnect the power steering lines from the right-hand side of the subframe.

18 Ideally, support the engine/transmission with a cradle on a trolley jack. Alternatively, two trolley jacks and the help of two assistants will be required.

19 Unscrew the bolts securing the transmission front mounting to the subframe. On petrol engine models, also unscrew the bolt securing the right-hand front mounting to the subframe.

20 Unscrew the subframe mounting bolts – note that the rear mounting brackets must be unbolted from the underbody **(see illustrations)**. Slightly lower the subframe until the power steering gear fluid lines can be unscrewed and detached from the steering gear. Place a suitable container beneath the steering gear to catch the fluid. Tape over or plug the lines to prevent entry of dust and dirt then tie them to one side.

21 Lower the subframe to the ground. Remove the lower suspension arms with reference to Section 7, the anti-roll bar with reference to Section 6, the rear engine mounting with reference to the appropriate part of Chapter 2, and the steering gear with reference to Section 21.

Refitting

22 Refitting is a reversal of removal, but tighten all nuts and bolts to the specified torque where necessary in the stages given. Make sure that the alignment holes in the subframe and underbody are correctly aligned before fully tightening the mounting bolts.

---

5 Front suspension strut – removal, overhaul and refitting

Note: *A balljoint separator tool will be required for this operation. Ideally, both front suspension struts should be renewed at the same time in order to maintain good steering and suspension characteristics. It is recommended that all mounting nuts and bolts are renewed.*

Removal

1 Apply the handbrake, then jack up the front of the vehicle and support it on axle stands (see *Jacking and vehicle support*). Remove the front wheel.

2 Unscrew the nut and disconnect the anti-roll bar link from the strut. Use a spanner on the special flats to hold the link while the nut is being loosened.

3 Pull out the clip and disconnect the brake hose from the bracket on the strut.

4 Unclip the brake pad wiring harness from the strut **(see illustration)**.

5 Mark the position of the strut on the hub carrier. This is important to maintain the camber setting.

6 Unscrew and remove the two bolts securing the hub carrier to the strut noting which way round they are fitted. With the two bolts removed, pull the hub carrier away from the strut and support on an axle stand **(see illustrations)**.

5.4 Unclipping the brake pad wiring harness from the strut

5.6a Counterhold the hub carrier-to-strut bolts when loosening the nut . . .

5.6b . . . then remove the bolt

5.6c Pull the hub carrier away from the strut

5.7a Remove the cap . . .

5.7b . . . then unscrew the upper mounting nut while counterholding the piston rod with a further spanner . . .

5.7c . . . and remove the nut . . .

5.7d . . . followed by the upper mounting

7 Support the strut beneath the front wing. In the engine compartment remove the cap then unscrew the strut upper mounting nut while counterholding the piston rod with a further spanner. Recover the upper mounting from the suspension tower (see illustrations).
8 Lower the strut and withdraw from under the front wing (see illustration).

Overhaul

Note: *A spring compressor tool will be required for this operation.*

9 With the suspension strut resting on a bench, or clamped in a vice, fit a spring compressor tool, and compress the coil spring to relieve the pressure on the spring seats. Ensure that the compressor tool is securely located on the spring, in accordance with the tool manufacturer's instructions (see illustrations).
10 Counterhold the strut piston rod with a spanner, and unscrew the piston rod nut (see illustration).
11 Remove the upper damping ring with support bearing, upper spring seat, and buffer (see illustrations).
12 Remove the spring from the strut (see illustration).

5.8 Withdrawing the front suspension strut from under the front wing

5.9a The front suspension strut removed from the vehicle

5.9b Make sure the spring compressor tool is safely fitted to the front coil spring

5.10 Remove the piston rod nut . . .

5.11a . . . upper damping ring and support bearing . . .

5.11b . . . upper spring seat . . .

5.11c . . . and buffer

5.12 Removing the coil spring from the strut

13 With the strut assembly now completely dismantled, examine all the components for wear, damage or deformation, and check the support bearing for smoothness of operation. Renew any of the components as necessary.

14 Examine the strut for signs of fluid leakage. Check the strut piston for signs of pitting along its entire length, and check the strut body for signs of damage. While holding it in an upright position, test the operation of the strut by moving the piston through a full stroke, and then through short strokes of 50 to 100 mm. In both cases, the resistance felt should be smooth and continuous. If the resistance is jerky or uneven or if there is any visible sign of wear or damage to the strut, renewal is necessary.

15 If any doubt exists as to the condition of the coil spring, carefully remove the spring compressors and check the spring for distortion and signs of cracking. Renew the spring if it is damaged or distorted, or if there is any doubt as to its condition.

16 Inspect all other components for damage or deterioration, and renew any that are suspect.

17 With the spring compressed with the compressor tool, locate the spring on the strut making sure that it is correctly seated with its lower end on the raised stop **(see illustration)**.

18 Refit the buffer, upper spring seat, support bearing and upper damping ring.

19 Refit the piston rod nut and tighten it to the specified torque while counterholding the piston rod with a spanner.

5.17 Raised coil spring stop on the front suspension strut

20 Slowly slacken the spring compressor tool to relieve the tension in the spring. Check that the ends of the spring locate correctly against the stops on the spring seats. If necessary, turn the spring and the upper seat so that the components locate correctly before the compressor tool is removed. Remove the compressor tool when the spring is fully seated.

Refitting

21 Refitting is a reversal of removal, bearing in mind the following points.
a) Renew the two bolts securing the hub carrier to the strut, also the piston rod upper nuts.
b) Tighten all nuts and bolts to the specified torque **(see illustration)**.
c) On completion have the camber setting checked and adjusted by a suitably-equipped garage.

5.21 Tightening the front suspension strut upper mounting nut with a torque wrench

6 Front suspension anti-roll bar and links – removal and refitting

Note: *It is recommended that all mounting nuts and bolts are renewed.*

Removal

1 Remove the front subframe as described in Section 4.

2 Identify the links side for side to ensure correct refitting, then unscrew the nuts and remove the links from the front suspension strut and anti-roll bar. Use a spanner on the special flats to hold the links while the nuts are being loosened **(see illustrations)**.

3 Unbolt the clamps securing the anti-roll bar to the subframe **(see illustration)**. **Note:** *If the bolts are rusted in position, they can be cut off*

6.2a Link connection to the anti-roll bar

6.2b Use a spanner to counterhold the anti-roll bar link stub while loosening the nut

6.2c Disconnecting the anti-roll bar link from the front suspension strut

6.3 Front suspension anti-roll bar mounting clamp

7.2 Clamp bolt securing the lower arm to the hub carrier

7.4a Front suspension lower arm front inner mounting bolt . . .

7.4b . . . and rear inner mounting bolt

and drilled out and new inserts fitted. Consult a Vauxhall/Opel dealer for more information.
4 Lift the anti-roll bar from the subframe.
5 Note the position of the rubber bushes, then prise them from the anti-roll bar.
6 Examine the anti-roll bar, links, and rubber bushes for wear and damage and renew them if necessary.

Refitting

7 Refitting is a reversal of removal, but note the following points.
 a) The slits of the rubber bushes must face forwards when fitted to the anti-roll bar.
 b) Tighten all nuts and bolts to the specified torque.
 c) Refit the front subframe with reference to Section 4.

7 Front suspension lower arm – removal, overhaul and refitting

Note: The lower arm inner pivot bolts must be renewed when refitting.

Removal

1 Apply the handbrake, then jack up the front of the vehicle and support it on axle stands (see Jacking and vehicle support). Remove the front wheel.
2 Unscrew and remove the clamp bolt securing the front suspension lower arm balljoint to the bottom of the hub carrier, noting which way round it is fitted **(see illustration)**.
3 Using a suitable lever, push down the lower arm and separate it from the hub carrier. When releasing the lower arm, take care not to damage the balljoint rubber boot on the bottom of the hub carrier; if necessary protect it with a piece of card or plastic. **Note:** If the balljoint stub is tight in the hub carrier, use a screwdriver or cold chisel as a wedge to force the clamp apart.
4 Note that the lower arm inner retaining bolt heads are facing the front of the vehicle. Unscrew and remove the bolts and withdraw the lower arm from the subframe **(see illustrations)**. It will be necessary to slightly press the arms to release the rubber mountings.

Overhaul

5 The lower balljoint may be renewed as described in Section 8. The rubber bushes are a tight fit in the arm and must be pressed out. If a press is not available, the bushes can be drawn out using a long bolt, nut, washers and a socket or length of metal tubing.
6 Prior to fitting the new bushes, coat them with silicone grease or soapy water. Press both bushes fully into the lower arm.

Refitting

7 Locate the lower arm on the subframe and fit the retaining bolts from the front of the vehicle. Hand tighten the bolts at this stage.
8 Locate the lower balljoint stub fully in the bottom of the hub carrier, then refit the clamp bolt and tighten to the specified torque. Make sure the bolt head is facing the front.
9 Refit the front wheel and lower the vehicle to the ground.
10 With the weight of the vehicle on the suspension, tighten the lower arm inner pivot bolts to the specified torque and in the stages given.

8 Front suspension lower balljoint – renewal

Note: The original balljoint is riveted to the lower arm, however service replacements are bolted in position.

1 Remove the front suspension lower arm as described in Section 7. **Note:** If the fitted balljoint is a service replacement, it is not necessary to completely remove the arm but only to disconnect the balljoint from the bottom of the hub carrier then unbolt the old balljoint.
2 Mount the lower arm in a vice, then drill the heads from the three rivets that secure the balljoint to the lower arm, using a 12.0 mm diameter drill **(see illustration)**.
3 If necessary, tap the rivets from the lower arm, then remove the balljoint.
4 Clean any rust from the rivet holes, and apply rust inhibitor.
5 The new balljoint must be fitted using three special bolts, spring washers and nuts, available from a Vauxhall/Opel parts centre.

6 Ensure that the balljoint is fitted the correct way up, noting that the securing nuts are positioned on the underside of the lower arm. Tighten the nuts to the specified torque.
7 Refit the front suspension lower arm as described in Section 7.

9 Rear hub and bracket – removal and refitting

Note: New nuts will be required when refitting the rear hub bracket to the trailing arm.

Removal

1 Remove the rear brake drum or disc as applicable as described in Chapter 9.
2 On the inside of the rear trailing arm, disconnect the wiring for the wheel speed sensor.

8.2 The original lower balljoint is riveted to the lower arm, but service replacements are bolted to the arm

9.3 Rear hub bracket mounting nuts on the trailing arm

3 Support the rear brake backplate and shoes on an axle stand, then support the rear hub and unscrew the mounting nuts on the inside of the trailing arm **(see illustration)**. Withdraw the hub bracket from the rear trailing arm. Note that the locating studs are spaced so that the hub bracket will only fit in one position. If required, the backplate and handbrake shoes may be removed with reference to Chapter 9.

Refitting

4 Where removed, refit the backplate with reference to Chapter 9, then locate the hub bracket in the trailing arm and fit new nuts to secure. Tighten the nuts to the specified torque and angles in the stages given.
5 Reconnect the wiring for the wheel speed sensor.

6 Refit the rear brake drum or disc as applicable as described in Chapter 9. Where necessary, adjust the handbrake as described in Chapter 9.

10 Rear wheel bearings – checking and renewal

1 Chock the front wheels, then jack up the rear of the vehicle and support on axle stands (see *Jacking and vehicle support*). Remove the rear wheels.
2 On models with rear brake drums, remove the drums as described in Chapter 9.
3 A dial test indicator (DTI) or datum bar and feeler blades will be required to measure the amount of play in the bearing. On disc brake models zero the DTI on the brake disc, and on brake drum models zero it on the hub flange. Alternatively, position the datum bar against the surface and use a feeler blade to measure the clearance.
4 Lever the hub in and out and measure the amount of play in the bearing.
5 Now measure the run-out of the bearing by turning the disc or drum flange.
6 The lateral run-out is measured by locating the probe on the outer diameter of the hub centre aperture.
7 If the play or run-out exceeds the specified amounts, renew the hub bearing and bracket as described in Section 9.

11 Rear suspension strut – removal, overhaul and refitting

Note: *A spring compressor tool will be required for this operation. Ideally both rear suspension struts should be renewed at the same time in order to maintain good suspension characteristics. It is recommended that all mounting nuts and bolts are renewed.*

Removal

1 Chock the front wheels, then jack up the rear of the vehicle and support on axle stands (see *Jacking and vehicle support*). Remove the rear roadwheel and support the trailing arm on an axle stand.
2 Remove the liner from under the rear wheelarch.
3 Unscrew and remove the strut lower mounting bolt and disconnect the strut from the trailing arm. Recover the washer from the inner side of the strut **(see illustration)**.
4 Support the strut, then loosen only the two upper mounting bolts and remove the lower mounting bolts securing the strut upper carrier bracket to the inner body panel. Note the location of the bracket on the lower rear bolt **(see illustrations)**.
5 Lift the strut from under the rear wheelarch **(see illustration)**.

Overhaul

Note: *A spring compressor tool is required for this operation. To ensure correct reassembly, note the position of the component parts as they are removed.*

6 With the suspension strut resting on a bench, or clamped in a vice, fit a spring compressor tool, and compress the coil spring to relieve the pressure on the spring seats. Ensure that the compressor tool is securely located on the spring, in accordance with the tool manufacturer's instructions **(see illustration)**.
7 Hold the piston rod stationary with a spanner on the hexagon, then unscrew and remove the nut from the top of the rod **(see illustrations)**.
8 Remove the shock absorber upper cup and bearing followed by the top carrier, lower bearing and sleeve, and lower cup **(see illustrations)**.

11.3 Rear suspension strut lower mounting bolt

11.4a Removing the rear suspension strut lower rear mounting bolt and bracket . . .

11.4b . . . and lower front mounting bolt

11.5 Lower the rear suspension strut from the loosened upper mounting bolts

11.6 Compressor tool fitted to the rear suspension coil spring

11.7a Counterhold the piston rod while loosening the nut . . .

11.7b . . . then remove the nut from the top of the piston rod

11.8a Remove the upper cup . . .

11.8b . . . bearing . . .

11.8c . . . then lift off the top carrier . . .

11.8d . . . and remove the lower bearing and sleeve . . .

9 Remove the buffer from the piston rod then remove the coil spring from the lower seat on the shock absorber **(see illustration)**.

10 Remove the coil spring seat from the top carrier **(see illustration)**.

11 On models fitted with an automatic self-levelling device, also remove the guard tube and damper ring from the shock absorber.

12 Note that the coil spring lower seat cannot be removed from the shock absorber.

13 With the strut assembly now completely dismantled, examine all the components for wear, damage or deformation. Renew the components as necessary.

14 Examine the strut for signs of fluid leakage. Check the strut piston for signs of pitting along its entire length, and check the strut body and carrier for signs of damage. While holding it in an upright position, test the operation of the strut by moving the piston through a full stroke, and then through short strokes of 50 to 100 mm. In both cases, the resistance felt should be smooth and continuous. If the resistance is jerky or uneven or if there is any visible sign of wear or damage to the strut, renewal is necessary.

15 If any doubt exists as to the condition of the coil spring, carefully remove the spring compressors and check the spring for distortion and signs of damage. Renew the spring if necessary.

16 Inspect all other components for damage or deterioration, and renew as necessary.

17 If the spring compressor tool has been removed from the spring, refit it and compress the spring sufficiently to enable it to be refitted to the strut.

18 On models fitted with an automatic self-

levelling device, refit the guard tube and damper ring to the shock absorber.

19 Locate the coil spring seat in the top carrier.

20 Locate the spring onto the shock absorber and position the lower end of the spring in the lower seat indentation.

21 Fit the buffer onto the piston rod.

22 To the shock absorber piston rod, fit the

11.8e . . . lower cup . . .

11.10 Removing the coil spring seat from the top carrier

lower cup followed by the lower bearing and sleeve.

23 Locate the top carrier over the piston rod and onto the coil spring making sure that the end of the coil spring is located in the seat indentation **(see illustration)**.

24 Fit the shock absorber upper bearing and cup.

11.9 . . . and buffer

11.23 Make sure the end of the coil spring is located in the seat indentation

11.27 Location stud for the rear suspension strut top carrier

12.2 Rear anti-roll bar link and bolt securing the link to the trailing arm

12.3 Rear anti-roll bar mounting bolt on the crossmember

25 Fit the nut to the top of the piston rod and tighten to the specified torque while holding the rod with a spanner on the hexagon.

26 Slowly slacken the spring compressor tool to relieve the tension in the spring. Check that the ends of the spring locate correctly against the indentations in the spring seats. Remove the compressor tool when the spring is fully seated.

Refitting

27 Refitting is a reversal of removal, but renew the strut-to-trailing arm lower mounting bolt. Hand-tighten the lower mounting bolt initially and tighten it to the specified torque with the weight of the vehicle on the suspension. The carrier mounting bolts can be fully tightened before lowering the vehicle to the ground but first lift the strut to the ends of the elongated slots in the carrier. Note also the location stud near the rear lower mounting bolt **(see illustration)**.

12 Rear suspension anti-roll bar and links – removal and refitting

Note: *It is recommended that all mounting nuts and bolts are renewed.*

Removal

1 Chock the front wheels, then jack up the rear of the vehicle and support on axle stands (see *Jacking and vehicle support*). Remove the rear wheels.

2 Note the fitted positions of the links, then

unscrew and remove the bolts securing the links to the tops of the trailing arms **(see illustration)**.

3 Unscrew the nuts securing the anti-roll bar support clamps to the crossmember, then tilt the anti-roll bar and withdraw it from under the vehicle **(see illustration)**.

4 Unhook and remove the clamps.

5 Unbolt the links from the anti-roll bar. To ensure correct reassembly, mark the links for position.

6 Remove the rubber mountings from the anti-roll bar.

7 Examine the anti-roll bar, links, and rubber bushes for wear and damage and renew them if necessary.

Refitting

8 Refitting is a reversal of removal, but tighten all nuts and bolts to the specified torque with the weight of the vehicle on the suspension.

13 Rear suspension upper arm – removal, overhaul and refitting

Note: *It is recommended that all mounting nuts and bolts are renewed.*

Removal

1 Chock the front wheels, then jack up the rear of the vehicle and support on axle stands (see *Jacking and vehicle support*). Remove the rear wheel on the relevant side of the vehicle.

2 Release the locking plate, then unscrew the

outer bolt securing the upper arm to the trailing arm **(see illustration)**.

3 Unscrew the inner bolt and withdraw the upper arm from the crossmember and trailing arm **(see illustration)**.

Overhaul

4 To renew the inner rubber bush, grip the arm in a vice then use a long threaded bar, nuts and metal tubing to press the rubber bush from the arm. Alternatively, use a press to remove the bush. Insert a spacer in the arm to prevent it from being crushed while removing the bush.

5 Press the new bush into the arm using the tool used for removal.

6 The outer rubber bush may be removed from the trailing arm with reference to Section 15.

Refitting

7 Refitting is a reversal of removal, but renew the locking plate and do not fully tighten the mounting bolts until the weight of the vehicle is on the suspension. Have the rear wheel toe-in setting checked and if necessary adjusted at the earliest opportunity.

14 Rear suspension lower arm – removal, overhaul and refitting

Note: *It is recommended that all mounting nuts and bolts are renewed.*

Removal

1 Chock the front wheels, then jack up the rear of the vehicle and support on axle stands (see *Jacking and vehicle support*). Remove the rear wheel on the relevant side of the vehicle.

2 Release the locking plate, then unscrew the outer bolt securing the lower arm to the trailing arm **(see illustration)**.

3 Unscrew the inner bolt and withdraw the lower arm from the crossmember and trailing arm **(see illustration)**.

Overhaul

4 To renew the inner rubber bush, grip the arm in a vice then use a long threaded bar, nuts and metal tubing to press the rubber bush from the arm. Alternatively, use a press

13.2 Rear suspension upper arm outer mounting bolt

13.3 Mounting bolts in the crossmember for the rear suspension upper and lower arms

to remove the bush. Insert a spacer in the arm to prevent it from being crushed while removing the bush.

5 Press the new bush into the arm using the tool used for removal.

6 The outer rubber bush may be removed from the trailing arm with reference to Section 15.

Refitting

7 Refitting is a reversal of removal, but renew the locking plate and do not fully tighten the mounting bolts until the weight of the vehicle is on the suspension. Have the rear wheel toe-in setting checked and if necessary adjusted at the earliest opportunity.

15 Rear suspension trailing arm – removal, overhaul and refitting

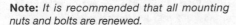

Note: *It is recommended that all mounting nuts and bolts are renewed.*

Removal

1 Chock the front wheels, then jack up the rear of the vehicle and support on axle stands (see *Jacking and vehicle support*). Remove the wheel on the relevant side of the vehicle.

2 With the handbrake released, disconnect the rear cable from the secondary cable by prising the fitting from the special clip.

3 Remove the secondary handbrake cable from the support on the trailing arm.

4 Remove the rear hub and bracket together with the brake backplate as described in Section 9.

5 Unbolt the brake hydraulic line support from the top of the trailing arm.

6 Release the ABS wheel speed sensor wiring from the trailing arm.

7 Unscrew the bolt securing the anti-roll bar link to the trailing arm.

8 Release the locking plates then unscrew the bolts securing the upper and lower arms to the trailing arm. Prise the arms free.

9 Unscrew the bolt securing the bottom of the strut to the trailing arm.

10 Accurately mark the position of the trailing arm front mounting plate on the underbody. This is important since the position of the plate determines the toe-in setting of the rear wheel.

11 Unscrew the front mounting bolts and withdraw the trailing arm from the underbody.

Overhaul

12 If it is required to remove the front mounting bracket from the trailing arm, first determine the rest position of the bracket in relation to the arm by measuring the distance from the rear of the bracket to the arm. Vauxhall/Opel technicians use a special tool to set the bracket position, however if the position of the bracket is noted before removal, the new bracket can be set to the same position.

13 Unscrew the bolt, noting which way round

14.2 Rear suspension lower arm outer mounting bolt

it is fitted, and separate the bracket from the arm.

14 To renew the rubber bushes, grip the arm in a vice then use a long threaded bar, nuts and metal tubing to press out the rubber bushes. Alternatively, use a press to remove the bushes.

15 Press in the new bushes using the tool used for removal.

16 Locate the bracket on the front of the trailing arm, and position it as noted during removal. Tighten the bolt to the specified torque and angle.

Refitting

17 Locate the trailing arm and front bracket on the underbody, and insert the bolts. Position the bracket as noted on removal, then tighten the bolts to the specified torque and angles.

18 Insert the bolt securing the bottom of the strut to the trailing arm and tighten to the specified torque and angles.

19 Locate the upper and lower arms on the trailing arm and insert the retaining bolts loosely at this stage.

20 Refit the anti-roll bar link and tighten the mounting bolt to the specified torque.

21 Attach the ABS wheel speed sensor wiring to the trailing arm.

22 Refit the brake hydraulic line support to the top of the trailing arm and tighten the bolt.

23 Refit the rear hub and bracket together with the brake backplate as described in Section 9.

24 Insert the handbrake secondary cable in the support, then connect the inner cable to

16.7 Trailing arm front mounting plate

14.3 Lower arm inner mounting on the rear crossmember

the rear cable by pressing the end fitting into the special clip.

25 Refit the wheel then lower the vehicle to the ground. Apply the handbrake.

26 With the weight of the vehicle on the suspension, fully tighten the upper and lower arm outer retaining bolts.

27 Have the rear wheel toe-in setting checked and if necessary adjusted at the earliest opportunity.

16 Rear suspension crossmember – removal and refitting

Note: *It is recommended that all mounting nuts and bolts are renewed.*

Removal

1 Chock the front wheels, then jack up the rear of the vehicle and support on axle stands (see *Jacking and vehicle support*). Remove both rear wheels.

2 Remove the rear exhaust system as described in the appropriate part of Chapter 4.

3 Clamp the brake rear hydraulic hoses using hose clamps, or alternatively remove the brake fluid reservoir cap and tighten it down onto a piece of polythene. This will prevent the loss of fluid while the brake lines are disconnected.

4 Unscrew the union nuts attaching the rigid brake lines to the flexible hoses on the trailing arms, then pull out the retaining spring clips and detach the hoses from the supports. Plug the hoses and lines to prevent entry of dust and dirt. Be prepared for some loss of fluid by placing cloth rags or a container beneath the hoses.

5 Disconnect the handbrake secondary cables from the rear cables by prising the cable fittings from the special clip.

6 Disconnect the wiring from the ABS wheel speed sensors on both sides of the vehicle.

7 Accurately mark the positions of the trailing arm front mounting plates on the underbody. This is important since the position of the plates determines the toe-in setting of the rear wheels. Working on each trailing arm in turn, unscrew and remove the bolts securing the arm front brackets to the underbody **(see illustration)**. Support the arms on axle stands.

16.10 Rear suspension crossmember mounting

8 Using a trolley jack, support the weight of the crossmember. If necessary, use a length of wood positioned beneath the crossmember.

9 Unscrew the bolts securing the bottom of the struts to the trailing arms on each side.

10 With the help of an assistant, unscrew the four mounting bolts and carefully lower the crossmember to the floor **(see illustration)**.

11 Remove the upper and lower arms from the crossmember together with the trailing arms and rear hubs, with reference to Sections 13 and 14.

12 Remove the anti-roll bar from the cross-member with reference to Section 12.

Refitting

13 Refitting is a reversal of removal, but note the following points.

a) *Before lifting the crossmember into position, check the condition of the*

captive mounting nuts in the underbody and renew them if necessary.

b) *Delay fully tightening the upper and lower arm inner bolts until the weight of the vehicle is on the suspension.*

c) *Bleed the brake hydraulic system as described in Chapter 9.*

d) *Have the rear wheel toe-in setting checked and if necessary adjusted at the earliest opportunity.*

17 Steering wheel – removal and refitting

Note: *A puller will be required to draw the steering wheel off the column splines. A new retaining nut lockwasher will be required when refitting.*

Models without an airbag

1 Disconnect the battery negative (earth) lead (see Chapter 5A).

2 Set the front wheels in the straight-ahead position, then remove the ignition key and lock the column by turning the steering wheel as required. Unlike earlier models which locked in the straight-ahead position, models from 1999 Model Year lock in a different position due to a modified intermediate shaft. Right-hand drive models lock with the steering wheel approximately 5° anti-clockwise, and left-hand drive models lock with the steering wheel approximately 45° clockwise.

3 Carefully ease the horn button out from the steering wheel, and disconnect its wiring.

4 Using a screwdriver, prise back the tabs on the retaining nut lockwasher.

5 Unscrew the retaining nut, and lift off the lockwasher. Discard the lockwasher; a new one should be used on refitting.

6 Make alignment marks between the steering wheel and steering column shaft.

7 A two-legged puller will now be required to free the steering wheel from its splines. Locate the legs of the puller in the holes in the centre of the wheel, and draw the steering wheel off the column splines. Lift off the steering wheel, and remove the spring from the column shaft.

8 Check that the indicator cancelling lug/horn button contact pad fitted to the rear of steering wheel is in good condition, and if necessary renew it. To release the pad, depress the two clips located inside the steering wheel. Apply a little copper grease to the contact pad before refitting it.

9 Ensure that the indicator switch stalk is in its central (OFF) position. Failure to do this could lead to the steering wheel lug breaking the switch tab as the steering wheel is refitted.

10 Fit the spring to the column, then locate the wheel on the column splines, aligning the marks made on removal.

11 Fit the new lockwasher, and screw on the retaining nut. Tighten the retaining nut to the specified torque, and secure it in position with the lockwasher tabs.

12 Reconnect the wiring connectors to the horn button, and refit the button in the centre of the steering wheel.

13 Reconnect the battery, and check the operation of the horn.

Models with an airbag

 Warning: *Before removing the steering wheel, observe the safety precautions given in Chapter 12 and in Section 1 of this Chapter.*

14 Disconnect the battery negative (earth) lead (see Chapter 5A).

Caution: Wait at least one minute before proceeding. This is necessary to allow the airbag condenser to fully discharge.

15 Set the front wheels in the straight-ahead position, then remove the ignition key and lock the column by turning the steering wheel as required. Unlike earlier models which locked in the straight-ahead position, models from 1999 Model Year lock in a different position due to a modified intermediate shaft. Right-hand drive models lock with the steering wheel approximately 5° anti-clockwise, and left-hand drive models lock with the steering wheel approximately 45° clockwise.

16 Unscrew and remove the two screws from the rear of the steering wheel and carefully lift the airbag/horn-push from the steering wheel. Disconnect the wiring from the airbag **(see illustrations)**. Position the airbag in a safe place where it cannot be tampered with, making sure that the padded side is facing upwards.

17 Where fitted, disconnect the wiring from the radio control switches **(see illustration)**.

17.16a Remove the screws from the steering wheel . . .

17.16b . . . then remove the airbag/horn-push . . .

17.16c . . . and disconnect the wiring

17.17 Disconnect the wiring from the radio control switches

17.18 Prise back the tabs on the retaining nut lockwasher . . .

17.19a . . . then loosen the steering wheel mounting nut . . .

17.19b . . . and remove it . . .

17.19c . . . together with the lockwasher

17.21a Using a two-legged puller to remove the steering wheel from the column

17.21b As the steering wheel is removed, feed the airbag wiring through the hole

18 Using a screwdriver, prise back the tabs on the retaining nut lockwasher **(see illustration)**.

19 Unscrew the retaining nut, and lift off the lockwasher **(see illustrations)**. Discard the lockwasher; a new one should be used on refitting.

20 Make alignment marks between the steering wheel and steering column shaft.

21 A two-legged puller will now be required to free the steering wheel from its splines. Locate the legs of the puller in the holes in the centre of the wheel, and draw the steering wheel off the column splines. Lift off the steering wheel, and remove the spring from the column shaft. As the steering wheel is removed, guide the wiring for the contact unit (and radio control if fitted) through the hole **(see illustrations)**.

22 With the steering wheel removed, do not disturb the contact unit. If necessary hold it in its central position with tape.

Right-hand drive models

23 Check that the contact unit is positioned with the arrows aligned with each other. If it has been disturbed, return it to its central position by depressing the detent and rotating it fully anti-clockwise then clockwise to determine the central position – instructions are given on the unit. The arrows must be aligned with each other before refitting the steering wheel.

24 Offer the steering wheel onto the column splines and guide the wiring for the contact unit (and radio control if fitted) through the hole. Vauxhall/Opel technicians use a special alignment card to ensure the steering wheel is

located 5° anti-clockwise, so that it will be in its straight-ahead position with the steering unlocked and the front wheels straight-ahead.

Left-hand drive models

25 Check that the contact unit is still positioned 40° clockwise from vertical – Vauxhall/Opel technicians use a special alignment card which locates in the shroud mounting screw holes to make this setting. If using the special tool, release the detent and turn the contact unit clockwise to the 40° position.

26 Offer the steering wheel onto the column splines and guide the wiring for the contact unit (and radio control if fitted) through the hole.

All models

27 Ensure that the indicator switch stalk is in its central (OFF) position, then refit the steering wheel to the column, aligning the marks made prior to removal. When locating the steering wheel on the splines, make sure that the contact unit is correctly engaged with both the steering column and indicator switch.

28 Fit the new lockwasher, and screw on the retaining nut. Tighten the retaining nut to the specified torque, and secure it in position with the lockwasher tabs.

29 Reconnect the wiring for the radio control switches where fitted.

30 Refit the airbag/horn-push and reconnect the wiring. Insert the two screws and tighten to the specified torque.

31 Release the steering lock, then reconnect the battery negative lead.

18 Steering column – removal and refitting

Note: *A new shear bolt must be used on refitting.*

Removal

1 Remove the steering wheel as described in Section 17. Alternatively, the steering wheel may remain in position, but it will have to be turned for access to the shroud end face screws.

2 Remove the steering column shrouds by unscrewing the tilt steering lever, then removing the two screws from the end face and three screws from the bottom shroud. Recover the ignition key position indicator from the ignition switch **(see illustrations)**.

18.2a Removing the tilt steering lever

18.2b With the steering wheel turned 90° from the straight-ahead position, undo the end face screws from the shrouds

18.2c Undo the three screws from the bottom of the shrouds

18.2d Removing the upper shroud . . .

18.2e . . . and lower shroud

18.2f Removing the ignition key position indicator

18.8 Clamp securing the intermediate shaft to the bottom of the upper column

3 On models with an airbag remove the contact unit as follows. Using a small screwdriver lift off the locking plate, then disconnect the wiring plug. Release the four rear clips and pull the contact unit from the top of the column. **Note:** *Make sure that the contact unit halves remain in their central position with the arrows aligned at the bottom. If necessary, apply tape to the halves to hold them.*

4 Unclip and remove the turn signal switch and wiper switch (refer to Chapter 12, Section 4, if necessary).

5 Remove the ignition switch and lock cylinder as described in Chapter 12, Section 4.

6 Remove the trim panel from under the driver's side of the facia, then pull out the air distribution duct leading to the heater unit.

7 Remove the screws and withdraw the driver's footwell inner trim panel for access to the steering column support brace. Unscrew the lower bolt and the upper nuts and remove the brace.

8 Mark the intermediate shaft in relation to the upper column. Unscrew and remove the clamp bolt and disconnect the column intermediate shaft from the splines on the bottom of the upper column **(see illustration)**.

9 The upper column mounting is secured with a shear bolt. Drill out the shear using a small cold chisel.

10 Unscrew the remaining mounting bolts and withdraw the steering column from the bulkhead. Remove the column from inside the vehicle.

Refitting

11 Commence refitting by locating the steering column on the bulkhead and inserting the mounting bolts loosely. Screw in the new shear bolt finger-tight.

12 Check that the column is correctly located then tighten the shear bolt until its head breaks off.

13 Slide the intermediate shaft onto the splines on the bottom of the upper column. Clean the threads of the clamp bolt then apply a little locking fluid to them. Position the intermediate shaft then insert the clamp bolt and tighten to the specified torque and angles.

14 Refit the steering column support brace and screw on the nuts loosely. Apply a little locking fluid to the threads of the bolt then insert it and tighten to the specified torque. Tighten the nuts to the specified torque.

15 Refit the air distribution duct and the trim panel to the driver's footwell.

16 Refit the ignition switch and lock cylinder as described in Chapter 12.

17 Refit the turn signal switch and wiper switch as described in Chapter 12.

18 On models with an airbag refit the contact unit to the top of the column (if necessary refer to Chapter 12). Make sure that the alignment arrows are positioned correctly and that the contact unit is not tilted but retained by the clips correctly.

19 Refit the steering column shrouds and tighten the retaining screws. Refit and tighten the tilt steering lever.

20 Refit the steering wheel (Section 17).

19 Steering column intermediate shaft – removal and refitting

Removal

1 Set the front wheels in the straight-ahead position, then remove the ignition key and lock the column by turning the steering wheel as required. Unlike earlier models which locked in the straight-ahead position, models from 1999 Model Year lock in a different position due to a modified intermediate shaft. Right-hand drive models lock with the steering wheel approximately 5° anti-clockwise, and left-hand drive models lock with the steering wheel approximately 45° clockwise.

2 Remove the trim panel from under the driver's side of the facia, then pull out the air distribution duct leading to the heater unit.

3 Using paint or a suitable marker pen, make alignment marks between the intermediate shaft joints and the steering column and steering gear pinion.

4 Unscrew and remove the upper and lower clamp bolts.

5 Disengage the shaft universal joint from the steering column, then slide the shaft from the steering gear pinion and remove it from the vehicle.

Inspection

6 Inspect the intermediate shaft universal joints for excessive wear or damage. If either joint is worn or damaged, the complete shaft assembly must be renewed.

Refitting

7 Check that the front wheels are still in the locked position, and that the steering wheel is correctly positioned.

8 Aligning the marks made on removal, engage the shaft universal joints with the steering gear pinion and column. Apply thread locking fluid to the clamp bolts, then insert them and tighten to the specified torque and angles. **Note:** *On all models from 10/98 (ie, 1999 Model Year) the larger diameter outer sleeve of the intermediate shaft is positioned downwards (ie, towards the steering gear. On earlier models the sleeve is positioned towards the steering column).*

9 Refit the air distribution duct and trim panel.

10 Make sure that the front wheels point straight-ahead with the steering wheel in the straight-ahead position. If not, reposition the steering wheel with reference to Section 17.

20 Steering gear rubber gaiters – renewal

1 Remove the relevant track rod end as described in Section 24.

2 Remove the inner and outer securing clips, then slide the gaiter off the end of the track rod **(see illustrations)**.

3 Thoroughly clean the track rod, then slide the new gaiter into position. Note that a groove is provided in the track rod for the outer end of the gaiter to locate in.

4 Fit the gaiter securing clips, using new clips if necessary, making sure that the gaiter is not twisted.

5 Refit the track rod end (Section 24).

6 Have the front wheel toe-in and camber setting checked and adjusted at the earliest opportunity.

21 Steering gear – removal and refitting

Removal

1 Set the front wheels in the straight-ahead position, then remove the ignition key and lock the column by turning the steering wheel as required. Unlike earlier models which locked in the straight-ahead position, models from 1999 Model Year, lock in a different position due to a modified intermediate shaft. Right-hand drive models lock with the steering wheel approximately 5° anti-clockwise, and left-hand drive models lock with the steering wheel approximately 45° clockwise.

2 Remove the front subframe as described in Section 4.

3 Unbolt the rear engine mounting bracket from the subframe.

4 Mark the steering gear mounting clamps for position to ensure correct refitting, then unscrew the mounting bolts and remove the clamps **(see illustration)**.

20.2a Steering gear rubber gaiter inner . . .

5 Lift the steering gear from the subframe.

6 Prise the rubber mountings from the steering gear, noting their fitted positions. Also remove the rubber grommet from the pinion **(see illustration)**.

7 Examine the mountings and rubber grommet for wear and damage and renew them if necessary.

Refitting

8 Locate the rubber mountings and grommet on the steering gear in the positions noted on removal.

9 Fit the clamps over the mountings, then insert the bolts and tighten to the specified torque.

10 Refit the rear engine mounting bracket and tighten the bolts to the specified torque.

11 Refit the front subframe as described in Section 4.

12 Have the front wheel toe-in and camber setting checked and adjusted at the earliest opportunity.

22 Power steering pump – removal and refitting

Petrol engine (except Z22SE)

Removal

1 Remove the air cleaner assembly as described in Chapter 4A. Where applicable, remove the engine top cover.

2 Unscrew the cap from the power steering

21.4 Steering gear mounting clamp

20.2b . . . and outer securing clips

fluid reservoir, then syphon the fluid into a container. An old poultry baster or hydrometer can be used to draw out the fluid.

3 Remove the auxiliary drivebelt as described in Chapter 1A. Mark the drivebelt with the direction of travel to ensure correct refitting.

4 On models with the Y16XE, Z16XE, Z18XE and Z18XEL engines, drain the cooling system as described in Chapter 1A, then loosen the clips and remove the radiator upper hose.

5 Position a container beneath the power steering pump to catch spilled fluid, then unscrew the union bolt and disconnect the pressure line from the pump. Release the pressure line from the support bracket.

6 On models with the Y16XE, Z16XE, Z18XE and Z18XEL engines, unbolt and remove the exhaust manifold/catalytic converter heat shield.

7 Release the clip and disconnect the return line from the bottom of the reservoir. Plug the fluid lines and openings to prevent entry of dust and dirt.

8 Unscrew the four mounting bolts and withdraw the power steering pump together with the fluid reservoir from the engine. Wrap the pump in cloth rags to prevent fluid being spilt on the vehicle paintwork.

Refitting

9 Locate the power steering pump on the mounting brackets, then insert the bolts and tighten to the specified torque.

10 Reconnect the return line to the bottom of the reservoir and fit the clip.

21.6 Rubber grommet on the steering gear pinion

22.17 Power steering pump (Z22SE engine)

11 Refit the exhaust manifold/catalytic converter heat shield on Z16XE, Z18XE and Z18XEL engine models.
12 Reconnect the pressure line and refit the union bolt. Tighten the union bolt to the specified torque, and locate the line in the support bracket.
13 On models with the Y16XE, Z16XE, Z18XE and Z18XEL engines, refit the radiator upper hose and tighten the clips, then refill and bleed the cooling system with reference to Chapters 3 and 1A.
14 Refit and tension the auxiliary drivebelt as described in Chapter 1A.
15 Refit the air cleaner assembly as described in Chapter 4A.
16 Fill the fluid reservoir with fresh fluid and bleed the system as described in Section 23.

Z22SE petrol engine

Removal

17 Remove the engine top cover and move aside the wiring loom from over the power steering pump **(see illustration)**.
18 Unscrew the cap from the power steering fluid reservoir, then syphon the fluid into a container. An old poultry baster or hydrometer can be used to draw out the fluid.
19 Position a container beneath the power steering pump to catch spilled fluid, then unscrew the union bolt and disconnect the pressure line from the pump. Unbolt the pressure line from the support bracket **(see illustration)**.
20 Unscrew the mounting bolts securing the pump to the left-hand end of the cylinder

22.21 Removing the power steering pump on the Z22SE engine

22.19 Power steering pump pressure line support bracket (Z22SE engine)

head, then loosen the clip and disconnect the fluid return hose. Plug the hose.
21 Wrap the pump in cloth rags to prevent fluid being spilt on the vehicle paintwork, then release the pressure line and withdraw the pump from the engine **(see illustration)**.
22 Hold the pump, then remove the retaining clips and detach the fluid reservoir from the pump. Check the sealing rings, and if necessary renew them.

Refitting

23 Locate the pump on the engine and insert the pressure line. Refit the fluid reservoir to the pump and secure with the clips.
24 Reconnect the fluid return hose and tighten the clip.
25 Insert the mounting bolts and tighten to the specified torque.
26 Refit the pressure line to the bracket and tighten the bolt.
27 Tighten the pressure line union bolt to the specified torque.
28 Fill the fluid reservoir with fresh fluid and bleed the system as described in Section 23.
29 Refit the engine top cover.

Diesel engine

Removal

Note: *New pumps are supplied together with the support bracket.*

30 Unclip the fuse/relay bracket from the air cleaner, then remove the air cleaner and inlet hose with reference to Chapter 4B.
31 Apply the handbrake, then jack up the front of the vehicle and support it on axle stands (see *Jacking and vehicle support*).

22.37 The power steering hydraulic fluid reservoir is mounted on the top of the radiator on diesel models

Remove the engine compartment undertray.
32 Drain the cooling system as described in Chapter 1B.
33 Loosen the clips and disconnect the coolant hoses from the thermostat housing.
34 Mark the running direction of the auxiliary drivebelt and note the routing around the pulleys, then loosen only the bolts securing the pulley to the power steering pump.
35 Using a socket on the hexagon, turn the tensioner anti-clockwise to release the tension on the belt, then remove the belt from the pulleys. Release the tensioner.
36 Unbolt the pulley from the power steering pump.
37 Using hose clamps, clamp both the supply and return hoses near the reservoir located over the radiator **(see illustration)**. Alternatively, unscrew the cap from the power steering fluid reservoir, then syphon the fluid into a container. An old poultry baster or hydrometer can be used to draw out the fluid.
38 Position a container beneath the power steering pump to catch spilled fluid, then unscrew the union bolt and disconnect the pressure line from the pump.
39 Release the clip and disconnect the return line from the pump. Plug the fluid lines and openings to prevent entry of dust and dirt.
40 Unscrew the mounting bolts and withdraw the pump from the bracket on the engine. Wrap the pump in cloth rags before removing it to prevent spilling fluid onto the paintwork. Remove the sealing rings and discard them; new ones must be obtained for refitting. If necessary, unbolt the bracket from the engine.

Refitting

41 If a new pump is being fitted, unbolt the transit kit and remove the transit sealing rings.
42 If removed, refit the bracket to the engine and tighten the bolts.
43 Apply silicone grease to the sealing rings and locate them on the pump. Make sure that the pump rear cover is located correctly in the guide pin and held with the retaining ring. Fit the pump to the bracket and progressively tighten the bolts initially by hand, then to the specified torque.
44 Refit the return line and tighten the clip.
45 Refit the pressure line and tighten the union bolt to the specified torque.
46 Remove the hose clamps, or top-up the fluid in the reservoir (as applicable).
47 Refit the pulley and tighten the bolts to the specified torque.
48 Using a socket, turn the tensioner hexagon anti-clockwise, then relocate the drivebelt on the pulleys, making sure it is the correct way around as noted during removal. Release the tensioner and check that the drivebelt is correctly located on the pulley grooves.
49 Refit the hoses to the thermostat housing and tighten the clips.
50 Refit the air cleaner and inlet hose, then clip the fuse/relay bracket to the air cleaner.

24.2 Remove rust from the track rod end mounting nut with a wire brush

24.4 Using a balljoint separator tool to release the track rod end from the steering arm

51 Refill and bleed the cooling system as described in Chapter 1B.
52 Bleed the power steering fluid circuit as described in Section 23.
53 Refit the engine compartment undertray and lower the car to the ground.

23 Power steering system – bleeding

1 Check and top-up the power steering fluid level to the MAX mark as described in *Weekly checks*.
2 Start the engine and allow it to idle, then *slowly* turn the steering wheel two or three times 45° to the left and right. Now turn the steering twice from lock-to-lock – do not hold the steering wheel on full lock for more than 15 seconds at a time.
3 Check the fluid level in the reservoir and top-up if necessary. Check for air bubbles in the fluid – if air bubbles are visible, the system requires further bleeding. **Note:** *The fluid reservoir must not be allowed to run dry*
4 Stop the engine and recheck the fluid level.
5 If air bubbles appear in the reservoir when the system is operated, or if the pump is noisy in operation (not to be confused with a slipping drivebelt), repeat the bleeding procedure.

24 Track rod end – removal and refitting

Note: *A balljoint separator tool will be required for this operation.*

Removal

1 Remove the relevant front wheel trim or the wheel centre plate (alloy wheels), then slacken the wheel nuts. Apply the handbrake, then jack up the front of the vehicle, and support

securely on axle stands (see *Jacking and vehicle support*). Remove the roadwheel.
2 Loosen the track rod end securing locknut on the track rod a quarter turn. If necessary, use a wire brush to remove rust from the nut and threads and lubricate the threads with penetrating oil before unscrewing the nut **(see illustration)**.
3 Unscrew and remove the track rod end balljoint nut.
4 Disconnect the track rod end balljoint from the steering arm on the hub carrier using a balljoint separator tool, taking care not to damage the balljoint boot. Once the balljoint has been released, remove the balljoint nut and remove the balljoint from the steering arm **(see illustration)**.
5 Unscrew the track rod end from the track rod, counting the number of turns necessary to remove it and taking care not to disturb the locknut.

Refitting

6 Screw the track rod end onto the track rod the number of turns noted during removal.
7 Insert the track rod end balljoint in the steering arm on the hub carrier, then fit the nut and tighten to the specified torque. If the balljoint stud turns as the nut is being tightened, press down on the track rod end to force the stud into the arm.
8 Tighten the track rod end securing locknut on the track rod to the specified torque.
9 Refit the roadwheel, then lower the vehicle to the ground, and tighten the wheel nuts.
10 Have the front wheel alignment checked and adjusted at the earliest opportunity.

25 Track rod – removal and refitting

Removal

1 Remove the steering gear as described in Section 21.

2 Remove the relevant track rod end with reference to Section 24.
3 Measure the distance from the track rod end locknut to the end of the track rod, then unscrew and remove the locknut.
4 Release the clips and remove the rubber bellows from the steering gear and track rod.
5 Locate the steering gear in a vice, then unscrew the inner balljoint from the rack and remove the track rod.

Refitting

6 Apply locking fluid to the threads, then screw the track rod inner balljoint on the rack and tighten to the specified torque.
7 Refit the bellows making sure that the inner end is pushed fully onto the steering gear and the outer end is seated in the groove on the track rod.
8 Screw on the locknut to the position noted on removal.
9 Refit the track rod end with reference to Section 24.
10 Refit the steering gear as described in Section 21.
11 Have the front wheel alignment checked and adjusted at the earliest opportunity.

26 Wheel alignment and steering angles – general information

1 Accurate wheel alignment is essential to good steering and for even tyre wear. Before considering the steering angles, check that the tyres are correctly inflated, that the front wheels are not buckled, the hub bearings are not worn and that the steering linkage is in good order without slackness or wear at the joints. The fuel tank must be half full and each front seat must be loaded with 70 kg.

26.2 Wheel alignment and steering angles

2 Wheel alignment consists of four factors **(see illustration):**

Camber is the angle at which the roadwheels are set from the vertical when viewed from the front or rear of the vehicle. Positive camber is the angle (in degrees) that the wheels are tilted outwards at the top from the vertical. Negative camber is the angle that the wheels are tilted inwards at the top from the vertical. The camber angle is adjusted by loosening the two bolts securing the bottom of the front suspension struts to the hub carriers, then lowering the weight of the vehicle onto the front wheels until the correct camber angle is achieved. The bolt holes are not slotted and only minimal adjustment is possible (±1°).

Castor is the angle between the steering axis and a vertical line when viewed from each side of the vehicle. Positive castor is indicated when the steering axis is inclined towards the rear of the vehicle at its upper end. This angle is not adjustable.

Steering axis inclination (kingpin inclination) is the angle, when viewed from the front or rear of the vehicle, between the vertical and an imaginary line drawn between the upper and lower front suspension strut mountings. This angle is not adjustable.

Toe is the angle between the wheel and the straight-ahead position, or the amount by which the distance between the front inside edges of the roadwheel rim differs from that between the rear inside edges. If the angle is positive, or the distance between the front edges is less than that at the rear, the wheels are said to toe-in. If the angle is negative, or the distance between the front inside edges is greater than that at the rear, the wheels toe-out.

3 Owing to the need for precision gauges to measure the small angles of the steering and suspension settings, it is preferable that all checking is left to a service station having the necessary equipment.

Chapter 11
Bodywork and fittings

Contents

Degrees of difficulty

Easy, suitable for novice with little experience	Fairly easy, suitable for beginner with some experience	Fairly difficult, suitable for competent DIY mechanic	Difficult, suitable for experienced DIY mechanic	Very difficult, suitable for expert DIY or professional

Specifications

Torque wrench settings	Nm	lbf ft
Bonnet striker locknut:		
Black coating	22	16
Galvanized coating	40	30
Front seat belt reel	35	26
Front seat belt tensioner	35	26
Front seat belt to seat	20	15
Front seat belt-to-B-pillar upper mounting bolt	35	26
Front seat mounting screws	20	15
Rear seat backrest hinge	20	15
Rear seat belt height adjuster to C-pillar	20	15
Rear seat belt mountings to floor	35	26
Rear seat belt reel	35	26
Sunroof glass side mounting screws	5	4

1 General information

The bodyshell is of five-door Hatchback, four-door Notchback, or Estate configuration, and is made of high-strength low alloy sheet metal sections. The sections are alloy-galvanized on one or both sides, depending on their position on the vehicle. Most components are welded together, but some use is made of structural adhesives. The front wings are bolted on.

The bonnet, doors and some other vulnerable panels are made of zinc-coated metal, and are further protected by being coated with an anti-chip primer prior to being sprayed. The front and rear doors incorporate safety bars as protection in the event of a side impact.

Electrically-operated front and rear windows are fitted according to model. The electric window mechanism incorporates a safety feature which stops the window if it meets an obstruction.

The central locking incorporates a 'deadlock' system as additional security, making it impossible to open the doors from inside the car with the doors locked.

Extensive use is made of plastic materials, mainly in the interior, but also in exterior components. The front and rear bumpers and the front grille are injection-moulded from a synthetic material which is very strong, and yet light. Plastic components such as wheelarch liners are fitted to the underside of the vehicle, to improve the body's resistance to corrosion.

2 Maintenance – bodywork and underframe

The general condition of a vehicle's bodywork is the one thing that significantly affects its value. Maintenance is easy, but needs to be regular. Neglect, particularly after minor damage, can lead quickly to further deterioration and costly repair bills. It is important also to keep watch on those parts of the vehicle not immediately visible, for instance the underside, inside all the wheel arches, and the lower part of the engine compartment.

The basic maintenance routine for the bodywork is washing – preferably with a lot of water, from a hose. This will remove all the loose solids which may have stuck to the vehicle. It is important to flush these off in such a way as to prevent grit from scratching the finish. The wheel arches and underframe need washing in the same way, to remove any accumulated mud which will retain moisture and tend to encourage rust. Paradoxically enough, the best time to clean the underframe and wheel arches is in wet weather, when the mud is thoroughly wet and soft. In very wet weather, the underframe is usually cleaned of large accumulations automatically, and this is a good time for inspection.

Periodically, except on vehicles with a wax-based underbody protective coating, it is a good idea to have the whole of the underframe of the vehicle steam-cleaned, engine compartment included, so that a thorough inspection can be carried out to see what minor repairs and renovations are necessary. Steam-cleaning is available at many garages, and is necessary for the removal of the accumulation of oily grime, which sometimes is allowed to become thick in certain areas. If steam-cleaning facilities are not available, there are one or two excellent grease solvents available, which can be brush-applied; the dirt can then be simply hosed off. Note that these methods should not be used on vehicles with wax-based underbody protective coating, or the coating will be removed. Such vehicles should be inspected annually, preferably just prior to Winter, when the underbody should be washed down, and any damage to the wax coating repaired. Ideally, a completely fresh coat should be applied. It would also be worth considering the use of such wax-based protection for injection into door panels, sills, box sections, etc, as an additional safeguard against rust damage, where such protection is not provided by the vehicle manufacturer.

After washing paintwork, wipe off with a chamois leather to give an unspotted clear finish. A coat of clear protective wax polish will give added protection against chemical pollutants in the air. If the paintwork sheen has dulled or oxidised, use a cleaner/polisher combination to restore the brilliance of the shine. This requires a little effort, but such dulling is usually caused because regular washing has been neglected. Care needs to be taken with metallic paintwork, as special non-abrasive cleaner/polisher is required to avoid damage to the finish. Always check that the door and ventilator opening drain holes and pipes are completely clear, so that water can be drained out. Brightwork should be treated in the same way as paintwork. Windscreens and windows can be kept clear of the smeary film which often appears, by the use of proprietary glass cleaner. Never use any form of wax or other body or chromium polish on glass.

3 Maintenance – upholstery and carpets

Mats and carpets should be brushed or vacuum-cleaned regularly, to keep them free of grit. If they are badly stained, remove them from the vehicle for scrubbing or sponging, and make quite sure they are dry before refitting. Seats and interior trim panels can be kept clean by wiping with a damp cloth. If they do become stained (which can be more apparent on light-coloured upholstery), use a little liquid detergent and a soft nail brush to scour the grime out of the grain of the material. Do not forget to keep the headlining clean in the same way as the upholstery. When using liquid cleaners inside the vehicle, do not over-wet the surfaces being cleaned. Excessive damp could get into the seams and padded interior, causing stains, offensive odours or even rot. If the inside of the vehicle gets wet accidentally, it is worthwhile taking some trouble to dry it out properly, particularly where carpets are involved. *Do not leave oil or electric heaters inside the vehicle for this purpose.*

4 Minor body damage – repair

Repairs of minor scratches in bodywork

If the scratch is very superficial, and does not penetrate to the metal of the bodywork, repair is very simple. Lightly rub the area of the scratch with a paintwork renovator, or a very fine cutting paste, to remove loose paint from the scratch, and to clear the surrounding bodywork of wax polish. Rinse the area with clean water.

Apply touch-up paint to the scratch using a fine paint brush; continue to apply fine layers of paint until the surface of the paint in the scratch is level with the surrounding paintwork. Allow the new paint at least two weeks to harden, then blend it into the surrounding paintwork by rubbing the scratch area with a paintwork renovator or a very fine cutting paste. Finally, apply wax polish.

Where the scratch has penetrated right through to the metal of the bodywork, causing the metal to rust, a different repair technique is required. Remove any loose rust from the bottom of the scratch with a penknife, then apply rust-inhibiting paint, to prevent the formation of rust in the future. Using a rubber or nylon applicator, fill the scratch with bodystopper paste. If required, this paste can be mixed with cellulose thinners, to provide a very thin paste which is ideal for filling narrow scratches. Before the stopper-paste in the scratch hardens, wrap a piece of smooth cotton rag around the top of a finger. Dip the finger in cellulose thinners, and quickly sweep it across the surface of the stopper-paste in the scratch; this will ensure that the surface of the stopper-paste is slightly hollowed. The scratch can now be painted over as described earlier in this Section.

Repairs of dents in bodywork

When deep denting of the vehicle's bodywork has taken place, the first task is to pull the dent out, until the affected bodywork almost attains its original shape. There is little point in trying to restore the original shape completely, as the metal in the damaged area will have stretched on impact, and cannot be reshaped fully to its original contour. It is better to bring the level of the dent up to a point which is about 3 mm below the level of the surrounding bodywork. In cases where the dent is very shallow anyway, it is not worth trying to pull it out at all. If the underside of the dent is accessible, it can be hammered out gently from behind, using a mallet with a wooden or plastic head. Whilst doing this, hold a suitable block of wood firmly against the outside of the panel, to absorb the impact from the hammer blows and thus prevent a large area of the bodywork from being 'belled-out'.

Should the dent be in a section of the bodywork which has a double skin, or some other factor making it inaccessible from behind, a different technique is called for. Drill several small holes through the metal inside the area – particularly in the deeper section. Then screw long self-tapping screws into the holes, just sufficiently for them to gain a good purchase in the metal. Now the dent can be pulled out by pulling on the protruding heads of the screws with a pair of pliers.

The next stage of the repair is the removal of the paint from the damaged area, and from an inch or so of the surrounding 'sound' bodywork. This is accomplished most easily by using a wire brush or abrasive pad on a power drill, although it can be done just as effectively by hand, using sheets of abrasive paper. To complete the preparation for filling, score the surface of the bare metal with a screwdriver or the tang of a file, or alternatively, drill small holes in the affected area. This will provide a really good 'key' for the filler paste.

To complete the repair, see the Section on filling and respraying.

Repairs of rust holes or gashes in bodywork

Remove all paint from the affected area, and from an inch or so of the surrounding 'sound' bodywork, using an abrasive pad or a wire brush on a power drill. If these are not available, a few sheets of abrasive paper will do the job most effectively. With the paint removed, you will be able to judge the severity of the corrosion, and therefore decide whether to renew the whole panel (if this is possible) or to repair the affected area. New body panels are not as expensive as most people think, and it is often quicker and more satisfactory to fit a new panel than to attempt to repair large areas of corrosion.

Remove all fittings from the affected area, except those which will act as a guide to the original shape of the damaged bodywork (eg headlamp shells etc). Then, using tin snips or a hacksaw blade, remove all loose metal and any other metal badly affected by corrosion. Hammer the edges of the hole inwards, in order to create a slight depression for the filler paste.

Wire-brush the affected area to remove the powdery rust from the surface of the remaining metal. Paint the affected area with rust-inhibiting paint; if the back of the rusted area is accessible, treat this also.

Before filling can take place, it will be necessary to block the hole in some way. This can be achieved by the use of aluminium or plastic mesh, or aluminium tape.

Aluminium or plastic mesh, or glass-fibre matting is probably the best material to use for a large hole. Cut a piece to the approximate size and shape of the hole to be filled, then position it in the hole so that its edges are below the level of the surrounding bodywork. It can be retained in position by several blobs of filler paste around its periphery.

Aluminium tape should be used for small or very narrow holes. Pull a piece off the roll, trim it to the approximate size and shape required, then pull off the backing paper (if used) and stick the tape over the hole; it can be overlapped if the thickness of one piece is insufficient. Burnish down the edges of the tape with the handle of a screwdriver or similar, to ensure that the tape is securely attached to the metal underneath.

Bodywork repairs – filling and respraying

Before using this Section, see the Sections on dent, deep scratch, rust holes and gash repairs.

Many types of bodyfiller are available, but generally speaking, those proprietary kits which contain a tin of filler paste and a tube of resin hardener are best for this type of repair. A wide, flexible plastic or nylon applicator will be found invaluable for imparting a smooth and well-contoured finish to the surface of the filler.

Mix up a little filler on a clean piece of card or board – measure the hardener carefully (follow the maker's instructions on the pack), otherwise the filler will set too rapidly or too slowly. Using the applicator, apply the filler paste to the prepared area; draw the applicator across the surface of the filler to achieve the correct contour and to level the surface. As soon as a contour that approximates to the correct one is achieved, stop working the paste – if you carry on too long, the paste will become sticky and begin to 'pick-up' on the applicator. Continue to add thin layers of filler paste at 20-minute intervals, until the level of the filler is just proud of the surrounding bodywork.

Once the filler has hardened, the excess can be removed using a metal plane or file. From then on, progressively-finer grades of abrasive paper should be used, starting with a 40-grade production paper, and finishing with a 400-grade wet-and-dry paper. Always wrap the abrasive paper around a flat rubber, cork, or wooden block – otherwise the surface of the filler will not be completely flat. During the smoothing of the filler surface, the wet-and-dry paper should be periodically rinsed in water. This will ensure that a very smooth finish is imparted to the filler at the final stage.

At this stage, the 'dent' should be surrounded by a ring of bare metal, which in turn should be encircled by the finely 'feathered' edge of the good paintwork. Rinse the repair area with clean water, until all of the dust produced by the rubbing-down operation has gone.

Spray the whole area with a light coat of – this will show up any imperfections in the surface of the filler. Repair these imperfections with fresh filler paste or bodystopper, and once more smooth the surface with abrasive paper. If bodystopper is used, it can be mixed with cellulose thinners, to form a really thin paste which is ideal for filling small holes. Repeat this spray-and-repair procedure until you are satisfied that the surface of the filler, and the feathered edge of the paintwork, are perfect. Clean the repair area with clean water, and allow to dry fully.

The repair area is now ready for final spraying. Paint spraying must be carried out in a warm, dry, windless and dust-free atmosphere. This condition can be created artificially if you have access to a large indoor working area, but if you are forced to work in the open, you will have to pick your day very carefully. If you are working indoors, dousing the floor in the work area with water will help to settle the dust which would otherwise be in the atmosphere. If the repair area is confined to one body panel, mask off the surrounding panels; this will help to minimise the effects of a slight mis-match in paint colours. Bodywork fittings (eg chrome strips, door handles etc) will also need to be masked off. Use genuine masking tape, and several thicknesses of newspaper, for the masking operations.

Before commencing to spray, agitate the aerosol can thoroughly, then spray a test area (an old tin, or similar) until the technique is mastered. Cover the repair area with a thick coat of primer; the thickness should be built up using several thin layers of paint, rather than one thick one. Using 400 grade wet-and-dry paper, rub down the surface of the primer until it is really smooth. While doing this, the work area should be thoroughly doused with water, and the wet-and-dry paper periodically rinsed in water. Allow to dry before spraying on more paint.

Spray on the top coat, again building up the thickness by using several thin layers of paint. Start spraying at one edge of the repair area, and then, using a side-to-side motion, work until the whole repair area and about 2 inches of the surrounding original paintwork is covered. Remove all masking material 10 to 15 minutes after spraying on the final coat of paint.

Allow the new paint at least two weeks to harden, then, using a paintwork renovator or a very fine cutting paste, blend the edges of the paint into the existing paintwork. Finally, apply wax polish.

6.2a Removing the side . . .

6.2b . . . and bottom Torx screws from the wheelarch liners

6.2c Removing the complete wheelarch liner

6.2d Removing the front bumper side mounting screws

Plastic components

With the use of more and more plastic body components by the vehicle manufacturers (eg bumpers. spoilers, and in some cases major body panels), rectification of more serious damage to such items has become a matter of either entrusting repair work to a specialist in this field, or renewing complete components. Repair of such damage by the DIY owner is not really feasible, owing to the cost of the equipment and materials required for effecting such repairs. The basic technique involves making a groove along the line of the crack in the plastic, using a rotary burr in a power drill. The damaged part is then welded back together, using a hot air gun to heat up and fuse a plastic filler rod into the groove. Any excess plastic is then removed, and the area rubbed down to a smooth finish. It is important that a filler rod of the correct plastic

is used, as body components can be made of a variety of different types (eg polycarbonate, ABS, polypropylene).

Damage of a less serious nature (abrasions, minor cracks etc) can be repaired by the DIY owner using a two-part epoxy filler repair. Once mixed in equal, this is used in similar fashion to the bodywork filler used on metal panels. The filler is usually cured in twenty to thirty minutes, ready for sanding and painting.

If the owner is renewing a complete component himself, or if he has repaired it with epoxy filler, he will be left with the problem of finding a suitable paint for finishing which is compatible with the type of plastic used. At one time, the use of a universal paint was not possible, owing to the complex range of plastics encountered in body component applications. Standard paints, generally speaking, will not bond to plastic or rubber satisfactorily, but suitable paints to match any

plastic or rubber finish, can be obtained from dealers. However, it is now possible to obtain a plastic body parts finishing kit which consists of a pre-primer treatment, a primer and coloured top coat. Full instructions are normally supplied with a kit, but basically, the method of use is to first apply the pre-primer to the component concerned, and allow it to dry for up to 30 minutes. Then the primer is applied, and left to dry for about an hour before finally applying the special-coloured top coat. The result is a correctly-coloured component, where the paint will flex with the plastic or rubber, a property that standard paint does not normally possess.

5 Major body damage – repair

Where serious damage has occurred, or large areas need renewal due to neglect, it means that complete new panels will need welding-in, and this is best left to professionals. If the damage is due to impact, it will also be necessary to check completely the alignment of the bodyshell, and this can only be carried out accurately by a Vauxhall/Opel dealer using special jigs. If the body is left misaligned, it is primarily dangerous, as the car will not handle properly, and secondly, uneven stresses will be imposed on the steering, suspension and possibly transmission, causing abnormal wear, or complete failure, particularly to such items as the tyres.

6 Bumpers – removal and refitting

Front bumper

Removal

1 Remove the radiator grille as described in Section 7.
2 Working beneath the front wheelarches, use a Torx key to remove the screws, then pull back the liners for access to the front bumper side mounting screws. If preferred, the liners can be completely removed by releasing the plastic retainers (press the centre pins through the clips). Unscrew and remove the bumper side mounting screws **(see illustrations)**.
3 Remove the plastic clips securing the bottom of the front bumper to the front valance. To do this, pull out the centre pins using a pair of pliers **(see illustrations)**.
4 Unscrew and remove the upper mounting bolts, then carefully withdraw the front bumper from the front of the vehicle **(see illustrations)**.
5 Where a spoiler is fitted, prise off the special clips then compress the lugs and separate the

6.3a Use a pair of pliers to pull out the centre pins . . .

6.3b . . . then pull the plastic clips from the bottom of the front bumper

spoiler from the front bumper. If the original spoiler is fitted, or to remove the air intakes, use a knife to separate the factory-made welding points. **Note:** *New front bumpers are supplied in base colour and require painting in the correct colour before fitting.*

Refitting

6 Refitting is a reversal of removal but tighten the screws securely. Special clips are available from Vauxhall/Opel dealers for refitting the air intakes.

Rear bumper

Removal

7 Open the bootlid or tailgate as applicable.
8 Pull up the weatherstrip to provide access to the rear bumper upper mounting screws.
9 Using a Torx key, unscrew the screws securing the front of the rear bumper to the rear wheelarch on both sides. On Estate models also remove the screws from the lower corners.
10 Using the key, unscrew the screws securing the bottom of the rear bumper to the rear valance.
11 Unscrew the upper mounting screws then carefully withdraw the rear bumper from the rear of the vehicle. On models fitted with the 'park pilot' aid, disconnect the wiring and where necessary remove the unit from the bumper. **Note:** *New rear bumpers are supplied in base colour and require painting in the correct colour before fitting.*
12 Where a spoiler is fitted, drill out the rivets, press out the tabs, and detach the spoiler lip from the bumper.
13 Where a trailer hitch is fitted, remove the impact absorber, lock mechanisms and small panel.

Refitting

14 Refitting is a reversal of removal but tighten the screws securely.

7 Radiator grille – removal and refitting

Removal

1 Open the bonnet, then unscrew the radiator grille upper mounting screws (see illustration).

8.2 Bonnet hinge and mounting bolts

6.4a Unscrew the upper mounting bolts . . .

7.1 Unscrew the upper mounting screws . . .

2 Lift the radiator grille and release the clips from the front bumper (see illustration).

Refitting

3 Refitting is a reversal of removal but tighten the screws securely.

8 Bonnet and support struts – removal, refitting and adjustment

Bonnet

Removal

1 Open the bonnet, and have an assistant support it.
2 Using a marker pen or paint, mark around the hinge positions on the bonnet (see illustration).

8.3 Windscreen washer fluid hose and clip on the bonnet

6.4b . . . and withdraw the front bumper

7.2 . . . then lift the radiator grille and release the clips from the front bumper

3 Disconnect the windscreen washer fluid hose at the connector and support (see illustration). Where applicable, also release the wiring loom.
4 With the aid of the assistant, unscrew the bolts securing the bonnet to the hinges on both sides (see illustration).
5 Lift off the bonnet taking care not to damage the vehicle paintwork.

Refitting

6 With the aid of the assistant, align the marks made on the bonnet before removal with the hinges, then refit and tighten the bonnet securing bolts.
7 Reconnect the windscreen washer fluid hose and, where applicable, the wiring loom.
8 Check the bonnet adjustment as follows.

Adjustment

9 Close the bonnet, and check that there is an equal gap (approximately 4.0 mm) at

8.4 Bolts securing the bonnet to the hinges

8.11a The bonnet rubber bump stops are located at the front corners

8.11b Bonnet striker and safety catch

8.13 Prise the spring clip from the bonnet support strut to disconnect it from the ball

each side, between the bonnet and the wing panels. Check also that the bonnet sits flush in relation to the surrounding body panels.

10 The bonnet should close smoothly and positively without excessive pressure. If this is not the case, adjustment will be required.

11 To adjust the bonnet alignment, loosen the bonnet-to-hinge mounting bolts, and move the bonnet on the bolts as required (the bolt holes in the hinges are enlarged). If necessary, the scissor-type hinge mounting bolts may be loosened as well. To adjust the bonnet front height in relation to the front wings, adjustable rubber bump stops are fitted to the front corners of the bonnet. These may be screwed in or out as necessary. After making an adjustment, the bonnet striker must be adjusted so that the lock spring holds the bonnet firmly against the rubber bump stops. Loosen the locknut and screw the striker in or out as necessary **(see illustrations)**.

Support struts

Removal

12 Open the bonnet, and have an assistant support it.

13 Using a screwdriver prise out the retaining spring clips and disconnect the strut from the bonnet and body. Note which way round the strut is fitted **(see illustration)**.

Refitting

14 Refitting is a reversal of removal.

11.2 Wiring connector on the front door

9 Bonnet release cable – removal and refitting

Removal

1 Remove the lower trim panel from under the driver's side of the facia.

2 Remove the radiator grille as described in Section 7.

3 Disconnect the front end of the release cable from the bonnet lock spring.

4 Disconnect the rear end of the release cable from the release lever in the driver's footwell. Access is very limited and the use of a mirror will help.

5 Release the cable from the support clips in the engine compartment, then withdraw the cable through the rubber grommet and withdraw into the engine compartment. As an aid to refitting, tie a length of string to the cable before removing it and leave the string in position ready for refitting.

Refitting

6 Refitting is a reversal of removal, but tie the string to the release lever end of the cable, and use the string to pull the cable into position. Ensure that the cable is routed as noted before removal, and make sure that the grommet is correctly seated.

10 Bonnet lock spring – removal and refitting

Removal

1 The bonnet is held in its locked position with a strong spring which engages with the striker on the front edge of the bonnet. The release cable is connected to the end of the spring.

2 The striker may be removed from the bonnet by unscrewing the locknut, however measure its fitted length first as a guide to refitting it.

3 To remove the lock spring, first remove the radiator grille (see Section 7) then disconnect the cable and unhook the spring from the front crossmember.

Refitting

4 Refitting is a reversal of removal.

11 Door – removal and refitting

Removal

1 The door hinges are welded onto the door frame and the body pillar. Where necessary, adjustment is carried out using special tools to bend the hinges.

2 Open the door to gain access to the wiring connector which is fitted to the front edge of the door. Disconnect the wiring connector from the front edge of the door. To do this, unscrew the connector locking ring, then pull the connector away from the door **(see illustration)**.

3 Unscrew and remove the bolt securing the door check link to the vehicle body **(see illustration)**.

4 Remove the plastic covers from the door hinge pins. Have an assistant support the door, then drive both hinge pins out of position using a hammer and suitable punch. **Note:** *Vauxhall/Opel technicians use a special hinge pin removal tool which acts like a slide hammer.* Remove the door from the vehicle.

5 Inspect the hinge pins for signs of wear or damage, and renew if necessary.

Refitting

6 Refitting is a reversal of removal, but check that when shut the door is positioned centrally

11.3 Front door check link

11.6 Rear door striker

12.2a Pull off the exterior mirror adjustment handle . . .

12.2b . . . then prise off the triangular plastic cover . . .

within the body aperture. If the hinge pins have been renewed and adjustment is still required, the hinges will have to be re-aligned using special tools. This work must be carried out by a Vauxhall/Opel dealer, however minor adjustment may be possible by physically lifting the door on its hinges. After adjustment, make sure that the door lock engages correctly with the striker on the body pillar. If necessary loosen the striker retaining screws using a Torx key, then reposition the striker and tighten the screws **(see illustration)**.

12 Door inner trim panel –
removal and refitting

> **Warning: The front door plastic membrane must be renewed after removal on all models fitted with**

side airbags; the operation of the side airbag relies on the integrity of the membrane.

Front door

Removal

1 Disconnect the battery negative (earth) lead (see Chapter 5A).
2 With the front door open carefully pull off the exterior mirror adjustment handle on models with a manually-adjustable exterior mirror. On all models, prise off the triangular plastic cover taking care not to damage the retaining clips. Remove the foam padding where fitted **(see illustrations)**.
3 Prise the plastic cover from the inside of the interior door handle grip. Also prise out the small plastic cover or electric mirror switch (as applicable) from the outside of the grip – disconnect the wiring where necessary **(see illustrations)**.

12.2c . . . and remove the foam padding

4 Prise off the small loudspeaker grille **(see illustration)**.
5 Undo the retaining screws and remove the door handle surround/grip. Disconnect the wiring from the loudspeaker **(see illustrations)**.

12.2d Removing the plastic cover on models with electrically-operated exterior mirrors

12.3a Prise off the plastic cover from the inside of the interior front door handle grip . . .

12.3b . . . then prise out the upper plastic cover from the outside of the grip

12.4 Prise off the small loudspeaker grille from the front door

12.5a Undo the retaining screws . . .

12.5b . . . and remove the front door handle surround/grip . . .

12.5c ... then disconnect the wiring from the loudspeaker

12.7a Undo the screws from the bottom edge of the front door trim panel ...

12.7b ... then prise out the panel clips and remove the trim panel from the door

12.7c Unhook the top of the panel from the locking knob

12.8a Peel the protective plastic membrane from the front door

12.8b Side airbag 'Warning' on the protective plastic membrane

6 On base models, remove the window regulator handle by first closing the window and noting the fitted angle of the handle. Using a piece of cloth rag inserted behind the handle, release the wire clip then withdraw the handle from the splined shaft.

7 Unscrew and remove the screws from the bottom edge of the trim panel, then use a wide-bladed screwdriver or removal tool to carefully prise the panel clips from the door. Unhook the top of the panel from the locking knob and remove it from the door **(see illustrations)**.

8 If necessary, carefully peel the protective plastic membrane from the door, but note the **Warning** at the beginning of this Section and renew it on models fitted with side airbags **(see illustrations)**. It may be necessary to cut the new membrane to size and use adhesive to attach it to the door.

Refitting

9 Refitting is a reversal of removal.

Rear door

Removal

10 Disconnect the battery negative (earth) lead (see Chapter 5A).

11 With the rear door open use a small screwdriver to carefully prise off the small loudspeaker grille **(see illustration)**.

12 Prise out the lower plastic plug and upper plug or electric window switch (as applicable) from the interior handle surround – disconnect the wiring where necessary **(see illustrations)**.

13 Unscrew and remove the retaining screws and remove the door handle surround/grip **(see illustrations)**.

14 Where a manual window regulator is fitted, fully close the window and note the position of the regulator handle. The handle must now be removed from the splined shaft. To do this, locate a cloth rag between the handle and the trim panel and pull it to one

12.11 Prise off the small loudspeaker grille from the rear door

12.12a Prise out the lower plastic plug ...

12.12b ... and the upper plastic plug from the rear door inner trim panel

12.13a Undo the retaining screws ...

12.13b . . . and remove the rear door handle surround/grip

12.14a Locate a cloth rag between the handle and the trim panel . . .

12.14b . . . then pull it to one side to release the spring clip, and remove the handle from the splined shaft . . .

12.14c . . . and remove the escutcheon

12.15 Prise off the triangular plastic cover from the upper rear of the rear door

12.16a Remove the screws from the bottom edge of the rear door . . .

side to release the spring clip. The handle can now be removed from the splined shaft and the escutcheon removed **(see illustrations)**.

15 Prise the triangular plastic cover from the upper rear of the trim panel **(see illustration)**.

16 Unscrew and remove the screws from the bottom edge of the trim panel, then use a wide-bladed screwdriver or removal tool to carefully prise the inner trim panel clips from the inside of the rear door. Unhook the top of

the panel from the locking knob and remove it from the door **(see illustrations)**.

17 As necessary, remove the window glass inner seal from the door.

18 If necessary, carefully peel the protective plastic membrane from the door **(see illustration)**.

Refitting

19 Refitting is a reversal of removal.

13 Door handles and lock components – removal and refitting

12.16b . . . then carefully prise away the inner trim panel . . .

12.16c . . . and unhook it from the locking knob

Door interior handle

Removal

1 Remove the door inner trim panel, and peel back the protective plastic sheeting as described in Section 12.

2 Press the interior handle forwards to release it from the elongated slots in the door panel.

3 Unhook the handle from the linkage **(see illustration)**.

Refitting

4 Refitting is a reversal of removal.

Front door exterior handle

Removal

5 Remove the door inner trim panel, and peel back the protective plastic sheeting as described in Section 12.

12.18 Peel the protective plastic membrane from the door

13.3 Unhook the interior handle from the linkage

13.6a Undo the upper mounting screw . . .

13.6b . . . and lower rear mounting screw . . .

13.6c . . . then withdraw the guide from the aperture in the door

13.7 Unscrew the nuts using a socket through the hole in the door . . .

13.8 . . . then withdraw the front door exterior handle from the outside of the door . . .

13.9a . . . unhook the linkage . . .

6 With the window closed, pull out the guide rubber then unscrew the retaining screws and lower the rear window guide from the window. Withdraw the guide from the aperture in the door **(see illustrations)**.

7 Unscrew the nuts from the rear of the exterior handle using a socket inserted through the aperture provided for access to the rear nut **(see illustration)**.

8 Carefully withdraw the exterior handle from

the door taking care not to damage the paintwork **(see illustration)**.

9 Unhook the linkage from the inner cover/lock cylinder housing and withdraw through the aperture in the door **(see illustrations)**.

Refitting

10 Refitting is a reversal of removal, but before refitting the inner trim panel, screw down the knurled nut on the handle linkage until it is free of play.

13.9b . . . and withdraw the handle through the aperture in the door

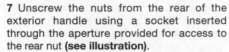

13.12 Pull the weatherstrip from the guide . . .

Rear door exterior handle

Removal

11 Remove the door inner trim panel, and peel back the protective plastic sheeting as described in Section 12.

12 Lower the rear window. Pull the window weatherstrip from the rear of the window aperture and pull it upwards from the window guide **(see illustration)**.

13 Unscrew the retaining screws and withdraw the window guide from the top of the door. Note the lower retaining screw is accessed through the special hole in the door **(see illustration)**.

14 Unscrew the nuts from the rear of the exterior handle using a socket inserted through the aperture provided for access to the rear nut. Withdraw the inner cover/security plate through the aperture in the door **(see illustrations)**.

15 Disconnect the linkage arms from the door lock by prising up the plastic clips.

13.13 . . . then unscrew the retaining screws and withdraw the guide

13.14a Unscrew the nuts . . .

13.14b . . . and withdraw the inner cover/security plate from the door

13.16 Withdraw the rear door exterior handle from the outside of the door

13.24 Use a screwdriver to lever up the plastic retainer in order to separate the central locking wiring from the lock

16 Withdraw the handle from the door taking care not to damage the paintwork **(see illustration)**.

Refitting

17 Refitting is a reversal of removal, but before refitting the inner trim panel, screw down the knurled nut on the handle linkage until it is free of play.

Front door lock cylinder (free-wheeling)

Removal

18 Remove the exterior handle as described previously in this Section.
19 Prise off the circlip and remove the arm together with the springs from the rear of the cylinder. Note the position of the arm to ensure correct refitting.

20 Using a suitable drift, drive out the retaining roll pin, then insert the ignition key and remove the housing followed by the lock cylinder. Recover the balls and coupling.

Refitting

21 Refitting is a reversal of removal, but after fitting the roll pin, use a punch to caulk it into the rear of the housing.

Front door lock

Removal

22 Remove the door inner trim panel, and peel back the protective plastic sheeting as described in Section 12.
23 With the window closed, unscrew the retaining screws and lower the rear window guide from the window. Withdraw the guide from the aperture in the door.

24 Where fitted, disconnect the central locking wiring from the lock by levering up the plastic retainer and separating the connector **(see illustration)**.
25 Undo the three retaining screws then disconnect the linkage arms for the outer door handle and lock cylinder from the lock.
26 Withdraw the lock from inside the door while guiding the locking knob through the hole provided **(see illustrations)**.
27 Disconnect the inner door handle cable.

Refitting

28 Refitting is a reversal of removal.

Rear door lock

Removal

29 Remove the door inner trim panel, and peel back the protective plastic sheeting as described in Section 12.
30 Remove the rear door exterior handle as described previously in this Section.
31 Disconnect the locking knob extension linkage from the lock by releasing the plastic clip **(see illustration)**.
32 Undo the screw and disconnect the front end of the locking knob cable from the intermediate lever. Release the cable from the support **(see illustrations)**.
33 Unscrew the lock mounting screws and withdraw the lock through the door inner aperture **(see illustrations)**.
34 Disconnect the central locking wiring by levering up the plastic retainer and separating the connector.

13.26a Guide the locking knob through the hole . . .

13.26b . . . while withdrawing the lock from the front door

13.31 Release the plastic clip and disconnect the locking knob extension from the rear door lock

13.32a Undo the screw and disconnect the front end of the locking knob cable from the intermediate lever . . .

13.32b . . . then release the cable from the support

13.33a Unscrew the mounting screws ...

13.33b ... and withdraw the lock through the rear door inner aperture

13.35 Removing the rear door locking knob intermediate lever

35 If necessary, remove the locking knob intermediate lever **(see illustration)**.

Refitting

36 Refitting is a reversal of removal.

14.3 Secure the window glass fully closed using strong adhesive tape

---

14 Door window regulator and glass – removal and refitting

Window regulator

Note: *New rivets will be required to secure the regulator mechanism to the door on refitting.*

Removal

1 Remove the door inner trim panel, and peel back the protective plastic membrane as described in Section 12.

⚠️ *Warning: On models fitted with side airbags, the membrane must be renewed; the operation of the side airbags relies on the integrity of the membrane.*

2 When removing the front regulator on models fitted with side airbags, remove the

side airbag sensor bracket with reference to Chapter 12, Section 24.

3 Using strong adhesive tape, secure the window fully closed **(see illustration)**.

4 On models with electric window regulators, disconnect the wiring connector by squeezing the retaining tags **(see illustration)**.

5 Mark the position of the regulator guide rail in the elongated slot, then unscrew and remove the adjustment screw **(see illustration)**.

6 Drill out the rivets then slide the arm extensions from the channel at the bottom of the glass **(see illustrations)**.

7 Manoeuvre the regulator mechanism out from the aperture in the door inner panel **(see illustrations)**.

Refitting

8 Refitting is a reversal of removal but use a pop riveter to secure the regulator with new

14.4 Disconnecting the wiring from the electric window regulator

14.5 Mark the position of the regulator guide rail in the elongated slot before unscrewing it

14.6a Drill out the rivets ...

14.6b ... then slide the arm extensions from the channel at the bottom of the glass

14.7a Removing a front door window regulator mechanism ...

14.7b ... and rear door window regulator mechanism

rivets **(see illustrations)**. Before refitting the inner trim panel and protective plastic sheeting, adjust the position of the regulator by inserting the adjustment screw hand-tight then raising and lowering the window fully. Tighten the adjustment screw and check that the window opens and closes correctly. Finally refit the inner trim panel and plastic sheeting.

9 On models with electric window regulators the winder must be reprogrammed as follows. Fully close the window then hold the switch down for a further 5 seconds.

Window glass

Removal

10 Remove the regulator as previously described in this Section.
11 Remove the window seal on the outer edge of the door, then tilt the window glass down at the front and carefully lift it upwards from the door **(see illustration)**.

Refitting

12 Refitting is a reversal of removal.

15 Rear quarter window glass – removal and refitting

Note: *This Section describes the removal of the rear quarter window glass on Notchback and Hatchback models only. On Estate models, the window glass is bonded in position (refer to Section 24).*

Removal

1 Remove the inner trim panel for access to the rear quarter window glass with reference to Section 29.
2 Unscrew the nuts and remove the window glass from the body. On Notchback models there are 4 nuts; on Hatchback models there are 7 nuts.

Refitting

3 Refitting is a reversal of removal.

16 Fuel filler flap lock and release cable – removal and refitting

Removal

1 Open the fuel flap and remove the filler cap.
2 Undo the two screws and withdraw the fuel filler flap.
3 Release the rubber boot from the body and withdraw it over the filler neck.
4 The catch can be removed after unscrewing the two screws.

Refitting

5 Refitting is a reversal of removal but use suitable adhesive to stick the rubber boot to the body. Clean away all old adhesive first.

14.8a Fit new pop rivets . . .

Note that a new flap must be painted with the body colour before fitting.

17 Bootlid – removal, refitting and adjustment

Removal

1 Open the bootlid, then disconnect the wiring at the connector.
2 Using a pencil or marker pen, mark around the hinges on the bootlid as a guide for refitting.
3 With the aid of an assistant, unscrew the mounting bolts then lift the bootlid from the hinges.
4 The hinges can be removed if required by unhooking the return springs and unbolting the hinges from the body.

Refitting and adjustment

5 Refitting is a reversal of removal, but make sure that the hinges are positioned as noted on removal and tighten the mounting bolts securely. With the bootlid closed, check that it is positioned centrally within the body aperture. If adjustment is necessary, loosen the mounting bolts and reposition the bootlid, then retighten the bolts. Check that the striker enters the lock centrally, and if necessary adjust the striker position by loosening the mounting bolt. Tighten the bolt on completion.

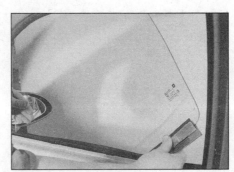
14.11 Removing a front door window glass

14.8b . . . and secure with a riveter

18 Bootlid lock components – removal and refitting

Lock

Removal

1 Open the bootlid then undo the screws and remove the trim panel by prising carefully using a wide-bladed screwdriver.
2 Disconnect the private lock linkage rod by prising up the plastic retainer.
3 Using a Torx key unscrew the mounting bolts, then withdraw the lock from inside the bootlid.

Refitting

4 Refitting is a reversal of removal. Check that when closed the bootlid lock engages the lock striker centrally. If necessary loosen the bolt and adjust the position of the striker, then tighten the bolt.

Lock cylinder

Removal

5 Open the bootlid and remove the trim panel as previously described.
6 Disconnect the central locking linkage rod by prising up the plastic retainer.
7 Unscrew the hexagon-headed mounting nuts, then unhook the lock cylinder from the lock linkage rod and remove from the bootlid.

Refitting

8 Refitting is a reversal of removal.

19 Tailgate and support struts – removal, refitting and adjustment

Tailgate (Hatchback models)

Removal

1 Disconnect the battery negative (earth) lead (see Chapter 5A).
2 Open the tailgate and disconnect the wiring harness at the connectors.
3 Disconnect the tailgate washer hose.
4 Have an assistant support the tailgate, then disconnect the tops of the support struts by

19.8a Undo the upper screws . . .

19.8b . . . and lower screws . . .

19.8c . . . then prise the trim panel from the inside of the tailgate (Estate models)

prising out the spring clips with a small screwdriver. Lower the struts to the body.

5 Extract the clips from the hinge pivot pins, then drive out the pins with a suitable drift while the assistant supports the tailgate. Withdraw the tailgate from the body.

Refitting

6 Refitting is a reversal of removal, but apply a little grease to the pivot pins, and check that when closed the tailgate is positioned centrally within the body aperture and flush with the surrounding bodywork. If necessary, remove the trim from the rear of the roof headlining and loosen the hinge mounting bolts. Reposition the tailgate then tighten the bolts and refit the trim. If necessary, adjust the position of the rubber supports so that the tailgate is flush with the surrounding bodywork. After making adjustments, check that the striker enters the lock centrally and if

necessary loosen the striker bolts to reposition it. Tighten the bolts on completion.

Tailgate (Estate models)

Removal

7 Disconnect the battery negative (earth) lead (see Chapter 5A).

8 Open the tailgate then remove the trim panel by removing the screws and carefully prising the panel free from the clips (see illustrations).

9 Disconnect the wiring at the connector just below the tailgate glass.

10 Release the cable ties and unbolt the earth cable.

11 Disconnect the wiring from the heated rear screen, interior light switch, number plate lamp, wiper motor, central door locking drive and anti-theft warning system switch.

12 Attach a piece of string to the end of the wiring harness, then withdraw it from the top of the tailgate. Untie the string and leave it in position inside the tailgate to aid refitting.

13 Disconnect the tailgate washer hose.

14 Have an assistant support the tailgate, then disconnect the tops of the support struts by prising out the spring clips with a small screwdriver. Lower the struts to the body.

15 Extract the clips from the hinge pivot pins, then drive out the pins with a suitable drift while the assistant supports the tailgate. Withdraw the tailgate from the body (see illustration).

Refitting

16 Refitting is a reversal of removal, but apply a little grease to the pivot pins, and check that when closed the tailgate is positioned centrally within the body aperture and flush with the surrounding bodywork. If necessary, remove the trim from the rear of the roof headlining and loosen the hinge mounting bolts. Reposition the tailgate then tighten the bolts and refit the trim. If necessary, adjust the position of the rubber supports so that the tailgate is flush with the surrounding bodywork. After making adjustments, check that the striker enters the lock centrally and if necessary loosen the striker bolts to reposition it. Remove the rear trim panel where necessary. Tighten the bolts and refit the trim on completion (see illustrations).

Support struts

Removal

17 Open the tailgate and note which way round the struts are fitted. Have an assistant support the tailgate in its open position.

18 Using a small screwdriver, prise the spring clip from the top of the strut and disconnect it from the ball on the tailgate (see illustration).

19 Similarly prise the spring clip from the bottom of the strut and disconnect it from the ball on the body. Withdraw the strut.

Refitting

20 Refitting is a reversal of removal but make sure that the exposed rod is at the top of the strut.

19.15 Location of clip securing the tailgate hinge pin (Estate models)

19.16a Undo the screws and remove the rear trim panel . . .

19.16b . . . for access to the tailgate lock striker

19.18 Use a screwdriver to prise out the spring clip from the top of the tailgate support strut

20.1a Prise out the plastic covers . . .

20.1b . . . and undo the retaining screws

20.1c The rear shelf strap hook screw also retains the rear shelf

20.3 Tailgate lock and mounting bolts

20.6 Tailgate lock cylinder and linkage

20.7a Unscrew the nuts . . .

20 Tailgate lock components – removal and refitting

Lock

Removal

1 Open the tailgate and remove the trim panel. To do this, prise out the plastic covers for access to the screws, remove the screws and carefully release the trim from the retaining clips, using a wide-bladed screwdriver or similar tool (see illustrations).
2 Disconnect the linkage by prising up the plastic retainer.
3 Using a Torx key unscrew the mounting bolts then withdraw the lock from the tailgate (see illustration).

Refitting

4 Refitting is a reversal of removal.

Lock cylinder assembly

Removal

5 Open the tailgate and remove the trim panel.
6 Disconnect the central locking linkage by prising up the plastic retainer (see illustration).
7 Unscrew the hexagon-headed mounting nuts, then unhook the lock cylinder assembly from the lock linkage rod and remove from the tailgate (see illustrations).

Refitting

8 Refitting is a reversal of removal.

21 Central locking system components – removal and refitting

Door servo motor

1 The servo motors are integral with the door locks. Refer to Section 13 for removal and refitting information.

Control unit

Note: *The central locking control unit is combined with the anti-theft warning system, and incorporates a safety feature whereby all locks are released in the event of a major front end collision. The unit incorporates a self-diagnosis and programming feature, requiring the use of the TECH1 diagnosis and programming tool only available to Vauxhall technicians.*
2 Remove the trim panel from the right-hand front footwell.
3 Release the catch and disconnect the wiring from the bottom of the control unit (see illustration).
4 Unscrew the mounting nuts and remove the control unit from inside the vehicle.
5 Refitting is a reversal of removal, but tighten the mounting nuts securely.

Bootlid servo motor

6 Open the bootlid, then disconnect the central locking linkage from the servo motor by prising up the plastic retainer.
7 Disconnect the wiring connector(s) from the motor.
8 Unscrew the mounting bolts and remove the servo motor from the bootlid.

21.3 Central locking control unit

20.7b . . . and withdraw the lock cylinder assembly from the tailgate

21.12 Unscrew the mounting bolts . . .

21.13 . . . and remove the servo motor from the tailgate

21.15 Fuel filler flap servo motor located behind the right-hand side luggage compartment side trim lid (Hatchback and Estate models)

9 Refitting is a reversal of removal, but tighten the mounting bolts securely.

Tailgate servo motor

10 Open the tailgate and remove the trim panel.
11 Disconnect the servo motor linkage from the lock cylinder by prising up the plastic retainer.
12 Unscrew the mounting bolts (see illustration).
13 Disconnect the wiring connector from the motor and remove the servo motor from the tailgate (see illustration).
14 Refitting is a reversal of removal, but tighten the mounting bolts securely.

Fuel filler flap servo motor

Hatchback and Estate models

15 Open the right-hand side luggage compartment trim lid, then disconnect the wiring plug from the servo motor (see illustration).
16 Unscrew the two mounting bolts and remove the servo motor from the rear quarter panel. Withdraw from inside the vehicle.
17 Refitting is a reversal of removal, but tighten the mounting bolts securely.

Notchback models

18 Open the right-hand side luggage compartment trim lid, then remove the jack.
19 Detach the interior trim panel then disconnect the wiring plug from the servo motor.
20 Unbolt the retainer and the servo motor and withdraw from inside the vehicle.

21 Refitting is a reversal of removal, but tighten the mounting bolts securely.

22 Electric window components – removal and refitting

Note: *After reconnecting the battery, renewing fuses or reconnecting the window winder wiring plugs, each window winder motor must be reprogrammed as described at the end of this Section.*

Centre console control switch

Removal

1 Carefully prise the storage compartment panel from under the handbrake lever on the centre console.
2 Disconnect the relevant wiring plug, then carefully lever out the control switch and remove it together with the wiring from the centre console.

Refitting

3 Refitting is a reversal of removal.

Rear door control switch

Removal

4 Using two small screwdrivers, carefully lever the rear door control switch from the plastic door grip. Also prise out the speaker grille and the lower plastic plug.
5 Unscrew the bolts and remove the door grip while feeding the switch wiring through.

23.1 Disconnect the wiring . . .

23.3a . . . then unscrew the mounting bolts . . .

6 Disconnect the wiring and remove the switch.

Refitting

7 Refitting is a reversal of removal.

Window winder motor

Removal

8 Remove the window regulator as described in Section 14.
9 Unbolt the motor from the regulator.

Refitting

10 Refitting is a reversal of removal.

Programming

11 After refitting a window winder motor or reconnecting the battery, each motor must be programmed with its fully closed position.
12 With the ignition switched on, close all doors.
13 Working on each window in turn, completely close the window by pressing and holding down the rocker switch, then hold the switch down for at least a further 2 seconds.

23 Exterior mirrors and associated components – removal and refitting

Exterior mirror

Removal

1 On models with electrically-controlled and heated exterior mirrors, remove the door inner trim panel as described in Section 12 then disconnect the wiring for the mirror (see illustration).
2 On models with non-electric exterior mirrors, carefully pull off the control knob then prise off the triangular trim from the inside of the exterior mirror and remove the padding.
3 Support the mirror then unscrew the three mounting bolts and lift the mirror from the door. Note that the front bolt is located on the edge of the door (see illustrations).

Refitting

4 Refitting is a reversal of removal. On non-electric mirrors, adjust the mirror rubber seal position as necessary by turning the eccentric bolt accessed through the hole beneath the mirror.

Mirror glass

Removal

5 Using a wad of cloth, press the upper inner corner of the glass inwards so that the glass is forced out from the centre retainer and control cable ends (see illustration).
6 Disconnect the mirror heating wiring and withdraw the mirror from the housing.

Refitting

7 Refitting is a reversal of removal. Carefully press the mirror into the housing until the centre retainer and control cable ends are engaged (see illustration).

Servo motor

Removal

8 Remove the mirror as described earlier in this Section.
9 Remove the mirror glass as described earlier in this Section.
10 Remove the front cover by prising out the upper and lower corners until the lug is released, then pulling the rear out of the eccentric. Lever out the wiring plug then undo the three screws and withdraw the servo motor.

Refitting

11 Refitting is a reversal of removal.

Mirror actuation switch

Removal

12 Prise the plastic cover from the inside of the interior door handle grip. Also prise out the small plastic cover or electric mirror switch (as applicable) from the outside of the grip – disconnect the wiring where necessary.
13 Prise off the small loudspeaker grille.
14 Unscrew and remove the retaining screws and remove the door handle surround/grip while feeding the switch wiring through the hole. Disconnect the wiring from the loudspeaker.
15 Disconnect the wiring and remove the switch.

23.5 Disconnecting the exterior mirror glass from the centre retainer and control cable ends

23.3b . . . and lift the exterior mirror from the front door

Refitting

16 Refitting is a reversal of removal.

Mirror adjusting cable

Removal

17 Remove the mirror glass as described earlier.
18 Detach the mounting bracket and covers from the housing.
19 Note the position of the guide grooves, then push the control cable guides apart and remove from the rear of the mirror housing. Note that the upper cable fitting is coloured white and the lower one is coloured black.

Refitting

20 Refitting is a reversal of removal, but note that the cable guides must be located in the second groove on the driver's side and in the first groove on the passenger's side.

24 Windscreen and fixed window glass – general information

The windscreen, rear/tailgate screen and rear quarter window glass (Estate models) are cemented in position with a special adhesive and require the use of specialist equipment for their removal and refitting. Renewal of such fixed glass is considered beyond the scope of the home mechanic. Owners are strongly advised to have the work carried out

23.7 When fitting a new glass, press it firmly into the housing until the centre retainer and control cable ends are engaged

by one of the many specialist windscreen fitting specialists.

On Estate models the rear quarter window glass incorporates a breakage sensor which is linked to the anti-theft security system, and the rear screen incorporates an aerial for the radio.

25 Sunroof components – removal and refitting

1 Either a manually-operated or electrically-operated sunroof may be fitted.

Sunroof glass

Removal

2 Slide back the sun screen and half open the sunroof.
3 Undo the screws from the rear edge of the sunroof and remove the trim.
4 Close the sunroof then unclip the side trim using a screwdriver.
5 Mark the position of the side screws then unscrew them and withdraw the glass.

Refitting

6 Refitting is a reversal of removal but adjust the height of the glass as follows. With the side screws loose, position the glass so that the front edge is flush with the front of the roof or a maximum of 1.0 mm below the roof and the rear edge is flush with the rear of the roof or a maximum of 1.0 mm above the roof. Tighten the screws to the specified torque with the glass in this position.

Sunroof screen

Removal

7 Remove the sunroof glass as described earlier.
8 Remove the water deflector panel.
9 Remove the front sliders, then pull the screen forwards and remove the rear sliders.
10 Withdraw the screen from the roof.

Refitting

11 Refitting is a reversal of removal.

Wind deflector

Removal

12 Half open the glass then use pliers to release the lugs at the front of the opening.
13 Lever off the retaining ring and extract the pin, then remove the deflector.

Refitting

14 Refitting is a reversal of removal.

Sunroof crank drive

Removal

15 Remove the interior lamp as described in Chapter 12, Section 6.
16 Undo the centre screw and remove the crank handle from the splined shaft.

17 Undo the screws and remove the control unit cover.
18 Undo the screws and remove the crank drive.

Refitting

19 Refitting is a reversal of removal, however first adjust the drive by temporarily locating the crank handle on the splines and turning the drive clockwise as far as possible. Now turn the handle back three full turns to the catch position. **Note:** *On manual versions, the crank handle stops after 8 turns clockwise after which the button must be depressed and the handle turned a further 2 turns for the glass to reach its end position.*

Sunroof electric drive unit

Removal

20 Remove the control unit panel then disconnect the wiring harness plug from the drive unit.
21 Unbolt and remove the electric drive unit.

Refitting

22 Refitting is a reversal of removal. It is recommended that new bolts are used to secure the drive unit.

Sunroof assembly and control cables

Removal and refitting

23 Removal and refitting of the complete sunroof assembly and control cables is considered beyond the scope of the average home mechanic as it involves the removal of

27.3 The front seats are secured to the floor with Torx screws

27.5b . . . and disconnect the wiring

27.1 Prise off the cover for access to the seat belt mounting on the front seat

the headlining. This work should be carried out by a Vauxhall/Opel dealer.

---

26 Body exterior fittings – removal and refitting

Scuttle cover panel

Removal

1 Open the bonnet then remove the wind-screen wiper arms as described in Chapter 12.
2 Pull the rubber weatherstrip from the front of the scuttle.
3 Release the side clips and withdraw the scuttle cover panel.

Refitting

4 Refitting is a reversal of removal.

27.5a Release the clip . . .

27.7 Rear seat cushion front hinge pins

Wheelarch liners

Removal and refitting

5 The wheelarch liners are secured by a combination of self-tapping screws, push-fit clips and nuts. Removal is self-evident after supporting the vehicle on axle stands and removing the roadwheel (see *Jacking and vehicle support*). The clips are removed by pushing the centre pins through, and are secured by inserting the pins and pushing them in flush.

Body trim strips and badges

Removal and refitting

6 The various body trim strips and badges are held in position with a special adhesive. Removal requires the trim/badge to be heated, to soften the adhesive, and then cut away from the surface. Due to the high risk of damage to the vehicle paintwork during this operation, it is recommended that this task should be entrusted to a Vauxhall/Opel dealer.

---

27 Seats – removal and refitting

Front seat

⚠ *Warning: The front seats are fitted with pyrotechnic seat belt tensioners which are triggered by the airbag control system. Before removing the front seats, disconnect the battery and wait at least 1 minute to allow the system capacitors to discharge.*

Removal

1 Carefully prise the cover from the outer side of the front seat **(see illustration)**.
2 Using a Torx key unscrew the mounting bolt and disconnect the belt from the front seat. Recover the special washer.
3 Adjust the seat fully forwards, then use the Torx key to unscrew the rear mounting screws **(see illustration)**.
4 Tilt the seat forward and release it from the front mountings.
5 Disconnect the wiring and remove the front seat from inside the vehicle **(see illustrations)**.

Refitting

6 Refitting is a reversal of removal but tighten the mounting screws to the specified torque.

Rear seat cushion

Removal

7 Fold the rear seat cushion forwards to expose the front hinge pins **(see illustration)**.
8 Extract the circlips then drive out the hinge pins using a suitable drift.
9 Withdraw the rear seat from inside the vehicle.

Refitting

10 Refitting is a reversal of removal.

Rear seat backrest

Removal

11 Fold the rear seat cushion forwards and detach the seat belt buckles from the backrest.

12 Where necessary detach the rubber cable.

13 Fold the backrest forwards then prise out the clips and pull back the carpet from the rear outer corners **(see illustrations)**.

14 Using a Torx key undo the screws and detach the side hinges.

15 Undo the screws and detach the centre hinges **(see illustration)**.

16 Withdraw the rear seat backrest from inside the vehicle.

Refitting

17 Refitting is a reversal of removal.

---

28 Seat belt components – removal and refitting

27.13a Use a screwdriver or removal tool . . .

27.13c . . . then pull back the carpet to expose the rear seat backrest side hinges

27.13b . . . to remove the plastic clips . . .

27.15 Rear seat backrest centre hinge mounting screws

> ⚠ **Warning: The front seats are fitted with pyrotechnic seat belt tensioners which are triggered by the airbag control system. Before removing a front seat belt, disconnect the battery and wait at least 1 minute to allow the system capacitors to discharge.**

Front belt and reel

Removal

1 Carefully prise the cover from the outer side of the front seat.

2 Using a Torx key unscrew the mounting bolt and disconnect the belt from the front seat. Recover the special washer.

3 Remove the upper trim panel from the B-pillar.

4 Unhook the seat belt from the shackle, then unscrew the upper mounting bolt and detach the seat belt – recover the special washer.

5 Remove the lower trim panel from the B-pillar.

6 Prise the cover from the lower outside of the B-pillar for access to the front seat belt reel mounting nut. Using a deep socket, unscrew the nut taking care not to drop it

inside the B-pillar. Note that an extension pin is provided to enable the nut to be removed safely.

7 With the nut removed, remove the reel from the inside of the pillar. As it is being removed, feed the belt through the hole in the trim panel.

Refitting

8 Refitting is a reversal of removal, but tighten the mounting bolts to the specified torque.

Front belt stalk and tensioner

Removal

9 Remove the front seat as described in Section 27.

10 Disconnect the wiring plug and release the cable tie, then unbolt and remove the tensioner **(see illustration)**.

Refitting

11 Refitting is a reversal of removal but tighten the mounting bolt to the specified torque.

Rear belt and reel

Removal

12 Open the rear door and pull the weatherstrip from the door aperture in the area of the wheelarch **(see illustration)**.

13 Remove the retaining clamp for the rear seat backrest, and remove the load compartment cover.

14 Undo the screws and remove the rear quarter inner panel, noting the location slots in the upper trim **(see illustrations)**.

15 Remove the cover (where fitted) from the seat belt reel, then unbolt and remove the reel

28.10 Front seat belt stalk and tensioner

28.12 Pull the weatherstrip from the door aperture and remove the trim

28.14a Remove the rear quarter inner panel . . .

28.14b . . . noting the location slots

28.16 Rear seat belt outer mounting on the floor

28.17a Removing the cover from the rear seat belt height adjuster

from behind the backrest. On Notchback models thread the seat belt through the inner panel.

16 Remove the sill inner trim panel, then unscrew the bolt securing the outer belt to the floor **(see illustration)**.

17 Remove the cover, then unscrew the bolt securing the seat belt to the height adjuster, noting the location of the spacers **(see illustrations)**.

18 Fold the rear seat cushion forwards, then unbolt the centre seat belt stalks from the floor **(see illustration)**.

Refitting

19 Refitting is a reversal of removal, but tighten the mounting bolts to the specified torque.

28.17b Unscrew the bolt securing the seat belt to the height adjuster

28.18 Rear seat belt centre stalks

---

29 Interior trim – removal and refitting

1 The interior trim panels are secured by a combination of clips and screws. Removal and refitting is generally self-explanatory, noting that it may be necessary to remove or loosen surrounding panels to allow a particular panel to be removed. The following paragraphs describe the removal and refitting of the major panels in more detail.

Front footwell side trim panel

2 Open the front door and pull the weatherstrip away from the side trim panel.

29.14 Removing the rear quarter glass trim panel

3 Undo the crosshead screw and press the centre pin through the clip, then remove the side trim panel.

4 Refitting is a reversal of removal.

B-pillar trim panel

5 Where fitted, carefully lever off the movement sensor and disconnect the wiring.

6 Unbolt the front seat belt from the height adjuster with reference to Section 28.

7 Pull the door weatherstrip away from the trim.

8 Prise the upper trim panel from the B-pillar and feed the seat belt through.

9 Remove the trim panel from the sill, then prise away the B-pillar trim.

10 Refitting is a reversal of removal.

Rear quarter glass trim panel

11 On Estate and Hatchback models remove the rear luggage compartment cover.

12 Pull the weatherstrip from the front of the trim panel.

13 Remove the rear seat belt from the C-pillar with reference to Section 28.

14 Carefully prise away the rear quarter glass trim panel **(see illustration)**. On Notchback models, feed the seat belt through the panel.

15 Refitting is a reversal of removal.

Sill inner trim panel

16 Remove the relevant front seat as described in Section 27.

17 Pull away the door weatherstrip from the top of the trim panel.

18 The trim panel is secured with 7 clips.

Carefully prise away the panel using a screwdriver to release the clips.

19 Refitting is a reversal of removal.

Luggage compartment side trim

Hatchback models

20 Remove the rear luggage compartment cover.

21 Fold the rear seat backrest forwards.

22 Undo the retaining screws, then prise out the trim panel using a screwdriver to release the retaining clips.

23 Disconnect the wiring for the interior lamp, and withdraw the trim panel.

24 Refitting is a reversal of removal.

Estate models

25 Remove the rear luggage compartment cover.

26 Undo the screws then prise out the side trim panel using a screwdriver to release the retaining clips.

27 Refitting is a reversal of removal.

Notchback models

28 Open the bootlid and remove the vehicle tools.

29 Remove the rear seat backrest release bracket, the rubber buffer and the hinge pin.

30 Remove the luggage compartment carpet.

31 The side trim panels are secured with clips and nuts. After removing them prise the panels away from the body.

32 Refitting is a reversal of removal.

Carpets

Removal

33 The front and rear carpets can be removed after removing the front seats, centre console and rear footwell air distribution ducts together with side trim panels and remaining brackets.

34 On Estate models the rear luggage compartment carpet can be removed by releasing the clips located on the backrest and rear valance then removing the tools and spare wheel cover.

Refitting

35 Refitting is a reversal of removal.

Headlining

36 The headlining is secured to the roof with clips and screws, and can be withdrawn once all fittings such as the grab handles, sun visors, sunroof, front, centre and rear pillar trim panels, and associated components have been removed. The door and tailgate aperture weatherseals will also have to be prised clear.

37 Note that headlining removal requires considerable skill and experience if it is to be carried out without damage, and is therefore best entrusted to an expert.

30 Centre console – removal and refitting

Removal

1 Disconnect the battery negative (earth) lead (see Chapter 5A).

2 Carefully prise out the oddments tray from under the handbrake lever then unclip the gaiter and surround and remove from the top of the handbrake lever (see illustrations).

3 Undo the screws and remove the gear lever/selector lever surround panel. Where necessary also disconnect the wiring from the electric window switches (see illustration).

4 Using a small screwdriver, carefully prise out the covers from the centre console side retaining screws then undo the screws. Two are located on each side of the front of the console and a further two are located at the rear of the console. Also unscrew the middle mounting screw (see illustrations).

5 Withdraw the console slightly from the facia, then carefully prise off the covers at each side of the ashtray.

6 Prise out the ashtray and can holder insert retaining clamp.

7 Disconnect the wiring for the ashtray illumination and cigar lighter.

8 Fully apply the handbrake lever, then withdraw the centre console upwards and remove from inside the vehicle (see illustration).

Refitting

9 Refitting is a reversal of removal.

30.2a Removing the oddments tray

30.3 Gear lever/selector lever surround panel securing screws (1) and centre console middle mounting screw (2)

31 Glovebox – removal and refitting

RHD models without passenger's airbag and CD changer

Removal

1 Disconnect the battery negative (earth) lead (see Chapter 5A).

2 With the glovebox open, undo the mounting screws securing the glovebox to the facia panel. There are two in the roof of the box, and two more on the lower front of the box.

3 Withdraw the glovebox from the facia, and at the same time, disconnect the illumination lamp wiring. disconnect disconnect

30.4b . . . and middle retaining screw

30.2b Removing the gaiter and surround from the handbrake lever

30.4a Unscrewing the side retaining screws . . .

Refitting

4 Refitting is a reversal of removal.

All other models

Removal

5 Open the glovebox lid and undo the two upper mounting screws securing the top of the glovebox to the facia panel.

6 Undo the two lower screws and withdraw the glovebox from the facia panel sufficient to disconnect the wiring from the illumination lamp.

7 Disconnect the wiring from the CD changer. On models fitted with air conditioning detach the hose from the cooling slider.

8 Withdraw the glovebox from inside the vehicle.

Refitting

9 Refitting is a reversal of removal.

30.8 Removing the centre console

32.7a Remove the clips . . .

32.7b . . . and remove the lower trim panel from under the facia on the driver's side

32.7c Prise out the air distribution duct

32 Facia assembly – removal and refitting

Removal

1 Disconnect the battery negative (earth) lead (see Chapter 5A).

 Warning: Wait for at least 1 minute after disconnecting the battery to allow the airbag control system capacitors to discharge.

2 Remove the steering wheel as described in Chapter 10.

3 Remove the airbag contact unit as described in Chapter 12, Section 24.

4 Remove the wiper and indicator switches from the steering column as described in Chapter 12, Section 4. Also remove the switch mounting bracket.

5 Remove the ignition switch as described in Chapter 12, Section 4.

6 Remove the immobiliser control unit as described in Chapter 12, Section 22.

7 On the driver's side remove the lower trim panel from under the facia then prise out the air distribution duct **(see illustrations)**.

8 Remove the radio as described in Chapter 12.

9 Remove the heating controls as described in Chapter 3.

10 Remove the centre air vents as described in Chapter 3, Section 10, and the instrument panel as described in Chapter 12.

11 Remove the glovebox as described in Section 31.

12 Remove the centre console with reference to Section 30.

13 Where fitted, remove the passenger side airbag as described in Chapter 12, Section 24.

14 Remove the inner panels from the A-pillars.

15 Remove the coolant line cover from under the facia.

16 Carefully prise the windscreen airflow cover from the front of the facia.

17 Remove the trim panels from the outer sides of each front footwell.

18 Remove the heating air ducts from the left- and right-hand sides.

19 Unclip the wiring loom and support then unbolt the support brace from below the centre of the facia assembly **(see illustrations)**.

20 Disconnect the wiring harness plug located in the right-hand side of the engine compartment.

21 Unscrew the bolt and disconnect the earth cable from the bottom of the A-pillar. Also detach the earth cable from the steering column bracket.

22 Where necessary, remove the brake ABS hydraulic modulator with reference to Chapter 9, Section 23, then disconnect the wiring harness plug and withdraw the wiring into the passenger compartment.

23 Remove the fusebox cover and unbolt the fusebox.

24 Unscrew the bolts securing the facia to the bulkhead and body, and withdraw it together with the wiring **(see illustration)**. Remove from inside the vehicle.

Refitting

25 Refitting is a reversal of removal, referring to the relevant Chapters where necessary. If a new facia assembly is fitted, make sure that the airbag warning stickers are transferred from the old facia

32.19a Release the clips . . .

32.19b . . . and remove the wiring support . . .

32.19c . . . then unscrew the support brace lower mounting nuts . . .

32.19d . . . and upper mounting screws

32.24 Facia panel lower mounting bolt

Chapter 12
Body electrical system

Contents

Degrees of difficulty

| **Easy,** suitable for novice with little experience | | **Fairly easy,** suitable for beginner with some experience | | **Fairly difficult,** suitable for competent DIY mechanic | | **Difficult,** suitable for experienced DIY mechanic | | **Very difficult,** suitable for expert DIY or professional | |

Specifications

System type .... 12 volt negative earth

Torque wrench settings	Nm	lbf ft
Airbag control unit	10	7
Airbag to steering wheel	8	6
Passenger side airbag and cover	5	4
Side airbag	5	4
Tailgate wiper motor retaining nut	10	7

1 General information and precautions

⚠️ **Warning: Before carrying out any work on the electrical system, read through the precautions given in Safety first! at the beginning of this manual, and in Chapter 5A.**

1 The electrical system is of 12 volt negative earth type. Power for the lights and all electrical accessories is supplied by a lead-acid type battery, which is charged by the alternator. The speedometer is of the electrical type, and uses the ABS wheel sensors or a speed sensor on the transmission to monitor the vehicle speed. There is no speedometer cable.

2 This Chapter covers repair and service procedures for the various electrical components not associated with the engine. Information on the battery, alternator and starter motor can be found in Chapter 5A.

3 It should be noted that, before working on any component in the electrical system, the battery negative terminal should first be disconnected, to prevent the possibility of electrical short-circuits and/or fires.

4 At regular intervals, check the routing of the wiring harness, ensuring that it is correctly secured by the clips or ties to prevent it chafing against other components. If evidence of chafing is found, repair the damage and ensure that the harness is secured or protected so that the problem cannot occur again.

Caution: If the radio/cassette player fitted to the vehicle is one with an anti-theft security code, refer to 'Radio/cassette unit anti-theft system' in the Reference Section of this manual before disconnecting the battery.

2 Electrical fault finding – general information

Note: *Refer to the precautions given in 'Safety first!' (at the beginning of this manual) and to Section 1 of this Chapter before starting work. The following tests relate to testing of the main electrical circuits, and should not be used to test delicate electronic circuits (such as anti-lock braking systems), particularly where an electronic control module is used.*

General

1 A typical electrical circuit consists of an electrical component, any switches, relays, motors, fuses, fusible links or circuit breakers related to that component, and the wiring and connectors that link the component to both the battery and the chassis. To help to pinpoint a problem in an electrical circuit, wiring diagrams are included at the end of this chapter.

2 Before attempting to diagnose an electrical fault, first study the appropriate wiring diagram to obtain a complete understanding of the components included in the particular circuit concerned. The possible sources of a fault can be narrowed down by noting whether other components related to the circuit are operating properly. If several components or circuits fail at one time, the problem is likely to be related to a shared fuse or earth connection.

3 Electrical problems usually stem from simple causes, such as loose or corroded connections, a faulty earth connection, a blown fuse, a melted fusible link, or a faulty relay (refer to Section 3 for details of testing relays). Visually inspect the condition of all fuses, wires and connections in a problem circuit before testing the components. Use the wiring diagrams to determine which terminal connections will need to be checked, to pinpoint the trouble-spot.

4 The basic tools required for electrical fault finding include the following:

a) *a circuit tester or voltmeter (a 12 volt bulb with a set of test leads can also be used for certain tests).*
b) *a self-powered test light (sometimes known as a continuity tester).*
c) *an ohmmeter (to measure resistance).*
d) *a battery.*
e) *a set of test leads.*
f) *a jumper wire, preferably with a circuit breaker or fuse incorporated, which can be used to bypass suspect wires or electrical components.*

Before attempting to locate a problem with test instruments, use the wiring diagram to determine where to make the connections.

5 To find the source of an intermittent wiring fault (usually due to a poor or dirty connection, or damaged wiring insulation), a 'wiggle' test can be performed on the wiring. This involves 'wiggling' the wiring by hand, to see if the fault occurs as the wiring is moved. It should be possible to narrow down the source of the fault to a particular section of wiring. This method of testing can be used in conjunction with any of the tests described in the following sub-Sections.

6 Apart from problems due to poor connections, two basic types of fault can occur in an electrical circuit – open-circuit and short-circuit.

7 Open-circuit faults are caused by a break somewhere in the circuit, which prevents current from flowing. An open-circuit fault will prevent a component from working, but will not cause the relevant circuit fuse to blow.

8 Short-circuit faults are caused by a 'short' somewhere in the circuit, which allows the current flowing in the circuit to 'escape' along an alternative route, usually to earth. Short-circuit faults are normally caused by a breakdown in wiring insulation, which allows a feed wire to touch either another wire, or an earthed component such as the bodyshell. A short-circuit fault will normally cause the relevant circuit fuse to blow.

Finding an open-circuit

9 To check for an open-circuit, connect one lead of a circuit tester or voltmeter to either the negative battery terminal or a known good earth.

10 Connect the other lead to a connector in the circuit being tested, preferably nearest to the battery or fuse.

11 Switch on the circuit, remembering that some circuits are live only when the ignition switch is moved to a particular position.

12 If voltage is present (indicated either by the tester bulb lighting or a voltmeter reading, as applicable), this means that the section of the circuit between the relevant connector and the battery is problem-free.

13 Continue to check the remainder of the circuit in the same fashion.

14 When a point is reached at which no voltage is present, the problem must lie between that point and the previous test point with voltage. Most problems can be traced to a broken, corroded or loose connection.

Finding a short-circuit

15 To check for a short-circuit, first disconnect the load(s) from the circuit (loads are the components that draw current from a circuit, such as bulbs, motors, heating elements, etc).

16 Remove the relevant fuse from the circuit, and connect a circuit tester or voltmeter to the fuse connections.

17 Switch on the circuit, remembering that some circuits are live only when the ignition switch is moved to a particular position.

18 If voltage is present (indicated either by the tester bulb lighting or a voltmeter reading, as applicable), this means that there is a short-circuit.

19 If no voltage is present, but the fuse still blows with the load(s) connected, this indicates an internal fault in the load(s).

Finding an earth fault

20 The battery negative terminal is connected to 'earth' (the metal of the engine/transmission and the car body), and most systems are wired so that they only receive a positive feed. The current returning through the metal of the car body. This means that the component mounting and the body form part of that circuit. Loose or corroded mountings can therefore cause a range of electrical faults, ranging from total failure of a circuit, to a puzzling partial fault. In particular, lights may shine dimly (especially when another circuit sharing the same earth point is in operation). Motors (eg, wiper motors or the radiator cooling fan motor) may run slowly, and the operation of one circuit may have an affect on another. Note that on many vehicles, earth straps are used between certain components, such as the engine/transmission and the body, usually where there is no metal-to-metal contact between components, due to flexible rubber mountings, etc.

21 To check whether a component is

3.2 The main fuses are located beneath a cover on the driver's side of the facia panel

3.5 Using the special tweezers to remove a fuse

properly earthed, disconnect the battery, and connect one lead of an ohmmeter to a known good earth point. Connect the other lead to the wire or earth connection being tested. The resistance reading should be zero; if not, check the connection as follows.

22 If an earth connection is thought to be faulty, dismantle the connection, and clean back to bare metal both the bodyshell and the wire terminal or the component earth connection mating surface. Be careful to remove all traces of dirt and corrosion, then use a knife to trim away any paint, so that a clean metal-to-metal joint is made. On reassembly, tighten the joint fasteners securely; if a wire terminal is being refitted, use serrated washers between the terminal and the bodyshell, to ensure a clean and secure connection. When the connection is remade, prevent the onset of corrosion in the future by applying a coat of petroleum jelly or silicone-based grease.

3 Fuses and relays –
general information

General

Fuses

1 Fuses are designed to break a circuit when a predetermined current is reached, to protect the components and wiring which could be damaged by excessive current flow. Any excessive current flow will be due to a fault in the circuit, usually a short-circuit (see Section 2).

2 The main fuses and relays are located in a panel beneath a cover at the right-hand end of the facia **(see illustration)**.

3 The circuits protected by the various fuses and relays are marked on the inside of the panel cover.

4 A blown fuse can be recognised from its melted or broken wire.

5 To remove a fuse, first ensure that the relevant circuit is switched off. Then open the cover and pull the relevant fuse from the panel using the tweezers supplied **(see illustration)**. If desired, the lower end of the panel can be tilted forwards, after releasing the retaining clip, to improve access.

6 Before renewing a blown fuse, trace and rectify the cause, and always use a fuse of the correct rating. Never substitute a fuse of a higher rating, or make temporary repairs using wire or metal foil, as more serious damage or even fire could result.

7 Spare fuses are generally provided in the blank terminal positions in the fusebox.

8 Note that the fuses are colour-coded as follows:

Light Brown	5A
Brown	7.5A
Red	10A
Light Blue	15A
Yellow	20A
Light Green	30A
Orange	40A

Refer to the wiring diagrams for details of the fuse ratings and the circuits protected.

Relays

9 A relay is an electrically-operated switch, which is used for the following reasons:
 a) A relay can switch a heavy current

remotely from the circuit in which the control current is flowing, allowing the use of lighter-gauge wiring and control switch contacts.
b) A relay can receive more than one control input, unlike a mechanical switch.
c) A relay can have a timer function.

10 The main relays are located on the main fusebox, although some engine-related relays are located in the engine compartment. The relay boxes are located in front of or to one side of the battery, and above the ABS control unit **(see illustration)**.

11 If a circuit or system controlled by a relay develops a fault, and the relay is suspect, operate the system. If the relay is functioning, it should be possible to hear it 'click' as it is energised. If this is the case, the fault lies with the components or wiring of the system. If the relay is not being energised, then either the relay is not receiving a main supply or a switching voltage, or the relay itself is faulty. Testing is by the substitution of a known good unit, but be careful – while some relays are identical in appearance and in operation, others look similar but perform different functions.

12 To remove a relay, first ensure that the relevant circuit is switched off. The relay can then simply be pulled out from the socket, and pushed back into position **(see illustration)**.

3.10 The engine related relays are located in front of the battery on diesel models

3.12 Removing a relay from the main fusebox

4.2a Undo the retaining screws (also on lower shroud) . . .

4.2b . . . and remove the steering column shrouds

4.3 Disconnecting the wiring from the anti-theft immobiliser transceiver

13 Incorporated in the fusebox is a multi-timer which combines the components and relays that were previously separate units. The timer slides into the side of the fusebox as a separate module.

4 Switches – removal and refitting

Steering column lock

1 Remove the steering wheel. Alternatively, the steering wheel may remain in position, but it will have to turned for access to the end face screws of the shrouds.

2 Remove the steering column shrouds by unscrewing the tilt steering lever, then removing the two screws from the end face and three screws from the bottom shroud

(see illustrations). Recover the ignition key position indicator from the ignition switch.
3 Withdraw the anti-theft immobiliser transceiver unit from the lock and disconnect the wiring (see illustration).
4 Insert the ignition key and turn it to position I.
5 Using a small screwdriver or pin punch, depress the locking pin through the hole in the top of the column, then withdraw the lock cylinder using the key (see illustrations).
6 To refit the lock cylinder, push the assembly into the lock housing, until the locking pin engages, then turn the ignition key to position 0 and withdraw the key. If the steering lock pin engages with the steering column as the cylinder is removed, it will not be possible to insert the cylinder so that the locking pin engages. In this case, use a screwdriver in the housing to press the steering lock pin down before inserting the lock cylinder (see illustration).

Ignition switch

7 To remove the ignition switch, disconnect the battery negative (earth) lead (see Chapter 5A) then remove the lock cylinder as previously described.
8 Undo the small grub screw and remove the switch from the steering column.
9 Disconnect the wiring from the switch, using a screwdriver to lever it out if necessary (see illustration).
10 Refitting is a reversal of removal.

Turn signal/wiper switch

11 The turn signal and wiper switch assemblies are removed identically.
12 Remove the steering wheel. Alternatively, the steering wheel may remain in position, but it will have to be turned for access to the end face screws of the shrouds.
13 Remove the steering column shrouds by unscrewing the tilt steering lever, then removing the two screws from the end face and three screws from the bottom shroud. Recover the ignition key position indicator from the ignition switch.
14 Depress the retaining clips, and carefully slide the switch from the top of the housing, then disconnect the wiring and remove it from the vehicle (see illustrations). On models with cruise control, disconnect the additional plugs.
15 Refitting is a reversal of removal.

Facia-mounted switches

Pushbutton (except hazard warning)

16 A small, hooked instrument or length of

4.5a Depress the locking pin . . .

4.5b . . . and withdraw the lock cylinder using the key

4.6 Pressing the steering lock pin down with a screwdriver before inserting the lock cylinder

4.9 Disconnecting the wiring from the ignition switch

4.14a Slide the turn signal/wiper switch from the top of the housing . . .

welding rod is required to pull the switch from the facia.

17 Carefully insert the hooked instrument between the switch and surround, then pull out the switch **(see illustration)**.

18 Disconnect the wiring from the switch.

19 Refitting is a reversal of removal.

Lighting and foglight switch

20 Using a small screwdriver, carefully prise the lighting switch from the facia **(see illustrations)**. Take care not to damage the facia by placing a wad of cloth beneath the screwdriver. If the switch is tight, use a screwdriver inserted on each side of the switch. Note that the terminals on the rear of the switch locate directly in the sockets in the housing. To remove the foglight switch, release the tab.

21 If necessary, the housing can be removed by removing the air vent, then undoing the screw and withdrawing the housing **(see illustration)**. Disconnect the wiring.

22 Refitting is a reversal of removal.

Hazard warning switch

23 It is easier to remove the hazard warning switch when in the ON position.

24 Insert screwdrivers into the channel on either side of the switch and carefully prise it from the facia, or use a small, hooked instrument or length of welding rod to remove the switch **(see illustration)**.

25 On some models the switch cover will separate from the switch, but removal is otherwise the same.

26 Refitting is a reversal of removal.

4.14b . . . and disconnect the wiring

4.20a Use a screwdriver and wad of cloth . . .

Heater blower motor switch

27 Refer to Chapter 3, Section 10.

Braking system switches

28 Refer to Chapter 9, Sections 20, 21 and 23.

4.17 Removing a facia-mounted pushbutton switch

4.20b . . . to prise out the lighting switch

Courtesy and luggage compartment light switches

29 Undo the retaining screw and withdraw the switch **(see illustrations)**.

30 Disconnect the wiring and tape it to the panel to prevent it dropping out of reach.

31 Make sure that the retaining screw makes good contact with the body and switch. If necessary clean the contact points.

32 Refitting is a reversal of removal.

Window switch

Centre console

33 Prise the small storage compartment from beneath the handbrake lever on the centre console.

34 Disconnect the relevant wiring plug.

35 Undo the two screws and lift out the gear lever surround.

36 Press the switch from the surround **(see illustration)**.

4.21 Removing the vent/switch rear housing from the facia

4.24 Use a hooked instrument to prise out the hazard switch

4.29a Undo the screw and remove the courtesy light switch . . .

4.29b . . . then disconnect the wiring

4.36 Press the window switch from the surround

5.3 Removing the cover from the rear of the headlight

37 Refitting is a reversal of removal.

Rear door

38 Using a small screwdriver, carefully prise the lighting switch from the rear door handgrip. Take care not to damage the trim by placing a wad of cloth beneath the screwdriver. If the switch is tight, use a screwdriver inserted on each side of the switch.
39 Prise out the circular panel next to the interior door handle.
40 Undo the screws and remove the handgrip.
41 Disconnect the wiring plug, using a screwdriver to depress the retaining tab, then withdraw the switch and wiring through the handgrip.
42 Refitting is a reversal of removal.

5.5a Depress and unhook the retaining clip . . .

5.9 Remove the cover . . .

5.4 Disconnecting the wiring plug from the headlight bulb

5 Bulbs (exterior lights) – renewal

1 Whenever a bulb is renewed, note the following points.
a) Remember that, if the light has just been in use, the bulb may be extremely hot.
b) Do not touch the bulb glass with the fingers, as this can result in early failure or a dull reflector.
c) Always check the bulb contacts and holder, ensuring that there is clean metal-to-metal contact between the bulb and its live(s) and earth. Clean off any corrosion or dirt before fitting a new bulb.
d) Ensure that the new bulb is of the correct rating.

5.5b . . . and withdraw the bulb

5.10 . . . withdraw the sidelight bulbholder . . .

Headlight

⚠️ **Warning: Xenon dipped beam headlights operate at very high voltage. Do not touch the associated wiring when the headlights are switched on.**

2 Where Xenon dipped beam headlights are fitted, make sure that the ignition is switched off, and also remove fuses F6 and F24 from the interior fusebox.
3 With the bonnet open, remove the cover from the rear of the relevant headlight **(see illustration)**. Note that the outer headlight is for dipped beam and the inner headlight is for the main beam. If working on the left-hand front headlight, it is necessary to temporarily remove the relay box from the front of the battery.
4 Disconnect the wiring plug from the bulb **(see illustration)**. On Xenon headlights, turn the plug anti-clockwise.
5 Where the conventional type headlight is fitted, depress and unhook the retaining clip, then withdraw the bulb from the headlight **(see illustrations)**. On the Xenon type, turn the retaining ring anti-clockwise and withdraw the bulb.
6 When handling the new bulb, use a tissue or clean cloth to avoid touching the glass with the fingers; moisture and grease from the skin can cause blackening and rapid failure of this type of bulb. If the glass is accidentally touched, wipe it clean using methylated spirit.
7 Fit the new bulb using a reversal of the removal procedure, but make sure that the bulb is seated correctly in the cut-outs in the headlight.
8 The remainder is a reversal of the removal procedure.

Front sidelight

9 The front sidelight bulb is located on the outer main beam headlight. First remove the cover from the rear of the headlight **(see illustration)**.
10 Withdraw the sidelight bulbholder from the rear of the headlight **(see illustration)**.
11 Remove the bulb from the holder **(see illustration)**.
12 Fit the new bulb using a reversal of the removal procedure.

5.11 . . . and remove the bulb

5.13 Disconnect the wiring from the front direction indicator bulbholder . . .

5.14a Twist the bulbholder anti-clockwise to remove it . . .

5.14b . . . then depress and turn the bulb from the bulbholder

5.16a Release the clip . . .

5.16b . . . and remove the cover from the rear of the foglight

5.17a Release the spring clip . . .

Front direction indicator

13 The front direction indicator light forms part of the main headlight unit. With the bonnet open, reach down to the rear of the headlight, and disconnect the wiring from the front direction indicator bulbholder **(see illustration)**.

14 Twist the bulbholder anti-clockwise to withdraw it from the headlight, then depress and turn the bulb to remove it **(see illustrations)**.

15 Fit the new bulb using a reversal of the removal procedure.

Front foglight

16 Release the clip and remove the cover from the rear of the foglight located behind the front bumper **(see illustrations)**.

17 Disconnect the wiring at the connector, then release the spring clip and remove the bulb from the foglight **(see illustrations)**.

18 Fit the new bulb using a reversal of the removal procedure. When handling the new bulb, use a tissue or clean cloth to avoid touching the glass with the fingers; moisture and grease from the skin can cause blackening and rapid failure of this type of bulb. If the glass is accidentally touched, wipe it clean using methylated spirit.

Direction indicator side repeater

19 Using a small screwdriver, carefully lever the side repeater light from the front wing moulding **(see illustration)**.

20 Hold the bulbholder, then twist the lens to remove it **(see illustration)**.

21 Pull the wedge-type bulb from the bulbholder **(see illustration)**.

22 Fit the new bulb using a reversal of the removal procedure.

5.17b . . . and remove the bulb from the foglight

5.20 . . . then twist the lens to remove it . . .

Rear light cluster

23 In the luggage compartment, remove the side trim cover. If working on the right-hand side, remove the first aid kit and warning

5.19 Prise the side repeater light from the front wing moulding . . .

5.21 . . . and pull out the wedge-type bulb

5.23a Removing the rear light cluster bulb cover from the left-hand side . . .

5.23b . . . and right-hand side

5.24 Depress the lug to remove the bulbholder

5.25 Depress and twist the relevant bulb to remove it

5.30a Prise out the plastic covers . . .

5.30b . . . and remove the vertical trim from the tailgate

triangle **(see illustrations)**. On Estate models, the left-hand cover is removed by twisting the fastener.

24 Depress the retaining lug in the middle of the rear light cluster, and withdraw the bulbholder from the rear light **(see illustration)**.

25 Depress and twist the relevant bulb to remove it **(see illustration)**.
26 Fit the new bulb using a reversal of the removal procedure.

Rear number plate light

27 Open the tailgate halfway, then undo the screws from the relevant light and withdraw the light unit from under the handle moulding.
28 Release the festoon-type bulb from the spring contacts.
29 Fit the new bulb using a reversal of the removal procedure. Make sure that the bulb is held firmly between the spring contacts, and if necessary pretension the contacts before fitting the bulb.

High-level stop-light

Notchback and Hatchback models

30 Prise out the plastic covers then undo the screws securing the right-hand vertical trim strip to the inside of the tailgate, and carefully release the trim from the retaining clips **(see illustrations)**.
31 Similarly, undo the screws and release the upper trim from its clips. Disconnect the wiring from the high-level stop-light and withdraw the trim **(see illustrations)**.
32 With the trim on the bench, release the clips and separate the stop-light **(see illustrations)**. It is not possible to renew the bulbs individually; renew the light unit complete.

5.31a Undo the screws . . .

5.31b . . . remove the trim . . .

5.31c . . . and disconnect the wiring from the high-level stop-light

5.32a Release the clips . . .

5.32b . . . and separate the stop-light from the trim

6.2a Use a screwdriver to prise out the front interior light . . .

33 Fit the new light unit using a reversal of the removal procedure.

Estate models

34 With the tailgate open, remove the inner trim panelling with reference to Chapter 11, Section 29.
35 Prise out the screw covers then undo the screws and remove the edging panel together with the high-level stop-light).
36 Unclip the stop-light from the panel.
37 Release the cover from the bulbholder then use a screwdriver to release the tabs and withdraw the bulb strip from the holder.
38 Disconnect the wiring and remove the bulb strip.
39 Fit the new bulb using a reversal of the removal procedure.

6 Bulbs (interior lights) – renewal

1 Whenever a bulb is renewed, note the following points.

a) Remember that, if the light has just been in use, the bulb may be extremely hot.

b) Do not touch the bulb glass with the fingers, as this can result in early failure or a dull reflector.

c) Always check the bulb contacts and holder, ensuring that there is clean metal-to-metal contact between the bulb and its live(s) and earth. Clean off any corrosion or dirt before fitting a new bulb.

d) Ensure that the new bulb is of the correct rating.

Front interior light

2 Carefully prise the interior light from the head-lining using a screwdriver (see illustrations).
3 Remove the festoon-type bulb from the spring contacts (see illustration).
4 Fit the new bulb using a reversal of the removal procedure. Make sure that the bulb is held firmly between the spring contacts. If necessary, pretension the contacts before fitting the bulb.

Rear interior light

5 Carefully prise the interior light from the trim (see illustration).
6 Remove the festoon-type bulb from the spring contacts (see illustration).
7 Fit the new bulb using a reversal of the removal procedure. Make sure that the bulb is held firmly between the spring contacts. If necessary, pretension the contacts before fitting the bulb.

Luggage compartment light

8 Carefully prise the light from the side trim (see illustration).
9 Remove the festoon-type bulb from the spring contacts (see illustration).

6.2b . . . and remove it from the headlining

6.3 Removing the festoon-type bulb from the front interior light

6.5 Prise the rear interior light from the trim

6.6 Rear interior light and festoon-type bulb

6.8 Prising the luggage compartment interior light from the side trim

6.9 Removing the festoon-type bulb from the luggage compartment interior light

6.26a Removing a small warning bulbholder . . .

6.26b . . . and large warning bulbholder from the instrument panel

6.26c The large bulbs can be removed from their bulbholders

10 Fit the new bulb using a reversal of the removal procedure. Make sure that the bulb is held firmly between the spring contacts. If necessary, pretension the contacts before fitting the bulb.

Glovebox light

11 With the glovebox open, carefully prise out the light unit.
12 Remove the festoon-type bulb from the spring contacts.
13 Fit the new bulb using a reversal of the removal procedure. Make sure that the bulb is held firmly between the spring contacts. If necessary, pretension the contacts before fitting the bulb.

Rear reading light

14 Undo the screws and remove the grip from the headlining.
15 Disconnect the wiring or remove the heat shield, then remove the bulb.
16 Fit the new bulb using a reversal of the removal procedure.

Door-mounted interior light

17 Carefully lever the light from the door trim panel.
18 Disconnect the wiring or remove the heat shield, then remove the festoon-type bulb from the spring contacts.
19 Fit the new bulb using a reversal of the removal procedure. Make sure that the bulb is held firmly between the spring contacts. If necessary, pretension the contacts before fitting the bulb.

Cigarette lighter bulb

20 Remove the centre console as described in Chapter 11.
21 Undo the screws and remove the storage compartment together with the ashtray.

22 Disconnect the upper wiring from the rear of the lighter, remove the bulbholder and remove the bulb.
23 Fit the new bulb using a reversal of the removal procedure.

Instrument illumination and warning lights

24 Remove the instrument panel as described in Section 9.
25 The central (white) bulbholders are for the instrument illumination and the lower (black) bulbholders on the circuit board are the warning lights. The centre lower (black) bulbholder is for the odometer display illumination and LCD illumination (according to model).
26 To remove the bulbs, twist and turn the bulbholder and remove from the instrument panel, then where possible remove the bulb from the bulbholder. Note that some bulbs cannot be removed from their bulbholders **(see illustrations)**.
27 Fit the new bulb using a reversal of the removal procedure.

Light switch illumination

28 Remove the light switch as described in Section 4.
29 Using a screwdriver, twist the bulbholder from the rear of the switch **(see illustration)**.
30 Fit the new bulb using a reversal of the removal procedure.

Clock/multi-function display unit

31 Remove the instrument panel as described in Section 9. The clock/multi-function display unit is located on the rear of the instrument panel.
32 Using a pair of pliers twist the relevant bulbholder from the rear of the display unit **(see illustrations)**.
33 Fit the new bulb using a reversal of the removal procedure.

Heater control illumination

34 Remove the heater control assembly as described in Chapter 3, Section 10.
35 Pull out the relevant wedge-type bulb from the assembly **(see illustration)**.
36 Fit the new bulb using a reversal of the removal procedure.

6.29 Removing the illumination bulb from the rear of the lighting switch

6.32a Use a pair of pliers . . .

6.32b . . . to remove the bulbholder from the clock/multi-function display unit

6.35 Removing a wedge-type bulb from the heater control assembly

7.2a Remove the side . . .

7.2b . . . and upper headlight mounting bolts

7.3a Withdraw the headlight unit from the front of the car . . .

7 Exterior light units – removal and refitting

Headlight/front indicator light

⚠️ **Warning: Xenon dipped beam headlights operate at very high voltage. Where fitted, do not touch the associated wiring when the headlights are switched on.**

Removal

1 Remove the radiator grille and the front bumper as described in Chapter 11.

2 Support the headlight/indicator unit, then unscrew and remove the three mounting bolts securing the unit to the front panel **(see illustrations)**.

3 Withdraw the unit from the front of the car, then disconnect the wiring from the beam adjustment servo unit, headlight and indicator **(see illustrations)**. Where Xenon headlights are fitted, disconnect the wiring for the control unit on the right-hand side, or remove the control unit on the left-hand side.

4 If necessary, the headlight range control servo may be removed by twisting it anti-clockwise **(see illustrations)**.

Refitting

5 Refitting is a reversal of removal, but make sure that the locating lug on the headlight engages with the corresponding hole in the front valance and, on completion, have the headlight beam alignment checked at the earliest opportunity.

Xenon headlight control unit

⚠️ **Warning: Xenon dipped beam headlights operate at very high voltage. Do not touch the associated wiring when the headlights are switched on.**

Removal

6 Make sure that the ignition is switched off, and also remove fuses F6 and F24 from the interior fusebox.

7 Remove the headlight as described earlier in this Section.

8 To remove the right-hand control unit, unscrew the two bolts and withdraw the unit together with the bracket.

9 The left-hand control unit is attached to the headlight. Undo the three bolts and withdraw the unit.

7.3b . . . then disconnect the wiring from the beam adjustment servo unit . . .

7.3c . . . headlight . . .

7.3d . . . and indicator

7.3e Headlight unit removed from the car

7.4a Twist the headlight range control servo . . .

7.4b . . . and remove it from the headlight

7.17a Unscrew the mounting nuts . . .

7.17b . . . and remove the rear light cluster

Refitting

10 Refitting is a reversal of removal, with reference to the headlight sub-section earlier.

Front foglight

Removal

11 Remove the front bumper as described in Chapter 11.

12 Unscrew the three mounting bolts and remove the foglight, then disconnect the wiring.

Refitting

13 Refitting is a reversal of removal.

Direction indicator side repeater

14 The procedure is described in Section 5.

Rear light cluster

Removal

15 In the luggage compartment, remove the

9.2 Using feeler blades to remove the centre air vents

side trim cover. If working on the right-hand side, remove the first aid kit and warning triangle. On Estate models, the left-hand cover is removed by twisting the fastener.

16 Depress the retaining lug in the middle of the rear light cluster, and withdraw the bulbholder from the rear light.

17 Unscrew the mounting nuts and withdraw the light cluster from the rear of the vehicle **(see illustrations)**. Take care not to damage the vehicle paintwork.

Refitting

18 Refitting is a reversal of removal.

Rear number plate light

19 The procedure is described in Section 5.

High-level stop-light

20 The procedure is described in Section 5.

| 8 | **Headlight beam alignment –** general information |

1 Accurate adjustment of the headlight beam is only possible using optical beam-setting equipment, and this work should therefore be carried out by a Vauxhall/Opel dealer or suitably-equipped workshop.

2 For reference, the headlights can be adjusted using the adjuster assemblies fitted to the front upper outer mounting and to the rear inner mounting. The inner screw is for horizontal adjustment and the outer one for vertical adjustment.

3 All models have an electrically-operated headlight beam adjustment range system, controlled via a switch in the facia. The recommended settings are as follows.

  0 Front seat(s) occupied.
  1 All seats occupied.
  2 All seats occupied, and load in luggage compartment.
  3 Driver's seat occupied and load in the luggage compartment.

Note: *When adjusting the headlight aim, ensure that the switch is set to position 0.*

4 On Estate models with automatic self-levelling control, the headlight range adjustment should be reduced by one setting after completing approximately 3 km (1.8 miles).

5 Some models fitted with Xenon headlights may have an automatic range adjustment system. If a fault occurs in the system, a warning symbol lights up on the instrument display unit.

| 9 | **Instrument panel –** removal and refitting | |

Removal

1 Remove the steering column shrouds. To do this, first remove the steering wheel. Alternatively, the steering wheel may remain in position, but it will have to turned for access to the end face screws of the shrouds. Unscrew the tilt steering lever, then remove the two screws from the end face and three screws from the bottom shroud. Remove the shrouds and recover the ignition key position indicator from the ignition switch.

2 Carefully prise the centre and driver's side air vents and housings from the facia, using a small screwdriver or alternatively feeler blades to depress the side clips **(see illustration)**. Where applicable, place a wad of cloth beneath the screwdriver to prevent damage.

3 Remove the light switch as described in Section 4.

4 Undo the mounting screws and remove the centre surround and side surround/light switch housing from the facia. Disconnect the wiring **(see illustrations)**.

9.4a Undo the inner screws . . .

9.4b . . . and the outer screws . . .

9.4c . . . then remove the surround

5 Undo the two mounting screws and withdraw the instrument panel from the facia **(see illustrations)**.

6 Disconnect the wiring from the rear of the instrument panel and withdraw the unit **(see illustration)**.

Refitting

7 Refitting is a reversal of removal, but check the operation of all the warning and illumination bulbs on completion.

10 Instrument panel components – removal and refitting

Removal

1 With the instrument panel removed as described in Section 9, remove the warning and illumination bulbs as described in Section 6.

2 Remove the multi-function display unit as described in Section 11.

3 Carefully release the clips using a screwdriver, then release the front frame from the main housing.

4 Further dismantling of the instrument panel is not recommended.

Refitting

5 Refitting is a reversal of removal.

11 Clock/multi-function display components – removal and refitting

Note: If fitting a new display unit, take the vehicle to a dealer for it to be programmed.

Removal

1 To remove the display unit, first remove the instrument panel as described in Section 9. Undo the screws and remove the multi-info display unit, the triple-info display unit, or the digital clock as required from the rear of the instrument panel.

2 To remove the ambient temperature sensor, remove the radiator grille as described in Chapter 11. Unclip the sensor from the retainer then disconnect the wiring.

3 To remove the bulb check sensor, first remove the glovebox as described in Chapter 11. Remove the sensor from the retainer on the bulkhead and disconnect the wiring. The trailer bulb control sensor is located above the bulb check sensor and may be pulled from its base if required.

4 The brake fluid level and coolant level sensors are part of the multi-function display. To remove the brake fluid level sensor, unscrew the filler cap from the brake hydraulic fluid reservoir and disconnect the wiring. To remove the coolant level sensor, unscrew and remove the filler cap from the expansion tank (note the precautions given in Chapter 3), and draw off the coolant until the level is just below the sensor. Remove the sensor from

9.4d The side surround/light switch housing screws

9.5b ... and withdraw the instrument panel from the facia

the tank. Refitting of the sensors is a reversal of the removal procedure.

Refitting

5 Refitting is a reversal of removal.

12 Cigarette lighter – removal and refitting

Removal

1 Remove the centre console as described in Chapter 11.

2 Undo the screws and remove the storage compartment together with the ashtray, then pull out the cigarette lighter element and disconnect the wiring from the rear of the lighter.

3 Using a small screwdriver, release the retainer and ring then remove the cigarette lighter.

14.1 The horn is located behind the front bumper on the right-hand side on RHD models

9.5a Undo the mounting screws ...

9.6 Disconnecting the wiring from the instrument panel

Refitting

4 Refitting is a reversal of removal.

13 Acoustic warning system – general

1 The acoustic warning system has three functions as described in the following paragraphs. The multi-timer incorporated within the fusebox operates the system.

2 If the parking or low beam lights are on and the front door is opened, a warning buzzer is sounded to prompt the driver to switch off the lights.

3 With the parking lights on (using the indicator switch), a warning buzzer is sounded for 2 seconds when the door is opened. This reminds the driver that the parking lights are on.

4 With the ignition key inserted in the steering lock, a warning buzzer is sounded when the door is opened to remind the driver that the ignition key is still inserted.

14 Horn(s) – removal and refitting

Removal

1 The horn is located behind the front bumper on the right-hand side on RHD models or on the left-hand side on LHD models **(see illustration)**.

On some models it is located in the left-hand side of the engine compartment next to the transmission. One or two horns are fitted according to model. First apply the handbrake, then jack up the front of the vehicle and support it on axle stands (see *Jacking and vehicle support*).

2 Disconnect the wiring from the horn.

3 Unscrew the mounting nut securing the horn to the bracket and remove the horn.

Refitting

4 Refitting is a reversal of removal.

15 Wiper arm – removal and refitting

Windscreen wiper arm

Removal

1 Operate the wiper motor, then switch it off so that the wiper arm returns to the at-rest position.

> **HAYNES HINT**
> *Stick a piece of masking tape on the windscreen, along the edge of the wiper blade, to use as an alignment aid on refitting.*

2 Using a screwdriver prise the cover from the spindle end of the wiper arm **(see illustrations)**.

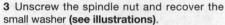

15.2a Use a screwdriver . . .

3 Unscrew the spindle nut and recover the small washer **(see illustrations)**.

4 Lift the blade off the glass, and pull the wiper arm off its spindle **(see illustration)**. Note that the wiper arms may be very tight on the spindle splines – if necessary, lever the arm off the spindle, using a flat-bladed screwdriver (take care not to damage the scuttle cover panel).

5 If necessary, remove the blade from the arm with reference to *Weekly checks*.

Refitting

6 If removed, refit the wiper blade to the arm at this stage. This will prevent any damage to the windscreen from the upper end of the arm.

7 Ensure that the wiper arm and spindle splines are clean and dry, then refit the arm to the spindle and align the blade with the previously noted rest position.

15.2b . . . to prise off the cover . . .

8 Refit the washer and spindle nut, and tighten it securely. Refit the cover.

Tailgate wiper arm

Removal

9 Operate the wiper motor, then switch it off so that the wiper arm returns to the at-rest position.

> **HAYNES HINT**
> *Stick a piece of masking tape on the window, along the edge of the wiper blade, to use as an alignment aid on refitting.*

10 Lift the cover from the base of the wiper arm and unscrew the retaining nut **(see illustrations)**.

11 Lift the blade off the glass, and pull the wiper arm off its spindle **(see illustration)**.

15.3a . . . then remove the nut . . .

15.3b . . . and small washer . . .

15.4 . . . and remove the wiper arm from the spindle

15.10a Lift the cover . . .

15.10b . . . then unscrew the retaining nut . . .

15.11 . . . and pull the tailgate wiper arm from the spindle splines

12 If necessary, remove the blade from the arm with reference to *Weekly checks*.

Refitting

13 If removed, refit the wiper blade to the arm at this stage. This will prevent any damage to the rear window from the upper end of the arm.

14 Ensure that the wiper arm and spindle splines are clean and dry, then refit the arm to the spindle and align the blade with the previously noted rest position.

15 Refit the spindle nut, and tighten it securely. Close the cover on the base of the arm.

16 Windscreen wiper motor and linkage – removal and refitting

Removal

1 Remove the wiper arms as described in Section 15.

2 Pull the rubber weatherstrip from the rear of the engine compartment, then unscrew the nuts securing the water deflector panel to the wiper spindle housings. Unclip and remove the panel **(see illustrations)**.

3 Disconnect the wiring at the wiper motor **(see illustration)**.

4 Unscrew the bolts securing the wiper motor assembly to the scuttle, and withdraw the assembly **(see illustrations)**.

5 The motor can be removed from the linkage assembly by prising free the rod from the crank and unbolting the motor. The remaining

16.2a Unscrew and remove the spindle housing nuts . . .

linkage rods can also be dismantled if necessary **(see illustrations)**.

6 Clean the assembly and examine the spindles and joints for wear and damage. Renew the components as required.

Refitting

7 Refitting is a reversal of removal, but lubricate the joints with a little grease before assembling them. Refit the wiper arms with reference to Section 15.

17 Tailgate wiper motor – removal and refitting

Removal

1 Remove the wiper arm from the tailgate as described in Section 15.

16.2b . . . then remove the water deflector panel

16.3 Disconnecting the wiring from the wiper motor

2 Remove the trim panelling from the inside of the tailgate with reference to Chapter 11, Section 29.

3 Remove the rubber cap from the wiper spindle **(see illustration)**.

16.4a Unscrew the central mounting bolt . . .

16.4b . . . and outer linkage mounting bolt . . .

16.4c . . . and withdraw the windscreen wiper motor and linkage from the scuttle

16.5a The windscreen wiper motor and linkage removed from the vehicle

16.5b Windscreen wiper motor and linkage mounting bolts/nut

17.3 Remove the rubber cap . . .

17.4a . . . then unscrew and remove the nut . . .

17.4b . . . remove the washer . . .

17.4c . . . and withdraw the rubber seal

17.5 Disconnecting the wiring from the tailgate wiper motor

17.6a Unscrew the mounting bolts . . .

17.6b . . . and withdraw the wiper motor from the tailgate

4 Unscrew the nut securing the spindle housing to the tailgate, and remove the washer and rubber seal **(see illustrations)**.
5 Disconnect the wiring at the plug **(see illustration)**.

6 Unscrew the mounting bolts and withdraw the wiper motor while sliding the spindle housing through the rubber grommet **(see illustrations)**.
7 If necessary remove the rubber grommet

17.6c Tailgate wiper motor location

18.3 Washer fluid reservoir and pump

from the tailgate. Examine the grommet for wear and damage and renew it if necessary.

Refitting

8 Refitting is a reversal of removal; tighten the mounting nut to the specified torque. Refit the wiper arm with reference to Section 15.

18 Washer system components – removal and refitting

Washer fluid reservoir

Removal

1 Remove the front bumper as described in Chapter 11.
2 Remove the left-hand front wheelarch liner as described in Chapter 11, Section 26.
3 Position a container beneath the washer fluid pump and reservoir to collect the fluid **(see illustration)**.
4 Disconnect the wiring from the top of the pump and position to one side **(see illustration)**.
5 Disconnect the hose from the pump and allow the fluid to drain into the container.
6 On models with a multi-function display unit, disconnect the wiring from the level sensor on the fluid reservoir.
7 On models with a headlight washer system, disconnect the wiring and hose from the additional pump on the reservoir.
8 Disconnect the filler neck(s) from the reservoir.
9 Release the wiring from the clips on top of the reservoir **(see illustration)**.

18.4 The washer fluid reservoir and pump is located behind the front bumper

18.9 Release the wiring from the top of the reservoir

10 Unscrew the mounting bolts and withdraw the reservoir from the front valance **(see illustration)**.

Refitting

11 Refitting is a reversal of removal. Fill the reservoir with washer fluid with reference to *Weekly checks*.

Washer fluid pump

Removal

12 Remove the front bumper as described in Chapter 11.

13 Remove the left-hand front wheelarch liner as described in Chapter 11, Section 26.

14 Position a suitable container beneath the washer fluid pump and reservoir to collect the fluid.

15 Disconnect the wiring from the top of the pump and position to one side.

16 Disconnect the hose from the pump and allow the fluid to drain into the container.

17 Pull the pump to the side and extract it from the reservoir.

18 If necessary, remove the grommet from the reservoir.

Refitting

19 Refitting is a reversal of removal. Fill the reservoir with washer fluid with reference to *Weekly checks*.

Windscreen washer nozzle

Removal

20 With the bonnet open, disconnect the wiring and supply hose from the bottom of the nozzle.

21 Release the nozzle from the bonnet and remove it upwards.

Refitting

22 Refitting is a reversal of removal.

Tailgate washer nozzle

Removal

23 On Hatchback models, carefully lever the nozzle out of the aerial base with a small screwdriver, then disconnect the nozzle from the hose.

24 On Estate models, carefully insert a small screwdriver between the nozzle and the

rubber seal. Depress the lugs and remove the nozzle from the tailgate.

25 Disconnect the nozzle from the hose.

Refitting

26 Refitting is a reversal of removal.

Headlight washer nozzle

Removal

27 Remove the headlight as described in Section 7.

28 Release the supply hose from the support and remove it from the nozzle.

29 Pull out the clip and remove the nozzle from the front bumper.

Refitting

30 Refitting is a reversal of removal.

---

19 Radio/cassette/CD player – removal and refitting

Note: *On models with a security-coded radio/cassette player, once the battery has been disconnected, the unit cannot be re-activated until the appropriate security code has been entered. Do not remove the unit unless the appropriate code is known. The following information applies to radio/cassette players having standard DIN fixings. Two DIN removal tools will be required for this operation.*

Radio/cassette player

Removal

1 Where fitted, use an Allen key to undo the grub screws from the four holes in each corner of the radio front face **(see illustration)**.

2 Insert the two DIN removal tools into the holes on each side of the radio until they are felt to engage with the retaining strips.

3 Press the DIN tools slightly outwards, then carefully withdraw the radio/cassette player from the facia **(see illustration)**.

4 Disconnect the wiring and aerial from the rear of the radio.

5 Remove the removal tools and refit the grub screws.

18.10 Washer fluid reservoir mounting bolt

Refitting

6 Reconnect the wiring plugs and the aerial lead, then push the unit into its housing until the securing clips engage.

7 On completion, enter the security code.

CD player

Removal

8 Remove the glovebox as described in Chapter 11.

9 Disconnect the wiring plug.

10 Unscrew the mounting bolts and withdraw the CD player from behind the facia.

Refitting

11 Refitting is a reversal of removal.

---

20 Loudspeakers – removal and refitting

Front door loudspeakers

Removal

1 Remove the front door inner trim panel, as described in Chapter 11, Section 12 **(see illustration)**.

2 Undo the mounting screws and withdraw the loudspeaker from the door inner panel **(see illustration)**.

3 Disconnect the wiring from the loudspeaker **(see illustration)**.

19.1 Removing the grub screws before fitting the DIN removal tools

19.3 Using the DIN removal tools to remove the radio/cassette player

20.1 Front door-mounted loudspeakers

20.2 Undo the mounting screws . . .

Refitting

4 Refitting is a reversal of removal.

Front door tweeters

Removal

5 Remove the front door inner handle grip with reference to Chapter 11, Section 12.
6 Disconnect the wiring, then release the loudspeaker from the grip.

Refitting

7 Refitting is a reversal of removal.

Rear door loudspeakers

Removal

8 Remove the rear door inner trim panel, as described in Chapter 11, Section 12.
9 Undo the mounting screws and withdraw the loudspeaker from the door inner panel **(see illustration)**.
10 Disconnect the wiring from the loudspeaker **(see illustration)**.

Refitting

11 Refitting is a reversal of removal.

21 Radio aerial – removal and refitting

Removal

1 Remove the headlining moulding from the rear of the luggage compartment.
2 On Hatchback models, remove the rear screen wash/wipe system hose.

20.9 Removing a rear door loudspeaker

20.3 . . . then disconnect the wiring from the rear of the loudspeaker

3 Disconnect the lead from the aerial.
4 Unscrew the nut and remove the aerial from the roof.

Refitting

5 Refitting is a reversal of removal.

22 Anti-theft alarm system and engine immobiliser – general information

1 All models have an engine immobiliser which effectively prevents the engine from being started when the ignition key is in the OFF position or removed from the steering lock. The system is activated by the ignition key and an electronic sensor mounted on the steering lock. The driver's door lock barrel is freewheeling – if an attempt is made to forcefully turn the lock without the correct key, it will just turn within its housing.
2 The anti-theft alarm system monitors the doors, bootlid or tailgate, bonnet, radio, ignition, and on some models the passenger compartment. The control unit for the system is located behind the outer trim panel on the right-hand side of the right-hand footwell. On higher specification models an ultrasonic sensor is located at the top of each B-pillar. The anti-theft alarm system horn is located on the bulkhead in the engine compartment and the power sounder is located beneath the left-hand front wing. On Estate models, a glass breakage detector is fitted to the luggage compartment rear side windows. The system is activated by locking the driver's door and

20.10 Disconnecting the wiring from the rear door loudspeaker

turning the ignition key towards the rear again within 10 seconds. It can also be activated by pressing the remote control unit two times with 10 seconds. Where passenger compartment ultrasonic sensors are fitted, this feature may be switched off (eg, when animals are in the vehicle) by depressing the sensor switch on the instrument panel before exiting the vehicle and locking the doors.
3 To remove the ultrasonic sensor, carefully lever it out of its housing on the B-pillar using a screwdriver, then disconnect the wiring.
4 To remove the warning horn from its location at the rear of the engine compartment, disconnect the wiring and unscrew the mounting nut.
5 To remove the bonnet contact on the left-hand side of the engine compartment, disconnect the wiring then detach the contact.
6 To remove the power sounder located beneath the left-hand wheelarch liner, disconnect the battery negative lead, as described in Chapter 5A, within 15 seconds of switching off the ignition. Remove the wheelarch liner from under the left-hand front wing, then disconnect the wiring and unbolt the bracket and power sounder.
7 Refitting of the components is a reversal of the removal procedure.
8 Any faults with the system should be referred to a Vauxhall/Opel dealer.

23 Airbag system – general information, precautions and system de-activation

General information

A driver's airbag is fitted as standard equipment to all models. The airbag is fitted to the steering wheel centre pad. A passenger's airbag is fitted as standard equipment, or as an option, according to model. Side airbags, located in the outer sections of the front seat backrests, may also be fitted.

The system is armed only when the ignition is switched on, however, a reserve power source maintains a power supply to the system in the event of a break in the main electrical supply. The system is activated by a 'g' sensor (deceleration sensor), incorporated in the electronic control unit. The electronic control unit also controls the front seat belt tensioners.

The airbags are inflated by gas generators, which force the bags out from their locations in the steering wheel, passenger side facia, or seat backrest, as applicable.

In the event of a fault occurring in the airbag system (warning light illuminated on the instrument panel), seek the advice of a Vauxhall/Opel dealer.

Precautions

⚠️ *Warning: The following precautions must be observed when working on vehicles equipped* with an airbag system, to prevent the possibility of personal injury.

General precautions

The following precautions **must** be observed when carrying out work on a vehicle equipped with an airbag.

a) *Following the deployment of an airbag in a collision, the control unit, all airbag units and the contact unit must be renewed.*

b) *Do not disconnect the battery with the engine running.*

c) *Before carrying out any work in the vicinity of the airbag, removal of any of the airbag components, or any welding work on the vehicle, de-activate the system as described in the following sub-Section.*

d) *Do not attempt to test any of the airbag system circuits using test meters or any other test equipment.*

e) *If the airbag warning light comes on, or any fault in the system is suspected, consult a Vauxhall/Opel dealer without delay. Do not attempt to carry out fault diagnosis, or any dismantling of the components.*

Precautions to be taken when handling an airbag

a) *Transport the airbag by itself, bag upward.*

b) *Do not put your arms around the airbag.*

c) *Carry the airbag close to the body, bag outward.*

d) *Do not drop the airbag or expose it to impacts.*

e) *Do not attempt to dismantle the airbag unit.*

f) *Do not connect any form of electrical equipment to any part of the airbag circuit.*

g) *Do not allow any solvents or cleaning agents to contact the airbag assembly. The unit must be cleaned using only a damp cloth.*

Precautions to be taken when storing an airbag unit

a) *Store the unit in a cupboard with the airbag upward.*

b) *Do not expose the airbag to temperatures above 90°C.*

c) *Do not expose the airbag to flames.*

d) *Do not attempt to dispose of the airbag – consult a Vauxhall/Opel dealer.*

e) *Never refit an airbag which is known to be faulty or damaged.*

De-activation of airbag system

The system must be de-activated as follows, before carrying out any work on the airbag components or surrounding area.

a) *Switch off the ignition.*

b) *Remove the ignition key.*

c) *Switch off all electrical equipment.*

d) *Disconnect the battery negative lead (see Chapter 5A).*

e) *Insulate the battery negative terminal and*

24.5a Release the clip . . .

the end of the battery negative lead to prevent any possibility of contact.

f) *Wait for at least one minute before carrying out any further work. This will allow the system capacitor to discharge.*

24 Airbag system components – removal and refitting

Driver's airbag unit

⚠ **Warning: Refer to the precautions given in Section 23 before attempting to carry out work on the airbag components.**

Removal

1 The airbag unit is an integral part of the steering wheel centre pad.

2 De-activate the airbag system as described in Section 23.

3 Set the front wheels in the straight-ahead position, then remove the ignition key and lock the column by turning the steering wheel as required. Unlike earlier models which locked in the straight-ahead position, models from 1999 Model Year lock in a different position due to a modified intermediate shaft. Right-hand drive models lock with the steering wheel approximately 5° anti-clockwise, and left-hand drive models lock with the steering wheel approximately 45° clockwise.

4 Unscrew and remove the two screws from the rear of the steering wheel and carefully lift the airbag/horn-push from the steering wheel.

5 Disconnect the wiring from the airbag **(see illustrations)**. Position the airbag in a safe place where it cannot be tampered with, making sure that the padded side is facing upwards.

Refitting

6 Refitting is a reversal of removal, but make sure that the wiring connector is securely reconnected and tighten the retaining screws to the specified torque.

Passenger's airbag unit

⚠ **Warning: Refer to the precautions given in Section 23 before attempting to carry out work on the airbag components.**

24.5b . . . and disconnect the wiring from the airbag

Removal

7 De-activate the airbag system as described in Section 23.

8 Remove the glovebox and passenger side air distribution duct from under the facia with reference to Chapter 11.

9 Unscrew the lower mounting screws and remove the airbag cover in an outwards direction.

10 Disconnect the wiring from the airbag.

11 Undo the three lower screws and lift the airbag from the facia. Discard the screws and obtain new ones for refitting.

Refitting

12 Refitting is a reversal of removal, but make sure that the wiring connector is securely reconnected and tighten the retaining screws to the specified torque. The screws must always be renewed after removal.

Side airbag unit

⚠ **Warning: Refer to the precautions given in Section 23 before attempting to carry out work on the airbag components.**

Removal

13 The side airbag is located in the front seat backrest. To remove it first de-activate the airbag system as described in Section 23.

14 Carefully pull back the upholstery on the sides and bottom, to expose the side airbag unit.

15 Disconnect the wiring from the airbag.

16 Unscrew the three securing nuts and remove the airbag from the seat backrest.

Refitting

17 Refitting is a reversal of removal, but make sure that the wiring connector is securely reconnected and tighten the retaining nuts to the specified torque.

Airbag contact unit (on steering column)

⚠ **Warning: Refer to the precautions given in Section 23 before attempting to carry out work on the airbag components.**

Removal

18 Remove the driver's airbag unit as described earlier in this Section.

24.22a Use a screwdriver to release the four rear clips . . .

24.22b . . . then remove the airbag contact unit from the top of the column

24.23 Centre position arrows on the airbag contact unit

19 Remove the steering wheel as described in Chapter 10.

20 Remove the steering column shrouds by unscrewing the tilt steering lever, then removing the two screws from the end face and three screws from the bottom shroud. Recover the ignition key position indicator from the ignition switch.

21 Using a small screwdriver lift off the locking plate, then disconnect the wiring plug.

22 Release the four rear clips and remove the contact unit from the top of the column **(see illustrations)**. **Note:** *Make sure that the contact unit halves remain in their central position with the arrows aligned at the bottom. If necessary, apply tape to the halves to hold them.*

Refitting

23 Before refitting the contact unit, if the centre position has been lost or if a new unit is being fitted, determine the centre position as follows. Depress the detent on top of the unit and carefully turn the centre part of the unit anti-clockwise until resistance is felt. Now turn it 2.5 turns clockwise and align the arrows on the centre part and outer edge **(see illustration)**.

24 If a new unit is fitted, first remove the transport clip.

25 Locate the contact unit on the top of the steering column making sure that the guide pins locate in the holes provided. Press the unit in until the clips engage **(see illustration)**.

Note: *The clips must not be damaged in any way. If they are, the unit must be renewed. Do not tilt the unit when fitting it.*

26 Reconnect the wiring while depressing the slider.

27 Refit the ignition key position indicator, then refit the steering column shrouds and tighten the securing screws. Refit and tighten the tilt steering lever.

28 Refit the steering wheel as described in Chapter 10.

29 Refit the driver's airbag unit as described earlier.

Electronic control unit

> ⚠ **Warning: Refer to the precautions given in Section 23 before attempting to carry out work on the airbag components.**

Removal

30 De-activate the airbag system as described in Section 23.

31 Remove the centre console as described in Chapter 11.

32 Disconnect the wiring from the control unit, then unscrew the mounting nuts and remove the unit from inside the vehicle **(see illustration)**.

Refitting

33 Refitting is a reversal of removal but tighten the mounting nuts to the specified torque.

Side airbag sensor

Note: *The airbag sensors are different for each front door. Make sure that the sensors are fitted to their correct sides.*

Removal

34 De-activate the airbag system as described in Section 23.

35 Remove the front door inner trim panel as described in Chapter 11, Section 12.

36 Pull back the water membrane for access to the sensor.

> ⚠ **Warning: If the membrane is damaged, it must be renewed; the operation of the side airbags relies on the integrity of the membrane.**

37 Disconnect the wiring, then unscrew the mounting bolts and remove the sensor.

Refitting

38 Refitting is a reversal of removal. Check and if necessary renew the membrane if damaged.

Side airbag sensor bracket

Removal

39 Remove the side airbag sensor as described in paragraphs 34 to 36.

40 Drill out the three rivets and release the bracket from the lower tags.

Refitting

41 Refitting is a reversal of removal. Use new rivets to secure the bracket.

24.25 Contact unit located on the top of the steering column

24.32 Airbag electronic control unit

Vectra wiring diagrams

Diagram 1

Key to symbols

Bulb	⊗
Flashing bulb	⊗
Switch	
Multiple contact switch (ganged)	
Fuse/fusible link and current rating	F5 30A
Resistor	
Variable resistor	
Variable resistor	
Wire splice or soldered joint	
Connecting wires	
Wire colour (brown with black tracer)	Bn/Bk
Screened cable	

Item no.	2
Single speed pump/motor	M
Twin speed pump/motor	M
Gauge/meter	
Earth point	
Diode	
Light emitting diode (LED)	
Solenoid actuator	
Heating element	

Dashed outline denotes part of a larger item, containing in this case an electronic or solid state device.

23 - connector pin identification

Key to circuits

Diagram 1	Information for wiring diagrams.
Diagram 2	Starting, charging, diagnostic socket, parking, tail & number plate lights.
Diagram 3	Headlights & headlight levelling.
Diagram 4	Stop & reversing lights, direction indicators & hazard warning lights.
Diagram 5	Front & rear foglights, trailer socket & heater blower.
Diagram 6	Wash/wipe & heated rear window.
Diagram 7	Instrument cluster.
Diagram 8	Cigar lighter, glovebox light, luggage compartment light, interior lighting.
Diagram 9	Safety restraint system, anti-lock brakes & traction control.
Diagram 10	Audio system, horn, cruise control & sunroof.
Diagram 11	Heated seats, electric mirrors & electric windows.
Diagram 12	Central locking & air conditioning.
Diagram 13	Engine management (X16XEL).
Diagram 14	Engine management (X18XE1).
Diagram 15	Engine management (X18XE/X20XEV).
Diagram 16	Engine management (X20DTL/X20DTH).
Diagram 17	Engine management (Z16XE).
Diagram 18	Engine management (Z18XE).
Diagram 19	Engine management (Z22SE).
Diagram 20	Engine management (Y20DTH/Y22DTR).

Typical passenger fusebox

Fuse	Rating	Circuit protected
F1	-	Spare
F2	30A	Air conditioning system, cooling fan
F3	40A	Heated rear window
F4	-	Spare
F5	-	Spare
F6	10/15A*	RH dipped beam, headlight levelling
F7	10A	RH parking & tail lights
F8	10A	RH main beam
F9	30A	Headlight washer
F10	20A	Horn
F11	30A	Central locking system
F12	20A	Fog lights
F13	-	Spare
F13*	10A	Interior light
F14	30A	Windscreen wiper
F15	-	Spare
F15*	5A	Reading lights
F16	10A	Rear fog light
F17	30A	Electric windows
F18	10A	Number plate light
F19	20A	Fuel pump
F19*	10A	Radio, carphone, infotainment system
F20	30A	Electric windows
F21	-	Spare
F21*	10A	Infotainment system, selector lever lock, central locking, hazard warning lights
F22	20A	Hazard warning lights, information display, trip computer, air conditioning, interior light, cooling fan, radio
F22*	20A	Hazard warning lights, information display, air conditioning, interior light, cooling fan, infotainment system
F23	-	Spare
F24	10A/15A*	LH dipped beam, headlight levelling
F25	10A	LH parking & tail lights
F26	10A	LH main beam
F27	-	Spare
F28	20A	Coolant heating (Diesel)
F29	10A	Hazard warning lights, electric mirrors, electric windows, sunroof, instruments, cruise control, interior light
F29*	10A	Hazard warning lights, dipped beam, reversing lights, electric mirrors, electric windows, sunroof, instruments, interior light
F30	30A	Sunroof
F31	-	Spare
F31*	30A	Interior light, instrument illumination
F32	10A	Daytime running lights (Scandinavia)
F33	10A/20A*	Constant supply for caravan/trailer
F34	10A	CD changer
F34*	20A	Instruments, radio, carphone, infotainment system
F35	10A	ABS, Traction control, automatic transmission
F36	20A	Air conditioning, heated front seats, cigar lighter
F36*	20A	Air conditioning, heated front seats
F37	-	Spare
F37*	10A	Cigar lighter
F38	10A	Stop & reversing lights, automatic transmission, cooling fan, information display, cruise control
F38*	10A	Stop lights, cooling fan, information display, cruise control
F39	10A	Automatic transmission
F40	10A	Cooling fan, air conditioning, heated rear window
F40*	10A	Cooling fan, air conditioning
F41	10A	Heated mirrors

* Models from '00

Earth locations

E1	LH front strut turret	E7	Behind LH headlight
E2	Near alternator	E8	Base of RH 'A' pilar
E3	Base of LH 'A' pilar	E9	On engine
E4	Bracket, steering column/crossmember	E10	On engine
E5	Transmission column - under handbrake	E11	oxygen sensor/ignition coil
E6	Boot rear crossmember (saloon/hatch) Behind LH rear light cluster (estate)	E12	LH side of tailgate

H32506

Wire colours

Bn	Brown	**Rd**	Red
Bu	Blue	**Bk**	Black
Ye	Yellow	**Wh**	White
Gn	Green	**Vt**	Violet
Gy	Grey	**Vi**	Mauve
Og	Orange	**DBu**	Dark blue
Pu	Purple	**LBu**	Light blue
Pk	Pink		

Key to items

1 Battery
2 Starter motor
3 Alternator
4 Ignition switch
5 Diagnostic socket
6 Light switch
　a = side/headlight
7 Combined indicator switch
　a = parking light

8 Filament failure module
9 Number plate light
10 LH parking light
11 RH parking light
12 LH tail light
13 RH tail light
14 Automatic transmission switch

Diagram 2

H32507

Starting & charging system

Diagnostic socket

Parking, tail & number plate lights

Wire colours

Bn	Brown	**Rd**	Red
Bu	Blue	**Bk**	Black
Ye	Yellow	**Wh**	White
Gn	Green	**Vt**	Violet
Gy	Grey	**Vi**	Mauve
Og	Orange	**DBu**	Dark blue
Pu	Purple	**LBu**	Light blue
Pk	Pink		

Key to items

1   Battery
4   Ignition switch
6   Light switch
   a = side/headlight
   b = headlight levelling
7   Combined indicator switch
   a = parking light
   b = dip/main/flasher
8   Filament failure module
16 LH main beam headlight
17 RH main beam headlight
18 LH dipped beam headlight

19 RH dipped beam headlight
20 LH headlight levelling motor
21 RH headlight levelling motor
22 Main beam relay
23 LH xenon headlight assembly
   a = low beam
   b = ignition module
   c = control unit
   d = headlight levelling motor
   e = main beam
   f = parking light

24 RH xenon headlight assembly
   a = low beam
   b = ignition module
   c = headlight levelling motor
   d = main beam
   e = parking light
   f = control unit
25 Front vehicle level sensor
26 Rear vehicle level sensor

Diagram 3

H32508

Headlights - models without xenon lights

Headlight levelling

Xenon lighting

Wire colours

Bn	Brown	**Rd**	Red
Bu	Blue	**Bk**	Black
Ye	Yellow	**Wh**	White
Gn	Green	**Vt**	Violet
Gy	Grey	**Vi**	Mauve
Og	Orange	**DBu**	Dark blue
Pu	Purple	**LBu**	Light blue
Pk	Pink		

Key to items

1	Battery
4	Ignition switch
7	Combined indicator switch
	c = direction indicator
14	Automatic transmission switch
30	Stop light switch (single contact)
31	Stop light switch (twin contact)
32	Reversing light switch
33	LH reversing light switch
34	RH reversing light switch
35	LH stop light
36	RH stop light
37	High level brake light
38	Hazard warning light switch
39	Direction indicator relay
40	Multitimer unit
41	LH front direction indicator
42	LH front indicator side repeater
43	LH rear direction indicator
44	RH front direction indicator
45	RH front indicator side repeater
46	RH rear direction indicator

Diagram 4

H32509

Stop & reversing lights

Direction indicators & hazard warning lights

Wire colours

Bn Brown Rd Red
Bu Blue Bk Black
Ye Yellow Wh White
Gn Green Vt Violet
Gy Grey Vi Mauve
Og Orange DBu Dark blue
Pu Purple LBu Light blue
Pk Pink

Key to items

1 Battery
4 Ignition switch
40 Multitimer unit
50 Front foglight relay
51 Rear foglight relay
52 LH front foglight
53 RH front foglight
54 LH rear foglight
55 RH rear foglight
56 Trailer socket
57 Trailer foglight switch
58 Body to trailer socket wiring connector
59 Heater blower switch
60 Heater blower motor/resistor pack
61 Recirculation switch
62 Recirculation valve

Diagram 5

H32510

Front & rear foglights

Trailer socket

Heater blower

Wire colours

Bn	Brown	**Rd**	Red
Bu	Blue	**Bk**	Black
Ye	Yellow	**Wh**	White
Gn	Green	**Vt**	Violet
Gy	Grey	**Vi**	Mauve
Og	Orange	**DBu**	Dark blue
Pu	Purple	**LBu**	Light blue
Pk	Pink		

Key to items

1 Battery
4 Ignition switch
40 Multitimer unit
65 Combined wash/wipe switch
   a = rear wiper & front/rear washer
   b = front wiper
66 Headlight washer relay
67 Headlight washer pump
68 Front/rear washer pump
69 Front wiper relay

70 Front wiper motor
71 Rear wiper relay
72 Rear wiper motor
73 Heated mirror relay
74 Heated rear window relay
75 Heated rear window/heated mirror switch
76 Heated rear window
77 Rear window antenna module

Diagram 6

H32511

Wash/wipe

Heated rear window

Wire colours

Bn	Brown	**Rd**	Red
Bu	Blue	**Bk**	Black
Ye	Yellow	**Wh**	White
Gn	Green	**Vt**	Violet
Gy	Grey	**Vi**	Mauve
Og	Orange	**DBu**	Dark blue
Pu	Purple	**LBu**	Light blue
Pk	Pink		

Key to items

1 = Battery
4 = Ignition switch
40 = Multitimer unit
80 = Instrument cluster
  a = direction ind. warning light
  b = trailer direction ind. warning light
  c = oil pressure warning light
  d = alternator warning light
  e = brake system warning light
  f = pre-heater warning light
  g = airbag warning light
  h = ABS warning light
  i = seatbelt warning light

80 Instrument cluster continued
  j = engine management warning light
  k = auto. trans. fault warning light
  l = TCS warning light
  m = low fuel warning light
  n = fuel gauge
  o = coolant temperature gauge
  p = speedometer
  q = tachometer
  r = instrument illumination
  s = high beam warning light
  t = rear foglight warning light
  u = front foglight warning light

80 Instrument cluster continued
  v = m/function indicator
     warning light
  w = LH indicator warning light
  x = RH indicator warning light
81 Handbrake switch
82 Low brake fluid switch
83 Oil pressure switch
84 Coolant temperature sensor
85 Fuel gauge sender unit

Diagram 7

H32512

Instrument cluster - models up to 1999

Instrument cluster - models from 1999

Wire colours

Bn	Brown	**Rd**	Red
Bu	Blue	**Bk**	Black
Ye	Yellow	**Wh**	White
Gn	Green	**Vt**	Violet
Gy	Grey	**Vi**	Mauve
Og	Orange	**DBu**	Dark blue
Pu	Purple	**LBu**	Light blue
Pk	Pink		

Key to items

1 Battery
4 Ignition switch
40 Multitimer unit
90 Cigar lighter
91 Glove box light/switch
92 Luggage compartment light
93 Lugage compartment light switch
94 LH rear reading light
95 RH rear reading light
96 LH vanity mirror illumination
97 RH vanity mirror illumination
98 Driver's door courtesy light
99 Passenger's door courtesy light
100 LH rear door courtesy light
101 RH rear door courtesy light
102 Front interior light
103 Driver's door switch
104 Passenger's door switch
105 LH rear door switch
106 RH rear door switch

Diagram 8

H32513

Cigar lighter

Glove box light

Luggage compartment light

Interior lighting

Models from '00
Models up to '00

See diagrams 11 & 12
Central locking & electric windows

See diagrams 11 & 12
Central locking & electric windows

Wire colours

Bn	Brown	**Rd**	Red
Bu	Blue	**Bk**	Black
Ye	Yellow	**Wh**	White
Gn	Green	**Vt**	Violet
Gy	Grey	**Vi**	Mauve
Og	Orange	**DBu**	Dark blue
Pu	Purple	**LBu**	Light blue
Pk	Pink		

Key to items

1	Battery
4	Ignition switch
40	Multitimer unit
110	SRS control unit
111	Passenger's seatbelt pretensioner
112	Driver's seatbelt pretensioner
113	Passenger's side airbag sensor
114	Driver's side airbag sensor
115	Passenger's side airbag
116	Driver's side airbag
117	Passenger's airbag
118	Driver's airbag
119	Steering wheel contact unit
120	ABS control unit
121	ABS/TCS control unit
122	LH front wheel sensor
123	RH front wheel sensor
124	LH rear wheel sensor
125	RH rear wheel sensor
126	Traction control system switch

Diagram 9

H32514

Safety restraint system

Anti-lock brakes

Anti-lock brakes/traction control

Wire colours

Bn Brown   **Rd** Red
Bu Blue   **Bk** Black
Ye Yellow   **Wh** White
Gn Green   **Vt** Violet
Gy Grey   **Vi** Mauve
Og Orange   **DBu** Dark blue
Pu Purple   **LBu** Light blue
Pk Pink

Key to items

1   Battery
4   Ignition switch
40   Multimer unit
119   Steering wheel contact unit
130   Audio unit
131   CD changer
132   Remote control switches
133   LH door speaker
134   LH front speaker

135   LH front tweeter
136   LH rear tweeter
137   LH rear speaker
138   RH door speaker
139   RH front speaker
140   RH front tweeter
141   RH rear tweeter
142   RH rear speaker
143   Horn relay

144   Horn switch
145   Horn
146   Cruise control ECU
147   Cruise control switch
148   Clutch switch
149   Sunroof motor
150   Sunroof switch

Diagram 10

H32515

Audio system

Horn

Cruise control - petrol models

Sunroof

Note:
See diagram 16
for Diesel models

Wire colours

Bn	Brown	**Rd**	Red
Bu	Blue	**Bk**	Black
Ye	Yellow	**Wh**	White
Gn	Green	**Vt**	Violet
Gy	Grey	**Vi**	Mauve
Og	Orange	**DBu**	Dark blue
Pu	Purple	**LBu**	Light blue
Pk	Pink		

Key to items

1	Battery
4	Ignition switch
40	Multitimer unit
155	LH heated seat switch
156	RH heated seat switch
157	LH front heated seat
158	RH front heated seat
159	Mirror control switch

160	LH mirror assembly
161	RH mirror assembly
162	Window switch assembly
	a = LH front
	b = LH rear
	c = rear window cut out
	d = RH front
	e = RH rear

163	LH rear door switch
164	RH rear door switch
165	LH front window motor
166	LH rear window motor
167	RH front window motor
168	RH rear window motor

Diagram 11

H32516

Wire colours

Bn	Brown	**Rd**	Red
Bu	Blue	**Bk**	Black
Ye	Yellow	**Wh**	White
Gn	Green	**Vt**	Violet
Gy	Grey	**Vi**	Mauve
Og	Orange	**DBu**	Dark blue
Pu	Purple	**LBu**	Light blue
Pk	Pink		

Key to items

1 Battery
4 Ignition switch
40 Multitimer unit
60 Heater blower motor/resistor pack
170 Central locking/alarm control unit
171 RH front door lock assembly
    a = door locking switch
    b = door locking motor
172 Tailgate locking motor
173 Fuel filler flap locking motor

174 LH front door locking motor
175 LH rear door locking motor
176 RH rear door locking motor
177 Blower/air cond. switch
    a = temperature lever limit switch
    b = defrost lever limit switch
178 Air cond. relay
179 Coolant solenoid valve
180 Recirculation switch
181 Recirculation solenoid

182 Air cond. switch
183 Air cond. pressure switch
184 Air cond. pressure relay
185 Blower relay
186 Compressor relay
187 Compressor clutch
188 Compressor clutch doide

Diagram 12

H32517

Central locking

Typical air conditioning

Wire colours

Bn	Brown	Rd	Red
Bu	Blue	Bk	Black
Ye	Yellow	Wh	White
Gn	Green	Vt	Violet
Gy	Grey	Vi	Mauve
Og	Orange	DBu	Dark blue
Pu	Purple	LBu	Light blue
Pk	Pink		

Key to items

1 Battery
4 Ignition switch
190 Fuel pump relay
191 Engine management control unit
192 Fuel pump
193 Camshaft sensor
194 Crankshaft sensor
195 Canister purge valve
196 Ignition coil
197 Spark plugs

198 Fuel injectors
199 Idle speed actuator
200 Throttle potentiometer
201 MAP sensor
202 Knock sensor
203 Inlet air temperature sensor
204 Coolant temperature sensor
205 EGR recirculation valve
206 Oxygen sensor

Diagram 13

H32518

Engine management - X16XEL

Wire colours

Bn	Brown	**Rd**	Red
Bu	Blue	**Bk**	Black
Ye	Yellow	**Wh**	White
Gn	Green	**Vt**	Violet
Gy	Grey	**Vi**	Mauve
Og	Orange	**DBu**	Dark blue
Pu	Purple	**LBu**	Light blue
Pk	Pink		

Key to items

1   Battery
4   Ignition switch
190   Fuel pump relay
191   Engine management control unit
192   Fuel pump
193   Camshaft sensor
194   Crankshaft sensor
195   Canister purge valve
196   Ignition coil
197   Spark plugs

198   Fuel injectors
202   Knock sensor
204   Coolant temperature sensor
205   EGR recirculation valve
206   Oxygen sensor
207   Inlet manifold changeover valve
208   Air mass meter
209   Throttle valve positioner

Diagram 14

H32519

Engine management - X18XE1

Wire colours

Bn	Brown	**Rd**	Red
Bu	Blue	**Bk**	Black
Ye	Yellow	**Wh**	White
Gn	Green	**Vt**	Violet
Gy	Grey	**Vi**	Mauve
Og	Orange	**DBu**	Dark blue
Pu	Purple	**LBu**	Light blue
Pk	Pink		

Key to items

1 Battery
4 Ignition switch
190 Fuel pump relay
191 Engine management control unit
192 Fuel pump
193 Camshaft sensor
194 Crankshaft sensor
195 Canister purge valve
196 Ignition coil
197 Spark plugs

198 Fuel injectors
200 Throttle potentiometer
202 Knock sensor
203 Inlet air temperature sensor
204 Coolant temperature sensor
205 EGR recirculation valve
206 Oxygen sensor
207 Inlet manifold changeover valve
208 Air mass meter
210 Idle speed actuator

211 Secondary air relay
212 Secondary air pump
213 Secondary air valve
214 Fuel injection relay

Diagram 15

H32520a

Engine management - X18XE/X20XEV

Wire colours

Bn	Brown	**Rd**	Red
Bu	Blue	**Bk**	Black
Ye	Yellow	**Wh**	White
Gn	Green	**Vt**	Violet
Gy	Grey	**Vi**	Mauve
Og	Orange	**DBu**	Dark blue
Pu	Purple	**LBu**	Light blue
Pk	Pink		

Key to items

1	Battery
4	Ignition switch
147	Cruise control switch
148	Clutch switch
191	Engine management control unit
194	Crankshaft sensor
204	Coolant temperature sensor
205	EGR recirculation valve
208	Air mass meter
215	Engine main relay
216	Swirl control valve
217	Boost control valve
218	Load pressure sensor
219	Load pressure sensor
220	Engine oil temperature sensor
221	Injection pump control unit
222	Fuel filter heater relay
223	Fuel filter heater
224	Preheater control unit
225	Glow plugs

Diagram 16

H32521

Engine management - X20DTL/X20DTH

Wire colours				Key to items			
Bn	Brown	**Rd**	Red	1	Battery	198	Fuel injectors
Bu	Blue	**Bk**	Black	4	Ignition switch	201	MAP sensor
Ye	Yellow	**Wh**	White	147	Cruise control switch	202	Knock sensor
Gn	Green	**Vt**	Violet	190	Fuel pump relay	203	Inlet air temperature sensor
Gy	Grey	**Vi**	Mauve	191	Engine management control unit	204	Coolant temperature sensor
Og	Orange	**DBu**	Dark blue	192	Fuel pump	205	EGR recirculation valve
Pu	Purple	**LBu**	Light blue	193	Camshaft sensor	206	Oxygen sensor
Pk	Pink			194	Crankshaft sensor	209	Throttle valve positioner
				195	Canister purge valve	215	Engine main relay
				196	Ignition coil	218	Pedal position sensor
				197	Spark plugs		

Diagram 17

H32531

Wire colours

Bn	Brown	**Rd**	Red
Bu	Blue	**Bk**	Black
Ye	Yellow	**Wh**	White
Gn	Green	**Vt**	Violet
Gy	Grey	**Vi**	Mauve
Og	Orange	**DBu**	Dark blue
Pu	Purple	**LBu**	Light blue
Pk	Pink		

Key to items

1 Battery
4 Ignition switch
147 Cruise control switch
190 Fuel pump relay
191 Engine management control unit
192 Fuel pump
193 Camshaft sensor
194 Crankshaft sensor
195 Canister purge valve
196 Ignition coil

197 Spark plugs
198 Fuel injectors
202 Knock sensor
204 Coolant temperature sensor
206 Oxygen sensor
207 Inlet manifold changeover valve
208 Air mass meter
209 Throttle valve positioner
215 Engine main relay
218 Pedal position sensor

Diagram 18

H32532

Engine management - Z18XE

Wire colours

Bn	Brown	**Rd**	Red
Bu	Blue	**Bk**	Black
Ye	Yellow	**Wh**	White
Gn	Green	**Vt**	Violet
Gy	Grey	**Vi**	Mauve
Og	Orange	**DBu**	Dark blue
Pu	Purple	**LBu**	Light blue
Pk	Pink		

Key to items

1   Battery
4   Ignition switch
147   Cruise control switch
190   Fuel pump relay
191   Engine management control unit
192   Fuel pump
194   Crankshaft sensor
195   Canister purge valve
196   Ignition coil
197   Spark plugs

198   Fuel injectors
201   MAP sensor
202   Knock sensor
203   Inlet air temperature sensor
204   Coolant temperature sensor
205   EGR recirculation valve
206   Oxygen sensor
209   Throttle valve positioner
211   Secondary air relay
212   Secondary air pump

215   Engine main relay
218   Pedal position sensor
230   A/C pressure sensor
231   Suppressor

Diagram 19

H32533

Engine management - Z22SE

Wire colours

Bn	Brown	**Rd**	Red
Bu	Blue	**Bk**	Black
Ye	Yellow	**Wh**	White
Gn	Green	**Vt**	Violet
Gy	Grey	**Vi**	Mauve
Og	Orange	**DBu**	Dark blue
Pu	Purple	**LBu**	Light blue
Pk	Pink		

Key to items

1 Battery
4 Ignition switch
147 Cruise control switch
191 Engine management control unit
194 Crankshaft sensor
204 Coolant temperature sensor
205 EGR recirculation valve
208 Air mass meter

215 Engine main relay
216 Swirl control valve
217 Boost control valve
218 Pedal position sensor
219 Load pressure sensor
220 Engine oil temperature sensor
221 Injection pump control unit
222 Fuel filter heater relay

223 Fuel filter heater
224 Preheater control unit
225 Glow plugs

Diagram 20

H32534

Engine management - Y20DTH/Y22DTR

Dimensions and weights

Note: *All figures are approximate, and vary according to model. Refer to manufacturer's data for exact figures.*

Dimensions

Overall length:
  Notchback and Hatchback .... 4495 mm
  Estate .... 4490 mm
Overall width:
  Excluding wing mirrors .... 1707 mm
  Including wing mirrors .... 1845 mm
Overall height (unladen):
  Notchback and Hatchback .... 1425 mm
  Estate:
    Excluding roof rail .... 1445 mm
    Including roof rail .... 1490 mm
Wheelbase .... 2637 mm
Track width:
  Front .... 1463 or 1483 mm
  Rear .... 1450 or 1478 mm

Weights

Kerb weight:
  1.6 litre petrol engine models:
    Notchback .... 1285 to 1300 kg
    Hatchback .... 1300 to 1315 kg
  1.8 litre petrol engine models:
    Notchback .... 1300 to 1342 kg
    Hatchback .... 1315 to 1372 kg
    Estate .... 1345 to 1390 kg
  2.0 litre petrol engine models:
    Notchback .... 1405 to 1447 kg
    Hatchback .... 1420 to 1462 kg
    Estate .... 1450 to 1492 kg
  2.2 litre petrol engine models:
    Notchback .... 1345 to 1390 kg
    Hatchback .... 1348 to 1390 kg
    Estate .... 1348 to 1405 kg
  2.0 litre diesel engine models:
    Notchback .... 1405 to 1447 kg
    Hatchback .... 1420 to 1462 kg
    Estate .... 1450 to 1492 kg
  2.2 litre diesel engine models:
    Notchback .... 1405 to 1447 kg
    Hatchback .... 1420 to 1462 kg
    Estate .... 1450 to 1492 kg
Maximum roof rack load .... 100 kg

Conversion factors

Length (distance)

Inches (in)	x 25.4	= Millimetres (mm)	x 0.0394	= Inches (in)
Feet (ft)	x 0.305	= Metres (m)	x 3.281	= Feet (ft)
Miles	x 1.609	= Kilometres (km)	x 0.621	= Miles

Volume (capacity)

Cubic inches (cu in; in³)	x 16.387	= Cubic centimetres (cc; cm³)	x 0.061	= Cubic inches (cu in; in³)
Imperial pints (Imp pt)	x 0.568	= Litres (l)	x 1.76	= Imperial pints (Imp pt)
Imperial quarts (Imp qt)	x 1.137	= Litres (l)	x 0.88	= Imperial quarts (Imp qt)
Imperial quarts (Imp qt)	x 1.201	= US quarts (US qt)	x 0.833	= Imperial quarts (Imp qt)
US quarts (US qt)	x 0.946	= Litres (l)	x 1.057	= US quarts (US qt)
Imperial gallons (Imp gal)	x 4.546	= Litres (l)	x 0.22	= Imperial gallons (Imp gal)
Imperial gallons (Imp gal)	x 1.201	= US gallons (US gal)	x 0.833	= Imperial gallons (Imp gal)
US gallons (US gal)	x 3.785	= Litres (l)	x 0.264	= US gallons (US gal)

Mass (weight)

Ounces (oz)	x 28.35	= Grams (g)	x 0.035	= Ounces (oz)
Pounds (lb)	x 0.454	= Kilograms (kg)	x 2.205	= Pounds (lb)

Force

Ounces-force (ozf; oz)	x 0.278	= Newtons (N)	x 3.6	= Ounces-force (ozf; oz)
Pounds-force (lbf; lb)	x 4.448	= Newtons (N)	x 0.225	= Pounds-force (lbf; lb)
Newtons (N)	x 0.1	= Kilograms-force (kgf; kg)	x 9.81	= Newtons (N)

Pressure

Pounds-force per square inch (psi; lbf/in²; lb/in²)	x 0.070	= Kilograms-force per square centimetre (kgf/cm²; kg/cm²)	x 14.223	= Pounds-force per square inch (psi; lbf/in²; lb/in²)
Pounds-force per square inch (psi; lbf/in²; lb/in²)	x 0.068	= Atmospheres (atm)	x 14.696	= Pounds-force per square inch (psi; lbf/in²; lb/in²)
Pounds-force per square inch (psi; lbf/in²; lb/in²)	x 0.069	= Bars	x 14.5	= Pounds-force per square inch (psi; lbf/in²; lb/in²)
Pounds-force per square inch (psi; lbf/in²; lb/in²)	x 6.895	= Kilopascals (kPa)	x 0.145	= Pounds-force per square inch (psi; lbf/in²; lb/in²)
Kilopascals (kPa)	x 0.01	= Kilograms-force per square centimetre (kgf/cm²; kg/cm²)	x 98.1	= Kilopascals (kPa)
Millibar (mbar)	x 100	= Pascals (Pa)	x 0.01	= Millibar (mbar)
Millibar (mbar)	x 0.0145	= Pounds-force per square inch (psi; lbf/in²; lb/in²)	x 68.947	= Millibar (mbar)
Millibar (mbar)	x 0.75	= Millimetres of mercury (mmHg)	x 1.333	= Millibar (mbar)
Millibar (mbar)	x 0.401	= Inches of water (inH₂O)	x 2.491	= Millibar (mbar)
Millimetres of mercury (mmHg)	x 0.535	= Inches of water (inH₂O)	x 1.868	= Millimetres of mercury (mmHg)
Inches of water (inH₂O)	x 0.036	= Pounds-force per square inch (psi; lbf/in²; lb/in²)	x 27.68	= Inches of water (inH₂O)

Torque (moment of force)

Pounds-force inches (lbf in; lb in)	x 1.152	= Kilograms-force centimetre (kgf cm; kg cm)	x 0.868	= Pounds-force inches (lbf in; lb in)
Pounds-force inches (lbf in; lb in)	x 0.113	= Newton metres (Nm)	x 8.85	= Pounds-force inches (lbf in; lb in)
Pounds-force inches (lbf in; lb in)	x 0.083	= Pounds-force feet (lbf ft; lb ft)	x 12	= Pounds-force inches (lbf in; lb in)
Pounds-force feet (lbf ft; lb ft)	x 0.138	= Kilograms-force metres (kgf m; kg m)	x 7.233	= Pounds-force feet (lbf ft; lb ft)
Pounds-force feet (lbf ft; lb ft)	x 1.356	= Newton metres (Nm)	x 0.738	= Pounds-force feet (lbf ft; lb ft)
Newton metres (Nm)	x 0.102	= Kilograms-force metres (kgf m; kg m)	x 9.804	= Newton metres (Nm)

Power

Horsepower (hp)	x 745.7	= Watts (W)	x 0.0013	= Horsepower (hp)

Velocity (speed)

Miles per hour (miles/hr; mph)	x 1.609	= Kilometres per hour (km/hr; kph)	x 0.621	= Miles per hour (miles/hr; mph)

Fuel consumption*

Miles per gallon, Imperial (mpg)	x 0.354	= Kilometres per litre (km/l)	x 2.825	= Miles per gallon, Imperial (mpg)
Miles per gallon, US (mpg)	x 0.425	= Kilometres per litre (km/l)	x 2.352	= Miles per gallon, US (mpg)

Temperature

Degrees Fahrenheit = (°C x 1.8) + 32   Degrees Celsius (Degrees Centigrade; °C) = (°F - 32) x 0.56

It is common practice to convert from miles per gallon (mpg) to litres/100 kilometres (l/100km), where mpg x l/100 km = 282

Spare parts are available from many sources, including maker's appointed garages, accessory shops, and motor factors. To be sure of obtaining the correct parts, it will sometimes be necessary to quote the vehicle identification number. If possible, it can also be useful to take the old parts along for positive identification. Items such as starter motors and alternators may be available under a service exchange scheme – any parts returned should be clean.

Our advice regarding spare parts is as follows.

Officially appointed garages

This is the best source of parts which are peculiar to your car, and which are not otherwise generally available (eg, badges, interior trim, certain body panels, etc). It is also the only place at which you should buy parts if the vehicle is still under warranty.

Accessory shops

These are very good places to buy materials and components needed for the maintenance of your car (oil, air and fuel filters, light bulbs, drivebelts, greases, brake pads, touch-up paint, etc). Components of this nature sold by a reputable shop are of the same standard as those used by the car manufacturer.

Besides components, these shops also sell tools and general accessories, usually have convenient opening hours, charge lower prices, and can often be found close to home. Some accessory shops have parts counters where components needed for almost any repair job can be purchased or ordered.

Motor factors

Good factors will stock all the more important components which wear out comparatively quickly, and can sometimes supply individual components needed for the overhaul of a larger assembly (eg, brake seals and hydraulic parts, bearing shells, pistons, valves). They may also handle work such as cylinder block reboring, crankshaft regrinding, etc.

Tyre and exhaust specialists

These outlets may be independent, or members of a local or national chain. They frequently offer competitive prices when compared with a main dealer or local garage, but it will pay to obtain several quotes before making a decision. When researching prices, also ask what 'extras' may be added – for instance fitting a new valve and balancing the wheel are both commonly charged on top of the price of a new tyre.

Other sources

Beware of parts or materials obtained from market stalls, car boot sales or similar outlets. Such items are not invariably sub-standard, but there is little chance of compensation if they do prove unsatisfactory. In the case of safety-critical components such as brake pads, there is the risk not only of financial loss, but also of an accident causing injury or death.

Second-hand components or assemblies obtained from a car breaker can be a good buy in some circumstances, but his sort of purchase is best made by the experienced DIY mechanic.

Modifications are a continuing and unpublicised process in vehicle manufacture, quite apart from major model changes. Spare parts manuals and lists are compiled upon a numerical basis, the individual vehicle identification numbers being essential to correct identification of the component concerned.

When ordering spare parts, always give as much information as possible. Quote the car model, year of manufacture, body and engine numbers as appropriate.

The *Vehicle Identification Number (VIN)* is stamped on a plate located either on the front of the right-hand side B-pillar or on the engine compartment front crossmember. It is also stamped into the body floor panel between the right-hand front seat and the door sill panel; lift the flap in the carpet to see it **(see illustrations)**.

The *Engine number* is stamped on the front left-hand side of the cylinder block on petrol engines, and on the front right-hand side of the cylinder block beneath the injection pump on diesel engines.

Note: *When new, the car is provided with a Car Pass (similar to a credit card) having all the vehicle's data recorded on a magnetic strip.*

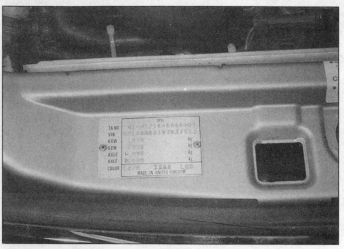

Vehicle Identification Number (VIN) stamped on a plate riveted to the engine compartment front crossmember

The VIN is also stamped into the body floor panel next to the right-hand front seat

Whenever servicing, repair or overhaul work is carried out on the car or its components, observe the following procedures and instructions. This will assist in carrying out the operation efficiently and to a professional standard of workmanship.

Joint mating faces and gaskets

When separating components at their mating faces, never insert screwdrivers or similar implements into the joint between the faces in order to prise them apart. This can cause severe damage which results in oil leaks, coolant leaks, etc upon reassembly. Separation is usually achieved by tapping along the joint with a soft-faced hammer in order to break the seal. However, note that this method may not be suitable where dowels are used for component location.

Where a gasket is used between the mating faces of two components, a new one must be fitted on reassembly; fit it dry unless otherwise stated in the repair procedure. Make sure that the mating faces are clean and dry, with all traces of old gasket removed. When cleaning a joint face, use a tool which is unlikely to score or damage the face, and remove any burrs or nicks with an oilstone or fine file.

Make sure that tapped holes are cleaned with a pipe cleaner, and keep them free of jointing compound, if this is being used, unless specifically instructed otherwise.

Ensure that all orifices, channels or pipes are clear, and blow through them, preferably using compressed air.

Oil seals

Oil seals can be removed by levering them out with a wide flat-bladed screwdriver or similar implement. Alternatively, a number of self-tapping screws may be screwed into the seal, and these used as a purchase for pliers or some similar device in order to pull the seal free.

Whenever an oil seal is removed from its working location, either individually or as part of an assembly, it should be renewed.

The very fine sealing lip of the seal is easily damaged, and will not seal if the surface it contacts is not completely clean and free from scratches, nicks or grooves. If the original sealing surface of the component cannot be restored, and the manufacturer has not made provision for slight relocation of the seal relative to the sealing surface, the component should be renewed.

Protect the lips of the seal from any surface which may damage them in the course of fitting. Use tape or a conical sleeve where possible. Lubricate the seal lips with oil before fitting and, on dual-lipped seals, fill the space between the lips with grease.

Unless otherwise stated, oil seals must be fitted with their sealing lips toward the lubricant to be sealed.

Use a tubular drift or block of wood of the appropriate size to install the seal and, if the seal housing is shouldered, drive the seal down to the shoulder. If the seal housing is unshouldered, the seal should be fitted with its face flush with the housing top face (unless otherwise instructed).

Screw threads and fastenings

Seized nuts, bolts and screws are quite a common occurrence where corrosion has set in, and the use of penetrating oil or releasing fluid will often overcome this problem if the offending item is soaked for a while before attempting to release it. The use of an impact driver may also provide a means of releasing such stubborn fastening devices, when used in conjunction with the appropriate screwdriver bit or socket. If none of these methods works, it may be necessary to resort to the careful application of heat, or the use of a hacksaw or nut splitter device.

Studs are usually removed by locking two nuts together on the threaded part, and then using a spanner on the lower nut to unscrew the stud. Studs or bolts which have broken off below the surface of the component in which they are mounted can sometimes be removed using a stud extractor. Always ensure that a blind tapped hole is completely free from oil, grease, water or other fluid before installing the bolt or stud. Failure to do this could cause the housing to crack due to the hydraulic action of the bolt or stud as it is screwed in.

When tightening a castellated nut to accept a split pin, tighten the nut to the specified torque, where applicable, and then tighten further to the next split pin hole. Never slacken the nut to align the split pin hole, unless stated in the repair procedure.

When checking or retightening a nut or bolt to a specified torque setting, slacken the nut or bolt by a quarter of a turn, and then retighten to the specified setting. However, this should not be attempted where angular tightening has been used.

For some screw fastenings, notably cylinder head bolts or nuts, torque wrench settings are no longer specified for the latter stages of tightening, "angle-tightening" being called up instead. Typically, a fairly low torque wrench setting will be applied to the bolts/nuts in the correct sequence, followed by one or more stages of tightening through specified angles.

Locknuts, locktabs and washers

Any fastening which will rotate against a component or housing during tightening should always have a washer between it and the relevant component or housing.

Spring or split washers should always be renewed when they are used to lock a critical component such as a big-end bearing retaining bolt or nut. Locktabs which are folded over to retain a nut or bolt should always be renewed.

Self-locking nuts can be re-used in non-critical areas, providing resistance can be felt when the locking portion passes over the bolt or stud thread. However, it should be noted that self-locking stiffnuts tend to lose their effectiveness after long periods of use, and should then be renewed as a matter of course.

Split pins must always be replaced with new ones of the correct size for the hole.

When thread-locking compound is found on the threads of a fastener which is to be re-used, it should be cleaned off with a wire brush and solvent, and fresh compound applied on reassembly.

Special tools

Some repair procedures in this manual entail the use of special tools such as a press, two or three-legged pullers, spring compressors, etc. Wherever possible, suitable readily-available alternatives to the manufacturer's special tools are described, and are shown in use. In some instances, where no alternative is possible, it has been necessary to resort to the use of a manufacturer's tool, and this has been done for reasons of safety as well as the efficient completion of the repair operation. Unless you are highly-skilled and have a thorough understanding of the procedures described, never attempt to bypass the use of any special tool when the procedure described specifies its use. Not only is there a very great risk of personal injury, but expensive damage could be caused to the components involved.

Environmental considerations

When disposing of used engine oil, brake fluid, antifreeze, etc, give due consideration to any detrimental environmental effects. Do not, for instance, pour any of the above liquids down drains into the general sewage system, or onto the ground to soak away. Many local council refuse tips provide a facility for waste oil disposal, as do some garages. If none of these facilities are available, consult your local Environmental Health Department, or the National Rivers Authority, for further advice.

With the universal tightening-up of legislation regarding the emission of environmentally-harmful substances from motor vehicles, most vehicles have tamperproof devices fitted to the main adjustment points of the fuel system. These devices are primarily designed to prevent unqualified persons from adjusting the fuel/air mixture, with the chance of a consequent increase in toxic emissions. If such devices are found during servicing or overhaul, they should, wherever possible, be renewed or refitted in accordance with the manufacturer's requirements or current legislation.

OIL CARE
FOLLOW THE CODE
OIL BANK LINE
0800 66 33 66
www.oilbankline.org.uk

Note: It is antisocial and illegal to dump oil down the drain. To find the location of your local oil recycling bank, call this number free.

The jack supplied with the vehicle tool kit should only be used for changing the roadwheels – see *Wheel changing* at the front of this manual. When carrying out any other kind of work, raise the vehicle using a hydraulic trolley jack, and always supplement the jack with axle stands positioned under the vehicle jacking points.

When using a trolley jack or axle stands, always position the jack head or axle stand head under, or adjacent to one of the relevant wheel changing jacking points under the sills. Use a block of wood between the jack or axle stand and the sill – the block of wood should have a groove cut into it, in which the welded flange of the sill will locate **(see illustrations).**

Do not attempt to jack the vehicle under the front crossmember, the sump, or any of the suspension components.

The jack supplied with the vehicle locates in the jacking points on the underside of the sills – see *Wheel changing* at the front of this manual. Ensure that the jack head is correctly engaged before attempting to raise the vehicle.

Never work under, around, or near a raised vehicle, unless it is adequately supported in at least two places.

Front jacking point for hydraulic jack or axle stands

Rear jacking point for hydraulic jack or axle stands

Pull out the cover to access the jacking point

The radio/cassette unit fitted may be equipped with a built-in security code, to deter thieves. If the power source to the unit is cut, the anti-theft system will activate. Even if the power source is immediately reconnected, the radio/cassette unit will not function until the correct security code has been entered. Therefore if you do not know the correct security code for the unit, **do not** disconnect the battery negative lead, or remove the radio/cassette unit from the vehicle.

If the security code is lost or forgotten, seek the advice of your Vauxhall dealer. On presentation of proof of ownership, a Vauxhall dealer will be able to provide you with a new security code.

Introduction

A selection of good tools is a fundamental requirement for anyone contemplating the maintenance and repair of a motor vehicle. For the owner who does not possess any, their purchase will prove a considerable expense, offsetting some of the savings made by doing-it-yourself. However, provided that the tools purchased meet the relevant national safety standards and are of good quality, they will last for many years and prove an extremely worthwhile investment.

To help the average owner to decide which tools are needed to carry out the various tasks detailed in this manual, we have compiled three lists of tools under the following headings: *Maintenance and minor repair, Repair and overhaul*, and *Special*. Newcomers to practical mechanics should start off with the *Maintenance and minor repair* tool kit, and confine themselves to the simpler jobs around the vehicle. Then, as confidence and experience grow, more difficult tasks can be undertaken, with extra tools being purchased as, and when, they are needed. In this way, a *Maintenance and minor repair* tool kit can be built up into a *Repair and overhaul* tool kit over a considerable period of time, without any major cash outlays. The experienced do-it-yourselfer will have a tool kit good enough for most repair and overhaul procedures, and will add tools from the *Special* category when it is felt that the expense is justified by the amount of use to which these tools will be put.

Maintenance and minor repair tool kit

The tools given in this list should be considered as a minimum requirement if routine maintenance, servicing and minor repair operations are to be undertaken. We recommend the purchase of combination spanners (ring one end, open-ended the other); although more expensive than open-ended ones, they do give the advantages of both types of spanner.

- ☐ *Combination spanners:*
  Metric - 8 to 19 mm inclusive
- ☐ *Adjustable spanner - 35 mm jaw (approx.)*
- ☐ *Spark plug spanner (with rubber insert) - petrol models*
- ☐ *Spark plug gap adjustment tool - petrol models*
- ☐ *Set of feeler gauges*
- ☐ *Brake bleed nipple spanner*
- ☐ *Screwdrivers:*
  Flat blade - 100 mm long x 6 mm dia
  Cross blade - 100 mm long x 6 mm dia
  Torx - various sizes (not all vehicles)
- ☐ *Combination pliers*
- ☐ *Hacksaw (junior)*
- ☐ *Tyre pump*
- ☐ *Tyre pressure gauge*
- ☐ *Oil can*
- ☐ *Oil filter removal tool*
- ☐ *Fine emery cloth*
- ☐ *Wire brush (small)*
- ☐ *Funnel (medium size)*
- ☐ *Sump drain plug key (not all vehicles)*

Repair and overhaul tool kit

These tools are virtually essential for anyone undertaking any major repairs to a motor vehicle, and are additional to those given in the *Maintenance and minor repair* list. Included in this list is a comprehensive set of sockets. Although these are expensive, they will be found invaluable as they are so versatile - particularly if various drives are included in the set. We recommend the half-inch square-drive type, as this can be used with most proprietary torque wrenches.

The tools in this list will sometimes need to be supplemented by tools from the *Special* list:

- ☐ *Sockets (or box spanners) to cover range in previous list (including Torx sockets)*
- ☐ *Reversible ratchet drive (for use with sockets)*
- ☐ *Extension piece, 250 mm (for use with sockets)*
- ☐ *Universal joint (for use with sockets)*
- ☐ *Flexible handle or sliding T "breaker bar" (for use with sockets)*
- ☐ *Torque wrench (for use with sockets)*
- ☐ *Self-locking grips*
- ☐ *Ball pein hammer*
- ☐ *Soft-faced mallet (plastic or rubber)*
- ☐ *Screwdrivers:*
  Flat blade - long & sturdy, short (chubby), and narrow (electrician's) types
  Cross blade - long & sturdy, and short (chubby) types
- ☐ *Pliers:*
  Long-nosed
  Side cutters (electrician's)
  Circlip (internal and external)
- ☐ *Cold chisel - 25 mm*
- ☐ *Scriber*
- ☐ *Scraper*
- ☐ *Centre-punch*
- ☐ *Pin punch*
- ☐ *Hacksaw*
- ☐ *Brake hose clamp*
- ☐ *Brake/clutch bleeding kit*
- ☐ *Selection of twist drills*
- ☐ *Steel rule/straight-edge*
- ☐ *Allen keys (inc. splined/Torx type)*
- ☐ *Selection of files*
- ☐ *Wire brush*
- ☐ *Axle stands*
- ☐ *Jack (strong trolley or hydraulic type)*
- ☐ *Light with extension lead*
- ☐ *Universal electrical multi-meter*

Sockets and reversible ratchet drive

Brake bleeding kit

Torx key, socket and bit

Hose clamp

Angular-tightening gauge

Special tools

The tools in this list are those which are not used regularly, are expensive to buy, or which need to be used in accordance with their manufacturers' instructions. Unless relatively difficult mechanical jobs are undertaken frequently, it will not be economic to buy many of these tools. Where this is the case, you could consider clubbing together with friends (or joining a motorists' club) to make a joint purchase, or borrowing the tools against a deposit from a local garage or tool hire specialist. It is worth noting that many of the larger DIY superstores now carry a large range of special tools for hire at modest rates.

The following list contains only those tools and instruments freely available to the public, and not those special tools produced by the vehicle manufacturer specifically for its dealer network. You will find occasional references to these manufacturers' special tools in the text of this manual. Generally, an alternative method of doing the job without the vehicle manufacturers' special tool is given. However, sometimes there is no alternative to using them. Where this is the case and the relevant tool cannot be bought or borrowed, you will have to entrust the work to a dealer.

- ☐ Angular-tightening gauge
- ☐ Valve spring compressor
- ☐ Valve grinding tool
- ☐ Piston ring compressor
- ☐ Piston ring removal/installation tool
- ☐ Cylinder bore hone
- ☐ Balljoint separator
- ☐ Coil spring compressors (where applicable)
- ☐ Two/three-legged hub and bearing puller
- ☐ Impact screwdriver
- ☐ Micrometer and/or vernier calipers
- ☐ Dial gauge
- ☐ Stroboscopic timing light
- ☐ Dwell angle meter/tachometer
- ☐ Fault code reader
- ☐ Cylinder compression gauge
- ☐ Hand-operated vacuum pump and gauge
- ☐ Clutch plate alignment set
- ☐ Brake shoe steady spring cup removal tool
- ☐ Bush and bearing removal/installation set
- ☐ Stud extractors
- ☐ Tap and die set
- ☐ Lifting tackle
- ☐ Trolley jack

Buying tools

Reputable motor accessory shops and superstores often offer excellent quality tools at discount prices, so it pays to shop around.

Remember, you don't have to buy the most expensive items on the shelf, but it is always advisable to steer clear of the very cheap tools. Beware of 'bargains' offered on market stalls or at car boot sales. There are plenty of good tools around at reasonable prices, but always aim to purchase items which meet the relevant national safety standards. If in doubt, ask the proprietor or manager of the shop for advice before making a purchase.

Care and maintenance of tools

Having purchased a reasonable tool kit, it is necessary to keep the tools in a clean and serviceable condition. After use, always wipe off any dirt, grease and metal particles using a clean, dry cloth, before putting the tools away. Never leave them lying around after they have been used. A simple tool rack on the garage or workshop wall for items such as screwdrivers and pliers is a good idea. Store all normal spanners and sockets in a metal box. Any measuring instruments, gauges, meters, etc, must be carefully stored where they cannot be damaged or become rusty.

Take a little care when tools are used. Hammer heads inevitably become marked, and screwdrivers lose the keen edge on their blades from time to time. A little timely attention with emery cloth or a file will soon restore items like this to a good finish.

Working facilities

Not to be forgotten when discussing tools is the workshop itself. If anything more than routine maintenance is to be carried out, a suitable working area becomes essential.

It is appreciated that many an owner-mechanic is forced by circumstances to remove an engine or similar item without the benefit of a garage or workshop. Having done this, any repairs should always be done under the cover of a roof.

Wherever possible, any dismantling should be done on a clean, flat workbench or table at a suitable working height.

Any workbench needs a vice; one with a jaw opening of 100 mm is suitable for most jobs. As mentioned previously, some clean dry storage space is also required for tools, as well as for any lubricants, cleaning fluids, touch-up paints etc, which become necessary.

Another item which may be required, and which has a much more general usage, is an electric drill with a chuck capacity of at least 8 mm. This, together with a good range of twist drills, is virtually essential for fitting accessories.

Last, but not least, always keep a supply of old newspapers and clean, lint-free rags available, and try to keep any working area as clean as possible.

Micrometers

Dial test indicator ("dial gauge")

Strap wrench

Compression tester

Fault code reader

This is a guide to getting your vehicle through the MOT test. Obviously it will not be possible to examine the vehicle to the same standard as the professional MOT tester. However, working through the following checks will enable you to identify any problem areas before submitting the vehicle for the test.

Where a testable component is in borderline condition, the tester has discretion in deciding whether to pass or fail it. The basis of such discretion is whether the tester would be happy for a close relative or friend to use the vehicle with the component in that condition. If the vehicle presented is clean and evidently well cared for, the tester may be more inclined to pass a borderline component than if the vehicle is scruffy and apparently neglected.

It has only been possible to summarise the test requirements here, based on the regulations in force at the time of printing. Test standards are becoming increasingly stringent, although there are some exemptions for older vehicles.

An assistant will be needed to help carry out some of these checks.

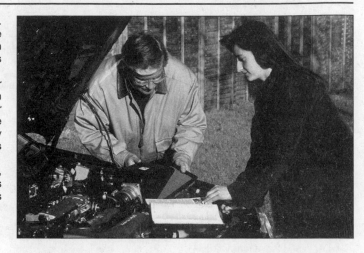

The checks have been sub-divided into four categories, as follows:

1 Checks carried out **FROM THE DRIVER'S SEAT**

2 Checks carried out **WITH THE VEHICLE ON THE GROUND**

3 Checks carried out **WITH THE VEHICLE RAISED AND THE WHEELS FREE TO TURN**

4 Checks carried out on **YOUR VEHICLE'S EXHAUST EMISSION SYSTEM**

1 Checks carried out **FROM THE DRIVER'S SEAT**

Handbrake

☐ Test the operation of the handbrake. Excessive travel (too many clicks) indicates incorrect brake or cable adjustment.

☐ Check that the handbrake cannot be released by tapping the lever sideways. Check the security of the lever mountings.

Footbrake

☐ Depress the brake pedal and check that it does not creep down to the floor, indicating a master cylinder fault. Release the pedal, wait a few seconds, then depress it again. If the pedal travels nearly to the floor before firm resistance is felt, brake adjustment or repair is necessary. If the pedal feels spongy, there is air in the hydraulic system which must be removed by bleeding.

☐ Check that the brake pedal is secure and in good condition. Check also for signs of fluid leaks on the pedal, floor or carpets, which would indicate failed seals in the brake master cylinder.

☐ Check the servo unit (when applicable) by operating the brake pedal several times, then keeping the pedal depressed and starting the engine. As the engine starts, the pedal will move down slightly. If not, the vacuum hose or the servo itself may be faulty.

Steering wheel and column

☐ Examine the steering wheel for fractures or looseness of the hub, spokes or rim.

☐ Move the steering wheel from side to side and then up and down. Check that the steering wheel is not loose on the column, indicating wear or a loose retaining nut. Continue moving the steering wheel as before, but also turn it slightly from left to right.

☐ Check that the steering wheel is not loose on the column, and that there is no abnormal

movement of the steering wheel, indicating wear in the column support bearings or couplings.

Windscreen, mirrors and sunvisor

☐ The windscreen must be free of cracks or other significant damage within the driver's field of view. (Small stone chips are acceptable.) Rear view mirrors must be secure, intact, and capable of being adjusted.

290mm

☐ The driver's sunvisor must be capable of being stored in the "up" position.

Seat belts and seats

Note: *The following checks are applicable to all seat belts, front and rear.*

☐ Examine the webbing of all the belts (including rear belts if fitted) for cuts, serious fraying or deterioration. Fasten and unfasten each belt to check the buckles. If applicable, check the retracting mechanism. Check the security of all seat belt mountings accessible from inside the vehicle.

☐ Seat belts with pre-tensioners, once activated, have a "flag" or similar showing on the seat belt stalk. This, in itself, is not a reason for test failure.

☐ The front seats themselves must be securely attached and the backrests must lock in the upright position.

Doors

☐ Both front doors must be able to be opened and closed from outside and inside, and must latch securely when closed.

2 Checks carried out WITH THE VEHICLE ON THE GROUND

Vehicle identification

☐ Number plates must be in good condition, secure and legible, with letters and numbers correctly spaced – spacing at (A) should be at least twice that at (B).

☐ The VIN plate and/or homologation plate must be legible.

Electrical equipment

☐ Switch on the ignition and check the operation of the horn.

☐ Check the windscreen washers and wipers, examining the wiper blades; renew damaged or perished blades. Also check the operation of the stop-lights.

☐ Check the operation of the sidelights and number plate lights. The lenses and reflectors must be secure, clean and undamaged.

☐ Check the operation and alignment of the headlights. The headlight reflectors must not be tarnished and the lenses must be undamaged.

☐ Switch on the ignition and check the operation of the direction indicators (including the instrument panel tell-tale) and the hazard warning lights. Operation of the sidelights and stop-lights must not affect the indicators - if it does, the cause is usually a bad earth at the rear light cluster.

☐ Check the operation of the rear foglight(s), including the warning light on the instrument panel or in the switch.

☐ The ABS warning light must illuminate in accordance with the manufacturers' design. For most vehicles, the ABS warning light should illuminate when the ignition is switched on, and (if the system is operating properly) extinguish after a few seconds. Refer to the owner's handbook.

Footbrake

☐ Examine the master cylinder, brake pipes and servo unit for leaks, loose mountings, corrosion or other damage.

☐ The fluid reservoir must be secure and the fluid level must be between the upper (A) and lower (B) markings.

☐ Inspect both front brake flexible hoses for cracks or deterioration of the rubber. Turn the steering from lock to lock, and ensure that the hoses do not contact the wheel, tyre, or any part of the steering or suspension mechanism. With the brake pedal firmly depressed, check the hoses for bulges or leaks under pressure.

Steering and suspension

☐ Have your assistant turn the steering wheel from side to side slightly, up to the point where the steering gear just begins to transmit this movement to the roadwheels. Check for excessive free play between the steering wheel and the steering gear, indicating wear or insecurity of the steering column joints, the column-to-steering gear coupling, or the steering gear itself.

☐ Have your assistant turn the steering wheel more vigorously in each direction, so that the roadwheels just begin to turn. As this is done, examine all the steering joints, linkages, fittings and attachments. Renew any component that shows signs of wear or damage. On vehicles with power steering, check the security and condition of the steering pump, drivebelt and hoses.

☐ Check that the vehicle is standing level, and at approximately the correct ride height.

Shock absorbers

☐ Depress each corner of the vehicle in turn, then release it. The vehicle should rise and then settle in its normal position. If the vehicle continues to rise and fall, the shock absorber is defective. A shock absorber which has seized will also cause the vehicle to fail.

Exhaust system

☐ Start the engine. With your assistant holding a rag over the tailpipe, check the entire system for leaks. Repair or renew leaking sections.

3 Checks carried out **WITH THE VEHICLE RAISED AND THE WHEELS FREE TO TURN**

Jack up the front and rear of the vehicle, and securely support it on axle stands. Position the stands clear of the suspension assemblies. Ensure that the wheels are clear of the ground and that the steering can be turned from lock to lock.

Steering mechanism

☐ Have your assistant turn the steering from lock to lock. Check that the steering turns smoothly, and that no part of the steering mechanism, including a wheel or tyre, fouls any brake hose or pipe or any part of the body structure.

☐ Examine the steering rack rubber gaiters for damage or insecurity of the retaining clips. If power steering is fitted, check for signs of damage or leakage of the fluid hoses, pipes or connections. Also check for excessive stiffness or binding of the steering, a missing split pin or locking device, or severe corrosion of the body structure within 30 cm of any steering component attachment point.

Front and rear suspension and wheel bearings

☐ Starting at the front right-hand side, grasp the roadwheel at the 3 o'clock and 9 o'clock positions and rock gently but firmly. Check for free play or insecurity at the wheel bearings, suspension balljoints, or suspension mountings, pivots and attachments.

☐ Now grasp the wheel at the 12 o'clock and 6 o'clock positions and repeat the previous inspection. Spin the wheel, and check for roughness or tightness of the front wheel bearing.

☐ If excess free play is suspected at a component pivot point, this can be confirmed by using a large screwdriver or similar tool and levering between the mounting and the component attachment. This will confirm whether the wear is in the pivot bush, its retaining bolt, or in the mounting itself (the bolt holes can often become elongated).

☐ Carry out all the above checks at the other front wheel, and then at both rear wheels.

Springs and shock absorbers

☐ Examine the suspension struts (when applicable) for serious fluid leakage, corrosion, or damage to the casing. Also check the security of the mounting points.

☐ If coil springs are fitted, check that the spring ends locate in their seats, and that the spring is not corroded, cracked or broken.

☐ If leaf springs are fitted, check that all leaves are intact, that the axle is securely attached to each spring, and that there is no deterioration of the spring eye mountings, bushes, and shackles.

☐ The same general checks apply to vehicles fitted with other suspension types, such as torsion bars, hydraulic displacer units, etc. Ensure that all mountings and attachments are secure, that there are no signs of excessive wear, corrosion or damage, and (on hydraulic types) that there are no fluid leaks or damaged pipes.

☐ Inspect the shock absorbers for signs of serious fluid leakage. Check for wear of the mounting bushes or attachments, or damage to the body of the unit.

Driveshafts
(fwd vehicles only)

☐ Rotate each front wheel in turn and inspect the constant velocity joint gaiters for splits or damage. Also check that each driveshaft is straight and undamaged.

Braking system

☐ If possible without dismantling, check brake pad wear and disc condition. Ensure that the friction lining material has not worn excessively, (A) and that the discs are not fractured, pitted, scored or badly worn (B).

☐ Examine all the rigid brake pipes underneath the vehicle, and the flexible hose(s) at the rear. Look for corrosion, chafing or insecurity of the pipes, and for signs of bulging under pressure, chafing, splits or deterioration of the flexible hoses.

☐ Look for signs of fluid leaks at the brake calipers or on the brake backplates. Repair or renew leaking components.

☐ Slowly spin each wheel, while your assistant depresses and releases the footbrake. Ensure that each brake is operating and does not bind when the pedal is released.

☐ Examine the handbrake mechanism, checking for frayed or broken cables, excessive corrosion, or wear or insecurity of the linkage. Check that the mechanism works on each relevant wheel, and releases fully, without binding.

☐ It is not possible to test brake efficiency without special equipment, but a road test can be carried out later to check that the vehicle pulls up in a straight line.

Fuel and exhaust systems

☐ Inspect the fuel tank (including the filler cap), fuel pipes, hoses and unions. All components must be secure and free from leaks.

☐ Examine the exhaust system over its entire length, checking for any damaged, broken or missing mountings, security of the retaining clamps and rust or corrosion.

Wheels and tyres

☐ Examine the sidewalls and tread area of each tyre in turn. Check for cuts, tears, lumps, bulges, separation of the tread, and exposure of the ply or cord due to wear or damage. Check that the tyre bead is correctly seated on the wheel rim, that the valve is sound and properly seated, and that the wheel is not distorted or damaged.

☐ Check that the tyres are of the correct size for the vehicle, that they are of the same size and type on each axle, and that the pressures are correct.

☐ Check the tyre tread depth. The legal minimum at the time of writing is 1.6 mm over at least three-quarters of the tread width. Abnormal tread wear may indicate incorrect front wheel alignment.

Body corrosion

☐ Check the condition of the entire vehicle structure for signs of corrosion in load-bearing areas. (These include chassis box sections, side sills, cross-members, pillars, and all suspension, steering, braking system and seat belt mountings and anchorages.) Any corrosion which has seriously reduced the thickness of a load-bearing area is likely to cause the vehicle to fail. In this case professional repairs are likely to be needed.

☐ Damage or corrosion which causes sharp or otherwise dangerous edges to be exposed will also cause the vehicle to fail.

4 Checks carried out on YOUR VEHICLE'S EXHAUST EMISSION SYSTEM

Petrol models

☐ Have the engine at normal operating temperature, and make sure that it is in good tune (ignition system in good order, air filter element clean, etc).

☐ Before any measurements are carried out, raise the engine speed to around 2500 rpm, and hold it at this speed for 20 seconds. Allow the engine speed to return to idle, and watch for smoke emissions from the exhaust tailpipe. If the idle speed is obviously much too high, or if dense blue or clearly-visible black smoke comes from the tailpipe for more than 5 seconds, the vehicle will fail. As a rule of thumb, blue smoke signifies oil being burnt (engine wear) while black smoke signifies unburnt fuel (dirty air cleaner element, or other carburettor or fuel system fault).

☐ An exhaust gas analyser capable of measuring carbon monoxide (CO) and hydrocarbons (HC) is now needed. If such an instrument cannot be hired or borrowed, a local garage may agree to perform the check for a small fee.

CO emissions (mixture)

☐ At the time of writing, for vehicles first used between 1st August 1975 and 31st July 1986 (P to C registration), the CO level must not exceed 4.5% by volume. For vehicles first used between 1st August 1986 and 31st July 1992 (D to J registration), the CO level must not exceed 3.5% by volume. Vehicles first

used after 1st August 1992 (K registration) must conform to the manufacturer's specification. The MOT tester has access to a DOT database or emissions handbook, which lists the CO and HC limits for each make and model of vehicle. The CO level is measured with the engine at idle speed, and at "fast idle". The following limits are given as a general guide:

At idle speed -
CO level no more than 0.5%
At "fast idle" (2500 to 3000 rpm) -
CO level no more than 0.3%
(Minimum oil temperature 60ºC)

☐ If the CO level cannot be reduced far enough to pass the test (and the fuel and ignition systems are otherwise in good condition) then the carburettor is badly worn, or there is some problem in the fuel injection system or catalytic converter (as applicable).

HC emissions

☐ With the CO within limits, HC emissions for vehicles first used between 1st August 1975 and 31st July 1992 (P to J registration) must not exceed 1200 ppm. Vehicles first used after 1st August 1992 (K registration) must conform to the manufacturer's specification. The MOT tester has access to a DOT database or emissions handbook, which lists the CO and HC limits for each make and model of vehicle. The HC level is measured with the engine at "fast idle". The following is given as a general guide:

At "fast idle" (2500 to 3000 rpm) -
HC level no more than 200 ppm
(Minimum oil temperature 60ºC)

☐ Excessive HC emissions are caused by incomplete combustion, the causes of which can include oil being burnt, mechanical wear and ignition/fuel system malfunction.

Diesel models

☐ The only emission test applicable to Diesel engines is the measuring of exhaust smoke density. The test involves accelerating the engine several times to its maximum unloaded speed.

Note: *It is of the utmost importance that the engine timing belt is in good condition before the test is carried out.*

☐ The limits for Diesel engine exhaust smoke, introduced in September 1995 are:
Vehicles first used before 1st August 1979:
Exempt from metered smoke testing, but must not emit "dense blue or clearly visible black smoke for a period of more than 5 seconds at idle" or "dense blue or clearly visible black smoke during acceleration which would obscure the view of other road users".
Non-turbocharged vehicles first used after 1st August 1979: 2.5m⁻¹
Turbocharged vehicles first used after 1st August 1979: 3.0m⁻¹

☐ Excessive smoke can be caused by a dirty air cleaner element. Otherwise, professional advice may be needed to find the cause.

Engine

- ☐ Engine fails to rotate when attempting to start
- ☐ Engine rotates, but will not start
- ☐ Engine difficult to start when cold
- ☐ Engine difficult to start when hot
- ☐ Starter motor noisy or excessively-rough in engagement
- ☐ Engine starts, but stops immediately
- ☐ Engine idles erratically
- ☐ Engine misfires at idle speed
- ☐ Engine misfires throughout the driving speed range
- ☐ Engine hesitates on acceleration
- ☐ Engine stalls
- ☐ Engine lacks power
- ☐ Engine backfires
- ☐ Oil pressure warning light illuminated with engine running
- ☐ Engine runs-on after switching off
- ☐ Engine noises

Cooling system

- ☐ Overheating
- ☐ Overcooling
- ☐ External coolant leakage
- ☐ Internal coolant leakage
- ☐ Corrosion

Fuel and exhaust systems

- ☐ Excessive fuel consumption
- ☐ Fuel leakage and/or fuel odour
- ☐ Excessive noise or fumes from the exhaust system

Clutch

- ☐ Pedal travels to floor – no pressure or very little resistance
- ☐ Clutch fails to disengage (unable to select gears)
- ☐ Clutch slips (engine speed increases, with no increase in vehicle speed)
- ☐ Judder as clutch is engaged
- ☐ Noise when depressing or releasing clutch pedal

Manual transmission

- ☐ Noisy in neutral with engine running
- ☐ Noisy in one particular gear
- ☐ Difficulty engaging gears
- ☐ Jumps out of gear
- ☐ Vibration
- ☐ Lubricant leaks

Automatic transmission

- ☐ Fluid leakage
- ☐ Transmission fluid brown, or has burned smell
- ☐ Engine will not start in any gear, or starts in gears other than Park or Neutral
- ☐ General gear selection problems
- ☐ Transmission will not downshift (kickdown) with accelerator pedal fully depressed
- ☐ Transmission slips, shifts roughly, is noisy, or has no drive in forward or reverse gears

Driveshafts

- ☐ Vibration when accelerating or decelerating
- ☐ Clicking or knocking noise on turns (at slow speed on full-lock)

Braking system

- ☐ Vehicle pulls to one side under braking
- ☐ Noise (grinding or high-pitched squeal) when brakes applied
- ☐ Excessive brake pedal travel
- ☐ Brake pedal feels spongy when depressed
- ☐ Excessive brake pedal effort required to stop vehicle
- ☐ Judder felt through brake pedal or steering wheel when braking
- ☐ Pedal pulsates when braking hard
- ☐ Brakes binding
- ☐ Rear wheels locking under normal braking

Steering and suspension

- ☐ Vehicle pulls to one side
- ☐ Wheel wobble and vibration
- ☐ Excessive pitching and/or rolling around corners, or during braking
- ☐ Wandering or general instability
- ☐ Excessively-stiff steering
- ☐ Excessive play in steering
- ☐ Lack of power assistance
- ☐ Tyre wear excessive

Electrical system

- ☐ Battery will not hold a charge for more than a few days
- ☐ Ignition/no-charge warning light remains illuminated with engine running
- ☐ Ignition/no-charge warning light fails to come on
- ☐ Lights inoperative
- ☐ Instrument readings inaccurate or erratic
- ☐ Horn inoperative, or unsatisfactory in operation
- ☐ Windscreen/tailgate wipers inoperative, or unsatisfactory in operation
- ☐ Windscreen/tailgate washers inoperative, or unsatisfactory in operation
- ☐ Electric windows inoperative, or unsatisfactory in operation
- ☐ Central locking system inoperative, or unsatisfactory in operation

Introduction

The vehicle owner who does his or her own maintenance according to the recommended service schedules should not have to use this section of the manual very often. Modern component reliability is such that, provided those items subject to wear or deterioration are inspected or renewed at the specified intervals, sudden failure is comparatively rare. Faults do not usually just happen as a result of sudden failure, but develop over a period of time. Major mechanical failures in particular are usually preceded by characteristic symptoms over hundreds or even thousands of miles. Those components which do occasionally fail without warning are often small and easily carried in the vehicle.

With any fault-finding, the first step is to decide where to begin investigations. Sometimes this is obvious, but on other occasions, a little detective work will be necessary. The owner who makes half a dozen haphazard adjustments or replacements may be successful in curing a fault (or its symptoms), but will be none the wiser if the fault recurs, and ultimately may have spent more time and money than was necessary. A calm and logical approach will be found to be more satisfactory in the long run. Always take into account any warning signs or abnormalities that may have been noticed in the period preceding the fault – power loss, high or low gauge readings, unusual smells, etc – and remember that failure of components such as fuses or spark plugs may only be pointers to some underlying fault.

The pages which follow provide an easy-reference guide to the more common problems which may occur during the operation of the vehicle. These problems and their possible causes are grouped under headings denoting various components or systems, such as Engine, Cooling system, etc. The general Chapter which deals with the problem is also shown in brackets; refer to the relevant part of that Chapter for system-specific information. Whatever the fault, certain basic principles apply. These are as follows:

Verify the fault. This is simply a matter of being sure that you know what the symptoms are before starting work. This is particularly important if you are investigating a fault for someone else, who may not have described it very accurately.

Don't overlook the obvious. For example, if the vehicle won't start, is there fuel in the tank? (Don't take anyone else's word on this particular point, and don't trust the fuel gauge either!) If an electrical fault is indicated, look for loose or broken wires before digging out the test gear.

Cure the disease, not the symptom. Substituting a flat battery with a fully-charged one will get you off the hard shoulder, but if the underlying cause is not attended to, the new battery will go the same way. Similarly, changing oil-fouled spark plugs for a new set will get you moving again, but remember that the reason for the fouling (if it wasn't simply an incorrect grade of plug) will have to be established and corrected.

Don't take anything for granted. Particularly, don't forget that a 'new' component may itself be defective (especially if it's been rattling around in the boot for months), and don't leave components out of a fault diagnosis sequence just because they are new or recently-fitted. When you do finally diagnose a difficult fault, you'll probably realise that all the evidence was there from the start.

Engine

Engine fails to rotate when attempting to start

☐ Battery terminal connections loose or corroded (see *Weekly checks*).
☐ Battery discharged or faulty (Chapter 5A).
☐ Broken, loose or disconnected wiring in the starting circuit (Chapter 5A).
☐ Defective starter solenoid or switch (Chapter 5A).
☐ Defective starter motor (Chapter 5A).
☐ Starter pinion or flywheel ring gear teeth loose or broken (Chapters 2 and 5A).
☐ Engine earth strap broken or disconnected (Chapter 5A).

Engine rotates, but will not start

☐ Fuel tank empty.
☐ Battery discharged (engine rotates slowly) (Chapter 5A).
☐ Battery terminal connections loose or corroded (see *Weekly checks*).
☐ Ignition components damp or damaged – petrol models (Chapters 1A and 5B).
☐ Broken, loose or disconnected wiring in the ignition circuit – petrol models (Chapters 1A and 5B).
☐ Worn, faulty or incorrectly-gapped spark plugs – petrol models (Chapter 1A).
☐ Preheating system faulty – diesel models (Chapter 5C).
☐ Fuel injection system faulty – petrol models (Chapter 4A).
☐ Stop solenoid faulty – diesel models (Chapter 4B).
☐ Air in fuel system – diesel models (Chapter 4B).
☐ Major mechanical failure (eg camshaft drive) (Chapter 2).

Engine difficult to start when cold

☐ Battery discharged (Chapter 5A).
☐ Battery terminal connections loose or corroded (see *Weekly checks*).
☐ Worn, faulty or incorrectly-gapped spark plugs – petrol models (Chapter 1A).
☐ Preheating system faulty – diesel models (Chapter 5C).
☐ Fuel injection system faulty – petrol models (Chapter 4A).
☐ Other ignition system fault – petrol models (Chapters 1A and 5B).
☐ Low cylinder compressions (Chapter 2).

Engine difficult to start when hot

☐ Air filter element dirty or clogged (Chapter 1).
☐ Fuel injection system faulty – petrol models (Chapter 4A).
☐ Low cylinder compressions (Chapter 2).

Starter motor noisy or excessively-rough in engagement

☐ Starter pinion or flywheel ring gear teeth loose or broken (Chapters 2 and 5A).
☐ Starter motor mounting bolts loose (Chapter 5A).
☐ Starter motor internal components worn or damaged (Chapter 5A).

Engine starts, but stops immediately

☐ Loose or faulty electrical connections in the ignition circuit – petrol models (Chapters 1A and 5B).
☐ Vacuum leak at the throttle body or inlet manifold – petrol models (Chapter 4A).
☐ Blocked injector/fuel injection system fault – petrol models (Chapter 4A).

Engine idles erratically

☐ Air filter element clogged (Chapter 1).
☐ Vacuum leak at the throttle body, inlet manifold or associated hoses – petrol models (Chapter 4A).
☐ Worn, faulty or incorrectly-gapped spark plugs – petrol models (Chapter 1A).
☐ Uneven or low cylinder compressions (Chapter 2).
☐ Camshaft lobes worn (Chapter 2).
☐ Timing belt/chain incorrectly fitted (Chapter 2).
☐ Blocked injector/fuel injection system fault – petrol models (Chapter 4A).
☐ Faulty injector(s) – diesel models (Chapter 4B).

Engine misfires at idle speed

☐ Worn, faulty or incorrectly-gapped spark plugs – petrol models (Chapter 1A).
☐ Faulty spark plug HT leads – petrol models (Chapter 1A).
☐ Vacuum leak at the throttle body, inlet manifold or associated hoses – petrol models (Chapter 4A).
☐ Blocked injector/fuel injection system fault – petrol models (Chapter 4A).
☐ Faulty injector(s) – diesel models (Chapter 4B).
☐ Uneven or low cylinder compressions (Chapter 2).
☐ Disconnected, leaking, or perished crankcase ventilation hoses (Chapter 4C).

Engine misfires throughout the driving speed range

☐ Fuel filter choked (Chapter 1).
☐ Fuel pump faulty, or delivery pressure low – petrol models (Chapter 4A).
☐ Fuel tank vent blocked, or fuel pipes restricted (Chapter 4).
☐ Vacuum leak at the throttle body, inlet manifold or associated hoses – petrol models (Chapter 4A).
☐ Worn, faulty or incorrectly-gapped spark plugs – petrol models (Chapter 1A).
☐ Faulty spark plug HT leads – petrol models (Chapter 1A).
☐ Faulty injector(s) – diesel models (Chapter 4B).
☐ Faulty ignition coil – petrol models (Chapter 5B).
☐ Uneven or low cylinder compressions (Chapter 2).
☐ Blocked injector/fuel injection system fault – petrol models (Chapter 4A).

Engine (continued)

Engine hesitates on acceleration

☐ Worn, faulty or incorrectly-gapped spark plugs – petrol models (Chapter 1A).
☐ Vacuum leak at the throttle body, inlet manifold or associated hoses – petrol models (Chapter 4A).
☐ Blocked injector/fuel injection system fault – petrol models (Chapter 4A).
☐ Faulty injector(s) – diesel models (Chapter 4B).

Engine stalls

☐ Vacuum leak at the throttle body, inlet manifold or associated hoses – petrol models (Chapter 4A).
☐ Fuel filter choked (Chapter 1).
☐ Fuel pump faulty, or delivery pressure low – petrol models (Chapter 4A).
☐ Fuel tank vent blocked, or fuel pipes restricted (Chapter 4).
☐ Blocked injector/fuel injection system fault – petrol models (Chapter 4A).
☐ Faulty injector(s) – diesel models (Chapter 4B).

Engine lacks power

☐ Timing belt/chain incorrectly fitted or tensioned (Chapter 2).
☐ Fuel filter choked (Chapter 1).
☐ Fuel pump faulty, or delivery pressure low – petrol models (Chapter 4A).
☐ Uneven or low cylinder compressions (Chapter 2).
☐ Worn, faulty or incorrectly-gapped spark plugs – petrol models (Chapter 1A).
☐ Vacuum leak at the throttle body, inlet manifold or associated hoses – petrol models (Chapter 4A).
☐ Blocked injector/fuel injection system fault – petrol models (Chapter 4A).
☐ Faulty injector(s) – diesel models (Chapter 4B).
☐ Injection pump timing incorrect – diesel models (Chapter 4B).
☐ Brakes binding (Chapters 1 and 9).
☐ Clutch slipping (Chapter 6).

Engine backfires

☐ Timing belt/chain incorrectly fitted or tensioned (Chapter 2).
☐ Vacuum leak at the throttle body, inlet manifold or associated hoses – petrol models (Chapter 4A).
☐ Blocked injector/fuel injection system fault – petrol models (Chapter 4A).

Oil pressure warning light illuminated with engine running

☐ Low oil level, or incorrect oil grade (Weekly checks).
☐ Faulty oil pressure sensor (Chapter 5A).
☐ Worn engine bearings and/or oil pump (Chapter 2).
☐ High engine operating temperature (Chapter 3).
☐ Oil pressure relief valve defective (Chapter 2).
☐ Oil pick-up strainer clogged (Chapter 2).

Engine runs-on after switching off

☐ Excessive carbon build-up in engine (Chapter 2).
☐ High engine operating temperature (Chapter 3).
☐ Fuel injection system faulty – petrol models (Chapter 4A).
☐ Faulty stop solenoid – diesel models (Chapter 4B).

Engine noises

Pre-ignition (pinking) or knocking during acceleration or under load

☐ Ignition timing incorrect/ignition system fault – petrol models (Chapters 1A and 5B).
☐ Incorrect grade of spark plug – petrol models (Chapter 1A).
☐ Incorrect grade of fuel (Chapter 4).
☐ Vacuum leak at the throttle body, inlet manifold or associated hoses – petrol models (Chapter 4A).
☐ Excessive carbon build-up in engine (Chapter 2).
☐ Blocked injector/fuel injection system fault – petrol models (Chapter 4A).

Whistling or wheezing noises

☐ Leaking inlet manifold or throttle body gasket – petrol models (Chapter 4A).
☐ Leaking exhaust manifold gasket or pipe-to-manifold joint (Chapter 4).
☐ Leaking vacuum hose (Chapters 4, 5 and 9).
☐ Blowing cylinder head gasket (Chapter 2).

Tapping or rattling noises

☐ Worn valve gear or camshaft (Chapter 2).
☐ Ancillary component fault (coolant pump, alternator, etc) (Chapters 3, 5, etc).

Knocking or thumping noises

☐ Worn big-end bearings (regular heavy knocking, perhaps less under load) (Chapter 2).
☐ Worn main bearings (rumbling and knocking, perhaps worsening under load) (Chapter 2).
☐ Piston slap (most noticeable when cold) (Chapter 2).
☐ Ancillary component fault (coolant pump, alternator, etc) (Chapters 3, 5, etc).

Cooling system

Overheating

☐ Insufficient coolant in system (*Weekly Checks*).
☐ Thermostat faulty (Chapter 3).
☐ Radiator core blocked, or grille restricted (Chapter 3).
☐ Electric cooling fan or thermostatic switch faulty (Chapter 3).
☐ Inaccurate temperature gauge sender unit (Chapter 3).
☐ Airlock in cooling system (Chapter 3).
☐ Expansion tank pressure cap faulty (Chapter 3).

Overcooling

☐ Thermostat faulty (Chapter 3).
☐ Inaccurate temperature gauge sender unit (Chapter 3).

External coolant leakage

☐ Deteriorated or damaged hoses or hose clips (Chapter 1).
☐ Radiator core or heater matrix leaking (Chapter 3).
☐ Pressure cap faulty (Chapter 3).
☐ Coolant pump internal seal leaking (Chapter 3).
☐ Coolant pump-to-block seal leaking (Chapter 3).
☐ Boiling due to overheating (Chapter 3).
☐ Core plug leaking (Chapter 2).

Internal coolant leakage

☐ Leaking cylinder head gasket (Chapter 2).
☐ Cracked cylinder head or cylinder block (Chapter 2).

Corrosion

☐ Infrequent draining and flushing (Chapter 1).
☐ Incorrect coolant mixture or inappropriate coolant type (see *Weekly checks*).

Fuel and exhaust systems

Excessive fuel consumption

☐ Air filter element dirty or clogged (Chapter 1).
☐ Fuel injection system faulty – petrol models (Chapter 4A).
☐ Faulty injector(s) – diesel models (Chapter 4B).
☐ Ignition timing incorrect/ignition system faulty – petrol models (Chapters 1A and 5B).
☐ Tyres under-inflated (see *Weekly checks*).

Fuel leakage and/or fuel odour

☐ Damaged or corroded fuel tank, pipes or connections (Chapter 4).

Excessive noise or fumes from the exhaust system

☐ Leaking exhaust system or manifold joints (Chapters 1 and 4).
☐ Leaking, corroded or damaged silencers or pipe (Chapters 1 and 4).
☐ Broken mountings causing body or suspension contact (Chapter 1).

Clutch

Pedal travels to floor – no pressure or very little resistance

- ☐ Air in hydraulic system/faulty master or slave cylinder (Chapter 6).
- ☐ Faulty hydraulic release system (Chapter 6).
- ☐ Broken clutch release bearing or arm (Chapter 6).
- ☐ Broken diaphragm spring in clutch pressure plate (Chapter 6).

Clutch fails to disengage (unable to select gears)

- ☐ Air in hydraulic system/faulty master or slave cylinder (Chapter 6).
- ☐ Faulty hydraulic release system (Chapter 6).
- ☐ Clutch disc sticking on gearbox input shaft splines (Chapter 6).
- ☐ Clutch disc sticking to flywheel or pressure plate (Chapter 6).
- ☐ Faulty pressure plate assembly (Chapter 6).
- ☐ Clutch release mechanism worn or incorrectly assembled (Chapter 6).

Clutch slips (engine speed increases, with no increase in vehicle speed)

- ☐ Faulty hydraulic release system (Chapter 6).
- ☐ Clutch disc linings excessively worn (Chapter 6).
- ☐ Clutch disc linings contaminated with oil or grease (Chapter 6).
- ☐ Faulty pressure plate or weak diaphragm spring (Chapter 6).

Judder as clutch is engaged

- ☐ Clutch disc linings contaminated with oil or grease (Chapter 6).
- ☐ Clutch disc linings excessively worn (Chapter 6).
- ☐ Faulty or distorted pressure plate or diaphragm spring (Chapter 6).
- ☐ Worn or loose engine or gearbox mountings (Chapter 2).
- ☐ Clutch disc hub or gearbox input shaft splines worn (Chapter 6).

Noise when depressing or releasing clutch pedal

- ☐ Worn clutch release bearing (Chapter 6).
- ☐ Worn or dry clutch pedal pivot (Chapter 6).
- ☐ Faulty pressure plate assembly (Chapter 6).
- ☐ Pressure plate diaphragm spring broken (Chapter 6).
- ☐ Broken clutch friction plate cushioning springs (Chapter 6).

Manual transmission

Noisy in neutral with engine running

- ☐ Input shaft bearings worn (noise apparent with clutch pedal released, but not when depressed) (Chapter 7A).*
- ☐ Clutch release bearing worn (noise apparent with clutch pedal depressed, possibly less when released) (Chapter 6).

Noisy in one particular gear

- ☐ Worn, damaged or chipped gear teeth (Chapter 7A).*

Difficulty engaging gears

- ☐ Clutch faulty (Chapter 6).
- ☐ Worn or damaged gear linkage (Chapter 7A).
- ☐ Worn synchroniser units (Chapter 7A).*

Jumps out of gear

- ☐ Worn or damaged gear linkage (Chapter 7A).
- ☐ Worn synchroniser units (Chapter 7A).*
- ☐ Worn selector forks (Chapter 7A).*

Vibration

- ☐ Lack of oil (Chapter 1).
- ☐ Worn bearings (Chapter 7A).*

Lubricant leaks

- ☐ Leaking oil seal (Chapter 7A).
- ☐ Leaking housing joint (Chapter 7A).*
- ☐ Leaking input shaft oil seal (Chapter 7A).*

Although the corrective action necessary to remedy the symptoms described is beyond the scope of the home mechanic, the above information should be helpful in isolating the cause of the condition, so that the owner can communicate clearly with a professional mechanic.

Automatic transmission

Note: *Due to the complexity of the automatic transmission, it is difficult for the home mechanic to properly diagnose and service this unit. For problems other than the following, the vehicle should be taken to a dealer service department or automatic transmission specialist. Do not be too hasty in removing the transmission if a fault is suspected, as most of the testing is carried out with the unit still fitted.*

Fluid leakage

☐ Automatic transmission fluid is usually dark in colour. Fluid leaks should not be confused with engine oil, which can easily be blown onto the transmission by airflow.

☐ To determine the source of a leak, first remove all built-up dirt and grime from the transmission housing and surrounding areas using a degreasing agent, or by steam-cleaning. Drive the vehicle at low speed, so airflow will not blow the leak far from its source. Raise and support the vehicle, and determine where the leak is coming from. The following are common areas of leakage:
a) *Oil pan (Chapter 1A and 7B).*
b) *Dipstick tube (Chapter 1A and 7B).*
c) *Transmission-to-fluid cooler pipes/unions (Chapter 7B).*

Transmission fluid brown, or has burned smell

☐ Transmission fluid level low, or fluid in need of renewal (Chapter 1A and 7B).

Engine will not start in any gear, or starts in gears other than Park or Neutral

☐ Incorrect starter/inhibitor switch adjustment (Chapter 7B).
☐ Incorrect selector cable adjustment (Chapter 7B).

General gear selection problems

☐ Chapter 7B deals with checking and adjusting the selector cable on automatic transmissions. The following are common problems which may be caused by a poorly-adjusted cable:
a) *Engine starting in gears other than Park or Neutral.*
b) *Indicator panel indicating a gear other than the one actually being used.*
c) *Vehicle moves when in Park or Neutral.*
d) *Poor gear shift quality or erratic gear changes.*
☐ Refer to Chapter 7B for the selector cable adjustment procedure.

Transmission will not downshift (kickdown) with accelerator pedal fully depressed

☐ Low transmission fluid level (Chapter 1A).
☐ Incorrect selector cable adjustment (Chapter 7B).

Transmission slips, shifts roughly, is noisy, or has no drive in forward or reverse gears

☐ There are many probable causes for the above problems, but the home mechanic should be concerned with only one possibility – fluid level. Before taking the vehicle to a dealer or transmission specialist, check the fluid level and condition of the fluid as described in Chapter 1A, or 7B, as applicable. Correct the fluid level as necessary, or change the fluid and filter if needed. If the problem persists, professional help will be necessary.

Driveshafts

Vibration when accelerating or decelerating

☐ Worn inner constant velocity joint (Chapter 8).
☐ Bent or distorted driveshaft (Chapter 8).
☐ Worn intermediate bearing – where applicable (Chapter 8).

Clicking or knocking noise on turns (at slow speed on full-lock)

☐ Worn outer constant velocity joint (Chapter 8).
☐ Lack of constant velocity joint lubricant, possibly due to damaged gaiter (Chapter 8).

Braking system

Note: *Before assuming that a brake problem exists, make sure that the tyres are in good condition and correctly inflated, that the front wheel alignment is correct, and that the vehicle is not loaded with weight in an unequal manner. Apart from checking the condition of all pipe and hose connections, any faults occurring on the anti-lock braking system should be referred to a Vauxhall/Opel dealer for diagnosis.*

Vehicle pulls to one side under braking

- ☐ Worn, defective, damaged or contaminated front or rear brake pads/shoes on one side (Chapters 1 and 9).
- ☐ Seized or partially-seized front or rear brake caliper/wheel cylinder piston (Chapter 9).
- ☐ A mixture of brake pad/shoe lining materials fitted between sides (Chapter 9).
- ☐ Brake caliper or rear brake backplate mounting bolts loose (Chapter 9).
- ☐ Worn or damaged steering or suspension components (Chapters 1 and 10).

Noise (grinding or high-pitched squeal) when brakes applied

- ☐ Brake pad/shoe friction lining material worn down to metal backing (Chapters 1 and 9).
- ☐ Excessive corrosion of brake disc or drum – may be apparent after the vehicle has been standing for some time (Chapters 1 and 9).
- ☐ Foreign object (stone chipping, etc) trapped between brake disc and shield (Chapters 1 and 9).

Excessive brake pedal travel

- ☐ Faulty rear drum brake self-adjust mechanism (Chapter 9).
- ☐ Faulty master cylinder (Chapter 9).
- ☐ Air in hydraulic system (Chapter 9).
- ☐ Faulty vacuum servo unit (Chapter 9).
- ☐ Faulty vacuum pump – diesel models (Chapter 9).

Brake pedal feels spongy when depressed

- ☐ Air in hydraulic system (Chapter 9).
- ☐ Deteriorated flexible rubber brake hoses (Chapters 1 and 9).
- ☐ Master cylinder mountings loose (Chapter 9).
- ☐ Faulty master cylinder (Chapter 9).

Excessive brake pedal effort required to stop vehicle

- ☐ Faulty vacuum servo unit (Chapter 9).
- ☐ Disconnected, damaged or insecure brake servo vacuum hose (Chapters 1 and 9).
- ☐ Faulty vacuum pump – diesel models (Chapter 9).
- ☐ Primary or secondary hydraulic circuit failure (Chapter 9).
- ☐ Seized brake caliper or wheel cylinder piston(s) (Chapter 9).
- ☐ Brake pads/shoes incorrectly fitted (Chapter 9).
- ☐ Incorrect grade of brake pads/shoes fitted (Chapter 9).
- ☐ Brake pads/shoe linings contaminated (Chapter 9).

Judder felt through brake pedal or steering wheel when braking

- ☐ Excessive run-out or distortion of brake disc(s) or drum(s) (Chapter 9).
- ☐ Brake pad/shoe linings worn (Chapters 1 and 9).
- ☐ Brake caliper or rear brake backplate mounting bolts loose (Chapter 9).
- ☐ Wear in suspension or steering components or mountings (Chapters 1 and 10).

Pedal pulsates when braking hard

- ☐ Normal feature of ABS – no fault

Brakes binding

- ☐ Seized brake caliper/wheel cylinder piston(s) (Chapter 9).
- ☐ Incorrectly-adjusted handbrake mechanism (Chapter 9).
- ☐ Faulty master cylinder (Chapter 9).

Rear wheels locking under normal braking

- ☐ Rear brake pad/shoe linings contaminated (Chapters 1 and 9).
- ☐ Rear brake discs/drums warped (Chapters 1 and 9).

Steering and suspension

Note: *Before diagnosing suspension or steering faults, be sure that the trouble is not due to incorrect tyre pressures, mixtures of tyre types, or binding brakes.*

Vehicle pulls to one side

☐ Defective tyre (see *Weekly checks*).
☐ Excessive wear in suspension or steering components (Chapters 1 and 10).
☐ Incorrect front wheel alignment (Chapter 10).
☐ Accident damage to steering or suspension components (Chapters 1 and 10).

Wheel wobble and vibration

☐ Front roadwheels out of balance (vibration felt mainly through the steering wheel) (Chapter 10).
☐ Rear roadwheels out of balance (vibration felt throughout the vehicle) (Chapter 10).
☐ Roadwheels damaged or distorted (Chapter 10).
☐ Faulty or damaged tyre (*Weekly Checks*).
☐ Worn steering or suspension joints, bushes or components (Chapters 1 and 10).
☐ Wheel bolts loose (Chapter 1 and 10).

Excessive pitching and/or rolling around corners, or during braking

☐ Defective shock absorbers (Chapters 1 and 10).
☐ Broken or weak coil spring and/or suspension component (Chapters 1 and 10).
☐ Worn or damaged anti-roll bar or mountings (Chapter 10).

Wandering or general instability

☐ Incorrect front wheel alignment (Chapter 10).
☐ Worn steering or suspension joints, bushes or components (Chapters 1 and 10).
☐ Roadwheels out of balance (Chapter 10).
☐ Faulty or damaged tyre (*Weekly Checks*).
☐ Wheel bolts loose (Chapter 10).
☐ Defective shock absorbers (Chapters 1 and 10).

Excessively-stiff steering

☐ Seized track rod end balljoint or suspension balljoint (Chapters 1 and 10).
☐ Broken or incorrectly adjusted auxiliary drivebelt (Chapter 1).
☐ Incorrect front wheel alignment (Chapter 10).
☐ Steering gear damaged (Chapter 10).

Excessive play in steering

☐ Worn steering column universal joint(s) (Chapter 10).
☐ Worn steering track rod end balljoints (Chapters 1 and 10).
☐ Worn steering gear (Chapter 10).
☐ Worn steering or suspension joints, bushes or components (Chapters 1 and 10).

Lack of power assistance

☐ Broken or incorrectly-adjusted auxiliary drivebelt (Chapter 1).
☐ Incorrect power steering fluid level (*Weekly Checks*).
☐ Restriction in power steering fluid hoses (Chapter 10).
☐ Faulty power steering pump (Chapter 10).
☐ Faulty steering gear (Chapter 10).

Tyre wear excessive

Tyres worn on inside or outside edges

☐ Tyres under-inflated (wear on both edges) (*Weekly Checks*).
☐ Incorrect camber or castor angles (wear on one edge only) (Chapter 10).
☐ Worn steering or suspension joints, bushes or components (Chapters 1 and 10).
☐ Excessively-hard cornering.
☐ Accident damage.

Tyre treads exhibit feathered edges

☐ Incorrect toe setting (Chapter 10).

Tyres worn in centre of tread

☐ Tyres over-inflated (*Weekly Checks*).

Tyres worn on inside and outside edges

☐ Tyres under-inflated (*Weekly Checks*).
☐ Worn shock absorbers (Chapter 10).

Tyres worn unevenly

☐ Tyres/wheels out of balance (*Weekly Checks*).
☐ Excessive wheel or tyre run-out (Chapter 10).
☐ Worn shock absorbers (Chapters 1 and 10).
☐ Faulty tyre (*Weekly Checks*).

Electrical system

Note: *For problems associated with the starting system, refer to the faults listed under 'Engine' earlier in this Section.*

Battery will not hold a charge for more than a few days

- ☐ Battery defective internally (Chapter 5A).
- ☐ Battery electrolyte level low – where applicable (*Weekly Checks*).
- ☐ Battery terminal connections loose or corroded (*Weekly Checks*).
- ☐ Auxiliary drivebelt worn – or incorrectly adjusted, where applicable (Chapter 1).
- ☐ Alternator not charging at correct output (Chapter 5A).
- ☐ Alternator or voltage regulator faulty (Chapter 5A).
- ☐ Short-circuit causing continual battery drain (Chapters 5 and 12).

Ignition/no-charge warning light remains illuminated with engine running

- ☐ Auxiliary drivebelt broken, worn, or incorrectly adjusted (Chapter 1).
- ☐ Internal fault in alternator or voltage regulator (Chapter 5A).
- ☐ Broken, disconnected, or loose wiring in charging circuit (Chapter 5A).

Ignition/no-charge warning light fails to come on

- ☐ Warning light bulb blown (Chapter 12).
- ☐ Broken, disconnected, or loose wiring in warning light circuit (Chapter 12).
- ☐ Alternator faulty (Chapter 5A).

Lights inoperative

- ☐ Bulb blown (Chapter 12).
- ☐ Corrosion of bulb or bulbholder contacts (Chapter 12).
- ☐ Blown fuse (Chapter 12).
- ☐ Faulty relay (Chapter 12).
- ☐ Broken, loose, or disconnected wiring (Chapter 12).
- ☐ Faulty switch (Chapter 12).

Instrument readings inaccurate or erratic

Instrument readings increase with engine speed

- ☐ Faulty voltage regulator (Chapter 12).

Fuel or temperature gauges give no reading

- ☐ Faulty gauge sender unit (Chapters 3 and 4).
- ☐ Wiring open-circuit (Chapter 12).
- ☐ Faulty gauge (Chapter 12).

Fuel or temperature gauges give continuous maximum reading

- ☐ Faulty gauge sender unit (Chapters 3 and 4).
- ☐ Wiring short-circuit (Chapter 12).
- ☐ Faulty gauge (Chapter 12).

Horn inoperative, or unsatisfactory in operation

Horn operates all the time

- ☐ Horn contacts permanently bridged or horn push stuck down (Chapter 12).

Horn fails to operate

- ☐ Blown fuse (Chapter 12).
- ☐ Cable or cable connections loose, broken or disconnected (Chapter 12).
- ☐ Faulty horn (Chapter 12).

Horn emits intermittent or unsatisfactory sound

- ☐ Cable connections loose (Chapter 12).
- ☐ Horn mountings loose (Chapter 12).
- ☐ Faulty horn (Chapter 12).

Windscreen/tailgate wipers inoperative, or unsatisfactory in operation

Wipers fail to operate, or operate very slowly

- ☐ Wiper blades stuck to screen, or linkage seized or binding (*Weekly Checks* and Chapter 12).
- ☐ Blown fuse (Chapter 12).
- ☐ Cable or cable connections loose, broken or disconnected (Chapter 12).
- ☐ Faulty relay (Chapter 12).
- ☐ Faulty wiper motor (Chapter 12).

Wiper blades sweep over too large or too small an area of the glass

- ☐ Wiper arms incorrectly positioned on spindles (Chapter 12).
- ☐ Excessive wear of wiper linkage (Chapter 12).
- ☐ Wiper motor or linkage mountings loose or insecure (Chapter 12).

Wiper blades fail to clean the glass effectively

- ☐ Wiper blade rubbers worn or perished (*Weekly Checks*).
- ☐ Wiper arm tension springs broken, or arm pivots seized (Chapter 12).
- ☐ Insufficient windscreen washer additive to adequately remove road film (*Weekly Checks*).

Electrical system (continued)

Windscreen/tailgate washers inoperative, or unsatisfactory in operation

One or more washer jets inoperative

☐ Blocked washer jet (Chapter 12).
☐ Disconnected, kinked or restricted fluid hose (Chapter 12).
☐ Insufficient fluid in washer reservoir (*Weekly Checks*).

Washer pump fails to operate

☐ Broken or disconnected wiring or connections (Chapter 12).
☐ Blown fuse (Chapter 12).
☐ Faulty washer switch (Chapter 12).
☐ Faulty washer pump (Chapter 12).

Washer pump runs for some time before fluid is emitted from jets

☐ Faulty one-way valve in fluid supply hose (Chapter 12).

Electric windows inoperative, or unsatisfactory in operation

Window glass will only move in one direction

☐ Faulty switch (Chapter 12).

Window glass slow to move

☐ Regulator seized or damaged, or in need of lubrication (Chapter 11).
☐ Door internal components or trim fouling regulator (Chapter 11).
☐ Faulty motor (Chapter 11).

Window glass fails to move

☐ Blown fuse (Chapter 12).
☐ Faulty relay (Chapter 12).
☐ Broken or disconnected wiring or connections (Chapter 12).
☐ Faulty motor (Chapter 12).

Central locking system inoperative, or unsatisfactory in operation

Complete system failure

☐ Blown fuse (Chapter 12).
☐ Faulty relay (Chapter 12).
☐ Broken or disconnected wiring or connections (Chapter 12).
☐ Faulty motor (Chapter 11).

Latch locks but will not unlock, or unlocks but will not lock

☐ Faulty switch (Chapter 12).
☐ Broken or disconnected latch operating rods or levers (Chapter 11).
☐ Faulty relay (Chapter 12).
☐ Faulty motor (Chapter 11).

One solenoid/motor fails to operate

☐ Broken or disconnected wiring or connections (Chapter 12).
☐ Faulty motor (Chapter 11).
☐ Broken, binding or disconnected lock operating rods or levers (Chapter 11).
☐ Fault in door lock (Chapter 11).

A

ABS (Anti-lock brake system) A system, usually electronically controlled, that senses incipient wheel lockup during braking and relieves hydraulic pressure at wheels that are about to skid.

Air bag An inflatable bag hidden in the steering wheel (driver's side) or the dash or glovebox (passenger side). In a head-on collision, the bags inflate, preventing the driver and front passenger from being thrown forward into the steering wheel or windscreen.

Air cleaner A metal or plastic housing, containing a filter element, which removes dust and dirt from the air being drawn into the engine.

Air filter element The actual filter in an air cleaner system, usually manufactured from pleated paper and requiring renewal at regular intervals.

Air filter

Allen key A hexagonal wrench which fits into a recessed hexagonal hole.

Alligator clip A long-nosed spring-loaded metal clip with meshing teeth. Used to make temporary electrical connections.

Alternator A component in the electrical system which converts mechanical energy from a drivebelt into electrical energy to charge the battery and to operate the starting system, ignition system and electrical accessories.

Alternator (exploded view)

Ampere (amp) A unit of measurement for the flow of electric current. One amp is the amount of current produced by one volt acting through a resistance of one ohm.

Anaerobic sealer A substance used to prevent bolts and screws from loosening. Anaerobic means that it does not require oxygen for activation. The Loctite brand is widely used.

Antifreeze A substance (usually ethylene glycol) mixed with water, and added to a vehicle's cooling system, to prevent freezing of the coolant in winter. Antifreeze also contains chemicals to inhibit corrosion and the formation of rust and other deposits that would tend to clog the radiator and coolant passages and reduce cooling efficiency.

Anti-seize compound A coating that reduces the risk of seizing on fasteners that are subjected to high temperatures, such as exhaust manifold bolts and nuts.

Anti-seize compound

Asbestos A natural fibrous mineral with great heat resistance, commonly used in the composition of brake friction materials. Asbestos is a health hazard and the dust created by brake systems should never be inhaled or ingested.

Axle A shaft on which a wheel revolves, or which revolves with a wheel. Also, a solid beam that connects the two wheels at one end of the vehicle. An axle which also transmits power to the wheels is known as a live axle.

Axle assembly

Axleshaft A single rotating shaft, on either side of the differential, which delivers power from the final drive assembly to the drive wheels. Also called a driveshaft or a halfshaft.

B

Ball bearing An anti-friction bearing consisting of a hardened inner and outer race with hardened steel balls between two races.

Bearing

Bearing The curved surface on a shaft or in a bore, or the part assembled into either, that permits relative motion between them with minimum wear and friction.

Big-end bearing The bearing in the end of the connecting rod that's attached to the crankshaft.

Bleed nipple A valve on a brake wheel cylinder, caliper or other hydraulic component that is opened to purge the hydraulic system of air. Also called a bleed screw.

Brake bleeding

Brake bleeding Procedure for removing air from lines of a hydraulic brake system.

Brake disc The component of a disc brake that rotates with the wheels.

Brake drum The component of a drum brake that rotates with the wheels.

Brake linings The friction material which contacts the brake disc or drum to retard the vehicle's speed. The linings are bonded or riveted to the brake pads or shoes.

Brake pads The replaceable friction pads that pinch the brake disc when the brakes are applied. Brake pads consist of a friction material bonded or riveted to a rigid backing plate.

Brake shoe The crescent-shaped carrier to which the brake linings are mounted and which forces the lining against the rotating drum during braking.

Braking systems For more information on braking systems, consult the *Haynes Automotive Brake Manual*.

Breaker bar A long socket wrench handle providing greater leverage.

Bulkhead The insulated partition between the engine and the passenger compartment.

C

Caliper The non-rotating part of a disc-brake assembly that straddles the disc and carries the brake pads. The caliper also contains the hydraulic components that cause the pads to pinch the disc when the brakes are applied. A caliper is also a measuring tool that can be set to measure inside or outside dimensions of an object.

Camshaft A rotating shaft on which a series of cam lobes operate the valve mechanisms. The camshaft may be driven by gears, by sprockets and chain or by sprockets and a belt.

Canister A container in an evaporative emission control system; contains activated charcoal granules to trap vapours from the fuel system.

Canister

Carburettor A device which mixes fuel with air in the proper proportions to provide a desired power output from a spark ignition internal combustion engine.

Carburettor

Castellated Resembling the parapets along the top of a castle wall. For example, a castellated balljoint stud nut.

Castellated nut

Castor In wheel alignment, the backward or forward tilt of the steering axis. Castor is positive when the steering axis is inclined rearward at the top.

Catalytic converter A silencer-like device in the exhaust system which converts certain pollutants in the exhaust gases into less harmful substances.

Catalytic converter

Circlip A ring-shaped clip used to prevent endwise movement of cylindrical parts and shafts. An internal circlip is installed in a groove in a housing; an external circlip fits into a groove on the outside of a cylindrical piece such as a shaft.

Clearance The amount of space between two parts. For example, between a piston and a cylinder, between a bearing and a journal, etc.

Coil spring A spiral of elastic steel found in various sizes throughout a vehicle, for example as a springing medium in the suspension and in the valve train.

Compression Reduction in volume, and increase in pressure and temperature, of a gas, caused by squeezing it into a smaller space.

Compression ratio The relationship between cylinder volume when the piston is at top dead centre and cylinder volume when the piston is at bottom dead centre.

Constant velocity (CV) joint A type of universal joint that cancels out vibrations caused by driving power being transmitted through an angle.

Core plug A disc or cup-shaped metal device inserted in a hole in a casting through which core was removed when the casting was formed. Also known as a freeze plug or expansion plug.

Crankcase The lower part of the engine block in which the crankshaft rotates.

Crankshaft The main rotating member, or shaft, running the length of the crankcase, with offset "throws" to which the connecting rods are attached.

Crankshaft assembly

Crocodile clip See Alligator clip

D

Diagnostic code Code numbers obtained by accessing the diagnostic mode of an engine management computer. This code can be used to determine the area in the system where a malfunction may be located.

Disc brake A brake design incorporating a rotating disc onto which brake pads are squeezed. The resulting friction converts the energy of a moving vehicle into heat.

Double-overhead cam (DOHC) An engine that uses two overhead camshafts, usually one for the intake valves and one for the exhaust valves.

Drivebelt(s) The belt(s) used to drive accessories such as the alternator, water pump, power steering pump, air conditioning compressor, etc. off the crankshaft pulley.

Accessory drivebelts

Driveshaft Any shaft used to transmit motion. Commonly used when referring to the axleshafts on a front wheel drive vehicle.

Driveshaft

Drum brake A type of brake using a drum-shaped metal cylinder attached to the inner surface of the wheel. When the brake pedal is pressed, curved brake shoes with friction linings press against the inside of the drum to slow or stop the vehicle.

Drum brake assembly

E

EGR valve A valve used to introduce exhaust gases into the intake air stream.

EGR valve

Electronic control unit (ECU) A computer which controls (for instance) ignition and fuel injection systems, or an anti-lock braking system. For more information refer to the *Haynes Automotive Electrical and Electronic Systems Manual.*

Electronic Fuel Injection (EFI) A computer controlled fuel system that distributes fuel through an injector located in each intake port of the engine.

Emergency brake A braking system, independent of the main hydraulic system, that can be used to slow or stop the vehicle if the primary brakes fail, or to hold the vehicle stationary even though the brake pedal isn't depressed. It usually consists of a hand lever that actuates either front or rear brakes mechanically through a series of cables and linkages. Also known as a handbrake or parking brake.

Endfloat The amount of lengthwise movement between two parts. As applied to a crankshaft, the distance that the crankshaft can move forward and back in the cylinder block.

Engine management system (EMS) A computer controlled system which manages the fuel injection and the ignition systems in an integrated fashion.

Exhaust manifold A part with several passages through which exhaust gases leave the engine combustion chambers and enter the exhaust pipe.

Exhaust manifold

F

Fan clutch A viscous (fluid) drive coupling device which permits variable engine fan speeds in relation to engine speeds.

Feeler blade A thin strip or blade of hardened steel, ground to an exact thickness, used to check or measure clearances between parts.

Feeler blade

Firing order The order in which the engine cylinders fire, or deliver their power strokes, beginning with the number one cylinder.

Flywheel A heavy spinning wheel in which energy is absorbed and stored by means of momentum. On cars, the flywheel is attached to the crankshaft to smooth out firing impulses.

Free play The amount of travel before any action takes place. The "looseness" in a linkage, or an assembly of parts, between the initial application of force and actual movement. For example, the distance the brake pedal moves before the pistons in the master cylinder are actuated.

Fuse An electrical device which protects a circuit against accidental overload. The typical fuse contains a soft piece of metal which is calibrated to melt at a predetermined current flow (expressed as amps) and break the circuit.

Fusible link A circuit protection device consisting of a conductor surrounded by heat-resistant insulation. The conductor is smaller than the wire it protects, so it acts as the weakest link in the circuit. Unlike a blown fuse, a failed fusible link must frequently be cut from the wire for replacement.

G

Gap The distance the spark must travel in jumping from the centre electrode to the side

Adjusting spark plug gap

electrode in a spark plug. Also refers to the spacing between the points in a contact breaker assembly in a conventional points-type ignition, or to the distance between the reluctor or rotor and the pickup coil in an electronic ignition.

Gasket Any thin, soft material - usually cork, cardboard, asbestos or soft metal - installed between two metal surfaces to ensure a good seal. For instance, the cylinder head gasket seals the joint between the block and the cylinder head.

Gasket

Gauge An instrument panel display used to monitor engine conditions. A gauge with a movable pointer on a dial or a fixed scale is an analogue gauge. A gauge with a numerical readout is called a digital gauge.

H

Halfshaft A rotating shaft that transmits power from the final drive unit to a drive wheel, usually when referring to a live rear axle.

Harmonic balancer A device designed to reduce torsion or twisting vibration in the crankshaft. May be incorporated in the crankshaft pulley. Also known as a vibration damper.

Hone An abrasive tool for correcting small irregularities or differences in diameter in an engine cylinder, brake cylinder, etc.

Hydraulic tappet A tappet that utilises hydraulic pressure from the engine's lubrication system to maintain zero clearance (constant contact with both camshaft and valve stem). Automatically adjusts to variation in valve stem length. Hydraulic tappets also reduce valve noise.

I

Ignition timing The moment at which the spark plug fires, usually expressed in the number of crankshaft degrees before the piston reaches the top of its stroke.

Inlet manifold A tube or housing with passages through which flows the air-fuel mixture (carburettor vehicles and vehicles with throttle body injection) or air only (port fuel-injected vehicles) to the port openings in the cylinder head.

J

Jump start Starting the engine of a vehicle with a discharged or weak battery by attaching jump leads from the weak battery to a charged or helper battery.

L

Load Sensing Proportioning Valve (LSPV) A brake hydraulic system control valve that works like a proportioning valve, but also takes into consideration the amount of weight carried by the rear axle.

Locknut A nut used to lock an adjustment nut, or other threaded component, in place. For example, a locknut is employed to keep the adjusting nut on the rocker arm in position.

Lockwasher A form of washer designed to prevent an attaching nut from working loose.

M

MacPherson strut A type of front suspension system devised by Earle MacPherson at Ford of England. In its original form, a simple lateral link with the anti-roll bar creates the lower control arm. A long strut - an integral coil spring and shock absorber - is mounted between the body and the steering knuckle. Many modern so-called MacPherson strut systems use a conventional lower A-arm and don't rely on the anti-roll bar for location.

Multimeter An electrical test instrument with the capability to measure voltage, current and resistance.

N

NOx Oxides of Nitrogen. A common toxic pollutant emitted by petrol and diesel engines at higher temperatures.

O

Ohm The unit of electrical resistance. One volt applied to a resistance of one ohm will produce a current of one amp.

Ohmmeter An instrument for measuring electrical resistance.

O-ring A type of sealing ring made of a special rubber-like material; in use, the O-ring is compressed into a groove to provide the sealing action.

O-ring

Overhead cam (ohc) engine An engine with the camshaft(s) located on top of the cylinder head(s).

Overhead valve (ohv) engine An engine with the valves located in the cylinder head, but with the camshaft located in the engine block.

Oxygen sensor A device installed in the engine exhaust manifold, which senses the oxygen content in the exhaust and converts this information into an electric current. Also called a Lambda sensor.

P

Phillips screw A type of screw head having a cross instead of a slot for a corresponding type of screwdriver.

Plastigage A thin strip of plastic thread, available in different sizes, used for measuring clearances. For example, a strip of Plastigage is laid across a bearing journal. The parts are assembled and dismantled; the width of the crushed strip indicates the clearance between journal and bearing.

Plastigage

Propeller shaft The long hollow tube with universal joints at both ends that carries power from the transmission to the differential on front-engined rear wheel drive vehicles.

Proportioning valve A hydraulic control valve which limits the amount of pressure to the rear brakes during panic stops to prevent wheel lock-up.

R

Rack-and-pinion steering A steering system with a pinion gear on the end of the steering shaft that mates with a rack (think of a geared wheel opened up and laid flat). When the steering wheel is turned, the pinion turns, moving the rack to the left or right. This movement is transmitted through the track rods to the steering arms at the wheels.

Radiator A liquid-to-air heat transfer device designed to reduce the temperature of the coolant in an internal combustion engine cooling system.

Refrigerant Any substance used as a heat transfer agent in an air-conditioning system. R-12 has been the principle refrigerant for many years; recently, however, manufacturers have begun using R-134a, a non-CFC substance that is considered less harmful to the ozone in the upper atmosphere.

Rocker arm A lever arm that rocks on a shaft or pivots on a stud. In an overhead valve engine, the rocker arm converts the upward movement of the pushrod into a downward movement to open a valve.

Rotor In a distributor, the rotating device inside the cap that connects the centre electrode and the outer terminals as it turns, distributing the high voltage from the coil secondary winding to the proper spark plug. Also, that part of an alternator which rotates inside the stator. Also, the rotating assembly of a turbocharger, including the compressor wheel, shaft and turbine wheel.

Runout The amount of wobble (in-and-out movement) of a gear or wheel as it's rotated. The amount a shaft rotates "out-of-true." The out-of-round condition of a rotating part.

S

Sealant A liquid or paste used to prevent leakage at a joint. Sometimes used in conjunction with a gasket.

Sealed beam lamp An older headlight design which integrates the reflector, lens and filaments into a hermetically-sealed one-piece unit. When a filament burns out or the lens cracks, the entire unit is simply replaced.

Serpentine drivebelt A single, long, wide accessory drivebelt that's used on some newer vehicles to drive all the accessories, instead of a series of smaller, shorter belts. Serpentine drivebelts are usually tensioned by an automatic tensioner.

Serpentine drivebelt

Shim Thin spacer, commonly used to adjust the clearance or relative positions between two parts. For example, shims inserted into or under bucket tappets control valve clearances. Clearance is adjusted by changing the thickness of the shim.

Slide hammer A special puller that screws into or hooks onto a component such as a shaft or bearing; a heavy sliding handle on the shaft bottoms against the end of the shaft to knock the component free.

Sprocket A tooth or projection on the periphery of a wheel, shaped to engage with a chain or drivebelt. Commonly used to refer to the sprocket wheel itself.

Starter inhibitor switch On vehicles with an automatic transmission, a switch that prevents starting if the vehicle is not in Neutral or Park.

Strut See MacPherson strut.

T

Tappet A cylindrical component which transmits motion from the cam to the valve stem, either directly or via a pushrod and rocker arm. Also called a cam follower.

Thermostat A heat-controlled valve that regulates the flow of coolant between the cylinder block and the radiator, so maintaining optimum engine operating temperature. A thermostat is also used in some air cleaners in which the temperature is regulated.

Thrust bearing The bearing in the clutch assembly that is moved in to the release levers by clutch pedal action to disengage the clutch. Also referred to as a release bearing.

Timing belt A toothed belt which drives the camshaft. Serious engine damage may result if it breaks in service.

Timing chain A chain which drives the camshaft.

Toe-in The amount the front wheels are closer together at the front than at the rear. On rear wheel drive vehicles, a slight amount of toe-in is usually specified to keep the front wheels running parallel on the road by offsetting other forces that tend to spread the wheels apart.

Toe-out The amount the front wheels are closer together at the rear than at the front. On front wheel drive vehicles, a slight amount of toe-out is usually specified.

Tools For full information on choosing and using tools, refer to the *Haynes Automotive Tools Manual*.

Tracer A stripe of a second colour applied to a wire insulator to distinguish that wire from another one with the same colour insulator.

Tune-up A process of accurate and careful adjustments and parts replacement to obtain the best possible engine performance.

Turbocharger A centrifugal device, driven by exhaust gases, that pressurises the intake air. Normally used to increase the power output from a given engine displacement, but can also be used primarily to reduce exhaust emissions (as on VW's "Umwelt" Diesel engine).

U

Universal joint or U-joint A double-pivoted connection for transmitting power from a driving to a driven shaft through an angle. A U-joint consists of two Y-shaped yokes and a cross-shaped member called the spider.

V

Valve A device through which the flow of liquid, gas, vacuum, or loose material in bulk may be started, stopped, or regulated by a movable part that opens, shuts, or partially obstructs one or more ports or passageways. A valve is also the movable part of such a device.

Valve clearance The clearance between the valve tip (the end of the valve stem) and the rocker arm or tappet. The valve clearance is measured when the valve is closed.

Vernier caliper A precision measuring instrument that measures inside and outside dimensions. Not quite as accurate as a micrometer, but more convenient.

Viscosity The thickness of a liquid or its resistance to flow.

Volt A unit for expressing electrical "pressure" in a circuit. One volt that will produce a current of one ampere through a resistance of one ohm.

W

Welding Various processes used to join metal items by heating the areas to be joined to a molten state and fusing them together. For more information refer to the *Haynes Automotive Welding Manual*.

Wiring diagram A drawing portraying the components and wires in a vehicle's electrical system, using standardised symbols. For more information refer to the *Haynes Automotive Electrical and Electronic Systems Manual*.

Note: *References throughout this index are in the form "**Chapter number**" • "**Page number**"*

S

T

Haynes Manuals – The Complete UK Car List

Title	Book No.
ALFA ROMEO Alfasud/Sprint (74 - 88) up to F *	0292
Alfa Romeo Alfetta (73 - 87) up to E *	0531
AUDI 80, 90 & Coupe Petrol (79 - Nov 88) up to F	0605
Audi 80, 90 & Coupe Petrol (Oct 86 - 90) D to H	1491
Audi 100 & 200 Petrol (Oct 82 - 90) up to H	0907
Audi 100 & A6 Petrol & Diesel (May 91 - May 97) H to P	3504
Audi A3 Petrol & Diesel (96 - May 03) P to 03	4253
Audi A4 Petrol & Diesel (95 - 00) M to X	3575
Audi A4 Petrol & Diesel (01 - 04) X to 54	4609
AUSTIN A35 & A40 (56 - 67) up to F *	0118
Austin/MG/Rover Maestro 1.3 & 1.6 Petrol (83 - 95) up to M	0922
Austin/MG Metro (80 - May 90) up to G	0718
Austin/Rover Montego 1.3 & 1.6 Petrol (84 - 94) A to L	1066
Austin/MG/Rover Montego 2.0 Petrol (84 - 95) A to M	1067
Mini (59 - 69) up to H *	0527
Mini (69 - 01) up to X	0646
Austin/Rover 2.0 litre Diesel Engine (86 - 93) C to L	1857
Austin Healey 100/6 & 3000 (56 - 68) up to G *	0049
BEDFORD CF Petrol (69 - 87) up to E	0163
Bedford/Vauxhall Rascal & Suzuki Supercarry (86 - Oct 94) C to M	3015
BMW 316, 320 & 320i (4-cyl) (75 - Feb 83) up to Y *	0276
BMW 320, 320i, 323i & 325i (6-cyl) (Oct 77 - Sept 87) up to E	0815
BMW 3- & 5-Series Petrol (81 - 91) up to J	1948
BMW 3-Series Petrol (Apr 91 - 99) H to V	3210
BMW 3-Series Petrol (Sept 98 - 03) S to 53	4067
BMW 520i & 525e (Oct 81 - June 88) up to E	1560
BMW 525, 528 & 528i (73 - Sept 81) up to X *	0632
BMW 5-Series 6-cyl Petrol (April 96 - Aug 03) N to 03	4151
BMW 1500, 1502, 1600, 1602, 2000 & 2002 (59 - 77) up to S *	0240
CHRYSLER PT Cruiser Petrol (00 - 03) W to 53	4058
CITROËN 2CV, Ami & Dyane (67 - 90) up to H	0196
Citroën AX Petrol & Diesel (87 - 97) D to P	3014
Citroën Berlingo & Peugeot Partner Petrol & Diesel (96 - 05) P to 55	4281
Citroën BX Petrol (83 - 94) A to L	0908
Citroën C15 Van Petrol & Diesel (89 - Oct 98) F to S	3509
Citroën C3 Petrol & Diesel (02 - 05) 51 to 05	4197
Citroen C5 Petrol & Diesel (01-08) Y to 08	4745
Citroën CX Petrol (75 - 88) up to F	0528
Citroën Saxo Petrol & Diesel (96 - 04) N to 54	3506
Citroën Visa Petrol (79 - 88) up to F	0620
Citroën Xantia Petrol & Diesel (93 - 01) K to Y	3082
Citroën XM Petrol & Diesel (89 - 00) G to X	3451
Citroën Xsara Petrol & Diesel (97 - Sept 00) R to W	3751
Citroën Xsara Picasso Petrol & Diesel (00 - 02) W to 52	3944
Citroen Xsara Picasso (03-08)	4784
Citroën ZX Diesel (91 - 98) J to S	1922
Citroën ZX Petrol (91 - 98) H to S	1881
Citroën 1.7 & 1.9 litre Diesel Engine (84 - 96) A to N	1379
FIAT 126 (73 - 87) up to E *	0305
Fiat 500 (57 - 73) up to M *	0090
Fiat Bravo & Brava Petrol (95 - 00) N to W	3572
Fiat Cinquecento (93 - 98) K to R	3501
Fiat Panda (81 - 95) up to M	0793
Fiat Punto Petrol & Diesel (94 - Oct 99) L to V	3251
Fiat Punto Petrol (Oct 99 - July 03) V to 03	4066
Fiat Punto Petrol (03-07) 03 to 07	4746
Fiat Regata Petrol (84 - 88) A to F	1167
Fiat Tipo Petrol (88 - 91) E to J	1625
Fiat Uno Petrol (83 - 95) up to M	0923
Fiat X1/9 (74 - 89) up to G *	0273
FORD Anglia (59 - 68) up to G *	0001

Title	Book No.
Ford Capri II (& III) 1.6 & 2.0 (74 - 87) up to E *	0283
Ford Capri II (& III) 2.8 & 3.0 V6 (74 - 87) up to E	1309
Ford Cortina Mk I & Corsair 1500 ('62 - '66) up to D*	0214
Ford Cortina Mk III 1300 & 1600 (70 - 76) up to P *	0070
Ford Escort Mk I 1100 & 1300 (68 - 74) up to N *	0171
Ford Escort Mk I Mexico, RS 1600 & RS 2000 (70 - 74) up to N *	0139
Ford Escort Mk II Mexico, RS 1800 & RS 2000 (75 - 80) up to W *	0735
Ford Escort (75 - Aug 80) up to V *	0280
Ford Escort Petrol (Sept 80 - Sept 90) up to H	0686
Ford Escort & Orion Petrol (Sept 90 - 00) H to X	1737
Ford Escort & Orion Diesel (Sept 90 - 00) H to X	4081
Ford Fiesta (76 - Aug 83) up to Y	0334
Ford Fiesta Petrol (Aug 83 - Feh 89) A to F	1030
Ford Fiesta Petrol (Feb 89 - Oct 95) F to N	1595
Ford Fiesta Petrol & Diesel (Oct 95 - Mar 02) N to 02	3397
Ford Fiesta Petrol & Diesel (Apr 02 - 07) 02 to 57	4170
Ford Focus Petrol & Diesel (98 - 01) S to Y	3759
Ford Focus Petrol & Diesel (Oct 01 - 05) 51 to 05	4167
Ford Galaxy Petrol & Diesel (95 - Aug 00) M to W	3984
Ford Granada Petrol (Sept 77 - Feb 85) up to B *	0481
Ford Granada & Scorpio Petrol (Mar 85 - 94) B to M	1245
Ford Ka (96 - 02) P to 52	3570
Ford Mondeo Petrol (93 - Sept 00) K to X	1923
Ford Mondeo Petrol & Diesel (Oct 00 - Jul 03) X to 03	3990
Ford Mondeo Petrol & Diesel (July 03 - 07) 03 to 56	4619
Ford Mondeo Diesel (93 - 96) L to N	3465
Ford Orion Petrol (83 - Sept 90) up to H	1009
Ford Sierra 4-cyl Petrol (82 - 93) up to K	0903
Ford Sierra V6 Petrol (82 - 91) up to J	0904
Ford Transit Petrol (Mk 2) (78 - Jan 86) up to C	0719
Ford Transit Petrol (Mk 3) (Feb 86 - 89) C to G	1468
Ford Transit Diesel (Feb 86 - 99) C to T	3019
Ford Transit Diesel (00-06)	4775
Ford 1.6 & 1.8 litre Diesel Engine (84 - 96) A to N	1172
Ford 2.1, 2.3 & 2.5 litre Diesel Engine (77 - 90) up to H	1606
FREIGHT ROVER Sherpa Petrol (74 - 87) up to E	0463
HILLMAN Avenger (70 - 82) up to Y	0037
Hillman Imp (63 - 76) up to R *	0022
HONDA Civic (Feb 84 - Oct 87) A to E	1226
Honda Civic (Nov 91 - 96) J to N	3199
Honda Civic Petrol (Mar 95 - 00) M to X	4050
Honda Civic Petrol & Diesel (01 - 05) X to 55	4611
Honda CR-V Petrol & Diesel (01-06)	4747
Honda Jazz (01 - Feb 08) 51 - 57	4735
HYUNDAI Pony (85 - 94) C to M	3398
JAGUAR E Type (61 - 72) up to L *	0140
Jaguar MkI & II, 240 & 340 (55 - 69) up to H *	0098
Jaguar XJ6, XJ & Sovereign; Daimler Sovereign (68 - Oct 86) up to D	0242
Jaguar XJ6 & Sovereign (Oct 86 - Sept 94) D to M	3261
Jaguar XJ12, XJS & Sovereign; Daimler Double Six (72 - 88) up to F	0478
JEEP Cherokee Petrol (93 - 96) K to N	1943
LADA 1200, 1300, 1500 & 1600 (74 - 91) up to J	0413
Lada Samara (87 - 91) D to J	1610
LAND ROVER 90, 110 & Defender Diesel (83 - 07) up to 56	3017
Land Rover Discovery Petrol & Diesel (89 - 98) G to S	3016
Land Rover Discovery Diesel (Nov 98 - Jul 04) S to 04	4606
Land Rover Freelander Petrol & Diesel (97 - Sept 03) R to 53	3929
Land Rover Freelander Petrol & Diesel (Oct 03 - Oct 06) 53 to 56	4623

Title	Book No.
Land Rover Series IIA & III Diesel (58 - 85) up to C	0529
Land Rover Series II, IIA & III 4-cyl Petrol (58 - 85) up to C	0314
MAZDA 323 (Mar 81 - Oct 89) up to G	1608
Mazda 323 (Oct 89 - 98) G to R	3455
Mazda 626 (May 83 - Sept 87) up to E	0929
Mazda B1600, B1800 & B2000 Pick-up Petrol (72 - 88) up to F	0267
Mazda RX-7 (79 - 85) up to C *	0460
MERCEDES-BENZ 190, 190E & 190D Petrol & Diesel (83 - 93) A to L	3450
Mercedes-Benz 200D, 240D, 240TD, 300D & 300TD 123 Series Diesel (Oct 76 - 85)	1114
Mercedes-Benz 250 & 280 (68 - 72) up to L *	0346
Mercedes-Benz 250 & 280 123 Series Petrol (Oct 76 - 84) up to B *	0677
Mercedes-Benz 124 Series Petrol & Diesel (85 - Aug 93) C to K	3253
Mercedes-Benz A-Class Petrol & Diesel (98-04) S to 54)	4748
Mercedes-Benz C-Class Petrol & Diesel (93 - Aug 00) L to W	3511
Mercedes-Benz C-Class (00-06)	4780
MGA (55 - 62) *	0475
MGB (62 - 80) up to W	0111
MG Midget & Austin-Healey Sprite (58 - 80) up to W *	0265
MINI Petrol (July 01 - 05) Y to 05	4273
MITSUBISHI Shogun & L200 Pick-Ups Petrol (83 - 94) up to M	1944
MORRIS Ital 1.3 (80 - 84) up to B	0705
Morris Minor 1000 (56 - 71) up to K	0024
NISSAN Almera Petrol (95 - Feb 00) N to V	4053
Nissan Almera & Tino Petrol (Feb 00 - 07) V to 56	4612
Nissan Bluebird (May 84 - Mar 86) A to C	1223
Nissan Bluebird Petrol (Mar 86 - 90) C to H	1473
Nissan Cherry (Sept 82 - 86) up to D	1031
Nissan Micra (83 - Jan 93) up to K	0931
Nissan Micra (93 - 02) K to 52	3254
Nissan Micra Petrol (03-07) 52 to 57	4734
Nissan Primera Petrol (90 - Aug 99) H to T	1851
Nissan Stanza (82 - 86) up to D	0824
Nissan Sunny Petrol (May 82 - Oct 86) up to D	0895
Nissan Sunny Petrol (Oct 86 - Mar 91) D to H	1378
Nissan Sunny Petrol (Apr 91 - 95) H to N	3219
OPEL Ascona & Manta (B Series) (Sept 75 - 88) up to F *	0316
Opel Ascona Petrol (81 - 88)	3215
Opel Astra Petrol (Oct 91 - Feb 98)	3156
Opel Corsa Petrol (83 - Mar 93)	3160
Opel Corsa Petrol (Mar 93 - 97)	3159
Opel Kadett Petrol (Nov 79 - Oct 84) up to B	0634
Opel Kadett Petrol (Oct 84 - Oct 91)	3196
Opel Omega & Senator Petrol (Nov 86 - 94)	3157
Opel Rekord Petrol (Feb 78 - Oct 86) up to D	0543
Opel Vectra Petrol (Oct 88 - Oct 95)	3158
PEUGEOT 106 Petrol & Diesel (91 - 04) J to 53	1882
Peugeot 205 Petrol (83 - 97) A to P	0932
Peugeot 206 Petrol & Diesel (98 - 01) S to X	3757
Peugeot 206 Petrol & Diesel (02 - 06) 51 to 06	4613
Peugeot 306 Petrol & Diesel (93 - 02) K to 02	3073
Peugeot 307 Petrol & Diesel (01 - 04) Y to 54	4147
Peugeot 309 Petrol (86 - 93) C to K	1266
Peugeot 405 Petrol (88 - 97) E to P	1559
Peugeot 405 Diesel (88 - 97) E to P	3198
Peugeot 406 Petrol & Diesel (96 - Mar 99) N to T	3394
Peugeot 406 Petrol & Diesel (Mar 99 - 02) T to 52	3982

* Classic reprint

Title	Book No.
Peugeot 505 Petrol (79 - 89) up to G	0762
Peugeot 1.7/1.8 & 1.9 litre Diesel Engine (82 - 96) up to N	0950
Peugeot 2.0, 2.1, 2.3 & 2.5 litre Diesel Engines (74 - 90) up to H	1607
PORSCHE 911 (65 - 85) up to C	0264
Porsche 924 & 924 Turbo (76 - 85) up to C	0397
PROTON (89 - 97) F to P	3255
RANGE ROVER V8 Petrol (70 - Oct 92) up to K	0606
RELIANT Robin & Kitten (73 - 83) up to A *	0436
RENAULT 4 (61 - 86) up to D *	0072
Renault 5 Petrol (Feb 85 - 96) B to N	1219
Renault 9 & 11 Petrol (82 - 89) up to F	0822
Renault 18 Petrol (79 - 86) up to D	0598
Renault 19 Petrol (89 - 96) F to N	1646
Renault 19 Diesel (89 - 96) F to N	1946
Renault 21 Petrol (86 - 94) C to M	1397
Renault 25 Petrol & Diesel (84 - 92) B to K	1228
Renault Clio Petrol (91 - May 98) H to R	1853
Renault Clio Diesel (91 - June 96) H to N	3031
Renault Clio Petrol & Diesel (May 98 - May 01) R to Y	3906
Renault Clio Petrol & Diesel (June '01 - '05) Y to 55	4168
Renault Espace Petrol & Diesel (85 - 96) C to N	3197
Renault Laguna Petrol & Diesel (94 - 00) L to W	3252
Renault Laguna Petrol & Diesel (Feb 01 - Feb 05) X to 54	4283
Renault Mégane & Scénic Petrol & Diesel (96 - 99) N to T	3395
Renault Mégane & Scénic Petrol & Diesel (Apr 99 - 02) T to 52	3916
Renault Megane Petrol & Diesel (Oct 02 - 05) 52 to 55	4284
Renault Scenic Petrol & Diesel (Sept 03 - 06) 53 to 06	4297
ROVER 213 & 216 (84 - 89) A to G	1116
Rover 214 & 414 Petrol (89 - 96) G to N	1689
Rover 216 & 416 Petrol (89 - 96) G to N	1830
Rover 211, 214, 216, 218 & 220 Petrol & Diesel (Dec 95 - 99) N to V	3399
Rover 25 & MG ZR Petrol & Diesel (Oct 99 - 04) V to 54	4145
Rover 414, 416 & 420 Petrol & Diesel (May 95 - 98) M to R	3453
Rover 45 / MG ZS Petrol & Diesel (99 - 05) V to 55	4384
Rover 618, 620 & 623 Petrol (93 - 97) K to P	3257
Rover 75 / MG ZT Petrol & Diesel (99 - 06) S to 06	4292
Rover 820, 825 & 827 Petrol (86 - 95) D to N	1380
Rover 3500 (76 - 87) up to E *	0365
Rover Metro, 111 & 114 Petrol (May 90 - 98) G to S	1711
SAAB 95 & 96 (66 - 76) up to R *	0198
Saab 90, 99 & 900 (79 - Oct 93) up to L	0765
Saab 900 (Oct 93 - 98) L to R	3512
Saab 9000 (4-cyl) (85 - 98) C to S	1686
Saab 9-3 Petrol & Diesel (98 - Aug 02) R to 02	4614
Saab 9-3 Petrol & Diesel (02-07) 52 to 57	4749
Saab 9-5 4-cyl Petrol (97 - 04) R to 54	4156
SEAT Ibiza & Cordoba Petrol & Diesel (Oct 93 - Oct 99) L to V	3571
Seat Ibiza & Malaga Petrol (85 - 92) B to K	1609
SKODA Estelle (77 - 89) up to G	0604
Skoda Fabia Petrol & Diesel (00 - 06) W to 06	4376
Skoda Favorit (89 - 96) F to N	1801
Skoda Felicia Petrol & Diesel (95 - 01) M to X	3505
Skoda Octavia Petrol & Diesel (98 - Apr 04) R to 04	4285
SUBARU 1600 & 1800 (Nov 79 - 90) up to H *	0995

Title	Book No.
SUNBEAM Alpine, Rapier & H120 (67 - 74) up to N *	0051
SUZUKI SJ Series, Samurai & Vitara (4-cyl) Petrol (82 - 97) up to P	1942
Suzuki Supercarry & Bedford/Vauxhall Rascal (86 - Oct 94) C to M	3015
TALBOT Alpine, Solara, Minx & Rapier (75 - 86) up to D	0337
Talbot Horizon Petrol (78 - 86) up to D	0473
Talbot Samba (82 - 86) up to D	0823
TOYOTA Avensis Petrol (98 - Jan 03) R to 52	4264
Toyota Carina E Petrol (May 92 - 97) J to P	3256
Toyota Corolla (80 - 85) up to C	0683
Toyota Corolla (Sept 83 - Sept 87) A to E	1024
Toyota Corolla (Sept 87 - Aug 92) E to K	1683
Toyota Corolla Petrol (Aug 92 - 97) K to P	3259
Toyota Corolla Petrol (July 97 - Feb 02) P to 51	4286
Toyota Hi-Ace & Hi-Lux Petrol (69 - Oct 83) up to A	0304
Toyota RAV4 Petrol & Diesel (94-06) L to 55	4750
Toyota Yaris Petrol (99 - 05) T to 05	4265
TRIUMPH GT6 & Vitesse (62 - 74) up to N *	0112
Triumph Herald (59 - 71) up to K *	0010
Triumph Spitfire (62 - 81) up to X	0113
Triumph Stag (70 - 78) up to T *	0441
Triumph TR2, TR3, TR3A, TR4 & TR4A (52 - 67) up to F *	0028
Triumph TR5 & 6 (67 - 75) up to P *	0031
Triumph TR7 (75 - 82) up to Y *	0322
VAUXHALL Astra Petrol (80 - Oct 84) up to B	0635
Vauxhall Astra & Belmont Petrol (Oct 84 - Oct 91) B to J	1136
Vauxhall Astra Petrol (Oct 91 - Feb 98) J to R	1832
Vauxhall/Opel Astra & Zafira Petrol (Feb 98 - Apr 04) R to 04	3758
Vauxhall/Opel Astra & Zafira Diesel (Feb 98 - Apr 04) R to 04	3797
Vauxhall/Opel Astra Petrol (04 - 08)	4732
Vauxhall/Opel Astra Diesel (04 - 08)	4733
Vauxhall/Opel Calibra (90 - 98) G to S	3502
Vauxhall Carlton Petrol (Oct 78 - Oct 86) up to D	0480
Vauxhall Carlton & Senator Petrol (Nov 86 - 94) D to L	1469
Vauxhall Cavalier Petrol (81 - Oct 88) up to F	0812
Vauxhall Cavalier Petrol (Oct 88 - 95) F to N	1570
Vauxhall Chevette (75 - 84) up to B	0285
Vauxhall/Opel Corsa Diesel (Mar 93 - Oct 00) K to X	4087
Vauxhall Corsa Petrol (Mar 93 - 97) K to R	1985
Vauxhall/Opel Corsa Petrol (Apr 97 - Oct 00) P to X	3921
Vauxhall/Opel Corsa Petrol & Diesel (Oct 00 - Sept 03) X to 53	4079
Vauxhall/Opel Corsa Petrol & Diesel (Oct 03 - Aug 06) 53 to 06	4617
Vauxhall/Opel Frontera Petrol & Diesel (91 - Sept 98) J to S	3454
Vauxhall Nova Petrol (83 - 93) up to K	0909
Vauxhall/Opel Omega Petrol (94 - 99) L to T	3510
Vauxhall/Opel Vectra Petrol & Diesel (95 - Feb 99) N to S	3396
Vauxhall/Opel Vectra Petrol & Diesel (Mar 99 - May 02) T to 02	3930
Vauxhall/Opel Vectra Petrol & Diesel (June 02 - Sept 05) 02 to 55	4618
Vauxhall/Opel 1.5, 1.6 & 1.7 litre Diesel Engine (82 - 96) up to N	1222
VW 411 & 412 (68 - 75) up to P *	0091
VW Beetle 1200 (54 - 77) up to S	0036
VW Beetle 1300 & 1500 (65 - 75) up to P	0039

Title	Book No.
VW 1302 & 1302S (70 - 72) up to L *	0110
VW Beetle 1303, 1303S & GT (72 - 75) up to P	0159
VW Beetle Petrol & Diesel (Apr 99 - 07) T to 57	3798
VW Golf & Jetta Mk 1 Petrol 1.1 & 1.3 (74 - 84) up to A	0716
VW Golf, Jetta & Scirocco Mk 1 Petrol 1.5, 1.6 & 1.8 (74 - 84) up to A	0726
VW Golf & Jetta Mk 1 Diesel (78 - 84) up to A	0451
VW Golf & Jetta Mk 2 Petrol (Mar 84 - Feb 92) A to J	1081
VW Golf & Vento Petrol & Diesel (Feb 92 - Mar 98) J to R	3097
VW Golf & Bora Petrol & Diesel (April 98 - 00) R to X	3727
VW Golf & Bora 4-cyl Petrol & Diesel (01 - 03) X to 53	4169
VW Golf & Jetta Petrol & Diesel (04 - 07) 53 to 07	4610
VW LT Petrol Vans & Light Trucks (76 - 87) up to E	0637
VW Passat & Santana Petrol (Sept 81 - May 88) up to E	0814
VW Passat 4-cyl Petrol & Diesel (May 88 - 96) E to P	3498
VW Passat 4-cyl Petrol & Diesel (Dec 96 - Nov 00) P to X	3917
VW Passat Petrol & Diesel (Dec 00 - May 05) X to 05	4279
VW Polo & Derby (76 - Jan 82) up to X	0335
VW Polo (82 - Oct 90) up to H	0813
VW Polo Petrol (Nov 90 - Aug 94) H to L	3245
VW Polo Hatchback Petrol & Diesel (94 - 99) M to S	3500
VW Polo Hatchback Petrol (00 - Jan 02) V to 51	4150
VW Polo Petrol & Diesel (02 - May 05) 51 to 05	4608
VW Scirocco (82 - 90) up to H *	1224
VW Transporter 1600 (68 - 79) up to V	0082
VW Transporter 1700, 1800 & 2000 (72 - 79) up to V *	0226
VW Transporter (air-cooled) Petrol (79 - 82) up to Y *	0638
VW Transporter (water-cooled) Petrol (82 - 90) up to H	3452
VW Type 3 (63 - 73) up to M *	0084
VOLVO 120 & 130 Series (& P1800) (61 - 73) up to M *	0203
Volvo 142, 144 & 145 (66 - 74) up to N *	0129
Volvo 240 Series Petrol (74 - 93) up to K	0270
Volvo 262, 264 & 260/265 (75 - 85) up to C *	0400
Volvo 340, 343, 345 & 360 (76 - 91) up to J	0715
Volvo 440, 460 & 480 Petrol (87 - 97) D to P	1691
Volvo 740 & 760 Petrol (82 - 91) up to J	1258
Volvo 850 Petrol (92 - 96) J to P	3260
Volvo 940 petrol (90 - 98) H to R	3249
Volvo S40 & V40 Petrol (96 - Mar 04) N to 04	3569
Volvo S40 & V50 Petrol & Diesel (Mar 04 - Jun 07) 04 to 07	4731
Volvo S60 Petrol & Diesel (01-08)	4793
Volvo S70, V70 & C70 Petrol (96 - 99) P to V	3573
Volvo V70 / S80 Petrol & Diesel (98 - 05) S to 55	4263

DIY MANUAL SERIES

Title	Book No.
The Haynes Air Conditioning Manual	4192
The Haynes Car Electrical Systems Manual	4251
The Haynes Manual on Bodywork	4198
The Haynes Manual on Brakes	4178
The Haynes Manual on Carburettors	4177
The Haynes Manual on Diesel Engines	4174
The Haynes Manual on Engine Management	4199
The Haynes Manual on Fault Codes	4175
The Haynes Manual on Practical Electrical Systems	4267
The Haynes Manual on Small Engines	4250
The Haynes Manual on Welding	4176

* Classic reprint

Preserving Our Motoring Heritage

< The Model J Duesenberg Derham Tourster. Only eight of these magnificent cars were ever built – this is the only example to be found outside the United States of America

Almost every car you've ever loved, loathed or desired is gathered under one roof at the Haynes Motor Museum. Over 300 immaculately presented cars and motorbikes represent every aspect of our motoring heritage, from elegant reminders of bygone days, such as the superb Model J Duesenberg to curiosities like the bug-eyed BMW Isetta. There are also many old friends and flames. Perhaps you remember the 1959 Ford Popular that you did your courting in? The magnificent 'Red Collection' is a spectacle of classic sports cars including AC, Alfa Romeo, Austin Healey, Ferrari, Lamborghini, Maserati, MG, Riley, Porsche and Triumph.

A Perfect Day Out

Each and every vehicle at the Haynes Motor Museum has played its part in the history and culture of Motoring. Today, they make a wonderful spectacle and a great day out for all the family. Bring the kids, bring Mum and Dad, but above all bring your camera to capture those golden memories for ever. You will also find an impressive array of motoring memorabilia, a comfortable 70 seat video cinema and one of the most extensive transport book shops in Britain. The Pit Stop Cafe serves everything from a cup of tea to wholesome, home-made meals or, if you prefer, you can enjoy the large picnic area nestled in the beautiful rural surroundings of Somerset.

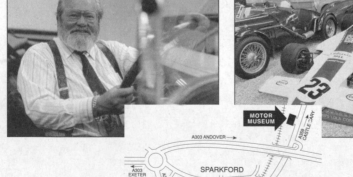

> John Haynes O.B.E., Founder and Chairman of the museum at the wheel of a Haynes Light 12.

< Graham Hill's Lola Cosworth Formula 1 car next to a 1934 Riley Sports.

The Museum is situated on the A359 Yeovil to Frome road at Sparkford, just off the A303 in Somerset. It is about 40 miles south of Bristol, and 25 minutes drive from the M5 intersection at Taunton.
Open 9.30am - 5.30pm (10.00am - 4.00pm Winter) 7 days a week, except Christmas Day, Boxing Day and New Years Day
Special rates available for schools, coach parties and outings Charitable Trust No. 292048